AUDREY HEPBURN

For the Erickson Family.

AUDREY HEPBURN

A LIFE OF BEAUTIFUL UNCERTAINTY

TOM SANTOPIETRO

THEATRE & CINEMA BOOKS

Essex, Connecticut

APPLAUSE
THEATRE & CINEMA BOOKS

An imprint of Globe Pequot, the trade division of
The Rowman & Littlefield Publishing Group, Inc.
4501 Forbes Blvd., Ste. 200
Lanham, MD 20706
www.rowman.com

Distributed by NATIONAL BOOK NETWORK

Title page photo © Pictorial Press Ltd./Alamy Stock Photo.

Library of Congress Cataloging-in-Publication Data

Names: Santopietro, Tom, author.
Title: Audrey Hepburn : a life of beautiful uncertainty / Tom Santopietro.
Description: Essex, Connecticut : Applause, [2024] | Includes
   bibliographical references and index.
Identifiers: LCCN 2024012750 (print) | LCCN 2024012751 (ebook) | ISBN
   9781493068081 (cloth) | ISBN 9781493068098 (epub)
Subjects: LCSH: Hepburn, Audrey, 1929-1993. | Motion picture actors and
   actresses--United States--Biography.
Classification: LCC PN2287.H43 S26 2024 (print) | LCC PN2287.H43 (ebook)
   | DDC 791.4302/8092 [B]--dc23/eng/20240614
LC record available at https://lccn.loc.gov/2024012750
LC ebook record available at https://lccn.loc.gov/2024012751

♾ ™ The paper used in this publication meets the minimum requirements of American National Standard for Information Sciences—Permanence of Paper for Printed Library Materials, ANSI/NISO Z39.48-1992.

Contents

ACT ONE

CODA/OVERTURE

Audrey's sculpted heavy lace Givenchy dress, worn while accepting her Academy Award *for Roman Holiday*. Givenchy designed this dress by re-working the Edith Head ballgown Audrey wore as Princess Anne in the film. *Time* magazine dubbed it the "Best Oscar Dress of All Time." Photo by Fred Duval/WireImage/Getty Images

Chapter One

A CLOSET, 1993

"She seemed so terribly different and sort of very angelic and sort of very ethereal. It was like some kind of fairy book person."

—Harry Belafonte

WHEN AUDREY HEPBURN DIED AT 8 P.M. on January 20, 1993, at the age of sixty-three, she left behind one Academy Award, two Tony Awards, dozens of lifetime achievement awards, her beloved sons Sean and Luca, companion Robert Wolders, millions of fans, universal acclaim as an indefatigable activist on behalf of the world's children, and one final surprise—a nearly empty closet.

This most stylish of actresses, muse for designer Hubert de Givenchy, perennial fixture on the Best-Dressed List, and idol of millions for her sense of style, had stored her endlessly discussed, dissected, and scrutinized clothing in the bedroom of her beloved "La Paisible" home in Tolochenaz, Switzerland. Ten double-paneled hand-painted doors in the light airy room held the promise of hidden couture treasures, perhaps original Givenchys or Ralph Laurens, and yet when the doors were opened, the closet was, in the words of Audrey's older son, Sean Ferrer, "not more than 20% full—with blue jeans, wool slacks, blazers, and t-shirts."

Where were the designer originals worth tens of thousands of dollars? The dazzling Cecil Beaton *My Fair Lady* gowns or the world-famous Givenchy Little Black Dress from *Breakfast at Tiffany's*? Why did Audrey Hepburn, of all people, have a nearly empty closet with nary a couture gown in sight? The answer proved both simple and profound, touching as it did upon every aspect of her life's journey, because during her last ten years, Audrey Hepburn kept ruthlessly paring away at her life until only the absolute essentials remained. Hollywood? Not interested. Fashion shows? Thank you, but no. There was simply no need for Givenchy gowns when trekking across drought-stricken portions of Africa on behalf of UNICEF and the starving children of the world.

She had walked away from the church of fame that rules Hollywood and ever-increasing swaths of the general public yet held onto that fame without even trying. Her elusiveness only increased public interest in her films and clothes as well as her life and loves, but Audrey Hepburn had grown uninterested in rehashing old tales of Hollywood glamour and legendary friends. In an industry which based its self-image on endless awards shows, she was, it was safe to say, the only screen idol about whom a son could convincingly state: "Being away from home to win an award was really a lost opportunity. Walking the dogs with her sons was a personal victory."

This turning away from surface fripperies occurred hand in hand with Audrey's inversion of the usual Hollywood worldview: far from dreading the years after age fifty, she had instead embraced them. With her sons grown and her priorities reordered, the freedom found in serving others had now granted her a belief in her own worth that she had sought, sometimes desperately, throughout her entire life.

In truth, if anyone had been paying strict attention to the substance beneath her oft-dazzling surface, they would have seen an indication of her ultimate direction as far back as 1959's *The Nun's Story*; speaking to her castmate Patricia Bosworth, she had, in an atypical piece of soul-bearing, explained: "I love fashion, you know. Really love it. But fashion has nothing to do with *me*." At which point, recalled Bosworth, Audrey touched her heart and emphasized: "The *me* in here . . . the private me, the interior me—inside I'm not fashionable at all."

As her acting abilities actually deepened—witness her moving cameo in her final film, Steven Spielberg's *Always*—she had, like all great artists, stripped away the extraneous and clever in search of the truth, seeking answers at last to the ultimate questions: Who am I, and where do I fit in? How can I make a difference? And with that personal expansion echoed in an evolution from couture clotheshorse to casual style icon to khaki-clad activist, only one constant remained: the vulnerability underneath the beautifully controlled and genuinely kind exterior.

Which brings us back to the bedroom closets: neatly painted, perfectly ordered, and nearly empty. Because by turning her back on the glamour—on the clothes, the awards, and the self-interest—by not just talking about giving back to others but actually doing so on an international scale unfathomable to others, Audrey Hepburn had actually deepened the bond with her fans of fifty years. How, they wondered, could anyone be filled with such loving kindness? Such unselfishness?

And while Audrey remained grateful for those who loved her films, after gracefully accepting compliments for her acting, she would politely but firmly switch the topic to her real, not reel, work: helping to save children through UNICEF. By now St. Audrey had become the focus of so much cultural heft placed upon her reed-thin frame that she had surpassed the boundaries imposed upon the very notion of stardom, becoming not just an inspirational figure but an aspirational one as well. A woman who made people feel better about themselves. A secular saint to many, she grew genuinely embarrassed by the attention heaped upon her and determinedly tried to focus that attention on others she felt had achieved so much more on behalf of children.

She had reinvented the entire third act of her life, not out of a wish for publicity or image polishing but, instead, out of a need to help others which had arisen from the most personal of experiences; having been saved from starvation at the end of World War II by the United Nations Relief and Rehabilitation Agency (UNRRA), Audrey could now, at last, pay it forward. And, in the process, fully come to terms with a Dutch childhood nearly suffocated by the Nazi occupiers of her homeland.

Because long before the dazzling turns in *Roman Holiday*, *Sabrina*, *Breakfast at Tiffany's*, and *My Fair Lady*, and decades before the awards and universal acclaim as a beautiful and charming trendsetter, there had been a childhood in which there had not been the slightest talk of acting and Hollywood stardom, a time when mere survival remained the only goal.

Audrey Kathleen van Heemstra Ruston. A face made for the camera. Photofest

Chapter Two

BEGINNINGS, 1929–1948

"Her life really is like a fairy tale because fairy tales are not just about good stuff. There are terrible things that happen on the way."

—Sean Hepburn Ferrer

ALTHOUGH AUDREY WAS TO DETERMINEDLY eschew all trappings of nobility, her mother Ella, born the third daughter of Baron Aarnoud van Heemstra, conducted her own life with a pronounced sense of aristocratic entitlement. Indeed, her marriage in 1920 to the Honourable Jon Hendrik Gustaaf Adolf Quarles van Ufford, Knight of the Order of Orange-Nassau, seemed socially fitting, began promisingly, and produced two sons, Ian and Alexander. But differing outlooks and two substantial egos ended the marriage after only five years, and Ella soon found the man with whom she felt destined to spend the rest of her married life, Joseph Ruston.

With his appropriately tweedy and aristocratic façade, the handsome and eleven-years-older Ruston seemed both well-heeled and well-connected. If Ella's own attractive features carried more than a hint of hauteur, for Ruston there was always the benefit of her title—Baroness Ella van Heemstra—to consider. A glider pilot and accomplished horseman, Ruston was smart—in the words of Ella and Joseph's grandson Sean, "He was a true dilettante and a brilliant one at that"—and he quickly divorced his wife to marry Ella.

After marrying on September 7, 1926, the couple soon settled in Brussels, where in the suburb of Ixelles, at 3 a.m. on May 24, 1929, they welcomed daughter Audrey—known to the family as Adrianntje. Almost immediately a crisis arose: at the age of three weeks Audrey caught whooping cough, and Ella, relying solely upon her Christian Science faith, did not take her to the doctor. When the crisis deepened and Audrey stopped breathing, Ella revived her infant daughter by spanking her back into life. In the view of Sean, the psychological effects of the incident upon his mother proved lifelong: "She saw life itself as a gift and saw her own survival as precious and a matter of chance."

Crisis averted, Ella and Joseph's infant daughter was now formally christened Audrey Kathleen van Heemstra Ruston. With a British father (Ireland was not yet an independent country when Joseph was born) and Dutch mother, infant Audrey, for purposes of citizenship, was deemed British. Her mixed heritage of Dutch, English, and Irish proved to be a big reason why Audrey never thought of herself as coming from any one country, laughingly stating in later years: "I'm half-Irish, half-Dutch and I was born in Belgium. If I was a dog, I'd be a hell of a mess."

As to the Hepburn name: by now, Joseph, who was descended from the engineer John Joseph Ruston, had concluded that he had Hepburn ancestors through his grandmother Isabella Hepburn and decided to add the Hepburn surname to Ruston. However, it had been John Joseph Ruston's second wife, Barbara Victoria Belha, who gave birth to his four children, his first wife Isabella Hepburn Ruston having died in 1857 without bearing any children. The provenance of the Hepburn surname may therefore remain questionable, but, said Audrey's cousin Walter Ruston, a family archivist: "I am convinced that, to her dying day, [Audrey] believed she was a Hepburn."

On the surface, all seemed fine in the Ruston household at the Castel Sainte-Cecile estate in the village of Linkebeek. Nanny Greta was on hand to help raise Audrey, and in the aftermath of the First World War, the Victorian era was quickly becoming a dusty relic. The 1920s had indeed begun to roar, with a burgeoning sense of personal freedom running right alongside a new consumer society stocked with automobiles, household appliances, and radios. Stocks soared ever higher and talking movies startled the world.

And yet.

Cracks soon began to appear in the façade. Three days after Audrey's birth, eight were killed in Berlin as Communists clashed with police, and the National Socialist Party continued to gain ground. A mere four years later, Adolf Hitler became chancellor of Germany, an ascendency which brought about a chapter in the Hepburn family history that was to haunt Audrey throughout her life: her parents' infatuation with fascism.

It was Joseph who first became enamored of the fascist movement in England, and after his boss, Montagu Norman, introduced him to friends like the notorious Hitler worshiper Unity Mitford, Joseph joined the circle surrounding the leader of the British Union of Fascists (BUF), Oswald Mosley. In the process, he inculcated a fervent support of the fascists in Ella.

Ella proceeded to publish several articles in *Blackshirt*, the BUF periodical, under the byline "Baroness Ella de Heemstra." The most notorious and unfortunate example of her writings ran on April 26, 1935, under the title "The Call of Fascism," in which she boldly extolled "those who have heard the call of Fascism, and have followed the light on the upward road to victory. . . ." More disturbing words were to come: "The Germany of today is a most present country, and the Germans, under Nazi rule, a splendid example to the white races of the world."

By now, Ella's fascination with Hitler extended well beyond the printed word, and she attended the Nazi Party conference in Nuremberg. It was, while it existed, a full-blown admiration for the fascist leader, and while she later renounced the Nazis, her undeniable early infatuation with Hitler and his associates was to prove anathema to Audrey, who loathed every aspect of the fascist movement.

Even a shared attraction to the fascists, however, could not paper over the increasing fissures in the Ruston marriage. Joseph, a self-proclaimed "financial broker," came to rely increasingly upon the van Heemstra money, and as the money vanished at an ever more rapid rate, quarrels between Joseph and Ella broke out frequently. Young Audrey took refuge in the one way that made sense to her six-year-old self: by hiding underneath the dining room table.

The Ruston marriage began to crumble amidst rumors of James's affair with a nanny, and ended for good when he walked out in 1935. Many assumed that the occasionally remote, aristocratic Ella suffered the separation and ultimate divorce in silence, but the opposite proved true. Stated Audrey in later years: "She cried day in, day out. I thought that she never would stop." Only six years old at the time, Audrey nonetheless took on a very adult role: "My mother would sob through the night. And I would just try and be with her."

For young Audrey, Joseph's abrupt departure proved devastating. Certainly, he was a remote father, but as his grandson Sean points out, he provided fun for young Audrey: "He was joyous—maybe not a warm father, not a joking father, but he spoke thirteen languages and as a gliding pilot he would take my mother gliding. When he left so abruptly it was almost as if he were going out for cigarettes and never came back."

The loss of her father gave birth to an emotional trauma which remained with Audrey for the rest of her life, and as late as 1989, the then-sixty-year-old Audrey bluntly termed Joseph's leaving "the most traumatic event in my life. . . . I was terrified. What was going to happen to me?" That upheaval proved the single most important reason why, when her own marriages to Mel Ferrer, father of Sean, and Andrea Dotti, father of Luca, ended, she insisted that both sons stay in close contact with their fathers: "[Children need] two parents for the equilibrium in life. I mean emotional equilibrium."

Joseph's move back to England, where he grew increasingly vocal about his fascist sympathies, marked the beginning of Audrey's peripatetic childhood, with Ella moving Audrey and her two brothers (Audrey was always to call them her brothers, no "half" about it) from their base in Brussels to Holland. Audrey also began living part of the year in England, starting school in 1935 at Miss Ridgen's in Elham, Kent, and when the divorce settlement between Joseph and Ella was finalized in 1938, part of the settlement decreed that Audrey was to continue her schooling in England. This portion of the decree was ostensibly included so that Audrey could reside part of every year near her father, but Joseph rarely came to visit his daughter.

Having been raised in Belgium and Holland, Audrey did not speak fluent English when she arrived in Elham, and when combined with the fact that she was, surprisingly enough, somewhat plump at that age, she experienced bouts of true loneliness. And yet, with her determination to rise above all obstacles, she later mused that it "turned out to be a good lesson in independence."

She soldiered on with her joyless school lessons, taking refuge in her own imagination and love of drawing: "I liked the children and my teachers but I never liked the process of learning. I was very restless and could never sit still for hours on end. . . . School in itself I found very dull, and I was happy when I was finished."

There was, however, one consolation which proved to be life altering: the introduction of dance into her life. A young dancer from London began traveling to Elham to teach ballet classes, and eight-year-old Audrey became utterly enthralled with dancing: both the artistic impulse that released her from her interior life and the disciplined, all-consuming dedication to her art dovetailed with Audrey's personality. Recalling those early dance lessons, she enthused: "I loved it, just loved it." In a revealing comment made over fifty years later, she explained: "I don't deal with words very well. I love music—dancing—it takes you out of yourself."

She found another life-altering experience in being sent every summer "to stay with a family (in England) whom I absolutely adored." Living with the coal-mining Butcher family in the summer months not only immersed Audrey in the English language but also provided her with a loving second family; in later years she was to keep a photo of the family's dog on her vanity.

Such was her bond with the Butchers that after gaining international fame as an Academy Award–winning movie star, she pursued a renewed connection with the family, and through her contacts at the United Nations joyfully aided one of the family members in adopting a baby.

Her ballet lessons and happy summers disappeared, however, when war broke out between Britain and Germany in September of 1939. Erroneously thinking that the Netherlands, unlike Britain, would never be invaded by the Germans, Ella decided that Audrey would be safer away from England, and on December 14, 1939, a DC-3 made the cross-channel flight with ten-year-old Audrey on board. It was, recalled Audrey, "really one of the last planes out."

Ella then moved her daughter and two sons to the van Heemstra home, Villa Beukenhof, in the village of Velp, where they began living with Ella's sister and father. Velp lay just outside the town of Arnhem, possessed the rail service deemed important to the Germans, and was situated only forty miles from the German border, yet in Ella's reasoning it would still prove safe because it was a good distance away from the front. Unfortunately, on May 17, 1940, the Germans crossed into Holland, marched directly into Arnhem, and instantly took complete control of the town. Said the adult Audrey: "There are so many images that will never go away. Tanks coming in for hours. Holland fell in 5 days." Still processing the loss of her father, Audrey was now also struggling to grasp the reality of the German invasion: "The second worst memory I have after my father's disappearance was my mother coming into my bedroom one morning, pulling back the curtains and saying, 'Wake up, the war's on.'" In later years, Audrey was to tell Sean: "From one day to the next everything you took for granted was gone. Eventually there was no food, no heat." And looming over it all, a complete and utter lack of freedom.

Noble antecedents meant nothing to the Nazis, and the remnants of the van Heemstra wealth—jewelry, stocks, and cash—all vanished. Audrey's brother Ian was sent to a labor camp in Germany while Alexander went into hiding and joined the resistance. Audrey's childhood innocence was over, and the knowledge of the horrors men were capable of inflicting upon one another was to haunt the shy youngster for the rest of her life.

Audrey, now age ten, was understandably confused about her nationality, and at the time she began school in the Netherlands felt "more English than Dutch." Enrolled in a Dutch public school, her English accent and rudimentary Dutch instantly marked her as an outsider: "Every time I opened my mouth, everyone was roaring with laughter." Concerned that the name Audrey sounded too British in occupied Holland, Ella changed two letters in her own name and for the duration of the occupation Audrey was henceforth known as Edda. (Curiously, she was still billed as Audrey Hepburn-Ruston in all programs for her Dansschool performances.)

Juggling different names and multiple countries meant that Audrey's desire and psychological need for a permanent home—a place of refuge, comfort and love—now took hold. As an adult, she explained it in the most basic of terms: "Maybe that's why I'm so attached to my own family. They are my roots."

Only eleven when she first glimpsed the horrors of the Nazi war machine, Audrey was unquestionably scarred for life by the atrocities she witnessed: "I saw families with little children, with babies, herded into meat wagons—trains of big wooden vans with just a little slat open at the top and all those faces peering out at you. . . . There would be families together and they would separate them, saying 'The men go there and the women go there.' Then they would take the babies . . ."

Joseph's disappearance had drawn Audrey and her mother closer, but it was closeness with a caveat: Ella was not demonstrative and rarely praised any of Audrey's efforts. Born June 12, 1900, and at her core a very Victorian aristocrat, Ella held the aristocratic view that it was unseemly in the extreme to make a spectacle of oneself. Said Robbie Wolders, Audrey's companion for the final thirteen years of her life: "Ella was a superior woman, very humorous… but critical of everyone, including Audrey. Biased. Intolerant." Deserted by her husband, and trying to raise a ten-year-old daughter under the shadow of the Nazis, Ella, out of necessity, developed a somewhat forbidding exterior. Wrote Luca of the war years: "Ella was her father figure and Meisje [her aunt] was her mother . . . Meisje was the one teaching her how to draw. It was really Meisje who made the magic come alive. Ella was about rules."

At the same time, however, it was Ella who recognized her daughter's attraction to the arts, and she encouraged Audrey's growing interest by taking her to concerts and to the ballet. The shy and impressionable youngster fell head over heels in love with the make believe, happily-ever-after world of the arts, where life was not only beautiful, but controllable. Design, lighting, action—it could all be practiced and perfected, with no room for unpleasant surprises like a beloved parent walking out.

It wasn't just thoughts of Audrey's welfare which motivated Ella, however, because underneath her very proper Victorian façade, Ella was, in fact more than a bit of a classic stage mother—a frustrated performer who lived out her dreams through her daughter. Said Audrey: "My mother desperately wanted to become an actress. Yet my grandfather strictly forbade her to go near the stage . . . I don't think my mother ever got over her disappointment in obeying him." In Ella's own words: "I tried to obey my father. But I grew up wanting more than anything else to be . . . well, English, slim, and an actress." Which makes it all the more interesting that in those last three words lies an exact description of Audrey. Said Luca: "Ella was the frustrated prima donna, born a century too soon." In the even more discerning assessment of Audrey herself: "My mother would have been better off in Vienna, or anywhere in Italy or France—anywhere where music and art were of equal importance to food and drink."

Ella, it turned out, was not going to let Audrey make the same mistake. If Audrey wanted to dance, then dance she would.

"I love music—dancing—it takes you out of yourself." Photofest

Chapter Three

WAR AND A LIFE OF DANCE, 1940–1947

"With her vivid style and incomparable elegance, Audrey Hepburn truly is the patron style saint of ballerinas."

— "Dance, Expression and Audrey Hepburn"

URGED ON BY ELLA, AT the age of eleven and a half, Audrey began studying ballet seriously at the Arnhemsche Muziekschool (Arnhem Music School) with Dutch ballerina Winja Marova. Her classes represented the beginning of a life of extraordinary self-discipline; whether expressed through hours at the barre, rehearsal on a film set, or in strict adherence to a notoriously spare diet, Audrey Hepburn's will soon came to play a very large role in her meteoric rise to fame. Explains Sean: "That discipline absolutely grew out of her training as a dancer. It's in the back, the posture, the arch, the frame. It's . . . how you move, how you step into a Givenchy dress and walk in it, but it's also your mind. Without that, it doesn't work."

Surrounded at home by people often two or three times her age, she was growing up fast. Explained Audrey in later years: "I was sixteen when the war finished, but I had been grown-up from the time I was twelve." In part as a survival mechanism—a way to take flight away from the horrors of the Nazis—and in part because she so loved music and dance, Audrey began immersing herself to an even greater degree in the fantasy world of the arts: "I was studying and dreaming of Pavlova and Diaghilev. To all intents and purposes, I had been cut off from the world of youngsters my age because the war had made me a prisoner not just physically but mentally, never allowing me to peep out to see what was really outside." Left to her own devices, she gravitated to music as a soundtrack to accompany her daydreams, and when combined with an introverted nature exemplified by a love of reading, drawing, and solitary walks, it all began to inform her very approach to life.

The relentless self-discipline of ballet may have felt natural to young Audrey, but the unending necessity of having to stare into the mirrors lining the rehearsal hall likely provided the first real step in her lifelong dissatisfaction with her own appearance. "I didn't think much of my looks. In fact, I thought I was such an ugly thing that no one would ever want me for a wife." Consistently lauded during her Hollywood years as a singular beauty, Audrey never fully surmounted a self-imposed focus on what she saw as her own physical imperfections: crooked teeth, wide jawline, flat chest, and big feet seemed to be all Audrey glimpsed in the mirror as she danced for hours. (In truth her feet were a size 8½ and certainly not huge.)

With all of life now up for grabs under the Nazi occupation, ballet provided a bedrock of certainty. Here, in this one area, the ground stopped shifting beneath her feet. Music, the barre, the mirror—all was in order, proving that beauty was still possible in a chaotic world. With its emphasis upon silhouette, ballet allowed Audrey to develop a preternatural grace, a floating, gliding walk which made it appear as if her feet never really touched the ground. Audrey may have noticed only her supposed defects, but that grace proved immediately apparent to all others, with Edouard Scheidius, a friend of Winja Marova, dubbing her "'Poezepas'—Dutch for cat-walk."

As she grew older, her much sought after, never to be successfully imitated walk evolved into a forward-gliding movement combining a fashion model's skimming-the-surface gait with the grace of a ballet dancer. Hours at the barre had resulted in a ramrod straight posture, the stuff of a designer's dreams. The end result was a walk that made clothes fall more softly, their clean lines displayed to best advantage by her ease of movement.

That walk was to remain with her for the rest of her life, and television interviewer Mo Rocca recalled his reaction when she visited Macy's, where he was then working: "I was twenty-three years old, behind the fragrance counter, in April 1992, and she walked by my counter. This is one of the biggest department stores in the world—and the entire floor fell silent. Even if cell phones had existed then you never would have taken your cell phone and shoved it in front of her face for a selfie. She floated by and people knew, this is Audrey Hepburn."

As a teenager, however, Audrey saw none of this, and grew self-conscious about her height. As the tallest girl in her ballet class, she had to undertake the male roles, lifting the little girls who were much shorter than she. How, she wondered, could she ever be a prima ballerina if she were taller than everyone else?

Although twelve-year-old Audrey had, in 1941, performed in ballet recitals in front of German officers at Arnhem's Wehrmachtheim, by age fifteen she had stopped dancing in any official or public capacity because she would have had to register as a member of the Dans Kultuurkamer, an artistic union that was part of the Reich. Instead of registering with the Dans Kultuurkamer, Audrey had begun helping Dr. Willem Visser 't Hooft, the unofficial head of the local resistance, whose daughter Annemarth was a dance pupil of Audrey's. The work was to prove dangerous, with fourteen-year-old Audrey at one point tapped to carry a Resistance message to an English parachutist hiding in the hills near Arnhem. After delivering the message, Audrey turned back toward home, only to be stopped by a German soldier. Having just picked flowers to fit her cover story of spending the day in the countryside, she smiled and gave the young German her bouquet of flowers. The soldier was charmed by the gesture, and Audrey, having succeeded in a first improvisation, smiled at the soldier and continued on her way home.

By 1944, she was actively helping the resistance as often as possible, telling an interviewer in 1951 that she had been "running around with food for the pilots" who had been shot down. She began delivering the resistance newspaper, *Oranjekrant*, which she described as half the size of a paper napkin; stuffing the newspapers in the woolen socks she wore with her wooden shoes, she biked around town to deliver the newspapers, an innocuous Dutch girl who thwarted the Germans under their very noses.

By now Ella had renounced her support of British fascism, her flirtation with the Nazis likely changed forever when the Germans shot Otto van Limburg Stirum, husband of her sister Miesje. Ella was certainly well aware of Audrey's role in helping Allied soldiers, but in typical fashion, Audrey always downplayed her own efforts. As late as 1988, she was to state in a television interview: "Stories about my contributions to the underground have been exaggerated. I took around messages a couple of times—but I was really too young."

Much worse was to come, however, when for the first time war was waged on the streets of Arnhem. So large was the scale of these operations that in the end, the Battle of Arnhem, which raged from September 17 to 26, 1944, proved to be the biggest air-land operation of World War II, resulting in more casualties than there had been on D-Day.

The exhausted and greatly undernourished Ella and Audrey now walked to Velp, where Audrey's grandfather was living at Castle Zijpendaal. Eventually, said Audrey, "we had thirty-seven people sleeping in our house as evacuees continued to arrive." The details of that unrelentingly harsh time never left Audrey: "We went for days at a time without anything to eat, and we sat and shivered in a house without heat or light. . . . We lived in a vacuum—no life, no news, no books, no soap."

As the war entered its sixth year, life in the Netherlands reached its nadir. In Audrey's own words: "Holland was one of the worst because it was occupied by the SS—not just the military." Faced with a shortage of soldiers and support personnel, the Germans took to literally grabbing women off the street to work in their military kitchens, and in March 1945, Audrey was "picked right off the street with a dozen others" by the notorious Dutch Green Police. She was now facing months of servitude, but when the truck stopped to force more women inside, Audrey jumped out of the truck and ran away: underneath that frail and shy exterior already lay the guts and determination that would serve her well in negotiating the perils of Hollywood. After this near escape, however, she did not, as legend has it, live by herself in the cellar of a bombed-out building for a month, but instead ran home and "stayed indoors for a month."

By now, Audrey was incapable of dancing because of malnutrition. Reduced to eating nettles, she developed both jaundice and anemia, and as a result, her resistance and strength were severely weakened. In that final winter of the war, 1944–1945, known as the "hunger winter," she, and tens of thousands of others, were living in a state of near starvation. The crushing reality of the time never left Audrey, and even near the end of her own life, she grimly recalled: "It was not on the scale of Somalia, but it was pretty bad too, you know. Children were always rummaging in the dust bins and people were dying of hunger and cold." In the end, the winter claimed nearly twenty-two thousand Dutch lives.

Shops were closed, electricity and heat nonexistent, and the Dutch were allowed to heat only one room in a house. Soap virtually disappeared, and the water supply was now unsafe. Fuel for cars and trucks was diverted to the German war machine, and all food confiscated by the Germans. Audrey was subsisting on turnips, bread made from peas and grass, and flour from tulip bulbs; her one meal per day featured a soup made from herbs and water. From the vantage point of later decades Audrey explained: "In those days I used to say to myself 'If only this comes to an end, I will never grumble about anything again.'"

With the war clearly lost, the Germans finally retreated, and as British and Canadian troops marched into Arnhem, Audrey "ran out to welcome the soldiers, I inhaled their petrol fumes as if it were a priceless perfume and I demanded a cigarette, even though it made me choke." A lifelong addiction to British cigarettes was born, right alongside an association of freedom with the smell of petrol and cigarettes. At age sixteen, she now held an unshakeable appreciation for freedom and liberty, remarking in later years: "That's why I say freedom has no price."

The British troops had marched into Arnhem on Audrey's sixteenth birthday, May 4, 1945, with the end of the war in Europe coming four days later. The cessation of hostilities was followed by an event which would forever change the course of Audrey's life: the arrival of the United Nations Relief and Rehabilitation Administration (UNRRA), a forerunner of the United Nations International Children's Emergency Fund (UNICEF). Alongside the Red Cross, UNRRA brought desperately needed food, medication, and clothing. The clothes, in fact, marked the beginning of Audrey's love affair with fashion, born as it was in the school classroom set up as the village clothing distribution center. Choosing from the donated clothes seemed like couture shopping to Audrey, who had been reduced to wearing her brother's shoes and skirts made of old curtains. For the rest of her life, she remembered the exact clothes she had picked out: "a white blouse with a Peter Pan collar and a navy-blue pleated skirt. There was a Saks Fifth Avenue label in the blouse. Hence my love ever since of fine clothes."

At war's end, Audrey stood five feet, seven inches tall, weighed a skeletal ninety pounds, and suffered from anemia, asthma, and jaundice. Explained Luca: "One thing my mother always talked about was that when the war was over, she was diagnosed as being two weeks away from death herself because of her malnutrition." Eventually, she gained twenty pounds, but throughout her adult life, her weight never rose above 110 pounds.

She had survived the war, a wise-beyond-her-years teenager who already understood at the core of her psyche exactly what mattered most in a successful life: "I came out of the war thankful to be alive, aware that human relationships matter more than wealth or career or even food. I matured quickly because, at a young age, I was made very aware of suffering and terror." She also now possessed a bone-deep belief that she could survive any ordeal, that her own intelligence and common sense would allow her to deal with whatever life threw her way. If Hitler's war machine could not kill or defeat her, nothing would. In her own pragmatic, tough worldview: "I think when you have problems and so forth, you can sense a loneliness because it is you that has to get it done or make a decision. We all have an innate loneliness because finally when the chips are down you are alone." And yet, after these horrific experiences in the war, her steel core remained tempered by a sense of optimism that may have been battered but still proved resilient: "I've been often through hell, but I've always come out at the other end."

While Audrey was surviving the war in the Netherlands, her father Joseph had lived out the entire war in a Brixton, England, prison. Having been arrested in July 1940 under Defense Regulation 18 B as an associate of foreign fascists, he did not gain release until April 1945. Once freed, he moved to Ireland (which had declared neutrality during the war), residing there for the rest of his life. At war's end, Audrey made no immediate attempt to find her father, although she knew where he had relocated: "I didn't try to reach him. By then the war had been over for months and he had never tried to reach me, nor had I ever heard from him in the ten months between my leaving England and Holland's occupation. So, the feelings of reaction were very strong, and I thought he didn't want to see me anymore."

Having survived the Nazis, in the postwar summer of 1945, Audrey worked as a volunteer nurse's aide in the Royal Military Invalids Home for veterans, and together with Ella soon relocated to Amsterdam. By now, dance teacher Winja Marova had recommended Audrey to

Sonia Gaskell, the founder of the Netherlands Dutch National Ballet, and as she gained strength and weight, Audrey began lessons with Gaskell at the state-run dance school, Balletstudio 45. Lack of money remained an enormous problem, so to fund her lessons, Audrey began making high-fashion hats, selling them to the wealthy women Ella met while peddling cosmetics door to door. So short of cash was Audrey that she even began making her own ballet tights out of Ace bandages dyed in water filled with red crepe paper.

Gaskell's methods proved grueling, and she drilled Audrey and her fellow pupils for hours on end until the steps morphed into muscle memory. Recalled Audrey: "Sonia taught me that if you really worked hard, you'd succeed." That hard work, in Audrey's view, helped make up for a multitude of sins: "I've been constantly in situations in my life and career where I've had no technique, but if you just feel enough, you will get away with murder."

She was now also training under the relentless eye of the Russian ballet teacher Olga Tarassova. Ironically, it was life with the "terribly strict" Ella that had prepared Audrey for Tarassova's exacting instructions: "I would train for two or three hours at a time and even if I were purple in the face and covered with sweat, she would shout 'Stand up, van Heemstra—don't slouch!' That gave me strength."

Her fellow dancers were the first to notice Audrey's inherent dramatic ability. Anneke van Wijk observed that Audrey possessed a remarkable ability to project emotion with her hands and eyes while dancing, and Ida de Jong then gave Audrey a crucial push toward a new life, insisting that she move to England: "You'll have a lot more opportunities there, and you don't have to ask to come in, because you are half English."

The seed for a move to England had been planted, but while Audrey still lived in Holland, the need for money loomed ever larger. When her ballet class was visited by the Dutch film director Charles Van der Linden, it was Audrey, "the tall, thin girl with the eyes" who captured his attention. On the lookout for attractive young women to cast in his film *Nederlands in Zeven Lessen* (*Dutch in Seven Lessons,* also known as *Dutch at the Double* in the English-language version), he offered Audrey a job. Delighted by the salary—by any salary—she quickly accepted. Grateful as she was, however, Audrey's reaction was mixed with a caveat for director Van der Linden: "I am not an actress. You will regret it."

Her matter-of-fact assessment notwithstanding, Audrey took on the role of a stewardess, imaginatively named . . . "Audrey." So low was the budget that her screen test, for which Audrey had worn her best dress, hat, and gloves, was included in the final edit of the film. Shot at the Schiphol airport in Amsterdam, the negligible film featured eighteen-year-old Audrey sporting a stewardess cap perched on top of her long, wavy hair. She was called upon to do little but smile, and after the film premiered on May 7, 1948, she discovered that her minimal dialogue had been edited out of the English-language version: she had been onscreen for fewer than sixty seconds.

She happily collected a paycheck of fifty guilders and spent little time thinking about a career in film. None of it mattered to her in the slightest because just over the horizon, London and the glamorous world of ballet beckoned.

1950: Posing for *Picture Post* magazine in Kew Gardens, London. This press shot, intended for one of London's Sunday papers, was clearly taken before Audrey's discovery of French couture. PictureLux/Alamy Stock Photo

Chapter Four

LONDON, 1948

> "Arthur Rubenstein had a difficult early life. He had to decide whether to reject life or to love it. He decided to love it unconditionally—and I believe in that."
>
> —Audrey Hepburn

AFTER SUCCESSFULLY AUDITIONING IN 1948 for the London based Marie Rambert School of Ballet, nineteen-year-old Audrey arrived in England armed with an officially stamped letter from B. E. F. Gage, counsellor at the British Embassy in the Hague. Dated April 10, 1948, and addressed "To Whom It May Concern," the letter stated that "Miss Audrey Hepburn-Ruston is known to me as a British subject. She has been for some time a student of ballet dancing and is proceeding to the United Kingdom to study at the Rambert School of Ballet Dancing."

Audrey gratefully accepted Rambert's offer of a partial scholarship, which allowed her to receive free room and board for six months. Along with the room came a flatmate, Christina Brooks, who nearly seventy years later remembered Audrey vividly: "She desperately wanted to be a dancer. You could recognize her star quality right away. She had a beautiful smile. And when she started to dance, she made everyone want to dance with her."

A new life was beginning, and with it came a new name: Audrey Hepburn-Ruston would henceforth be known as Audrey Hepburn. She had a new name, little money, and no definite career prospects, but she was ecstatic to taste the freedom found in England: "The world was functioning again. Above all there was a wonderful quality of hope, born from relief and gratitude for those greatest of all luxuries—freedom and peace."

Audrey, however, lagged far behind the other students. Five years of near starvation had left her with a deficit in technique and too much ground to make up. At five feet, seven inches, she proved too tall to be paired with many of the male dancers; as Rambert explained, Audrey might be able to join the corps de ballet, but she would never graduate to the rank of prima ballerina.

The news proved a devastating blow, and in later years Audrey confessed to her son Sean that as she walked home after her talk with Rambert, she all at once realized that "her dream had died." She was crushed, but rather than wait around for any scraps the ballet world might toss her way, she reacted with a characteristic combination of sadness and practicality. She would look for and accept any sort of work that might come her way: "I might have to slave for years (in ballet) to achieve only limited success. I couldn't wait years. I needed money badly."

To supplement her income, Audrey began modeling for photographers, and in the process learned the first practical tools which would stand her in good stead onscreen: "bright colors overpower me and wash me out." Print ads started coming her way, the most prominent being a stint for photographer Angus McBean as the face of Lacto-Calamine powder, with the ads featuring the oddball tagline: "A powder base by day, a skin food by night."

By now, Ella had also moved to London, undertaking a wide assortment of jobs unthinkable in her prewar life. Work was the key, and if it meant jobs ranging from florist, cook, and beautician to manager of an apartment building and door to door saleswoman of cosmetics, then that's exactly what she would do. Grandson Sean gives all credit to Ella: "Ella was a single mom who after the war moved to London with no money, helped my mother get a scholarship at Marie Rambert and undertook any job possible to help make ends meet. If it meant washing stairs, then that is what she did." With Ella rushing from one job to another, and Audrey facing a life without ballet, a practical decision had to be reached: how could Audrey actually earn a living while still dancing?

An unexpected answer now popped up: Audrey Kathleen Hepburn would begin dancing in London's West End. As a musical comedy chorine.

Chorus girl in *Sauce Piquante*: "I was very ambitious and took every opportunity. I wanted to learn and I wanted to be seen." PA Images/Alamy Stock Photo

Chapter Five

CHORUS GIRL, 1948–1949

"I tried always to do better: saw always a little further. I tried to stretch myself."
—Audrey Hepburn

AUDREY HEPBURN, WHOSE ETHEREAL AIR could not have been more different from that of the standard jaded West End dancer, seemed an unlikely candidate for an eight-times-a-week, sell-it-to-the-last-row job as a chorus girl, but in December of 1948 she landed a job in the London production of the Broadway musical hit *High Button Shoes*. Had Audrey's dancing instantly wowed the director and choreographer? Not in the least. But her personality, that aristocratic but approachable persona, had successfully carried the day. Wrote co-producer Jack Hylton on her audition card: "Lousy dancer. Great verve." The job was hers.

She had one line, the immortal "Have they all gone?" Well, it was a start—and for now, she was delighted to be in a show, embracing the camaraderie of dancing in a bright, splashy musical comedy: "I loved being in a musical show. For the first time, I felt the pure joy of living."

Cecil Landau, a producer of musical revues, saw Audrey in *High Button Shoes* and noticed her at once. Far from being the anonymous second chorus girl from the left, she registered with surprising impact: "I saw a girl come running across the stage. I remember two black eyes and a fringe. I got very excited." He quickly cast her in the 1949 revue *Sauce Tartare*, where she would be one of five dancing girls and participate in the show's series of satirical sketches. If the material was not exactly worthy of Chekhov—in one she played a "Boogie Woogie Yoga Follower"—Landau nonetheless provided encouragement and cast her again in the next year's follow up revue, *Sauce Piquante*, where the quality of both her roles and salary increased: from boogie woogie yoga follower to Dresden shepherdess, and from ten pounds weekly to fifteen.

It was during *Sauce Piquante* that for the first and last time ever, Audrey allowed herself to be talked into a slight adjustment of her natural look. Press agent Frederic Mullally had set up a photo shoot featuring the then de rigueur glamour shots at his offices in Mayfair. Told that these would be pin-up pictures, and that she should arrive in shorts and a low-necked sweater, Audrey arrived with shorts—and a high-necked sweater. Mullally's partner Suzanne Warner took one look and blanched. In her own words: "The trouble was that the sweater was certainly doing nothing for Audrey—and Audrey was doing as near as nothing to the sweater!" Pulling Audrey aside, Suzanne suggested that she employ falsies to build up her bosom. Audrey refused. Mullally and Warner pleaded, and the young Audrey at last agreed—very reluctantly. The ensuing photos of Audrey sporting an adjusted appearance were published in the London Sunday newspapers. Wrote Audrey's biographer Ian Woodward: "A copy of the picture went into Mullally's office files, with the caption: 'Audrey Hepburn—and friends.'" The youngster had capitulated this one time, but in the future, no matter the pressure or the budget, she would never again change her appearance.

She was, however, determined to improve herself, and she signed up to take acting classes with Betty and Philip Buchell, as well as elocution lessons with actor Felix Aylmer (Polonius to Laurence Olivier's Hamlet). It was Aylmer who provided Audrey with a lesson that would serve her well, not just onstage but also in her still nascent film career: the value of stillness. Let the audience come to you.

Her ambition was palpable, as was her work ethic, and while performing in *High Button Shoes*, taking ballet classes, and studying with both Aylmer and the Buchells, she was also performing in *Sauce Tartare* and an additional show entitled *Christmas Party*. Arriving home in the early hours of the morning, Audrey would eat, sleep, and step right back into rehearsal at 10 a.m.: "I was very ambitious and took every opportunity. I wanted to learn and I wanted to be seen."

If, in future years, acting never brought her the all-encompassing joy that dancing did, Audrey's practical bent overrode all; as late as the 1980s, when asked in a television interview if she was disappointed by her failure to make a career of ballet, she answered: "Deep down, ballet was my dream. I still get a lump in my throat from watching dance—I'm terribly moved. But I can't say today how disappointed I am because I've had such good fortune—been given so much."

In son Sean's view: "Acting was in effect a default choice because she had to work. As she gained great success, she remained very thankful to be self-supporting; she was, for parts of my childhood, a single mother who raised me and earned her own way. At that time, in certain countries women couldn't even wear pants or open a bank account without their husbands, but by choosing a career as an actor she forged her own path." Several years after her initial success in *Roman Holiday*, Audrey herself bluntly observed: "Only the absolutely determined people succeed." In the words of her soon-to-be-director William Wyler: "She struck me as being very alert, very smart, very talented, very ambitious."

Actor and aspiring director Richard Attenborough saw her in one of the *Sauce* revues and later said, "Everybody knew there was something totally remarkable about her and that sooner or later, she was going to become a major, major, movie star." If this statement rings of after-the-fact hyperbole, it nonetheless confirmed what everyone already felt: Audrey Hepburn was an original. But an original what?

1951's *Laughter in Paradise*. After foolishly turning down the lead, Audrey ended up with a cameo and one less-than-immortal line: "Who wants a ciggy?" World History Archive/Alamy Stock Photo

Chapter Six

A STAR IS (NOT QUITE YET) BORN, 1950–1951

"Even in her early films, her height, her skinniness and her wistfulness combined to get her noticed."

— "Audrey Hepburn: An Iconic Problem," *The Guardian*

AUDREY'S FOCUS MAY HAVE REMAINED on dance and theatre, but with her driving ambition, she certainly did not rule out future film appearances, so when the opportunity to audition came about, her attitude was one of why not? Which is how, in the summer of 1950, she came to audition for the role of Lygia in the MGM big budget epic *Quo Vadis*. Director Mervyn LeRoy thought her test terrific; the powers at MGM did not.

A screen test for *Lady Godiva Rides Again* went nowhere. She tested for the forgettable *Valley of the Eagles* and struck out once again, yet just as happened with Mervyn LeRoy, *Eagles* director Terence Young fell for Audrey, pronouncing her "utterly enchanting." In later years he explained: "I thought she was going to make it, and I hoped one day she would remember me, and get me to direct." Seventeen years hence, Young's wish would be granted—twice.

It was at the time of these unsuccessful screen tests that John McCallum and his wife, actress Googie Withers, stopped by Ciro's, where Audrey was performing in the short-lived revue *Summer Night*. Instantly struck by Audrey's charisma, they recommended her to casting director Robert Lennard at Associated British Pictures Corporation (ABC). The highly regarded Lennard, who cast films for both John Huston and Fred Zinnemann, had seen and liked Audrey in *Sauce Piquante*, and with the guidance of her recently acquired agent Jack Dunfee, Audrey now signed a three-picture contract. She would be paid 500 pounds for a first film, before jumping to 1,500 pounds for the remaining films.

Audrey was off and running, but unfortunately right into films of dubious quality. In addition to an August television appearance in "The Silent Village" on *BBC Night Theatre*, there were four very brief appearances in 1951 alone. She was first loaned out for the forgettable *One Wild Oat,* a movie which occupied her for exactly three days and resulted in a twenty-second appearance as a hotel receptionist exclaiming: "Good afternoon, this is the Regency Hotel." (Thirteen years later, she was to be reunited with the star of *One Wild Oat*, Stanley Holloway, on the infinitely more rewarding *My Fair Lady*.)

Even with this blink-and-you'll-miss-her appearance, casting director Lennard was taken with the twenty-two-year-old Audrey and brought Italian film director Mario Zampi to see her at Ciro's. So impressed was Zampi that he offered her the lead role in his new movie *Laughter in Paradise.* It was an unexpected and impressive offer for a newcomer, but the newly in love Audrey wanted to pursue a possible tour with her then boyfriend Marcel LeBon, and declined the role, writing Zampi: "I'm sorry. I've just signed to do a short tour in a show. I can't break the contract. It wouldn't be fair." Due to a lack of financing, the tour bookings with LeBon then fell through, and, upset that she had turned down a film to accommodate his plans, Audrey began to argue with LeBon. In the words of Warren Harris: "A battle royal ensued, ending with the hot-blooded Frenchman severing the relationship by signing up for a nitery revue being sent to the United States and Canada." A chastened Audrey returned to Zampi in hopes that his offer still stood. It did not, the part having been given to Beatrice Campbell. Offered a bit part instead—Zampi barked, "You start and finish on the same day"—she immediately said yes. Playing a cigarette girl who is glimpsed wearing a white apron over a short dress, she addresses ladies' man Guy Middleton with a saucy: "Hello! Who wants a ciggy?" That one line was followed shortly thereafter by, "Don't I count as a woman?" End of appearance.

Her third film of 1951, *Young Wives Tale* proved flimsy in the extreme, with Audrey playing a single woman working as a typist while living in an extremely crowded boardinghouse. This time she appeared in seven scenes, but the scenes and the film itself are of negligible import, landing with little or no impact. The movie may actually be most noteworthy as the one film in which Audrey quarreled with her director, in this instance, Henry Cass. Audrey, for reasons unknown to everyone but Cass, was the object of his constant criticism, and she later admitted: "He had it in for me. It was the only unhappy experience I ever had making a picture." In what would prove to be a typically generous and self-deprecating analysis, Audrey refused to assign blame to Cass, adding, "I was probably dreadful in it!"

Onward.

Lavender Hill Mob with Alec Guinness. Audrey had only one line, but, said Guinness: "Her faunlike beauty and presence were remarkable." Universal Pictures/Photofest © Universal Pictures

Chapter Seven

A SINGLE LINE AND ALEC GUINNESS, 1951–1952

"We all have our blind spots . . . I paid no particular attention to her."

Sir Michael Balcon, chair of Ealing Studios

ONE MONTH AFTER *YOUNG WIVES TALES* was released, Audrey appeared briefly in Ealing Studio's *Lavender Hill Mob*, an amusing tale about a shipping clerk who devises a plan for stealing one million pounds in gold from the Bank of England. The film proved a big hit, winning an Academy Award for T. E. B. Clarke's screenplay and a nod as the "Best British Film" of the year from the British Film Academy.

Audrey had exactly two lines as "Chiquita," but she made them count. Greeting star Alec Guinness at the airport after he gives her a goodbye present of cash to "get yourself a little birthday present," Chiquita delightedly responds "Oh, but how sweet of you! Thank you." That may have been the end of Audrey's screen time, but even while Guinness proved rather unimpressed by her acting ability, he was captivated by her star personality: "She only had half a line to say, and I don't think she said it in any particular or interesting way. But her fawnlike beauty and presence were remarkable."

Not that everyone else immediately saw Audrey's potential. It wasn't just Ealing Studios chairman Sir Michael Balcon who saw little promise in the newcomer; screenwriter Tibby Clarke claimed that Audrey "struck nobody as star material." But Balcon and Clarke aside, even in these miniscule parts, Audrey Hepburn did in fact register, and for one crucial reason common to all movie stars: the camera loved her. The cheekbones, the soulful eyes, and the vivid intelligence all registered with remarkable impact.

In Audrey's own assessment, the six movies she made between 1950 and 1951 "made a total of one quick appearance," but she had impressed Alec Guinness to such an extent that he personally recommended her to Hollywood power Mervyn LeRoy, who later recalled: "I never remember Guinness recommending anyone else to me, before or since. He even said he didn't think she could act, but that she was beautiful, so delicate, it didn't matter. Those are interesting words coming from a consummate actor! . . . I wanted to see this amazing creature myself." Raved Peter Ustinov, "With the perfect bone structure of her face, she seemed to possess the secret of a youth verging on the eternal, and yet the poise of maturity was already with her from a very early age." Flowery, yes—but also true.

And then, in November 1950, Audrey was tested by Thorold Dickinson for her first substantial role, that of "Nora Brentano," in Ealing Studio's *The Secret People*. If cast, Audrey would be playing not only the second female lead in the movie, but also a role she could slip into with great ease—that of a ballet student. The female lead in the film, political exile "Maria Brent," was to be played by the estimable Valentina Cortese, who proved to be an early ally of Audrey's. Cortese had looked at the tests of the four girls vying for the role of Nora and was instantly struck by the unknown-to-her Audrey: "a beautiful little thing, like a little deer, with this long neck and those big eyes." Won over by Audrey's modesty (she naively asked Valentina off camera—"Do you think I have a chance?"), Cortese quickly advised the newcomer to take off her shoes so that she wouldn't appear too tall on camera. The part was hers.

Filmed in 1951 and released in 1952, *The Secret People* centered around an assassination in a European country and gave Audrey a chance to dance onscreen. Her dancing is solid, although it's interesting to note that while her dancing in the classroom scenes is on full point, in the film's actual ballet sequences, she only dances on half-point. Perhaps the years of dancing in West End shows and revues had left her less than confident in her ballet technique, and Sidney Cole, the film's producer, later theorized that "the ballet scenes were a great strain for her—far greater a challenge, in a way, than the scenes calling for acting and spoken dialogue."

Her hard-to-place accent, replete with hints of English, French, and Dutch, intrigues, but also makes it seem highly unlikely that she was raised in the same family as her Italian-accented "sister" Cortese. She does, however, make the most of her close-ups, the first proof positive of her ability to project complex emotions on camera. Accents and the heavy-handed plot aside, Audrey is, for the first time, noticeable onscreen, and even in this relatively small part, she snagged above the title billing. Said critic Pauline Kael in later years: "With the young Audrey Hepburn in a sizable role, it's rather like seeing Cinderella before the transformation."

She was gaining in confidence and learning the intricacies of script construction. The film had reunited her with fellow revue performer Bob Monkhouse, who was now spending his spare time on set banging out multiple scripts for three radio shows. In a telling and humorous anecdote, while Monkhouse worked on a routine about his very poor childhood, Audrey observed him struggling for the right jokes, and finally suggested a "poverty" joke of her own: Monkhouse's family was so poor that they didn't have cheese to put in their mousetrap, and instead had to draw a picture of cheese to put in the trap. Monkhouse liked the gag but explained it wasn't a full joke, at which point Audrey instantly supplied the capper: "All right . . . you could then say that you then caught a picture of a mouse." Setup, joke, and payoff: she was beginning to understand all of it.

Serious at heart, she still found humor in everyday situations; Alfred Shaughnessy, who went on to become the principal writer on television's *Upstairs, Downstairs*, was trying to convince Audrey to play the part of "Petronilla" in his new script entitled *Brandy for the Parson*. Visiting Audrey on the set of *Secret People*, he gave her his script, which she returned the very next day, explaining with a smile that she liked the script but "couldn't play Scene 42. The censor wouldn't allow it." Puzzled by Audrey's reaction to what he felt was a very wholesome script, he raced to scene 42, which read:

Scene 42. Int. Cabin of Yacht. Day (Studio)
Petronilla is awake, dressed in Bill's pyjamas. She is peeing out of the porthole.

Laughed Shaughnessy: "The ladies in the script-typing pool had omitted the letter 'r,' either by accident or design."

Audrey, in fact, was interested in the role of Petronilla, but the film was to shoot at the same time as *Monte Carlo Baby*, to which she had already committed.

While *Secret People* was to prove an important steppingstone in Audrey's film career, perhaps its greatest impact on her life came from her interaction with stars Serge Reggiani and Valentina Cortese. From Reggiani she learned the value of not discussing one's personal life with the press; after stardom came her way, she proved unfailingly polite with journalists but would firmly, albeit with a smile, change the subject when it came to in-depth probing of personal matters. At the same time, from Valentina she learned the value of taking a cautious, distanced approach when dealing with Hollywood. Regarding the hothouse atmosphere of that one industry town, Cortese advised: "Think hard before you sign a long-term contract. Liberty is the most wonderful thing of all."

Cortese's advice ultimately changed the trajectory of Audrey's personal and professional lives, but after completing *The Secret People*, Audrey's focus remained upon her contractual obligation to shoot *Monte Carlo Baby* (also known as *Baby Beats the Band*). Audrey knew the script was mere fluff and once again asked Valentina Cortese for advice. Should she actually make the film? Recalled Cortese: "I said, 'If the cast is No. 1, if the director is No. 1, even if the part is not No. 1—do it. Maybe something else comes out of it.'"

Audrey had doubts, but, she rationalized, the film meant a trip to Monte Carlo with her mother, as well as the chance to keep a Dior dress she was scheduled to wear in the film. With her fluent command of French, Audrey was also the only cast member scheduled to appear in both the French- (*Nous Irons a Monte Carlo*) and English-language versions of the film. As it turned out, when the film was released in 1954 after *Roman Holiday* had established her as a star of the first rank, Oscar Godbout of the *New York Times* wrote: "She made this one before she became a [movie star] in reality. It is rather astonishing how she stands out in that seared desert of mediocrity. Miss Hepburn saves *Monte Carlo Baby* from being completely worthless."

Monte Carlo Baby may have registered as a by the numbers low budget programmer, but it was to prove a decisive turning point in Audrey's life when the location shoot brought her into the direct gaze of novelist and flinty-eyed observer Sidonie-Gabrielle Colette. Colette's "discovery" of Audrey soon became legendary, but whichever version of the legend is actually true, one fact remains: the events in question played out in such a wildly improbable who-could-make-this-up fashion that it made *A Star Is Born* look like cinema verité.

Audrey's first Broadway show, *Gigi*, in 1951. Shown here wearing a demure peignoir, Audrey garnered a Tony Award nomination and declared: "Oh dear—and I still have to learn how to act!." Photofest

Chapter Eight

DISCOVERY BY COLETTE, 1951–1952

"With no actress cast, Colette became a 'compulsive Gigi spotter' across France and often shouted, 'There! She's the one! She's my Gigi!'"

—Robert Matzen

WHEN VALENTINA CORTESE URGED AUDREY to occasionally accept lesser roles because "maybe something else comes out of it," she was, in fact, speaking of *Monte Carlo Baby*, an eminently forgettable film if ever there was one. But even the worldly Cortese could never have predicted that while shooting this trifle in Monte Carlo, Audrey would fall under the scrutiny of Colette, who was focused on finding just the right young woman to star in the stage adaptation of her most famous novel, *Gigi*.

Gigi, first published in 1944, had in fact already been turned into a 1948 French film starring Daniele Delorme. The blockbuster Academy Award–winning MGM musical film of the same title was to arrive in 1958, but in 1951, Colette was focused upon finding a theater actress to bring her creation to life. Who had the skill and personal charisma to help audiences accept a story centering around a charming young adolescent who is being groomed for the life of a courtesan? Given the iffy nature of the material, it was, to be certain, a tall order.

With Colette's approval, producer Gilbert Miller had enlisted Anita Loos of *Gentlemen Prefer Blondes* fame to script the adaptation, and top Hollywood director George Cukor had even agreed to return to his theatrical roots and direct. It was, however, Colette herself who held veto power over cast and script, and as the start of rehearsals loomed, no actress Colette deemed acceptable had been glimpsed, let alone signed.

It was at just this juncture that the author, who was staying at the marble and gold-mirrored Hotel de Paris as the guest of Prince Rainier, observed a pretty young girl with rather sparkling eyes and a dazzling smile dancing around a group of musicians during a break in the filming of *Nous Irons a Monte Carlo*. The battle-toughened Colette was instantaneously charmed, later recalling her reaction as a startled "Voila! There is my Gigi! This unknown young woman was my own thoroughly French Gigi come alive!" Never mind that Colette had felt the same way about numerous other Gigis that she had spotted in her travels—this young girl held her interest.

Beckoning Audrey over to her wheelchair, Colette conversed in French with the fluent youngster, firing off a series of questions: "What is your name?" "Are you a part of this movie?" "Are you the star of the movie?" Audrey, shy yet amused at the thought of being considered the possible star of the movie, responded with a smiling "Non, Madame." With Audrey called back to the set, a by now thoroughly charmed Colette dispatched her husband Maurice Goudeket to send a telegram to Gilbert Miller: "Do Not Cast Your Gigi Until You Read My Letter."

The letter in question proved to be a missive detailing what were, in Colette's mind, Audrey's rather extraordinary charms: "This would be a very good Gigi . . . I believe she has had little experience on the stage, but she is very pretty and has that piquant quality necessary for the part." "Piquant" was the first of the many adjectives, nouns, and adverbs writers were to willingly employ in an attempt to describe Audrey's unique charms: doe-eyed, elfin, will-o'-the-wisp, ethereal—all of these were to come, but for now Colette pronounced herself charmed—and Audrey piquant.

It all makes for a terrific story, but was this really how Audrey was discovered? If everyone who claimed to have been present when Colette first laid eyes on Audrey had actually been in Monte Carlo, the Hotel de Paris would have been bursting at the seams. It was, in the end, Audrey herself who best relayed the tale, recounting the events with characteristic understatement. In Audrey's recall, there was no dramatic scene of Colette shouting "Voila—Here is my Gigi," but instead, a straightforward acknowledgment that "Colette was very ill with arthritis or rheumatism and was in a wheelchair, in a corner of the hall. I was standing in the lobby and Colette said to her husband, 'Maybe this is the girl that's right.'" The novelist considered her a possibility. A definite maybe.

Did Audrey leap at the opportunity, assuring Colette that she wouldn't regret her choice? Not a bit. Instead, she asked Colette how she, Audrey, could possibly perform in a play when she had never created a dramatic role in the theatre. As to the mere idea of Colette suggesting it, why "what a crazy thing to say . . ." Colette was undeterred, telling the youngster: "You're a dancer. You know how to work hard." Yes, Audrey admitted, she was a dancer, and yes, as Madame could hear, she was fluent in French. Plusses to be sure, but what intrigued Colette even more was Audrey's very evident sangfroid and continental flair, qualities in short supply with the young American women who had been considered for the role.

Audrey remained uncertain. Turning to fellow *Monte Carlo Baby* cast member Marcel Dalio for advice, she was told: "Follow your instincts. If it feels right, it will *be* right." With Colette continuing to express interest, Audrey, sensing that the author was not just curious but actually engaged, demurred no longer: if Madame believed in her, then she would certainly do her best.

Did Audrey have doubts about the material itself? The plot and very themes did present underlying problems, but such were the times that material which strikes modern audiences as smarmy in the extreme was, in 1951, considered charmingly adult and naughty. In the words of Anita Loos: "It's a Cinderella story told in terms of sex. The play loses everything unless the actress looks like an absolute child. Yet she has to have the kind of charm that would make a worldly man fall in love with a sixteen-year-old girl." One generation's charming roue, another generation's criminal . . .

But for now, Audrey had to complete her roles in both *Nous Irons a Monte Carlo* and *Monte Carlo Baby*. Playing a movie star chasing after her missing baby in a series of comedic set pieces did not exactly plum unexpected depths in Audrey's acting, but the twelve-minute role had brought her to Monte Carlo, and, she rationalized, who knew what might happen with *Gigi*.

At the conclusion of filming, she returned to London and was immediately contacted by *Gigi*'s producer, Gilbert Miller. A deal was struck. Thirteen years later, Audrey would be paid $1 million to star in the film version of *My Fair Lady,* but for now she would play eight performances of *Gigi* each week for a salary of $500. And oh yes, she would have to pay for all of her own living accommodations in New York City.

Paying for her own housing wouldn't stop her, but what might do so were her ever-growing self-doubts. Had she made a terrible mistake by saying yes? Could she really handle the role? What if Colette thought her story was ruined because of Audrey? The doubts plaguing Audrey would continue throughout her career, but neither Colette nor her husband harbored any such reservations, with Goudeket forthrightly stating: "She is greatly thought of by film people generally and considered a future star of the first magnitude."

Audrey arrived in New York in October of 1951 for the start of rehearsals, and for the first and last time in her adult life, appeared to be overweight. Having feasted on the luxurious and plentiful meals on the transatlantic crossing, Audrey's appearance shocked Gilbert Miller and his general manager Morton Gottlieb. Was this rather sturdy young woman appearing in front of them the youngster they had been informed was downright sylph-like? Taking matters in hand, Gottlieb immediately placed Audrey on a diet, whereupon she lost the weight and never gained it back.

The real problems, however, began at the start of rehearsals, with the inexperienced Audrey floundering badly. She could not be heard beyond the first three rows of the orchestra, had only a rudimentary understanding of appropriate onstage body language, and had trouble memorizing her rather lengthy part. It was stage veteran Cathleen Nesbitt, playing Gigi's "Aunt Alicia," who took Audrey under her wing and saved her. Said Nesbitt, who in later years gained nationwide fame on television's *The Farmer's Daughter*: "Audrey didn't have much idea of phrasing, and even less of how to project. But she had that rare thing—audience authority—that makes everybody look at you."

By now, the delays in production had caused the in-demand George Cukor to depart, and he had been replaced by the Belgian Raymond Rouleau. Rouleau was not impressed by Audrey, indeed often despairing of her sketchy theatrical skills, and the rehearsal process was further complicated by the fact that Rouleau's shaky command of English made it virtually impossible for him to direct the cast. A solution was jerry-rigged: because everyone in the cast spoke French, Anita Loos translated her play into French for Rouleau. He then directed in French, and the cast spoke their lines in French, while simultaneously trying to translate words and actions into English for the upcoming Broadway audiences.

To help Audrey find her bearing onstage, Rouleau began coaching her in how to move about the stage, hoping that her liquid grace and natural charm would, as Loos herself stated, "blind the audience to her deficiencies." Continued Loos: "He staged the play practically like a ballet." Rouleau was not shy about accepting credit for the end result, and after his death, his widow wrote Charles Higham to relay Rouleau's statement that "the actors all followed me so completely that if I had asked them to throw themselves in the Hudson they would happily had done so."

Problems and all, Audrey already thoroughly understood the importance of her look onstage, and she layered her performance through use of the period clothes as well as the styled fall of her shoulder-length hair. Looking the part helped her feel the part: "Once you're in a three-quarter-length dress, with a rustling petticoat underneath and with high button shoes on your feet, you feel something. You walk differently, sit differently . . . I truly felt like sixteen, so I was halfway there."

Audrey may have been frightened, but she was also exhilarated and unquestionably self-aware. Her publicity photos for *Gigi* were to be taken by Richard Avedon himself, and while their paths were to cross again on more equal terms six years later on *Funny Face*, for now the neophyte recognized the value in listening to the master. In a lesson that was to stay with Audrey throughout her extraordinary run as a magazine cover girl, it was Avedon who was the first to suggest she try to pose in three-quarter profile, her head angled "so that her high cheekbones slimmed the lower part of her face." Audrey complied, and just as they usually did, Avedon's photos caused an immediate stir. The twenty-one-year-old Broadway newcomer may have been both unknown and untested, but she was already proving herself a master at self-presentation.

As *Gigi* underwent a grueling out-of-town tryout in Philadelphia, producer Gilbert Miller remained so dismayed by Audrey's performance that he contemplated firing her, refraining from doing so only because there was no one to replace her on such short notice. Rehearsing endlessly, Audrey slowly gained in confidence, her projection and command of the stage improving with each performance, and by the time the play opened at New York City's Fulton Theatre on November 24, 1951, she had gained enormously in onstage authority.

While the critics may have been very mixed as to the quality of the play itself, their praise for Audrey proved fulsome: Enthused Richard Watts Jr.: "The delightful Miss Hepburn obviously is not an experienced actress. But her quality is so winning and so right that she is the success of the evening. . . . Miss Hepburn is as fresh and frisky as a puppy out of a tub." The highly esteemed Elliot Norton, writing in the *Boston Post*, trumpeted: "She was at ease on the stage as though she had been born to it," and her personal triumph was sealed by the all-important *New York Times* who called her "a young actress of charm, honesty and talent."

In addition to winning a 1952 Theatre World Award, Audrey was nominated for a Tony Award as Best Actress in a Play alongside three genuine legends: Helen Hayes for *Mrs. McThing*, Jessica Tandy in *The Fourposter*, and Julie Harris (the winner) for *I Am a Camera* (Harris, in fact, had once been mentioned to play Gigi). So rapturous were the notices that with the agreement of Cathleen Nesbitt, only one week after the play opened, Audrey's name was placed in lights above the title. A marquee reading "GIGI with Audrey Hepburn" had quickly become "AUDREY HEPBURN in GIGI." Said Audrey: "Oh, dear, and I still have to learn how to act."

This was not a bit of well-timed self-deprecating humor aimed at scoring favor but rather the manifestation of a deeply ingrained self-doubt. She continued to take dance classes, and in her own candid self-assessment: "I'm halfway between a dancer and an actress. I've got to learn." As her career gathered force and the adulation began, far from reveling in the attention coming her way, she plaintively commented: "All I feel is a responsibility to live up to success."

Audiences raved as much as critics, but not everyone was impressed, and Audrey came in for the same sort of sniping from Noël Coward as had better-known actors. In a typical diary entry, he noted of *Gigi*: "An orgy of overacting and a vulgar script . . . Audrey Hepburn inexperienced and rather too noisy, and the whole thing badly directed." Coward, however, represented a decided minority, and the show quickly assumed sellout status. Colette pronounced herself thrilled, inscribing a photo to Audrey: "To Audrey Hepburn, the treasure I found on the beach."

It was all heady stuff, but having been brought up in the Ella van Heemstra school of "Don't talk about yourself—you're no better than anyone else," Audrey's feet remained planted firmly on the ground. Asked about her newly found fame, Audrey replied: "I thought being the 'Toast of Broadway' might mean people standing up and raising champagne glasses. But no one has ever done that. I thought it might mean sailing into restaurants when they were full and getting a table with just a smile at the head waiter. But Jimmy didn't risk it—he booked in advance."

Gigi seemed set for a long and lucrative run, yet producer Miller was asked if he would close the show by May 31, 1952. Why? Because Paramount Pictures wanted Audrey Hepburn to star in its upcoming William Wyler–directed production of *Roman Holiday*. Miller agreed—on two conditions: (1) He was to be compensated handsomely, the agreed-upon figure being $50,000 ($550,000 in today's money) and (2) Shooting of *Roman Holiday* had to finish by the end of September 1952, in order for Audrey to star in a national tour of *Gigi*. With Miller's demands satisfied, Paramount now announced that Broadway's newest star would play the lead in William Wyler's *Roman Holiday*.

Suddenly the unknown, self-described "inexperienced and untutored" actress was one of the hottest commodities in show business. And "commodity" was the word: Audrey had rehearsed and opened in *Gigi*, and at that same time made a striking appearance on the television show *We the People*. She also found time on February 10, 1952, to perform a scene from *Nine Days a Queen* with Rex Harrison on Ed Sullivan's television show *Toast of the Town*, followed by both the April CBS telecast of "Rainy Day in Paradise Junction" and the Betty Crocker Star Matinee episode "The Stove Won't Light." She topped off her run by rushing to Europe to film *Roman Holiday*, starred in a whirlwind national tour of *Gigi*—and exhausted herself into a severely needed rest cure.

That, however, is getting ahead of the story, and in 1952, one giant obstacle remained in Audrey's path on her lightning-fast rush to international stardom. How could an actress with just one Broadway credit and a handful of glorified screen cameos land the leading role in a high-profile Paramount Pictures production to be directed by the notoriously demanding William Wyler?

The answer: With a little luck, a lot of talent, and an exquisite sense of timing.

ACT TWO

WHAT PRICE HOLLYWOOD

1953: *Roman Holiday* and an Academy Award in her very first starring role. Audrey and veteran Oscar-winning designer Edith Head mutually decided on thick belts, no sleeveless blouses, and the use of scarves to accessorize. Always polite, Audrey stood up to the battle-hardened Head, who grudgingly admitted: "Audrey knows more about fashion than any actress save Dietrich." Paramount Pictures/Photofest © Paramount Pictures

Chapter Nine

ROMAN HOLIDAY, 1951–1953

"I was born with something that appealed to audiences at that particular time. It has never ceased to puzzle and dazzle me, in a way, that this happened."

—Audrey Hepburn

ROMAN HOLIDAY BEGAN LIFE AS the rare film whose star—in this case, screenwriter Dalton Trumbo—could not be acknowledged. A go-to screenwriter with credits ranging from soap opera (the Oscar-winning *Kitty Foyle* 1940) to the taut and nasty *Gun Crazy* (1950), Trumbo was the rarest of creatures in Hollywood—the screenwriter as star. He was also, in the early 1950s, a man being investigated by the House Un-American Activities Committee (HUAC) for his supposed Communist leanings; with an all-but-certain jail term awaiting him, he needed to write a blatantly commercial film to support his family while he was away. Inspired by the headline-generating romance of Britain's Princess Margaret and Peter Townsend, he set to work.

Aware that his name was politically radioactive, Trumbo requested that his story of an overly protected youthful princess who yearns for a life of freedom be submitted to Paramount under the name of his friend, screenwriter Ian McLellan Hunter. When Paramount subsequently bought the property for the film's original director, Frank Capra, Hunter then gave Trumbo the $50,000 fee paid by Paramount. Capra, however, proved ill at ease with Hunter's and Trumbo's politics, and after squabbling with Paramount over the $1.5 million budget, soon departed the film. Gone with him was his idea of co-starring Cary Grant alongside Elizabeth Taylor.

It was only then that the name of two-time Academy Award–winning director William Wyler came to the fore. Eager to make a comedy after fifteen years spent directing dramatic fare ranging from *The Little Foxes* (1941) to *The Heiress* (1949), Wyler sensed that there was a postwar audience hungry for the film's charming reverse fairy tale of a story—that of a princess escaping royal duties so that she can spend a day in Rome frolicking like an everyday tourist. Once Wyler was hired, Hunter, who had written his own screenplay from Trumbo's story, left the film, while Wyler, disappointed with a script submitted by Ben Hecht, next hired the British writer John Dighton to undertake additional revisions.

Given Wyler's participation, Paramount Pictures remained high on *Roman Holiday*, particularly if dependable, handsome box office draw Gregory Peck signed on as the male lead.

In future years, Wyler relayed that Peck first turned down the role, complaining that Princess Ann's was the best part. Said Wyler: "You surprise me. If you said the picture wasn't good, okay. But because somebody else's part is a little better than yours, that's no reason. I didn't think you were that kind of actor." Peck's own recall proved to be utterly at odds with Wyler's: "I have no recollection of hesitating at all. The idea of going to Rome and making a romantic comedy after some of the heavier stuff I'd been doing appealed to me immensely. Even more than that, I liked the idea of working with Willy . . . His sensitivity and artistry were recognized. You don't hesitate—at least I didn't."

What was needed to make the fairy tale believable, Wyler thought, was an actress "without an American accent—someone you could believe was brought up as a princess"—a young woman capable of projecting a believably aristocratic air while remaining warmly approachable. Someone European. To the manner born, yet down to earth. An unknown who could pull off royal behavior as easily as Roman hijinks and move easily between drama, comedy, and a heartfelt unrequited romance. A tall order.

Wyler's first choice to play the princess, the very British Jean Simmons, proved unavailable when Howard Hughes, who owned the actress's contract, refused to release her. At this point Richard Mealand, Paramount's London production chief, wrote studio headquarters in Hollywood: "I have another candidate for *Roman Holiday*—Audrey Hepburn. I was struck by her playing of a bit-part in *Laughter in Paradise*."

When Audrey returned to London for a two-week vacation after the conclusion of filming *Monte Carlo Baby*, Wyler, in her words, "met with me for a few minutes to check me out." However, not wanting to remain in London to test the five young women being considered for the role of Princess Ann, he assigned the screen tests to another director. Which is where fortune smiled upon Audrey Hepburn, because William Wyler asked Thorold Dickinson to direct Audrey's test, the same Thorold Dickinson who had directed Audrey in *Secret People*, and with whom she had developed a warm friendship.

A test was set for September 18, 1951, at Pinewood Studios, London. Dickinson began the test with a shot of Audrey, her back to the camera, slowly turning around to face forward. She read scenes from the script but seemed to score most strongly with an improvised wink. In later years Dickinson stated of the wink: "The minute you saw it, you knew she would get the part."

A second scheduled scene required Princess Ann to test the mattress of her bed, but Dickinson kept the camera rolling past his cry of "Cut!" and unaware that the camera was still running, Audrey giggled and exclaimed: "Oh, is it over now? Oh, good." Dickinson was so charmed by the moment that he included it in the final test reel he sent to Wyler and Paramount executives. In Wyler's slightly different retelling of this pivotal moment, Audrey exclaimed: "How was it? Was I any good?" and when she realized that the camera was still running, her spontaneous, laughing reaction to the deception was also captured.

While Audrey's very accent spoke of European, not American lineage, no one could quite define the origins of that accent, a puzzle which only added to her allure. Her perfect enunciation seemed to contain more than a hint of upper-crust British, a bit of continental savoir faire, and yes, perhaps just a touch of American-ese. The very timbre of the voice only added to her appeal: low, inviting, occasionally confidential, and capable of climbing up the scale in moments of great emotion. She clearly wasn't American, yet never exuded a whiff of European snobbery. It was as if all countries wanted to claim her—and none could.

As it turned out, Dickinson's biggest concern was fulfilling Paramount's request that he film Audrey talking about herself; while Audrey changed back into her own clothes, he loaded the camera with a thousand feet of film, and when she returned, under gentle prodding, she began talking about her life under the horrors of Nazi occupation. In Audrey's words: "Talking to Thorold, I forgot about the camera."

In later years, Audrey herself downplayed this conversation, claiming: "I was so green I didn't really know what to do, and I think Thorold got a little desperate." Legend has it that when viewing the test footage in Rome, grizzled veteran Wyler was immediately smitten: "Acting, looks, and personality! She was absolutely enchanting, and we said, 'That's the girl!'" In reality, however, Wyler's wife Talli related that while the director was "very intrigued" by Audrey, he still wanted to test Suzanne Cloutier as well, cabling Paramount: "Please tell Dickinson he did an excellent job. I would like very much to see Suzanne Cloutier tested exactly the same way, however—would give us an excellent opportunity to compare the two girls."

Ironically, in Audrey's own somewhat startling retelling, Wyler was far from completely sold on her: "I remember him saying to me he wasn't all that keen. He said, 'I thought you were a bit fat.' Which was absolutely true. I ate everything in sight, having been undernourished during the war. You know, whole boxes of chocolates. I was ten pounds more than I ever weighed in my life." Her eating, in fact, was not limited only to chocolates: "When the war was over and rations started pouring in I started to eat. By the time I was 20 I was tubby. I used to eat my way through whole pots of jam." Musing about that atypical bit of eating, Audrey smiled: "It's funny to think I might not have gotten the part because I was too fat, because from then on everybody thought I was too thin."

In truth, even a clod, let alone the great Wyler, could see that as with all true movie stars, the camera loved Audrey. She photographed beautifully, with light hitting her sculpted cheekbones and her seemingly translucent eyes flashing with life. The eyes that in real life allowed her to make an immediate connection with others registered just as vitally on film. Conflicting emotions darted across those eyes, because underneath the effortlessly charming exterior lay a genuine if muted sadness.

The nose and nostrils may have looked a bit large and the teeth slightly crooked, but they blended beautifully into a package of endlessly interesting contrasts. In later years, one of Audrey's favorite cinematographers, Franz Planer (*Roman Holiday*, *Breakfast at Tiffany's*, *The Nun's Story*, *The Unforgiven*) would smartly remark that her supposed faults were precisely what made Audrey a star: "Thick eyebrows, uneven teeth. She doesn't mind if her hair is disheveled or if she falls into a pot of soup. She is a real girl."

All of which meant that in the end, there really was no other choice for the role of Princess Ann. Yes, Wyler did describe Audrey as a bit "self-conscious," but at the same time, in a distinctly un-Wyler-like phrase, he found her "absolutely delicious."

Over the decades, the myth has sprung up that upon viewing the test footage, Paramount instantly capitulated and offered Audrey the role. In truth, Paramount struck a deal only after *Gigi* opened in November of 1951 and Audrey became the toast of Broadway. Stardom on Broadway reassured Paramount that Audrey could not only act but also connect directly with an audience. Wyler was happy, Gregory Peck, who had approval of his leading lady, was just as happy, and the part of Princess Ann was now officially Audrey's. She was thrilled, and characteristically, genuinely frightened: "Lord, help me live up to all of this."

A deal was struck: $12,500 for twelve weeks of work. Per diem expenses of no more than $250 per week. It was a respectable deal for a relatively unknown actress, but by way of contrast, Gregory Peck received a salary of $100,000, as well as $1,000 per week in expenses. The disparity in the deals made eminent Hollywood sense: *Roman Holiday* was Peck's twentieth film, and with several Academy Award nominations already under his belt, he was considered the film's box office draw.

Much of the film would be shot on location in Rome, a state of affairs that was still enough of a novelty in 1952 that the credits actually trumpeted the fact that "*Roman Holiday* was filmed on location in Rome." Audrey felt at home in Rome and loved staying at the luxurious Hassler Roma Hotel that figured in a less well-reported instance of the Hepburn legend; such was the unimpeachable character of the fledgling star that at the end of filming *Roman Holiday*, when she was contractually required to give Paramount a complete report of her daily expenses, she returned the unspent portion of her per diem. Safe to assume, that action has never been repeated by another star, and Paramount, smartly, had the good grace not to accept Audrey's check.

Rome enchanted Audrey, but shooting in the city proper proved difficult in the extreme. The Eternal City remained consistently noisy, with both exuberant natives and thousands of tourists filling the streets and clogging traffic, no matter the time of day or night. Wyler had not previously undertaken much location work, let alone in a city as chaotic as Rome, and the autocratic director, used to the perfectly controlled environs of a Hollywood soundstage, encountered a steep learning curve. Certainly, he had never previously faced the sort of wardrobe and hair malfunctions caused by the intense Roman summer heat that melted the actors' makeup. Said Audrey: "Now I know what it's like to be a star—it's warmer, more uncomfortable, and the hours are longer."

Problems and all, Rome itself was emerging as the third star of the film: the ancient ruins, the Pantheon, the Castel San Angel, Barberini Palazzi—it all added up to the perfect setting for a movie that is, when all is said and done, more about discovering the world than it is about falling in love. It is a bright film in both tone and look, and the many outdoor scenes unfolding throughout Rome help the transformation of Princess Ann seem even bigger and brighter—the world is opening up right before her eyes.

Audrey seemed to fit the role of Princess Ann smoothly from day one, and it quickly became apparent that the combination of her European sophistication and curiously winning naivete fit the role far more comfortably than would have proved the case with an American actress. The outlandish but cagey fashion maven Diana Vreeland understood that naivete perfectly: "She's a darling girl, enchanting, just adorable. If she loves a friend, she loves like a child. She's not at all worldly."

Playing the European "Princess Ann"—the character's country of origin is never specified—Hepburn's regal bearing was inescapable. When that grace of movement was combined with the genuine interest in others that her mother insisted proved the essence of good manners, Audrey appeared to be of the same—no, more rarified—lineage as any member of real-life European nobility. Said Sean after his mother's death: "I never saw anyone misbehave in her presence in social situations. She always gave you the sense that there were boundaries that were not to be crossed. I remember hearing that, upon meeting her, Britain's Queen Mother murmured, 'She is one of us.'"

When, early in the film, Princess Ann is referred to as "Her Royal Highness," Audrey's bearing makes anyone and everyone believe she is a queen in waiting. Lines that would sound laughable if delivered by many stars of the 1950s—"That will be all, Countess. Thank you"— come across as quintessentially blue-blooded and understanding in Hepburn's mid-Atlantic purr. Audrey, like Princess Ann, looked innocent but proved wise beyond her years; character and actress alike remained elusive, which only intrigued audiences all the more.

It was the film's rather unexpected take on a fairy-tale myth that further endeared *Roman Holiday* and Audrey to audiences: here was a big-screen Cinderella undergoing a reverse journey from princess to commoner before sadly returning to life as a princess. This particular Cinderella's ball was not another formal royal gala but was instead found in the freedom to dance on a houseboat and wander through Rome like thousands of other footloose tourists.

Audrey did not have a reservoir of acting technique to fall back upon, but Wyler's direction to just exist in the moment, to avoid "acting," resonated with her. His well-documented penchant for dozens of takes actually helped Audrey relax, making her feel secure in the knowledge that if she made mistakes, she would have additional chances to perfect a scene. Under Wyler's tutelage, she inherently understood that she should never play to the camera, but instead, dig within herself to convey the required emotion: her childhood sense of abandonment, the will of iron demanded by the world of ballet, and even the instinctive good manners—these all constituted elements that Audrey could and did readily access. Asked in later years what she had learned from Wyler, Audrey replied with feeling: "Almost everything. His attitude was that only simplicity and the truth count. It has to come from the inside. You can't fake it. That is something I long remembered."

Decades later, her admiration remained just as strong: "He was so dear to me. He never made me feel he had to teach me anything. He just said go ahead and do it. Therefore, I felt very relaxed. . . . I was never aware of being put through my paces or that what I did wasn't good enough. He'd say, 'Well, let's just do it again.'" Speaking of her great fortune in filming her first two starring roles under the direction of Wyler and Billy Wilder, she explained: "These directors realized there was enough there for them to draw out. I never really became an actress. I never did the repertoire in the theatre . . ."

Only once did Wyler become upset with his leading lady. When the Princess realizes that adherence to duty must trump any romance with Joe Bradley, the American newspaperman with whom she has shared her day of freedom, she is devastated. Try as she might, however, Audrey could not cry on cue, and after multiple ruined takes, Wyler finally yelled: "We can't stay here all night. Can't you cry, for God's sake?" Audrey was so upset over being yelled at, so unaccustomed to the harsh words which reminded her of parental arguments, that she burst into tears. Said co-star Peck: "It was embarrassing and frightened her and shook her up, but she did it perfectly the very next time. On screen it looked like it was because she was parting from me, but actually it was because Wyler had just scared the wits out of her."

As it turned out, Peck had his own issues with Wyler about farewell tears; tapping into the emotions at play in the scene, Peck's tears began coursing down his cheeks, only to have Wyler insist: "No, Greg, don't get upset. Get angry! Angry! Angry!" Following Wyler's instructions, Peck played the scene with a sense of anger that he would never see Princess Ann again, ultimately relaying to his friend Roger Moore that the entire incident constituted "one of the defining moments of his career . . . he realized just how important listening to a director like

Wyler could be." Peck, in fact, remained a big fan of his director: "Willy sensed the interplay between actors. There's a whole parade of moments, with nuances and subtexts . . . it's why so many actors won Oscars with Willy, because he recognized the moments that brought them alive on the screen."

In this first starring role, Audrey manages the not inconsiderable trick of appealing to men and women alike, and when she wakes up in Joe's apartment after her night on the town, she exudes innocence tinged with more than a hint of sensuality. This is one princess who looks as sensational in Joe Bradley's pajamas and robe as she does in a ball gown and tiara. It's no wonder the hardened reporter smilingly tells her: "You should always wear my clothes."

In fact, if clothes make the man, then in the case of Audrey Hepburn, clothes made the superstar. Combining the height and waistline of a model with the legs and rear end of a ballet dancer, Audrey's ultra-sleek build enabled her to move on film with a dancer's grace, lightly skimming the surface of the ground as she walked. She was, it was already clear, a clotheshorse par excellence.

Her ability to make this instantaneous impact was greatly enhanced both by landing at Paramount, the most style-conscious of the major studios, and by working with the formidable Edith Head, the studio's leading designer. The very first meeting between Edith and Audrey had taken place near the end of *Gigi*'s run on Broadway, and it was Head who decided to use clothing to deliberately broaden Audrey's shoulders, thereby minimizing any concerns over her rather square jaw. In order to camouflage Audrey's neck and collarbone, jewelry and scarves were utilized as accessories, and it was quickly decided that because of her ultra-slim physique, Audrey should not be photographed in sleeveless blouses.

Head quickly recognized Audrey's unique sense of fashion, and over time grudgingly came to appreciate not only her charm and grace but also her will of iron. Audrey may have been young, but with her innate sense of style she was able to stand up to Head, politely insisting upon thicker belts not just for the long, full-flared skirt she would wear throughout much of the film but also for all of her onscreen dresses (excepting the white and silver brocade formal gown).

Edith Head, queen of Hollywood costume design, was not used to having her dictums challenged, and there's more than a hint of irritation in her recollection of meeting with Audrey to discuss *Roman Holiday*: "[She] had the assurance of a veteran. She would laugh and curl up on the floor . . . and then she would say, with a sweetness that cut like a knife to the heart of the problem, 'I don't think the princess would be quite so shrewd, Edith darling, as to use that particular décolletage!' And I would think, 'Oh, my God, if she doesn't get to the top I'll eat Hedda Hopper's hats!'" Just to make sure no one missed the point, Head not so casually added that fittings with Audrey were "of the ten hour, not ten minute, kind."

In the designer's own words: "What I liked best about her is that she calculated all her business decisions, but made it look as if she didn't have a clue." The winner of eight Oscars for best costume design had, it seemed, little chance against the firm opinion and charm offensive of a twenty-two-year-old actress with a whim of iron. In the words of Head: "Audrey knows more about fashion than any actress save Dietrich."

Head had proven herself a past master of calculated studio politicking in service of her own position, but the difference between the methods of the two women lay in the fact that Head could never make it look as if she didn't have a clue. Which is not to say that Head was immune to Audrey's charms; writer-director Nora Ephron once related the story that when she visited Edith Head's fitting room with its famed thirty-six panels of mirror (one for every ten degrees), Head told her that only one person ever looked good in all thirty-six mirrors—Audrey Hepburn. In the designer's words: "Audrey was the perfect figure model: very slim and tall—5′6 ¾″."

Audrey's strong sense of self meant that she felt comfortable expressing her opinions to the crusty Head, but at the same time, surrounded as she was by the best of golden age Hollywood craftsmen and women, she also listened and followed advice. The look of those almond-shaped eyes that stared out at the world with intelligence and curiosity? It all came courtesy of Alberto De Rossi, whose wife Grazia served as Audrey's hair designer. One look at Audrey's eyes onscreen and women instantly wondered, "What was the trick?" Could they have "Audrey Hepburn eyes" of their own? The answer was yes—with a lot of time and patience. Alberto, it turned out, first applied mascara, and then separated each individual eyelash with a safety pin. Eyeliner was applied on the top lid only, while eyebrows remained thick and styled upward.

Alberto also played a key role in de-emphasizing Audrey's somewhat square jaw. Said the designer: "In a sense I reversed her face by emphasizing her temples. Except for that, she has such beautiful bone structure that her features need very little shading."

Paramount executives viewing the dailies were more than happy—in fact nearly entranced if such hard-boiled characters were ever capable of enthusiasm. Audrey Hepburn seemed to glow on film, and while part of that was her own natural intelligence and beauty, credit was again due to Alberto De Rossi. He would clean her face with soap and water, apply foundation and powder, spray on water for just a few minutes and then blot it all carefully before she faced the cameras. The result appeared minimalistic compared to the pancake-heavy makeup styles so prevalent during the 1940s, and it's a key reason why Audrey's look and style remain appealing to twenty-first-century audiences; like Ingrid Bergman's rather timeless hairstyle in *Casablanca*—no 1940s upswept pompadour in sight—Audrey's aesthetic belongs to no single decade.

So completely did Audrey come to rely upon Alberto that in the recall of Sean Ferrer: "I remember her saying when he died, crying as though she had lost a brother, that she would rather not work again. I have sweet memories of going to the soccer games with him. Grazia still lives in a beautiful area outside Rome, and I consider her a member of my family." In fact, when Alberto died, Audrey was so distraught that her then husband Andrea Dotti declared that her mourning was out of proportion to the event itself, criticizing her behavior in what can, with hindsight, easily be read as another sign of an unraveling marriage.

Feeling protected by Wyler, cinematographer Planer (who, after falling ill, was replaced by Henri Alekan), De Rossi, Grazia, and even Edith Head, Audrey relaxed, delivering a performance of great natural charm. By turns wistful and determined, her eyes convey the excitement of Anne's dual existence as princess and commoner. With her slight physique, Audrey reads onscreen as vulnerable and physically frail, and yet audiences still felt that she could and would take care of herself.

Roman Holiday, however, remains far from a one-woman show, and not enough has been said about why the chemistry between Hepburn and Gregory Peck reads as so natural and unforced. The biggest reason is simple: Hepburn relaxes the sometimes overly stiff Peck. There is a lightness to his performance in the film which is often absent in his Mount Rushmore Arrow

Collar Man portrayals. He is utterly at ease with Audrey, and the result was one of his very best turns. That onscreen chemistry carried over off set as well, and there were rumors that the two stars were personally involved. In later years Audrey addressed the issue with characteristic delicacy: "If there was anything going on, it didn't last long because most of our time was taken up with work. It's true that I had an enormous crush on him. But I was engaged at the time, and I even had my wedding gown hanging in the wardrobe of my Roman hotel room. And Greg was married to Greta. I knew that he wasn't happy, that his marriage was not good. . . . Maybe he did feel something for me, maybe there was a little chemistry between us that made our scenes work. I was in Rome, being treated like a princess, and it was not difficult for me to believe I was the princess in the film, and it was not difficult for me to believe I was in love with Gregory Peck."

Enthusing further, she added: "Greg . . . was the gentlest person I'd ever known, and he never made me feel self-conscious." The feelings were reciprocated, and in later years Peck referred to his time with Audrey with a graceful compliment: "It was my good luck, during that wonderful summer in Rome, to be the first of her screen fellows, to hold out my hand, and help her keep her balance as she did her spins and pirouettes." He continued: "Everyone on the set of *Roman Holiday* was in love with Audrey. We did that one picture together, and I think it was the happiest experience I ever had on a movie set."

So relaxed was Peck that it was he who conspired with Wyler to surprise Audrey with an improvised piece of slapstick at the ancient "Mouth of Truth." As Joe Bradley whisks Princess Ann on a whirlwind tour of Rome, they stop at the famous monument with its open gargoyle mouth. When Peck stuck his hand inside the mouth, he pushed his hand up his sleeve so that when he displayed it to Hepburn it looked chopped off, causing her to let out a scream of genuine surprise—she had no idea that the duo had cooked up this inspired piece of business. Laughed Audrey: "It was the only scene Wyler ever did in one take."

Besides the charm of the Hepburn-Peck team, *Roman Holiday* scores with audiences by conveying an infectious spirit of release. Gone are the stuffy rituals of Princess Ann's court life, replaced by impulse and whimsy in a celebration of change. The film's most famous scene of transformation occurs when, on the spur of the moment, Princess Ann has her long hair cut off in an Italian barber shop. The barber is uncertain as to the wisdom of such a move, but the princess is insistent, and it is at this moment, right before the viewer's eyes, that the Audrey Hepburn look is born on film. When the movie was released in 1953, young women all over the world not only made mental note of Audrey's sleek, short hairstyle but responded viscerally to the sight of a young woman taking charge of her own life. As Princess Ann breaks out of her ossified court life, her smile widens in delight, and that million-dollar smile, the one Audrey felt showed her crooked teeth, made goners of men and women alike.

By the end of the film, even though the audience has spent two hours rooting for the princess to enjoy her freedom, that same audience understands the necessity of the sorry-grateful conclusion; a newspaperman and a princess can never stay together because in Princess Ann's world, duty trumps all. There is no happy ending to this tale of mismatched lovers, but as Paramount studio executive A. C. Lyles enthused: "Audrey had it in her to be the sugar coating on a bad-tasting pill."

With its rueful and bittersweet romance, *Roman Holiday* was setting the template for a key component of the Audrey Hepburn filmography: romantic attraction trumps physical passion.

Apart from *Two for the Road*, physical expression and sexuality are kept to a minimum in all her major films, replaced instead by romantic yearning, preferably expressed while dressed in the highest of fashions.

It was Princess Ann's yearning that drove the film, so when the Paramount publicity machine went into overdrive ahead of *Roman Holiday*'s August 27, 1953, release, it made a certain kind of sense that the relatively unknown Audrey Hepburn was billed above the title in the boldest of letters: "Gregory Peck—Audrey Hepburn in *Roman Holiday*." And yet—how had Audrey secured above-the-title billing alongside a certified movie star like Gregory Peck? Was her agent really that good?

The story of Audrey's billing almost immediately became a part of her Cinderella story, with a widely repeated story making the rounds that Gregory Peck himself insisted upon the billing by telling his agent: "The real star of this picture is Audrey Hepburn. [Tell] the studio I want Audrey Hepburn to be billed on the same line." In reality, gentlemanly as Peck was, the production files for *Roman Holiday* show that it was Wyler and the studio personnel at Paramount who had the idea of billing Audrey above the title alongside Peck, although "they realized this was a delicate matter because of the actor's contract." Peck was approached and quickly agreed to the change. In her first starring role, Audrey Hepburn was now billed above the title, right alongside a bona fide movie star.

As the final edit of *Roman Holiday* was locked in, word began circulating on the Paramount lot that this new Hepburn might just prove to be as memorable and downright unique as the older, equally patrician Katharine Hepburn. The publicity buildup began, at which point Audrey Hepburn did something very unusual for a contract actress in the studio system days: she stood up to the studio brass. In an era when names, background, and appearance were still routinely invented by the studios, Arthur Wilde, the Paramount publicist assigned to build up Hepburn and *Roman Holiday*, had informed her that given her rather flat-chested appearance, the studio might ask her to wear falsies. Her answer? Nothing doing. "She was adamant that she would change nothing in her appearance—she would be herself or no one at all." Her instincts were, as so often proved to be the case, correct, and after her untimely death, the *New York Times* eulogized: "What a burden she lifted from women. There was proof that looking good need not be synonymous with looking bimbo. Thanks to their first glimpse of Audrey Hepburn in *Roman Holiday*, half a generation of young females stopped stuffing their bras and teetering on stiletto heels."

She then refused a second studio request, emphatically rejecting the suggestion that she ditch the surname of Hepburn in order to avoid confusion with Katharine. Drawing a contrast between the two Hepburns, film historian Jeanine Basinger explains: "For quite a while, especially at the beginning, there were many people who did not like Katharine Hepburn—they found her too brittle. She's an exterior actress, unlike Audrey. But the biggest difference is that everyone loved Audrey right from the start." If, during the Red Scare, Lillian Hellman would not "cut her conscience to fit the standards of the day," then Audrey would not cut out the most essential part of herself—her name.

When *Roman Holiday* opened at Radio City Music Hall, the acclaim proved immediate both for the film and for Audrey. Bosley Crowther of the *New York Times*, who was to remain Audrey's biggest cheerleader throughout his tenure at the paper, described her as "alternately regal and childlike . . . Hepburn is the discovery of the decade." Who cared that *Roman*

Holiday's story could be called contrived? It was, in the words of A. H. Weiler of the *New York Times*, a "bittersweet legend with laughs that leave the spirits soaring."

In an era when the cover of *Time* magazine meant a great deal, Audrey found herself in that sought after position a mere four days after the film opened, with the story inside toasting her in glowing terms worthy of the Hollywood star machine at its best: "Amid the rhinestone glitter of *Roman Holiday*'s make-believe, Paramount's new star sparkles and glows with the fire of a newly cut diamond." Then U.S. senator John F. Kennedy pronounced it his favorite film, and as revealed by William Wyler's biographer Jan Herman, during the October 1962 Cuban missile crisis, it was *Roman Holiday* that President Kennedy requested be screened at the White House while awaiting the Soviet Union's response. The president watched the movie on October 27, the day before the Soviets agreed to remove their missiles from Cuba.

Jeanine Basinger points out that Audrey's explosive impact was a particularly American phenomenon; people in the UK and Europe had gained a gradual familiarity with the star through her turns in *Lavender Hill Mob*, *Monte Carlo Baby*, and *Secret People*, but in the United States, "when you are introduced in a high-quality film like *Roman Holiday*, starring with Gregory Peck and directed by William Wyler, people notice. And this film would not have been the same with anyone else. You could take the same script, production design and location work but it's Audrey that elevated it. She was so distinct in her look and dress. You can't locate her exact personality, so you remain intrigued. She was 'the other' and yet seemed real. She wasn't an alien being—she was completely and totally fresh. And—an exceptional talent. She's very, very good, and perfectly cast as a young princess."

With *Roman Holiday*'s critical acclaim matched by its box office success, it was no surprise that the film garnered ten Academy Award nominations: Best Picture, Director, Actress, Supporting Actor (Eddie Albert), Cinematography Black and White (Franz Planer), Best Adapted Screenplay (Ian McLellan Hunter), Art Direction Black and White (Hal Pereira), and Film Editing (Robert Swink).

Roman Holiday may have lost the Best Picture award to *From Here to Eternity*, but it won for Best Costume Design, Black and White (Edith Head) and Best Writing, Original Motion Picture Story. Dalton Trumbo, however, still a figure of suspicion, proved to be persona non grata at the Academy Awards. Instead, *Roman Holiday*'s award for Best Story was "won" by John Dighton and Ian McLellan Hunter (the duo was also nominated for Best Screenplay, losing to Daniel Taradash for *From Here to Eternity*), and it took another forty years before the deceased Trumbo's rightful Oscar was presented to his children and widow Cleo. In Ian Hunter's recall: "I was given an Academy Award for a story that was clearly not mine. Had it [the award] been for the screenplay, I could have convinced myself that I had done most of it."

Unlike Trumbo, Audrey was very much in evidence on Oscar night of March 25, 1954, but in New York City, where she was starring in the Broadway production of *Ondine*. After scoring wins as Best Actress with the New York Film Critics Circle, the Golden Globes, and the British Academy of Film and Television Arts (BAFTA), Audrey was considered one of the favorites for the Academy Award but remained too busy with *Ondine* to obsess over the idea of winning an Oscar. No one expected Maggie McNamara to win for *The Moon Is Blue*, with the film's most notable contribution to film history lying in its status as the first mainstream Hollywood film to utilize the word "virgin." Ava Gardner cared little about either Hollywood or winning for *Mogambo*, and Leslie Caron's performance in *Lili* was charming, but the film considered a trifle.

No, Audrey's real competition lay with Deborah Kerr for her unexpected turn as an adulterous wife in *From Here to Eternity*.

As the telecast entered its third hour, the list of nominees for Best Actress was read by Gary Cooper from a location shoot in Mexico. In a move certain to torture the five nominated actresses, he did not then read the name of the winner and instead turned the telecast back over to Hollywood host Donald O'Connor. O'Connor joked about not reading out the winner's name, before finally exclaiming: "In New York, Miss Audrey Hepburn for *Roman Holiday*!" Seated in the NBC Century Theatre, Audrey bounded out of her seat and up to the stage, and in her excitement immediately exited stage right instead of accepting her award. Her winningly innocent move having further endeared her to everyone in the theatre and the tens of millions watching at home, she then crossed to center stage in a white Givenchy gown adorned with appliqued flowers, a dress so flattering that in 1995, two years after her death, *Time* magazine voted it "the best Oscar dress of all time."

A beaming Audrey received her Oscar from producer Jean Hersholt, keeping her speech to a bare minimum and simply proclaiming: "It's too much. I want to say thank you to everybody who these past months and years have helped, guided, and given so much. I'm truly, truly, grateful, and terribly happy."

Her entire life had just changed, and yet somehow, she herself never did. In the words of British ballerina Darcey Bussell: "She was always very real, one of those natural stars who never tried to be anything other than who she was. It's hard to stay true to yourself and it's rare, especially today."

Audrey's own reaction to her newly found top-of-the-world public persona? "It's easier to be a shy dancer than a shy actress."

Pretty in pink: Audrey, photographed wearing one of her signature colors, proved a fresh antidote to the hyper sex symbols of the early 1950s. The demure dress with its gentle A-line skirt and fitted waist is typical of Givenchy's work for Audrey. Photofest

Chapter Ten

RIGHT GIRL, RIGHT PLACE, RIGHT TIME—the 1950s

"With her skinny waist, short hair, and thick eyebrows, she single-handedly changed the way leading ladies looked in Hollywood."

—medium.com

AS THE IMMEDIATE ACCLAIM FOR *Roman Holiday* made clear, Audrey had proven to be the right girl, in the right place, at the right time, the beneficiary of arriving on the scene while the Hollywood studio system still retained power. By signing her contract with Paramount Pictures, she was now receiving a buildup from a phalanx of studio publicists toiling to put her decidedly unchanged name in front of the public. And when that publicity machine went into high gear, the press agents were delighted to find that the general population was genuinely interested in the Hepburn story, from her years aiding the underground to her discovery by Colette. When combined with a flair for fashion that instantly struck a chord, she began to be promoted not as a sex symbol but as a star with whom other women could identify.

Just like Jean Simmons, Audrey registered as the antidote to the beautiful but blatantly sexual personae of Marilyn Monroe and Elizabeth Taylor. Women could never see themselves wearing a startling white halter dress while standing over a subway grate like Marilyn Monroe in *The Seven Year Itch*, but Audrey, dark haired, flat chested, and gazellelike in movement, seemed within reach—utterly approachable, aristocratic bearing and all. Right there on the thirty-foot silver screen, gamboling about Rome, was a comforting symbol for girls who had not yet grown into women; for those not ready to think of themselves as sexual beings, Audrey presented a warm, nonthreatening image.

America, indeed, the world, was ready for the new type of postwar woman Audrey represented. Her very background, in fact, proved to be an essential part of her appeal to the many Americans longing for a brand of European sophistication rather than American WASP hauteur. Her intriguing persona seemed a bundle of contradictions straight out of a fairy tale: The daughter of a baroness, yet a woman who seemed to want no part of the aristocracy. Tomboyish yet utterly feminine. A ballerina by training who forsook the rarified world of ballet for musical theatre and Hollywood. A beauty with the bearing of a model, but one who remained friendly to all.

She now seemed to be everywhere at once, her influence ranging from haute couture—she displayed the perfect silhouetted figure for Dior's New Look—to animation, with Disney Studios animator Tom Oreb reportedly basing his original 1959 conception sketch for *Sleeping Beauty*'s Princess Aurora on Audrey. Her chic was even said to influence Maria Callas, with some commentators definitively stating that it was after seeing *Roman Holiday* that Callas decided to transform herself from a stereotypically overweight opera diva into a slim, ultra-chic jet-setter.

Audiences who connected more deeply with Gregory Peck's persona when the interesting cracks behind the handsome exterior were exposed in films like *12 O'Clock High* similarly seemed to grasp the near palpable sadness underneath Audrey's beautiful exterior. Thin to the point of audience concern, Audrey was still somehow strong enough to hoist those concerns onto her own shoulders and run with the audience's trust. Hers was a resolute spirit neither as overtly determined as Katharine Hepburn's nor as desperate as Joan Crawford's. She dealt with setbacks by never giving up, striking a note of delicacy alongside the inner strength, and proving altogether unique in her postwar ability to inspire hope. Among post–World War II stars, only Doris Day inspired a similar, much more American, and down-to-earth belief.

Audrey's European sensibility was, in all ways, the antithesis of the hard sell, and if Doris Day was in the process of establishing herself as 1950s America's favorite girl next door, then Audrey Hepburn was securing a place as the princess next door. Said shrewd observer Cecil Beaton, ten years before he and Audrey were to work together so memorably on *My Fair Lady*: "It took the rubble of Belgium, an English accent, and an American success to launch the striking personality that best exemplifies our new zeitgeist."

It all seemed new—and irresistible to men and women alike. Regal bearing and all, underneath that voice and perfect posture was a woman who still seemed like a whole lot of fun. She was, as Peck characterized her, "wacky and funny, a very lovable girl who was always making faces and doing backflips and clowning around"—"a sophisticated elf." Even in *Roman Holiday*, her own sense of humor about herself and others, an acknowledgment of the universal foibles that make up a major part of the human condition, read beautifully onscreen. As her final life partner Robert Wolders put it in later years: "Her sense of appropriateness and decorum was happily mixed with a sense of irony and humor—not taking herself too seriously, but seriously enough."

Audrey Hepburn, it seemed, could do no wrong.

Yet.

With then-fiancée James Hanson in 1952. Running into billionaire Hanson decades later, Audrey smiled: "Haven't we done well for ourselves." PA Images/Alamy Stock Photo.

Chapter Eleven

A FIRST LOVE, 1950–1952

"For a year I thought it possible to make our combined lives and careers work out . . ."
—Audrey Hepburn

ON THE MISGUIDED 2000 TELEVISION movie *The Audrey Hepburn Story*, fifth billing had been granted to Peter Giles in the role of "James Hanson." The actors and characters billed above Giles were recognizable to any devotees of Audrey's life story: Frances Fisher as Ella van Heemstra, Keir Dullea playing Joseph Ruston, and Gabriel Macht in the role of William Holden. But who exactly was James Hanson? The short answer: a very successful businessman who almost landed a real-life role as the first Mr. Audrey Hepburn.

It was in the summer of 1950, soon after completing her role in *The Lavender Hill Mob*, that Audrey first met James Hanson. Seven years older than the twenty-one-year-old Audrey, Hanson, a handsome six-foot, four-inch man about town, was the scion of a Huddersfield, Yorkshire, family that had made a sizable fortune in the trucking industry. The Hanson money was serious: not just comfortable, not just millionaire-level serious, but rather, as one commentator had it, "net worth . . . in the tens of millions of pounds sterling."

Decades down the line, Hanson would become Lord Hanson, the chair of Hanson PLC, a "17 billion dollar global conglomerate," but for now he was a rich, impeccably mannered playboy who fell hard for Audrey. In his decades-later assessment: "Everybody saw in her this wonderful life and brightness and terrific strength of character." Hanson, in fact, met and charmed the formidable Ella, and contrary to reports, he reported that Baroness van Heemstra "thought we were well suited."

The charming and good-looking duo fell in love and were noticed about London: Beauty and the Handsome Rich Man. It all played out as a storybook romance, with an engagement and announcement in the "Forthcoming Marriages" column of the *London Times* following on December 4, 1951. Hanson was listed as the son of Mr. and Mrs. Robert Hanson of Norwood Grange, Huddersfield, Yorkshire, while Audrey appeared in print as the "daughter of Baroness Ella van Heemstra, of 65 South Audley Street, London, W.1." The name of James Ruston was nowhere to be found.

So far, so good. The Fontana sisters, highly acclaimed designers based in Rome, created the wedding dress of Audrey's dreams, an elegant, streamlined confection of ivory silk with a bow underneath the bust; given Audrey's ever-increasing public profile, a photo of her in that gown appeared in papers well before the wedding. Two hundred guests received invitations to the event at Huddersfield, where there would be flowers, champagne, and music. With the war finally in the rearview mirror, life was returning to normal. Or as normal as a wedding between a multimillionaire and a new Broadway star could be.

But . . .

Busy with *Gigi* and the proposed filming of *Roman Holiday*, Audrey found it increasingly difficult to find time alone for and with Hanson. Visitors to her backstage dressing room at the Fulton Theatre noticed that Audrey spoke less and less of her fiancé—and soon realized that his photo had disappeared from her dressing room. Nothing to be concerned about, explained Audrey; she simply felt the photo was too public a display of affection for what she deemed a private matter of the heart. But, it started to seem like the romance was unraveling, and no one was exactly shocked when, during *Gigi*'s road tour, a printed cancellation card was issued which read: "Baroness Ella van Heemstra much regrets to announce that the wedding of her daughter Audrey Hepburn to James Hanson, arranged to take place on 30th September, 1952, at Huddersfield Parish Church, is unavoidably postponed and will take place in New York later this year." It was all adding up to a romantic misfire, and shortly thereafter, halfway through the eight-month tour of *Gigi*, the *London Times* matrimonial column officially announced: "The engagement between Mr. James Hanson and Miss Audrey Hepburn has been broken."

Uncharacteristically, Audrey spoke with the *New York Daily News* in November of 1952 about this private matter: "Jimmy and I talked it over two weeks ago, and we decided we weren't made for each other. When I'm married I want to be very much married. I want people to look at me and know they never need ask, 'Were you ever married?' . . . We agreed to break things off—it was mutual." Hanson's discreet comment: "Our work kept us apart more and more." Audrey, who throughout her life could display a surprisingly practical bent, bluntly stated: "When I found out that I didn't even have time to attend to the furnishing of our London flat, I suddenly knew I would make a pretty bad wife. I would forever have to be studying parts, fitting costumes and giving interviews. What a humiliating spot to put my husband in—making him stand by, holding my coat while I signed autographs."

Decades later, and in his nineties, Hanson allowed as how the decision to call things off was mutual, recalling that Audrey told him: "'I really don't think I want to get married at this time. I hate to do this to you. I love your family.' There was disappointment, yes, but there was no rift or rupture, just a natural decision made by both sides." Indeed, all those decades later, Hanson remained fully on board in terms of Audrey's career: "Had she married me, Audrey would have continued with her career. No doubt about it. I believed in that. There was never any 'either/or' marriage/career problem. She was somebody whose star and whose destiny had been set by her talent."

The marriage was off, and the wedding gown given away, with Audrey telling the Fontana sisters to donate the dress: "I want my dress to be worn by another girl for her wedding, perhaps someone who couldn't ever afford a dress like mine, the most beautiful poor Italian girl you can find." In the end, the dress was worn by Amiable Altobella at her farm wedding, and when sold at auction in London in 2009 it brought in $23,000. Said Altobella: "I have had a happy marriage, so the dress brought me luck."

The friendship between Audrey and Hanson endured through the decades, and when they saw each other again many years later, their mutual affection remained; unexpectedly meeting at the opening of the Aga Khan's Costa Smeralda Hotel in Sardinia, Audrey spotted Hanson, who had recently been knighted, and in his recall, gave him "a little smile and said, 'Haven't we done well!' That's how she was, always gracious and fun." That same grace informed her relationship with another former beau, millionaire yachtsman and theatrical producer Michael Butler, with whom she had spent time in the early 1950s. Said Butler, long after the end of their relationship: "Anything positive you have heard is not an exaggeration—she was one of the loveliest human beings I've known in my life—very bright, intelligent, great fun."

There were to be casual romances post-Hanson, and Audrey occasionally dated an up-and-coming United States senator from Massachusetts by the name of John F. Kennedy. (Some twenty plus years later, another United States president, Jimmy Carter, declared to Audrey: "I have admired and loved you at a distance.") But for now, no additional matters of the heart proved serious. Work was all, even if Audrey didn't necessarily want it that way. In fact, she definitely did not want it that way, but after her smash debut in *Roman Holiday* she was the in-demand it girl of the moment. And that moment dictated *Sabrina*. Humphrey Bogart. Billy Wilder.

And William Holden.

Audrey in her bateau-neckline Givenchy cocktail dress from Sabrina. This style became a favorite of both Givenchy and Audrey because it emphasized her swan-like neck. Audrey was very discerning, indeed hyper self-critical, about her looks, thinking her nose too prominent, her neck too long, and her feet too big (hence the lower-heeled plain shoes she usually wore). The moviegoing public adamantly disagreed. Paramount Pictures/Photofest © Paramount Pictures.

Chapter Twelve

SABRINA, BOGIE, and WILLIAM HOLDEN, 1953–1954

"This girl, singlehanded, will make bosoms a thing of the past."

—Billy Wilder

ROME, BRUSSELS, AND LONDON SUITED Audrey Hepburn in a way Los Angeles never could, but looming above every other city in her life was the magical connection she felt to Paris, a love affair on film which began with the 1953 filming of *Sabrina*. Yes, this was a Hollywood soundstage version of Paris, unlike the location shooting which would dazzle in *Funny Face*, but even here, Audrey felt at home. For a fashionista who was fluent in French, any iteration of Paris would do very nicely indeed. It was the idea of Paris which would play a key role in this all-important follow-up to *Roman Holiday*, and if, as Dizzy Gillespie had it, the professional is the guy who can do it twice, then the question at the heart of the matter remained clear: Was Audrey a one-hit wonder, or could lightning strike twice?

The movie's source material, the play *Sabrina Fair* by Samuel Taylor, had opened on Broadway in November 1953, but at Audrey's urging, Paramount (which had taken over her contract from ABC) had bought rights to the play even before it opened, in fact before rehearsals had even begun. Billy Wilder eventually claimed that he was the one who had asked Paramount to buy the rights, but whomever urged Paramount, the director already knew that he wanted to work with Audrey: "We first saw a test that was made with her. She looked like a princess."

Audrey felt simpatico with this particular Cinderella story as soon as she read the Wilder–Ernest Lehman–Samuel Taylor screenplay's very first words: "Once upon a time, on the North Shore of Long Island." The film, now simply titled *Sabrina*, would center around the romantic misadventures of Sabrina, the daughter of a chauffeur working for the wealthy Larrabee family. Growing up in love with David Larrabee, the handsome ne'er-do-well younger son who barely notices her existence, Sabrina is sent to Paris for "finishing" after an inept suicide attempt fueled by her romantic despair. Unlike her future films *Funny Face* and *My Fair Lady*, in which her character undergoes a transformation initiated by others, here in *Sabrina*, Audrey's character would oversee the transformation herself, with no man necessary.

Returning to Long Island a polished and poised couture-wearing sophisticate, Sabrina, like all true Cinderellas, breaks down barriers while wowing a black-tie crowd at the Larrabees' formal dinner dance. The Larrabees represent American royalty, and Sabrina is every inch their equal—it just takes her the entire film to figure out that she has had the wrong Prince Charming in mind. It's David's older brother Linus, a hard-charging, successful business tycoon, who ultimately proves the one man worthy of Sabrina's love.

The seemingly ageless Cary Grant seemed a perfect fit to play opposite Audrey as the strait-laced but ultimately charming Linus. Indeed, even at this early stage of Audrey's career, people had already begun clamoring for a pairing with Cary Grant, but at fifty, Grant, always vigilant about his screen image, thought himself too old for the role; the twenty-five-year age gap with Audrey made him feel more than a little like a dirty old man. The role was then offered to the fifty-four-year-old Humphrey Bogart, who not only looked a good decade older than Grant, but also had never been celebrated for his way with romantic comedy. Perhaps attracted by the substantial fee of $300,000, Bogart accepted the role, as did the Academy Award-winning William Holden, who, for a fee of $150,000, signed on to play David Larrabee. Audrey's fee? $15,000.

Sabrina may have been set on the North Shore of Long Island, but this daughter of a very British-sounding chauffeur (played by John Williams) seemed to speak with a rather aristocratic mid-Atlantic accent. Where exactly had she been raised? She definitely did not sound like a New Yorker, but in the end no one much cared, because what had always been crystal clear was that stardom, allotted to a precious few, made its own rules. Audiences would make all sorts of concessions when it came to their favorite stars, be it Audrey Hepburn or Julie Andrews, with whom Audrey's life and career would soon begin to intersect in all manner of interesting and headline-making ways. Julie would ultimately play the title character in 1967's all-American musical *Thoroughly Modern Millie*, and while her Millie from the heartland of the USA spoke with an entirely out-of-place crisp English accent, not one person in the audience cared. They just wanted to hear Julie Andrews sing.

Varying accents and all, filming on *Sabrina* began in September, with location shooting taking place in Mamaroneck, New York, at the estate of Barney Balaban, chief of production at Paramount. After additional filming on Long Island, the most notable set being the swimming pool of CBS chairman William Paley and his socialite wife Babe, the film returned to Paramount for two months of interior shooting. Production ended on December 5, eleven days behind schedule, at a total cost of $2.2 million.

It was the end of a rather arduous shoot, with Wilder and screenwriter Lehman often writing scenes the night before they were to be filmed. Occasionally starting the day without enough pages for a full day's filming, director Wilder would ask Audrey to help him stall so that he could continue writing. Approaching Audrey on set he explained: "Look, you have to fumble a line, you have to misread the line. I'm terribly sorry, you have to help me, we cannot shoot more than a page and a half. . . . And she said, 'I'll do it.' She said, 'Oh, I have a terrible headache, let me lie down a bit.' And then she was fifteen minutes, an hour, so I just barely ran out of stuff, the page and half by six o'clock. . . . She was helping me. . . . She just did it."

Whether on location in Long Island or back in Hollywood, Audrey Hepburn had charmed the entire crew, and even the extraordinarily cynical Wilder, survivor of both the Nazis and the Hollywood dream factory, found himself happily surrendering to his star: "After so many drive-in waitresses in movies (it has been a real drought) here is class—somebody who went to school, can spell, and possibly play the piano. The other class girl is Katharine Hepburn. There is nobody else—just a lot of drive-in waitresses off to the races, wriggling their behinds at the

3-D camera." Speaking of Audrey's dancing ability, he rated her: "Great. . . . She was a good *everything*."

With Wilder, Audrey immediately formed a lifelong friendship. Her relationship with Bogie? Tricky. Her partnership with Holden? Romantic. In the extreme.

Ahh—William Holden. The uber-handsome leading man of American cinema who had started out playing the violinist turned boxer in *Golden Boy* (1939). Untutored but possessed of a vivid screen presence, Holden had been nurtured by co-star Barbara Stanwyck in that first starring role, and after the film's success, began receiving increasingly important roles. In short order he seemed to corner the market on characters suggesting the dark strains underneath an all-American exterior, turning in a first-rate performance in Wilder's brilliant *Sunset Boulevard* (1950) and winning an Oscar as a prisoner of war in *Stalag 17* (1953). Holden proved masculine enough to appease men while still enough of a heartthrob to set female hearts fluttering. On *Sabrina*, however, it was the married Holden's heart that took a tumble: one look at Audrey, one heart-to-heart talk in that endearingly intimate way of hers, and the nine-years-older Holden was a goner. So too, at least for a brief and very intense period, was Audrey.

The atmosphere proved intoxicating: two stars living in the rarified hothouse of a first-class Hollywood production with every whim catered to in a cocoon of intimacy. The rest of the world registered only as an intrusion and there was talk of Holden leaving his wife and two sons for a life with Audrey. At which point came the one piece of news the child-loving Audrey could not overcome: Holden had undergone a vasectomy and could not father any more children. His decision flew directly in the face of Audrey's deepest desires, because Audrey wanted children far more than she ever wanted a career in Hollywood: "The one thing I dreamed of in my life was to have children of my own. It always boils down to the same thing. Not only receiving love but wanting desperately to give it . . . almost needing to give it."

In one telling of the story, Holden blamed his vasectomy on both Audrey and his own drinking: "The constant talk of marriage and babies was getting on my nerves, so I went out and got a vasectomy—I was half-drunk at the time. I did it to shut her up talking about babies. Audrey was shocked. She broke down and cried and our romance crashed." She broke off the involvement, and any desperate hopes Holden held of rekindling the romance were forever dashed when she announced her plan to marry Mel Ferrer, announced it in fact, on the very evening she and Mel were out on a double date with Holden and his wife Ardis. The message was received by a heartbroken Holden, but not happily. His later comment: "I was in a jealous rage."

It was not just Holden who was thoroughly smitten with Audrey, however, with her affect causing the most jaded of Hollywood observers to happily capitulate. Said veteran Hollywood photographer Bob Willoughby, on assignment to take still photographs of Audrey for publicity use: "I was talking to Bud Fraker, waiting for the arrival of the subject, when out of the dressing room floated this vision swathed in voile. Bud caught my look of admiration and helped me to close my open mouth." Willoughby, by then seemingly inured to the artifice of Hollywood, was a goner: "She took my hand and dazzled me with a smile that God designed to melt mortal men's hearts. She had a voice filled with smiles."

Tradition may have held that stars sometimes give gifts to co-stars or favored members of the crew, but on *Sabrina*, it was the crew who gave Audrey a silver box with the inscription: "To Audrey Hepburn. With sincere love and great admiration from the entire *Sabrina Fair* crew. Hollywood—1953." Crew members taking up a collection to give a gift to the star? It's as unheard of in Hollywood as a star trying to give back part of her per diem . . .

The crew may have loved Audrey, but her relations with Humphrey Bogart did not always run quite as smoothly. There were rumors of friction, all of which seemed to center around Bogie objecting to Audrey's style of acting. Asked by Clifton Webb about working with Audrey, Bogie responded: "She's OK if you like to do 36 takes." (In later years, Wilder instantly debunked an even lower number of supposed takes: "Twenty-six takes? Audrey Hepburn? Twenty-six, no. That was Marilyn Monroe, before we could get the line straight.") In Stephen Bogart's memoir of his father, he bluntly writes: "Dad also did not care for Audrey Hepburn. Though he said gracious things about her in interviews, he privately thought that she was unprofessional." The charge is unexpected and seems rather out of place, "professional" being the one word repeatedly utilized by Audrey's colleagues to describe her work ethic.

Explaining further, Stephen Bogart writes: "Even on this movie, which he was unhappy about, Dad knew his lines cold, and he often got impatient with Holden and Hepburn, both of whom had a tendency to blow lines." Given Audrey's thorough daily preparation, it seems a strange charge, but then again, Bogart was unhappy on the movie. Upset that he was Wilder's second choice for the role of Linus Larrabee, Bogart, in the recall of his agent Phil Gersh, complained vociferously about Wilder: "'Look, this guy is shooting the back of my head, I don't even have to put my hairpiece on; I'm not in this picture.'" Such was Bogart's unhappiness that Gersh, in his own recall, "went to Billy Wilder and told him, 'Look, Bogie is very unhappy, he's going to walk.'"

Bogart did not walk, but in Ernest Lehman's estimation, there was yet another element at play, particularly when Wilder shot the scene of Bogart and Audrey dancing in the indoor tennis court: "What happened in that scene is that Billy Wilder fell in love with Audrey's image onscreen." Director Wilder wanted to present his star at her most beautiful, and if Bogart's feathers were ruffled in the process, Wilder figured let the chips fall where they may. Even the great Bogart, it seemed, could not compete with Audrey at her most beautiful.

Audrey in later years dismissed the rumors of friction: "I adored Bogie. If he didn't like me he certainly never showed it. He had his problems with drinking." Any tension between Audrey and Bogart may also have been the result of his rumored wish that wife Lauren Bacall be hired to play Sabrina, an idea which fortunately went nowhere, it being a noticeable stretch for Bacall to ever have played an innocent. (Interestingly, Jeanine Basinger points out a parallel between Bacall and Audrey: "Like Audrey, Lauren Bacall was one of the very few others who seemed to appear out of nowhere. She was nineteen, there had been no prior sightings aside from some modeling pictures, and she too was placed with a great male star—Bogart—in a showy role in *The Big Sleep*. Bacall with her voice and seen it all look at age nineteen was also new and different, but at the time she first hit the scene, she didn't hit the heights of stardom the way Audrey did, as much as she did in publicity.")

As it was, while all those around him praised Audrey, the best Bogie could mutter was: "With Audrey it's kind of unpredictable. She's like a good tennis player—she varies her shots." Pressed further, he managed: "She's disciplined, like all those ballet dames." Bogart's lukewarm comments are noteworthy because they represent the exception to fulsome praise from co-stars ranging from Gregory Peck, William Holden, and Gary Cooper to Fred Astaire and Albert Finney. Audrey never did have many detractors—it's as if audience and co-workers alike understood the sincerity of her effort. In the case of Bogart, part of the tension may simply have resulted from his awareness that at thirty years Audrey's senior, he looked more like her father than beau. Tough guy or not, Bogart, like all stars, possessed a finely tuned awareness of exactly how old he appeared on screen, and in his canny professionalism, he was instantly aware of Wilder's plethora of over-the-shoulder shots focusing on Audrey's beautiful, unlined face.

In the end, the relationship between Bogart and Audrey is probably best summed up by her comment of later years: "I was rather terrified of Humphrey Bogart—and he knew it. [But] if he didn't like me he certainly never showed it." Speaking to Robert Wolders, she did characterize the relationship with Bogart as filled with Bogie's "jovial roughness," and in typically modest fashion, she told Sean that she and Bogie got along "okay" but that she sensed he didn't think a great deal of her as an actress. Loyal son Sean called Bogie's assessment unfair, at which point, he smilingly recalled, she "looked straight at me and said he probably had reason to."

In truth the real friction on the set of *Sabrina* lay between Bogie and Billy Wilder. Their collaboration proved to be a clash between two tough, cynical men, and although Bogart had begun by making fun of Audrey's accent, he soon took to imitating Wilder's German-accented English, asking bystanders to translate Wilder's comments into English. Bogart then upped the friction, calling Wilder a "Nazi son of a bitch"—this, jokingly or not, to a man who lost his mother and stepfather at Auschwitz.

Not one to be fazed by an actor, Wilder retorted: "I look at you, Bogie, and beneath the surface of an apparent shit, I see the face of a real shit." Agent Swifty Lazar characterized the relationship in terms of Bogart's demands: "Bogart thought that a director must humble himself before Bogart. But on a Billy Wilder picture there is no star but Billy Wilder." It proved no surprise that the two men never worked together again, and yet decades later, Wilder managed to put the relationship in perspective and achieve a reconciliation: "Unfortunately, Bogart knew he was my second choice. All through the shooting of *Sabrina*, he would bring up Cary Grant. He was very mean to me and I was very annoyed with him. For that role, after all, who wouldn't have wanted Cary Grant? But when Bogart was dying, I went to visit him at his home. He was very brave and, in the end, I forgave him everything and held him in the highest esteem." Summing up his star, Wilder explained: "He always played the hero, but he never was . . . until the end."

When the final edit of *Sabrina* was completed, it was clear that the film belonged to no one but Audrey. Yes, Holden was handsome, and Bogie was, well, Bogie, trying his best to overcome the fish-out-of-water aspect of having to mutter, "Oh, you look lovely Sabrina." But as it turned out, even as the billing listed the three stars in alphabetical order, the scales were tipped in Audrey's favor as soon as the words "Once upon a time" were uttered. Stars though they were, there was nothing "Once Upon a Time" about either Humphrey Bogart or William Holden.

In fact, the film's overt fairy-tale roots caused a pitched battle between screenwriters Lehman and Wilder. Wilder demanded that Sabrina and Linus sleep together in Linus's apartment. Lehman refused: "I absolutely wouldn't let Billy do it. . . . He was furious. He said, 'You're a middle-class Jewish prude.' I said, 'You just can't do it—I'll never forgive you.' And I stubbornly prevailed."

And yet, when all was said and done, Bogart may have ultimately proven the correct choice for the role of Linus; if in fact the role had been played by Cary Grant, the optics would have dazzled but all romantic suspense instantly torpedoed—the audience would have known from the start that Audrey would choose Cary Grant. Anything else would have been unimaginable.

It may have been Bogie and not Cary Grant onscreen, but the success of the film was evident right from the terrific opening shot of Audrey/Sabrina in a tree, gazing at the Larrabees' ball and desperately wanting to be a part of that enchanted scene. Barefoot and dressed down, a vulnerable-to-love Audrey Hepburn embodied the yearning, hope, and promise of youth and first love. (Concerning the wan 1994 remake of *Sabrina* starring Julia Ormond, Wilder dismissively stated: "But in the remake, there was a cold fish in that tree. She was not right, she was not *in love*.")

With her fairy tale aura, Audrey unsurprisingly provided the film's most alluring moments. To wit:

- Standing in the Long Island train station after she returns from Paris, a newly sophisticated Sabrina is revealed. The sequence is made all the more effective by the fact that Sabrina's Parisian transformation has been deliberately withheld from the audience until this point. Aside from the opening sequence, Sabrina has only been glimpsed while washing cars with her father or attending a cooking class in Paris. But now, back on American soil at the Glen Cove train station, the distance traveled in her transformation is fully on display: with her short hair, pleated turban, heels, and gold hoop earrings, Audrey's appearance is specifically designed to accent her Givenchy-designed ottoman tailleur suit with cinch waist. As the camera pans from shoes to hat and the soundtrack swells with "La Vie en Rose," it's no surprise to find that William Holden's David Larrabee screeches to a halt as he drives by, clearly wondering who this exotic creature could be.

- Originally, David was to recognize Sabrina right away, but it was screenwriter Ernest Lehman who smartly realized, "The scene needed a concept, a gimmick, a trick"—the concept being that Sabrina was now so sophisticated in appearance that she proved unrecognizable to someone who had watched her grow up. As the camera pulls back, the sense of fashion's transformative power, courtesy of Hubert de Givenchy and Audrey Hepburn, dazzles.

The camera, in fact, seems to caress the suit's very fabric, the beautifully sensual garment wordlessly conveying that this new Sabrina is no longer a girl—she is her own, very interesting, woman. The suit is not just a matter of appearance because Sabrina is hereby announcing the change in her economic status and, by extension, her sexual status. If clothes make the man, then they here define the woman. It's a trope played out nearly forty years later by one of Hepburn's Hollywood successors, Julia Roberts, in her 1990 megahit *Pretty Woman*; trading in her tacky hooker clothes for an elaborate ball gown and jewels, Julia Roberts faced forward, flashed her trademark megawatt smile, and the entire moviegoing audience capitulated.

A second dazzling scene—

- Sabrina/Audrey floats by in her extraordinary, paneled Givenchy gown, blithely asking her lifelong crush David Larrabee (Holden), "Would you like to kiss me?" Her impossibly thin waist and impeccable posture complete the picture all on their own, and the audience supplies its own highly affirmative answer.

Sabrina has wowed not only both Larrabee brothers but also all their aristocratic friends attending the ball, and in the process arrived at the key moment in her personal journey. This former schoolgirl is now a woman of formidable charm, beauty, and self-possession, sophisticated yet still full of joy—two women in one (it is no accident that when Sabrina later cooks for Linus in his office kitchen, her shadow is fragmented, the top forming a separate piece from the bottom).

And finally—

- Having figured out that it is the businesslike sardonic Linus who is worthy of her attentions, Sabrina finally kisses the curmudgeonly older man, and in a series of beautiful but fleeting images, her face registers shock, awe, and the sheer pleasure of being alive and fully in love. If that reaction took, to use Bogart's expression, thirty-six takes, then it was worth the wait.

Part of the reason for Audrey's rather seismic leap to stardom in her first two films lay not just in her unparalleled ability to portray a Cinderella figure but also in her very apparent gift at conveying a real sense of wonder at the foibles of the human race. No one else on the scene possessed such an acute ability to convey wistfulness, and after just two starring roles she was beginning to solidify and refine a singular screen persona. If Katharine Hepburn projected aristocratic Yankee independence brought down to earth by salt of the earth Spencer Tracy, then Audrey Hepburn personified a vulnerable girl morphing into a woman while gliding elegantly, if sometimes uncertainly, through life on her own terms. Sensuous, the very definition of lithe, and perhaps a bit untouchable, she consistently projected a feeling of "I need you." Eager to protect her, audiences willingly surrendered, their acquiescence never dissipating even when they realized that Audrey was, in fact, more than capable of taking care of herself.

With *Sabrina*, Audrey had now triumphed for a second time, but Hollywood columnist Dorothy Manners sounded what turned out to be a prescient, cautionary note: "I am beginning to believe she is not the easiest actress in the world to cast. In a lovely, charged, breathless way she is almost as stylized as the other Miss Hepburn . . ." Stylization had never hindered Katharine Hepburn, and it would not stop Audrey from rising to the pinnacle of Hollywood, but Manners was onto something. Audrey had to exercise extreme care in choosing her roles. She was believable as a Cinderella figure, and seemed right at home in aristocratic circles, but would she ring true in, say, a western?

That answer would come five years later with *The Unforgiven*, but with the opening of *Sabrina*, the chorus singing her praises continued to swell by leaps and bounds. In the words of journalist Louis Sobol: "You'll feel like buying Paramount stock after viewing *Sabrina* with three stars named Audrey Hepburn, Humphrey Bogart and Bill Holden. The play was great— the picture is great—and Audrey is the greatest . . ."

In the words of Jeanine Basinger: "*Sabrina* would not work without Audrey, or at the least, not work in the same way, as we saw with the remake. Sabrina herself is like the older sister of Princess Ann in *Roman Holiday*, but it's reversed: instead of a princess stuck in the castle, it's the chauffeur's daughter trapped in the role designated to her by society. The key is that both women are trapped, and it works because Sabrina is here 'trapped' in an elegant, witty, hilarious script."

Audrey's ability to project a sense of down-to-earth royalty allowed audiences to believe in her both as the daydreaming girl on Long Island as well as the ultrasophisticated young woman returning from Paris. Cosmopolitan she is, but she hasn't lost the wistful quality of the girl she was. In Basinger's smart words: "Audrey Hepburn is here sporting a totally original and spectacular look. This level of fashion is really fashion-fashion, not movie fashion. She's the only one who could successfully pull that off—wearing fashion-fashion in a way that still allows her to define the character." In Audrey's acute self-assessment: "What has always helped me are the clothes. It was often an enormous help to know you looked the part—then the rest wasn't so tough anymore. . . . Clothes have often given me the confidence I needed because I was insecure about myself."

In an odd way, for all its success, *Sabrina* is an underrated film, the kneejerk reaction reducing the charm of the film to that of a comedy starring the enviably thin Audrey Hepburn in fashion plate mode. But when this fashion plate puts on her beautiful Givenchy dresses, her character is fleshed out, not reduced. Audrey Hepburn wears the couture with ease—the gowns never wear her.

Audrey still doubted her own startling success, but even her reservations were swept aside in the wake of the film's six Oscar nominations: Audrey—Best Actress; Wilder—Best Director; Wilder, Taylor, and Lehman—Best Screenplay; Edith Head—Costume Design; Charles Lang—Cinematography; Hal Pereira and Walter Tyler—Art Direction. On Oscar night, only Edith Head triumphed, and it was the manner of the win, or more precisely the acceptance speech, which actually upset Audrey; her own loss to Grace Kelly for *The Country Girl* could be shrugged off, but Audrey knew better than anyone that Edith Head had not designed any of those attention-grabbing haute couture outfits the Academy members had acknowledged with their votes.

No, those dresses had been created, start to finish, by the man with whom Audrey had just embarked upon the longest, most fulfilling "romance" of her life—Hubert de Givenchy.

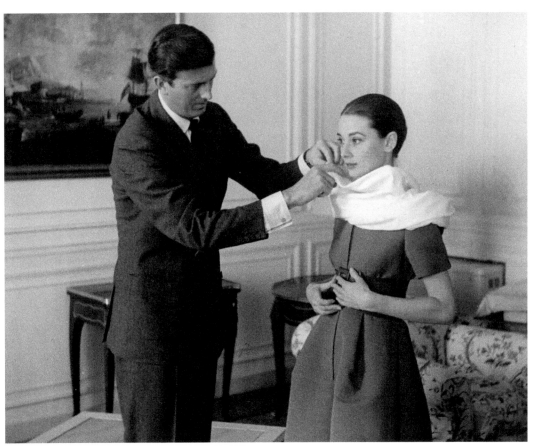

Givenchy at a fitting with Audrey early in their decades-long friendship. The severity of the daytime woolen dress is contrasted with the draped cowl neckline. Their friendship grew into a loving sibling-like relationship. Pictorial Press Ltd./Alamy Stock Photo.

Chapter Thirteen

SOUL MATES, 1953–1993

"They were just way up there in the sky, you know, and I'm sure if he dies, he's gonna look her up."
—Billy Wilder on the relationship between Hubert de Givenchy and Audrey Hepburn

ABOUT THOSE SHOW-STOPPING CLOTHES IN *Sabrina.*

Edith Head—solid, reliable, award-winning Edith Head—had actually been assigned to design Audrey's clothes for *Sabrina*. Which was all well and good after their successful collaboration on *Roman Holiday*, but Audrey had something else in mind for *Sabrina*. Something more European, something and someone from Paris.

Who did she have in mind? No one less than the famed Spanish-born couturiere Cristóbal Balenciaga. The competitive Edith Head was not pleased, but ever the politician, she figured that when Audrey came back to Hollywood with her high-fashion gowns, it would be a straightforward affair to show all parties involved that the haute couture gowns would not work for the demands of a movie. Who would then save the day? Edith Head. Or so she thought.

Off to Paris went Audrey. It was summer, 1953, and she was free and footloose in the world's most glamorous city. The Parisian lights beckoned—especially with a Hollywood studio footing the bill. As documented by Sam Wasson in his book *Fifth Avenue, 5 A.M.: Audrey Hepburn, Breakfast at Tiffany's, and the Dawn of the Modern Woman*, Frank Caffey, Paramount studio manager, wrote Russell Holman, a lawyer in Paramount's New York office, informing him that Audrey would now shop in Paris for a dark suit, blouses, hats, and a "very smart French day dress."

The ever-practical studio noted that the clothes were to be bought as part of Audrey's private wardrobe, thereby ensuring that no duty need be paid when she returned to the United States. And in that letter from Caffey to Holman lay one key sentence: "Obviously we cannot afford to give any screen credit and the clothes as selected and modified by Hepburn should be under the guise of her own wardrobe without reference to Paramount." No matter—who was even thinking about wardrobe screen credit at the time? Audrey was simply going to pick up a dark suit and one oh-so-chic French day dress.

But a rather large hiccup now arose. Balenciaga, it turned out, was simply too pressed for time to be of service. His suggestion: speak to Hubert de Givenchy. That all seemed to make sense, because Audrey's shopping would be overseen by Gladys de Segonzac, the wife of the head of Paramount's Paris office—and a woman who knew Givenchy from his time working at the salon of the legendary Elsa Schiaparelli. In fact, the now twenty-six-year-old Givenchy had served as the director of Schiaparelli's boutique for four years, leaving the fashion doyenne only when he decided to open his own salon. Courtly and elegant, the six-foot, four-inch Givenchy was never seen at work without a white linen smock draped over his own suit, a gentle giant who nonetheless possessed a will of iron, the only designer who dared ban the press from attending his shows.

Well, Gladys thought, the combination of Hepburn and Givenchy might prove an excellent pairing of styles. Audrey, she knew, shared Givenchy's love of clean lines, and a meeting was quickly arranged at Givenchy's salon. To meet the imposing Givenchy, Audrey dressed not up, not down, but as herself, in clothes that expressed the singular nature of her own personality: plain pants, ballet flats, and a t-shirt, the outfit accented by a straw hat emblazoned with the legend "Venezia." Stylish, whimsical, and her own woman.

Givenchy appeared more than a bit startled by this twenty-four-year-old apparition in the grand salon of the House of Givenchy. (In later years he admitted to thinking, "This is too much!") Not that his eye didn't instantly take in the singular nature of the woman standing before him. It was just that he thought an appointment with "Miss Hepburn" meant Katharine Hepburn, and instead of the athletic all-American Kate, he was faced with a lovely, charming young woman who wanted to order wardrobe for a new film entitled *Sabrina*. (The Katharine/Audrey confusion would be reversed in humorous fashion when Katharine Hepburn starred in her one and only Broadway musical *Coco*, based upon the life of Coco Chanel. Given Katharine's noticeable lack of singing and dancing skills, Broadway wags circulated the rumor that on the first day of rehearsal, choreographer Michael Bennett exclaimed: "I wanted Audrey Hepburn, not Katharine!")

At the time of their first meeting, however, Audrey struck Givenchy "like a very fragile animal. She had such beautiful eyes, she was so slender—and she wore no makeup!" Dreda Mele, the directrice of Givenchy, instantly grasped Audrey's special quality: "[She] was like the arrival of a summer flower. She was lumineuse—radiant, in both a physical and spiritual sense. I felt immediately how lovely she was, inside and out."

The legendary Katharine Hepburn she wasn't, but Givenchy was nonetheless captivated by the flat-chested beauty with the saucer eyes, military posture, and slicked-back hair. He sensed a kindred spirit: both were aristocratic in bearing, nominally Protestant, and definitely European.

Instinctively, he realized that her spare lines were a perfect match for his pared-down sense of design. It was too bad then, Hubert explained, that he was simply too busy and could not undertake the job of costuming the actress for her film. Audrey pleaded—could she please just take a moment to look through his designs? Givenchy relented—yes, she could look. But he was still too busy.

Audrey's eyes lit upon a gray wool suit and tried it on. The designer instantly capitulated, in later years recalling: "The change from the little girl who arrived that morning was unbelievable. The way she moved in the suit, she was so happy. She said that it was exactly what she wanted for the movie. She gave a life to the clothes—she had a way of installing herself in them that I have seen in no one else since." *Vanity Fair* would lovingly detail the suit as "an Oxford-gray wool-ottoman tailleur with a cinch-waisted, double-breasted scoop-neck jacket and a slim, calf-length vented skirt." To Audrey, it was joyfully "jazzy."

A total of three outfits were instantly chosen: the first was the "jazzy" gray suit. The second, much to Audrey's delight, was a black silk cocktail dress cut low in the back, with tiny bows on each shoulder, and a square cut neckline that eventually came to be called "decollete Sabrina." Always self-conscious about her prominent collarbone, Audrey found that the high "Sabrina neckline" suited her taste perfectly. Collarbone covered, the emphasis now lay upon her throat and—there was no other word for it—swanlike neck. In later years, that very feature would be memorialized in a well-received novel by Alan Brown entitled *Audrey Hepburn's Neck*, and it even found its way into the 1981 Neil Simon movie *Only When I Laugh*, with overweight actor "Jimmy" (James Coco) plaintively sighing: "I always wanted to have a neck like Audrey Hepburn."

Hubert's dress, thought Audrey, was nearly perfect—it just needed one finishing touch, which she quickly decided should be a hat. The entire outfit was now topped by a toque which Audrey herself found in Givenchy's salon, one studded with rhinestones, and completed by a series of idiosyncratic peaks that made it look more than a little like a crown. Said Givenchy: "She always puts the finishing touch on my work." As Sean Ferrer pointed out, it was a true collaboration: "Givenchy always said they had to figure out how to adapt his clothes to the character she was portraying in the films. He didn't have time to design all the clothes from scratch, and my mother always knew what was best for her. It was a lifelong collaboration and friendship. Wonderful."

But it was the third of the Givenchy creations chosen by Audrey for *Sabrina* that proved the stunner, a perfect blend of spare shapes and pure colors signaling the arrival of a woman who could triumphantly meet the Larrabees on their home ground. This ball gown would serve as the official crowning of Sabrina Fairchild as Cinderella, and prove to be of far more import than any glass slipper. How could an ordinary glass slipper compete with a white strapless organdy gown with detachable overskirt, accented by an embroidery of jet beads on both the top and skirt?

If Givenchy's idol Balenciaga had once said "the secret of elegance is elimination," then Hubert had here delivered the ultimate proof of the maestro's maxim. No feathers, no swirling ornamentation—just a dress of rich fabric designed along classical lines, one capable of enhancing character by announcing the arrival of the new Sabrina and, not so coincidentally, of Givenchy himself. In this, their first film together, Audrey and Givenchy had already achieved symbiosis. Said French fashionista Dreda Mele: "She was attracted by the image he could give her. And she entered that image totally. She entered into his dream, too. I repeat; they were made for each other."

So special did the gown prove to be, not just to the moviegoing audience eagerly awaiting Sabrina's final transformation but also to Audrey herself, that while shooting *The Nun's Story* five years later*,* Audrey told her castmate Patricia Bosworth that the gown was her very favorite of all: "Yes, it was heaven. An angelic bouffant layered gown . . ." To Bosworth, who had avidly watched *Sabrina* in a movie theatre, the dress singlehandedly captured Audrey's essence: "The slim boyish figure with the airborne femininity. When Audrey walked in it, it was if she were walking on air."

Even such perfectly tailored Givenchy designs, however, were never only about Audrey's body, but instead about the lines of the fabric, lines best exhibited when draped on Audrey's model-thin torso. In her own words: "Somehow his clothes have always been right for me, for my body. It's never elegant and pompous." With her one-of-a-kind beauty defined by the features she herself found so irregular, the clothes not only proved to be co-stars of sorts, but they also helped to make her seem approachable, the friendly, dazzling, and popular nice girl of fantasy.

Audrey intuitively grasped that the designer's clothes completed her own essential self because Hubert made a virtue out of what others might have considered deficiencies. If Audrey was tall and extremely thin, then cinched waists and narrow-cut pants would even things out—flaws turned into virtues. At the same time, she enhanced Givenchy's designs in ways even the designer himself could not have anticipated, explaining: "There's a wonderful French word—depouille—without ornament—with everything stripped away. There's a purity about his clothes but always with a sense of humor."

Here was fashion which allowed Audrey to show her own distinctive personality. Said Givenchy: "In film after film, Audrey wore clothes with such talent and flair that she created a style, which in turn had a major impact on fashion. Her chic, her youth, her bearing, and her silhouette grew evermore celebrated, enveloping me in a kind of aura or radiance that I could never have hoped for."

In a fulsome, heartfelt tribute, Audrey explained: "His are the only clothes in which I am myself. He is far more than couturiere, he is a creator of personality." But Audrey herself is not fully accurate here, because by the time she met Hubert, her own talent and loving yet determined personality were already blossoming—the extraordinary Givenchy wardrobe simply enhanced the package. Audrey's three-time director Stanley Donen once remarked, somewhat unkindly, "Audrey was almost more about fashion than movies or acting," but that assessment is at once inaccurate and slightly ungenerous: it was her singing and dancing in his *Funny Face* and her tough yet vulnerable performance in the Donen-directed *Two for the Road*, that made us remember the clothes, not the reverse.

No Hollywood actress has ever worn clothes with more of an instinctive flair for fashion than Audrey Hepburn, and all the Givenchy dresses in the world would not make audiences pay attention seventy years later if not for Audrey's own style and personality. It's the totality of her persona to which audiences have always responded; if it weren't, those audiences might as well be collectively mooning over pictures of Babe Paley, who in the mid-twentieth century was repeatedly voted the best dressed woman of the year, yet in the twenty-first century remains a social footnote, the leading "swan" among Truman Capote's coterie of wealthy female friends.

As Audrey and Hubert's friendship evolved, equal parts designer/client, best friends, and brother/sister, their relationship affected both profoundly. Said Audrey: "Hubert and I are very much alike. We love the same things. We're hurt by the same things. I think we're both very sensitive." In Sean's words: "They consulted with each other on everything."

Their friendship deepened so quickly that Hepburn took to sometimes calling Givenchy simply to tell him how much she loved him—"and then she'd say bye-bye and hang up. She remained from that time on absolutely, unbelievably loyal to me and everyone here at the house. The entire staff adored her, everyone had enormous respect for her—she became part of the family. . . . I have always considered her my sister."

Yet close as the two were, even Hubert sensed that certain closed-off, private parts of Audrey's life remained: "She shared her joy with friends, but kept her unhappy moments to herself." In a rather revealing interview given in 1954 right after she had first burst upon the scene, Audrey explained her attitude toward dealing with questions about her private life: "It's hard work, really, harder than preparing for a play. You keep giving performances all the time."

But with Hubert, Audrey could lower her guard, and from their first meeting onward, their friendship/collaboration succeeded so beautifully that Edith Head's plan to point out the deficiencies in the Givenchy designs fizzled on the spot. Her contribution to Audrey's look in the film was now limited to designing Sabrina's pre-makeover clothes and executing the black cocktail dress and hat from Givenchy's sketch. Interviewed in the 1970s, Hepburn explained "Edith was very good about it," but, writes Head's biographer David Chierichetti, if Audrey actually believed that, then "Edith was a better actress than most, for she was seething, even thirty years later when I asked her about it."

Head's contribution may have been extremely limited, but at the Academy Awards of 1955 she was nonetheless anointed the winner for Best Costume design. It was an Oscar that actually brought Audrey unhappiness, because, it was eminently clear, the Academy voters were really rewarding Head for the most memorable and striking of the film's clothes: the suit Sabrina wore at the Glen Cove train station, the little black dress seen at the cocktail party, and above all, the embroidered flowing gown which stunned everyone at the Larrabee ball. Clothes all designed by Hubert de Givenchy.

As the ironclad Hollywood contract made clear, however, Edith Head would be the only designer receiving credit on *Sabrina*. Never once would the name Hubert de Givenchy be mentioned, even on the evening of March 30, 1955, when Head willingly accepted the Academy Award for *Sabrina*. Loathe to grant credit to even her most trusted assistants, Head not only refused to recognize Givenchy on the night of the Academy Awards but until her death continued to claim credit for designing both the famous ball gown and the black cocktail dress. Wrote David Chierichetti: "Unknowingly I used a picture of the ballgown in *Hollywood Costume Design* and gave Edith credit for it, and she did not correct me when she reviewed my manuscript." When he subsequently brought up this error to Head, she barked: "I lied. So what? If I bought a sweater at Bullock's Wilshire, do I have to give them credit too?"

Perhaps Head convinced herself that she had actually designed the dress, and Givenchy himself remarked that the lack of mention must have been the result of "an oversight." Even decades later he would only allow himself to wonder: "Imagine if I had received credit for *Sabrina* then, at the beginning of my career. It would have helped. But it doesn't matter—a few years passed, and then everyone knew. Anyway, what could I do? I didn't really care. I was so pleased to dress Miss Hepburn."

In the future, Givenchy would, at Audrey's insistence, always receive screen credit for all the designs she wore onscreen in *Funny Face, Love in the Afternoon, Breakfast at Tiffany's, Charade, Paris When It Sizzles, How to Steal a Million, Bloodline,* and *Love Among Thieves*. Never again, decreed Audrey, would there be a debacle à la *Sabrina*. She wanted the world to know of the beautiful work done by her friend—"the single person I know with the greatest integrity." Hubert, whose status subsequently grew to the point that he provided Jacqueline Kennedy's dress for the funeral of President Kennedy, returned the compliment: "She kept her promise. This was one of the most marvelous things about her. She thought constantly of others."

Their professional relationship eventually expanded far beyond the world of Hollywood. It was Hubert who designed the dress for her wedding to second husband Andrea Dotti, as well as the christening gowns used at the baptisms of her sons Sean and Luca. Such was her loyalty to

Hubert that she wore his designs with such frequency that they began to fray: "I don't replace clothes until they can't be worn. I'll wear the skirt of an old suit with sweaters. I had a red coat—the one in *Charade*—by Hubert, of course. I wore it until the threads began to separate and it was all shiny on the edges."

Small wonder then, that their enduring friendship, a very real, platonic love affair, lasted throughout Audrey's life. When she turned sixty in 1989, Givenchy had sixty pink rosebushes planted in the garden of her beloved home, La Paisible, and very purposefully, Audrey asked him to serve as an executor of her estate.

Till death do us part—or the threads begin to separate.

For her September 1954 wedding to Mel Ferrer, Audrey wore an organdy Pierre Balmain tea-length gown. Demure and covered up, this shirtwaist style perfectly fit the intimate Swiss wedding and Audrey's own understated persona. PA Images/Alamy Stock Photo.

Chapter Fourteen

MEETING MEL, 1953–1968

"When I fell in love and married, I lived in a constant fear of being left. I was terrified that someone else would take them away from me. I learned that you can't love without the fear of losing."

—Audrey Hepburn

AUDREY'S PROFESSIONAL AND PERSONAL RELATIONSHIP with Givenchy proved to be the most solid and long-lasting male friendship of her entire life, but by the time of their life-altering platonic liaison, she had already begun her first serious relationship since the departure of James Hanson. It was, in fact, a marriage-serious romance which dated back to the time of *Roman Holiday*'s London premiere in 1953.

Audrey had greatly admired Mel Ferrer's performance as the bitter, handicapped puppeteer in *Lili*, a small, charming film which starred the gamine-like Leslie Caron and featured the award winning song "Hi-Lili Hi-Lo." Caron, in fact, reminded many of Audrey herself: a trained dancer who had skyrocketed to stardom starring opposite Gene Kelly in *An American in Paris*, Caron would go on to play Audrey's titular roles in both *Gigi* (stage and film) and *Ondine* (stage). Caron and Ferrer had clicked together nicely onscreen, his height and craggy good looks registering with decided impact opposite the petite Caron, and while Audrey may not have known Ferrer, his onscreen *Lili* alter ego "Paul" attracted her enormously.

Twelve years older than Audrey, Ferrer, like James Hanson, nicely fit Audrey's preference for older men who could serve as protective father figures. He was a six-foot, three-inch tall native of New Jersey, with striking, though not classically handsome, looks. Confident he was, but with a well-hidden vulnerability resulting from a childhood bout with polio. Princeton educated, with a Cuban surgeon father, a socialite mother, and a physician sister, Mel was at ease in any social setting and projected confidence at all turns.

Having begun his career as a dancer—Clifton Webb taught him how to tap dance—Mel shared Audrey's facility with languages and spoke fluent Spanish, French, and English. When the politically liberal Audrey found out that Ferrer had made a successful movie of striking social conscience, *Lost Boundaries* (1949), her interest heightened further. Based upon an article written by William L. White, a light-skinned African American physician, Ferrer starred in the film as "Dr. Scott Mason Carter," who, unable to find work as a black physician, reluctantly decides to pass as white until events reveal his true identity.

The film, produced for a mere $250,000, grossed over $5 million, and after being shown at the White House during its initial release, it helped inspire President Truman to push legislation allowing African Americans to become officers in the U.S. Navy. In Mel's own view, the film proved to be "light years ahead" of the socially conscious *Pinky* and *Home of the Brave*, which were released in the same year, and he remained proud of the film, stating "I still consider it the best movie I was ever lucky enough to be in."

Wildly ambitious from the start, Mel had set his eyes on concurrent careers as a director/producer as well as actor, and by the time he met Audrey, he had directed José Ferrer (no relation) in *Cyrano de Bergerac* (1946) on Broadway. As it turned out, another director had ultimately restaged parts of *Cyrano*, but Mel's desire to also direct a movie had remained, and he subsequently directed two smaller films, *The Girl of the Limberlost* (1945), and *Secret Fury* (1950). Neither film made much of an impact, but he nursed his directing ambitions while continuing to act in high-profile films like 1953's *Knights of the Round Table* (playing King Arthur to Ava Gardner's Queen Guinevere).

By now, Audrey's friendship with Gregory Peck had deepened to the point where she felt free to approach him with a personal request at the July 1953 London premiere of *Roman Holiday*: Could he help her meet Mel Ferrer? Peck performed the introductions, with Audrey explaining to Mel: "I saw you in *Lili*—I loved it. That's why I asked Greg Peck to introduce you to me." Her reaction to this in-person meeting proved muted: "The thing I remember most about that first meeting was that he was so serious. He didn't smile. I liked him . . . but that was all."

The two actors struck up a wide-ranging conversation and Audrey grew intrigued; Mel was educated and cultured, able to converse about political matters of the day as easily as Hollywood grosses, and with his older, grave mien, exuded an aura of confidence and all-encompassing protection. The affection between the two grew daily, and like grew into love. This, she was convinced, was the real thing. Plans were made, and Audrey gave Mel a platinum watch engraved with the Noël Coward song title "Mad About the Boy."

By this time, Ferrer had already been married three times, twice to Frances Pilchard, with whom he had a son and daughter, as well as once to Barbara Tripp, with whom he also had a son and daughter. His self-assurance and drive appealed to Audrey, and as the demands for her time and attention grew daily in the face of her acclaimed performance in *Roman Holiday*, the need for a protector loomed large. Analyzed Robert Wolders: "She was in part attracted to Mel because he was like a father figure to her. . . . It's true that he took over her life, but she wanted to be protected and she trusted Mel. In a sense, she did that with me as well." And even if Ella remained displeased with Mel's previous marital history (said Audrey in later years—"It ate away at me that they couldn't get along."), Audrey herself remained blissfully happy.

Ella may have disapproved of Mel's multiple previous marriages, but one year after that first Gregory Peck–arranged meeting, Audrey and Mel married on September 24, 1954, in a civil ceremony at the mayor's home in Buochs, Switzerland. The vows were repeated the next day in a religious ceremony held at a thirteenth-century chapel in Bürgenstock, Switzerland. On a very foggy day, Audrey wore a high-necked, tea-length Pierre Balmain dress, with a satin sash tied in the back, her hair accented by a crown of white roses. She pronounced herself blissfully happy.

Desperate not to repeat the mistakes of her parents, Audrey spoke of a determination to make her marriage every bit as important as her career: "I think marriage and art can develop together. The thing to remember is that you have to work at both. . . . When I got married to Mel I decided that if I worked for, say, three months on my own career, I would save another three months for being a married woman and a proper wife." Not for Audrey the shortcoming she viewed as inherent in American style marriage: "American women have a tendency to take over too much and in that way they miss out on a lot of fun that their European sisters have."

Audrey held a British passport while Mel remained a citizen of the United States, but a mutual decision was made to apply for residency in Switzerland. Audrey could and did appreciate aspects of life in the United States and the United Kingdom, but she held a lifelong self-identification as European and wanted to remain living on the continent where she had grown up. Practical matters figured in the decision as well: if the couple had settled in the UK, they would have been faced with a 90 percent tax rate on their rapidly increasing earnings.

Audrey quickly embraced the sense of quietude found in their home on the Bürgenstock mountain in Switzerland; that pricey hideaway, which maintained its own police force, consisted of three hotels situated on five hundred acres high above Lake Lucerne and came complete with a golf course, tennis courts, and pool. If it did not, in Audrey's mind, represent a permanent residence, it was one she felt could still serve as a home base. Except when she and Mel were on the road—which was, given their careers, all of the time.

For Audrey, who had grown up in three different countries in the midst of World War II, the four-star hotels they stayed in while filming on location still had to exude a semblance of home. She wanted to be surrounded by her own belongings, not the hotel's, which meant that the Hepburn-Ferrer caravan consisted of no fewer than fifty fully packed trunks and suitcases, marked by a clearly delineated division of labor: Mel made all the arrangements, Audrey did the packing, and, she emphasized, "carried my own bags." With constant moves from film set to film set, hotel to hotel, and even continent to continent, detailed, numbered lists were typed for each trunk and suitcase, with all of the lists clipped into a binder where Audrey could locate every object at a moment's notice.

This near obsessive attention to detail unfolded as an elaborate, extraordinarily upscale traveling sideshow, the trunks filled with Audrey's own china, books, candelabra, cashmere blankets, white silk pillows, family photographs, lamps, and silverware. Especially in Paris, where the Raphael Hotel proved home base during the filming of *Funny Face* and *Love in the Afternoon*, it seemed as if the entire contents of the Bürgenstock villa had been transported over the borders. The desire to control by creating order out of chaos persisted until the end of her life, and in an interview conducted after Audrey had passed away, Sean commented: "When she would get time off, between her UNICEF trips, she would spend a lot of time upstairs in the house organizing her things. Really, when she passed away, everything was perfectly ordered."

There were, inevitably, stresses and strains which accompanied the ceaseless moving, with one inescapable irony underlying it all: Mel was far more career focused, indeed driven, than Audrey, but it was Audrey who remained the internationally popular and adored star. That balance was to remain wildly uneven throughout their marriage, a bitter pill that was not easy for Mel to swallow. If Audrey had eclipsed Gregory Peck in *Roman Holiday*, and both Bogart and Holden in *Sabrina*, what kind of chance did the committed but less-skilled Mel have? As it was, within the first years of marriage the not-so-quiet whispers began: Mel was playing Svengali, insistently telling Audrey what to do and when. Audrey demurred: "He is a protective husband, and I like it. Most women do."

Determined to bolster her husband and make the marriage work, Audrey even gave Mel credit for part of her famous fashion sense: "I'm fortunate to be married to a fashion-conscious man by the name of Mel Ferrer, whom I think has infallible taste." But try as she might to equalize their professional status with such public praise, the imbalance remained.

This was, after all, the 1950s, and with explicitly defined gender roles—men providing and women staying home—the problem seemed to grow larger, not smaller, by the day. Mel and Audrey could ignore the problem, talk around it, or even barrel on full steam ahead, but it loomed large on stage and thirty-foot-tall movie screens alike. Staring anyone who paid close attention to their three joint undertakings right in the face.

Audrey sketching on the set of 1956's *War and Peace*, in one of the costumes designed by Maria De Matteis and Giulio Ferrari. As the nineteenth-century Russian aristocracy was enamored of all things French, women took their style cues from the French, including the high-waisted Empire line of dresses. Paramount Pictures/Photofest © Paramount Pictures.

Chapter Fifteen

EXHIBITS A-B-C, 1954–1957

"Mel's success in Lili did not bear the fruits that he might have hoped for and in the course of time, he was not pleased to be Mr. Hepburn."

—Actor Robert Flemyng

Exhibit A: *Ondine*
Exhibit B: *War and Peace*
Exhibit C: *Mayerling*

Exhibit A: *Ondine*—At the beginning of married life, Mel began to envision his partnership with Audrey as a new iteration of Laurence Olivier and Vivien Leigh—a married couple united onstage and off. First up: Audrey's post–*Roman Holiday* return to Broadway in Jean Giradoux's *Ondine*, in which she would play the titular character of an androgynous otherworldly aquatic sprite.

Ondine would be directed by the estimable Alfred Lunt, with original music composed by Virgil Thomson. With the buzz about *Roman Holiday* increasing by the day, advance box office sales for *Ondine* began to leap toward sellout status, but one rather large problem loomed: playing Ondine's love interest, "Hans Ritter," would be Mel Ferrer, and Mel Ferrer was, if nothing else, cocksure of his own opinions.

At the start, the experience registered as bright, even exciting, with the play itself seeming all but handcrafted for Audrey: set in the Middle Ages, the Giradoux play, translated into English by Maurice Valency, was based upon a German legend that had already served as the basis for two operas. Ondine, a water nymph with supernatural powers, falls in love with a knight, and the subsequent blurring of boundaries between the water world and the kingdom of man ends in the death of the knight. Even Audrey's very physicality seemed tailor-made for the role of Ondine, a presence half of the corporeal world and half of the sea. This Ondine could jump from a standing to a sitting position, leaving audiences gasping aloud as she leapt directly into co-star Ferrer's lap. (That same show-stopping move would be repeated ten years later in *My Fair Lady*, while Audrey exclaimed that she "Could Have Danced All Night.")

And yet, fitting as the role seemed for Audrey, problems arose as soon as rehearsals began. Not with Audrey, whose work ethic remained impeccable. As explained by son Sean in later years: "She could not understand why people wanted her . . . and what they thought was so special about her. So she made up for it by working extra hard." No, the problem lay with Mel, who chafed under Alfred Lunt's direction and, it quickly proved clear, wanted to direct Audrey himself. The tension-filled rehearsal period proved frustrating for Lunt and Ferrer alike, as well as upsetting for Audrey. The entire weight of the production was resting upon her shoulders, and precious rehearsal time was being eaten up with arguments between her husband/co-star and the show's director. Said Lunt in later years: "Ferrer used Audrey's crush on him to rule her with an iron fist."

Upset or not, however, Audrey had gained in confidence in the three years since she had appeared onstage in *Gigi*. Now earning $2,500 per week, this time around she believed that she did indeed belong on a Broadway stage. There were no worries about voice projection, no anxiety over remembering lines. Said fellow cast member, the Tony Award–winning actress Marian Seldes: "I loved watching her rehearse and act. How beautiful she made other people feel! That was her magic on and off the screen." (Seldes was more reserved in her assessment of Baroness Ella, who had by now appeared on the scene: "She was very correct, beautifully dressed and coiffed—but daunting, rather aloof, and undemonstrative.")

Whatever affection Ella withheld from Audrey was more than made up for by critics and audiences alike, and after a tryout in Boston, when the play opened on Broadway, the tough-to-please New York City critics fell over themselves in their rush to praise Audrey. Richard Watts in the *New York Post* called her performance "irresistible," going on to write: "Magic it seems to me, is exactly the right word to apply to Miss Hepburn . . . she manages to make her role at once immensely moving and eerily unworldly." The dean of theatrical critics, Brooks Atkinson of the *New York Times*, capitulated entirely: "She gives a pulsing performance that is all grace and enchantment, disciplined by an instinct for the realities of the stage." The ultimate tribute, however, came from Walter Kerr in the *New York Herald Tribune*, who wittily wrote: "She is every man's dream of the nymph he once planned to meet."

Amidst this wild acclaim, grumbles were heard on opening night. Not about Audrey, who modestly accepted the audience's shower of approval, but rather about the actual curtain calls. Why, people wondered, did Audrey, who carried the confection of a story entirely upon her own shoulders, forego a solo curtain call and instead take her bows with Mel? In the immediate aftermath of the opening, whispers began that Mel had insisted upon a joint curtain call, and the chorus of disapproval grew louder, until, "six weeks later, Audrey was once again taking solo curtain calls."

Ondine opened on February 18, 1954. Two months later Audrey won the Academy Award for *Roman Holiday*. One week after that she won the Tony Award as Best Actress for *Ondine*. By winning the Oscar and the Tony in the same year, she had equaled a feat achieved only by Shirley Booth and, in the future, Bob Fosse.

The world was Audrey's oyster.

But she wasn't happy.

Grateful—yes. Full of praise for her teammates—and she thought of them all as a team—on the play. She was exhausted, however, worn down by three years of solid work. A new set of whispers began: Audrey was having a nervous breakdown from the strain. A breakdown? Untrue.

But she was, in fact, depressed. Even at this high point of her career, happiness remained elusive. The feeling of having been deserted by her father had never fully vanished and the near starvation and horror of living under the Nazis haunted her memory.

Remaining optimistic remained an act of willpower for Audrey. She put on a brave face, and her manners, the desire to put others at ease, remained impeccable. But much as she liked the theatre, insisting that her contract with Paramount allow her twelve months between films for the theatre—"I have learned the little I know about acting from my stage work, and I think I'll continue to learn from the theatre"—she left Broadway and the standing-room-only audiences at *Ondine* to spend the summer recuperating in Switzerland. She felt guilty that the play would now close—it was impossible to envision audiences accepting any other actress as a replacement for her. But under the strain she had lost even more weight from her alarmingly thin frame, and her anemia had returned with a vengeance. A rest was not just needed, but mandatory.

There would be rumors of other stage work throughout the ensuing years, talk that she might star in the title role of Maxwell Anderson's *Mary of Scotland*, with Helen Hayes playing Queen Elizabeth. Another trial balloon: Would Audrey play Juliet at Stratford-upon-Avon? Perhaps a turn as either Ariel or Miranda in *The Tempest*. Even better: Audrey playing half the week as Ariel, and the other half as Miranda.

Nothing ever came of any of it. For now she would rest and relax in Switzerland. Mull over possible film scripts. But most of all she wanted a baby, knowing with rock ribbed certainty that she would not feel complete until she became a mother.

She would never return to the Broadway stage.

Exhibit B: *War and Peace*—Wanting to keep busy, in 1955 Audrey allowed herself to be wooed back to work. The film that beckoned was nothing less than *War and Peace*. The Mount Everest of novels was being turned into a Hollywood epic, and if Audrey could not yet have the family she so desired, then she wanted to be a part of *War and Peace*, to prove that she was capable of stretching herself as an actress.

A savvy reader, Audrey knew a great role when she saw it: Natasha Rostova, a lighthearted pretty girl in early nineteenth-century Russia, buffeted by war and the death of loved ones, evolves from spoiled girl to a woman of surprising fortitude over the course of the novel's twelve hundred pages, proving capable of surviving Napoleon's invasion of her homeland just as the teenage Audrey outlasted the Nazis. Survival trumped all.

Like others associated with the film, Audrey was also struck by the fact that Tolstoy's very description of Natasha sounded a great deal like Audrey herself: "This black-eyed, wide mouthed girl, not pretty but full of life, with childish bare shoulders . . . black curls tossed backwards, thin bare arms and feet in low slippers." Even Prince Andrei's declaration of love for Natasha sounds like what Mel—or more likely William Holden—would have said of Audrey herself: "What a joy it is to dance with her. Like holding springtime in your arms. Like holding a branch of lilac or a kitten."

Audrey was tempted: a complex character, a first film in color, and one additional inducement: the chance to be directed by another certifiable Hollywood legend, King Vidor. With a career ranging from the days of the silent classics *The Big Parade* (1925) and *The Crowd* (1928) to acclaimed sound movies like *Stella Dallas* (1937), Vidor had remained a major player in Hollywood for thirty years, one who had even worked uncredited on the Kansas sequences in *The Wizard of Oz*. Nominated for a total of five Oscars (he would win an honorary Oscar in 1979), he would here be taking on the biggest movie of his career. The elements unfolding under his supervision: Napoleon's army. The March on Moscow. The upheaval of an entire nation. An international extravaganza, one produced in Rome by the duo of Dino De Laurentiis and Carlo Ponti, with a screenplay by six writers from three different countries. This United Nations approach to the film included British cinematographer Jack Cardiff, Italian composer Nino Rota, and the British-Dutch-Belgian Audrey. Added to the mix: a $6 million budget ($67 million today), seven thousand costumes, several tons of artificial snow flown in from England, five thousand guns, one hundred thousand buttons, and, in those pre-CGI days, hundreds of extras.

Although she had not yet formally signed her contract, Audrey hoped that Gregory Peck would be free to play the role of Pierre, but when her *Roman Holiday* co-star proved unavailable, the role went to Henry Fonda. For the role of Prince Andrei: Mel Ferrer. Would Audrey have made the film without Mel? Most likely, yes, but they did not like to be apart for long periods of time, and Audrey, exercising her gentle but iron will, pushed for Mel. Negotiations to sign both husband and wife ran not just back and forth but up and down, as well as backward and forward, conducted as only the volatile De Laurentiis could; in the end, a high-speed chase found De Laurentiis's car following Audrey and Mel's, until contracts held out the car window were signed. In the words of a *New York World Telegram* headline: "*War & Peace* Settled in Two Speeding Autos."

The salaries: Audrey: $350,000. Mel: $100,000. When told of her record-setting salary, Audrey murmured to her agent: "I'm not worth it. It's impossible. Please don't tell anyone." In the Hollywood universe where stars often insisted upon press releases trumpeting their record-setting salaries, Audrey's wish that her salary not be publicized represented nothing so much as a new version of giving back unspent per diem. Not publicizing her record-setting salary? With publicity-mad moguls Dino De Laurentiis and Carlo Ponti producing? The chances for silence remained zero.

Although increasingly common by the mid-1950s, Technicolor features were still far from a given for ever-cost-conscious producers, but the idea of shooting the epic *War and Peace* in black and white was never seriously considered. Which meant that with Audrey facing her first ever Technicolor feature, the call went out to her favorite cinematographer, Franz Planer. Planer proved unavailable, but given Audrey's love of the virulently colored *Red Shoes* and *Black Narcissus*, inquiries were made about Jack Cardiff, the estimable director of photography on those two Michael Powell–directed masterpieces.

Cardiff, then in the midst of fashioning one of the all-time great careers in cinematography, understood the unique demands of filming camera-conscious leading ladies. Having expertly photographed Ava Gardner in *Pandora and the Flying Dutchman* (1951) and *The Barefoot Contessa* (1954), as well as Katharine Hepburn in *The African Queen* (1951), he now began by taking as many photographs of Audrey as possible, studying her face from all possible angles while analyzing flaws and virtues alike. Said Cardiff: "Her problem is the jawline. It doesn't photograph well. You must concentrate on those great big brown eyes."

After photographing Audrey for the film, he opined: "Audrey has made a symbol of her eyebrows, emphasized to make them thick and black. I filmed her in *War and Peace,* and they didn't seem right for the period. I asked her to soften the bold effects that characterized her success. She agreed." In the end, Cardiff came to understand the same dichotomy between Audrey's genteel looks and determined personality noted by so many who worked closely with her: "She has steel determination and delicacy that girl." He did, however, hold a rather jaundiced view of Mel, explaining that Mel was "like a manager with her as well as a husband. 'Is the car ready for Miss Hepburn?' . . . 'The costume is wrong for Miss Hepburn' . . . 'It is too hot (or too cold) for Miss Hepburn.'"

Filming began in July 1955 and did not conclude until November. Worldwide press interest remained high, but Audrey's sense of privacy remained inviolate: it may have been only her third starring role, but she did not want any press on the set. Nor, she added, did she want to submit to any interviews off set, even with the then all-powerful gossip queen Louella Parsons. When urged by the studio, however, she ultimately agreed to chat with the columnist on the telephone. Already a very savvy player in the Hollywood publicity sweepstakes, Audrey knew that in order to win over Parsons she should send a present; Parsons's yearly haul of Christmas presents sent by sycophantic stars and studio executives was already legendary, so Audrey sent the columnist a basket of flowers—but not just any basket. These flowers did not come in the form of a stiff, formal arrangement from a tony Beverly Hills florist. Instead, Audrey had flowers sent from her own garden. Parsons was impressed—she had been kept at arm's length yet still felt personally honored. Veteran studio publicists, it appeared, could learn a thing or two from Audrey.

Unlike *Roman Holiday* and *Sabrina*, *War and Peace* would not be shot in sequence, the logistics on such an epic dictating otherwise. It all added up to a sizable challenge for Audrey, with each shooting day bringing a different Natasha. Was she the young carefree Natasha or war-weary, disillusioned Natasha? Was she just getting to know Prince Andrei, or had she already lost him? Tiring as the process was, and exhausting as De Laurentiis could be, Audrey liked filming in Rome, enjoyed eating with the crew, and felt she had the support of a bona fide Team Audrey in Vidor, Cardiff, and makeup artist Alberto De Rossi. Pan-European as she was, she thoroughly enjoyed the international flavor of the film: shot in English, manned by Italians, and eventually dubbed into French, German, and Spanish.

A first cut of the film ran to five hours. Trims were ordered, with the final edit whittled down to 208 minutes. The verdict from critics? An international mixed bag featuring moments of beauty juxtaposed with a hard-to-follow narrative and wildly varying acting styles.

At its worst, the film features performances by Audrey, Mel, and Henry Fonda that seem to have been spliced together from three different films. Which is not to say that the film is without virtues, beginning with Audrey's graceful performance and Jack Cardiff's stunningly composed mise-en-scènes. Cardiff favored a chiaroscuro approach—the screen morphing from light to dark and then back to light again, with Audrey's porcelain white skin deliberately placed against the darkest of backgrounds. There are startlingly effective shots of dark crowds huddled against the white landscape of snowy Russia, and one singularly beautiful shot of Audrey's face in the darkness during the retreat from Moscow resembles a painting by an old master. Sequences of French soldiers retreating through mud and snow convey the horrors of battle in powerfully affecting fashion and provide moments of beauty that helped audiences forgive some noticeably artificial-looking sets.

In the Audrey universe, however, what is most noteworthy here are the relative shortcomings of Mel Ferrer as a leading man. He's attractive in an offbeat way, but more often than not he appears stiff rather than alive with passion. One always senses an awareness of the camera on Mel's part, an inability to let go and show true emotion. While the camera seems to all but caress Audrey's cheekbones and soulful eyes, with Mel the camera simply appears to be paying a courtesy call, noting his presence via an occasional close-up or two. There is no star heat on display, none of the overt sex appeal that makes audiences stop in their tracks and pay attention. Called upon to utter grand declamations as Russia collapses about him, he can't overcome that inherent woodenness. He's better in the quiet moments, but unlike Audrey, he appears incapable of totally giving himself over to the camera. He's a man of decided talent who often received short shrift in comparison to Audrey, but although he is better here than the miscast Fonda, one senses a talent better suited behind the camera than in the center of the frame.

War and Peace represented Vidor's penultimate film, and he received an Academy Award nomination for his work, as did costume designer Maria De Matteis. Vidor also received a Golden Globe nomination, one which was accompanied by additional nods for the film itself as Best Picture, Oskar Homolka (playing Field Marshal Kutuzov) as Supporting Actor, and Audrey as Best Actress. Audrey's Golden Globe nomination was matched by a BAFTA Award as "Best British Actress," and the passage of time has revealed that she is in fact the most effective presence in the film, her physical grace and wounded expression conveying character in far better fashion than Fonda's surprisingly wan turn and Mel's too often wooden mien. She downplayed her own efforts: "I had no technique, so I had to make believe like children do," but through her fragile determination, the audience is able to process how the formerly spoiled Natasha has endured the hardships that have changed her into a complex, recognizable human being.

In the end, however, it's simply too difficult for the film to achieve any textual consistency when the accents on display range from aristocratic British to Midwestern American, with a stop along the way for a touch of cockney. The story moves in fits and starts, a seeming casualty of six screenwriters from multiple countries laboring over the same script.

Strange as it is to say about the overflowing-with-passion story of *War and Peace*, the film seems to simply fade away whenever Audrey is offscreen, flickering back to life only when she returns for the next twist in Natasha's story. Her warmth and passion inject the intermittently moving but ultimately misshapen multinational enterprise with the much-needed vitality that involves an audience—but only for as long as she is onscreen.

Perhaps the ultimate compliment to her performance came when *War and Peace* was filmed once again in 1966, on a budget of $100 million supplied entirely by the Soviet government; in that monumental rendering of this quintessential Russian story, the role of Natasha was played by ballerina Lyudmila Savelyeva, who looked like no one so much as Audrey's lost-at-birth twin sister.

Exhibit C: *Mayerling*—One year after *War and Peace*, Audrey and Mel co-starred again, this time in a 1957 television adaptation of *Mayerling*, the oft-told real-life tale of Austria's Crown Prince Rudolf and his teenage mistress, Baroness Maria Vetsera. The mystery of how the two lovers died together at his hunting lodge in January 1889 has never been solved, a fact which did not stop either the 1936 movie starring Danielle Darrieux and Charles Boyer or this television production from positing their own solutions: forced to marry another woman, Prince Rudolf could not stop himself from continuing to meet his beloved Maria, and realizing the impossibility of their relationship, he shoots her before committing suicide. So much for couples counseling.

Mayerling, theorizes Sean Ferrer, appealed to his father's "dramatic sense of theatre," which is understandable given the story's hold on the popular imagination. Marveled Billy

Wilder: "When I was in Vienna, in the '20s, every week in the Sunday supplements there was a new story about what really happened at Mayerling with Prince Rudolf of Hapsburg and his mistress, Marie Vetsera. Did they commit suicide in 1888 or didn't they?" With that widespread interest in mind, this production was budgeted at the very hefty for live television sum of $620,000, and while, just as on *War and Peace*, Audrey would receive a greater salary than Mel, the disparity this time was not so great: Audrey would receive $150,000 and Mel $100,000.

The live telecast was set for February 4, 1957, but even with the esteemed Anatole Litvak directing, after three weeks of rehearsal, including five full days for the television crew, this *Mayerling* remained stubbornly inert. On paper, the appeal of the role proved easy to spot: Audrey would be playing a beautiful young woman who mingles with the highest levels of society and dances at the royal ball with her own Prince Charming. At age twenty-seven, Audrey could still pass for a teenager, there are beautiful costumes courtesy of Dorothy Jeakins, and even courtly dances staged by Marc Breaux of *Sound of Music* fame. But just as happened with the then married Elizabeth Taylor and Richard Burton in *The Sandpiper* and *Hammersmith Is Out*, Audrey and Mel simply generated no heat together.

Making matters worse is the fact that in a production that runs only seventy-five minutes, audiences were forced to wait fifteen minutes for Audrey's first appearance. Center stage is instead ceded to Mel, who unfortunately proves stiff in both body language and delivery. He is frequently dour, and as a result even Audrey appears a bit strained, mildly earthbound while playing opposite her real-life love.

Mel's is a modern sensibility, and it's hard to credit him as a nineteenth-century European aristocrat. He was not without talent as an actor, but when all was said and done, he remained a bit of a cool customer for women in the viewing audience. That audience watched with the knowledge that Mel and Audrey were husband and wife in real life, but this pairing played out as a slightly unsettling live television rendering of *A Star is Born*, with a startlingly talented younger wife eclipsing her older, more experienced husband.

The ratings were impressive—by some estimates as many as fifty million watched—and the production was actually released in theatres overseas, but the critics remained unimpressed. In an acerbic yet not wholly inaccurate review, syndicated columnist Sheilah Graham laid it on the line: "The lovers seemed more fated to bore each other to death than to end their illicit alliance in a murder-suicide pact."

Even Audrey herself voiced frustration days after the airing: "I'm not sorry I did it. But television has certain drawbacks. We had only three weeks to rehearse—actually two weeks and four days—and much of the time was consumed by technicians. That isn't enough time to put on a ninety-minute play."

Audrey was right, but she was to be in more congenial territory—and much less rushed—with her next film, the effortlessly chic *Funny Face*. There might not have been a career with the Paris ballet in store for Audrey, but there would be a glorious Paris-set Technicolor Hollywood musical with a score by the Gershwins, a first-ever teaming with director Stanley Donen, and floating above the entire inspired outing, the greatest dancer of them all—Fred Astaire.

Audrey as Jo Stockton in *Funny Face*, wearing Givenchy's red column strapless gown with separate train and chiffon stole. This dress, and the photo sequence in particular, emphasized how Audrey's character had metamorphosed into a chic and knowing high fashion model: "I don't want to stop—Take the picture, take the picture!" Paramount Pictures/Photofest © Paramount Pictures

Chapter Sixteen

BONJOUR, PARIS! 1956–1957

"Paris is always a good idea."

—Audrey Hepburn

RIDING HIGH AFTER *ROMAN HOLIDAY* (1953) and the hugely popular *Sabrina* (1954), Audrey had let it be known that she'd "love to do a musical one day." Enter *Funny Face*. Said Audrey: "I read it in Paris and I fell in love with it. It was a charming story."

The charm of the story may have seemed effortless, but the task of bringing it to the screen more closely resembled the Hundred Years' War. Originally a 1920s Broadway musical starring Fred and Adele Astaire, *Funny Face* had been completely revamped, and now featured a screenplay by Leonard Gershe based upon his own unproduced movie *Wedding Day*. It had been producer Roger Edens's inspired idea to combine Gershe's script with Gershwin music and lyrics, reasoning, accurately enough, that little could go wrong with Stanley Donen, Audrey Hepburn, and the Gershwins. There was just one very big problem: MGM owned both the rights to the script and the contract of producer Roger Edens, but Paramount held Audrey Hepburn's contract.

A deal was struck: MGM would grant Paramount the *Funny Face* rights and the services of the illustrious Roger Edens, in return for Paramount loaning out Audrey for a future film at MGM. In the end, Paramount ended up with the beautiful *Funny Face*, and MGM with the monumental turkey *Green Mansions*, but that latter film lay two years in the future, and for now, both studios were pleased with the deal. As was Audrey, who, although under contract to Paramount, proved to be far from a mere pawn in the negotiations; said Roger Edens: "Miss Hepburn was all shrewd businesswoman till the deal was signed by a long-drawn-out process, believe me." Audrey's salary? 75,000 pounds, along with a few other essentials: A suite at the Ritz Hotel in Paris during location shooting. Per diem allowance. Permanent possession of her Givenchy wardrobe. By the estimation of director Donen, when toting up the cost of all the deals negotiated for actors, screenplay, and world-famous Gershwin songs, $1 million had been spent before a single frame had been shot.

Audrey would here be cast as "Jo Stockton," a self-serious young woman who doesn't believe that appearances matter until she arrives in Paris and metamorphoses from bookstore clerk to photographer Dick Avery's fashion muse. Most important of all to Audrey, however, was the fact that Dick Avery would be played by her dream co-star, Fred Astaire. Said Astaire: "They had her and she said, 'well, I'll do it if you get Fred Astaire.' And that was the biggest compliment you can get, you know." As eager to make the film as Audrey, Astaire even agreed to second billing.

Just as in *Sabrina* three years earlier, Audrey would here be playing Cinderella to a much older man. She was twenty-seven to Astaire's fifty-seven, but the thirty-year difference did not concern her in the slightest. Astaire, everyone agreed, was ageless. Not to mention possessing the ability to dance circles around men thirty years his junior. Said Audrey: "Who cares how old he is? He's Fred Astaire! And if anyone doesn't like it, he can go jump in the lake."

In fact, inside Audrey's humorous comment lies an essential truth: her pairings here with Astaire and seven years later with the twenty-five years older Cary Grant, worked because both men appeared to be just as sophisticated as she, and even more importantly, possessed the same abundant charm that made audiences believe in the possibility of happily ever after. Said Audrey in later years: "Was Fred good looking? I think so, because charm is the best-looking thing in the world, isn't it?"

The film's technical advisor, famed fashion photographer Richard Avedon, actually served as the inspiration for the character of Dick Avery, while Audrey's character was based in part upon famed model Dorcas "Doe" Norwell, Avedon's first wife. For a fee of $10,000, the world-famous Avedon would provide the title credits and backgrounds, tips on lighting, and the film's cutting edge freeze-frame photographs. Avedon, who had always idolized Astaire, smilingly related: "I learned how to be me by pretending to be him," before adding, "then I had to teach him how to pretend to be me."

With the start of official rehearsals looming, and the Academy Award–winning Audrey feeling as nervous as a schoolgirl at the mere thought of dancing with Astaire, she began rehearsing with dance director Eugene Loring. Feeling, in her own words, that "it's every woman's dream to dance with Fred Astaire," Audrey later recalled their first rehearsal together: "One look at this most debonair and elegant and distinguished of legends, and I could feel myself turn into solid lead while my heart sank into my two left feet." Astaire, sensing her nerves, gently smiled: "Come on, let's have a little go together." Audrey's reaction: "It was such fun, it was so divine." The sense memory of the thrill lingered for decades: ". . . suddenly I felt a hand around my waist, and with his inimitable grace and lightness Fred literally swept me off my feet."

The two perfectionists proved kindred spirits: "He gave me such confidence. We practiced a lot, which is an understatement. For hours, and hours, and hours, and hours, and hours. . . .With that wonderful nonchalance of his, you didn't want it to end." The ever-chic Audrey was even a bit in awe of the way the uber dapper Astaire dressed for rehearsals: impeccably groomed and wearing a pair of gray flannel slacks which were often belted with a necktie. So taken was Audrey with Fred's style that she asked her co-star for a photograph of himself, and, following her own flawless instincts for effortless style, had a gray flannel frame custom made for the photo.

Shooting began in Hollywood in April of 1956, followed by a month of location filming in Paris. And if money was going to be spent filming in Paris, then all of Paris was going to be utilized: the film would feature no fewer than thirty-five locations, from the Louvre and Eiffel Tower to Notre Dame and the Arc de Triomphe. For Audrey, it was to be Paris experienced while decked out in a wardrobe by Givenchy, one that would provide her with the biggest fashion statement yet of her burgeoning career. In fact, although the credit of "Miss Hepburn's Paris Wardrobe by Hubert de Givenchy" would seem to imply that her clothes for the New York City sequences were designed by Paramount's Edith Head, Stanley Donen remembered that even those clothes were Givenchy's.

Analyzed fashion author Pamela Clarke Keogh of this quintessential Hepburn-Givenchy collaboration: "They were two very special individuals. The talent was so unique it was almost like gold. You can't reduce it, can't take it away, you can't refine it—it is what it is." Or, in the words of designer Jeffrey Banks: "They were both modern masters of their métier."

There was to be far more than the dazzling clothes on display however, because Audrey at long last would be able to fulfill her deep desire to appear in a musical, singing classic Gershwin songs in her own small but effective mezzo soprano ("Soft, gentle, but dear" in the words of Stanley Donen). Best of all as far as Audrey was concerned: she would have no fewer than three opportunities to dance with Fred Astaire, on the songs "Funny Face," "Bonjour, Paris!" and the film ending "S'Wonderful." In Sean Ferrer's beautifully judged phrase: "She took off on a dance whirlwind that had been bottled up for years."

About her musical numbers:

"How Long Has This Been Going On"—Jo would be discovered clerking in a drab Manhattan bookstore. Minions from *Quality* magazine descend on the store to stage a fashion shoot, wreaking havoc before leaving as quickly as they arrived. Beginning to clean up their mess while alone in a dark, dusty room, Audrey begins to sing "How Long Has This Been Going On" in a sweet voice at once intimate and confiding. Donen, collaborating with cinematographer Ray June, filmed the number utilizing high angles, with Audrey half in darkness, the yellow and orange scarf she wrapped around her hat the only daub of color in the frame. Evocative, painterly, and character defining all at once.

"Basal Metabolism"—Audrey in head-to-toe black, dancing in a nightclub and mocking the beatnik culture of the day, all while delivering a terrific routine which shows off her still-beautiful line. In control, even when cutting loose.

Her outfit: a high-necked black sweater paired with slim-fitting black pants, a look still copied today. No one may think of copying fashions from dozens of terrific 1940s and '50s musicals produced by the famed Freed Unit at MGM, but it's a fact of style that Audrey's *Funny Face* look captivates in the twenty-first century as easily as it did in 1957.

That chic look, however, came with its own set of problems, and proved the source of a rare, heated dispute between star and director. Donen insisted that the black sweater and fitted black pants be topped off by white socks, the better to draw attention to her light, fast footwork. Audrey wanted to be clad entirely in black from head to toe—black socks, not white. In the retelling, Donen insisted that Audrey cried over the socks. Audrey disagreed emphatically while adding: "But what I did not tell Stanley until years later was that there was something he did not realize at the time about why I was so upset. You see, as a little girl I had a terrible complex about my big feet—I wear eight and a half—and I'd grown up with ballerinas who were little things." A great Hollywood star was now living out her fantasies by dancing with Astaire, but the little girl who felt white socks would draw attention to her galumphing feet was now, and forever after, present. The feeling never did leave, and even while promoting her 1987 television movie *Love Among Thieves*, when asked if she would change anything about her appearance, Audrey immediately responded: "I'd like to have had smaller feet. My friends have pretty feet and wear such pretty shoes." Such feelings of self-consciousness could not have been helped by Ella's comment, instantly recalled by Audrey, in that same interview: "Years ago my mother said I looked like Olive Oyl—thin legs and big feet."

Feelings were hurt by the disagreement with Donen, until Audrey saw a rough cut of the number and sent her director a note: "You were right about the socks." As the sometimes-curmudgeonly Donen admitted in later years: "When she realized you appreciated her gifts and were doing all in your power to make her look as good as possible—and with Audrey that was very, very good—she entrusted herself to you completely. I admit, though, it was something she made you earn."

For all of her nerves, Audrey was having a great time in her make-believe world: High fashion. Gershwin. Fred Astaire. Even her mother got into the act—look quickly, and yes, that is Baroness Ella van Heemstra in the role of a sidewalk café customer. A family affair.

Highlighting the location shooting was a tour de force trip around Paris with Audrey/Jo photographed by Astaire/Avery in a succession of dazzling Givenchy creations:

- Audrey all in black chasing balloons in the Tuileries. Even the inevitable location shoot accidents seemed to aid the film: it rained during the filming of this sequence, yet the rain falling among the gently floating umbrellas somehow made it look all the more special, like a delirious Technicolor dream. Everyone's best idea of Paris.
- Audrey sporting white pedal pushers while fishing on the Seine. In the words of Jeffrey Banks: "The white pants, the little cropped top and pink sash—it was slightly bohemian, very chic—and very Audrey Hepburn."

Ingenuity proved the order of the day when it came time to capture this tour de force sequence in freeze frames. Instead of facing the normal freeze-frame distortion which occurs when a frame is printed repeatedly, Donen solved the problem by placing a two-way mirror over the lens; the movie camera then shot through the mirror "while Avedon focused on the mirror, and the lab later matched the still photo with the film frame." This was all ahead of its time—experimenting with freeze frames and negative still photos was not standard 1950s movie musical fare—but the catch-you-by-surprise technique is one of many reasons why the film has held up so beautifully over the decades.

Yes, the "Bonjour, Paris!" number was certainly splashy and fun, but what audiences remember most vividly sixty years on is the extraordinary sequence of Audrey materializing from behind the statue of "Winged Victory"; swathed in a strapless red chiffon evening gown, diamond necklace glittering around her throat and red shawl floating behind her, she runs, no, skims, down the white marble staircase as the melody of "Funny Face" wafts through the air. Arms held high, simultaneously hurrying and floating—this is one Cinderella at the ball who stuns the prince. The ugly duckling has become a swan among swans, melding style with substance in a joyful elegance that seems at once both otherworldly and yet surprisingly accessible. Running down the sweeping Daru staircase, she joyfully cries out "I don't want to stop it. I like it! Take the picture. Take the picture. Take the picture!" (With typical modesty Audrey recalled: "I did it once and I didn't break my neck. Just good luck. I could not look down.") Yes, all credit to cinematographer Ray June, whose lighting brilliantly contrasts the statue, the rich red gown, and the white opera-length gloves, but nearly seventy years later this showstopping moment remains pure Audrey. Gorgeously sophisticated yet full of fun and laughter. Unique.

Funny Face's fairy-tale plot was capped by a film-ending wedding at a nineteenth-century Chantilly hunting lodge—complete with swans. It's the only time in Audrey's filmography where she's filmed wearing a wedding dress, her chic femininity all the more noticeable when compared with the deliberately androgynous black outfit she sports when dancing "Basal Metabolism." Says Jeffrey Banks of that wedding dress: "It had a dropped torso, and it was not floor length. It was very daring for its time and yet it's timeless. People still want to look like that fifty years later."

Just to complete the misty-water-colored memory, it's not just the swans who float on the water—so too do Hepburn and Astaire, off to the far horizon on a raft surrounded by the swans. At which point the realization hits that all of Audrey's fairy-tale endings prove appealing precisely because of their oft-times surprising complexity: In *Roman Holiday* she forsakes love for the throne, in *Sabrina* Prince Charming turns out to be a grumpy older man in the person of Humphrey Bogart, and in *My Fair Lady* the future remains ambiguous. Only here in *Funny Face* was she provided with a true fairy-tale ending, blissfully floating away with Fred Astaire.

Happily ever after.

Except.

Kay Thompson, playing "Maggie Prescott" (a character based upon *Vogue* editor Diana Vreeland) took a slightly more jaundiced view of the filming, particularly that ethereal ending. Two straight weeks of rain had turned the ground to thick, goopy mud, and in the brittle yet effective Thompson's telling, it had also turned Fred Astaire into a demanding fussbudget. Angular, talented, and a bit of a bulldozer, Thompson shared a mutual respect with Astaire, but in the end, they remained two artists who simply did not match up as people. In her recall, Astaire grew increasingly impatient about the muddy conditions, bluntly informing Donen: "I can't dance in that. Fix it. . . . Put down a wood floor and paint it green." Even more, she claimed, Astaire grew querulous with Audrey while filming on the raft, snapping at her: "What are you doing?"

So severe were the muddy conditions that Audrey had no fewer than nine pairs of white satin dancing pumps made in Paris, with the continuous rain making each pair progressively dirtier and more unusable. In Thompson's version of events, as Astaire grew grumpier, she counseled Audrey to "remember the camera is on you and whatever he says is unimportant. Don't listen." Claimed Thompson, Audrey responded to her counsel by replying: "Yes, well, it is a bit of a strain." Audrey's own genteel retelling provides a different take on any possible contretemps with Astaire: "I never saw him cross, never. I've never even heard he was difficult."

In the end, the two women simply possessed very different recall of the events, but Thompson only had praise for Audrey, calling her "very serious. There was no coziness, no demanding to speak to Stanley on the side, no secret conversations, no anything like that." Whichever version is accurate, what is indisputable is that Audrey broke the tension over the mud by quipping: "Here I have waited twenty years to dance with Fred Astaire, and what do I get? Mud!" A smiling Astaire recalled the quip as "my favorite remark of all time."

Whatever Kay Thompson's opinion, Hepburn, Astaire, and Donen hit it off remarkably well, and in a nicely written puff piece which appeared three days before the opening of the film, Donen opined: "It soon became apparent to me in directing the new Paramount musical *Funny*

Face that Miss Hepburn, who co-stars with Fred Astaire, has the disturbing facility of doing everything so well that it almost seems a shame ever to let the camera leave her."

Astaire's reaction to his director offering such fulsome praise only for Audrey remains unknown, but of his pairing with Audrey there can be no doubt. Their lithe bodies, the seemingly lighter-than-air charm that both possess, help each of them complete the other. She reassures him of his continued vitality, just as he is effectively telling her: "Yes, you really can dance." If, in *Sabrina*, Audrey seemed to possess two times the energy of Humphrey Bogart, in *Funny Face* Astaire proves a match for her every step of the way.

In a strange bit of advertising, the print ads for the film's February 13, 1957, premiere featured Audrey in the black "Basal Metabolism" outfit under the headline: "Audrey's Hep!" There is no mention of Hollywood's leading fashion icon swanning through Paris in Givenchy. No touting of the dances with Astaire or even the music of Gershwin. Critical reception nonetheless proved highly favorable, with *Film and Filming* terming it "the most original screen musical since *Seven Brides for Seven Brothers* and possibly the most enjoyable since *Singin' in the Rain*." Perhaps the ad copy threw people off, because the initial box office reception proved nothing more than mildly favorable for a film which has now firmly attained the rank of cult classic.

Cult classic or not, the ever-critical André Previn positioned himself as one of the few dissenters, terming the film: "Too chic . . . I didn't think it had any muscle in it. It was all so precious." Most, however, agreed with Frank Sinatra: "[Working with Audrey] is still an unfulfilled ambition of mine. She's the kind of girl you know mother would love, the kind they build musicals around."

In a number of ways, *Funny Face* remains the film which speaks most intensely to the joy in performing which Audrey sought and here actually obtained. If *Breakfast at Tiffany's* is the film people most prominently associate with Audrey, it is *Funny Face* which speaks to her essential screen self, mixing the largest fashion show of her film career with the biggest artistic love of her life—dancing. That she was singing Gershwin and dancing with Astaire proved the icing on the cake. Said the *New York Times*, "Miss Hepburn has the meek charm of a wallflower turned into a rueful butterfly."

It's a nicely turned phrase, one which reaches to the very essence of Audrey Hepburn onscreen, because there proved to be no more glorious sight than this particular Cinderella-in-waiting transforming into a butterfly. That she remained rueful in the process, acknowledging her own vulnerability amidst her triumph, made viewers around the world love her even more. As those audiences now realized, there simply was no one else like her.

Wearing one of Hubert de Givenchy's frothy daytime confections for 1957's *Love in the Afternoon*. Like many of Givenchy's designs from this era, it has a lightness and youthful appeal that sets it apart from his contemporaries like Dior and Balenciaga. Allied Artists/Photofest © Allied Artists.

Chapter Seventeen

LOVE IN THE AFTERNOON, 1957

"An over-long and only spasmodically amusing romantic comedy . . ."
—Geoff Andrew, *Time Out*

AFTER COMPLETING FUNNY FACE, AND following four weeks' vacation in Bürgenstock, Audrey began shooting *Love in the Afternoon* in August 1956.

Forever sad about her father's disappearance, Audrey was here once again gravitating toward the idea/figure of a decidedly older man in her choice of material. The most prominent motif present in these early films was not the fact of romance itself but rather the presence of that significantly older male as her love interest, a protective father figure capable of providing room in which to spread her wings. Romantic, yes, but always with an undercurrent of temporal sadness.

What was it about the Hepburn screen persona which made writers and directors alike concoct films which were not just battles of the sexes but, even more noticeably, skirmishes between the generations? Was it her youthful appearance and air of schoolgirl innocence? Was Audrey herself attracted to such films as an attempt to recreate her own missing father-daughter relationship? (Barbra Streisand did precisely that in her directorial and screenwriting debut, 1983's *Yentl.*) Or was it simply the case of a savvy new Hollywood star realizing exactly what her audiences wanted to see? Whatever the reason, and it mostly likely was a combination of all three, when approached by Billy Wilder shortly after their smashing success with *Sabrina,* Audrey had immediately said yes to *Love in the Afternoon.*

Here was the first-ever soon-to-become-famous collaboration between Billy Wilder and his new writing partner, I. A. L. Diamond. Based upon the Claude Anet novel *Ariane,* the story for *Love in the Afternoon* had already been filmed in both German (*Ariane,* 1931) and French (*Ariane, jeune fille russe,* 1932). Wilder, however, was so determined to cast Audrey in the leading role of this new version that he had sent her a cable in December 1954 explaining that he wanted to buy the rights to *Ariane* but would not commit without her promise to star in the film. Read the telegram: "Ariane without you unthinkable." Eager to work with Wilder again, and happy at the prospect of filming at the Studios de Boulogne in Paris, Audrey signed on for the film a full year before it was to begin production, committing herself to the movie before she had even begun filming *War and Peace*.

Love in the Afternoon, whose plot bore more than a passing resemblance to the Wilder-scripted *Bluebird's Eighth Wife*, found Audrey playing Ariane, the schoolgirlish daughter of Claude Chavasse (Maurice Chevalier). While still living with her father, Ariane develops a hopeless crush upon the much older womanizing American business tycoon Frank Flanagan and attempts to interest the high-living Flanagan by inventing a nonexistent romantic past.

And who would play Ariane's love interest, a paragon of masculine appeal old enough to be Ariane's father? Cary Grant (fifty-two years old) proved unavailable. So too did Yul Brynner (at forty-one, Brynner was thirteen years older than Audrey). Thoughts then turned to Gary Cooper, who at fifty-five was only three years older than Grant (and five years older than Wilder himself.) Cooper was still a very big star, a recent winner of the Best Actor Oscar for *High Noon* (1952), and he quickly expressed interest in the role. Just one big obstacle loomed: Gary Cooper looked every one of his fifty-five years—and then some.

That problem becomes immediately apparent upon Cooper's first, long-delayed (thirty minutes) entrance into the film. Still handsome but filmed in heavy shadows which can't fully disguise the bags under his eyes, Cooper is always a welcome sight onscreen, but viewers could not help but be distracted by Wilder's overt use of filters. Echoing the technique he had utilized in filming Humphrey Bogart, he here employs the same plethora of shots from behind Cooper's shoulders. There may still be heat generated in the close-ups of Cooper and Hepburn together, but the age discrepancy becomes more of an issue here than it ever was with Astaire or Bogart, precisely because of the filmmakers' strenuous efforts to distract viewers from what is staring them right in the face. Cooper looks nothing so much as tired, an essentially shy but genuinely nice man who seems a bit fatigued, wondering, perhaps, what all the fuss is about. If he wonders, then so too does the audience, and as a result, his aw-shucks charm proves harder than usual to swallow.

Decades later, Wilder himself admitted that this casting lay at the heart of the film's problem: "But the mistake there was that my beloved friend Gary Cooper, whom I miss terribly, was the wrong casting, you know? . . . He photographed like a decent, tough marshal from *High Noon*."

It's not that Cooper and Audrey didn't like each other or find an easygoing rapport. In fact, the veteran Cooper pronounced himself smitten: "I've been in pictures over thirty years, but I've never had a more exciting leading lady than Audrey. She puts more life and energy into her acting than anyone I've ever met." The affection proved mutual, with Audrey, not someone associated with the ethos of the Friars Club, even participating in a Friar's Club roast of Cooper on January 9, 1961, four months before the actor's death. Listening to the reaction of the crowd, it's almost as if Audrey's mere presence makes the boozed-up, blue-humored participants straighten up and fly right; eschewing the typical Friar's Club brand of biting and often X-rated humor, Audrey contributed her own gentle poem, entitled "What Is a Gary Cooper?" In a series of rhyming stanzas, she extolled the actor's virtues, enumerating:

It's cheerful, charming
Charitable and disarming
Bewitching, unaffected,
Enriching and unexpected.

Great as the affection between Audrey and Cooper was, however, the problem onscreen lay in the fact that the much more believable relationship on display was that between Audrey and her screen father Chevalier, the two actors exuding a similar and decidedly continental sophistication. In the case of Chevalier, however, the eye-catching surface hid a decidedly shallow interior, and in the words of Billy Wilder's wife Audrey Wilder: "His only topic of conversation from morning to night was himself."

Chevalier, in fact, figured prominently in a fascinating "what if" moment that occurred during filming, when Alan Jay Lerner stopped by the set to discuss a planned musical film adaptation of *Gigi*. Lerner, who was writing the screenplay as well as the lyrics, inquired if Chevalier was interested in the role of the older roue Honoré Lachaille? And more to the point, was Audrey interested in recreating her star-making role—and in a Lerner and Lowe, Vincente Minnelli–directed, MGM Technicolor extravaganza to boot? Audrey's response proved typically polite and thoughtful, but negative. At twenty-eight she felt she was too old for the role, and the part was ultimately played with great success by Audrey's near doppelganger, Leslie Caron, whose singing was largely dubbed, albeit with none of the attendant controversy that swamped Audrey seven years later on *My Fair Lady*.

By the time filming began on what was now her fifth starring role, Audrey had developed enough onscreen skills to make you believe in her relationships with both papa Chevalier and ladies' man Cooper. She may have exuded an air of girlishness, but she still displayed a maturity that allowed her to go toe to toe with the scene-stealing Chevalier and the revered Cooper. Audrey made her onscreen romances with older men work because she conveyed the idea that no matter how youthful her character, she was a young woman who wanted to be treated as an equal. Said Billy Wilder: "She made it so clear that her acting partners had to react the proper way. She drew them into reality."

Romantically eager in her pursuit of Flanagan yet never bulldozer strong, Audrey's Ariane was sensitive yet full of self-confidence, a combination which allowed audiences to feel genuinely protective while rooting for her success. Just as moviegoers agreed with Spencer Tracy's assessment of Katharine Hepburn in *Pat and Mike*—"Not much meat on her . . . [but] what's there is cherce"—they here agree with Flanagan's response when Audrey enumerates a seemingly autobiographical list of Ariane's faults: "I'm too thin and my ears stick out and my teeth are crooked and my neck's much too long." Cooper's smiling reply? "Maybe so—but I love the way it all hangs together." To the delight of audiences everywhere, it was the male characters—not only Frank Flanagan in *Love in the Afternoon* but also Joe Bradley in *Roman Holiday*, Linus Larrabee in *Sabrina*, and even Henry Higgins in *My Fair Lady*—who would act as fairy godfathers in the emergence of each film's beautiful young Cinderella-like character played by Audrey.

Perhaps if Cooper were ten years younger, or if the role of Frank Flanagan had been played by Cary Grant with his studied nonchalance and unbeatable charm, it might have worked. The problem, however, lies not only with Cooper but in the very concept at the heart of the film. Frank Flanagan is not just more than twice Ariane's age—he's off-putting in his pride that he forgets the names of his previous amorous conquests. Is he a charming rascal or, more likely, a full-fledged male chauvinist?

Struggling to overcome this desultory premise, the film remains unbalanced, with Audrey and Chevalier supplying charm but Cooper inspiring an occasional sense of unease. Flickering to life only intermittently, the film moves in fits and starts, and at two hours and ten minutes proves at least twenty minutes too long. And yet, there are several moments in the film which display the patented Wilder touch, most notably Audrey's silent dance with her cello, a dance which gracefully explains both Ariane's musical studies as well as her private character and fantasies.

The problem, however, remains in the fact that for every amusing moment of a mood-setting string quartet following Flanagan into the Turkish bath, there is a stretched-to-the-breaking-point gag about Ariane trying to hide her interest in Flanagan from her father. Even when the trademark Wilder humor begins to take off, any sensible viewer is yanked out of emotional involvement with the realization that for an unemployed student, Ariane appears to be awfully well-off; how is a mere student able to afford the Givenchy outfits she sports in each scene? (The same question pops into the head of anyone watching *Sabrina*, but it simply doesn't matter, such is the charm of that film.)

Love in the Afternoon does recapture some lost ground with a wonderful finale in which the towering Cooper sweeps Audrey up and onto a train hurtling out of Paris. In later years, however, Wilder related the interesting story that his good friend William Wyler told him that Audrey's character should not have spoken to Cooper as his train was departing at film's end: "Wyler said, 'Make it silent.' But I couldn't because her lips were moving." Asked if he would have made the finale silent if he could have, Wilder explains: "Yes. I would have had her start to follow and then he leaves, then she runs parallel with the train, and then he grabs her. But I had too many words there . . . she's already said goodbye to him. She should shut up at the moment and should just keep running, and then he *grabs* her."

As it turned out, even the inspired finale caused its own share of controversy, with the still powerful Legion of Decency threatening a "C" for "Condemned" rating if the unmarried Ariane and Flanagan rode off into the distance together; as a result, instead of a wordless final shot of Cooper sweeping her up onto the train, Chevalier now announced in voiceover: "They are now married, serving a life sentence in New York." The tagline, however, succeeded only in nudging the film toward a "B" rating: "Morally objectionable in part for all."

Yes, *Love in the Afternoon* proved amusing in its cynicism, but only intermittently so, with nearly all of the scattered moments of charm supplied by Audrey, who received a Golden Globe Nomination for Best Motion Pictures Actress, Musical/Comedy. Her star brand may have been slightly dinged by the film's shaky virtues, but for now it remained unassailable.

In the end, the film sputtered at the box office, eking out a mediocre gross that did not return a profit to Allied Artists. In the early 1980s, the idea of a *Love in the Afternoon* remake starring the then popular Nastassja Kinski was bruited about, and although Wilder and Diamond were not sure who could play the male lead, they liked the idea. However, when Wilder's last ever film, *Buddy, Buddy* (1981), failed at the box office, all talk of a *Love in the Afternoon* remake disappeared.

Love in the Afternoon had not reproduced the Hepburn-Wilder magic found in *Sabrina*, but studios still wanted to be in the Audrey Hepburn business, and with Mel continuing to play an important part in deciding which films she would make, a new joint Hepburn-Ferrer movie was now proposed. It was, however, one with a caveat: How about a feature film starring Audrey, but with Mel in the director's chair rather than onscreen as co-star? Mel, it turned out, had just the project in mind—an exotic extravaganza titled *Green Mansions*.

Audrey as the ethereal forest dweller Rima in the surpassingly strange *Green Mansions*, directed by Mel Ferrer.
Photo by Silver Screen Collection/Getty Images.

Chapter Eighteen

FEATURE FILM MISTAKE #1—*GREEN MANSIONS*, 1958–1959

"Filmization of W. H. Hudson's novel has been approached with reverence and taste but fantastic elements puzzle and annoy."

—Variety

BASED UPON W. H. HUDSON'S 1904 novel of the same name, *Green Mansions* was to star Audrey as Rima, a naïve habitue of the jungle who lives with her grandfather and the wild animals who serve as her only companions. This once popular, and very strange story—a jungle-land version of Audrey's Tony Award–winning role as the sea-dwelling *Ondine*—was now being turned into a multimillion-dollar Hollywood feature for one reason only: Audrey Hepburn had agreed to star in the film.

A story of gauzy mysticism, *Green Mansions* had been bruited about for the big screen as far back as the 1930s, when it was first proposed as a star vehicle for Dolores del Rio. Two decades later, it had been talked up once again, this time as a feature film for the delicate Pier Angeli. Neither version came close to production, but MGM, Mel, and Audrey all chose to ignore the warning signals that the story's gossamer tone seemed ill suited to the interests of a more demanding postwar moviegoing audience. In the novel Rima is depicted as both younger and wilder than Audrey, but Audrey's preternatural grace of movement did seem to make her the only actress anyone would accept as a fawnlike innocent; unfortunately, no one seemed to stop and ask the most basic of questions: who exactly wanted to see the beautiful Audrey Hepburn wearing a sackcloth outfit while playing a queen of the jungle?

But with Mel fixated upon the Cinderella-of-the-jungle story, and with his ironclad belief that he could guide Audrey to a fully realized performance, the studio expressed interest. Granted, none of the black-and-white feature films Mel directed had turned out to be hits— not *Vendetta*, *The Secret Fury*, or *Girl of the Limberlost*—but then again, none of those films had starred Audrey Hepburn in Technicolor. The studio acquiesced—*Green Mansions* would complete the *Funny Face*/Paramount/MGM quid pro quo agreed to two years earlier—and a $3 million budget was granted.

Off Mel went to Latin America to film background footage and scout prospective locations. The jungle locales he found proved undeniably beautiful, but they were also deemed too inaccessible for the physical requirements of a major Hollywood production. A decision was made:

although some of that background footage would be incorporated into the final film, the movie itself would be shot in Hollywood, with large portions of the MGM backlot being turned into a jungle, courtesy of art director Preston Ames.

Ames utilized hundreds of plants that Mel had shipped back from his Latin American trip to turn football-stadium-sized areas of the MGM back lot into a jungle playground for Audrey/Rima and her pet deer. *Mansions* producer Edmund Grainger had in fact spoken with Clarence Brown, director of *The Yearling*, about his experiences dealing with that film's deer, and it was Brown who suggested that a deer be adopted by Audrey right after its birth; with Audrey bottle-feeding the fawn, the deer would look upon Audrey as its actual mother. Such a plan would likely never pass muster in the animal-safety-conscious Hollywood of the twenty-first century, but in the late 1950s, anything was deemed possible when it came to a star of Audrey's stature. Adopt the fawn she did, naming him Ip, after the sound he made while calling for attention.

Down the line, there would be regrets about this adoption, because as Ip grew to full size, it became clear that a new home would have to be found for him at a zoo. Seeing and hearing how Ip cried when she left, Audrey realized that she had made a mistake in domesticating a wild animal—"She never forgave herself," reported her son Luca. That particular trauma lay several months in the future, however, and for now, as the start of filming drew near, wherever Audrey went, so too did Ip. When Audrey and Mel ate in the dining room of their well-appointed rental home, Ip would eat in the dining room right along with them. Sleeping accommodations? No problem at all: While Audrey and Mel slept in their bedroom, Ip would simply sleep in the adjacent bathroom.

Ip did indeed now think of Audrey as his mother, and as the press continued to refer to Audrey as faunlike and the possessor of doe eyes, there were now snapshots of mother and fawn cavorting in the backyard or shopping together in a Beverly Hills supermarket. It proves even more surprising, then, to watch *Green Mansions* and realize how little footage of Ip made it into the final film. All that time Audrey spent with Ip seemed to result in nothing more than three minutes of screen time.

But it was not the exact timing of Ip's footage that proved of primary concern during filming. Instead, it was Audrey, ever her own worst critic, who grew very upset with the first week's footage. Feeling that the much wider ratio (2.33 to 1) of the film's CinemaScope process only emphasized what she considered the shortcomings of her square features, Audrey, in her best iron-fist-inside-a-velvet-glove-fashion, let it be known that MGM must fix the distorted images—pronto. Emergency calls were put out, and Robert E. Gottschalk, the original developer of the anamorphic lens, brought his own brand-new lens to MGM and shot test footage. Gottschalk, MGM fixer-in-chief Eddie Mannix, Audrey, and Mel assembled in the screening room to watch this newly shot footage, and when the Panavision camera closed in on Audrey's face as she peered out from behind jungle foliage, a collective sigh of relief was followed by a round of applause. The lens difficulties had been solved; now it was just the story itself that began growing into an ever-larger problem.

In the finished film, audiences are denied a glimpse of Audrey until a full twenty-eight minutes have elapsed, and her first words are not uttered until forty minutes into the film's one hour and forty-four minutes running time. So uninvolving is the drama, so nonexistent the chemistry between Audrey and leading man Anthony Perkins ("Abel"), that the viewer is left to idly wonder how Rima keeps her one and only outfit so pristinely clean and pressed in the middle of the jungle. Perkins, three years younger than Audrey, is himself too much of a naif to provide any contrast to Audrey, and while he liked Audrey a great deal—"She was wonderful to work with, like a real person, almost a sister"—he was saddled with lines which would stymie Olivier himself, squeaking out "I've got to live!" as a high point of emotion. Even the film's thundering score by Bronislau Kaper distracts, underlining every forced emotion several times, just in case any youngster in the audience missed the point.

Mel's direction registers as competent, but his decision to regularly utilize a green tint proves disorienting. While the footage from his trip to Latin America is impressive, noticeably artificial sets representing the cave of Rima's grandfather Nuflo (a hammy Lee J. Cobb) further add to audience disconnection. Perhaps the film might have fared better back in the '30s when it was first mentioned as a possible feature, but sophisticated 1950s audiences weren't buying this particular brand of whimsy.

Tony Perkins felt that the film failed commercially "because it was good but unusual," but Sean Ferrer provides the most nuanced take on why his parents' film didn't score: "In some ways it seems like more of an idea than a fully realized story. My father didn't get the budget to really sell it and they had to make do with big plants on a studio set—those sets look artificial and pull you out of the fantasy. The story seems a bit stale, but they also didn't let my father take it as far as he could have. And maybe he had doubts and didn't have the courage to take the material all the way."

For nearly two hours the audience watches Rima run around the jungle while trying to find true love with Abel, yet in the end she is killed, only to reappear as a cross between a flower and an apparition. Where exactly was the audience for an Audrey Hepburn film in which she plays a jungle spirit who is burned alive at the climax? It's a denouement to which the only logical reaction is "Huh? Audrey's dead but now she's a flower?!" Audiences were not impressed, and neither were the critics. Even Audrey's fan Bosley Crowther struggled for words of praise, only managing to write: "Even so, Miss Hepburn conducts herself all through it with grace and dignity, making Rima both poignant and idyllic, if not in the least logical." More typically, however, "D.B." in *Monthly Film Bulletin* bluntly stated: "A piece of irritating and often risible hokum."

The film flopped, and Mel Ferrer never again directed either Audrey or a Hollywood feature film. Noting the failure of *Green Mansions*, as well as the lackluster *Mayerling*, Paramount did not exercise its option on three other proposed Hepburn/Ferrer films: Thomas Wolfe's *Look Homeward, Angel* and Jean Anouilh's *The Lark*, as well as a Ferrer-directed version of *L'Aiglon*. Mel's dream of teaming with Audrey to become the postwar version of the Oliviers was fading fast, the score for their five years/four joint projects falling far below their hoped-for goal:

Ondine—A Tony Award for Audrey, grumblings about Mel's misplaced ego.
War and Peace—Praise for Audrey but indifference toward Mel.
Mayerling—Nobody's idea of a good time.
Green Mansions—Best forgotten by everyone involved.

But while *Green Mansions* may have failed financially, Audrey's star was soon to reach its zenith with the next year's release of an extraordinary film, one which contained the finest acting of her career. The performance, in fact, that Audrey preferred over any other in her filmography.

Audrey Kathleen Hepburn, the ultimate fashion icon, would be trading in Givenchy for the habit of a cloistered nun.

Her finest performance: 1959's beautifully wrought *The Nun's Story*. Entertainment Pictures/Alamy Stock Photo.

Chapter Nineteen

THE NUN'S STORY, 1959

"A transcendent film, comparable more to Bergman or Bresson than to anything in the American cinema."

—John Fitzpatrick

FRESH OFF THE FAILURE OF *Green Mansions* and still desperately wanting a child, Audrey looked at work as a welcome distraction from her personal disappointments. If she couldn't yet have a family of her own, she would still have a chance to stretch her acting muscles with a role as far from her normal screen fare as possible: that of a young woman who enters the cloistered world of the convent, only to experience a life-altering crisis of faith. *The Nun's Story.*

Based upon the best-selling novel of the same name by Kathryn Hulme, *The Nun's Story* told the story of the real-life Marie Louise Habets (here named Gabrielle van der Mal), who was known as Sister Luke after taking the veil. Audrey had first become aware of the book when her sister-in-law enthusiastically recommended it to Mel, who immediately saw the story as an opportunity for Audrey to expand her range as an actress; when the idea of a movie based upon Hulme's novel had first been broached, it was pitched as a vehicle for Ingrid Bergman, who was now back in public favor after the scandal of her out-of-wedlock pregnancy with Italian director Roberto Rossellini. Bergman, however, felt she was too old for the role and suggested Audrey to play Sister Luke.

The movie's screenwriter, Robert Anderson, was immediately interested in the idea of casting Audrey and asked his agent Kay Brown to call Audrey's agent Kurt Frings. Audrey was intrigued, quickly realizing that Anderson, famous for his play *Tea and Sympathy*, had written a psychologically complex script of surprising depth. (As it turned out, Anderson and Audrey had a discreet and relatively short-term personal involvement that he wrote about, in slightly disguised fashion, in his novel *After*.)

Anderson's first-rate screenplay considered issues of faith against a background stretching from a sheltered convent to Africa, and from 1920s Belgium to the Europe of World War II. Here was a script that grappled with nothing less than the biggest of questions—in the striking words of Hillel utilized by Anderson in his screenplay: "If I am not for myself, who will be for me? And if I am for myself alone, what am I?"

Audrey felt an immediate kinship with the character of Sister Luke: both women were born in Belgium, lost their fathers at a young age, left their native countries, experienced suffering during the Second World War while working for the underground, and had brothers sent to labor camps during the war. Sean believes that what attracted Audrey to the part was the chance to investigate the life of "someone who had the courage to choose humanity over ideology. The system of ideology was preventing the nun from doing what she really wanted her life to be about—helping people. That struck a chord with my mother. . . . I think the experience of filming parts of *Nun's Story* in Africa also helped plant the seeds of her UNICEF work later in life."

Gabrielle's onscreen journey would take her from privileged Belgian schoolgirl to cloistered nun before she grows disillusioned and leaves the order. This was all far from the world of *The Sound of Music* or even *Dialogue of the Carmelites*; in the words of the film's Oscar-winning director Fred Zinnemann (*From Here to Eternity*, 1953), Sister Luke's story was "not a crisis of faith, but a crisis of worthiness," feelings to which the perpetually self-doubting Audrey could relate.

Still, Audrey hesitated. The idea intrigued, but at this same time, she was once again considering the ongoing request that she star in the film adaptation of *The Diary of Anne Frank*. Contrary to the accepted story that Audrey had instantaneously turned down the idea of starring in *Anne Frank* because it rang too close to her own wartime experience, she now wrote to Fred Zinnemann that Kurt Frings and George Stevens were in fact trying to "work out a schedule whereby *Anne Frank* could possibly be done before the *Nun*, but I can see no way of doing this without jeopardizing your and my preparations." Audrey was now juggling two highly prestigious properties in *Anne Frank* and *The Nun's Story*—it was all a very long way from *Monte Carlo Baby*.

Mel and Kurt Frings began pushing Audrey to accept *The Nun's Story*. Yes, they acknowledged, location filming in the Belgian Congo might prove to be very uncomfortable. Yes, this was a decidedly different role for her, but therein lay the attraction. Why not journey out of her comfort zone? Hungering after more substantial onscreen fare, Audrey agreed to take on the role.

Her deal in place—a fee of $200,000 plus an additional ten percent of the gross after her salary had been recouped—Audrey grew enthusiastic. Here was a meaty dramatic role and the chance to work with yet another Academy Award–winning director. In only her seventh starring role, she would now be guided by her fifth certified legend, with Zinnemann following in the footsteps of Wyler, Wilder (twice), Vidor, and Donen.

The underpinnings of *The Nun's Story* seemed a natural fit for Zinnemann, who instinctively gravitated toward films centering around a personal journey of self-discovery. In movies ranging from *The Men* (1950) to *High Noon* (1952) and *The Member of the Wedding* (1952), his filmography, in the words of Zinnemann scholar Gene D. Phillips, constituted a cinematic search for the "self-knowledge that enables [the character] to find his place in the community in which he lives."

The erudite Zinnemann, who had first been sent Hulme's novel by his friend Gary Cooper, would here be working with color for only the second time in his career (the first was on *Oklahoma!* in 1955) while functioning in the dual capacities of director and executive producer. Esteemed throughout Hollywood he may have been, but Zinnemann was the first to admit that *The Nun's Story* was greenlit for production for only one reason—the involvement of Audrey Hepburn. Said Zinnemann of the time spent pitching the film to various studios: "Unhappily, my enthusiasm was not shared by any of the studios. . . . But when Audrey said she wanted to do it the studios suddenly became intensely interested," and Warner Bros. committed to a top-tier budget of $3.5 million. In the director's own words: "With the exception of Ingrid Bergman, there was at that time no star as incandescent as Audrey. She was shy, coltish, and intelligent; she looked delicate, but there was a hint of iron in the jawline that signified a stubborn will. I thought she would be ideal."

The feeling proved mutual, with Audrey commenting in later years: "I was very fortunate to fall into a period of moviemaking when these directors were around and wanted me. That's the miracle of my career because I haven't made that many pictures." Just as proved the case with both William Wyler and Billy Wilder, a lifelong friendship with Zinnemann followed, and eight years later he expressed a desire to cast her as Sir Thomas More's daughter in his film version of Robert Bolt's *A Man for All Seasons*; the idea never gained traction, however, both because of scheduling problems and because Audrey, nearly forty by the time of production, was too old for the role.

Favorite cinematographer Franz Planer would be on board for *The Nun's Story*, as would production designer Alexandre Trauner, who had recently worked with Audrey on *Love in the Afternoon*. After the bishop of Bruges nixed location shooting at the actual Sisters of Charity convent in Belgium, the highly skilled and detail-oriented Trauner set about recreating Sister Luke's convent and chapel at the Centro Sperimentale and Cinecitta studios. By shooting these interiors in Rome rather than Hollywood, the production would save $1 million while also remaining near Santa Sabina, the Mother House of the Dominican Order whose members served as advisers on the film.

Given that real nuns were not allowed to be photographed, the location shooting in Rome meant that extras were utilized for the ceremonial scenes of religious processions. Explained Zinnemann: "In the end, twenty dancers were borrowed from the ballet corps of the Rome Opera and were drilled by two Dominican nuns, one of them a university professor." For close-ups of the nuns, Zinnemann looked for faces of "great character and personality" and found them, surprisingly, among the Roman aristocracy. Wrote the director: "A lot of principessas and contessas would turn up in their Rolls-Royces or Mercedes at five in the morning. Dressed as nuns they looked marvelous."

Far from trying to populate the film with real-life Roman Catholics, Zinnemann preferred not to use such true believers: "It seemed important to keep an objective approach to the work, without the emotional involvement a faithful believer would bring to it, as this would create a private sentimental quality I wanted to avoid at all costs." Robert Anderson, a Protestant, Edith Evans and Audrey as Christian Scientists, and Peggy Ashcroft as an agnostic, all passed this test.

Given the fact that Audrey would spend most of the film clad in a habit, the services of Givenchy were not required, but wanting the security blanket of advice from her trusted friend, Audrey asked that Hubert review Marjorie Best's designs. Sister Luke's simple habit would, she felt, require attention to detail that would help define her character. She wanted to test the movement of the fabric while walking and kneeling, and sought to develop a sense memory of just how the garment changed her posture and demeanor. Even the manner in which the nuns held the skirts of their habits influenced her interpretation and inventiveness, and when Sister Luke walks out of the convent at film's end, it was Audrey who decided that she would instinctively move to hold her skirt "and then realize she no longer has that kind of skirt."

Given Audrey's image as an avatar of fashion chic, it may have come as a surprise to some—but not to Zinnemann—how devoted she was to her craft. Before filming began, Audrey, Edith Evans and Peggy Ashcroft stayed at a convent in order to fully experience the life of a nun. Beginning each day with prayers at 5:30 a.m., Audrey learned firsthand how a cloistered silent life replete with closed doors and grills affected one's own psychological outlook. How, she wondered, did Gabrielle feel when she lost her own name and acquired the name Sister Luke? How did it feel for Sister Luke to be referred to as #1072?

Contacting Marie Louise Habets in order to gain further understanding of the nun's life, Audrey formed a friendship with the former nun which grew into a genuinely close relationship. She peppered Marie Louise with questions about surgical nursing: How were instruments handled? What were the proper sterilization procedures?

Wanting to acquire firsthand experience, she attended several operations, but her most intensive preparation revolved around her collaboration with Zinnemann. It has been claimed that Audrey closely studied Carl Dreyer's highly regarded 1928 silent film, *The Passion of Joan of Arc*, although Zinnemann himself denied ever studying the film for insight. What is certain, however, is that actress and director spent great periods of time talking about how Sister Luke developed and changed in her reactions to others both in and outside of the convent. In Zinnemann's words: "It took many hours of going into lots of details. I always work that way with almost all actors. Then when we are rehearsing, I always want to see what the actor brings to the part, without telling him what to do . . ."

Given the power of the Catholic Church in 1958, the filmmakers deliberately sought the church's approval regarding Anderson's script. The church remained wary, uneasy about Sister Luke's status as someone incapable of accepting the church's edict forbidding any involvement in the war effort. The filmmakers' discussions with nuns had revealed that obedience remained the hardest vow of all to follow, and the church powers remained displeased with the screenplay's declaration "Dear Lord, forgive me, but I cannot obey anymore." Here was a nun for whom the German occupation and her father's murder—temporal, human events—trumped faith in the Almighty, a message the church disliked.

So intense were the lengthy discussions with the Dominican Order heading the Cinema Office of the Catholic Church, that in his autobiography Zinnemann details a two-hour discussion regarding a single line spoken by the mother superior: "The life of a nun is a life against nature." The Dominican advisers insisted that the line be changed to "a life *above* nature," until a Jesuit friend of Zinnemann's suggested a compromise: "*In many ways* it's a life *against* nature." In the end, Edith Evans delivered the line with a slight adjustment: "In a way, it's a life against nature."

Audrey herself struck a diplomatic balance, insisting: "The story is not pro-catholic nor is it anti-catholic. It is simply a story, and a very warm and interesting one." In a smart, analytical letter to Mel dated January 20, 1958, she explained the stakes at play: "In the story we find examples of the Order trying to make her conform to obedience first, something which to Sister Luke remains secondary until the last; her impulses are always to give and serve first. The coldness she is shown when this honest and courageous woman finally leaves the convent with sorrow in her eyes, yet great faith in her heart, should make for an acutely believable finish."

What the church insisted upon most strongly of all, however, was that any suggestion of an attraction between Sister Luke and the tough dedicated Dr. Fortunati (Peter Finch) be excised. The mere hint of a possible romance was tamped down, but Hepburn and Finch nonetheless imbued their roles with a subtext of sensuality; to Peter Ustinov, who worked with Fred Zinnemann on *The Sundowners*, their abstinence "became an erotic barometer and the unrequited longings of the protagonists kept hovering on the brink of obscenity." The film, of course, proved the furthest thing from obscene, but it was nonetheless Dr. Fortunati who pushed Sister Luke toward a greater awareness of her own true beliefs. In his blunt admonition to Sister Luke: "I've seen nuns come and go and I tell you this—you are not like them. You have not got the vocation."

With all script compromises finally hammered out, location shooting began in Stanleyville, Belgian Congo, with four days spent filming at the Yalisombo leper colony on an island in the middle of the Congo River. To members of the cast and crew concerned over their proximity to leprosy, Stanley Browne, the colony's doctor, insisted: "You have less risk of getting leprosy here than catching a cold in the New York subway." As detailed by Zinnemann, at the end of the four days of shooting, Browne did, however, cheekily add, "Of course you have to understand that the incubation period for leprosy is seventeen years."

Attending church at the colony, Audrey felt awestruck at service's end when all assembled began singing Beethoven's "Ode to Joy" in a mix of English, French, Lingala, and Swahili. Deeply moved by the sight of men and women who responded to their difficult lives with joy and deep faith, Audrey began a period of intense self-questioning that would take her thirty years to fully answer, in part by circling back to Africa through her work with UNICEF. How could she, who led a life of such privilege, most effectively give back to those who had so little? Certainly, she seemed to feel, there had to be work of greater import than making movies.

For now, however, the immediate problem lay in managing the extremely difficult conditions. An expensive sequence featuring three men drowning in quicksand during a torrential rainstorm involved wind machines and the building of a man-made island complete with mini elevators, but the night before shooting, the river fell by two feet, and in Zinnemann's baffled explanation, "all the chicken-wire and cement holding the 'quicksand' was glaringly exposed. Unfortunately, no one knew why the river had shrunk so suddenly or when it might rise again. The scene was never shot."

Nor did Zinnemann's tantalizing proposal to shoot the European sections of the film in black-and-white but the African sections in vibrant color, ever see the light of day. The proposal was vetoed by Jack Warner who thought the idea "too tricky and too far ahead of popular imagination." It was a poor decision on Warner's part, given the effectiveness with which it would have underscored the dichotomy between austere life in Belgium and the technicolor fecundity of Africa.

The way the film leaps forward when it reaches Africa, the screen filling with an aerial shot of a river slicing through the green and vibrant landscape, makes it clear that the contrast with Europe, the sense of greater freedom Africa provides Sister Luke, would have been even more profound if these first shots of Africa had also represented the film's first shots in color. Refused Warner's permission, Zinnemann had to compensate by shooting the European scenes in a more washed-out color palette.

Hot as it was to film a movie in equatorial Africa while wearing a heavy nun's habit, Audrey remained energized and spoke of her determination to make the best of whatever came her way: "In the Congo, a cool day was 100 and the temperature was often 130. People ask me if I didn't swelter in my nun's habit. I didn't. Actually, all that covering keeps the heat out." The ever-chic Audrey Hepburn roughing it in Africa? The mere idea was grist for Hollywood gossip columnists who began circulating a rumor that Audrey was demanding that a bidet be sent to Africa. Audrey's exasperated response to the lie? "How and where would you hook it up?" (Zinnemann did detail a request for an air conditioner, which was sent from California to no effect—instead of an air conditioner, the studio sent a humidifier . . .) Said Zinnemann: "I have never seen anyone more disciplined, more gracious, or more dedicated to her work than Audrey. There was no ego, no asking for extra favors; there was the greatest consideration for her co-workers."

Ironically, Audrey survived the noticeable hardships of Africa without incident, but became extremely ill with painful kidney stones when the film returned to Cinecitta Studios for interior shooting. Informed of her daughter's illness, Ella jetted in from London, while Mel immediately dropped all his work and flew to Rome.

Upon recovering from the attack, Audrey returned to filming with an even more determined focus, as if her own illness had helped her understand the difficulties faced by Sister Luke's patients. It was at this point in the filming that Robert F. Hawkins of the *New York Times* Rome bureau visited the Cinecitta set, ending his visit with a surprised respect for Audrey's intense preparation; she possessed, he found, "a brilliant grasp of the end result wanted. What seemed nearly effortless was doubtlessly the product of much private thought, and of hard work." By this point, so immersed was Audrey in the role that during filming she would neither look in the mirror nor listen to records, explaining: "My character would never do these things." Said castmate Patricia Bosworth, Audrey "seemed almost transfixed."

Audrey also consulted in detail with trusted hairdresser Grazia De Rossi about the character defining sequence in which Gabrielle's long hair is cut after she enters the convent. As in *Roman Holiday*, the hair cutting would serve to illustrate her character's brand-new persona, but the scene carried its own technical challenges: How could Audrey's long wig be cut on camera without the wig being pulled off balance? The neat solution: Grazia De Rossi herself would play the nun in charge of cutting the postulants' hair. As Sister Luke sits in profile, awaiting the haircut with her eyes closed, we instantly understand what this symbolic loss of hair is costing her—it is all present in the stiffness of Audrey's neck, in the flickering dismay and resistance under her partially closed eyelids. The resulting sequence contained a particularly beautiful shot in which Zinnemann's camera focuses upon a large piece of Gabrielle's hair falling onto a gold platter. She is, as a postulant, fully rejecting worldly concerns about beauty and appearance, and yet as the close-ups reveal, she has never looked more beautiful.

Audrey always did go to see her daily rushes—"There might be something I can still correct"—and *The Nun's Story* daily rushes soon revealed a performance of far more skill, maturity, and understanding than any she had previously delivered. The convent sequences found her more than holding her own—indeed at times surpassing—the formidable trio of Mildred Dunnock, Dame Peggy Ashcroft, and Dame Edith Evans. With her body shrouded in the voluminous nun's habit and only her eyes and mouth revealed, Audrey was able to convey Sister Luke's metamorphosis from naïve, hopeful girl to tired nun simply through the increasing sadness found in her eyes. In the recall of Patricia Bosworth, before filming the goodbye scene between Sister Luke and best friend Sister Simone (Bosworth): "Audrey drifted over to me and took my hands in hers. 'Patti,' she said softly and intensely, don't *do* anything. Above all, don't *act*. The camera picks up everything. But do mean what you say."

Audrey Hepburn, Hollywood star, had completely disappeared, replaced by a nun exemplifying the ineffable qualities of faith, disappointment, and the determination to endure. By means of subtle shifts in her body language, as well as the glimpses of frustration flashing silently across her face, Audrey is able to show Sister Luke's evolution from submission to resistance. She wants to escape the stifling dictates of the ruling cardinals in Rome as surely as she wants to help people escape the Germans.

Audrey is aided immeasurably throughout by Zinnemann's beautiful direction. At the end of the movie, as Sister Luke meets with Mother Emmanuel regarding her request to leave the convent, Zinnemann films the two women in front of a glass wall, the solitary tree seen in the rain outside clearly standing as a metaphor for Sister Luke. When the mother superior comes to understand that Sister Luke is no longer capable of "obedience without question, without inner murmuring," Zinnemann frames Audrey alone on a bench in the middle of the frame. She is a solitary figure, about to lose the protection of the convent, and in the next sequence, when she takes off her robes, she will be leaving the convent without anyone bidding her farewell.

That final scene, an extraordinarily effective four-minute sequence which begins with Sister Luke exchanging her habit for street clothes, works beautifully because of all the information Audrey is able to silently convey. She removes her wimple, and the camera pans upward to an image of a cross, the next shot finding her dressed in a gray suit and removing the ring symbolizing her marriage to Christ. The film has now come full circle, the removal of the ring acting as a mirror image to the removal of her own ring when she left home for the convent. Placing her hat in a suitcase, she hears a buzzed click signaling that the door to leave the convent has opened. Zinnemann's camera frames Sister Luke in the doorway and she slowly walks down the street—hesitates—and then turns right. Nothing is wrapped up in a neat and tidy Hollywood ending. The ability of one nun's story to impart universality to the life choices made by all has reached its ultimate conclusion, and done so in complete silence.

That silence, in fact, came as the result of an intense argument between Zinnemann and Jack Warner. The film's composer, Franz Waxman, was, in Zinnemann's view, anti-Catholic: "What I didn't know was that he had a strong dislike of the Catholic Church. When we listened to his music it sounded like the background for the dungeons of *The Count of Monte Cristo*. I decided not to use very much of it. Franz was outraged and complained to Jack Warner."

Zinnemann's removal of Waxman's music from the final scene triggered an intense disagreement with Jack Warner, who argued that "every Warner Brothers picture has music at the end." Forcefully explaining that the inclusion of music would send a message to the audience that "Warner Brothers congratulate the nun on quitting the convent," Zinnemann pointedly asked the mogul: "Is that what you want? If the music is heavy the audience will be depressed; I don't see how you can win." Warner acquiesced, if grudgingly, and the camera focused on Gabrielle's retreating figure without a single note of musical accompaniment.

Zinnemann's style of editing also helped to increase the film's effectiveness given his notable use of more fragmented scenes toward the end of the film, "partly because of the tension and the war, and partly because the tempo of life intensifies. It's no longer the idyllic Congo." Just as the outside world has fallen apart, so too has Sister Luke's private interior world, and in the end, when she leaves the convent, the film has once again reverted to the longer takes utilized in the first half of the film: the storytelling itself has come full circle.

So complete is the film's quiet study of religious vocation and loss of faith that its few short-comings do not detract from its overall effectiveness. By the time of Sister Luke's departure from the convent, close to twenty years have elapsed between the 1920s-era start of the film and the hostilities of World War II, but you wouldn't know it by looking at Audrey's seemingly identical hair. Since nunneries are not exactly known as a center of hair dyeing and beauty treatments, a few, or several, strands of gray hair would have gone a long way toward silently indicating that passage of time.

Such a misstep is a small quibble, however, in the face of what Zinnemann and Audrey have achieved: an absorbing, effective inquiry into the very nature of faith and God. Said an impressed Marie Louise Habets after attending the screening of a four-hour rough cut: "I'm never going to see it again because if I do I'm going to run right back to the convent. . . . I could just sit there and cry my eyes out, not with regret, but because of the beauty of it. It is a beautiful life, the religious life, if you . . . can accept it without murmuring all the time."

Warner Bros., however, remained very uneasy about the film's prospects, unsure if anyone wanted to see a film about a nun's life, starring Audrey Hepburn in the most atypical role of her career. Their answer came in the form of grosses which made it the most successful Warner Bros. film of the year, with a cumulative worldwide gross of $11.5 million against a cost of only $3.5 million. (Given the canny deal struck by Kurt Frings which gave Audrey a percentage of the film's profits, this would prove to be the most personally profitable film she ever made.)

The Nun's Story would go on to earn eight Academy Award nominations, including Best Picture, Best Actress (Audrey's third nomination), Best Director (Zinnemann), Screenplay (Robert Anderson), Cinematography (Franz Planer), Editing, Score, and Sound. And, while the film would not win any of the Oscars for which it was nominated, Audrey, who was also nominated for a Golden Globe Award, did win a Best Actress award from the New York Film Critics; in a close race between Audrey and Simone Signoret (who would win the Oscar for *Room at the Top)*, the New York Film Critics ultimately selected Audrey as Best Actress on the sixth ballot. Audrey would also go on to win the BAFTA award as Best Actress and Zinnemann won honors as Best Director from both the New York Film Critics and the National Board of Review.

Regarding Audrey's performance, there remains near unanimous agreement. Says Jeanine Basinger: "Audrey Hepburn here gives one of the great performances by an actress in the history of film. I don't say that lightly because normally if the film involves nuns I run for the hills. I think I was frightened as a child by *The Song of Bernadette!* The film is beautifully directed by Zinnemann—he was a very intelligent director, never flashy, who adjusted his style according to the material. Sister Luke's inner struggle is very different from Gary Cooper's sheriff in *High Noon,* but Zinnemann brings the same sensitivity to both films. This film is the true test of Audrey Hepburn as a superb actress. There is no fashion in sight—she's in a nun's habit and that's it. She is here presenting herself bare—there's not even a hint of a movie star wearing a nun's habit. Her face is so beautifully expressive, and her intelligence is on full display. The performance is in total service to the character. Look at how different Sister Luke is from Joanna in *Two for the Road*—it takes a real actress to encompass that range. She really should have won the Academy Award for her performance as Sister Luke."

Said Zinnemann in later years: "Looking at the film again, after more than twenty-five years, I am struck by the fine, firm line of development in Audrey's performance. The subconscious quality of independence is present in all her actions." The feeling of admiration proved mutual, with Audrey in later years exclaiming: "Fred Zinnemann is a perfectionist. It was wonderful!"

Without any couture fashion in sight and featuring long stretches of silence that deepen its consideration of religious dedication, *The Nun's Story* featured an Audrey whose performance, in the words of Henry Hart in *Film in Review*, should "forever silence those who have thought her less an actress than a symbol of the sophisticated child-woman." Said her son Sean: "I think my mother was proudest of *The Nun's Story* . . . she thought it was an important film."

Decades later, it was Robert Wolders who best expressed the import of *The Nun's Story* in Audrey's filmography, unexpectedly yet logically explaining that the character of Sister Luke represented the woman closest to the real Audrey Hepburn: "What I see in the film and in the character is so close to Audrey in those moments when she was in turmoil, when there was something she could not resolve." By drawing deeply upon her own conflicted personality and feelings, Audrey had achieved not just her best performance, but her deepest personal expression of art's universality and power to heal.

A pensive Audrey in the only western of her career, John Huston's wildly uneven *The Unforgiven,* 1960. MGM-UA/ Photofest © MGM-UA.

Chapter Twenty

FEATURE FILM MISTAKE #2—*THE UNFORGIVEN*, 1960

"Some of my pictures I don't care for. This one I actively dislike."

—Director John Huston

AFTER THE WORLDWIDE SUCCESS OF *The Nun's Story,* Audrey Hepburn was more in demand than ever, with her slightest signal of attraction to the material serving to greenlight virtually any film that captured her interest. And yet, just as with any topflight Hollywood actress, Audrey occasionally undertook roles that left audiences wondering, "What was she thinking?" Which meant that if *Green Mansions*, the bizarre fantasy that found Audrey traipsing around the jungle, represented her first head-scratcher, then her second walloping mistake came with John Huston's *The Unforgiven* (1960).

What was Audrey doing in the midst of Huston's surpassingly strange western? For an actress indelibly associated with high fashion and romantic comedies, playing a nineteenth-century Native American woman proved odd indeed. This was not terra firma for Audrey, a state of affairs proven literally true when, during location filming in Durango, she fell off an Arabian stallion once owned by Cuban dictator Fulgencio Batista and ended up in the hospital for weeks.

Which is getting ahead of a story, where, in the very beginning, Audrey expressed an interest in filming a western. After reading the Ben Maddow *Unforgiven* screenplay (based upon Alan Le May's novel of the same name), Audrey decided to take a leap of faith; perhaps it was the chance to spread her wings acting-wise that made her agree to play "Rachel Zachary," a Kiowa Indian "rescued" in childhood and raised by a white family in the Texas panhandle of the 1860s. Only Rachel's "mother" (Lillian Gish) knows that she is a full-blooded Kiowa Indian, and the simmering racial tensions on display finally explode at film's end, in a shootout led by Rachel's brother Ben (Burt Lancaster).

It all seemed a questionable setting for such a sophisticated and continental actress, but Audrey was, understandably enough, drawn to the idea of working with award-winning director John Huston. Add in a paycheck for $200,000 and a $6 million budget, which made the film one of the most expensive westerns ever made, and it all shaped up as a promising endeavor. What could really go wrong? As it turned out, plenty.

For starters, director Huston and star/producer Burt Lancaster clashed throughout filming. Both men proved wildly egocentric, and while Huston called the shots behind the camera, Lancaster held the ultimate financial power as the film's producer. As soon as shooting began, Huston grew increasingly disgruntled when he realized that Lancaster and his producing partner James Hill wanted to make a traditional western, ignoring the considerations of racism that had intrigued Huston in the first place.

Sporting long hair which fell down her back, Audrey was covered in reddish-dark makeup which did little to help convince the viewer that she was Native American, and her comfort level was not helped by the fact that she disliked the hot, dusty location conditions. More disconcertingly, the skin makeup seemed to disappear from one scene to another, leaving all viewers puzzled as to exactly where Rachel was living; she's shown riding horses outdoors in the scorched plains of the west, but in the next scene her reddish skin tone appears to have become all white. Had Rachel gone to the Alps to escape the heat? In her own life, Audrey thrived in the outdoors, taking long hikes through the mountainous Swiss countryside, but here she appears nothing so much as ill at ease. Whether on horseback or not, she had to indulge in the most un-Audrey-like of activities: firing a shotgun!

Beautifully photographed throughout by Franz Planer, Audrey nonetheless proves disconcerting every time she must speak the pedestrian dialogue. She of the perfectly modulated speaking voice was now declaiming: "I never seen you before . . . I'm dreamin', ain't I?" The wildly uneven screenplay makes it impossible to take Rachel's supposedly homespun wisdom seriously: contemplating a flock of geese, Audrey exclaims: "They jest fly a mite higher than us." There is simply no way that this Rachel, for all of her "ain'ts" and "jests," registers as a believable Kiowa Native American.

Huston's directorial methods also left Audrey more than a bit at sea, and while they got along well, their director-actress collaboration proved to be an uneasy mix of styles. Used to the exacting precision of Wyler, Wilder, and Donen, Audrey found that Huston "makes the artist take a lot of responsibility and that is like a challenge."

Filming plodded along, and Audrey remained uneasy over the amount of time she had to spend riding horses. She had, in fact, developed a fear of riding after breaking her collarbone when thrown from a horse at age eleven, but during the making of *War and Peace*, Mel had helped her conquer that fear. Then, in the midst of *Unforgiven*'s mix of bad weather, warring egos, and cornpone dialogue, came a terrible accident. On January 28, 1959, while riding her horse "Diablo," Audrey took a bad fall and landed on her back, fracturing four vertebrae in the process. She lay unconscious for five minutes, and Mel flew in with her personal doctor, Howard Mendelson. She was eventually flown back to Los Angeles via ambulance plane, and Marie Louise Habets, the real life "Sister Luke" of *The Nun's Story*, spent three weeks nursing her back to health.

As noted by Marie Louise, Audrey refused to take any narcotics or sedatives, no matter how great her discomfort. Taking her first steps again on February 15, she quickly returned to the set and gamely hoisted herself back onto Diablo to complete the aborted riding scene. By now, however, the production seemed cursed: co-star Audie Murphy nearly drowned in a duck-hunting accident, and three crew members were killed in a plane crash.

When all was said and done, the film remained too uneven for any coherent audience response. For every beautifully photographed outdoor scene, there is a strangely truncated consideration of the plight facing Native Americans, until the entire story bogs down in a strange mishmash of styles and oddball psychology. At the story's climax, with the Zachary family under siege from the Kiowas, Rachel asks her brother Ben (Lancaster) if he would "fancy her" if they weren't related—he answers the question by kissing her while surrounded by Native Americans trying to kill them both. How does Rachel solve this conundrum? By shooting and killing her actual Native American brother. Even Sigmund Freud would throw up his hands at this one.

Planer's lighting of the landscape proved capable of explaining the film's story and subtext far more eloquently than does the screenplay, but unevenness of tone and style does the film in. Burdened with an inappropriately jaunty score by Dimitri Tiomkin, the film led Huston to conclude in later years that "the overall tone is bombastic and overinflated. Everybody in it is bigger than life. . . . But Hepburn was a trouper and I wished I had used her to better advantage. She could have carried the picture if I let her."

The film proved unsuccessful with critics and audiences alike and earned Audrey a rare outright pan from critic Dwight Macdonald: "She is not an actress, she is a model, with her stiff meagre body and her blank face full of good bone structure. She has the model's narcissism, not the actress's introversion." Countered Huston, who had already triumphed directing Katharine Hepburn in *The African Queen* (1951): "She's as good as the other Hepburn."

Yes, Audrey appreciated Huston's support, but there was, she felt, only one part in life that warranted her full and total commitment. Audrey Hepburn Ferrer desperately wanted to be a mother.

Blissfully happy with the birth of son Sean Hepburn Ferrer, July 17, 1960. Bettmann/Getty Images.

Chapter Twenty-One

MOTHERHOOD, 1960

"My mother wanted to have a kid because she wanted to right the wrongs of her childhood."
—Sean Hepburn Ferrer

AMID THE UPS AND DOWNS of a world-famous Hollywood career, ranging from the triumph of *The Nun's Story* to the failure of *The Unforgiven*, one element remained constant for Audrey: family mattered more to her than did any career. In an interesting choice of words redolent of the 1950s and early 1960s, she opined: "My greatest ambition is to have a career without becoming a career woman."

Audrey's yearning for a child of her own had taken hold when she was still a young girl, when the loss of her father, the war-enforced disappearances of her brothers, the uncertainty of her own continued existence, and the rather muted love displayed by Ella, all combined to instill a sense that only having her own children would bring her unconditional love and stability. Nothing else would allow her to lavish the love she so desperately wanted to express, which made what ultimately proved to be four miscarriages, including the loss of a little girl she carried almost to midterm, all the more painful: "From the earliest time I can remember, the thing I most wanted was babies. My miscarriages were more painful to me than anything ever, including my parents' divorce and the disappearance of my father." In Sean's view, his mother's overwhelming desire to have children was in fact tied directly to that fractured relationship with her father: "I think it was part of the healing from her father having left the family when she was so young."

Still without the baby she longed for, Audrey told a friend at Christmas of 1959: "I must work to forget. Only work can help me; holidays give me time to think and that's bad for me." Two years later Audrey would return to work in the most iconic role of her career, as Holly Golightly in *Breakfast at Tiffany's*, but first came the happiest news of all: a successful pregnancy and the birth of her first child.

A son, Sean Hepburn Ferrer, was born July 17, 1960, complete with a highly impressive list of credits: Place of birth—Lucerne, Switzerland. Christened by the same Pastor Endiguer who had married Audrey and Mel six years earlier. Godparents: Audrey's brother Ian and Mel's sister Terry. Christening gown courtesy of Hubert de Givenchy. An American passport, accompanied by an American flag, personally delivered by the U.S. ambassador to Switzerland. It all made for an impressive A-list welcome, but then again, it's not every newborn whose birth is deemed worldwide news worthy of a maternal press conference.

Said Audrey: "I would like to mix Sean with all kinds of people in all countries. . . . If he's the right kind of person, he should take his own small part in making the world a better place."

For the first time since earliest childhood she felt complete, even granting interviews to discuss her newfound happiness as a mother: "I'm sure it's wonderful when you're 18. But if you wait years, the joy is impossible to describe." After all her miscarriages, Audrey was ecstatic to be a mother, and her past history, in Sean's view, helped explain why mother and son formed such a close bond: "I think when she finally had me, it was more than just the desire of having a child. It was also a healing from those experiences. I know it was very, very hard for her. That she did talk about."

With a child now completing their family, Audrey and Mel began to explore additional options about where to bring up their son. They did in fact utilize Bürgenstock as their home base for a decade, which meant that for the first years of his life, Sean was brought up at that exclusive mountain resort. Bürgenstock may have proved a bit too far removed from the show business hubbub for Mel's taste, but to Audrey's delight, Sean would now grow up far from Hollywood, in the countryside setting she loved. The fresh mountain air was even proving to help with Audrey's own lifelong case of asthma.

That Bürgenstock villa, decorated according to Audrey's own exacting standards, even met with approval from the ever-spiky Cecil Beaton. Writing in his diaries of a March 1964 visit to the Ferrers' chalet, he enthused: "To step inside this Swiss doll's house was to realize what I had missed in St. Moritz. Everything was white, and of a clean simplicity; white cotton covers on chairs, long white net curtains and white Swiss linen everywhere; huge bouquets of white tulips or yellow flowers to complement the orange and yellow sofas; an incredible impeccability—in the modern white china, the embroidered napkin wrapping the brown-bread toast, the array of books, the Picasso drawing, the Modigliani figure, the Matisse head. The bedrooms with their covers and huge pillows were of a mountain-water cleanliness. This was something more nourishing than a good steak, for it was food for the spirit. . . . Audrey is very proud of her home and everything in it. . . . The infinite trouble and the finesse she manages strike me as being extraordinary."

Her privacy maintained in Bürgenstock, Audrey began to form new friendships, including a blossoming acquaintance with Sophia Loren, who had recently moved to Switzerland. Both women experienced great difficulty in bearing children, with Sophia's first child, Carlo Ponti Jr., born five years after Sean. When Sophia would visit Audrey, the two young but already legendary actresses would talk shop, husbands, and parenting, and in a neat reversal of the expected, it was Audrey who would cook pasta for Sophia.

She wanted to stay home. Take care of Sean. Movies were nice, but decidedly not the priority. Except—Hollywood kept knocking at her door, offering enormous salaries. Perks. And the role of a lifetime.

Which she didn't want.

Audrey in the columnar black Givenchy evening dress that launched a thousand copies, complete with its daring racer-like back neckline. Paramount Pictures/Photofest © Paramount Pictures.

Chapter Twenty-Two

WHEN AUDREY MET HOLLY, 1961

"Everything you have read, heard or wished to be true about Audrey Hepburn doesn't come close to how wonderful she was. . . . She was just an extraordinary, extraordinary person. Everyone should know that."

—Richard Shepard, producer of *Breakfast at Tiffany's*

IF, IN THE LIFE OF every Hollywood superstar, there is one career defining role that solidifies image, fame, and career—Streisand with *Funny Girl* or Bogart with *Casablanca*—then in the life of Audrey Hepburn, such a moment arrived in 1961 with *Breakfast at Tiffany's*. That reality is rather paradoxical since Audrey had to be dragged kicking and screaming to the set, a state of affairs which in the Hepburn universe means that she had politely explained her resistance to the role more than once.

The fact that the image of Audrey standing in front of Tiffany's glitters more brightly than any portrait of Eliza Doolittle or Sabrina ever could is even more ironic in light of the fact that Truman Capote, author of the novella upon which *Breakfast at Tiffany's* was based, felt that Audrey Hepburn was a terrible choice to play his beloved Holly Golightly. Yet out of the mix of Audrey's reluctance and Capote's disapproval came—and it is not too strong a phrase—movie magic that continues to resonate around the world sixty plus years after the film's initial release.

When Capote introduced Holly Golightly to the world in his 1959 novella *Breakfast at Tiffany's (And Other Stories)*, even the egocentric author himself could not have fully anticipated the lasting impact his creation would have. What would have irked him more than a little, royalty checks notwithstanding, is that the long shadow Holly casts has come courtesy of Audrey Hepburn more than from his own novella. Because much as Capote admired Audrey Hepburn and considered her his friend, she did not match his own vision of Lulamae Barnes, the backwoods girl who descends upon New York City in the late 1940s and reinvents herself as glamorous, sophisticated Holly Golightly.

In structure and tone, *Breakfast at Tiffany's* certainly seems strikingly similar to Christopher Isherwood's *Berlin Stories* (1945), another collection which featured a "kooky" heroine and a male narrator of uncertain sexuality. Knowing that Isherwood's stories had been successfully adapted into both a Broadway play and a movie (1955's *I Am a Camera*), when Capote's novella grew into a national best-seller, Hollywood came calling in the form of independent producers

Martin Jurow and Richard Shepherd. Would Capote sell the film rights? A lunch was arranged, with Capote making an entrance worthy of Holly herself. Quipped Jurow: "Only Mae West could have made a bigger production out of his entrance than did Capote." The author, a fan of sizable Hollywood paychecks, was definitely interested, but insisted that there was only one Hollywood star who could portray Holly—Marilyn Monroe.

In fact, Capote emphasized, Marilyn wanted the role so much that she had "worked up" two scenes to perform only for Capote. Given the author's status as an inveterate spinner of tall tales in which he figured as everyone's all-knowing confidante, the truth of that assertion is unknown, but what is certain is that he pushed wholeheartedly for Marilyn to play Holly. That tantalizing possibility, however, was not to be.

Two competing versions of Monroe's non-participation have circulated through the years. The first has Monroe's Svengali/acting coach Paula Strasberg saying: "Marilyn Monroe will not play a lady of the evening." The second finds producers Jurow and Shepherd refusing to consider Monroe for the role, explaining that they simply could not see Marilyn Monroe successfully portraying a self-invented sophisticate who window shops at Tiffany's. (At this point Marilyn was not the only actress talked about for the role; Jane Fonda had been mentioned as a possibility, and Shirley MacLaine, then in the process of cornering the market on portraying kooks [*Some Came Running*, 1958, and *Two for the Seesaw*, 1962] seemed a real possibility but proved unavailable.)

It all provides a fascinating question of "what if" because Marilyn, with her trademark mixture of breathy sexuality and naivete was, in many ways, right for the role of Holly. If Audrey Hepburn is still, somehow, innocent by film's end, Marilyn Monroe would have provided a more palpable layer of sadness, so overwhelming was her fragility onscreen and off. Monroe was the only actress capable of conveying a quality of yearning as skillfully as did Audrey, but hers was of a more wounded and desperate variety than Hepburn's ever was.

What Shepherd and Jurow understood was that Audrey was respected in her films in ways Marilyn never was. Men did not take Audrey for granted and never put overt sexual pressure upon her, and those were qualities which would go a long way toward making the fact of Holly's prostitution more palatable in the America of 1961. It was Audrey's onscreen persona, one which embodied the battle between a desire for true love and the need to maintain freedom, that had struck a chord with women around the world, and it was that friction which lay at the core of *Breakfast at Tiffany's*.

In the end, perhaps the best summary of the different qualities the two stars would bring to the role was provided by Robert Wolders: "Marilyn Monroe would probably have been allowed to play the character as created in the book, but they unfortunately wouldn't allow Hepburn to do that. I've found myself wishing she could have done the part as written. People don't know how earthy and how true to life Audrey could be." And yet, in Wolders's view, it was Audrey's essential persona that allowed her to successfully portray Holly: "She had a way of showing us who she really was. She had a way of making you look into her soul. And you see it whether she played a princess or a nun or a flower girl or Holly Golightly."

Given Capote's resistance to Audrey, it's ironic that in his novella the description of a Holly figurine seems to bear a noticeable resemblance to Audrey herself: "an elongated carving of a head, a girl's, hair sleek and short as a young man's, her smooth wood eyes too large and tilted in the tapering face, her mouth wide." Even the narrator's first glimpse of Holly seems to have been written with Audrey in mind, as he describes her wearing a "slim cool black dress, black sandals, a pearl choker. For all her chic thinness she had an almost breakfast cereal air of health . . . her mouth was large. . . . A pair of dark glasses blotted out her eyes. It was a face beyond childhood, yet this side of belonging to a woman."

Once the rights to Capote's novella had been secured, Shepherd and Jurow focused upon finding a screenwriter capable of capturing Holly's essence while sanitizing Capote's novella for mass consumption. Given Hollywood's lingering prudery regarding matters of sex, the job required a delicate, nearly floating touch; it was George Axelrod, who had scored successes with his screenplays for *The Seven Year Itch* (1955), *Bus Stop* (1956), and *Will Success Spoil Rock Hunter?* (1957), who struck Jurow and Shepherd as the best choice to navigate the required thin line between fidelity to story and censorship.

Axelrod's solution to those competing demands was to follow many of the novella's set pieces while at the same time adding a love story between Holly and her neighbor Paul Varjak. Gone was Varjak's questionable sexuality and in came a love story between Holly and her handsome neighbor. Paul was now presented as avowedly heterosexual, albeit a kept man, courtesy of the wealthy woman known as "2E Failenson." Said producer Shepherd of casting Patricia Neal as "2E": "We wanted someone who was no-nonsense, who could play that strong subterranean sexual role. Pat Neal was a fan of Audrey's, and it was a very good role." Between 2E Failenson and Holly, Paul would now be one busy man, because in Axelrod's telling, Holly and Paul also go to bed—he's just so exhausted that it turns into a non-event. Why exhausted? Because according to the dictates of 1961 Hollywood, romance must come before sex.

As written by Axelrod, Holly is still a call girl—it's just that her profession is never directly referenced. For Jurow and Shepherd it proved to be a clear-cut case of rationalization: neither of them, they explained, had ever thought of Holly as a prostitute. She was simply "a woman who defied definition." Translation: Holly on screen would be less complicated than in the novella, with all rough edges and quirks sanded down for widespread consumption.

Given the opposition to Monroe, Audrey's name began to be mentioned for the role of Holly with increasing frequency. Blissfully happy as the mother of one-year-old Sean, she nonetheless still maintained an interest in making select film appearances. She knew this film would garner a great deal of attention from the press, but the thought of playing a prostitute gave her pause. Audrey, who yearned for roots, her own home, and children, playing the completely rootless Holly? She hesitated—and then hesitated again. Because for all her stardom and awards, Audrey Hepburn remained riddled with genuine self-doubt, going so far as to tell one interviewer: "I have often thought of myself as quite ugly. To be frank, I've often been depressed and deeply disappointed in myself. You can even say that I hated myself at certain periods."

Perhaps that is why Audrey responded so well to the duality of Lulamae Barnes and Holly Golightly. Savvy about her own onscreen persona, Audrey knew that audiences enjoyed watching her turn into Cinderella, whether in *Roman Holiday*, *Sabrina*, or *Funny Face*. At the same time, she realized, in *Breakfast at Tiffany's* the transformation came with a twist: unlike Princess Ann and Sabrina, Holly's Cinderella-like metamorphosis into a chic sophisticate was already complete at the film's outset.

Holly's new persona, however, remained tinged with desperation. For all the bon mots— "A girl can't read without her lipstick"—Holly still yearns. She's just not sure for what. Her assured exterior masked a fragile psyche, and that, thought Audrey, could give her something very real to play. Maybe yes—maybe no—she hesitated again. Kurt Frings pressed her. Say yes. Mmm—possibly . . .

At which point Mel Ferrer, always savvy about Audrey's career, urged her to take the chance. Say yes—step toward the unknown. Added producer Jurow: "Audrey still had qualms about playing the role until I said that it was not a lady of the evening that we sought but a lopsided romantic, a dreamer of dreams." Lulamae Barnes spinning her own dreams while sitting by the fire escape. Or the backwoods river. Waiting 'round the bend . . .

OK—Audrey would do it, distraught though she was at having to leave Sean in Switzerland while filming in New York City and Hollywood. Audrey's yes, however, came with conditions: prostitute or not, Holy's clothes would be designed by Givenchy, and that requirement was nonnegotiable. Holly had to have some plainer clothes for daily life, and those would be provided by the redoubtable Edith Head, but the glamorous gowns were to be Givenchy's, start to finish. Thought—and negotiation—went into the credit: "Miss Hepburn's wardrobe principally by Hubert de Givenchy, Miss Neal's wardrobe principally by Pauline Trigere, costume supervision by Edith Head."

The ever-practical Head now supervised making copies of the soon-to-be-famous Givenchy gowns. Any feelings that such a job was beneath her were banished by her knowledge that Audrey was then in talks for *Summer and Smoke*, and, writes Head biographer David Chierichetti, "since Givenchy had not before designed period costumes, Edith was sure the job would go to her. In his autobiography, [producer] Hal Wallis says that the matter of who would design the costumes was the reason that Hepburn did not star in *Summer and Smoke*." For Audrey, loyalty to Givenchy trumped any role.

As it turned out, Audrey's last encounter with Head came in the Universal Studios commissary in the 1970s, and when Audrey exclaimed: "Why Edith, you haven't changed a bit," Head abruptly replied: "I haven't had time to, I've been too busy working." Chierichetti, who observed the interaction, felt that with this comment Head had directed a dig at Audrey's then ongoing retirement from films. Ultimately, however, even Head recognized Audrey's extraordinary fashion intelligence and simply stated: "Audrey could have been a designer herself, she had such perfect taste."

It was at this point that Truman Capote weighed in on the casting of Holly, writing to Audrey shortly after Sean was born: "I have no opinion of the film script, never having had the opportunity to read it. But since Audrey and Holly are both such wonderful girls, I feel nothing can defeat either of them." Nice words. Perhaps he even meant them. But still the whispers about the author's preference for Monroe persisted.

Whoever directed the film would need both skill and an above average sensitivity to navigate the screenplay's balancing act between appearance (New York City sophisticate) and reality (prostitute) and the producers began pushing for the up-and-coming John Frankenheimer to land the job. Not familiar with his work, and used to Hollywood heavyweights like Wilder and Wyler, Audrey nixed the choice. Recounted Frankenheimer: "I was fired because of course she had never heard of me. I had directed a lot of television but only one film—so I was canned." Frankenheimer, who triumphed one year later with the extraordinary *Manchurian Candidate*, would undoubtedly have made a darker film, one closer in spirit to the book, but in 1961, no one was interested in dark when it came to Audrey Hepburn, New York City, and Tiffany's.

Enter Blake Edwards.

A veteran television director of the highly successful *Peter Gunn*, Edwards had by this time also helmed the amusing feature film *Operation Petticoat* (1959) with Cary Grant and Tony Curtis. He could handle stars, and his modern sensibility seemed sympatico with the film's deliberate update from the New York City of the '40s and '50s to Kennedy-era Manhattan. One further element: Blake Edwards wanted this job—badly. "I would have done it if I had to crawl all the way up the walk of fame. It was a big opportunity for me."

Audrey began expressing her concerns to Edwards, who realized that "in Audrey's mind it was a big jump from Capote's Holly to our film's Holly. . . . I told her I thought she would be absolutely great. She would not be the Holly of Truman's book. . . . I don't think the majority of the audience thought of Audrey as a call girl." Fully convinced by Blake's assurance that Holly would be "purified by the style in which he would shoot the picture," Audrey capitulated, explaining: "It was Blake Edwards who finally persuaded me (to become Holly). He at least is perfectly cast as a director, and I discovered his approach emphasizes the same sort of spontaneity as my own."

Her happiness grew when he agreed to hire Franz Planer as cinematographer. Ever worried about her teeth, her feet, her square jaw, her everything, Audrey knew that after his Academy Award–nominated triumphs on *Roman Holiday* and *The Nun's Story*, as well as his work on *The Unforgiven*, Planer could and would protect her. In fact, whatever the problems with *The Unforgiven*—and they were legion—none of them, Audrey felt, could be blamed on Planer. Franz Planer made Audrey Hepburn feel secure.

The casting of Audrey's leading man remained problematic until George Peppard's name began to pop up with increasing frequency. Extraordinarily handsome, the Actors Studio–trained, self-serious Peppard, born one year before Audrey, would become only the second leading man in Audrey's career whose age approximated her own (the other being Anthony Perkins in *Green Mansions*). Ruminating about the casting of Peppard decades later, Blake Edwards explained: "We liked each other as human beings. He liked me and admired me greatly, I found out, as a director—and I didn't want him in the movie! If you would ask me if I would cast him now, I doubt I would. He just didn't have what I wanted—just wasn't my cup of tea." Nonetheless, cast Peppard he did, and while troubles with the actor did seem to rumble beneath the surface even during preproduction, they would not fully burst forth until shooting began. For now, it was actually the complicated shooting schedule that was causing problems.

Interiors would be shot in Hollywood, but the filming would begin with eight days of location shooting in New York, because alongside Audrey and George Peppard, the third star of the movie remained New York City, or more specifically, the very idea of New York. Where everyone who doesn't fit in elsewhere belongs. The pulse, heat, and overwhelming human energy of Manhattan would be faked on a studio set at the risk of disaster because, in the words of Truman Capote: "[New York City] is like living inside an electric light bulb." New York City it would be. The Women's House of Detention. Central Park. Fifth Avenue. The New York Public Library. Tiffany's.

The press couldn't get enough: Audrey as a hooker? Not if Paramount had anything to say about it: Holly would be a kook, not a prostitute. After all, who else but a kook would eat breakfast in front of Tiffany's and keep a fish in a birdcage? The publicity machine ramped up: "Kook is not, as everybody associated with *Breakfast at Tiffany's* knows, a beatnik term. Couldn't be. The star is Audrey Hepburn, not Tawdry Hepburn."

Audrey herself weighed in: "It's true we've left sex ambiguous in the script. Too many people think of Holly as a tramp, when actually she's just putting on an act for shock effect, because she's very young. Besides I know Truman Capote very well, and much of what is good and delicate about his writing is his elusiveness."

October 2, 1960. The first day of shooting. Dawn breaking over the nearly silent Manhattan streets as a still-dressed-from-the-night-before Holly nibbles her breakfast while gazing in the window at Tiffany's. The title sequence of the film, the entire metaphorical underpinnings of the story, would now be shot as the very first scene on the very first day. No time for a warm-up. Time to do or die—for Audrey and Blake alike.

"Quiet please"—and then: "Action!"

Holly/Audrey floats out of a cab into the early quiet of 5ᵗʰ Avenue, the streaks of dawn seeming to burnish her extraordinary, nearly translucent beauty, the famous swanlike neck wrapped in a five-strand pearl necklace. Soothing herself after being up all night, Holly fights the "mean reds" by gazing at the priceless jewels in the Tiffany windows.

Never mind that in real life the jewels would likely not have been left out overnight in the display window. This is fantasy time, that of a couture-clad liberated woman who has not yet been to bed and is now drinking coffee out of a paper cup while eating a Danish pastry. In front of Tiffany's. The viewer is instantly captivated. Who is this woman? What is her story?

It's a breathtaking sequence, because in the atypically peaceful New York City of early morning, the world is literally and figuratively seen in a different light. No dialogue or voiceover narration intrudes upon the hushed atmosphere, and viewers are instantly pulled in—pulled in, that is, because it's Tiffany's, and especially because it's Audrey Hepburn. With blond-streaked hair piled high anchored by a tiara-like jewel. The jewel—a seemingly over-the-top look only a self-assured fashionista like Audrey could pull off, and the perfect accessory for Holly's dress.

The dress.

Actually, two of them. One for Audrey's walk up to the window display, and a second designed by Givenchy for standing in front of that window. A dress fitted so snugly that even wafer-thin Audrey could not walk in it.

Audiences looked. And then looked again, memorizing the details. It was all in the details—a discreet slit right down the side. Nothing to spoil the line. This was not Coco Chanel's circa 1920 suitable-for-mourning little black dress. Here was sophisticated elegance, the viewer's eye drawn to Audrey's neck, her arms swathed in black opera-length evening gloves. Even the wing eyebrows so carefully drawn to follow the curve of her jaw took second place to the dress.

Yes, there was another little black dress glimpsed later in the film, short in length and accessorized with a wide-brim hat. Worn while visiting gangster Sally Tomato at Sing Sing Prison. But it was the dress that opened the film—that stole the film—that imprinted itself upon the world's collective memory. Plain when viewed from the front, the surprise lay in the low-cut back. Every woman watching that scene knew she could never be as impossibly thin or as wonderfully glamorous, mysterious, and sad as the ethereal creature gazing in the window, but when Holly/Audrey eats a pedestrian Danish (and not the ice cream cone Audrey requested but was denied by Edwards) it grounded Holly in a reality with which everyone could identify. As noted by author Sam Wasson in his definitive study of the making of the film, *Fifth Avenue,*

Five A.M.: "After *Tiffany's* anyone, no matter what their financial situation, could be chic every day and everywhere."

"Cut!"

Blake smiled. Audrey exhaled. Commented Edwards years later about the iconic scene: "It was as if God said, I'm going to give you a break now, but for the rest of your career you're going to have to live off this one."

A rapport quickly developed between Audrey and Blake. At the end of each shooting day he would rehearse her next day's scenes in order to give her a foundation for the upcoming work. It all seemed agreeable—until shooting would begin the next morning and Audrey would head off in directions they had never discussed. Decades later, Edwards, who seemed to suspect Mel of secretly directing Audrey, explained the on-set situation: "Audrey and I never had a disagreement that I can remember. People would advise Audrey and we'd rehearse one night, and she'd come back the next day and do something totally different. [I said] 'there's only one director and he may not be the best, but that's what you got. You either go along with what we agree on together or you gotta get another director.' It changed right then. She was some kind of spectacular lady."

Said Edwards of his star: "She was funny, dear, disciplined, joyous, a hard worker and yet you always felt comfortable because she made it easy. The camera loved her—she just glowed."

Audrey and Blake grew sympatico, her gentleness softening his hard-edged, black humor, but Peppard proved a tougher nut for Blake, in fact for everyone on the set. With his mannered Method intensity and his need to constantly question Edwards, clashes ensued, and even Audrey seemed to find her leading man difficult. Loathe as she was to speak poorly of a fellow actor, she never commented publicly, and Peppard did pay smiling homage to Audrey decades later at her Lincoln Center Film Society tribute. Said Patricia Neal of Peppard's modus operandi: "We got along superbly at the Actors Studio. I was so thrilled to do this film with him. But, he had been spoiled—he wanted things as he wanted them." Put more bluntly by producer Dick Shepherd: "I must say there wasn't a human being that Audrey Hepburn didn't have a kind word for, except George Peppard. She didn't like him at all. She thought he was pompous."

Filming progressed toward the movie's biggest set piece: Holly's raucous party—a whiskey soaked bacchanal and a Blake Edwards specialty: "The script didn't delineate that much in terms of party shenanigans, so I was going to have to invent it." There would be dozens of extras, oceans of booze, and cigarettes—the very quintessence of early 1960s New York sophistication. Audrey clad in a sheet, languidly smoking through a foot-long black cigarette holder. A phone ringing inside a suitcase. A woman's hat set on fire. Witty dialogue: "She's a phony, but she's a real phony. You know why? Because she honestly believes all this phony junk she believes in." Which seemed to describe half of Hollywood itself.

Filming of the party took a full week, giving several of the actors time to observe Audrey up close. In an era when above-the-title stars kept to themselves and away from the crowd, Audrey, explained Miriam Nelson ("Party Guest in Gold Dress") was "so nice. She would sit around and talk to us between shots." The more thorough scrutiny, however, came from Joan Staley, the party's "Blonde in Low-Cut Cream Dress": "Audrey was amazing. You could see her soul through her eyes. She was gentle, and calm, and deep. And very much herself."

In fact, such was the power of Audrey's appeal—Peppard called her "the most innocent call girl you ever saw"—that it could even surmount the biggest flaw in the movie, one so egregious that it comes close to shredding the fabric of the entire film: the casting of Mickey Rooney as Holly's Japanese neighbor Mr. Yunioshi. Such were the times in early 1960s Hollywood that Rooney's casting as an Asian man did not even generate a great deal of comment. Mused Blake Edwards years later: "I didn't really think it out. I'm not sure I would have changed my mind anyway but looking back I wish I'd never done that. At the time, no one criticized me—it was perfectly OK. I would give anything to be able to recast it."

In the light of the twenty-first century, however, Rooney's portrayal proves nothing short of cringeworthy, his Caucasian features scrunched into a cartoon version of an Asian American, all buck teeth and thick glasses. As the years passed and changing notions of authenticity in casting caused the controversy over Rooney's portrayal to grow, Rooney himself wrote in his autobiography that he was "downright ashamed" of his role as Mr. Yunioshi. Strangely, however, he explains that his shame arises only from the flaws he finds in his acting: "I was too cute. And the whole damn movie was just too, too precious."

Sean Ferrer, who admires much of his mother's signature film—"She elevates the part out of typecasting and transforms it"—expresses his dismay over Rooney's portrayal: "*Breakfast at Tiffany's* is treated as her most sacred film, but the casting of Mickey Rooney is a real detriment. Yes, World War II had ended only fifteen years before, but there is no need to have Mickey, with fake teeth, screaming over the staircase at Holly. Maybe one day, in a full-scale restoration, we can get those scenes taken out. Nowadays we're taking down offensive statues—maybe we can excise that racist portrayal of a Japanese-American."

Rooney's Yunioshi is, in fact, a squirm-inducing portrayal for any twenty-first-century audience, with the most even-handed summary of the character coming from Phil Lee, the president of Media Action Network for Asian Americans. Calling the film "beloved and charming . . . in other ways," he allows that if someone young was seeing the film, "you'd explain the painful historical context and how stereotypes prevent people from seeing reality. This is how I see the movie. I look on it not only as a movie people enjoy, but as a learning opportunity."

Putting aside Mr. Yunioshi, if, as producer Jarow had it, this Holly was a lopsided romantic, then what about the song called for in Axelrod's script? Singing a song was no time for wearing a little black dress—this required the real Holly/Lulamae to be dressed down in blue jeans, strumming a guitar. Needing an intimate song for a big moment, Edwards turned to Henry Mancini, with whom he had happily worked on the previous year's Bing Crosby vehicle *High Time*. With dozens of films already to the thirty-six-year-old Mancini's credit, his skills as composer, arranger, and conductor had established him as a rising musical star in Hollywood. There was just one problem: the song wouldn't come. A week went by. Two weeks. A month. And without Mancini's melody, lyricist Johnny Mercer was stuck in limbo. Used to soaring melodies and lush orchestrations, Mancini struggled to answer the film's musical question: What would this southern transplant turned New York sophisticate be singing about on a fire escape? Henry Mancini was blocked.

Until—thinking of Audrey's wistfulness and what he termed her "slight sadness," he hit on a simple, slightly mournful three-note introduction, and out it all flowed, nestling perfectly into Audrey's eight-note range. Written in the same key as that utilized for her gentle rendition of *Funny Face*'s "How Long Has This Been Going On," the song was, said Mancini, "Very, very simple . . . a sophisticated country song. You can play it all on the white keys . . . a trick that I wasn't aware of—it just happened." With the brilliant and occasionally difficult Johnny Mercer now supplying a letter-perfect lyric, a song of disarming simplicity was turned into a three-act play. Touching, vulnerable, and a distillation of longing both wistful and melancholy. It worked for Holly, and it worked for Audrey, because both onscreen and in real life Audrey Hepburn, better than almost any other actor, instinctively understood the inherently human condition of being perpetually sorry-grateful.

Hubert de Givenchy once paid tribute to his great friend by noting that even after coming face-to-face with the horrors of war, Audrey had somehow clung to a certain optimism, explaining: "Despite the difficulties of life, Audrey always knew how to preserve in herself a part of childhood." Givenchy had it right, because in the near universal desire to hold onto at least some tendrils of childhood belief, audiences around the world recognized that very same quality in Audrey's tender singing of "Moon River"; melancholy yet somehow hopeful, the song resonated precisely because underneath its deceptive surface simplicity, Audrey was able to locate and access a certain lingering sadness she also held within herself.

Shooting completed, Edwards and editor Howard Smith cut, trimmed, and rearranged right up until a first sneak preview. It all seemed to be unspooling beautifully, the audience swept along as soon as they glimpsed Audrey gliding up to Tiffany's, a harmonica plaintively whispering "Moon River" before melting into the sound of a full orchestra swirling around the gorgeous melody. Kudos all around, until the post-screening meeting, where Paramount executive Marty Rackin fulminated "the fucking song has to go." At which point, in the Blake Edwards version of the meeting, gentle Audrey rose up to announce in ringing tones: "Over my dead body." In the telling of others, it was producer Dick Shepherd who said: "You'll cut that song over my dead body!" Whichever the accurate account, the bottom line remained clear: the song stayed.

"Moon River" was the start of a beautifully understated love fest between Mancini and Audrey, with the composer following up this collaboration with elegant, mood-setting songs for *Charade* and *Two for the Road*. When it came to "Moon River," however, even after the number of recorded versions of the song exceeded one thousand, Mancini's thoughts remained happily focused on only one version: "To this day, no one has done it with more feeling or understanding . . . hers is unquestionably the greatest." Mancini is right; when Audrey sings "We're after the same rainbow's end/ waiting 'round the bend/ My huckleberry friend," she is not just singing about Holly being swept along by the currents of life. She is singing to and about everyone.

In an elegant note written to Mancini, Audrey returned his compliment—with interest: "A movie without music is a little bit like an aeroplane without fuel. However beautifully the job is done, we are still on the ground and in a world of reality. Your music has lifted us all up and sent us soaring. Everything we cannot say with words or show with action you have expressed for us."

As the general release date of October 1961 approached, twelve months had passed since the start of shooting, and yet only now had the movie's artwork been finalized. There would be small figures of Audrey and George Peppard locked in embrace at the righthand side of the poster, a way of letting the audience know that Audrey/Holly was romantic, not a prostitute. But the image that would sell this film all around the world was a Robert McGinnis illustration running from top to bottom: Audrey in the film-opening black dress, her leg exposed, jewels around her neck, the personification of glamour with a foot-long cigarette holder and opera-length gloves. And yet, it was the inclusion of a cat draped around her neck that provided the ne plus ultra, grounding the poster with an everyday image to which all could relate. Sure, Holly's beautiful and a kook—but she loves her cat so how crazy could she be?! (In an amusing aside, Blake Edwards said of the cat's performance in the film-ending rainstorm: "Man, did that cat smell!")

Paramount publicists went into overdrive: Audrey lookalike contests! Product tie-ins! Be a kook like Audrey at Tiffany's! By now everyone had heard about the movie, but one key question remained: Was it any good?

Yes. And no.

- On the plus side—Audrey. Not just because of the magical opening and the tender version of "Moon River." There was real acting on display: hearing the news that her brother has died, Holly Golightly drops the sophisticated veneer and reveals the scared and vulnerable Lulamae, a young woman who is heartsick over losing her brother. It's a remarkable piece of screen acting that is often overlooked in the collective rush to worship, indeed almost fetishize, Audrey's uber-glamorous look. Equally effective is the near end of the film, when Holly stands sobbing in the rain after pushing her cat out of a taxi. The sequence retains undiminished power sixty years later because, in the words of the 50th Anniversary Companion book to the film: "The sheer pain of letting love in is written on her face."
- On the negative side of the ledger—Mickey Rooney. Wildly overacting, he makes an audience uncomfortable every time he shows up on screen.
- In the middle—George Peppard. More than a bit wooden, but so extraordinarily handsome in his early 1960s *Mad Men* kind of way that the audience roots for him to successfully woo Holly.

In other words, when scored to a fare-thee-well by Henry Mancini, the sight of beautiful people in the midst of a glamorously pulsating New York City can go a long way toward overcoming flaws in the spinning of cinematic dreams.

And how do those very beautiful people end up? In Capote's novella, the bittersweet story concludes with Holly having left New York City for Africa. But here, in Hollywoodland, there is, instead, a very traditional happy ending; it may not make sense, but the audience wants and needs the sight of two ridiculously attractive people kissing in the rain, reunited with Holly's "Cat" while "Moon River" swells on the soundtrack. And on the most elemental of levels it actually works, because unrealistic as that happy ending is, the audience sees behind the bluster, and understands not just Holly but also Audrey's own personal tenderness.

The critics now weighed in, with A. H. Weiler of the *New York Times* smartly noting: "A completely unbelievable but wholly captivating flight into fancy." For all the quibbles, nearly all the critics seemed charmed by Audrey, with even the hard-to-please Judith Crist noting: "Audrey Hepburn may not be your (or Truman Capote's) notion of the amoral and pixyish Holly Golightly, but she's still enchanting enough to make *Breakfast at Tiffany's* worth watching."

For better or worse, this film, then, was the version of the story that audiences around the world would know best—not to mention the version that would help keep the novella in print and Capote in royalties.

Through the decades, Truman retained his fondness for Audrey while never approving of either the film, Mickey Rooney, or Blake Edwards: "The book was really rather bitter. The movie became a mawkish valentine to New York City and as a result was thin and pretty whereas it should have been rich and ugly." In an interview years later with Lawrence Grobel, he minced no words: "Although I'm very fond of Audrey Hepburn, she's an extremely good friend of mine, I was shocked and terribly annoyed when she was cast in that part. It was high treachery on the part of the producers. They didn't do a single thing they promised. . . . The day I signed the contract they turned around and did exactly the reverse. They got a lousy director like Blake Edwards, who I could spit on!" This represents more than a bit of revisionist history on Capote's part; there was no sign of shock or outrage in his acceptance of royalty checks or in his letter to Audrey written shortly before filming began. It was simply a part of doing business with Truman Capote to realize that he always needed the last word. (Capote may not have liked the movie, but he ultimately proved even less fond of a 1963 Broadway musical adaptation which, despite the combined talents of Nunnally Johnson, Edward Albee, Mary Tyler Moore, and Richard Chamberlain, was closed by producer David Merrick before the official opening night. Capote heartily disliked both the score and Mary Tyler Moore, and seemed to concur with Merrick's assessment to close it "rather than subject the public to an excruciatingly boring evening.")

Whatever Capote's quibbles, the film soon earned five Academy Award nominations, including nods for Best Screenplay and Art Direction, as well as a nomination for Audrey as Best Actress. Audrey flew to Los Angeles but had a sore throat and stayed in her hotel rather than attend the ceremony. It was just as well—she lost to good friend Sophia Loren for her performance in *Two Women*. *Tiffany's* did not go away empty-handed, however, notching wins for Best Song and Best Score, wins that seemed only fitting given that aside from the hypnotic opening sequence, the takeaway moment from the film remained Audrey's heartfelt singing of "Moon River."

Famous as the film is now, it is easy to forget that *Breakfast at Tiffany's* was not a blockbuster at the time of its release. In the United States, it proved more popular in big cities than in small towns and suburbs, and its $4 million domestic gross was topped by a more substantial $6 million gross in Europe. (In France the film carried the snazzy title: *Diamonds on Toaste*.) The film's success was enough to wipe out any lingering audience memories of the twin failures of *Green Mansions* and *The Unforgiven*, and it remains a steady seller on home video, its appeal continuing to grow through repeated television broadcasts.

That growing appeal has been boosted immeasurably by the allure of the Givenchy black dress, or more specifically, the Givenchy black dress as worn by Audrey Hepburn. Which leads to an interesting question: Why is the image of Audrey standing in front of Tiffany's the single most iconic image of her career and persona? Why not Audrey in *Sabrina*, dressed in the Givenchy ball gown? Why not Audrey in any one of the spectacular outfits she wears throughout *Charade*?

The answer begins with the title, because the name Tiffany instantly conjures up dazzling images of glamour and New York sophistication. Audrey Hepburn in front of the Tiffany's window is a confluence of all the elements that made her a star of the highest order: She's mysterious and extraordinarily beautiful, but the paper cup and the Danish pastry ground the image—here is a sophisticate who still retains warmth and girlishness.

Says Jeanine Basinger: "Film history works in mysterious ways. By the time of *Breakfast at Tiffany's* everyone knew Audrey Hepburn. She already was iconic, and when she pulls up in the taxi, walks to the Tiffany's window in the highest of high fashion and wearing dark glasses, it's the most arresting of images. If Audrey Hepburn isn't already Audrey Hepburn—the star associated with high fashion—this film is going nowhere. It's either one of the greatest starts in film history or it dies right there. And this image pulls together Audrey's high-class fashion with the human being right beneath the dazzling surface. You need Audrey Hepburn to make this work. She has become meaning as image—she's associated with high fashion yet so likeable as a human being in her acting roles that the image and role become part of the culture. Audrey herself becomes culture—she's an emoji."

And now, thanks to the combined talents of Audrey and Hubert de Givenchy, black was no longer associated only with butlers and maids but was instead turning into the color of power, one that signified rule breaking. A visual representation of independence. A woman in a black couture gown who ate breakfast at Tiffany's followed her own dictates and was a woman worthy of attention. Holly may have started out by running away from any sign of responsibility, but Audrey's own inherently grounded persona signaled to the audience that Holly Golightly remained in charge of her own destiny.

With the dawning of the women's movement, young women on the cusp of adulthood identified ever more strongly with Holly's desire for freedom, one typified by her plea to erstwhile husband "Doc" (a nicely subdued Buddy Ebsen): "Please Doc. Please understand. I love you but I'm just not Lulamae anymore. I'm not." Amid changing times, Holly's plea that others allow her to be her true self, to let her grow, change, and control her own life, continued to resonate.

The reach of the film grew in ever-widening circles around the globe, and decades after the film's original release, singer/actress Cher wrote a note to Audrey which detailed: "I so wanted to be like you in *Breakfast at Tiffany's* that I put my hair in two ponytails, bought huge sunglasses and wore the closest thing to you I could put together. I got suspended from school for the sunglasses."

With *Breakfast at Tiffany's*, Audrey Hepburn had once again proved to be the right actress in the right film at exactly the right time. As pointed out in Sam Wasson's study of the film, *Breakfast at Tiffany's* did a lot to demolish the Eisenhower-era complacency of Hollywood studio films, pointing the way to a more mature treatment of sex and female independence. In reality, however, the stronger blow was likely struck by the previous year's Academy Award-winning *The Apartment*, a cynically entertaining look at corporate politics, adultery, and relationships. That extraordinarily stylish and witty Billy Wilder film had landed with such force that it led Judith Crist to proclaim: "With that film we became grownups." With the popularity of the late 1960s films *Bonnie and Clyde* (1967), *The Graduate* (1967), and *Midnight Cowboy* (1969), the last vestiges of censorship crumbled, but it was *The Apartment* and *Breakfast at Tiffany's* that fired the opening shots in the culture wars.

In the end, through its curious but unbeatable combination of glamour, romance, and wistful sadness, *Breakfast at Tiffany's* provided Audrey with *the* signature role of her career. After seeing the final cut, Audrey told agent Kurt Frings: "This is the best thing I've ever done. . . ." As she explained to interviewers, "I'm an introvert . . . playing the extroverted girl in *Breakfast at Tiffany's* was the hardest thing I ever did."

Always her own least-impressed fan, when musing about the film decades later she commented: "It's the easiest of my pictures for me to look at. It's the one I'm least embarrassed by." And yet, she detailed, "the two things I always think of when I see it are: 1. How could I have abandoned my cat? and 2. Truman Capote really wanted Marilyn Monroe for the part."

Audrey is here undercutting her own considerable achievement. What connects viewers to Holly is Audrey's ability to convey the palpable sense of loneliness underneath the bravado. Here were the lingering effects of Audrey's war-torn childhood, and viewers sensed that despite seeming to have it all—beauty, money, glamour, and fame—she too was searching for a huckleberry friend. In her own words: "I had very little real youth, few friends, little fun in the usual teenage way, and no security. Is it any wonder I became an interior sort of person?"

As the decades passed and the cult of Holly/Audrey steadily gained power, Audrey's continuing friendship with director Blake Edwards and his wife Julie Andrews provided a pleasant reminder of a unique time in all of their lives. In a touchingly humorous recollection after Audrey died, Edwards explained that he last saw Audrey at a flower shop in Gstaad, Switzerland. Running after her to say hello, he slipped and broke his ankle. Cried Audrey: "'Oh, dear, Blackie, what have you done?'" Said Edwards in response: "Obviously I'm not the first or the last person to fall at your feet."

They were never to see each other again.

With friends and co-stars Shirley MacLaine and James Garner in the overly timid 1961 film version of Lillian Hellman's *The Children's Hour*. PA Images/Alamy Stock Photo.

Chapter Twenty-Three

FROM HOLLY TO KAREN, 1961

> "She knew how to love. You didn't have to be in constant contact with her to feel you had a friend. We always picked up right where we left off."
>
> —Shirley MacLaine on Audrey Hepburn

HOW WOULD AUDREY FOLLOW UP the success of *Breakfast at Tiffany's*? With a musical? An out-and-out romantic comedy? Eschewing the easy choice, she instead chose what was, on paper, potentially the most controversial of all her films. *The Children's Hour*. The subject: Lesbianism. The outcome? Not what anyone expected.

Certainly the material came with an impressive pedigree: based upon Lillian Hellman's play of the same name, the story had previously been filmed as *These Three,* directed by William Wyler and starring Miriam Hopkins, Merle Oberon, and Joel McCrea. That 1936 movie had changed the play's subject matter of a possibly lesbian affair among schoolteachers to a rumored adulterous heterosexual affair, but with the slow loosening of societal restrictions over the next twenty-five years, it was decided that the remake would revert to the play's original subject matter.

In light of the recently concluded nightmare of the House Un-American Activities Committee, the politically minded Wyler leapt at the chance to reexamine a story centering around the power of a lie. For her part, Audrey was so eager to work once again with Wyler that in a letter dated August 5, 1960, she accepted the role of Karen before the screenplay had even been completed: "I'm just thrilled and so terribly happy. . . . Man, oh man." Audrey's contract called for a fee of $500,000 against ten percent of the gross, with her salary burnished by substantial perks: a car with chauffeur, $1,000 per week in personal expenses, 100,000 lira for the services of her Italian hairdresser, and direct payment of all travel expenses incurred by her personal secretary.

When scheduling problems prevented Lillian Hellman from fulfilling director Wyler's request that she write the screenplay, the film was assigned to John Michael Hayes, who had found great success writing the Hitchcock films *Rear Window* (1954), *To Catch a Thief* (1955), and *The Man Who Knew Too Much* (1956). Through no fault of Hayes, the screenplay was hampered right from the start when it was decreed that no Production Code Seal of Approval would be forthcoming if the word "lesbian" was uttered. Suggested, yes. Stated aloud, no. Translation: the entire idea behind the film was neutered before production ever started. Such general uneasiness was even reflected in the list of all the titles that were considered for the film: *Infamous*, *With Sinful Knowledge*, *Strange Awareness*, and *Whispers in the Dark*. (When the film was released in the UK, it was known, none too subtly, as *The Loudest Whisper*.)

Nonetheless, hopes remained high, and a top-tier trio of stars was signed: co-starring with the top billed Audrey (playing "Karen Wright") were Shirley MacLaine ("Martha Dobie") and James Garner ("Dr. Joe Cardin"). The three stars immediately took to one another—or more precisely, in the case of MacLaine, "immediately" translated into a three-hour trial period: "I had plenty of qualms when I met Audrey for the first rehearsal for *The Children's Hour*. It took me quite a while to thaw her out—about three hours. From then on, it was one big kick." The two women worked together easily, and in the humorous recall of Shirley, it was decided that between takes Audrey would teach Shirley how to dress, while "I tried to teach her how to be eloquently profane." Those differences in personality were reflected in their approach to acting, with Wyler pointing out: "Audrey, like most actresses, will require a moment to get herself in the proper mood for the scene, but Shirley—she will make jokes and clown it up until the last second. And then, when the camera starts, she will be right in it. It's often disconcerting for the other people around."

Garner, cast in the somewhat thankless role of Audrey's boyfriend, admired her skill and, in his own words, "fell in love with her. She was quiet and demure, a very proper lady, though she had a great sense of humor." He was, not, however, a fan of Mel Ferrer's: "I could never figure out how she could have married that guy Mel Ferrer. She was way too good for him."

Mutual respect between the stars did not, however, ease the trials of filming. The role of Karen Wright proved intense, and with few laughs to leaven the proceedings, Wyler's endless retakes proved exhausting. Wrote the film's stills photographer Bob Willoughby of Audrey's on-set routine: "She would just disappear, and when I went looking, I would find her hidden away in an unlit part of the set. She needed to get away from all the distractions and prepare herself to face the scene again."

In the early 1960s the story of lives being destroyed by a malicious child spreading unfounded rumors of a lesbian affair was still ahead of its time, and the film was weakened by Wyler's surprisingly skittish treatment of the idea. In subsequent years, Shirley MacLaine stated that Wyler, fearing the wrath of the Production Code, became very uneasy at any mention of lesbianism, and cut the scenes showing Martha brushing Karen's hair and taking care of her clothes. In typically blunt fashion she emphasized that Wyler "chickened out" and "gutted scenes in the middle of the picture which showed that Martha was in love with Karen." MacLaine did, however, blame herself for part of the film's resulting blandness: "I should have fought more with Willie Wyler to investigate the lesbian relationship. John Michael Hayes had not pulled any punches in the script. In one scene, I baked a chocolate cake for Audrey, cut it like a work of art, placed the slices on doilies just so. Every nuance was the act of a lover."

Yes, the film's timidness hurts, but it is misguided to criticize the film through a twenty-first-century prism that, in E. P. Thompson's apt phrase, represents the enormous condescension of posterity. If the fact that Martha commits suicide at the end of the film because she is gay continues to rankle today, it is still noteworthy that in the early 1960s, even hinting at homosexuality, let alone discussing it boldly, constituted a genuine step forward in Hollywood.

Given the Production Code's straitjacket, the film still contains some moments of surprising effectiveness. When Karen (Audrey) finds out that everyone is withdrawing their children from the school because of rumors of lesbianism, there is no over-the-top emoting. Instead, Wyler stages the scene silently, shooting at a distance, and thereby underscoring the difficulties faced in confronting whispered half-truths and innuendos: everyone hears and interprets the events differently. Similarly, the confrontation between Grandmother Amelia Tilford (a first-rate Fay Bainter) and the two girls spreading the rumors is powerful and rings true.

Even better is the moment when Karen realizes that Martha may have committed suicide; she runs back to the house and the door is battered down, but Martha is already dead. Making the scene all the more powerful is the fact that overt histrionics are eschewed by means of an immediate and highly effective cut to Martha's funeral. Karen's school has been destroyed, her engagement to Dr. Joe called off, and she has lost her best friend to suicide; the power of lies to destroy lives has been solidly conveyed. Why then, does the film refuse to hang together?

The biggest reason: these high points prove too intermittent to be effective, and the film's screenplay proves a big hindrance. For all of his talent, Hayes's sensibility is not a natural fit for the material, and the bowdlerization of the material made his task all the more difficult. Said Hellman of the final script: "[It is] mostly workable [but] . . . has a strange flat quality. Mr. Hayes has a bad ear."

The usually estimable Alex North, a fifteen-time Oscar nominee, turns in a rather ponderous score, and while Audrey is solid if not particularly memorable, she does rely too heavily upon her tested bag of tricks, signaling a tried-and-true moist-eyed concern rather than a conflicted young woman. MacLaine does better by the frustrated-in-love Karen, but it's a surprise that the skill Wyler displayed guiding Audrey in *Roman Holiday* was here in short supply, perhaps done in by the necessity of tiptoeing around the subject of homosexuality. Hollywood, it was clear, had not yet fully grown up.

Most damaging of all, however, the film is irrevocably thrown off balance by the screeching performance of newcomer Karen Balkin as the young girl who starts the rumors. It is unfortunate that first choice Hayley Mills was not available because Balkin's performance remains a mere shadow of Bonita Granville's highly effective turn in *These Three*. Telegraphing every move in advance, Balkin's characterization is rendered at such an over-the-top pitch that she ultimately comes to represent a juvenile version of F. Scott Fitzgerald's quip about writing for Joan Crawford: "You can never give her such a stage direction as 'telling a lie' because if you did, she would practically give a representation of Benedict Arnold selling West Point to the British." Wyler's failure to reign in Balkin, a shortcoming made worse by filming many of her tantrums in close-up, ruins the very heart of the film.

As the film geared up for its premiere on December 19, 1961, the finalized artwork told the story of pulled punches: against a shocking pink background, MacLaine and Hepburn are represented by stylized drawings, the former in profile, the latter facing forward with demurely lowered eyes. Between the two women lies one word: "Different." Off to the side under the title lies a warning: "Because of the nature of the theme—this movie is not recommended for children." Or for anyone else according to the blandly negative reviews. (Wyler biographer Jan Herman unearthed a humorously titled negative review headlined: "The Lesbian Said the Better.") Respect was accorded the two stars, but after praising MacLaine, *Time* magazine, lit into Audrey: "But Audrey Hepburn gives her standard frail, indomitable characterization, which is to say that her eyes water constantly (frailty) and her chin is forever cantilevered forward."

Wyler himself knew he had not succeeded, later calling the film "a disaster." He was exaggerating for effect, but he did agree with Hellman's criticism that he had been "too faithful to the original and made no attempt to modernize and bring it up to date. . . . She said that if she had done the screenplay she would have changed a lot of things . . ."

Surprisingly, the film received five Academy Award nominations, although not for the three stars. Instead, Fay Bainter was nominated for her skillful performance as Grandmother Amelia, and additional nominations were scored by Franz Planer (Black and White Cinematography), Art Direction, Sound Design, and surprisingly, Costume Design; given the downbeat, nearly one-set look of the film, Audrey had agreed to forego Givenchy and instead work with Dorothy Jeakins for the third time. Karen's bland, utilitarian wardrobe would certainly not do anything for Audrey's reputation as one of the world's leading fashion plates, and nomination or not, it was clear by now that the talented Oscar-winning Jeakins played second fiddle to Givenchy when it came to costuming Audrey on film: Givenchy nabbed *Sabrina*, *Charade*, and *How to Steal a Million* while Jeakins was stuck with *Green Mansions*, *The Unforgiven*, and *The Children's Hour*.

In the end, *The Children's Hour* proved to be a case of good intentions and misplaced results, the situation best summed up by James Garner post-opening: "If I was taking part at this moment, I doubt that I'd take that on. But I wasn't really looking for the part so much as the association. I wanted to be in good company."

The somber end results had simply proved too uneven for audiences to derive any sustained pleasure from the movie, which meant that a quick change of pace back to the congenial territory of romantic comedy seemed exactly the right shot in the arm for Audrey's career. Next up—*Paris When It Sizzles*: a combination of Paris and Givenchy, not to mention an onscreen reunion with William Holden.

Hopes ran high—at least at the start.

Audrey wearing a classic sherbet colored Givenchy sleeveless sheath dress, typical of the kinds of daytime dresses he made for her. This style, like so many of Givenchy's simpler designs, was copied by mass dress manufacturers for its chic lady-like appeal. Paramount Pictures/Photofest © Paramount Pictures.

Chapter Twenty-Four

PARIS WHEN IT FIZZLES, 1962–1964

"The trouble is that *Paris When It Sizzles* seems constantly on the verge of hilarity, but it never gets entirely into it."

—*Hollywood Reporter*, April 8, 1964

AFTER THE BIRTH OF SEAN, Audrey had pronounced herself happier at home than on any film set. Which meant that if she were going to spend time away from home making a movie, the material in question had to provide either a sense of fun or a thought-provoking message. In that light, *Breakfast at Tiffany's* and *Charade* made perfect sense, but her choice of *Paris When It Sizzles* produces only one reaction: Why? Why spend time away from home on an ill-advised reunion with an alcoholic William Holden who still carried the torch for her?

Top billed over Audrey, Holden was here playing "Richard Benson," a hard-drinking screenwriter who must write an overdue screenplay in only forty-eight hours. Given the parallel between the character and Holden's own alcoholic personal life, the conceit underlying the entire story should have raised alarm signals, yet that problem was conveniently ignored in the studio's pursuit of hoped-for box office glory. Perhaps the powers that be held such blind faith in Audrey's star power that they felt audiences would turn out to see a reunion of *Sabrina*'s romantic leads, but as written, Audrey's role of "Gabrielle Simpson," a secretary hired to help Benson overcome his writer's block, should have immediately told them otherwise. Extensive as her skills were, even Audrey could not ring much charm out of a secretary co-opted into playing out the fantasies Benson dreams up for his screenplay.

Screenwriter George Axelrod had proved himself a talented writer with both *Breakfast at Tiffany's* and especially the brilliant *Manchurian Candidate* (1962), but he came a cropper here. His screenplay, based upon the 1951 French film *La Fete a Henriette*, and intended as a spoof of both moviemaking and sex farces, was stuffed with forced shenanigans in which Audrey and Holden pranced around exotic locations in a wild mix of spy chase, traffic accidents, and love story. The only thing missing was coherence.

Although by 1962 Audrey's marriage to Mel Ferrer was under increasing strain, she now proved dismayed, not enchanted, by the protestations of love still coming from Holden on the set of *Paris When It Sizzles*. Audrey, it seemed, felt nothing so much as sorrow about what had happened to her former love. Frequently inebriated, Holden caused delays on the set and took to drunken nighttime attempts at rekindling his love affair with Audrey. It was clear by now that the uber-masculine but surprisingly insecure Holden had never fully grown up, while the seemingly fragile Audrey Hepburn was all about growing up, moving forward, and taking charge of her own life.

In fact, matters appeared jinxed right from the start when, during filming, Audrey's house in Switzerland was burglarized and her Academy Award stolen. The Oscar, which was eventually found in nearby woods, had been stolen by Jean-Claude Thouroude, an obsessed twenty-two-year-old fan who had moved to Switzerland to be near his idol. Audrey took the burglary in stride, but what she did not take in stride during the filming of *Sizzles* was her displeasure with the work of cinematographer Claude Renoir (grandson of painter Pierre-Auguste Renoir). In the words of the film's director Richard Quine: "Audrey's strong, very strong, and she was not happy with the way she looked. . . . *Paris When It Sizzles* called for a lot of movement and use of key lights, and as a result he got unsettled and photographed Audrey very roughly."

Renoir was replaced by Charles Lang, whom Audrey had favored ever since his work on *Sabrina*, and while, thanks to Lang's skills and key lighting, Audrey ended up looking nearly as youthful as she had eight years earlier on that film, Lang could do nothing to disguise the toll that Holden's years of hard drinking had taken; in the end, special lighting and all, Holden's weathered visage—a golden boy no longer—causes concern, not envy, in the viewer's mind.

This Paris did not so much sizzle as strain laboriously, with the stars valiantly trying to breathe life into a premise that needed a lighter-than-air approach and instead slammed viewers over the head as if to shout: "Are you having fun yet?" By now the thirty-three-year-old Audrey was too old and smart to play the type of naif she is saddled with here, and the plot, which features digs at Method actors and avant-garde films, at one point found Audrey playing a fighter pilot, the tone of the sequence resembling nothing so much as a subpar *Saturday Night Live* skit.

Axelrod, who had successfully walked a very fine line with his script for *Breakfast at Tiffany's*, could not solve his story's conceptual problems, and to help gin up the proceedings, director Quine resorted to the use of star cameos. Marlene Dietrich, Tony Curtis, Mel Ferrer, and Noël Coward all whiz by, and at times it seems as if the crème de la crème of 1960s Hollywood had shown up to help out. Nelson Riddle provides the score, Frank Sinatra sings one line of the title song for the film within a film—*The Girl Who Stole the Eiffel Tower*—and Fred Astaire even sings "That Face," his charming vocal synced with a close-up of Audrey's face. It was all for naught.

The labored and rather leaden shenanigans of *Paris When It Sizzles* ultimately reduce the number of pleasurable moments to a very fleeting few: amusing inside references to *Funny Face* and *Breakfast at Tiffany's*, as well as the sight of Audrey crossing the room in a nightgown as if floating on air, grace intact even in the midst of utter nonsense. But everyone tries too hard, and the wild party meant to echo the bacchanal in *Breakfast at Tiffany's* plays out as desperate rather than enticing. In the end, the finished film most closely resembles a soufflé which stubbornly refuses to rise, and when a single onscreen credit for perfume generated more interest among critics than the film itself, a doomed outcome was guaranteed.

As to that perfume. Givenchy, who here outfitted Audrey in a series of dazzling creations constituting the one visually appealing aspect of the film, received his standard separate credit. This time, however, it was credit with a difference: "Miss Hepburn's wardrobe and perfume by

Hubert de Givenchy." Which means that *Paris When It Sizzles*'s claim to film history lies in its status as possibly the first ever film to display a separate credit for a fragrance.

In the words of the film's publicists, the perfume, christened "L'Interdit"—French for "forbidden"—represented a creation "in the image of Audrey Hepburn as a tribute to her beauty and as something interdit to others and thereby exclusive." Audrey Hepburn, and not a single other person, would wear Givenchy's scent. Although advertised in the *New Yorker* as far back as June of 1963, the perfume was not released to the public until 1967, and while television viewers in the twenty-first century may be inured to the endless advertisements for celebrity perfumes, in the early 1960s, the novelty of the idea proved startling.

L'Interdit did not represent the first Audrey-sanctioned endorsement; she had, at the time of *Funny Face*, already endorsed Lux Soap. But she chose and controlled her few endorsements with great care; when she agreed to film commercials for a Japanese wig company in 1976—with her dark hair and eyes, exquisite manners, and soft-spoken mien, Audrey remained immensely popular in Japan—she made certain that the ads could never be shown anywhere but in Japan.

Filming on *Paris When It Sizzles* was completed in 1962, but faced with a farce they knew was a flop, Paramount did not release the film until 1964, when they hoped to capitalize upon the enormous recent success of *Charade*. The attempt did not work, box office receipts proved soggy, and the film quickly disappeared. Said Sean diplomatically after his mother's death: "She didn't care much for *Paris When It Sizzles*."

The film may have flopped, but even in the face of such disappointment, director Quine remained an ardent fan of Audrey's: "Audrey . . . was the charmer of the world. Of all the people I've worked with in my life, Audrey and Jack Lemmon were my favorites. They don't have a false bone in their bodies, absolutely not a flaw, professional, kind, gentle, considerate, no temperament at all."

Kind and gentle she was, but what Audrey Hepburn needed was a better script and a hit film. She landed both, and then some, with her next film, her long-anticipated pairing with Cary Grant in *Charade*. Together again—for the very first time—were cinema's two most stylish purveyors of movie star chic.

Charade, it turned out, would register as that rarest of cinematic feats—a confection of undiluted charm.

Wearing Givenchy's rolled collar pom-pom trimmed merlot-colored wool boucle suit for her role as Regina Lampley in *Charade*. This slightly fitted tailleur was typical of Givenchy's flair for gentle tailoring and exuberant color. Moviestore Collection Ltd./Alamy Stock Photo.

Chapter Twenty-Five

CHARADE, 1962–1963

"Cary Grant and Audrey Hepburn are two people who will never be bettered on the screen— the epitome of beauty and handsomeness and culture."

—Stanley Donen

WHEN PRODUCTION ON *CHARADE* BEGAN in October of 1962, the general reaction to the teaming of Cary Grant and Audrey Hepburn seemed to be a smiling exclamation of "What took so long?" It certainly hadn't been for lack of trying, with the duo having previously been mentioned as possible co-stars for *Roman Holiday, Sabrina*, and *Love in the Afternoon.* And yet, none of those proposed pairings had come close to happening because of Grant's reservations regarding both the scripts and the twenty-five-year gap in their ages.

Most notably, with both *Sabrina* and *Love in the Afternoon*, Grant's hesitation about working with Billy Wilder had tipped the scales. Said Grant to Wilder at the time of *Love in the Afternoon*: "Don't persist. Look, I like you, Wilder, but I cannot explain it. I just . . . the wrong signals come up in me." Grant's well-known antipathy toward autocratic directors (he had disliked working with the overbearing Michael Curtiz on *Night and Day* in 1946) meant that he had not welcomed the prospect of a months-long shoot with Wilder. In the star's own words: "I'd heard he didn't like actors very much and I'd already worked with enough of those kinds of directors to last a lifetime. Humphrey Bogart did *Sabrina* and he looks very unhappy all the way through."

Wilder, however, was not attached to *Charade*, and although writer Peter Stone had failed to interest any publisher in *Charade* as a novel, Stanley Donen had glimpsed the story's potential as a film, writing Stone that it "might make a very interesting suspense action film, if one was fortunate enough to get an extremely good screenplay, and, of course, a marvelous woman to play the leading part. I have in mind Audrey Hepburn, and I am hopeful that I will be able to interest her in doing it."

Donen paid Stone $750 per week plus expenses to write a script based upon his novel, with Stone finishing his draft in 1962. Grant liked Stone's script, had worked well with Donen on *Indiscreet* (1958) and *The Grass Is Greener* (1960), and having passed on the Howard Hawks–directed *Man's Favorite Sport* (1964), the stars finally aligned for his much-anticipated teaming with Audrey.

Said Donen: "I don't know anyone who lived in those years who doesn't think of Audrey and Cary as the most enchanting people, and to be able to have them together in a movie was beyond anyone's dreams." The wait had been so worthwhile that Audrey accepted second billing without a quibble.

Stone's witty script, an entertaining mixture of comedy and thrills, cast Audrey against type as the suddenly widowed "Reggie Lambert," who finds herself broke, homeless, and chased by no fewer than three men. When "Peter Joshua" shows up in the person of Cary Grant, the games begin in earnest. Is Peter a friend or a wolf in sheep's clothing? The issue would only be solved at the very end of the film's one hundred and thirteen minutes, the solution nearly taking second place to the dazzling clothes, gorgeous European locales, and witty byplay between Grant and Hepburn.

With small tweaks made to the script, Grant's reservations about being a dirty old man twenty-five years Audrey's senior had soon disappeared. It was Audrey's character of Reggie who would be the romantic aggressor; charmingly forthright in her seduction of Grant, Audrey projected a mix of girlish pluck and womanly assertiveness, and in the process provided a perfect foil for Grant's exasperated reactions. She is upfront about her romantic feelings but is neither overly aggressive nor operating from a fear of rejection. In the end, the ageless charm of Grant gave *Charade* a romantic fizz that had eluded the pairings of Audrey with Gary Cooper and Henry Fonda, and yet for a film which has acquired a reputation as a romantic classic, the surprise lies in the fact that Grant and Hepburn never kiss.

Instead, the script doles out witty lines to both stars, their romantic sparring escalating with each scenic chase and shoot-out. As Reggie contemplates Peter's face, zeroing in on Grant's famously cleft chin, she wonders aloud:

Reggie: How do you shave in there?
Peter: Like porcupines make love. Very carefully!

It's deft, sexy, and never vulgar, yet the soon to crumble Production Code still would not allow the line, deeming it too suggestive. Instead, the exchange was reduced to:

Reggie: How do you shave in there?
Peter: Very carefully!

The affection the stars held for each other is palpable on screen, and there is a lightness to both of their performances throughout. As Audrey perceptively noted: "While you might not think it, Cary was a vulnerable man, and he recognized my own vulnerability. We had that in common." Grant, a long-established past master of the romantic comedy opposite actresses ranging from Katharine Hepburn to Doris Day, seemed to revel in the screenplay's playful structure. Time after time a romantic build-up was deftly undercut by an often-subversive quip, lending the film a tone of chuckles, not belly laughs, that fit both stars to a T.

What looked effortless and chic as they dazzled onscreen was of course achieved with hard work and a mutual understanding which deepened their onscreen affect. In a comment which Audrey never forgot, Grant one day leaned over to her on the set between shots and gently informed his ever-nervous co-star: "You've got to learn to like yourself a little more." Audrey's intimates knew of her constant self-criticism, but it was not every co-star who recognized the worries underneath the glittering surface. It was this mutual awareness that helped to inform their spirited repartee, and in a further burst of candid appraisal, Grant summarized: "In spite of her fragile appearance she's like steel. She may bend, but she never breaks."

That combination of fragility and steel was beautifully captured by the Givenchy wardrobe, which presented Audrey as the epitome of European chic in a whirlwind of collarless jackets, sleek-fitting dresses, oversized sunglasses, and pillbox hats. So noticeable are Givenchy's designs that in retrospect it seems as if accurate advertisements for the film should have boldly proclaimed: "Cary Grant, Audrey Hepburn, and Hubert de Givenchy in *Charade*!"

After *Sabrina, Funny Face, Love in the Afternoon*, and *Paris When It Sizzles, Charade* represented Audrey's fifth film set in Paris. Part of Paris's dazzle was thanks to the painterly cinematography of Charles Lang, here reunited with Audrey after their collaboration on *Sabrina* (*Wait Until Dark* was to follow). Lang's photography caught Paris at its most alluring, and when combined with a Givenchy-clad Audrey, titles by the great Maurice Binder, and a haunting score by Henry Mancini, *Charade* ended up a glossy, satisfying, and effortless bauble of the type thought of as "typical Hollywood" but rarely achieved. It's a confection, but with just enough substance beneath the admittedly glittering surface to linger in the memory.

That charm is encapsulated in the Mancini/Johnny Mercer title tune which perfectly captures the lingering sadness underneath the film's—and Audrey's—gaiety:

Best on the bill, lovers until
Love left the masquerade

Said Mancini himself: "I think *Charade* is the best work John (Mercer) and I ever did together."

Charade may not have broken any new ground, and yes, the plot occasionally registers as convoluted, but with the larger-than-life personalities of the two stars, and the charm with which the material is presented, audiences, as one commentator accurately pegged it, "feel in on the joke." In typical fashion, Audrey praised her director while deflecting any thought that she contributed substantially to the film's success: "I was bloody lucky, let's face it. With Stanley, certainly, and with practically all my co-stars and directors, but with Stanley on a somewhat more personal level. I do know that my private life was not always happy, but with Stanley I would always be happy on the set. Stanley made me laugh, and that, for me, was an enormous turn-on."

Donen knew Audrey's strengths as an actress, and in this second pairing there was an ease of method and communication. Explains Sean Ferrer: "Of course the directors listened to her input, and with the directors she worked with frequently, like Donen, it was very easy for the director to make slight adjustments—more color here, greater emphasis there. It was like a recipe. If the pancake is too thick you add a little milk and it becomes a crepe."

For his part, Donen, who could turn surprisingly acerbic with others, praised Audrey extravagantly; he was more than a little bit in love with his three-time leading lady, while still perceptively noting: "I longed to get closer, to get behind whatever was the invisible, but decidedly present, barrier between her and the rest of us, but I never got to the deepest part of Audrey . . . she always kept a little of herself in reserve which was hers alone. . . . She was the pot of gold at the end of the rainbow."

The sixth of Audrey's films to premiere at Radio City Music Hall, *Charade* proved to be a big hit, one that even the often-exasperated Pauline Kael deemed "probably the best American film of last year—as artificial and enjoyable in its way as *The Big Sleep* . . . [containing] a freshness and spirit that make them unlike the films of any other country." For her efforts, Audrey received a Golden Globe nomination as well as a third Best Actress BAFTA.

Grant, not often easily pleased with his own efforts, had found the pairing with Audrey so enjoyable that he wanted her as his co-star in the upcoming *Father Goose* (that film ultimately brought *Charade* screenwriter Peter Stone an Oscar). Audrey, alas, said no, and was, unsurprisingly, replaced by Leslie Caron. For all her gamine charm, Caron appeared noticeably tougher than Audrey and perhaps fit the movie's stranded on an island routine more comfortably. Throughout the next decade, studios continued their attempts to reteam Hepburn and Grant, and MGM did in fact ask them to co-star in its 1969 musical remake of *Goodbye, Mr. Chips*. The resulting film, which ultimately co-starred Peter O'Toole and Petula Clark, did contain a few pleasant songs but remained stubbornly earthbound. It was better for all concerned that Grant was not tempted out of retirement for that musical extravaganza.

Audrey's mutual admiration society with Cary Grant continued throughout the years, with Grant once stating: "All I want for Christmas is another picture with Audrey Hepburn." Audrey gracefully returned the compliment: "Cary was a lovely souvenir in my life"—but perhaps the best summary of their magical pairing comes in the words of Peter Stone's screenplay:

Reggie: Do you know what's wrong with you?
Peter: What?
Reggie: Nothing!

Audiences for sixty years seemed to agree.

In the garden at home in Tolochenaz, Switzerland, wearing one of her perpetual go-to's: capri pants in white with a Breton striped casual sweater. This is a variation on the capri pants and bateau-neck top Audrey wore when she first met Givenchy. Album/Alamy Stock Photo.

Chapter Twenty-Six

HOME, 1963–1993

"It's going to sound like a thumping bore, but my idea of heaven is Robert and my two sons at home—I hate separations—and the dogs, a good movie, a wonderful meal, and great television all coming together. . . . As a child I wanted a house with a garden, which I have today. This is what I dreamed of."

—Audrey Hepburn

THE SUCCESS OF *CHARADE* HAD more than made up for the twin disappointments of *The Children's Hour* and *Paris When It Sizzles*, but Audrey's focus remained not on her career but on achieving her one remaining heart's desire: finding a permanent home.

After decades spent traveling from country to country, with rental properties leased one right after another in dizzying profusion—in 1965 alone Mel and Audrey were to rent houses in Rome, Madrid, and Paris—Audrey wanted a permanent home. She was nearing forty, a wife and mother, and tired of packing and unpacking dozens upon dozens of trunks. Mel, immersed in the show business swim as actor, director, and producer, liked constantly being on the move, but Audrey wanted roots. Deep ones.

She had loved Switzerland from the start. Bürgenstock did provide an oasis of natural beauty, one far more restful than glamorous Gstaad, but it still felt like less than a permanent answer. The intense mountainside winters had also proved so extreme that Audrey longed for a more temperate climate, albeit while still residing in Switzerland.

She had already learned that her privacy would be honored by the courteous and respectful Swiss. With an always polite, seemingly friendly, but reserved demeanor arising out of an inherent sense of self-protection, Audrey was proving to be a unicorn among film stars: a worldwide celebrity whose space and privacy the public inherently respected. In the words of Stanley Donen: "She had the ability to keep people at a distance without being in the least bit rough or unkind." More than any other actress of her time, she maintained a highly private life, but one that was blended with a sometimes startling emotional availability.

An intensive search for the proper house began. Starting point of the search: still haunted by memories of the war, Audrey refused to reside in the German-speaking part of Switzerland. Home had to lie in another part of the country, which meant that month after month, when slivers of free time could be snatched, Audrey and Mel headed out on scouting expeditions, driving for hours through country lanes dotted with homes that looked promising yet never proved fully suitable.

After months of fruitless searching by Audrey and Mel, friends now weighed in, telling Audrey that there was a farmhouse which might be for sale in the small town of Tolochenaz-sur-Morges, a short ten-minute drive from Lausanne. On a clear autumn day, Mel and Audrey drove as close as possible to the property, with Audrey standing on the hood of their car to better take in the house and surrounding property. In Sean's words: "She ended up on the wrong side of the house at the bottom of the garden. The cherry trees were in bloom—she could barely see the house. But she just had a feeling."

What she did see, set on two and a half acres of property lined with fruit trees, was an eighteenth-century Vaudois farmhouse, with shutters framing the windows of a two-story dwelling built of peach-colored brick. A stone wall fronting on the town's only street, the Route de Biere, marked the property line. Audrey gazed at the slate roof, at the house's clean lines and knew: it was as if she had been attempting to navigate the world in a foreign language—or in Audrey's case, five foreign languages—and had suddenly found herself in the homeland of her native tongue. A girl born in Brussels, raised in the Netherlands and England, who spoke five languages and worked in Africa, Mexico, France, Italy, and the United States, had found the home of her dreams in Switzerland. It was 1963, and in the words of Sean, the thirty-four-year-old Audrey "remembered feeling butterflies in her stomach and felt she had come home."

Papers were signed, and for 18,500 pounds the house was now hers. The farmhouse, Audrey decided, would be known as La Paisible—the peaceful place. Private. Surrounded by mountains and rolling countryside, and far from Hollywood and its incessant talk of box office grosses. Here lay small-town life with room for Sean to grow and explore, far removed from the glare of her celebrity. Yes, there would still be happy weeks spent at a condominium in Gstaad, but Tolochenaz was, now and forever after, home.

Says Sean: "When my parents found the house in Tolochenaz, near Lake Leman in the French-speaking part of Switzerland, it seemed just right. It was near where Yul Brynner, Elizabeth Taylor, and Noël Coward were living. It was really a farmhouse with animals living right there. It was stone with relatively low ceilings, seven or eight feet—and my mother converted the entire house. The work was really accomplished in record time."

In Audrey's hands, the décor throughout the eight-bedroom house proved to be high end but comfortable. Scattered throughout was her favorite color, cyan—a subtle, clean, and cool blue/green shade that looks remarkably similar to the color of Tiffany boxes. There were to be cyan accents on her linens, her pillows, and even the shutters of the house. The living room couches were a cheerful yellow or pink, their bright colors offset by the white interior walls. In Audrey's own words: "Simple, homey, cottagey."

Her Academy Award was nestled in the middle of a shelf of books in the playroom, far from the living room where visitors would have seen it. Said Luca: "My mother chose to keep the acknowledgements she received for her humanitarian work in the living room, as ultimately, they meant far more to her."

Shortly after moving in, she excitedly went to work on her garden, hiring a professional to redesign it yet happy to do quite a bit of the work herself. Out went any red flowers, and in went a sea of white bulbs, centering around the white Dutch tulips sent by brothers Ian and Alex. So well-known did Audrey's love of flowers grow to be that two flowers were named after her in Holland: the white and long-necked Audrey Hepburn Tulip (cultivated in 1990) and the Audrey Hepburn Rose. Exclaimed Audrey about her namesake tulip: "This was the single most romantic thing to happen in my life." Luca describes the Audrey Hepburn roses as "beautiful . . . because they are a deep pink in bud, but when they open up they become a softer pink and then almost white. My mother positively loved them so much as she grew them in her garden and because if you make a bouquet, you can have lots of different hues."

Vegetable and cutting gardens, as well as orchards and meadows, all made for a sense of peace and safety. Nearing forty, and even with her career still in high gear, she liked the idea of slowing down and living in Tolochenaz with Sean. Staying home because she finally had a home. In her own very evocative phrase: "The more there is, the less I want. The more man flies to the moon, the more I want to look at a tree." It was almost as if Audrey, like Robinson Crusoe, felt that one had to be in actual contact with nature—to literally hear the birds and smell the flowers—in order to fully know and understand oneself, to attempt the impossible task of being fully grateful for each day.

Beautiful as La Paisible was in its classical simplicity, it was the countryside itself that spoke even more strongly to Audrey. Said Luca: "My mother was at the very deep of her heart a farm girl. . . . She grew up with a great love for everything linked to the countryside—furniture, style. That's why at the end she chose to live in Switzerland in the middle of the fields." This was not a Hollywood star playacting at the farm life, and in Luca's words: "We had a lot of fruit trees and with those we made and ate freshly made marmalade, apple juice and we had a vegetable garden too. During the winter the tomatoes were frozen to be used fresh. We spent a lot of time preparing the preserves and marmalades—which is something that is now back into fashion."

She took long walks through the secluded Swiss countryside—the legacy of her childhood war years caused her to "hate anything that crowds me." Still looking upon her own fame, in the words of Sean, as a freak accident of nature, she was happy in her solitude, and the townspeople of Tolochenaz left her to her own devices, granting her privacy on the trips to the market that she so enjoyed. Said Luca: "She loved going to the market herself. It was very important to know the people she was buying from, talking to them, taking advice, making conversation." Shopping and cooking assumed pride of place for Audrey, with Luca further recalling "she had a true passion for enormous supermarkets where she could now push her cart around at will, fascinated by the abundant offerings."

There was help and plenty of it: maid/companion Giovanna Orunesu, the gardener-chauffeur Giovanni and his wife Rucchita, their two children Marilena and Pierluigi, housekeeper Engracia de la Rocha, and when living in Italy, a nanny for Luca. But in Sean's words: "My mother didn't order people around. She chose to do a lot of the housework herself."

Never one to frequent a gym, she did not play sports but kept fit through her long walks. Said Sean: "Throughout her formative years she was dancing constantly and as an adult she remained very active. She had a wonderful figure because she walked everywhere." The walks, in fact, were conducted at such a brisk clip that her companions would find themselves nearly trotting in order to keep up with her. Asked by Sean why she walked so quickly, she replied, "I just want to get there," but perhaps an even deeper reason lay in a later conversation when she confessed that her ultra-brisk pace grew out of a reaction to her own mother's studied and leisurely pace.

The food she loved to cook? At the top of the list—pasta. Spaghetti al pomodoro reigned as her all-time favorite. Explained Sean: "She was a wonderful, talented, very healthy cook. We didn't know as much then about food groups and nutrition, but she said eating a plate of all white isn't very interesting, so it can't be very good for you."

Simple foods, like the clean lines of her home and clothes.

Whiskey—yes. Cigarettes—unfortunately. A smoker her entire life, the more nervous she became, the less she ate and the more she smoked. She knew she shouldn't, and yet she could not stop; as far back as the 1958 filming of *The Nun's Story*, she had chastised her castmate and friend Patricia Bosworth for smoking too much, leading Bosworth to recall their on-set conversation: "'I get nervous. I smoke too, you know,' [Audrey] told me quietly. 'It doesn't do any good.'"

Having spent a working lifetime surrounded by hair and makeup artists who poked, dabbed, and painted her into big-screen perfection, she spent little time on her makeup at home—a clean, scrubbed face and a touch of lipstick or eyeliner were all she needed or wanted. Spending a long time looking at herself in the mirror was, she felt, nothing so much as a big bore.

Her dress: casual. Putting aside the Givenchy gowns she wore for the most formal of occasions, Audrey found herself happiest when wearing tailored slacks, Lacoste shirts, and loafers—comfort clothes. As recounted by documentary filmmakers Joan Kramer and David Helley, Audrey, having happily agreed to narrate their 1991 television documentary *The Fred Astaire Songbook*, pronounced herself thrilled when they asked her to dress casually for the filming in slacks, shirt, and sweater. With no need for Givenchy, she perched on a sofa, her feet tucked underneath, happy to be comfortable while talking about her legendary co-star.

A perfect evening at home? Cooking a simple supper and then curling up on the sofa to watch television.

Movies she liked:

- *Witness*
- *Ferris Bueller's Day Off*
- *E.T.*
- *The Princess Bride*
- *Cyrano*
- *The Mission*

And—most surprisingly:

- *Prizzi's Honor*

Movies she didn't like watching:

- Anything violent, having seen enough real-life carnage in World War II to last her a lifetime.

Regarding Stanley Kubrick's *A Clockwork Orange*, she pulled no punches: "One of the most brutal, heartless things I've ever had to sit through." Which makes it all the more ironic that Kubrick himself asked Audrey to star as Empress Josephine in his long-planned film on the life of Napoleon. (A 2019 British film exhibit about Kubrick's exhaustive research and preparation for the epic, never-filmed movie contained a gracious, handwritten note from Audrey to "Mr. Kubrick" declining the role of Josephine.)

- Her own films.

(Not one to spend much time contemplating her own screen legacy, when pressed as to her favorite among her own movies, she sometimes allowed as how she felt particularly proud of *The Nun's Story*, while "the film that meant the most to me emotionally was *Roman Holiday*.")

Movies she longed for:

- Romantic comedies. The world, she felt, was now a "darker, less secure place . . . no longer very funny."

Actresses she admired:

- Meryl Streep
- Julia Roberts

And surprisingly:

- Cher: "Cher has an enormous scale of emotions and total lack of inhibition, which I haven't."

Performances that elicited her highest admiration:

- Liv Ullmann and Ingrid Bergman in the Ingmar Bergman masterpiece *Autumn Sonata*.

Not surprisingly, it was the role of the repressed daughter portrayed by Liv Ullmann that affected her most deeply.

Favorite television shows:

- *L.A. Law*
- *Dynasty*—Why? For the chuckles.

And while Audrey loved staying home with three-year-old Sean—in fact nothing made her happier—she could still be tempted by a juicy film role. Which meant that when Jack Warner let it be known that he was very interested in the idea of casting Audrey Hepburn as Eliza Doolittle in the film version of *My Fair Lady*, Audrey Hepburn let it be known that she was very interested in playing Eliza Doolittle.

The most famous postwar musical of them all. A brilliant score. And a role considered the personal property of Julie Andrews.

My Fair Lady: Cecil Beaton's masterful Edwardian lace fitted gown with its bold black-and-white ribbon trim and large ostrich feather and ribbon hat. The touch of colored flowers on the hat and matching cloth purse were the only vivid colors in the entire black, white, and gray Ascot sequence. Warner Bros./Photofest © Warner Bros.

Audrey's embassy ballgown had a delicately beaded bodice and cap sleeve with a beaded chiffon overlay skirt. The scoop neckline was emphasized by the elaborate dog collar jeweled necklace. This dress has been copied by the Givenchy Maison in an updated sheer version worn by Kendall Jenner in 2021 at the Met Gala. Warner Bros./Photofest © Warner Bros.

Audrey's pale mauve organza tea dress was a marvel of dress making, with Cecil Beaton declaring that it was to look as though there were absolutely no seams in the dress. The high-neck ruffled collar accentuated Audrey's swan-like visage. PictureLux/The Hollywood Archive/Alamy Stock Photo.

Chapter Twenty-Seven

MY FAIR LADY, 1963–1964

"And, finally, my thanks to a man who made a wonderful movie and who made all this possible in the first place, Mr. Jack Warner."
—Julie Andrews accepting her Best Actress Academy Award for *Mary Poppins*

JUST HOW MUCH DID AUDREY HEPBURN want to play "Eliza Doolittle" in *My Fair Lady*? Consider her answer to a reporter when, just as *Breakfast at Tiffany's* finished shooting, he inquired as to what role she would like to play next. Quick as a shot the answer came back: "That's easy to answer. I'd do anything to play Eliza Doolittle in *My Fair Lady*. There's no other role I'm dying to do; I just want to be Eliza."

And after two years of back and forth, public debate, and will she or won't she, that ideal role came to pass. Audrey was ecstatic—but as Saint Teresa of Avila once had it, "More tears are shed over answered prayers than unanswered ones."

The most popular postwar Broadway musical of its era, 1956's *My Fair Lady* had occasioned a furious bidding war for film rights, with the victory ultimately claimed by Warner Bros. to the tune of $5.5 million (over $50 million in today's money). With that huge investment in mind, Jack Warner was not interested in hiring the then unknown-to-film Julie Andrews to recreate her acclaimed Broadway turn as Eliza. Never mind that the original cast album had reigned as number one on the charts for months on end and that the role had landed Andrews on the then all-important cover of *LIFE* magazine. As far as Jack Warner was concerned, Julie Andrews was an unknown, and therefore suspect, quantity.

According to one biographer, Jack Warner and Julie Andrews actually talked about the film version of *My Fair Lady* on the phone, with Warner asking her to screen-test for the role. Andrews's reply: "Screen test? You've seen me do the part. You know I can do a good job." Warner shot back: "You've never made a movie and I'm investing a lot of money in this. I have to be sure you photograph and project well. Films are a different medium." Andrews refused the test. The ever-cost-conscious Warner was not even swayed by Andrews's extremely modest demand for a $75,000 salary. Julie Andrews would not play Eliza.

Jack Warner, it turned out, had his eye on Audrey Hepburn. *The Nun's Story* had been a huge success for Warner Bros., and Audrey was as big a star in Europe and Japan as in the

United States. It was Audrey Hepburn, and not Julie Andrews, who represented the box office insurance Warner insisted upon.

And yet, even though Audrey coveted the role, she still thought Julie Andrews should be given a fair shake at recreating her signature role. To that end, as reported in the family-approved *The Audrey Hepburn Treasures* scrapbook: "She actually hosted a dinner party for some of the studio executives in order to further convince them that Julie should be hired for the role."

The answer? No dice. And when Audrey saw that Jack Warner would not, under any circumstances, sign Julie Andrews to play Eliza, and that he was considering other actresses for the role, she let it be known, via agent Kurt Frings, that she was interested in playing the role of Eliza Doolittle. Very interested: "If I turned it down they would offer it to another movie actress and I thought I was entitled to do it as much as the third girl, so then I did accept." Audrey may have received letters from people angry at her for "taking" Julie Andrews's role, but knowing that Julie was never going to be offered the part, she very logically rationalized: "It was a plum role, the script was terrific, and so I accepted the offer." In later years, relates Sean, when Julie Andrews and Blake Edwards would visit Audrey in Switzerland, Julie would joke: "Thank God I didn't get that part, because instead I got the Oscar for *Mary Poppins* and made *The Sound of Music*."

A deal was struck in May of 1962: for six weeks of rehearsal and three and a half months of filming, Audrey would receive a salary of $1 million, a sum equaled at that point only by Elizabeth Taylor (*Cleopatra*), Marlon Brando, and Sophia Loren. To mitigate the tax consequences, payment would be spread out over seven years, with Audrey receiving $142,957.15 on July 1 of each year from 1963 through 1969. With additional bonuses, Audrey would end up earning some $1.1 million. There were, however, other tax ramifications still to be considered; with *My Fair Lady* being shot entirely on the Warner Bros. lot, Audrey would be subject to the high United States tax rates, and as a result, explained Sean, Audrey sold her percentages back to the studio for $1 million.

In addition to her $1 million fee, Warner Bros. would also pay all of Audrey's living expenses while in Hollywood, the cost of her travel to and from Switzerland, and the salary for her personal secretary. The choice of cameraman, still photographer, hairdressers and makeup artists were hers alone, as was veto power over all of her costumes. Perhaps even more important in Audrey's view, the film would be shot in sequence, a rarity for any production, but one Audrey felt crucial in order to help her fully develop Eliza's transformation from cockney flower seller to grand lady. It all added up to one incontrovertible fact: with every one of her wishes granted, Audrey Hepburn had now arrived at the very top of the Hollywood pecking order.

Deal in place, one question dwarfed all others: Could Audrey handle the vocal demands of the role? The Lerner and Loewe score, which most of America knew from the wildly successful original cast recording, covered an enormous range of styles, from the humorous "Just You Wait" to the joy-filled "I Could Have Danced All Night," all of it part of a unique musical structure: the principals do not ever share a love song, and the emotional thrust of the love story is kept subterranean, emerging only at movie's end when phonetics professor Henry Higgins grudgingly admits "I've Grown Accustomed to Her Face." Before filming began, a disappointed Julie Andrews was quoted as saying that she felt Audrey would be "enormously successful" in the role but that she should be aware that "two of the songs [in particular], 'Just You Wait,

'Enry 'Iggins' and 'I Could Have Danced All Night' are not easy. [The former] requires a lot of power, [the latter] has a great range [of notes]."

Hinting at questions of vocal ability as they did, Andrews's comments still paled in comparison to those running rampant in the press: the snubbing of Julie Andrews was big news and the all-powerful columnists of the day now weighed in, with Hedda Hopper vehemently castigating Warner for not giving the role of Eliza to Julie. Columnists Earl Wilson and Leonard Lyons staked out opposing positions; according to Wilson, Audrey could and would sing the score, but to Lyons, it was all but certain Audrey would not sing it. The volume of press about Audrey's singing ability grew by the day.

Well aware of the vocal pitfalls to which Andrews had referred, Audrey felt reassured by the knowledge that it was the legendary George Cukor who would be directing the astronomically budgeted $17 million film, then the most expensive musical of all time. Ironically, even with four previous Academy Award nominations to his credit, Cukor had not been the first choice to direct the film. Instead, it was Vincente Minnelli, the renowned director of the classic movie musicals *Gigi*, *The Bandwagon*, and *Meet Me in St. Louis*, who had ranked as Jack Warner's number-one choice.

Cukor, however, was less expensive than Minnelli, a big plus in the view of the notoriously tightfisted Warner, and unlike Minnelli, Cukor did not insist upon the right of final cut. Minnelli had no peer when it came to color and design, but it was Cukor, the famed "women's director" (code for gay), who possessed a solid gold reputation when it came to eliciting award-winning performances. Cukor, who had hoped to direct Audrey's Broadway production of *Gigi* before scheduling conflicts interfered, was coming off the disastrous Sophia Loren vehicle *Heller in Pink Tights* (1960), as well as the disappointing *The Chapman Report* (1962). He needed a hit, wanted the *My Fair Lady* job, and was not going to make contractual demands to Warner.

Thrilled to finally be working with Audrey, he gladly accepted Warner's offer of $300,000 for fifty-two weeks of work. Cukor and Audrey quickly struck up a great friendship, and ever loyal to his new star, after watching *Mary Poppins*, he privately weighed in: "I am not mean spirited or envious but me no like." He found *Poppins* to be without any notable style, and opined that although Andrews sang nicely, he found her "earthbound and prim."

Who best to star opposite Audrey as the Svengali-like phonetics professor Henry Higgins? Rex Harrison, twenty-one years older than Audrey, and the original star of the Broadway production, was a known quantity on film even if not a box office star of the first rank, but while he may have appeared to be the logical choice, Jack Warner had other ideas and offered the part to Cary Grant. Warner considered Grant a much better box office bet than Harrison, but Grant immediately declined the role. After stating that he felt his friend Audrey was an inspired choice for the role of Eliza, Grant added that the part of Higgins belonged to Rex Harrison. In fact, not only did he refuse the part, but, he added, he also would not even see the film unless Rex Harrison played Higgins.

Peter O'Toole was then seriously considered for the role, and Cukor even visited him on the set of *Lawrence of Arabia* to discuss the possibility. So serious were the discussions that Cukor wrote Jack Warner's aide Steve Trilling on September 24, 1962: "I hope O'Toole was liked—I think he is our man." But just as happened with Vincente Minnelli, O'Toole's agent asked for too much money, and the idea of casting the Irish actor was dropped. (O'Toole did eventually play Henry Higgins in a 1987 Broadway revival of *Pygmalion* opposite Amanda Plummer.)

Asked to screen-test for the role, Harrison declined, and instead, at the suggestion of his wife Rachel Roberts, cheekily sent Cukor two nude photos, one with a conveniently placed Chianti bottle in front of his torso, and the other featuring a strategically displayed copy of the *New Statesman*. It was all designed to show that he was still more than capable of playing the role, and either the pictures or common sense on Warner's part did the trick, because the part was Harrison's—for a salary of $250,000 and a promise from Cukor to return the photographs.

Harrison immediately began exercising his star prerogatives, shipping his own Rolls-Royce from London to New York, where it was picked up and driven cross-country. In Harrison's grand reasoning: "When I flew into Los Angeles I was met at the airport by my own car."

Such demands were not out of character for Harrison, and in an amusing aside about the film's casting, the often-acerbic André Previn reported that Rex didn't care if Eliza was played by Julie or Audrey because in Harrison's opinion, "Nobody was interested in the girl. They were only interested in *him*."

Even in his autobiography, the best Harrison could manage about his three-year onstage relationship with Julie Andrews was to state: "In the three years we played together we never had a cross word of any kind," adding only, "we had had an extremely good working relationship, leading separate private lives and meeting only onstage." As to the differences between his two Eliza Doolittles, Harrison opined: "I think there's a lot of steel in [Julie], more steel than in Audrey."

Harrison was right about his two Elizas: both women exuded charm, both were consummate professionals, and both treated their co-workers with unfailing respect. The difference lay in their affect. Julie Andrews's genuine niceness was tempered by the wariness anyone would have acquired after a childhood spent working in vaudeville, and she remained friendly, polite—and guarded. Audrey, for all her veneer of sophistication, remained strikingly vulnerable, self-effacing, and eager to please. Having interviewed both women in the 1980s for his authorized biography of Cecil Beaton, Hugo Vickers smartly described the difference in his telephone calls with the two Elizas: "The difference between talking to [Julie] and talking to Audrey Hepburn was that I felt this one was sitting bolt upright or even standing, while Audrey would have been lying with her feet up. Julie Andrews was more factual and precise, Audrey Hepburn more dreamy." It was, in effect, the difference between a charming nanny and a wistful gamine.

Harrison's extraordinary ego was made clear in his exasperated statement about the musicians with whom he'd be working: "Why the musicians will have to follow me. They are my servants." Wrote Cecil Beaton to a friend: "Audrey is just as marvellous as he [Rex] is awful!" By now Beaton and Audrey had formed a genuine friendship, one which had begun tentatively at the time of Broadway's *Gigi*, when the worldly Beaton had photographed the nervous new star at the behest of Diana Vreeland. The two aesthetes had instantly hit it off, and Audrey took to calling him whenever she found herself in London. Speaking years after Beaton died, Audrey made it clear that her love for Beaton had not diminished: "My feeling about Cecil—I really did love him. I'm not gushing when I say that. I really adored him because he was very tender with me . . ."

Love Audrey he did, but Beaton disdained Harrison, a feeling shared by Mona Washbourne, who was cast in the film as Higgins's housekeeper Mrs. Pearce. Wrote Hugo Vickers of his encounter with Washbourne: "She loved Audrey Hepburn, and she said that someone rang to ask her about Rex Harrison. He asked, 'Is there something nice you could say about him?' 'No,' she replied."

Small wonder then that Harrison stated: "Filming *My Fair Lady* was not at all a piece of cake."

At the early stages of preproduction, however, Audrey remained thrilled with everything about *My Fair Lady*, and on April 6, 1963, she wrote to Cukor after receiving the script. On pale blue stationery embossed with a small crest in the upper lefthand corner, she enthused at length: "As I was just off for a few days in Madrid with Mel, I took it with me and read it one afternoon, resting in bed. There are not words! It's <u>MARVELLOUS</u>, I am beyond myself with happiness and excitement!"

Careful to defer to Cukor and Beaton, she nonetheless gently suggested that the musical numbers be staged by Gene Loring, who had choreographed her "Basal Metabolism" "beatnik" dance in *Funny Face*: "The reason I dare to even make the suggestion is that I know him and you. You would like him. He is totally without the kind of 'ego' that would make him insist on his way if you know what I mean. . . . I do think he can do any kind of style required and you would find him wonderfully easy to work with." Even Audrey's genteel power had limits, however, and the choreography was ultimately entrusted to Fred Astaire's righthand man, Hermes Pan.

Aware that her not inconsiderable task was to suggest a cockney flower seller while still rendering the words understandable, Audrey began studying cockney dialect with Peter Ladefoged, a professor of phonetics at the University of Southern California. Said Audrey months later: "I worked on the accent, worked on the lines. In the beginning the cockney was too thick and people on the set couldn't understand it. If you speak cockney fast, it's very hard for non-cockney ears." (The very title *My Fair Lady*, after all, comes from the cockney pronunciation of Mayfair Lady.)

Amid all this activity, the elephant in the room grew larger by the day: Would Audrey really be allowed to sing all of her songs? This had been the subject of much discussion even before she arrived in California for preproduction, and in his diary entry of May 16, 1963, two days before Audrey flew in from Switzerland, Cecil Beaton noted that "after lunch, we accompanied him [Alan Jay Lerner] to listen to a girl singing Eliza's songs, in case Audrey's voice proves to be too frail for one or two of the more operatic arias, and a few notes have to be dubbed." Audrey's contract gave the studio the right to substitute another singing voice for hers if they felt it necessary, but since she fully intended to do all her own singing, she began six weeks of vocal training in the summer of 1963 with Sue Seaton and pianist Harper MacKay, while simultaneously working with Hermes Pan and musical supervisor André Previn.

That "girl singing Eliza's songs" was actress/singer Marni Nixon, who had already dubbed the singing voices of Deborah Kerr in *The King and I* and Natalie Wood in *West Side Story*. Her audition, held in Beaton's bungalow on the Warner Bros. lot, was attended by George Cukor, production designer Gene Allen, and Harper MacKay (with whom Nixon had worked on *The King and I*). Surprisingly absent was Nixon's friend André Previn. Remarked Previn in later years: "Marni had this peculiar, chameleonlike quality: She could 'do' everybody. You would hand her a piece of music and say, the first four bars are cockney, then it gets French. It made no difference; she could do it."

Marni Nixon wanted this job—if, in fact, it turned into a job. Not having heard a word after her audition, she called the New York offices of Warner Bros. to inform them that she was in town and glad to audition once again. For her efforts, she was rather condescendingly turned down: "We can't have any native 'Californian' to do *this* dubbing." Aware that André Previn was greatly displeased he had not even been told about her test, she was not surprised to soon receive a call from Warner Bros. asking her to come in and audition again. This audition took place not in Cukor's bungalow but in a dark sound booth, where she could not see any of those listening.

After the audition went off without a hitch, she was still uncertain as to whether the job was hers. Cukor and Previn remained undecided as well, at which point Jack Warner called the film's post production supervisor Rudi Fehr. In Nixon's retelling, it was Fehr who emphatically told Warner: "The only one who can do this part is Marni Nixon." Replied Warner: "Fine, it's done! Hire her!"

Even with Nixon on tap, at this stage it still remained unclear just how much of the score would be sung by Audrey and how much supplied by Nixon. In fact, on the day of Audrey's arrival in Los Angeles, Cukor, Lerner, and Beaton paid Audrey a visit at her rented house, and while tea was being dispensed, Audrey queried lyricist Alan J. Lerner if hers would be the voice heard singing the entire score; she then asked the same question of Cecil Beaton, and, most notably, of Cukor himself. The director gave his reply: Yes, Audrey's voice would be used, but it might well be mixed with another voice for the higher notes, an approach that had worked very well with Leslie Caron's vocals in *Gigi*. Replied Audrey: "I'll understand if you do, but in any case, I'll work hard on my voice, have as many lessons as you like. It's all part of the business, to learn to sing and dance." Noted Beaton in his diary entry for June 27, seven weeks before the start of filming: "Having worked on it like a Trojan ever since her arrival, her voice has improved to such an extent that she will be singing most of Eliza's songs."

It soon became clear, however, that Frederick Loewe and Alan Jay Lerner did not feel that Audrey's pleasant but thin singing voice could handle their demanding score, particularly on the soaring final notes of "I Could Have Danced All Night." André Previn granted an after-the-fact window into the composers' decision-making process, pointing out that even if Audrey was not the greatest singer in the world, "it wasn't such a crime. But you can imagine how Lerner and Loewe felt. . . . This was their statement for the ages." In fact, Lerner, who doubled as the film's screenwriter as well as lyricist, is one of the few to ever criticize Audrey's professionalism, in later years telling Hugo Vickers that his original idea for Eliza's entrance was for a cart piled high with vegetables and flowers to crash through a big puddle and drench Eliza. In Lerner's telling, Audrey refused the entrance, claiming that her fans would not like it, leading Lerner to deem her attitude "unprofessional."

What made the *My Fair Lady* musical experience unique and daunting for both Audrey and Marni was that even with a final decision not yet made, Nixon was actually present while Audrey sang for Sue Seaton, the better to learn Audrey's speech patterns and breathing techniques. Explained Nixon: "The most crucial criterion was for the basic timbre of the voice to not only match Audrey Hepburn's, but also be flexible enough to complement her acting style. . . It was a matter of my singing the songs with her accent, and then her imitating me. She had to have a lot of trust in me. The thrill I have is that I was able to pick up on Audrey and her style. I really felt fused with her." The work required a microscopic attention to detail: "Audrey seemed to have a lower, wider-shaped hard palate than mine, which was narrower and higher in shape. These anatomic differences can affect the high partials in the resonance and the overtones in any voice."

During these joint rehearsals, whatever Audrey's private feelings, she gave no indication of any discomfort with Nixon's presence, going so far as to pick Nixon up each morning en route to the studio. Related Marni: "Who had ever heard of such a thing? Audrey Hepburn had! . . . She was absolutely charming and real, but you still had the sense of her being very aristocratic. When she spoke, it was with carefully chosen words."

As their daily rides together increased in number, their talks became more personal, touching upon husbands, marriage, and children. A sense of trust was developing, which ultimately informed Nixon's work: "The more I know a person the more chameleonlike I can be and the better I can serve the character being created."

With the question of dubbing still undecided, both Audrey and Nixon continued to rehearse Eliza's songs. For "Just You Wait" Audrey would begin the song, with Marni taking over in the midsection before Audrey's voice returned for the final stanza in which Eliza joyfully imagines Higgins's demise. For "The Rain in Spain," Audrey now spoke the introductory lines before Marni chimed in. Both women recorded vocal tracks, with Marni "trying to sing it as I thought she would have, and then she would correct my pronunciation. It was really a technical thing. She had to have a lot of trust in me."

Singing rehearsals were held on the Warner's soundstage in front of Cukor, Beaton, Hermes Pan, Previn, and dialect coach Peter Ladefoged (in Nixon's humorous recall, Audrey referred to Ladefoged as: "An American who probably knows London like I know Peking"). As the hybrid rehearsals continued, Nixon would often begin to sing one of the songs, only to be stopped by Cukor, who wanted to coach Audrey as to what Eliza was thinking at this point in the story. Direction completed, Nixon would begin to sing again, this time incorporating all the instructions Cukor had given Audrey.

Added into the mix was the question of the proper cockney accent to be used in the earliest songs, specifically "Wouldn't It Be Lovely" and "Just You Wait." According to Nixon, Audrey insisted upon waiting for the arrival of Stanley Holloway, cast as Eliza's incorrigible father, so that she could imitate the cockney accent he would be using. The score, however, needed to be recorded before his arrival, leading Nixon to state, "Ultimately Audrey [and I] listened carefully to all the opinions, then it seemed to me she just did it her own way."

Recording sessions began on July 4, 1963, at Goldwyn Studios. Ever the perfectionist, Audrey worked tirelessly on her singing, and after each recording, pleaded to rerecord the song. Observed Nixon: "She felt that now that she heard how it *should* be done, she could actually do it." To Cecil Beaton, the recording session proved "an ordeal" for Audrey, but she worked her way through "Wouldn't It Be Loverly," and when actual filming began, lip-synced to her own vocal of the song.

While Audrey prerecorded the score in the studio, Harrison insisted upon performing his numbers live on set via a shortwave radio microphone placed under his tie. The problem with this early prototype lay in the fact that it kept picking up audio traffic being broadcast on the same wavelength, including, most memorably, a talk by the mayor of Miami.

With Harrison's audio problems corrected, filming began on schedule. While Harrison concentrated on adjusting his performance for the all-seeing eye of the camera, Audrey worked at deepening her characterization. Of the film's very first scene, in which a bedraggled Eliza attempts to sell flowers, Beaton noted: "[Audrey] didn't get into the right groove; had been too strident, her eyes bugged, and she hadn't felt deeply enough. Audrey realized her own mistake, commenting 'Unless you know a character so well that you can relax completely, it somehow doesn't work. I see what it should be now that it's too late. . . .'" Fortunately for all involved, the scene was later reshot.

My Fair Lady was deemed a closed set, and each one of the six sound stages utilized for filming sported signs stating, "Positively no visitors." Consumed with preparation for the marathon role, Audrey hung a sign on the white picket fence erected around her dressing room: "Positively Do Not Disturb." The only people allowed onto the Warners soundstages while Audrey was working were Mel Ferrer, Doris Brynner, and Hubert de Givenchy. Givenchy did not contribute any costumes—*My Fair Lady* had been Beaton's exclusive property since its theatrical premiere in 1956—but as Audrey's trusted confidante, he was a welcome presence for the highly stressed star. She was, as always, pleasant to all involved with the film, but between scenes she studied her script and people did not speak to her. So tense was Audrey that she decreed she did not want anyone in her "eyeline range" during filming, claiming it threw her "off balance." To keep his star happy, Cukor set up baffles with peepholes, just as he had done when directing Greta Garbo in *Camille* (1936).

The pressure Audrey felt resulted not only from the issue of whether her singing would be dubbed but also from the scope of such a massive undertaking. In the costume department alone, ninety-three full-time assistants labored to help create over 1,000 costumes, at a total cost of $500,000. Executing the designs of the gifted, often difficult Cecil Beaton, these assistants stitched together Edwardian-style gowns for the women and suits and top hats for the men, the nearly 1,100 costumes complimented by an extraordinary array of long-out-of-style hats and caps.

Audrey loved Beaton's designs and paid tribute to his talent in an interview with a reporter from *Vogue* magazine: "He makes you look the way you have always wanted to look . . . I adore the hats; they seem to be always in motion . . . the dress becomes a stem to the hat." Their relationship grew into one of total and mutual admiration; Audrey felt that Beaton understood her personally as well as professionally, and Beaton always did comprehend the joyful/sad dichotomy in her personality. Even without mascara and shadow, he noted, her eyes "are like those in a Flemish painting and are even more appealing—young and sad."

With her typical modesty, Audrey explained to Hugo Vickers: "I really adored him because he was always very tender with me, very sweet to me. There's nothing terribly unusual about me, but perhaps there was a sensitivity about him, and I think he understood me. . . . If somebody loves you very much then they make you feel beautiful and he did it with his tenderness, but also with his art." Beaton, whose waspish imperiousness could intimidate and wound, let down his guard with Audrey, responding to such an extent that, as Vickers relayed to Audrey, in the designer's diaries "every time he mentioned you—I don't know if he published it—he describes you as an 'angel of goodness.'" Responded Audrey: "We did understand each other. And I loved him very much. That he understood."

Beaton, who was to work happily with Barbra Streisand on 1970's *On a Clear Day You Can See Forever*, incisively described Audrey's approach to stardom, especially in contrast to Streisand's. There were, he felt, two types of superstars—"The coolly detached and the fanatically involved." Audrey, he felt, embodied the first and Streisand the second. In both *My Fair Lady* and *On a Clear Day*, the two stars portrayed characters who morphed from bedraggled urchins to regal ladies, and he took pleasure in designing accordingly: "Both women were marvelous at conveying this earthiness and seemed to relish the chance to wear rags and carry on like craven guttersnipes. But as grand ladies, dressed to the hilt, they were truly in their element, aware that everything had been building up to that moment—neither had a lack of confidence in their ability to act regal and look monumental, despite their widely varying types and images."

Ever the clotheshorse, Audrey fell in love with the gowns Beaton had designed for the film, and realizing that Eliza spent half the movie costumed as a bedraggled flower girl, she asked to try on some of the gowns created for the extras. Knowing a potential publicity bonanza when he saw it, Jack Warner granted permission for Beaton to spend two days taking still photos, and Audrey happily spent June 5 and 6, 1963, trying on dozens of different dresses. Beaton took upwards of one thousand photos, and as detailed by the designer in his diary, "the combination of Audrey and these exaggerated clothes created comic magic. She wanted to pose for photographs in every one of them. 'I don't want to play Eliza! She doesn't have enough pretty clothes. I want to parade in all these.' And she did: they will never look so well on anybody else." (So beautifully did Audrey play to the lenses of dozens of still photographers that it is no great surprise to learn that a rough estimate finds her having spent a combined total of two years of her life shooting some 650 magazine covers.)

Julie Andrews may still be associated with the role of Eliza because of her spectacular singing, but even she never inhabited the newly respectable "Miss Eliza Doolittle" of the embassy ball quite so thoroughly as did Audrey, for the simple reason that she never exuded the love of finery that emanated from Audrey. Andrews dutifully wore the beautiful society clothes, and with her great figure looked the part, but whether in *My Fair Lady*, *Camelot*, or *Thoroughly Modern Millie*, one always had a sense that as a thorough professional she would certainly parade in the clothes but deep down longed to take off the fancy hats and briskly clap her hands for everyone to return to the business at hand. Coolly efficient she was, which made her ideal to play a governess or two.

Wanting to give Beaton a present for allowing her to play dress-up, Audrey did not buy him an expensive Beverly Hills bibelot but instead gifted him with a more personal present: roses flown in from her own garden. Inscribing a photo to Beaton, she wrote: "Dearest C.B.: Ever since I can remember I have always so badly wanted to be beautiful. Looking at those photographs last night I saw that, for a short time at least, I am, all because of you." Drawing a heart, she signed the note "Audrey."

Audrey's son Sean, in fact, gives great credit to Beaton for the success of the film: "He created the look of the film with his production design, designed all the clothes, and as part of his duties took those amazing black-and-white photographs of my mother in all the incredible clothes. For me Beaton's photographs—not just of my mother but all of his work—are the entertainment industry equivalent of Ansel Adams's photographs of El Capitan. He also wrote extraordinary articles—he was like a modern-day Leonardo."

Audrey and Beaton may have formed a deep and lasting friendship, but Beaton and Cukor certainly did not. Both men were talented, highly opinionated, creative, and gay, each accustomed to always having his own way; working in such close proximity for months on end inevitably made for a clash of egos, with Cukor not wanting Beaton to bother Audrey with portrait sittings, while Beaton felt his contribution was being undervalued. Wrote the designer of the women cast as extras: "The glittering capes were for tall women who should have looked like birds of paradise. Here was a dreary gang of runts. They might have been dressed from any old, tarnished rag-bag."

On July 17, two months into filming, tempers boiled over, with Max Bercutt, the director of publicity, informing Beaton: "Mr. Cukor doesn't want you to take pictures of Audrey while they are fixing the lights. . . . Mr. Cukor does not want you to photograph her on the set during any of her working days." Wrote Beaton in his diary: "I was later told that it took George Cukor two hours to recover from his displeasure with me enough to continue."

Although Audrey remained oblivious to the conflict—"it was something I was not aware of during the picture"—ten days later relations between the two men had disintegrated to the point where Beaton further confided: "I have begun to feel like a trespasser on the sets that I have designed." In reality, however, while Beaton received credit for the film's production design, only the costumes were completely his; the true production design credit properly belonged to the veteran Gene Allen, who ultimately received billing as co-production designer for having done the lion's share of the work.

On November 22, his final day on the film, Beaton managed to say goodbye to Cukor, but the two men never spent another day working together. Still, Beaton had managed to remain the only still photographer allowed on set, with a tense Audrey explaining to her friend Bob Willoughby that while the movie camera did not disturb her, the smaller lens of a still camera simply distracted her too much for anyone other than Beaton to be present.

Cukor drove Audrey without let-up—in the blunt words of Willoughby, "He was unrelenting." Audrey grew exhausted, and after three months of shooting, the pressures grew crushing; in one weekend alone, she revealed to Beaton, her son Sean had been sick with a temperature of 103 degrees, her canary had flown away, and her diamond wedding ring had been stolen from her mobile dressing room. The necessity of getting up at 5:30 a.m. for six months in a row had left her worn out, and Beaton felt that if shooting were to continue "three days longer than she is geared for, total collapse would be inevitable."

And yet, even though Cukor drove Audrey mercilessly, the two remained staunch friends, and for years after, Audrey would often stay at his home when in Hollywood. Their close relationship was to continue until his death in 1983, and in a letter he wrote her on February 25, 1965, six weeks before that year's controversial Academy Awards, he gushed: "Dearest, dearest Audrey, you're lovely, talented, intelligent, distinguished, capable only of beautiful behavior. You're possessed of all the graces and virtues including the rarest of all—simple kindness and plain goodness." In a humorous ending to the letter, he added: "I hope all this praise doesn't make you become insufferable."

As the months of filming continued, Audrey remained under the illusion that all of her own vocals might be used, with just an occasional interpolated high note from Marni Nixon. But now, with a final decision made, Cukor had to inform Audrey, in the midst of a day's shooting, that Nixon would be dubbing her songs. Audrey let out a startled "Oh!" and for the first and last time in her career left the set during the day's shooting. Returning the next day, she apologized for what she termed her "wicked" behavior. There were no histrionics, simply a muttered "oh" that nonetheless conveyed a world of disappointment. Such was diva-dom, Audrey Hepburn style.

What actually bothered Audrey most about the dubbing fiasco was that in stringing her along and allowing her to believe she would be heard on the majority of the songs, the filmmakers had not been honest: "I felt used. And I was angry. I was really angry. But I didn't show it outright. I just kept it inside. . . ." Her anger, in fact, had proved justified, a fact underscored by Marni Nixon: "Rudi Fehr, who was with Warner all the time, has said that they just let her record her tracks to placate her. They never had any serious intention of using her voice. Never."

In André Previn's blunt analysis: "Marni blabbed all over town that she was going to more or less 'save' the movie," but in the end, although Nixon received royalties from the successful soundtrack, she did not receive any screen credit. A talented and warm woman, she would go on to play Eliza herself in a May 1964 New York City Center revival of *My Fair Lady*, receiving special coaching for the role from Julie Andrews when the two were filming *The Sound of Music*. Said Nixon about playing the role: "Having to really play the whole role (as opposed to just singing it) made me respect Audrey Hepburn even more—if that was possible—than I had before."

Speaking about the dubbing controversy in 2003, Marni allowed as how she "felt bad for Audrey: she could tell that she wasn't quite getting it." In her telling, when she ran into Audrey's son Sean shortly after Audrey's death, "He told me that his mother admired me and every day she would come home from the studio and say how talented I was." It's a nice story but somewhat undercut by the fact that at the time *My Fair Lady* was filmed, Sean was four years old, and likely not conversant with the intricacies of film dubbing.

In truth, Audrey could have handled songs like "Loverly," "The Rain in Spain," and "Show Me," and the DVD for the film's beautiful $600,000 restoration in 1994 included bonus tracks of Audrey's own vocals on "Wouldn't It Be Loverly" and "Show Me." Everyone can now be the judge, and "Loverly" in fact sounds, well, just that; Audrey's small true voice hits all the notes while conveying the song's meaning—she is at home vocally because the song is not a big belting number along the lines of "I Could Have Danced All Night."

Says Sean: "I used to think that *My Fair Lady* had aged as a film but with time I've come to reverse my feelings. It's such a beautifully structured musical—maybe the greatest ever. I hate the fact that they dubbed my mother. You can hear how good she sounds on the restoration extras. I hear two small places where she sounds slightly offkey but if it were today, they could have let her sing and then gone back after the recording was completed and fixed it via ADR. I think her singing is great."

Audrey's singing is, in fact, charming and true to character, but these same tracks reveal that the high notes, the real money notes at the end of "I Could Have Danced All Night" would have been beyond her reach; she simply did not have the vocal range to soar up to the final burst of enthusiasm exclaiming "I could have danced, danced, danced—all night!" Those are the notes that provide the audience with an emotional catharsis to match Eliza's, and the powerful belt necessary to push the drama spinning forward would have eluded her.

Still, it's likely that only those elusive high notes need have been dubbed, and with Audrey's own voice utilized, the film would have gained in levels of authenticity. Instead, the powers that be decided that Audrey's own singing would be heard only in snippets: a fair amount of "Just You Wait" as well as scattered phrases in "Wouldn't It Be Loverly" and "Show Me" utilized Audrey's vocals, but the total amounted to no more than ten percent of Eliza's songs. Understandably enough, it remained a bit of a sore subject for Audrey, and in a 1991 interview on *Larry King Live*, when asked who had done the singing for her, she surprisingly replied: "I've forgotten her name, a lovely girl," before adding, "I sang a *bit* of it Larry!"

As for the personal relationship between Audrey and Rex Harrison, it was, at least on Audrey's part, entirely cordial and professional. It was known that Harrison had not been particularly kind or effusive with Julie Andrews on Broadway, but with her impeccable manners, Andrews has never spoken ill of Harrison. In the retelling of Roger Moore, however, Harrison "hated [Andrews] with a passion." As it was, Harrison began shooting the film with an attitude toward Audrey that was "wary at first." As biographer Charles Higham has pointed out, however, when Audrey stated that she had known Kay Kendall (Harrison's deceased wife) at the Marie Rambert ballet school, he soon grew friendlier, and genuinely appreciated Audrey's gift of a red bicycle to ride around the studio lot.

In his autobiography, Harrison struck a tactful note about *My Fair Lady*, writing "Audrey is a very gentle and sweet person, and we get on very well. She was terribly thin, and in the habit of eating only raw vegetables, which I always thought could not give her enough energy." In a second autobiography, he added: "Audrey also had to weather a great deal of adverse press publicity about how much she was being paid, for most of the press had sided with Julie . . . Audrey is a very sensitive person and could not fail to feel all this."

Harrison himself was, in fact, a brilliant performer, with a rapier-like ability to elevate any drawing-room comedy or witty bit of dialogue. But as a person? In the words of André Previn, although Harrison "gave one of the most transcendental performances ever, [he] was—and I don't say this lightly—the most appalling human being I ever worked with. He was charming and funny and a great raconteur, but Jesus Christ, what he did to people. Rex didn't like Audrey very much. He was mean about her, not to her. That was very much more his style."

As to the dubbing controversy, Harrison appeared to mostly look upon it as an inconvenience to himself: "[Audrey] had to be dubbed, and she mouthed the words while somebody else sang it, and I found it quite difficult to make the film with her like this, because I'd grown used to Julie singing her numbers at me every night on stage for three whole years." Referring to Julie having won the Oscar for *Mary Poppins*, Harrison pronounced himself delighted before adding: "The only thing I was not delighted with was that [Julie] didn't do the film with me, and that was only partly because it would have been much easier for me if she had."

In Previn's amusing analysis, Rex's "outward self-assurance was only a cover-up for an even greater self-assurance underneath. There seemed to be only two ways to approach any problem: his way and the wrong way. . . ." During the course of filming, it was Previn who grew ever fonder of Audrey, admitting to feeling awestruck by her beauty, and on one occasion stared at her until she said: "'What's the matter, what are you looking at?'" Previn's reply: "'Audrey you're just so beautiful I can't stand it.' She giggled and took my hand and said, 'Come to dinner.' I said, 'Okay.' It was wonderfully done."

What became clear as filming progressed was that Audrey appeared more at home as Miss Doolittle, the genteel lady, than as Eliza, the bedraggled guttersnipe of a flower girl. Even so, if her own natural elegance could not help but peep through at times, it was not for lack of trying to appear disheveled; her hair was curled every day in order to make it look frizzy, then coated with Vaseline to make it appear matted. The entire transformation was then topped off by the application of dirt on her face and Fuller's Earth on her unflattering, multilayered grimy clothing. Said Geoff Allan, the film's expert at aging clothes: "I gave Audrey's coat seven different dyeings to make it look as old as that." (Muttered Stanley Holloway to Cecil Beaton: "It is remarkable that this scraggy little girl has a green face and then on the screen looks like a million dollars.") So dirty was Audrey after all of these "preparations" that she did not even want Mel to visit her on set while she was wearing such filthy clothes. She did, however, find one way around the dirt by spraying herself with Joy, a very exclusive and expensive perfume: "I may look dirty,' she'd say, 'But I'm going to smell pretty.'"

Whatever the uneasiness about Audrey's believability as a raggedy flower girl, there was none about her transformation into an elegant lady. When, after a triumphant celebration of her linguistic mastery on "The Rain in Spain," she blossoms into a refined, beautifully dressed young woman, she positively soars. Her own physical characteristics, the ramrod straight ballet posture, model's figure, and graceful walk, all expertly conveyed Eliza's transformation into a "tower of strength" without a word being spoken. This newly minted lady of impeccable bearing appears aristocratic to the bone, and the memory of her flower-selling days remains present only in the open-hearted tenderness of her gaze.

Overshadowing every other aspect of this transformation was the audience's first glimpse of Eliza as she departs for the embassy ball. In one of the most iconic moments in film history, Audrey silently appears at the top of the stairs in a beautiful Empire-style antique white gown. Discovered in a shop by Beaton, the dress was, in his words, "quite as beautiful as snow and ice on trees in Switzerland." With her hair piled high and a diamond tiara in the middle of the upsweep, Audrey's ultra-glamorous look, completed by white opera gloves and a glittering diamond necklace, is so startling that for all involved, the only conceivable reaction was one of total capitulation. Which is precisely why the jaded *My Fair Lady* film crew broke into applause upon their first glimpse of this vision: "When she entered the set for the first time in it, she looked so beautiful the crew and the rest of the cast stood silently gazing at her, then broke out with applause and cheers." It's a show-stopping moment and yet Audrey immediately gave full credit for the effect to Cecil Beaton: "In that absolutely sublime dress, with my hair dressed to kill, and diamonds everywhere, I felt super!" In typically modest fashion she further analyzed: "All I had to do was walk down the stairs. How could I miss?"

Standing regally in the Higgins home, a mixture of pride and hesitation flitting across her face as she determinedly waits for Higgins to offer his arm, Audrey represents nothing less than the quintessence of Hollywood stardom. In the words of Cecil Beaton: "The little princess of *Roman Holiday* had grown into a queen's estate."

After all the Sturm und Drang of the dubbing controversy, the shooting of the film, tightly controlled by George Cukor, proceeded in relatively smooth fashion. There was, however, one big jolt which occurred six weeks into filming, when President Kennedy was assassinated on November 22, 1963. It was Audrey who relayed the news to the entire cast and crew, and after her announcement, shooting was canceled for the rest of the day. Filming soon resumed, continuing on its relatively obstacle-free path until the final shots were captured right before Christmas. Postproduction began in January 1964, with a release date of October 21, 1964, locked in.

Critical reaction to the final cut of two hours and fifty minutes proved highly favorable, with Bosley Crowther of the *New York Times* leading the applause: "They've made a superlative film from the musical stage show *My Fair Lady*. . . . The happiest single thing about it is that Audrey Hepburn superbly justifies the decision of the producer Jack L. Warner to get her to play the title role that Julie Andrews so charmingly and popularly originated on the stage." In the *New York Journal American*, the response proved even more emphatic: "Audrey Hepburn is an enchanting Eliza Doolittle."

In the end, the veteran Cukor does makes *My Fair Lady* work; it may not be sensational and it's not original, but it is thoroughly professional, expansively produced, and if not always transporting, highly enjoyable. The flaws remain mostly a result of a failure to fully mask the theatrical origins of the piece. The deliberately stylized Ascot sequences prove jarring in their affect, and while Beaton's costumes are, indeed, showstoppers; in an odd way they prove to be asset and detriment at the very same time. They are so beautiful in form and detail that the viewer's eye is captured and pleased, yet they almost literally stop the show. Especially in the Ascot scene, it's almost as if Cecil Beaton is pushing Cukor aside to say: "Stop the horses! I'm bringing out my costumes." They're beautiful in the extreme, but as Jeanine Basinger has pointed out, the viewer may also want to ask: "That's all very nice—but can we please get back to the story?"

The lack of movement in so many musical sequences proves more noticeable on screen than it ever did on stage, but the story still delivers, and the cumulative effect remains surprisingly powerful. While the role of a bedraggled cockney flower seller is not a natural fit for Audrey, Cukor skillfully works around this by repeatedly cutting to Rex Harrison for his horrified reactions to Eliza's caterwauling. More to the point, as sensitively directed by Cukor and photographed in loving close-up by Hollywood legend Harry Stradling, Audrey is still able to gamely strut through the first half of the film. Far from being the ersatz cockney of legend, she is often quite touching as the desperate-for-a-better-life Eliza.

It is, of course, after Eliza's transformation into a couture-wearing elegant lady that Audrey's performance fully takes off, but it's not just that the metamorphosis grants Audrey a chance to wear beautiful clothes and talk like a member of the aristocracy. It's that she is superb at conveying Eliza's emotional devastation at being cast aside after her triumph at the ball. If every person, male and female alike, continually tries to answer the age-old question of "Where do I fit in?" then where does the ladylike Eliza now belong in life? In her own words, "What's to become of me?" That overwhelming feeling of abandonment, one which Audrey had experienced in her own life, underscored her portrayal of an Eliza whose despair registers with a surprising emotional wallop.

Eliza was now caught between two worlds while belonging to neither, a sense of displacement that coursed through many of Audrey's films all the way back to *Roman Holiday* and *Sabrina*. When Sabrina's own father says of her: "She doesn't belong in a mansion, but then again she doesn't belong in the garage either," it established the motif that ran with great impact not only throughout Audrey's filmography, but also in her personal life. Where in fact did the young Audrey Hepburn fit in after her father disappeared from her life? Who, she continually asked both onscreen and off, would love her?

George Cukor knew how to frame and underscore this essential and appealing quality of Audrey's in order to make an audience care about Eliza's fate, just as he knew how to help Rex Harrison adjust and tamp down his stage performance for the different demands of the screen. Given how misogynistic and unpleasant Professor Higgins can be, one can never be sure how much the audience cares about his fate, which means that if the audience is not invested in Eliza's journey, *My Fair Lady* remains an object of audience indifference. But Audrey here lifts the film above the level of a mere stage adaptation, giving the film its heart and elevating the entire sweep of events above the somewhat stagey first half until the viewer is emotionally invested in Eliza's fate.

In many ways, the interplay between Eliza's fate and Audrey's own vulnerable personality infuses the entire film. The genuine tenderness Audrey displays throughout is rare to behold in any movie star because it's not put upon—it's raw. Any open-hearted sensitivity with which a star may have begun her ascent in golden age Hollywood often started to fracture beneath the sometimes crushing demands of stardom, but in rare cases, the vulnerability remained and could be displayed to sometimes hypnotic effect. Such proved to be the case with Marilyn Monroe, but her fragility often seemed on the verge of collapsing under the weight of her own desperation. Watching Marilyn, particularly at the end of her career, became not just poignant but sometimes uncomfortable, because no one seemed able to save her. In the case of Audrey Hepburn, however, the fragility was leavened by an audience's sense that she, like Eliza, would persevere and triumph, no matter how desperate the circumstances.

That mix of the professional persona with the intimately personal is precisely why, in the words of Bosley Crowther, Audrey's Eliza proved "almost unbearably poignant in the later scenes when she hungers for love." In the end, Eliza, Sabrina, and *Roman Holiday*'s Princess Ann share one crucial desire with Audrey herself: in the words of E. M. Forster, to "only connect."

Audrey plunged wholeheartedly into *My Fair Lady*'s promotional whirl, attending no fewer than ten premieres in London, Paris, Rome, Madrid, New York, and Hollywood. For the much ballyhooed Hollywood premiere on October 24, 1964, she continued her newfound friendship with George Cukor by happily accepting his invitation to stay at his home. Like comrades who have survived a fierce battle, they arrived back at Cukor's at 3 a.m., and she smilingly said to him: "Let's put up our feet and just sit and enjoy it." Star and director were to remain lifelong friends, and Cukor was saddened that neither his plan to direct Audrey as Peter Pan nor a proposed remake of his own 1936 version of *Romeo and Juliet*, to star Audrey with either Terence Stamp or Albert Finney, ever came to fruition.

With *My Fair Lady* riding the wave of multiple rave reviews, it proved no surprise when, early in the new year, the film scored twelve Academy Award nominations, second only to *Mary Poppins*'s thirteen nods. And yet, amid the fanfare heralding a heated competition between *My Fair Lady* and *Mary Poppins* for Best Film of the Year, it was one missing nomination that seemed to garner more attention than all of the others put together: Audrey Hepburn was nowhere to be seen in the race for Best Actress. Oh yes, Julie Andrews had been nominated for playing Mary Poppins, but Audrey, who had carried *My Fair Lady* through nearly every scene, had, it seemed, been rather deliberately overlooked.

Everyone, it seemed, had a theory as to why Audrey had not been nominated. Certainly, Julie Andrews's underdog status helped to turn sentiment against Audrey, no matter how unreasonably. The fact that Audrey's songs were dubbed played right into the sympathy underlying the "Julie was wronged" school of thought, and even Rex Harrison got into the act, stating of the dubbing controversy: "I think this may have been why she was not even nominated for an Academy Award, because in my opinion she gave a superb performance."

Audrey's case was also not helped by the fact that she had recently dismissed her longtime press representative, Henry Rogers, who, if on the scene, could have provided counsel in the lead-up to the announcement of nominations. That squabble with Rogers centered around Audrey's appearance as the public face of Givenchy's L'Interdit perfume.

Audrey had neither asked for nor received any fee or percentage in regard to the fragrance because, in Givenchy's words years later: "She never considered ours a business relationship." But the lack of fee had gnawed at Mel Ferrer, who then asked Rogers to discuss the matter with Jean-Claude de Givenchy, Hubert's brother and business manager. At the very same time, Audrey had been invited to the opening of the annual Cannes Film Festival, and Rogers had taken it upon himself to tell the organizers that it would be most welcome if Audrey were to receive a special award. The Cannes festival director, Robert Favre Le Bret, felt coerced by this "request" and told Audrey herself, who knew nothing of the exchange. Extremely upset, Audrey dismissed Rogers, a Hollywood veteran who was very well-known within the industry. Although Audrey and Rogers eventually patched up their differences, at the time of the buildup to the Academy Award nominations, he was not on hand to offer counsel about handling the press.

As it was, during the time of screenings and the traditional push for nominations, Audrey was back in Switzerland. Her desire to lead a personal life led to accusations that she remained aloof, but her Oscar snub may also have been deliberately aimed at the ever-cantankerous, notoriously combative and penny-pinching Jack L. Warner. The studio chief had personally produced *My Fair Lady*, and when antipathy toward Warner was combined with sympathy for Julie and miscues from Rogers, Audrey's nomination was doomed.

Audrey did in fact receive a David di Donatello Best Foreign Actress Award, a Golden Globe nomination, and a New York Film Critics Circle Best Actress Award for her Eliza Doolittle, but the missing Oscar nomination dominated all talk. It proved to be such a startling oversight that the *Los Angeles Times* ran a front-page headline trumpeting: "Julie Andrews Chosen, Audrey Hepburn Omitted." As stated bluntly in *Variety*: "Hepburn did the acting, but Marni Nixon subbed for her in the singing department and that's what undoubtedly led to her erasure."

Nixon herself wrote that André Previn and George Cukor blamed her for Audrey not being nominated, stating that both men claimed she had "blabbed too much to the press." Nixon had at first remained silent about the dubbing controversy, but as time passed, she began to feel that the longer she refused to comment, the more the discord grew. As a result, she began speaking out about her work on the film, later analyzing: "One thing I never wanted was to hurt Audrey, but the can was open and that was that." By this stage, the debate had grown so well known that even comedians had horned in on the act, with Marni relaying Shecky Greene's joke that he "dreamed last night that I made a date with Audrey Hepburn, but Marni Nixon showed up."

Audrey's own comment about the Oscar nomination controversy was characteristically honest: "I'm happy for Julie but sad and disappointed for myself—but that's the way the members voted. Many other people who gave great performances were not nominated either." Said Julie Andrews: "I think Audrey should have been nominated. I'm very sorry she wasn't."

Writing frankly to Cukor in a letter dated March 8, 1965, Audrey mused: "I think I am the only one who is not in the dark. . . . It seems to me it is all very simple—my performance was not up to snuff. . . . If people wanted to ensure Julie Andrews's Oscar, their sentiments would have automatically been cancelled out had my bravura been worthy. . . . Because *My Fair Lady* meant so terribly much to me, I had sort of secretly hoped for a nomination but never, never counted on the Oscar. There, disappointed I is, but not astounded like my chums seem to be or a lot of the press for that matter. What does amaze me is the hullabaloo which ensued and the constant pressure which was brought about for almost a week to get me to come to California for the big night . . ."

In the end, the funniest reaction to the controversy may have come from Katharine Hepburn, who, although not related to Audrey, was known to refer to Audrey as her "little daughter." In typically blunt Katharine Hepburn–speak, she fired off a telegram to Audrey: "Don't worry about not being nominated. Someday you'll get it for a part that doesn't rate it."

On the night of the Oscars, after scooping up wins for scoring, sound, and cinematography, *My Fair Lady* notched two more Oscars when Cecil Beaton won for costume design and art direction. Beaton was not at the ceremonies, but Audrey soon wrote him a highly affectionate note: "Darling C.B. Just to say how happy happy happy happy I am that you received your Oscar. I wish you could have heard the applause. All my love Audrey xxx." The film then scored an even bigger victory when George Cukor was announced as Best Director. Cukor had previously failed to win for *Little Women* (1933), *Philadelphia Story* (1940), *A Double Life* (1947), and *Born Yesterday* (1950), but after winning both a Golden Globe and the Director's Guild of America award for *My Fair Lady*, Cukor had arrived at the Oscars as the favorite; delighted by his win, he bounded up to the stage and proclaimed his thanks with "a deep bow to Mr. Rex Harrison and to adorable Audrey Hepburn."

In a surreal twist that seemed right out of a Hollywood screenplay, it was Audrey herself who was called upon to then present the Best Actor Oscar; by Academy tradition, the Oscar should have been presented by the previous year's Best Actress, Patricia Neal, but Neal was dealing with severe health problems at the time, and Audrey was asked to fill in as her replacement. As Julie Andrews anxiously waited to find out if she had won the Best Actress Award for *Mary Poppins*, Audrey received thunderous applause as she strode briskly onto the stage in order to announce that the Best Actor of the Year was . . . Rex Harrison for *My Fair Lady*. Taking the stage, Harrison and Audrey hugged and kissed repeatedly, and when Harrison looked at Audrey to proclaim: "I feel in a way I should split this in half," Audrey murmured, "You deserve it all yourself." Concluding his remarks, and well aware that Julie Andrews was mere feet away, Harrison gracefully proclaimed "Deep love to, uh, well, two fair ladies." For the egocentric Harrison, winning the Oscar represented a bit of revenge on Jack Warner for not initially wanting to cast him in the role, and he later wrote: "There he was, having wanted to recast the whole thing for the film, watching me, whom he hadn't wanted, collect my Oscar, and not Audrey, whom he had wanted, while the girl he'd turned down for Eliza, Julie Andrews, won one for another studio."

Such were the times that no matter what Audrey did when it came to *My Fair Lady*, she was criticized; the day after the Oscars, Patricia Neal pronounced herself "a little hurt and disappointed" that Audrey had not mentioned her on the telecast, but it was actually Neal's then husband, the acerbic Roald Dahl, who was most upset, proclaiming: "She and Audrey have known each other a long time. And Audrey didn't even call until the day after the ceremonies—and that was after I think someone told her that Pat was hurt. Audrey had to leave on a 1 o'clock plane, so she didn't have time to see Pat either." It was an unintentional oversight on Audrey's part, but Dahl's comments were picked up around the world.

After Julie Andrews received her Oscar, she and Audrey posed backstage hugging each other, with Audrey proclaiming "I'm thrilled for her, of course." In Julie's recall of the evening: "All the winners and presenters were asked to pose for photographs together. I stood next to Audrey, who looked absolutely gorgeous. She quietly said to me, 'Julie, you really should have done *My Fair Lady* . . . but I didn't have the guts to turn it down.' I told her that I completely understood, and in the years that followed, we became good friends."

Disappointed as she was not to be nominated, Audrey was surely heartened by Harrison's backstage words about Julie's win: "I wouldn't consider it poetic justice. Julie was marvelous onstage, but Audrey was wonderful too." Explaining further, he added: "Actually I think that in the end, Audrey gave an enchanting performance on film, and there's no doubt that she contributed greatly to the film's enormous success and lasting popularity." Addressing the differences between his two Eliza Doolittles, he added: "There are very few similarities between the two girls, except that they both have extraordinary charm." John Gielgud, however, went one—or several—steps further than Harrison, bluntly stating that Audrey was "much better than Julie Andrews."

The fact was, Audrey did seem genuinely happy for her friend Julie. The two women had long since formed a real friendship, and those in the press hoping for a Joan Crawford/Bette Davis–style feud remained sorely disappointed. In fact, when Julie and her husband Blake Edwards spent part of each winter in Gstaad, Switzerland, they always visited Audrey. By that time Audrey's son Luca was eight, and while he may not have fully understood who a celebrity was and exactly what that meant, he did understand that when Julie Andrews visited his house, he was eating dinner with Mary Poppins, and that realization interested him greatly. Writing in his book of reminiscences, he explained: "Julie Andrews put everyone at ease and immediately broke the ice, teaching me to whistle through my lower teeth."

Nonetheless, the Audrey-Julie dubbing controversy continued through the decades, although eventually with a more humorous edge; when Alan Jay Lerner died in June of 1986, a memorial service was held at New York's Shubert Theatre and included an appearance by Julie Andrews. Andrews was to be introduced via a film clip, but inexplicably, her *My Fair Lady* connection to Lerner was delivered by a clip from the film version, one complete with Audrey Hepburn lip-syncing to Marni Nixon. Clip completed, Julie Andrews walked onstage and forthrightly ad-libbed: "Hello, everyone, I'm Marni Nixon!"

In the end, the contretemps over Audrey's casting and lip-syncing overshadowed the significance of her achievement in the role, a state of affairs made all the more ironic when placed in the perspective of movie history. Rita Hayworth's world-famous and iconic "Put The Blame on Mame" in *Gilda* (1946) was voiced by Anita Ellis, not Rita, yet that has not stopped the song and dance from becoming the most famous striptease in film history. No one made a fuss over Marni Nixon dubbing Deborah's Kerr's vocals in *The King and I*, just as no one grew exercised over Carol Lawrence's signature role of Maria in *West Side Story* being given to Natalie Wood. The fact that the Russian-American Natalie Wood was playing the Puerto Rican Maria came in for scant comment, nor did the redoubtable Nixon's dubbing of Wood's voice. But, in the case of *My Fair Lady*, Julie Andrews had proved an overwhelmingly sympathetic figure, and even though it was against her wishes to be dubbed, Audrey was pilloried for that very fact.

Fifty-six years later, when Rami Malek portrayed famed rock singer Freddie Mercury in *Bohemian Rhapsody* (2018), he lip-synced every song to Mercury's own vocals—and received an Academy Award as Best Actor for his efforts.

Tempus fugit.

VOGUE

**AUDREY HEPBURN
CHEZ GIVENCHY**

VOS ROBES VACANCES
VOS VOYAGES:
BARBADES
MAROC
TUNISIE
ALLEMAGNE
HOLLANDE
JAPON
SIAM
HONG KONG

PARIS:
SES SNOBS
PAR DANINOS

MAI 1963·6F

Beautiful yet vulnerable, Audrey is here dressed in a cocoon of a pale peach tulle strapless Givenchy dress with nacre and jewel embroidery between the layers. This photo shoot later yielded the advertising art for Givenchy's L'Interdit perfume, which he created exclusively for Audrey. Jean Stockton/Alamy Stock Photo.

Chapter Twenty-Eight

WHAT COULD GO WRONG? 1960s

"I knew how difficult it had to be to be married to a world celebrity, recognised everywhere, second billed on the screen and in real life. How Mel suffered. But believe me, I put my career second."

—Audrey Hepburn

IN THE MONTHS AND YEARS following Sean's birth, the whispers of the Hollywood gossip-mongers had grown into a chorus: "Mel is holding Audrey back, Mel controls every one of Audrey's decisions." And yet for the time being, the marriage endured, because in their rush to judgment, Mel's detractors ignored one not so insignificant fact: Audrey Hepburn was a very smart woman, and if she trusted Mel, then there was a solid reason for that: he was an intelligent man and the possessor of show business savvy, a smart, steadying partner whose instincts helped Audrey shape her career choices. Oft forgotten in the contretemps, in fact, was that the control issue cut both ways. As one of Mel's friends noted in regards to Audrey's influence on the peripatetic Mel: "You won't believe this but he has actually begun to sit still."

It was Mel who advised Audrey to hire Henry Rogers as her press agent, and even more significantly, to employ the ex-boxer and ski instructor Kurt Frings as her agent. Frings, who at one point had represented both Olivia de Havilland and Elizabeth Taylor, had originally been recommended by his poker buddy, Billy Wilder, and contrary to the merry-go-round of Hollywood agentry, Audrey stayed the course with Frings throughout her career. Says Sean: "Based on what I saw and what she told me, my parents would discuss the creative aspects of a film she was considering—the script and the contents and packaging. Kurt then came in for the financial deal: he was a bulldog who would go after the money. . . . Once the first deal had been set by Kurt—choice of makeup artist, hair stylist, travel—those aspects would be repeated in every agreement. It then became a matter of how much she received up front and what percentage of the gross. My mother was able to separate: my father advised on the artistic front and Kurt dealt with the business."

Even Robert Wolders gave Mel solid credit for helping Audrey's career, noting: "People conveniently forget that they made a lot of good choices together." In the end, however, it may just be that the most perceptive analysis of the supposed Mel-Audrey, Svengali-Trilby relationship came from the still pining William Holden: "I think Audrey allows Mel to think he influences her."

Audrey certainly trusted Mel's judgment, so how exactly did their marriage begin to unravel? In the words of Ernest Hemingway on the subject of bankruptcy, it happened in two ways: "Gradually and then suddenly." After six years of marriage, times were changing rapidly: the seemingly quiescent Eisenhower years had given way to the vibrant presidency of JFK, and the strict societal roles assigned to men and women were now loosening up. But while Audrey maintained her status as one of the most successful actresses in the world, landing lead roles in feature films was proving increasingly difficult for Mel. As Audrey scored an Oscar nomination for *The Nun's Story* (1959) and nabbed the most sought-after role of the decade in *My Fair Lady* (1964), Mel was reduced to filming cameos in Audrey's films *Charade* (1963) and *Paris When It Sizzles* (1964), before moving into guest star appearances on television.

The problem lay in the fact that Mel's greatest talent seemed to lie not in acting but as a producer, a job in which his network of relationships and understanding of how Hollywood worked stood him in great stead. Audrey, in fact, told Sean years later: "Your father was the producer of my career." Explained Sean: "He was a good producer because he had done it all. He was a dancer, an actor, assistant producer, director, and veteran of radio. He could ride horses, fence, knew many people—he had a complete vision of the industry. He had started when he was eighteen and when my parents met, my mother was twenty-three and he was thirty-seven. He was smart and a show business veteran, advising her on possible films. He pushed for her to do *Nun's Story* and chose Terence Young as director for *Wait Until Dark*. He had a breadth of experience that was very helpful to my mother."

But Mel wanted to act, and because he was married to one of the biggest stars in the world, his career was constantly compared to his wife's, and inevitably found wanting. In show business terms, he lacked the X factor of appeal which defines any onscreen star, and when the marriage was breaking up, Yul Brynner, whose second wife Doris was among Audrey's closest friends, bluntly opined: "I'm sure that, above everything, Mel was jealous of her success, and he could not reconcile himself to the cold facts of life. She was much better than he in every way, so he was taking it out on her." Expounding further, Brynner added: "Finally she couldn't take it any longer. God knows, she did everything a woman could do to save her marriage."

Brynner had a vested interest in this analysis, given wife Doris's close friendship with Audrey; one need only look at newsreel footage of Audrey, returning to Switzerland after the 1965 *My Fair Lady* Oscars, happily bounding down airplane steps and giving Doris a big hug, to know how deep that friendship had grown. But was Yul Brynner right? Was Mel actually jealous of Audrey's success? Speaking in 1996, three years after Audrey's death, Mel stated: "I don't think anybody could compete with Audrey and there was no sense in trying to. I had a great deal to do with her career, and I'm delighted I was able to contribute. But I didn't benefit from it. . . ." Continuing his self-analysis he emphatically concluded: "I was not competitive nor was I controlling."

Mel seemed more aware of the problems found in living with a superstar wife than did anyone else: "It's a problem when the wife outshines the husband as Audrey does me. I'm pretty sensitive when producers call and say they want to discuss a film with me, when in reality they're angling for Audrey and using me as bait." Commented Audrey's longtime publicist Harry Rogers about the marriage at this time: "Rarely did I ever see her happy. . . . It seemed to me that she loved him more than he loved her, and it was frustrating. . . . She was filled with love. Mel was filled with ambition, for his wife and for himself."

The difficult times now seemed to occur more and more frequently, and Mel's domineering ways and surprisingly straitlaced code of behavior did not help matters. Billy Wilder's smart and stylish wife Audrey claimed that as far back as the filming of 1957's *Love in the Afternoon*, when Audrey spilled a drink and muttered "Shit!" at her own clumsiness, Mel was so incensed at this profanity that he stalked out of the restaurant in which they were all dining.

Still, Audrey tried to keep her marriage intact for Sean's sake, and when the disagreements occurred more frequently, she redoubled her efforts. She even spoke of the commitment to her marriage in the same breath as her all-out work-until-you-drop approach to *My Fair Lady*: "I also told myself . . . if you have a grain of energy or thought or emotion left in you, you're not giving this role enough. And that philosophy holds true not only for my work, but for my marriage too."

She had turned down any possible return to Broadway in order to be with Mel, explaining at the time of *My Fair Lady*'s premiere: "I would love to do another play or musical, but it presents tremendous problems with the mix of private life and career. Being in a play for months on end is very tough. We don't live in New York, and I like to follow my husband wherever he goes." She had, in fact, made no fewer than sixteen trips in eight months "through every part of Europe in order that Mel never be left alone." Rumors of Mel's infidelity now began floating around show business circles, and eventually the talk of divorce turned into a dull roar that prompted then powerful New York City gossip columnist Earl Wilson to call Audrey in Switzerland at 5 a.m. What, he wondered, was the state of Audrey's marriage?

In truth, there had been no scandals, no drunken binges or out-of-control behavior. The problems were simply too big to overcome: the fact that Audrey's career greatly eclipsed Mel's, as well as Mel's need, likely compensatory in nature, to exert control—even his desire to reside right in the center of the show business action while Audrey preferred the remote European countryside—it all added to the weight of a crumbling marriage until the cumulative pressure left their union hanging by a thread.

"Ip" the faun from *Green Mansions* took up residence inside the house with Audrey and Mel. Audrey's Yorkshire terrier "Mr. Famous" grew notably jealous. Photofest.

Chapter Twenty-Nine

FOR THE LOVE OF ANIMALS, 1957–1993

"I walk my dogs to keep me fit. I talk to my dogs, which keeps me sane. I can't think of anything that makes one happier than to cuddle and play and start the day with a warm puppy."

—Audrey Hepburn

UNHAPPY IN HER MARRIAGE AUDREY may have been, but even with her marriage to Mel growing more fragile by the day, Audrey still found an abundance of personal joy in two places: with Sean and in her life-changing companionship with her pets.

It was during the filming of *Love in the Afternoon* (1957) that Mel gave Audrey a Yorkshire terrier whom she immediately named "Mr. Famous." Not yet a mother at the time and possessed of an instinct to protect the most vulnerable members of society, Audrey poured all of her pent-up affection onto her new companion, who quickly lived up to his name and became one of the most well-known dogs on the planet.

He also proved to be noticeably ill behaved, with Audrey Wilder reporting that he urinated on her Louis XIV chairs. Perhaps the accident should have come as no surprise, given that Mr. Famous was already on tranquilizers due to his nervous behavior when having to cross any road. So quickly did Mr. Famous come to rule the roost that he became noticeably jealous when Ip, the *Green Mansions* fawn, came to live in the house. If Ip could, and did, eat his meals in the house, well then Mr. Famous would begin sleeping on Audrey's bed.

This overt love of animals permeated all aspects of Audrey's life, with John Isaac, the UNICEF photographer who accompanied Audrey on many of her charitable trips observing: "Whenever we saw cats or dogs she would straight away go and pet them even if they were on the street."

By this time Audrey's image was so pristine that it came as an hilarious surprise to learn that during her London chorus girl days, when a stray theatre cat was taken home by her friend Bob Monkhouse, she suggested that the cat be called "Tomorrow"; a puzzled Monkhouse asked her about the name, and a guileless Audrey explained that the cat had been castrated, and "you know what they say about tomorrow never coming." A highly amused Monkhouse allowed as how "Audrey was rather good with jokes." Said the acerbic and witty Billy Wilder: "She was kind of a little frivolous, you know, in her jokes. She was not all Virgin Mary. It's just that when it came out of her mouth, it was twice as funny."

In the midst of her failing marriage, it was dogs for whom Audrey professed unadulterated love: "Who thinks you're as fantastic as your dog does?" Audrey understood and related to a dog's fragility: "No person, and few children . . . are as unpremeditated, as understanding . . . they only ask to survive . . . completely vulnerable. And this complete vulnerability is what enables you to open up your heart completely, which you rarely do in a human being." People disappointed, but dogs never did.

So central a part did the dogs come to play in her life that although the number-one reason she began to work less frequently lay in her determination to be fully present for her sons, her dogs constituted the second major reason for her screen absences: she simply did not want to spend more than two weeks away from home because she—and her late-in-life companion Robbie Wolders—did not want to leave their dogs. A cameo in Steven Spielberg's 1989 film *Always*? Fine. Her entire role could be shot in four days. An extended three-month shooting schedule away from Switzerland and her dogs? No thank you.

Home and dogs helped Audrey feel grounded. And as a mother and pet lover, how did 1960s-era Hollywood make her feel?

Modest. Grateful.

Uncertain.

In the words of granddaughter Emma Ferrer: "I think she was chasing unconditional love her whole life." Science History Images/Alamy Stock Photos.

Chapter Thirty

A BEAUTIFUL UNCERTAINTY

"I'm terribly uncomfortable seeing myself onscreen. Terribly critical of myself. I don't like what I see. That's why my success is a miracle to me—the audience sees something that I don't see."

—Audrey Hepburn

GIVEN THE STRATOSPHERIC LEVEL OF Hollywood stardom Audrey occupied, the extraordinary thing about her personality and concern for others was that she categorically refused to indulge in even the slightest bit of "I'm a star" behavior. Observers on set were startled to realize that she remained filled with self-doubt even while immersed in a lifestyle so rarified that her *Nun's Story* castmate Patricia Bosworth recounted an afternoon on set when Audrey's assistant approached her to quietly whisper: "Miss Hepburn would like you to join her for tea tomorrow. Givenchy is flying in from Paris to show her his new collection and she thought you'd enjoy seeing it with her."

The unknown gamine clad in ballet slippers and a "Venezia" boater was now being personally shown Hubert de Givenchy's latest collection. It was enough to turn anyone's head, and yet it never did affect Audrey—not at the beginning of her career, not at her peak, and absolutely never at the end. Billy Wilder, never a pushover, called her bracingly modest, and the self-doubt she felt throughout her entire career proved genuine. When speaking to her friend Dominick Dunne about the acclaim that routinely fell her way, she remarked: "And you sort of don't believe any of it, and yet you're terribly grateful."

That sense of gratitude and modesty remained with her for life; nearly every interview from the 1950s through the 1980s is peppered with constant references to the luck she felt in having worked with great directors ranging from Wyler and Wilder to Stanley Donen and Steven Spielberg. Hers was a professional's astute awareness that she had come along at exactly the right time, arriving in a more innocent world where her fairy-tale Hollywood films could be crafted as the epitome of wish fulfillment.

Audrey's least impressed fan always remained Audrey herself, but then again, given her upbringing, how could it be otherwise? Ella was disconcerted enough that Audrey made a living by making a spectacle of herself, but bragging about it simply would never pass muster. No, adherence to Ella's mantra that concern for others was most important remained with Audrey at all times. Said Audrey herself: "You can tell more about a person by what he says about others than you can by what others say about him." Uninterested in Hollywood gossip, she focused her gaze and undivided attention upon her friends, with close friend Anna Cataldi observing: "After five minutes with Audrey you forgot who she was for everybody else." Connie Wald's son Andrew explained Audrey's fame and down-to-earth affect in show business terms: "Being around her was like traveling with a rock star who was nice to you."

It was this note of genuine interest in others that was immediately apparent to award-winning fashion designer Jeffrey Banks, whose lifelong fascination with Audrey grew into a strong friendship of many years standing:

I had been in love with Audrey since I was nine or ten years old. As a young boy I thought she was the most beautiful, charming, gorgeous creature ever. I thought "Maybe someday I'll be lucky enough to be in the same room with her."

I would go to the library in Washington, D.C., and pull every magazine and article I could find about Audrey, particularly if it was about *Funny Face*. I finally saw it at a revival house in D.C. on a double bill with *Lili*—and I made my mother sit through *Lili* a second time because of *Funny Face*! It's my favorite movie of all time: It has fashion, Paris, Avedon, Astaire, and above all else, Audrey. Years later when I received an email asking if I'd be interested in providing fashion commentary for the fiftieth anniversary DVD release, I instantly wrote back: "Yes! And you don't have to pay me!" I shouldn't have said that.

So, when I first met John Rizzuto, who was the VP of Givenchy Fragrances in the U.S., I instantly blurted out: "Do you know Audrey Hepburn?" He did and nicely said, "I'll call you when she's next in the United States." This was in the 1980s, and one month later he called me and said Audrey would be in New York for a celebration of Givenchy's career at the Fashion Institute of Technology (FIT).

I called FIT and told them I would buy a whole table if it was next to Audrey's. Then I called my friend Renny Reynolds, the florist, and said: "I want one dozen red roses— no two dozen—no four dozen! I want them for Audrey Hepburn." He put together what amounted to a small tree of roses—it was so big I got to the dinner early and hid it underneath the skirt of the table.

Between the first and second courses John introduced me to Audrey and when I brought out the red roses she was definitely startled. Of course, I hadn't given any thought to how she was going to transport this tree of roses and she was very gracious but had a faraway look in her eyes. I had built up our meeting so much in my imagination that I was somewhat dismayed.

My friends could see I was disappointed, and the next morning John called me and said: "I could tell you were not thrilled, but you must know Audrey was not herself last night. Her mother had just slipped and broken a hip at Audrey's home in Switzerland, and Audrey was so concerned about her mother that she almost didn't come to New York. But—she didn't want to disappoint Hubert and all the people who had bought tickets, so she took a train to Paris, the Concorde to New York, and then this morning turned around and did the same thing in reverse. Next time you meet her it will be completely different."

That next time came when I was invited to the taping of the Turner Classic Movies salute to Audrey. I assumed I'd be a part of the audience at the studio on 23rd Street. Well, there was no audience—it was just the crew, Audrey, Robbie Wolders, and me. I was thrilled, and she was charming, gracious—everything you could hope for.

After that I started sending her flowers every time she came to New York. When she received the Film Society of New York Charlie Chaplin award in 1991, I had flowers sent to her hotel suite. The night of the gala I was entering the theatre and heard someone calling my name. It was Audrey who came over, arms outstretched, and gave me what seemed like fourteen kisses on my checks, thanking me for the flowers. This was her night—a lifetime achievement award—and yet she was more concerned with thanking me for some flowers. That says everything about her.

When the Council of Fashion Designers of America (CFDA) gave their first lifetime achievement award to Ralph Lauren, Audrey was asked to present the award, so I picked Audrey and Robbie up at the airport and brought them to their hotel. We sat and talked in their suite, and she literally didn't talk one bit about herself. That didn't interest her. She asked about me and her concern was honest. When you were with her, she made you feel like you were the only person in the world who mattered. She had perfect manners. I'm a designer, and Audrey is the ultimate style icon, and yet we rarely talked about fashion. We talked about her work with UNICEF. Working with UNICEF gave her purpose and joy.

After I left, I called my friend Renny again, and I went on and on saying I wanted to send her lilies of the valley, peonies, I need this and I need that, and finally as I was running on and on he said: "Jeffrey you haven't told me how much you want to spend," and I said: "It's for Audrey Hepburn. Money is no object!" Which was not a smart answer for me to give to a very expensive florist. . . . The last time I saw Audrey, when she received an award at the Waldorf Astoria, she leaned over to me at dinner and said: "Jeffrey—the flowers have to stop. It's too much." I said to her: "It's never enough for you," and we both laughed.

The one other famous person who struck me the same way in her concern for others was when I met Princess Diana. I told her that I had been to the London Lighthouse AIDS hospice because I knew she had often visited patients there. She took my hand, looked me in the eye, and said: "Besides my children, that is my life's work." She really made me think of Audrey. They both connected to you in an immediate way.

The parallel to Princess Diana proved apt. Both women endured painful marriages and were devoted to their two sons. Both were revered as fashion icons of such extraordinary appeal that their dresses sold for $1 million nearly a quarter century after they died. Most notably, however, each woman found personal fulfillment in dedication to social causes: Diana with the campaign against land mines and Audrey in working for UNICEF. Using their startlingly intuitive emotional intelligence, both icons possessed the uncanny ability to make hundreds of people gathered in a ballroom feel as if they were being addressed one-on-one, and in the process raised millions for charity.

That genuine interest in others, the ability to forge a strong connection, was exactly what Cecil Beaton's biographer Hugo Vickers experienced when he interviewed Audrey in March of

1983. Accustomed to moving in the highest circles of society, Vickers was nonetheless reduced to awestruck admiration by their conversation, writing in his diary: "There are moments when the world seems suddenly to stand very still and this is one of them. I have just talked for twenty-five minutes to Audrey Hepburn. She was so sweet and adorable and so nice about Cecil. . . . From her very first 'hello' she was the total embodiment of all that I've always admired in her. . . . After her call there was a still and calmness in the flat. Nobody rang up for half an hour. And I was alone on an elevated plane."

Audrey's interest in the welfare of others and the care with which she responded to her friends' concerns welled up out of her own fragile self, her gorgeous exterior hiding a still shy little girl who, in her oft-repeated and self-revealing words, wanted desperately to both give and receive love. Says her granddaughter Emma Ferrer, born six months after Audrey died: "I think she was chasing unconditional love her whole life. She wanted to love and be loved. And I think she got it in her life, but I don't think she got it from a lot of people. For a woman who's the most loved in the world to have such a lack of love is so sad."

It was the mixture of joie de vivre and bone-deep sadness, her insistence upon finding joy among the world's many disappointments that proved so compelling to audiences and friends alike. When any of Audrey's characters appeared sad onscreen, every audience member understood that she wasn't pretending. Drawing upon her own disappointments and upsets allowed her instinctive gifts as an actress to flower, enabling her to express the pain felt by Sister Luke in *The Nun's Story* or the hurt felt by a cast-aside Eliza Doolittle in *My Fair Lady*. Audiences intuited that secrets and uncertainty remained, her darkest memories withheld lest they disrupt or prove too painful in the revelation. As with Garbo, a mystery remained, and audiences respected and understood her need to withhold. Wrote Patricia Bosworth: "She's something of a mystery. Enigmatic, detached, but irresistible."

Delving deeper into the extraordinary effect Audrey's presence had on the most hardened of Hollywood veterans, Bosworth continued: "I watched spellbound as she glided across the floor toward me, her feet barely touching the ground. . . . She greeted me as if she'd been waiting to meet me all her life, which I suspect is how she greeted everyone. [Her face] radiated such beauty and sadness." In the perfectly judged words of her *Nun's Story* co-star, the formidable Dame Edith Evans: "It's as if she's from another world."

ACT THREE

ICON

Paramount Pictures/Photofest © Paramount Pictures

Jacqueline Kennedy admitted the influence of Audrey's subtle and sophisticated style. That influence is clearly apparent in Jackie's ivory silk twill Oleg Cassini gown, highly reminiscent of Givenchy's cotton velvet and silk satin gown worn by Audrey in *Funny Face's* "Bird of Paradise" transformation sequence. Photo by Getty Images.

Chapter Thirty-One

THE NATURE OF THE APPEAL, 1953–1993

Audrey, Grace, Doris, and Jackie

"Over the years we chose three style icons from the twentieth century to write about: Audrey Hepburn, Grace Kelly, and Jacqueline Onassis. People enjoyed reading about all three, but the greatest response, hands down, was to Audrey."

—Pamela Fiori, editor in chief, *Town and Country*

TO FRIENDS AND CO-STARS RANGING from Dame Edith Evans to Harry Belafonte, Audrey may have appeared to be paying a visit from another world, but to American women in the 1950s and 1960s, her look in the 1950s and 1960s appealed precisely because the bandanas, capri pants, and ballet flats she favored all seemed notably un-American in style. Main Street USA was no longer in favor, and for upscale postwar American women, chic, European Audrey pointed the way to a different look. Yes, there was a touch of the American sporty WASP ethos in the Lacoste shirts with upturned collars that she favored, but everything Audrey wore was overlaid with a refined, modern European flair. Uncertain she remained in her professional life, but never when it came to her clothes.

Audrey may have been wearing the most expensive designer dresses on the planet, and her natural style of movement may have suggested that she was about to step onstage into the rarified world of *Swan Lake*, but for men and women alike, she still exuded a sense of playfulness. Forget the Givenchy she's wearing in *Sabrina*—when she spins around in Linus's chair before sprawling onto the conference room table, there isn't a trace of aristocratic hauteur: this girl was fun, and audiences knew it right away. If there's such a creature as a down-to-earth elitist, then Audrey Hepburn is it: European in style but mixed with a distinctly American playfulness. Which makes it a loss for everyone that she never had the opportunity to play the role of the goddess Venus in the Kurt Weill musical *One Touch of Venus*. Mixing elegance and comic situations, this Venus would have floated around the soundstage, dressed by Givenchy while singing "I'm a Stranger Here Myself" and "Speak Low." Oh, what might have been.

The appeal of this particular Venus began not with the designer clothes but instead with her confiding persona, the warmth in her eyes transmitting to women in the audience the feeling that she would make a real and trustworthy friend, one worthy of the most personal of confidences.

The invitation to confide was inherent in that mysterious voice, an unidentifiable continental accent mixing her British and Dutch backgrounds into drawn-out vowels and crisply enunciated consonants, all of it anchored by emphases upon unexpected syllables (a decided part of the appeal in her banter with Cary Grant in *Charade*). Her speech proved inviting, even mysterious, but, in Audrey's own analysis, having grown up speaking Dutch in her house, French in the outside world, and English during her years of schooling in Kent, "There is no speech I can relax into when I'm tired, because my ear has never been accustomed to one intonation. It's because I have no mother tongue that the critics accuse me of curious speech."

Far from being an affectation, her quiet, nearly confessional voice was a natural reflection of a childhood spent in multiple European countries as well as a reaction to the years spent listening to her parents' raised voices. If F. Scott Fitzgerald's Daisy Buchanan always spoke with a voice full of money, then Audrey's voice, in Cecil Beaton's memorable phrase, always possessed "the quality of heartbreak."

Just like another actress named Hepburn, absolutely no one else sounded quite like Audrey. Never raising her voice, she effortlessly invited any viewer or audience member to lean in and establish a connection. Said Stanley Donen: "To me, Ella Fitzgerald has the most tranquilizing singing voice on earth, and Audrey has the most tranquilizing speaking one." Clearly under the spell of Audrey's voice, he added: "Her voice was enough to soothe your jangled nerves . . . she surrounded (her words) with the consistency of honey. She captivated even in the dark."

Audiences remained intrigued and then, it is not too hyperbolic a claim, grew enthralled, the alluring voice made all the more effective when accompanied by a megawatt smile.

Capable of conveying the sheer joy found in simply being alive, Audrey's smile was nonetheless often tinged with sadness. Julia Roberts may possess an equally famous and all-encompassing smile, but there is never any sadness about it. She is simply too sturdy and upright to convey genuine heartbreak, while Audrey had to consciously work toward banishing her feelings of sadness; no matter the situation, she felt a need to put her best foot forward, and in the process will herself toward optimism: "Happy girls are the prettiest girls" she famously said—and meant. She would, unceasingly, march straight through her sadness, declaring "Nothing's impossible. The word itself says 'I'm possible!'"

That smile, chic, and cool beauty would seem to bring about an immediate comparison to another legendary Hollywood beauty, Grace Kelly, who, like Audrey, was born in 1929, established herself as a paragon of style, and also died a tragically early death—in her case at age 52. Audrey and Grace did share Hollywood history and the winning of Academy Awards, but they operated in completely different ways within the Hollywood hothouse. Each possessed a genuine beauty and exquisite manners, but even though layers of passion existed beneath their respective controlled exteriors, Kelly possessed a coolness unknown to Audrey, a sense that the world was her oyster never conveyed by Audrey.

The more interesting comparison is with Audrey's contemporary in Hollywood stardom, Doris Day. In fact, Audrey's declaration that other women could easily look like her was, in its own way, as pleasantly preposterous a statement as calling Doris Day the girl next door; no girl next door looked like Doris Day, sang like a million dollars, and could dance and act for and with everyone from Alfred Hitchcock to Bob Fosse and James Cagney. The beauty of Doris and Audrey's mutual affect lay in the fact that both women made it look so easy that audiences thought that they too could conquer Hollywood with just a little effort.

Both Day and Hepburn felt a lifelong loss from their fathers walking out when they were still very young, both reached their peak years of popularity in the 1950s and early 1960s, and even more notably, both managed the neat trick of appealing equally to men and women. Just as Audrey's beauty and sense of fun made her worthy of admiration by both sexes, Doris's forthright career-woman independence appealed to 1950s homebound women at the same time that men were attracted to her sunshiny girl next door sex appeal. In the words of their mutual co-star James Garner: "Doris exuded sex, but she made you smile about it."

Audrey never did function as a fantasy figure in the manner of Marilyn Monroe, Elizabeth Taylor, or Rita Hayworth. Yes, men found her to be warm and intelligent, but her sex appeal surfaced in a lowkey, simmering, back-burner kind of way. In her own words: "I'm not as well-stacked as Sophia Loren or Gina Lollobrigida . . . there is more to sex appeal than just measurements. I don't need a bedroom to prove my womanliness. I can convey just as much appeal fully clothed, picking apples off a tree or standing in the rain." Said Billy Wilder: "When she stood before the cameras she became Miss Audrey Hepburn. And she could put it on a little bit, the sexiness, and the effect was really something."

Men responded to Audrey's intelligence and impeccable bearing, sensing that she expected a certain standard of good behavior. For all of the tomboy attributes of short hair and a relatively flat chest, Audrey remained intensely feminine, and the fact that she did not self-consciously display an overt sexuality à la Monroe helped make the age differences with her legendary and older leading men seem palatable. Men wanted to protect her, but not because they felt she would fall apart at any moment like Monroe. No—for all her apparent fragility and air of needing protection, she always projected a core of inner strength that deepened the appeal, speaking as it did to the sense of a very equal partnership.

It was that sense of equal partnership that similarly informed Day's pairings with a who's-who of Hollywood's biggest stars: James Garner, Frank Sinatra, and Clark Gable. In her most famous screen partnership of all, her three comedies with Rock Hudson, Day too morphed into a fashion icon, an independent career woman decked out in the latest fashions designed by Jean Louis and Irene. The similarities with Audrey did not stop with fashion but in fact extended to their professional and personal lives as well. Like Audrey, Doris had begun decades of hard work while still a teenager, singing on the road with big bands just as Audrey danced in the chorus of West End musicals. Both worked nonstop through their peak years, with Day making thirty-nine movies and recording over six hundred songs.

Most notably of all, however, each woman walked away from Hollywood on her own terms: Audrey after *Wait Until Dark* in the late '60s, and Doris in the mid-'70s after the successful five-year run of her television series. For all the differences between Day's all-American pep and Audrey's continental-flavored sophistication, not only did both women seem incapable of lying, but they also shared a refusal to view the world through the protective prism of irony. Instead, both led with their heart, and if hurt by those close to them (Doris weathered four unsuccessful marriages), they shared a combination of vulnerability and strength that made audiences embrace them as friends, women who instilled confidence about life's possibilities. Maybe, both women seemed to suggest, happiness really did lie just around the corner.

It seemed fitting that both Audrey and Doris found happiness and a sense of peace in the final acts of their lives, away from the Hollywood machine: Audrey with UNICEF, Doris in her work on behalf of animal welfare. Beloved by their co-stars, each woman exuded a genuine sense of modesty. If Doris famously stated, "If I can do it, anyone can do it," and if Audrey never did understand the fuss about her appearance—"I see the problems when I get up in the morning and I do my best to do well"—their mutual self-deprecation came from a place of genuine modesty.

Audrey always did remain the one star capable of convincingly stating, "I'm not in love with my looks." In fact, she often went much further when asked what she would like to change about her appearance: "Oh I'd like to be not so flat-chested. I'd like not to have . . . such big feet, such a big nose." In typical Audrey fashion she gracefully added: "Actually I'm very grateful for what God's given me. I've done pretty well," but in her blithe estimation: "No, I don't think girls would like to look like me. Maybe they would like to be an actress like me. Who would I like to be? Elizabeth Taylor is the one I would like to look like. I think most females would; she's so beautiful."

There was no faux modesty in Audrey's self-analysis because she genuinely believed that she was not beautiful. So self-critical was she that she even found her shoulders to be subpar, telling Hedda Hopper in 1953: "I've always wanted really feminine shoulders that sort of slope down."

Interviewed by Cecil Beaton's biographer Hugo Vickers, in one brief span she put down her own extraordinary beauty no fewer than three times: "Oh, there's nothing terribly unusual about me. . . . There's not something all that special about me. . . . There's nothing very flamboyant about me or anything terribly beautiful or anything." Billy Wilder, for one, disagreed strongly, stating in later years: "Audrey Hepburn was something special because she was not 'pretty.' She was very beautiful."

Wilder was right and Audrey was wrong because no other Hollywood star ever quite harnessed that singular combination of grace, voice, and intelligence. Her appearance and style seemed at once unexpected and yet always present—as if she had burst forth fully formed, sui generis.

Said Sean in later years: "[She was] the perfect package of imperfections," a phrase that to him seemed to encompass both her beauty and a genuine sense of modesty, not only because she possessed a heightened sense of her own imperfections, but also because "the definition of beauty is not knowing that you are so special."

Where others saw a style icon, Audrey simply wanted to go her own way. And if she was, in her looks and style, utterly unique, did she have any peers when it came to setting fashion trends?

Perhaps only one: Jacqueline Bouvier Kennedy.

It is ironic then, that the connection between Audrey Hepburn and the Kennedy family had begun with John F. Kennedy, not Jackie, when, back in 1952, Audrey met the then senator who quickly declared her his favorite actress. The duo even managed an innocuous date before their respective romantic interests turned elsewhere, and it was Audrey who, at President Kennedy's request, sang "Happy [Forty-Sixth] Birthday" to him in May of 1963 at the Waldorf-Astoria Hotel, in celebration of what turned out to be his final birthday.

But it was Jackie with whom Audrey was ceaselessly compared over the decades, their images and fame continually mingling in interesting and complicated ways. Both women were highly involved mothers of two children. Each endured a pair of troubled marriages to men who proved difficult and self-involved, until both found lasting love and happiness with men they did not marry—financier Maurice Tempelsman for Jackie, actor Robert Wolders for Audrey.

Audrey and Jackie both possessed the now-vanished quality of allure, and notwithstanding Jackie's American citizenship, each managed the rather non-American quality of holding part of herself in reserve. Here were two women who functioned most happily just out of the spotlight but found themselves on the covers of hundreds, indeed thousands, of magazines. Both remained clotheshorses who set global trends, and yet, notably, it was Jackie who followed Audrey's lead. Said Givenchy of Audrey: "Her style was born as we now know it: the sophisticated sheath, the shoulder grazing decollete, the full skirt, a scarf tied around the head, and the pillbox hat that were immediately adopted by many clients, most notably by Jackie Kennedy." Jacqueline Kennedy Onassis, fashionista, was clandestinely looking to Audrey for fashion tips.

Audrey, it turned out, remained a lifelong subject of fascination for both Jackie and her close friend, singer Carly Simon. Writing about that attraction in her memoir *Touched by the Sun*, Simon relates that the two women actually discussed how each reminded the other of Audrey: "For me Jackie was the Audrey Hepburn of *War and Peace* and *My Fair Lady*. For Jackie, I was the Audrey Hepburn of *Funny Face*. I wore the *Funny Face* black turtleneck and ballet slippers look, while she was the very incarnation of Audrey's final persona in *My Fair Lady*, as perfect as if she were created by Henry Higgins."

Jackie and Audrey met only once, in the late 1980s, by chance at the Carlyle Hotel in New York City. Alas, the subjects discussed remained known only to the two women, but each would have recognized in the other not just a fellow fashion icon but the possessor of a similar bedrock refusal to talk about one's personal life. Jackie chose the gilded life of New York City, where her every move and outfit were dissected at close range, but she would retreat to her compound on Martha's Vineyard to rest and restore, just as Audrey returned to La Paisible at every possible opportunity.

The underlying link between the two women, the fascinating connection, is that for all of their worldwide fame and status as fashion trendsetters, it was their self-perceived flaws that informed their very self-images. Both women proved to be genuinely modest about their looks, plagued by self-doubt about their appearance. Both felt self-conscious about their (supposedly) large hands and feet, each was relatively flat chested, and just as Audrey worried about her nose and irregular teeth, Jackie felt her eyes were set too far apart.

Jackie might confess her self-doubts to intimates, but never to others, while Audrey simply discussed her supposed flaws before anyone else could. This need to list all of her own shortcomings remained with Audrey her entire life, and in the end, only increased her connection to her female fans. She never could understand the praise for her looks but nonetheless remained grateful for all that had come her way. Said Sean: "She felt honored and thankful for the attention, which is why she was always on time, she always knew her lines, and she always treated everyone around her with courtesy and respect."

A down-to-earth movie goddess. *One Touch of Venus* in the flesh.

Beautifully dressed in Givenchy's garnet silk satin and lacquered Coq feathers with a beaded corset-like inset, worn to present a Council of Fashion Designers Award to Richard Avedon. Audrey made quite the entrance in this gown, and even wore it a second time at an awards ceremony in California. Media Punch Inc./Alamy Stock Photo.

Chapter Thirty-Two

FASHIONISTA, 1953–1993

"She created her very own style, in which I am proud to have played a part—a style that remains both modern and yet timeless. Audrey was the epitome of elegance, in both body and soul."

—Hubert de Givenchy

THE APPEAL OF AUDREY'S PERSONA was of course heightened by the fashions she chose, clothes worn with such style and flair that by the mid-1950s, her first name alone served as fashion shorthand: anyone hearing the words "That's so Audrey!" immediately understood the reference.

And what exactly did "That's so Audrey!" mean? In the most basic terms, it served as shorthand for an elegant clean look that would not date. In Sean's words: "Beautiful evening dresses by Givenchy and Valentino. Pea coats in winter with the collars turned up, spread-toe boots in the '70s, cotton pants and Lacoste in the summer, ballet slippers and robe around the house in the morning." Avatar of high fashion she may have been, but Audrey brought the highest of fashion down to earth, and in the words of one commentator, made it "emotionally accessible" to the moviegoing audience.

Even if her emotional accessibility arrived via the world's most expensive clothing, women still felt the look was readily available, a view Audrey endorsed: "My look is attainable. Women can look like Audrey Hepburn by flipping out their hair, buying the large sunglasses, and the little sleeveless dresses."

Her body: a rail-thin model's frame: 32″-20″-35″, 5 feet, 7 inches tall, and 110 pounds—110 pounds, no matter her age and no matter her diet. Likely the most famous waistline since Scarlett O'Hara's; according to playwright Anita Loos, Audrey's hat size of 21 inches was wider than her waist, and to prove just how slim Audrey remained, a friend once used Audrey's belt as a collar for her St. Bernard dog. It fit.

With a waistline that thin, the whispers began—and never really ceased: Was Audrey Hepburn anorexic? Claims to that effect were made by author Diana Maychick in her 1993 biography *Audrey Hepburn*, but Maychick's claims of inside information garnered directly from Audrey were disputed by Audrey's entire family, with Robert Wolders definitively stating: "Never, ever did Audrey speak with her."

The answer to the question of Audrey's anorexia? An emphatic no. Her metabolism never did fully recover from the war years of near starvation, and she suffered lifelong effects from the anemia, edema, and jaundice that had ensued. The war-induced malnutrition meant that her muscular development had not proceeded in normal fashion, and nothing could ever fully repair the damage.

Did she pay attention to what she ate? Yes. There were lots of vegetables, no desserts, and a sparing consumption of alcohol, but then again, that disciplined approach to food is the norm for any dancer. She found pleasure in eating; when visiting great friend Connie Wald in Los Angeles, dinner would consist of "Audrey's favorite: my chicken salad. Before dinner she'd have her Scotch and a cigarette. She usually wanted a green apple for dessert, and she loved chocolates." Careful she was, savoring exactly one square of chocolate as a treat at the end of meals, but such discipline never prevented her from appreciating her food. As summed up by Jeffrey Banks: "She would eat anything and everything, but she wouldn't eat huge quantities of it."

She enjoyed a well-cooked steak because in her own words: "When you have had the strength to survive starvation, you never again send back a steak simply because it's underdone." Speaking of family meals Audrey shared with her two sons, Sean laughed: "She could eat us both under the table!"

The issue of her weight and how much she ate was simply not something she dwelt upon at length. In Sean's view, his mother wasn't even overly skinny; her upper body, "especially her thoracic cage" was thinner than normal, leading to her noticeably slender waist, but ballet had made her arms and legs athletic. It was simply her upper body that was skinny, what Audrey herself took to calling "fake thin."

Added to the years of malnutrition was the matter of genetics, with Audrey claiming that she possessed the same figure as her paternal grandmother. She seemed unable to gain weight even when she drank beer for just that purpose—and her willowy body would have been enough for others to despise her, if only she weren't so consistently, genuinely nice . . .

It was decidedly a model's body, perfectly structured for all of those world-famous designer clothes. Acres of print have been spilled over Audrey's work with Givenchy, but it was their mutual attraction to clean lines that made the partnership work so beautifully. Like the greatest artists—and Audrey undisputedly proved an artist with clothes—she and Givenchy stripped away everything extraneous in a search for the truth: the clothes should not draw attention to themselves but instead flatter the woman wearing them.

To wit: The *Breakfast at Tiffany's* little black dress with a neckline that plunged in the back, not the front. Accessorized with oversized Oliver Goldsmith tortoiseshell sunglasses and streaked highlights. A pearl-and-diamante necklace with matching tiara completed the look, proving that what looked de trop on anyone else looked effortlessly chic on Audrey.

Like Astaire when he danced, she made the clothes and movement appear effortless, a result achieved after endless practice and consideration. The amount of such practice always proved extraordinary; Hubert would visit with highlights from his latest couture collections, Audrey would try on the dresses—and then the real work would commence. This was not a case of Audrey standing in front of the mirror and pronouncing yea or nay. She would instead slip on the dress and then proceed to sit, walk, and turn, fully assessing both the look of the fabric and how the clothes lay on her body as she moved. Said Hubert: "The underthings, the shoes, the hats, the gloves or whatever else she wore with them—once she worked out the mechanics, she was happy. Sometimes this took ten minutes, sometimes ten hours." Her approach filled the designer with admiration: "She was so disciplined, so organized, she never was once late for a fitting."

In the early 1960s, when men and women still made an effort at dressing up, Audrey planned her wardrobe with meticulous care: "I prepare a clothes chart for the coming seasons, just as I do when handed a script of a new movie. I start writing down all the things I have and then eliminating the ones I feel I've worn out or are outdated."

Women gravitated toward the fashions Audrey wore onscreen and off, yet she was the first to in effect state: "Don't compare yourself to me or anyone else. . . . Focus on being yourself." The starting point of that focus was always an acute self-awareness of both assets and flaws: "You have to look at yourself objectively. Analyze yourself like an instrument. You have to be absolutely frank with yourself. Face your handicaps, don't try to hide them. Instead develop something else."

And develop something else she did, exerting an influence upon fashion never equaled by another Hollywood star. Combining a style impervious to trends with an utterly unique point of view, Audrey Hepburn dressed to please herself. Says Sean: "Elegance starts within. If you don't design or cultivate your mind there are no clothes that are going to help that. You're going to make a mistake at some point. My mother knew what worked for her and felt comfortable with her very personal choices. She used to say, 'I dress more like an English gentleman than a woman.' When she found the look that worked for her—for instance hacking jackets—she stuck with it for the rest of her life. If you look at her in any decade it's the same cut and look. It's an extension of who she was."

Which in effect led to How to Dress for Success, Audrey Hepburn style:

Clothes for Comfort:
Men's shirts tied around the waist, usually at the side, not the front
Fitted tops
Chinos
Lacoste shirts
Headscarves tied under the chin
Headscarves worn as bandanas

Shoes:
Ballet flats as everyday footwear

If ballet flats would have looked like an affectation on others, on Audrey they worked precisely because she had studied ballet for years, and people knew it. The first public figure to wear ballet slippers in public, Audrey wore the shoes not only to remember her first dream of dancing but also as a very practical reminder to pay attention to her walk.

Heels—minimum height kitten heels. Audrey did not want to add to her 5-foot, 7-inch frame.

If not small heels, then loafers. The key was comfortable shoes capable of completing a properly stylized look, especially when worn with capri pants. Said Pamela Fiori: "Casually dressed in capri pants and ballet flats, Audrey looked more elegant than anyone else all dressed up."

Accessories:
Baskets serving as a purse

Oversized sunglasses—a must, not just as shield and disguise, but because the frames helped to round out what she considered to be her square face. Confiding in Doris Brynner, Audrey explained that she had "'truly small eyes.' Her legendary wide-eyed look, she told her friend, 'was only a trick of makeup carried out expressly for the camera.'"

The Art of Minimalism:
Jewelry—Very little. Oval drop earrings often sufficed. "I like to wear very little jewelry. . . . It should never look as if the woman is wearing it to show off that she has it. I like jewelry best after 6 p.m."

For serious jewelry, the choice was pearls—either pearl earrings or the pearl necklace that was a gift from then husband Mel. Pearls, unlike the watches she deemed "cold," were "warm."

Makeup:
Just enough to bring attention to her cheekbones and silhouette
A hint of eyeliner on the top of the eye; completing the look: pale-colored lipstick

Fashion Don'ts:
No belts—unless specifically worn to accent dresses.
Wristwatches—never. An avoidance of cold metal or weight against her skin.

Hiding One's Flaws:
Tops with boatnecks. There was no better way, she felt, to divert attention away from her protruding collarbone.
No padded or squared shoulders: "I often cheat on my armholes and collars to give an illusion of narrow rather than wide shoulders."

Safety with Colors:
Black and white, beige, soft pinks, or greens—those were the colors of choice: "My coloring lacks definition. Bright colors overpower me and wash me out . . . beige or black . . . will look right at almost any hour of the day or evening and in almost any weather. . . . I have only black or beige shoes and bags and wear only white three-quarter length gloves."

A Mixture of High Fashion with Practicality:
A 1963 article on her worldwide fashion influence found her in the midst of buying a reversible poplin parka: olive green on one side and white on the other, complete with a hood and drawstring waistline for "walking the mountains." To be sure, not many in her audience spent great swaths of time walking the mountains, but of the reversible coat's appeal there was no doubt.

Stick with What You Know and Like:
When it came time for a new raincoat, Audrey asked Givenchy to make her a new coat, but only if lined with the same mink she had worn for ten years under another raincoat. She liked the

fur out of sight, worn for comfort rather than to impress. Besides, "It sounds terribly snobby, but fur is much warmer when it is against you."

Four Rules for the Hepburn Look:
1. Look for simplicity of line—aim for timeless, rather than the latest trend.
2. Buy quality rather than quantity.
3. Wear sports clothes that look lived-in rather than brand-new. The Fred Astaire approach to clothes.
4. Wear the right outfit at the right time. In other words—plan ahead.

The Art of Aging Gracefully:
As the years passed, her methods and preparation were pared down to the essentials because the prospect of aging held no fear. Growing older was, she felt, the most natural of processes, and a part of life to be enjoyed and treated with respect. To wit:

- Hair Care—Why color her hair? As Audrey aged and some of her chestnut hair turned gray, she let it be, simply pulling it back in a ponytail. The naturally graying hair and minimalist makeup seemed only to add to her beauty, the lack of artifice emphasizing her bone structure and cheekbones.
- Eyebrows—Without resorting to artificial means, she felt one should simply adjust to advancing age through small, meaningful changes. Having started with heavy dark brows, as the decades passed Audrey modified her eyebrows to appear lighter in color and thickness.
- Beauty Regimen—Virtually nonexistent. Shampoo from Philip Kingsley. Makeup courtesy of Dr. Ernő László's skin protective products. End of regimen.
- Cosmetic Surgery. Audrey never did have a facelift, but saw "nothing wrong with that, either for an actress or any woman who feels she needs it." Said Sean in an interview with the *Mail Online* after her death: "My mother thought everybody should be allowed to make their own choices and be allowed to feel more beautiful. I don't know if she would have had surgery herself, but maybe, and in her general style it would have been minor."

For all the acclaim directed her way as a fashion idol par excellence, her self-assessment remained humorously modest: "Put me in furs and jewels and I look like something off a barrel organ. I'm much happier in my favorite costume: tight red slacks and a pink Brooks shirt."

Explained Robert Wolders: "[She was] almost like a child in that she refused to believe how good she looked. She was extraordinarily modest . . . and it wasn't a kind of false modesty."

Ultimately, it never really was about high fashion or makeup, because in the words of Audrey's favorite essay, Sam Levenson's "Time Tested Beauty Tips," which she herself adapted into a poem:

The beauty of a woman is not in the clothes she wears, the figure
that she carries, or the way she combs her hair.
The beauty of a woman must be seen from in her eyes, because that is
the doorway to her heart, the place where love resides.

Wearing the 9/10 Tattersall coat, dress, and matching jaunty fedora in a publicity still for *How to Steal a Million*. In the final film, the fedora was switched to a draped navy pillbox. 20th Century-Fox Film Corporation/Photofest © 20th Century-Fox Film Corporation.

Chapter Thirty-Three

ONCE MORE WITH FEELING, 1966

"As a child I was taught that it was bad manners to bring attention to yourself, and never, ever make a spectacle of yourself. . . . All of which I've earned a living doing."

—Audrey Hepburn

WITH AUDREY'S FASHION INFLUENCE AT an all-time high after the triumphs of *Charade* and *My Fair Lady*, Hollywood now fell back on its default "creative" position: if a film works, repeat the formula with the fewest possible variations. In other words, when in doubt pair Audrey Hepburn with Paris and Hubert de Givenchy. *Sabrina*, *Funny Face*, *Charade*—the Hepburn-Paris combination couldn't be beat. Forget about *Paris When It Sizzles*—that was the exception that proved the rule. Instead, let Audrey reunite not just with Paris but also with Givenchy and director William Wyler. The vehicle? 1966's whimsical *How to Steal a Million* (original title: *Venus Rising*). As it turned out, not much went wrong, but then again, not much went particularly right either.

The "might-as-well-keep-busy-and-have-a-few-laughs" air which pervades the film seemed to have originated with Wyler's own shrugging acceptance of the assignment. In later years Wyler's wife Talli explained: "Willy took that picture at that moment because he didn't have anything better to do. . . . He took it because of his longtime friendship with Zanuck and because he felt he *ought* to do another movie." His shrugging acceptance of the assignment was reflected in the casting of Audrey herself; in conversation with his longtime editor Robert Swink, Wyler allowed that he deliberately asked for Audrey because he was sure Richard Zanuck would be unable to secure her as the film's star.

But secure her he did, and with Audrey on board, everyone proceeded with at least a degree of enthusiasm. On paper, the screenplay by Harry Kurnitz seemed promising, even if reminiscent of snippets of *Charade* and *Sabrina*; this time around, the story line would reverse the *My Fair Lady* transformation, with Audrey ("Nicole Bonnet") starting out wealthy before masquerading as a cleaning lady in order to pull off a successful museum heist. Nicole's partner in crime, handsome, charming "Simon Dermot," would be played by handsome, charming Peter O'Toole. Old friend and esteemed colleague Charles Lang would provide the cinematography, and Givenchy the wardrobe. Wyler, Lang, O'Toole, Paris, Givenchy: the omens for success all seemed to be in place.

In fact, O'Toole and Audrey did thoroughly enjoy each other's company on set, and although O'Toole, who was three years younger than Audrey, felt a bit intimidated by her "stern and formidable" façade, he developed a bit of a crush, even while perceptively noting the underlying layer of disappointment that seemed to cling to his co-star, no matter how strenuous her efforts to banish it through laughter: "There was a modesty and a sadness about her." Doffing his hat to Audrey, O'Toole admiringly stated: "She was the one—and I think only—actor who could soften [Wyler's] resolve."

As it turned out, the film's premise of a daring heist was mirrored in real life, when five robbers tied up the movie studio's concierge on a Saturday morning, cracked the safe, and escaped with the following week's $20,000 payroll. The crime was never solved, and that offscreen problem was soon mirrored on set by difficulties that centered around the role of wealthy American art collector "Davis Leland." Wyler's first choice, Walter Matthau, had priced himself out of the supporting role by demanding $200,000—twice the studio's offer—as well as above-the-title billing. Turning next to George C. Scott, Wyler was pleased to begin filming with the talented if temperamental award winner. Within the first week of filming, however, Scott's drinking caused delays in production, and Wyler fired Scott, replacing him with dependable veteran Eli Wallach. (Like Scott, O'Toole himself was also known to imbibe frequently, but he never caused delays in filming, and Wyler grew fond of the actor. Said Talli Wyler: "He knew his lines and knew what he was doing. Willy was even more impressed by his abilities.")

There were two additional members of the production team who also seemed to function as Audrey's co-stars: Hubert de Givenchy and production designer Alexandre Trauner. With Wyler unable to film in an actual museum for fear the crew would damage priceless paintings, Trauner, who by now had won an Academy Award for Billy Wilder's *The Apartment*, created a stunningly accurate depiction of an art museum and then hired seven painters, at a total cost of $100,000, to forge Monets, Goyas, Van Goghs, and Picassos.

But even more eye-catching than the paintings was Audrey's Givenchy-designed wardrobe. Her look was now changing: patterned tights, shorter skirts, and oversized bubble sunglasses dominated her onscreen appearance, and there was a different hairstyle featured as well, a layered beehive with sideburns, bouffant on top with bangs set to one side. Audrey was sporting a great deal more eyeliner than usual, and while this head-to-toe remake was striking on its own terms, it ultimately seemed like the filmmakers' attempt to keep up with the groovy 1960s.

At times the entire movie feels like one long parade of clothes, beginning with Audrey's first appearance in a "mod" hat and oversized sunglasses. Pastel outfits accessorized with belts, diamond earrings, sequined eyeliner and even a drop-dead black dress accented by a see-through mask all made an appearance. When plot machinations found O'Toole trying to steal art from the apartment Nicole shares with her art forger father Charles (Hugh Griffith), Audrey is seen swanning about in a pink nightgown under a shocking pink, perfectly tailored coat. It's an outfit which encapsulates the inherent imbalance found in the film: the viewer's attention is held far more by the extravagant wardrobe than it is by the silly and sometimes forced shenanigans playing out onscreen. The film was to prove Audrey's last notable onscreen pairing with Givenchy, with the outfits he was to design for *Bloodline* and the television movie *Love Among Thieves* playing out more like "guest appearance by Hubert de Givenchy" than as essential parts of the Hepburn-Givenchy filmography.

The collaboration between star and designer had unquestionably elevated both of their careers and resulted in an achievement that has survived the changing fashions and whims of the past half century. At their most dazzling, in *Sabrina, Funny Face, Breakfast at Tiffany's*, and *Charade*, Givenchy and Audrey inspired each other to extraordinary heights. By the time of *How to Steal a Million* (1966), however, Hollywood was changing. The studio system was crumbling, and expensive, elaborate wardrobes seemed a thing of the past—couture creations in an off-the-rack world.

By now, so well-known had the collaboration between Audrey and Givenchy become that Hubert's name even supplied one of *How to Steal a Million*'s punchlines; hiding in the museum closet, Nicole/Audrey changes into her cleaning lady clothes in order to pull off the heist. Studying Audrey's drab washerwoman garb closely, Peter O'Toole suddenly exclaims: "That does it!"

"What?"

"Well, it gives Givenchy the night off."

It's a mildly amusing line but suffers from being uttered during a wildly overlong sequence which finds Nicole and Simon crammed into a tiny closet. The budding romance between the duo within the confines of the close quarters should have made for a humorous ratcheting up of suspense and sexual tension a la Joel McCrea's and Jean Arthur's sensual bantering on the rooming house steps in 1943's *The More the Merrier*; instead, an inherently humorous situation grows flabby when stretched to twice its proper running time. That overlong running time is even reflected in the rather obtrusive Johnny Williams score, which thunders along during a Keystone Cops–like finale overstuffed with security guards running amok through the museum.

Yes, Audrey's sense of timing remained impeccable, as displayed by her response to the question: "Did this ruffian molest you in any way?" Pondering the question, she answers with a perfectly calibrated "Not much," a two-word line reading which tells you that this woman can take excellent care of herself, thank you very much. Hepburn and O'Toole spar nicely, and they certainly make for a great-looking couple. The film even includes a nicely judged in-joke which shows Audrey/Nicole in bed reading a magazine about Alfred Hitchcock, a knowing reference to the aborted Hitchcock-Hepburn collaboration on *No Time for the Jury*.

But in the end, Wyler seems nothing so much as stymied by the material, and it all lends a feeling of inevitability to the fact that after *How to Steal a Million* he directed only two more films: *Funny Girl* (1968) and *The Liberation of LB Jones* (1970). Reviews were mixed, but even though the *New York Times*'s Bosley Crowther smilingly termed it a "wholly ingratiating film that should leave everyone who sees it feeling kindlier about deceit," the film feels like a ten-years-later version of *Love in the Afternoon*. With its glossy look and reliance upon the charm of two larger-than-life stars, *How to Steal a Million* seems a relic from the late 1950s rather than a release aimed at the increasingly permissive marketplace found at the time of its July 1966 premiere. Still, it scored at the box office, grossing a very solid $10 million and causing producer Fred Kohlmar to smilingly proclaim: "If every picture that Fox made came out like that, there would never be anything to worry about."

It's a frustrating film to watch because it promises so much more than it delivers. But if the end product did nothing to particularly advance Audrey's career, it soon didn't matter, because Audrey Hepburn was about to give what is, along with her portrayal of Sister Luke in *The Nun's Story*, the finest performance of her entire career.

Two for the Road. A movie about a complicated marriage. A movie that, even with her marriage to Mel Ferrer in trouble, she made in part because Mel urged her to do so.

He always did give her valuable career advice.

Director Stanley Donen thought Givenchy would not be appropriate for Audrey's character in *Two for the Road*. Instead, Audrey's wardrobe was supervised by Clare Rendlesham, with specific items designed by Ken Scott, Michele Rosier, Mary Quant, and Foale & Tuffin. Playing the sophisticated and weary Joanna Wallace, Audrey wears Paco Rabanne's metal disc minidress at the end of the film. This was an entirely new, modern-era sexy Audrey, freed from her heretofore elegant lady-like attire. Allstar Picture Library Limited/Alamy Stock Photo

Chapter Thirty-Four

TWO FOR THE ROAD, 1967

"Donen and his associates . . . make 'Two for the Road' two things: a Hollywood-style romance between beautiful people, and an honest story about recognizable human beings. I'd call it 'A Man and a Woman' for grown-ups."

—Roger Ebert

WHEN FREDERIC RAPHAEL, FRESH FROM winning an Academy Award for *Darling* (1965), showed Stanley Donen his new, original screenplay charting the ups and downs of a married couple over the course of twelve years, the director had two immediate reactions: (1) He insisted upon directing the film. (2) He quickly called Audrey, saying "I'm sending you a treatment." Audrey's initial reaction upon reading the treatment: "It's too complicated." Donen, undaunted, simply replied: "You have to make this film."

Off Donen and Raphael flew to Switzerland to plead their case directly. After further consideration, Audrey said: "I'll do it. It's wonderful. I was wrong." Raphael recalled Audrey as "gracious, entirely sweet, and unassuming," but her marriage was encountering difficulties at the time, and he found Mel Ferrer to be a "one-hundred percent pain in the ass, very boring." Unsurprisingly, Mel's account of their meeting reads very differently: "Audrey usually makes up her own mind about what she's going to do, but when I read the script of *Two for the Road*, I told her to make it—right away."

In Raphael's architecturally complex script, every scene of the film finds Mark and Joanna Wallace on holiday, with the cars in which they journey essentially becoming their homes. These multiple holidays unfold over the course of twelve years, and by eschewing chronological storytelling, the screenplay is able to jump back and forth in time to reveal the entire story of a marriage: a scene detailing the unraveling of the Wallaces' partnership is followed by a painful reconciliation, only to then flash back to the beginning of the couple's relationship. The concept, in Raphael's words, sprang from his idea of how strange it would be to drive and "overtake ourselves—pass our old selves on the road and look back and see how the people we were then had become the people we are now."

A tentative deal for production and distribution was set up at Universal, but the studio soon pulled out, their skittishness echoed in the negative reaction from all of the other majors: the storytelling, they all felt, was just too complicated for American audiences. With none of the major Hollywood studios willing to bankroll the film, it remained stalled until the producing team of Richard Zanuck and David Brown expressed interest. Then just starting out on a partnership which would peak with *The Sting* (1973) and *Jaws* (1975), Zanuck and Brown forged a production and distribution deal with 20th Century Fox, and the film was greenlit.

With Audrey having signaled her willingness to star, the biggest casting decision now lay in finding the right actor to play Mark, Joanna's successful architect husband. Who possessed the necessary charisma and masculine appeal that would render Joanna's decision to stay with the oft-times unpleasant Mark understandable? Donen's first choice, Paul Newman, was not interested, and Michael Caine proved to be unavailable (when asked in later years if there were any roles that he wished he had played, Caine instantly replied "Yes, the Albert Finney role with Audrey Hepburn in *Two for the Road*").

With Caine out of the picture, the name of Albert Finney was mentioned—and then mentioned again. Hot off the Academy Award–winning *Tom Jones* (1963), as well as *Night Must Fall* (1964), Finney possessed an earthy sex appeal based upon a rugged masculinity that was laced with humor. A lunch meeting with Audrey was arranged in Paris, where Finney, for reasons best known to himself, decided to impersonate a homosexual interior decorator, complete with highly effeminate mannerisms. Said Donen: "The entire lunch Audrey's jaw kept dropping and she'd be looking at me, her eyes growing larger by the minute and she never saying a word, although obviously thinking: how ever am I going to play a love story with this man?" The ruse was dropped, a relieved Audrey laughed, and an instant friendship was formed.

The old, manicured style of dress favored by golden age Hollywood actresses was giving way to the more natural look of Julie Christie, Jacqueline Bisset, and Jeanne Moreau, and Audrey's role in *Two for the Road* now provided her with a chance to bridge the two worlds. Which meant—no Givenchy. Which also meant that her comfort zone—the clothes that gave her both a sense of protection and "a confidence I don't have on my own"—would be missing. Difficult as it was for Audrey to tell Hubert that she couldn't use him for the film, she knew the script demanded just such a change. (Ever loyal, shortly before the film's premiere, she pointedly noted: "I buy just as many things from Hubert as ever . . . my couture things are his.")

Off-the-rack clothes it would be, a new approach that found Audrey, Mel, and Donen shopping for two hours in Paris boutiques, browsing the racks until an exhausted Audrey told her husband and director: "You two know what's right for me, you do the shopping. I'll try on whatever you bring me. But in a nice, comfortable hotel suite."

Ninety outfits were purchased, with Audrey choosing twenty-nine for the first half of the film. Donen's wife then suggested that Ken Scott, an American who had set up shop in Rome, design clothes for the remaining portion of the film, and Audrey acquiesced to the choice, with the proviso that there be "no bright colors, no prints." Audrey spent two days in Milan trying on dozens of designs, but for Scott the collaboration proved difficult, and he called Audrey "extremely rigid" in her refusal to wear anything red. Exit Ken Scott, enter Lady Clare Rendlesham, who brought in seventy outfits for Donen's and Audrey's joint approval. Together, they selected miniskirts and swimsuits designed by both Mary Quant and Michele Rosier, "the 'vinyl girl,' who designed for the ready to wear French house of V de V." Rounding out the international flavor of the wardrobe were outfits designed by Spanish designer Paco Rabanne, then working out of Paris.

Part and parcel of the contemporary wardrobe were the new hairstyles chosen to help define the more casual look of Audrey's character. London expert Patricia Thomas was flown to Paris, and with strong input from Audrey, a variety of hairstyles were designed to convey the twelve years covered by the script. Less commented upon but just as noticeable was the change in Audrey's eyebrows. Gone were the trademark thick dark brows and in their place a thinner, more subtle look, all designed by her trusted makeup artist Alberto De Rossi: "Audrey's eyebrows are twice as thin now as when she made her first film. Then they were immense—but you never noticed how I brought them down, film by film. I've given her completely new eyes for this film."

Thin eyebrows. No couture glamour. A new Audrey playing a new type of modern, sexual woman.

In working with Albert Finney, Audrey would be playing opposite a much younger (seven years) leading man for the first time. Finney's palpable masculinity relaxed Audrey, and the co-stars enjoyed each other's company so much that Audrey discarded her usual practice of keeping to herself on set. Donen was the first to note the marked difference in her behavior, contrasting the Audrey of *Two for the Road* with the Audrey he had directed in *Funny Face* and *Charade*: "She was so free, so happy. I never saw her like that. So young!" Along with the ease came a contagious laughter, all of it underscoring Audrey's own pronouncement: "I love people who make me laugh. It's probably the most important thing in a person."

So well did Audrey get along with Finney that rumors of an affair quickly began. Seven years old at the time, Sean has memories of the filming: "I was on the set and my father came to visit—we have some lovely pictures from the south of France. But her relationship with my father was ending and she had a fling with 'Fin' as everyone called him. She always said, 'I stayed in my marriage seventeen years but that was maybe too long.' She overstayed because she so wanted it to work."

Robert Wolders expressed the most nuanced perspective on what that new relationship with Finney meant for Audrey: "Audrey cared for Finney a great deal. He represented a whole new freedom and closeness for her. It was the beginning of a new period in her life." Finney's thoughts? "Performing with Audrey was quite disturbing, actually. Playing a love scene with a woman as sexy as Audrey, you sometimes get to the edge where make believe and reality are blurred." Novelist Irwin Shaw, on set for parts of the filming, approvingly noted: "She and Albie had this wonderful thing to see. They were like a couple of kids."

Perhaps that sense of freedom resulted from the fact that with the notable exception of a studio set built for the raucous party scene near the end of the movie, the entire film was shot on locations throughout Europe. The realism of those locations was further matched by the true-to-life no-holds-barred dialogue, and audiences knew they were in for a different sort of ride as soon as they heard the first lines of dialogue:

Joanna: They don't look very happy.
Mark: Why should they? They just got married.

Tough, often bitchy dialogue received as much play as witty repartee, and for the first time in her career, Audrey Hepburn was now playing a woman who desired sex as much as romance.

The movie toggled back and forth in time, with one event nudging the film backward before it quickly flashed forward a full decade. Relationships stumbled along uncertain paths, with the younger versions of Mark and Joanna shadowed by their older selves. Movement proved constant because director Donen wanted "a lot of dialogue and lots of moving at the same time. I wanted it to be different from real life but feel like real life." In the words of *I Do and I Don't*, Jeanine Basinger's definitive history of marriage in the movies, "By removing all transitions and indications of change and by juxtaposing time frames ironically, the movie speaks cinematically about what happens in a marriage: as time passes, it gets edited and loses its original frame of reference."

With its winding back-and-forth temporal framework, *Two for the Road* slowly made it clear that there was never going to be a turning point leading to happily ever after land. Love scenes were juxtaposed against sequences of Audrey and Finney swearing and throwing verbal darts at one another, each set piece exposing raw nerve ends in its examination of how and when a marriage could spin off the tracks. Says Joanna: "You don't give me everything I want . . . you give me everything you want to give me."

Here was a movie not about the problems faced in getting married, but of staying married. Observed Donen: "Most of Audrey's pictures were about the euphoric feeling of falling in love. This was about the difficulties after that euphoria."

The deliberate, occasionally byzantine pacing built inexorably to one of the most powerful and unexpected scenes in the entire Hepburn filmography; when Joanna returns to her husband after having an affair with another man, husband Mark glances at her and very deliberately states: "Are you sure you remember which one I am?" It's not just the unexpected cruelty of the scene that lands, it's the conflicting emotions that play across Hepburn's face. Anger, sadness, rueful self-recognition—they're all silently displayed in a matter of seconds. It is no surprise, then, to learn that filming this adultery-centric sequence proved extremely difficult for Donen, Finney, and Hepburn alike. Commented the director: "All of us had things in our lives that it reminded us of, so we really suffered. When I look at it, I see extreme pain."

But for the most part, so happy did Audrey feel on set that she even faced down two of her lifelong fears: driving and being submerged in water. Eight years earlier in Beverly Hills, Audrey had rented a car, and while trying to swerve around an oncoming vehicle had crashed into a parked car. Audrey was not hurt but Joan Lora, a twenty-two-year-old actress and dancer, was injured. Claiming neck and back injuries because of the accident, she filed suit against Audrey for $45,000 in lost earnings. Audrey eventually paid only ten percent of that total but vowed never to drive again. Now, perhaps encouraged by the controlled conditions of a film set, she undertook sequences which found her behind the wheel of a car, successfully completing all of the driving without a hitch.

Of more import, however, was her willingness to confront her phobia about being pushed underwater. The scene in question called for Joanna to be thrown into a pool, and given Audrey's lifelong fear of the water, Donen reassured her that two assistant directors would be standing just out of camera range, poised to quickly snatch her out of the water. Cameras rolled, the action was captured to Donen's satisfaction, and he happily yelled "Cut!"—at which point he realized that in the rush to protect Audrey, one of the assistant directors had inadvertently stepped into the shot. With the sequence needing to be completely reshot, Audrey's hair had to be dried, her wardrobe repurposed, and the cameras reset, until, with tension growing by the minute, she prepared herself for another dunking. Donen yelled "Action!" Audrey steeled herself and this time the scene was captured perfectly. Said Donen: "It was very courageous of her to do it. Twice."

Finney and Hepburn's mutual regard continued to deepen with the passing weeks, as did their ease in playing off each other. Said Donen: "They worked well as a team. They both loved the parts. They were serious actors who worked hard." Donen's was a point well taken; Audrey's onscreen charm was such that people often failed to realize just how hard she worked at her craft. Said screenwriter Raphael: "I remember hearing her give Stanley eight different readings of the words 'Hello, darling.' Number six, she thought, was the right one. Always needed to be perfect, that was Audrey."

Shooting completed, Donen grew particularly anxious to hear not just the Henry Mancini score but especially the title tune he was writing with longtime collaborator Johnny Mercer. Into his studio Mancini disappeared, eventually emerging with a theme he thought fit the tone of the picture beautifully. Donen's reaction? "I don't think it's right for the movie." A disappointed Mancini returned one week later with a new and haunting theme, the lyrics by Mercer dovetailing perfectly with the pensive melody.

The song's bittersweet mix of melancholy sound and wondering lyric matched the finished film because, as Mancini explained: "If you listen to those songs—('Moon River,' 'Charade,' 'Two for the Road')—you can almost tell who inspired them, because they all have Audrey's quality of wistfulness—a kind of slight sadness." Mancini, an individual of great sensitivity, had caught the subtext of Audrey's persona: underneath the beautiful and gracious exterior lay an understanding of exactly how difficult life could be, with moments of beauty running headlong into acres of hurt. In the words of novelist Pat Conroy (*The Prince of Tides*), who spent a lifetime mining his own often tormented personal life in search of emotional truth: "Love had always issued out of the places that hurt the most."

Entering the editing room with Madeleine Gug and Richard Marden, Donen brought with him more footage than he had on any of his previous nineteen films. It all represented a deliberate choice, one that fit the roller coaster of emotions expressed by both husband and wife in the film: "On earlier pictures I camera cut the film—there was virtually no film left over after editing. Here, I shot so that I had a choice of who to focus in on."

What he now encountered in the editing room was an actress possessed of not just native talent but also extraordinary skill: "The role required a depth of emotion, care, yearning and maturity that Audrey had never played before." This, Donen felt, was the performance of Audrey's career. The naïve young Joanna in a red jersey is a very different woman from the hardened sophisticate in the flashy but cold metal dress found at film's end, and yet the progression makes sense. Audrey's control over her characterization remained total.

Whether imitating a traffic signal by wildly rotating her arms, impersonating the sounds of sheep and chickens, or even grappling with a recalcitrant faucet, there was a freedom about Audrey's performance that signaled a new level of skill in her acting. At age thirty-seven she was digging deeper within, exposing herself emotionally in an unprecedented manner by drawing upon her complicated feelings about the end of her own marriage. Meeting every challenge head-on, she appeared completely at home throughout a comically disturbing film which ends with husband and wife looking at each other and murmuring, "Bitch," "Bastard." Mark and Joanna will be staying together—but for how long is anyone's guess. Audrey, it was clear, had traveled a very great distance from the fairy tale land of *Sabrina* into the real-life landscape of twentieth-century marriage. Says Jeanine Basinger: "It really is one of the greatest, most fully realized, three dimensional portraits of a married woman ever put on film." A rare take on marriage in the Hollywood of 1967, *Two for the Road* would remain anomalous in the same way as does 2019's *Marriage Story*—as an unflinchingly intimate depiction of the realities of marriage.

Perhaps it had been Audrey's charm of manner, or the fact that she was a beautiful clothes-horse with a gift for light comedy, that had led to her having been underrated as an actress, but this time around, even the critics seemed favorably disposed, with Judith Crist describing a "new (mod and non-Givenchy) Audrey Hepburn displaying her too-long-neglected depths and scope as an actress . . ." Raved *Variety*: "Helped partially by variations in her hairdos but mostly by her facial expressions, she's completely believable, lovable and totally delightful."

The film proved a moderate box office success in the United States, but a bigger hit overseas. Part of the limited appeal for American audiences may have resulted from every American in the movie proving obnoxious in the extreme, from an overbearing guest at the final cocktail party to the mother, father, and little girl with whom Joanna and Mark travel for part of the film. The young girl, in fact, is the most unpleasant child glimpsed onscreen since, well, *The Children's Hour*.

Yes, the film is a little too self-consciously hip, and the mod late '60s clothes insist on drawing attention to themselves, but even when wearing the eye-catching metal dress near film's end, Audrey dominates it, wearing it in service to Joanna and the brittle, wounded survivor she has become. In Audrey's hands, Joanna remains a recognizably complicated woman of charm and battered strength, but the reaction to Finney's occasionally grating character proves a bit more complicated. Do all architects yell so incessantly? Whether that character trait is present in Raphael's screenplay or is simply how Finney approached the character is hard to discern, but even director Donen subsequently admitted: "It came out a little one-sided, like he's a shit, and he wasn't supposed to be."

Screenwriter Raphael termed the experience of making the film "sublime," and although he lost the Best Screenplay Oscar to William Rose's top-heavy script for *Guess Who's Coming to Dinner*, audiences ultimately accepted the finished film precisely because of the story's very complexity. Here was a married couple who laughed and then cried over their relationship, only to ultimately embrace it even while sometimes hating it. In other words, this was marriage in all its recognizable and universal contradictions.

Donen himself summed up the film's multilayered approach in accurate, rather gimlet-eyed terms: "This isn't happily ever after. The movie says this is how they loved ever after. Neither one is completely happy or sad. It's the closest we could get to the way marriages survive. They have grown together." It is more than likely that *Two for the Road*'s moderate returns at the box office resulted precisely because of this realistic view; die-hard Audrey fans preferred their heroine as the perennially beautiful princess moving gracefully through life toward a happily-ever-after ending. But in breaking that template, in digging deep to limn the essence of a woman not so very different from herself and millions of others, Audrey had provided audiences with a welcome look at her own artistic maturity.

Two for the Road proved to be the last hit of Donen's feature film career, the next four decades filled mostly with television work and feature-length misfires like *Lucky Lady* (1975). Audrey herself, by now the veteran of a three-film, ten-year collaboration with Donen, provided an interesting, thoughtful analysis of his filmography: "Stanley had his career when he was a young man. Perhaps careers really can only last a certain amount of time . . ."

With this statement, was Audrey also ruminating about her own career? As it developed, in the twenty-six years between *Two for the Road* and her own untimely death, she was to appear in only seven more films, including one cameo (*Always*), one talking head appearance (*Directed by William Wyler*), and one television movie (*Love Among Thieves*). The best of those additional seven films, *Wait Until Dark*, was released a mere six months after *Two for the Road*.

Audrey Hepburn had, with *Two for the Road*, banished all talk of the perennial ingénue, her remarkable talent and long-lasting appeal nowhere better summed up than by the words spoken early in the film, after Joanna and Mark make love for the first time:

Mark: Who are you?
Joanna: Some girl.

That she was.

A Givenchy-less Audrey wearing an off -the-rack jacquard safari style jacket for *Wait Until Dark*. Novelist Stephen King called the film "the scariest movie of all time." Pictorial Press Ltd./Alamy Stock Photo.

Chapter Thirty-Five

ALONE IN THE DARK, 1967–1968

"When the lights go out at the end of the film, so did the lights in the movie theaters. Terence Young's tense cinematic adaptation so ruthlessly tightens the screws of tension that one could be forgiven for not noticing an earthquake, much less dimmed house lights."

—*Slant Magazine*

IN THEIR BY NOW ALMOST desperate determination to stay together, Audrey and Mel decided upon one final joint venture, a film version of the Broadway thriller *Wait Until Dark*, to be produced by Mel and star Audrey. The story of a blind woman terrorized by murderous thugs who are after a drug-filled doll she doesn't even know she possesses was a far cry from the world of *Funny Face*, and that was, in fact, part of the allure. Disappointed she may have been by the unraveling of her marriage, but Audrey still recognized the possibilities inherent in *Wait Until Dark*, and at Mel's urging she said yes. Together again on a film set for one last time.

A hit play on Broadway written by Frederick Knott and starring Lee Remick, *Wait Until Dark* (1966) had been bought by Warner Bros. as a vehicle for Audrey for the princely sum of $1 million. Although the film was not to be released until 1967, negotiations for the rights had actually begun in 1965, before the play had even officially opened. In Mel's recall, Audrey knew as soon as she read the script that she wanted to play the role of Susy Hendrix: blind and vulnerable yet strong and determined, Susy outwits a psychopathic murderer through guts and brains. Here was material that represented a chance for Audrey to expand her range.

After Warner Bros. finalized the deal for the rights, agent Kurt Frings was able to land Audrey a top-of-the-line deal: in addition to veto power over her director, Audrey would receive a salary of $900,000, a percentage of the gross, and per diem of $1,000 per week throughout shooting.

Mel's salary as producer was fixed at $50,000, and it was at Mel's recommendation that Audrey's old friend Terence Young was tapped to direct. An extremely hot property after directing the James Bond hits *Dr. No* (1962) and *From Russia with Love* (1963), Young knew Audrey not only from the world of movies but also because twenty-three years earlier, as a young British soldier, he had been wounded at the Battle of Arnhem and Audrey and Ella had helped take care of him. Audrey's delight at working with Young was heightened by the knowledge that Charles Lang, the cinematographer on *Sabrina*, had signed on as the director of photography.

With Mel, Terence, and Charles, she would be surrounded by a team with whom she felt comfortable and protected.

During preproduction, Young asked that Audrey wear contact lenses to suggest the character's blindness, but Audrey thought they would make her face appear too rigid, and instead decided that she would study at the New York City Lighthouse for the Blind. By immersing herself in the environment of the Lighthouse, she learned the elemental lessons acquired by blind people living in a sighted world: How to navigate by sense of touch. The best means by which to differentiate sounds and textures. The way in which to use a special telephone. She soon met a young sightless woman at the Lighthouse whom she called "a blessing. . . . I said, 'Do something for me, find your way around this room.' And I sat on my chair and just watched her. She had beautiful eyes, dark shiny eyes. There was no way of knowing that she couldn't see."

To Audrey, the use of contacts or dark glasses would "draw attention to the fact that I am not blind. My hope was to do it from the inside out. To somehow convince the audience—for a fleeting moment—that I could create an illusion of blindness . . ." It was to Sean a prime example of his mother's acting ability: "She stayed very instinctive in terms of accessing her emotions for the role, and yet she would also fully prepare."

Like the play, the film would take place almost entirely in Susy Hendrix's apartment, and given the stripped-down nature of the production, there would be no Givenchy-designed wardrobe. Throughout the film's nearly two-hour running time, Audrey would be seen in only two outfits, both of them consisting of slacks and turtleneck, and the final cut of the film would contain no credit for costume design.

Alan Arkin, cast as the psychopathic "Roat" who terrorizes Susy, had made an initial splash in the previous year's *The Russians Are Coming, The Russians Are Coming*, but playing a killer was a new step for the then thirty-three-year-old actor: "I was coming out of a rough period in Chicago—I had met low lifes and I had seen drug addicts. It all influenced me in my approach to the role and I don't think either the director, Terence Young, or the producer 'got' what I was doing—until the moment I pulled out the knife. I was like a snake in hiding and all of a sudden it all clicked into place—people saw what I was after."

Arkin may have been playing a psychopath, but his memory of the film centers around Audrey's genteel insistence that the crew break for tea every afternoon: "An umbrella would be placed outside the set with nice chairs and a table, and five or six of us would sit around and talk. I was almost embarrassed because I hated being cruel to Audrey, hated playing such an awful character. It caused me to keep to myself a bit on set, but I would always sit for tea!"

Reflecting decades later about his time with Audrey, Arkin explained: "She had a regality about her but was utterly unaffected. Terrific to work with. Nothing about her demanded that anyone treat her in a special way, and she was never aloof. She was right in there, every day, making this scary film. In an odd way I think a problem throughout her career was that it was difficult to lower herself to play the characters she was assigned because her own character was so impeccable. Some think of this as a flaw, but I thought it was an asset. It was like working with royalty."

When Young and editor Gene Milford previewed a rough cut for the Warner Bros. brass, all assembled felt they had the makings of a major box office hit, and an extremely effective two-pronged marketing ploy was hatched: All print ads would carry the creepily effective taglines

"The blinds moving up and down . . . the squeaking shoes . . . and then the knife whistling past her ear." In addition, advertisements would also carry the warning that all lights in the theatre would be shut off during the climactic fifteen minutes, the better to heighten the sense of audience dread while Roat stalks Susy. This lights-out approach did in fact work brilliantly; in the climactic moments of the film, after Susy smashes all of the lights in her apartment so that her battle with Roat can be joined on equal ground, the injured Roat leaps out of the dark to kill her. Sitting in pitch-black theatres, audiences around the world never failed to scream.

Said Arkin fifty years after the film's premiere: "At the time I certainly had no idea we were making such a good film. You don't think that way during the process of making the movie, you don't think of being great. I just wanted to complete the work. But it's a film that really is first rate. It was basically one set, with the addition of the airport scene and one in the parking lot, but even with ninety percent of the film taking place in the apartment, it never feels like a stage play or like the camera is plopped in the fifth-row center.

"The funny thing is that Terence Young, the director, always seemed to be on the phone more than he was on the set! I felt he was not particularly paying attention, that he just wanted to get on with it. He always seemed to be talking with his agent or with his wife, so I'm kind of astonished at how well it turned out. I've seen it a couple of times in the years since we made it and I'm actually enormously impressed by how well made it is."

So effective was Arkin's malevolence that it allowed audiences to overlook gaps in the film's logic; since Susy is blind, why does Roat bother to change clothes and disguises each time he comes back to the apartment in search of the drug-filled doll? In the end, however, the audience's involvement in Susy's survival proved so intense that it didn't matter in the slightest, and in his book *Danse Macabre*, horror king novelist Stephen King called *Wait Until Dark* the scariest movie of all time.

The film proved an enormous box office hit and scored Audrey her fifth and final Academy Award nomination as Best Actress (she lost to Katharine Hepburn for *Guess Who's Coming to Dinner*). With her slight physique and understated technique, Audrey made audiences forget that the terrorized woman onscreen was Hollywood superstar Audrey Hepburn. Through a combination of meticulous preparation and skillfully displayed vulnerability, she had succeeded in delivering what is, along with *The Nun's Story*, the most unexpected characterization of her career. Thrilled she was by her Academy Award nomination, but ever the perfectionist, she later stated with a smile: "I was nominated for *Wait Until Dark* when I liked myself better in *Two for the Road* that year." She's right; effective as she was in *Wait Until Dark*, in that film she was portraying a woman who, while navigating an admittedly overwhelming situation, was doing so over the course of a single afternoon. In *Two for the Road*, she was portraying one woman in her various incarnations as newlywed, young wife, and jaded sophisticate, and managed to make each stage of her character's life separate and distinct.

After the worldwide success of *Wait Until Dark*, there was talk that Mel and Audrey would join forces once again for a feature-film remake of *Mayerling*. Terence Young was paged to direct, and Mel spent large chunks of time organizing the production, but it soon foundered. MGM had always wanted Omar Sharif to play the male lead, and Audrey decided against the film, in large part because she felt it was too soon after *Wait Until Dark* to work again with Mel. In the end, Catherine Deneuve was cast in the lead role opposite Sharif, and by then, the Ferrers had moved on—separately.

After thirteen years of marriage, four depressing and debilitating miscarriages, and one much-loved son, in September 1967 it was publicly announced by Audrey's mother Ella that "Audrey Hepburn, thirty-eight, and Mel Ferrer, fifty, have separated after thirteen years of marriage. Ferrer is in Paris and Miss Hepburn is at their home in Switzerland with their son, Sean, seven."

Sean heard the news directly from his mother: "She sat me down in the bedroom and gave me the news. Then she took me to see *The Jungle Book*, so as far as I was concerned, it was a good conclusion." Adding an interesting perspective in later years, Sean explained: "My parents never argued in front of me, but I was aware from quite a young age that something just wasn't right. . . . When she told me, I was very upset, naturally because I loved them both, but I was also relieved in a way, because it explained why things didn't feel quite right at home."

Said Audrey in later years: "I hung on in there as long as I could. For the child's sake is why we hang on. Also, out of respect for the marriage and for love of the person that you once loved. You always hope that if you love somebody enough that everything will be ok and things will come together again, but it isn't always true. . . . When a marriage doesn't work anymore then everything becomes destructive."

Remembering all too well the upset of never seeing her own father, Audrey made certain that Sean maintained consistent contact with Mel: "The feeling of family is terribly important. I think it's essential. I learned as a child that it's terribly important for a child to have a father. . . ." Sean would continue to see his father, but Audrey cut off her own direct contact with Mel; in 1984, sixteen years after the divorce, Mel simply stated: "I don't hear from Audrey, and I respect that. Audrey asked for the divorce." In later years, he amplified that statement, albeit adding somewhat disingenuously: "I still don't know what the difficulties were. Audrey's the one who asked for the divorce and started the affair with Andrea Dotti."

Mel's casual utterance constituted a rare overt public comment on a very private matter, but Audrey never did comment publicly, content in the ensuing years to simply state that she had tried to hold her marriage together for as long as possible. Said Sean: "My father spent the rest of his life regretting that he had let that relationship go. That was the relationship of his life. The woman of his life—no doubt about it."

As it was, during the next twenty-five years, the only times Audrey spoke directly with Mel were at Sean's school graduation and at his 1985 wedding to fashion designer Marina Spada-fora. By that time, Mel had remarried, Audrey was living happily with Robert Wolders, and at the reception, Audrey and Mel did dance together as parents of the groom.

They did not, however, share the first dance with each other, and Peter Bogdanovich relates the odd but strangely moving anecdote that after Sean and Marina danced together, Audrey walked onto the dance floor with her movie star friend James Stewart: "For obvious dramatic and strangely romantic reasons—it being Hollywood, after all—the star team that night was Stewart and Hepburn. And it certainly was a memorably electric, mythic moment: two of the last classic movie stars, who never did a picture together—but should have, you're thinking as you watch them—both tall, trim, and graceful, dancing cheek to check to a slow tune in the misty light."

As it turned out, even after the divorce, Audrey kept in close contact with her in-laws, as well as with Mel's sister Mary and Mary's son Joe. Said Joe of Audrey: "She was an exceptional person, kind, caring, involved and strong. She was someone you wished you could be like—a person who, so far as I could see, was even better than she appeared to be."

Used to sharing his parents with the world, it is Sean, accurately describing himself as his mother's "spiritual biographer," who offers a remarkably clear-eyed view as to how both of his parents shared blame for the difficulties: "They were both responsible for the failed marriage, she for projecting onto it something that wasn't, and he for not being able to get over himself at some level. . . . He wasn't an easy man, by any stretch of the imagination, even though he was extremely talented, well read, and educated." Loving but unblinking in his assessment, he added: "He was a perfectionist and although graced with a great mind and heart, he had a difficult and temperamental personality."

Explaining further, he reached for vivid metaphorical terms: "She was hoping that real love would come in the form of flowers that are sent, not requested. And when that proved to be a disappointment, things started to come apart. . . . There was a lot of love and a lot of difficulty."

Yes, the widely accepted view is that Mel stifled Audrey, turning his Svengali tendencies into suffocating control, but Audrey maintained a will of her own, and Sean seems to fully understand his mother's role in the breakup as well: "Mostly—it's on both sides. If you don't work through the baggage you're carrying around you go round and round and can't get to the next level." Reflecting on the break up in later years he analyzed: "What she didn't do was to speak up and be heard when she needed to, and she didn't put up healthy boundaries. Exhausted by an authoritarian mother, she wished for a world where caring and love came freely."

His final analysis? "She stayed too long in the marriage, and it had a toxic effect on her—she kept reacting over and over to the failure of the marriage."

When the divorce became final in November of 1968, a new life began for Audrey as a single mother. And with that new life came a different look, a new hairstyle. This did not, however, mean a casual trip to the neighborhood salon in her Swiss village. No, Audrey's hair would be cut by none other than the world's most famous stylist—Alexandre de Paris, and her process provides insight into her status as a painstaking fashionista who nonetheless strove to make it all look effortless. Ever the perfectionist, she first tried on wigs to decide on the style she liked best. Alexandre then cut and set her hair four times until it was very short, with "each strand . . . blunt cut, then thinned diagonally with a razor from root to tip . . . polished with a scissors cut on the bias." Then and only then was Audrey comfortable enough to debut her new look.

In that cataclysmic year of 1968, one suffused with assassinations, ferment, and loud cries demanding social change, Audrey Hepburn would keep step with the times. A single woman raising her son. Working rarely and enjoying life far from the Hollywood spotlight. Keeping tabs on her mother. Hiking in the Swiss countryside and puttering in her beloved garden.

Because, after losing her father and surviving miscarriages, divorce, and a world war, Audrey Hepburn knew with absolute certainty that tomorrow was not promised to anyone.

Seize the day.

Marriage to Andrea Dotti on January 18, 1969. Audrey is wearing the pale pink wool jersey cowlneck minidress and matching kerchief that Hubert de Givenchy designed for her. Quite the departure from her earlier Givenchy dresses, the simple youthful style, along with her newly cropped Alexandre coiffed hair, signaled a freer Audrey embarking on a brand new life. Photofest.

Chapter Thirty-Six

A DIFFERENT ROMAN HOLIDAY, 1969–1979

"She took her dogs for walks, navigated the city's grocery stores, and cooked her favorite dish: spaghetti al pomodoro. Her life in Rome was, by all means, normal. The city and its people were fond of her, and let her be . . ."

—Asia London Palomba

CERTAINLY THE MID-1960S HAD CEMENTED Audrey's place at the top of the Hollywood A list, with *Charade*, *My Fair Lady*, *Two for the Road*, and *Wait Until Dark* all garnering critical acclaim and audience approval. And yet, nice as the approbation was, exactly how much did the acclaim of total strangers actually mean? In Audrey's case, the answer was "not much"—and certainly not enough to offset the hurt resulting from the breakup of her marriage to Mel.

A failed marriage, not a box office bomb like *Paris When It Sizzles*, was what upset Audrey, and to escape her deepening sense of failure, she decided upon a change of scenery. The solution? A two-week Mediterranean cruise in June of 1968 with her friends Princess Olimpia Torlonia and her husband, Paul-Annik Weiller. A cruise upon which she met a close friend of her hosts, the dashing, worldly Italian psychiatrist, Andrea Dotti.

Audrey and Andrea had crossed paths without actually meeting some seven years earlier, at the Italian premiere of *Breakfast at Tiffany's*. This time, however, introductions were made, and an immediate spark struck; Audrey was attracted by the nine-years-younger Dotti's intelligence and stylish manner, Dotti by Audrey's glamour and unaffected air. The duo quickly made plans to spend time together in Turkey later that summer, with that trip proving so successful that two months after Audrey's divorce from Mel became final (on November 21, 1968) and seven months to the day they first met, Audrey and Andrea were married at the town hall in Morges, Switzerland, on January 18, 1969.

A Swiss wedding was not just a case of making it easy for eight-year-old Sean to attend the ceremony, but also a practical solution to the problem of the Catholic Dotti marrying the divorced and Protestant Audrey; a civil ceremony in a predominantly Protestant country sidestepped the religious issues which would have arisen in Roman Catholic Italy. Wearing an original Givenchy pink minidress accented by a matching headscarf, Audrey, attended by Doris Brynner and Capucine, was now, for the first time in years, smiling broadly out of sheer personal happiness.

Audrey would keep her house in Switzerland, but with Andrea's family living in Rome, she would divide her time between the two countries. Andrea's successful and high-profile practice was based in Rome, which meant that he would spend the majority of his time in Italy, a state of affairs which suited his formidable mother Paola's expectations nicely. Highly educated and interested in the arts and culture much more than in homemaking, Paola had divorced Andrea's father when her son was still young and then married Vero Roberti, the London-based correspondent for a Milan newspaper. Audrey and Paola developed a deep mutual affection, with Paola recognizing in Audrey a will as formidable as her own. Audrey, it was clear, would live her own life and raise her children exactly as she saw fit.

Said Robbie Wolders of Audrey's embrace of Dotti's large extended family: "To become part of a family was extremely important to her. Her own family had lacked that kind of closeness." She grew particularly close to her father-in-law Vero Roberti, who had fought the Nazis during the war and proved a decidedly more low-key presence than Paola. When he suffered a severe stroke and Paola, in Luca's term, "lost her mind" and relegated him to a third-rate hospital, Luca and Audrey went to visit him, only to find themselves horrified by the conditions. Trying to place him in a better location, Audrey called another facility and was turned down for lack of space. An upset Luca exclaimed to his mother: "For once in your life, Mummy use your name." Such was her affection for Roberto that Audrey acted against her own self-imposed code of conduct and called the facility once again, this time not as Signora Dotti, but as Audrey Hepburn of Hollywood fame. In Luca's nicely understated summary: "Suddenly there was room."

In Wolders's view, Audrey liked spending time with Dotti because "he made her laugh, he made her feel good about herself." Said her close friend Anna Cataldi: "At the beginning of the marriage she was so happy to be the wife of a doctor. They were so different but the bond was so strong." The sights, sounds, and smells of Rome, as well as the Italian propensity for an open emotional response to life's events so unlike the reserved Dutch approach, all appealed. Away from the confines of film sets, Audrey had the time to appreciate the small details of everyday life, and in a charming reminiscence, Luca recalled: "Every spring, especially here in Rome, you have this smell of orange blossom in the air. Spring is coming and it was her favorite season. It makes me think of her."

Although the Milan-based Cataldi stated, "People in Rome, they were not nice to Audrey. . . . She needed desperately to have friends and warmth. People were absolutely awful," others have spoken of a love affair between Audrey and the Eternal City. In the words of Andrew Wald, the son of Audrey's great friend Connie Wald: "She loved Rome and Rome loved her."

Having already spent weeks and even months in Rome while making *Roman Holiday, War and Peace*, and *The Nun's Story*, Audrey felt at home, responding to the culture and glorious history with an enthusiasm she had never felt for Hollywood. In fact, the idea of living in Hollywood had never even been seriously considered. Yes, Audrey liked the film crews and enjoyed seeing her friends, but the glitzy trappings held little allure. On nights of gala events she would often plaintively tell her sons: "I'd give anything to eat in the kitchen with you boys and go to bed early." It all fed a determination that her children not grow up in Hollywood's overly privileged atmosphere. Said Sean: "We didn't grow up in 'Hollywood,' not the place, not the state of mind. Our mother never watched her own films. Once they were done, that was it."

(Sean, in fact, discovered his mother's films on his own, projecting 16-millimeter copies of the films on a sheet in the attic of the house in Tolochenaz: "Remember, there was no VHS, no

DVDs, no YouTube. I put up a sheet and had a Bell & Howell projector. There was that tick-tick-tick sound of the film which somehow added to it—it all added up to a kind of magical experience because it was watching real film.")

Living the life of a "civilian" in Rome proved remarkably easy for Audrey. She had felt at sea in the fast-changing Hollywood of the late 1960s and early 1970s, where she was surrounded by films awash with violence and a new sexual permissiveness. Aware that her trademark Cinderella-style roles were not only inappropriate for a woman well into her forties but also falling out of favor at the box office, Audrey had surprisingly little difficulty walking away. A life out of the spotlight, and especially one in Rome with her husband and his family, began to suit her remarkably well.

Certainly, it was not difficult to stay at home in the palatial penthouse apartment she and Andrea had found by Ponte Vittorio, some five hundred meters away from Paola's three-story villa. In Sean's recall: "[It] had high ceilings and frescoes. It must have been 12,000 to 15,000 square feet." The Dottis eventually moved to another apartment, this one located in Rome's Parioli district, and they actually included their telephone number in the phone book, a state of affairs matched among show business luminaries only by Bob Fosse's willingness to list his number and address in the New York City phone book.

Audrey now felt free enough to embrace Roman fashion, specifically that of Valentino, and she formed a fast friendship with the designer. She still wore Givenchy—now and forever—but she embraced the Roman fashions of the times: maxi coats, capes, bell-bottom trousers, silk blouses, and oversized cardigan sweaters. Shopping for food or strolling through her neighborhood, she sported driving loafers from Gucci and flats from Ferragamo, with traces of the hippie era showing up in her clothes—it was just hippiedom as filtered through Gucci and Valentino. Related Givenchy: "When she needed things that I did not make—a sweater or maybe a trench coat—she'd take me shopping with her . . . when she was married to Dr. Dotti and living in Rome, sometimes she needed something immediately and would go to Valentino. But she'd call me up first and say, 'Hubert, please don't be furious with me!'" Added Givenchy, unsurprisingly, "We never together had an argument."

Audrey Hepburn, internationally famous movie star, did not employ a secretary and answered her own phone. She was now known in the neighborhood as Signora Dotti. In reality, she could have been addressed as Countess Dotti because of the title held by Andrea's father, but neither Audrey nor Dotti were interested in titles or honorariums. Ella may have liked being known as Baroness van Heemstra, but for Audrey, titles were out of the question. Years after his mother's death, Sean noted Audrey's resentment toward both her parents "for their political and social views, which is also why she let all of the family's title of nobility die and be buried with my grandmother."

Happy as Audrey and Andrea appeared to be, there were differences to be accommodated, and not just because Audrey was nine years older than her husband. A country girl at heart, Audrey now found herself living in the middle of one of the world's busiest cities, and her husband was often not at home, busy with both his private practice and as a professor of psychopharmacology at the University of Rome. Of more note, however, it quickly became clear that while Audrey may have preferred to cook dinner and watch television at home, Andrea was always happiest when out at the restaurants and clubs favored by Rome's smart set.

The noise, heat, chic, and passion of the Eternal City stimulated a constant excitement in Andrea, and he grew to like the press attention Audrey's stardom brought him. As a Roman psychiatrist, Dotti would not have been deemed especially newsworthy by himself, but as the husband of Audrey Hepburn he most definitely was, and when Audrey was in Switzerland, and Dotti was photographed out and about in Rome with beautiful women on his arm, well, that too was news.

When Audrey soon became pregnant, it seemed as if her most fervent wish had been answered. Forty years old, and with a history of miscarriages behind her, Audrey took great care in her preparations; aside from time spent pursuing her lifelong love of painting, she was confined to bed rest even as the whispers about Andrea's behavior grew louder. When Andrew Wald visited in Rome, Andrea's idea of hospitality was to take the young man clubbing in Rome, which, allowed Wald, "I didn't think was the best idea."

But genuine happiness abounded when son Luca (named after Andrea's brother) was born via C-section on February 8, 1970, at Cantonal Hospital in Lausanne, Switzerland. Luca may have been born in Switzerland, but he would grow up in Italy, surrounded by the extended Dotti clan. Italian became his first language, and as a youngster, he did not speak English; conversations at home were conducted in a mix of French and Italian. As Luca progressed from infant to youngster to schoolboy, and with Audrey hoping for more children (she suffered another miscarriage in 1974), there was still no sign of her returning to the world of movies. Sean was now a full-time student, and without planning it out in advance, Audrey rather easily made a life-altering decision: "I began to resent the time I spent away from him on location. That was always the real me. The movies were fairy tales. I withdrew to stay home with my children. I was very happy. It is not as if I was sitting at home, frustrated, biting my nails. Like all mothers, I am crazy about my two boys."

Home remained the anchor, not movies. Wrote Cecil Beaton as far back as a 1964 visit to Mel and Audrey in Bürgenstock: "Her success is astonishing and not only financially. Yet she never allows herself to regard it except as her professional career; it comes second to her private life." Twenty plus years later, when promoting *Love Among Thieves*, her 1987 television movie co-starring Robert Wagner, she sounded the same note when asked how much she had wanted to work during the 1970s and 1980s: "Not at all. Not at all. As I think everyone knows, I wanted to be with my sons."

Unlike Ella, who was so sparing with her praise, Audrey spoke with great love about her sons, and right on television; asked by a Dutch television interviewer what sprang to mind when she heard the name "Sean," she smilingly answered: "He is my best friend—he has been a rock in my life. Enormous support. Marvelous nature. I think he's one of the nicest human beings I've ever met." The feeling of course proved mutual, and when shown the video of that interview after his mother had passed away, Sean commented: "We had a tremendous relationship. We were really connected—sort of like soul mates. We understood each other and had a similar sensibility yet respected each other's boundaries. We were two sensitive people who had the same language. We were from the same tribe. She lacked the moral support, the love of one parent in her own life—her mother was pretty tough. Yet she was able to take all that and transform it into the ability to say something so lovely about us."

Audrey certainly proved to be a hands-on mother, one who limited her young children to one half hour of television at night, and one soda per week. She enforced the usual parental discipline, but with memories of her parents' own loud arguments still fresh in her mind, when she became upset, she would not yell or even raise her voice. Instead, says Luca, she "showed her displeasure. And she knew how to make you feel really bad. . . . I became tired of feeling guilt and let it all out by raising my voice; 'Enough! I'm fed up with your always being unhappy with me! It would be better if you smacked me!'" Said Sean: "She was, as some like to call her, 'a steel hand in a velvet glove.'"

That phrase, in effect another iteration of the phrase "steel magnolia" that has been particularly applied to southern women ranging from Dolly Parton to Rosalynn Carter, was, as Sean points out, a necessity, particularly for women fending for themselves in the tough patriarchal show business world of the 1950s and 60s: "Behind the spritely persona there was an iron fist—there were rules. You don't get to where she was without some steel. You have to have a core of iron if you maintain that stardom for decades, and she did—but she still was always thoughtful and gracious to people." Mulling over the phrase further, he adds: "It applied to her both professionally and personally. She was herself all the time and was very clear in what was right and wrong. She was not going to waver about it but felt how you say things, your tone and manner, mattered greatly."

As the boys grew older, life between mother and sons expanded, often around the kitchen table. Rising early, Audrey would walk downstairs in her bathrobe, alternating her lifelong breakfast of coffee, two boiled eggs, and whole wheat toast with a caffe latte and madeleine, sit at the table and talk with her sons.

Luca's reminiscences, a self-described "kitchen table biography" entitled *Audrey at Home: Memories of My Mother's Kitchen,* mixes recipes and personal stories, revealing that Audrey could and would now speak more openly about her experiences in the war. The trigger for that openness had actually occurred when the eleven-year-old Luca had bought an alarm clock manufactured by Krups, and when Audrey saw the name on the clock, so reminiscent of the word "Krupp" painted on the side of German tanks during the war, she exploded. In Luca's own words: "She completely flipped out. I couldn't understand—it was like she found a loaded gun under my pillow." When Luca explained he had no idea whatsoever about the name similarity, Audrey thawed, "and from that day she started talking more about the war."

There were philosophical discussions that touched on surprising topics. Recalled Luca: "We talked about so many things, even politics or euthanasia or prostitution. Whatever was in the news. And she had a way of making you see things from a different perspective. She said about prostitution: 'OK, but let's imagine it didn't exist. This way there would be so many ugly men who would never meet a nice lady, and this would only make them more frustrated and even aggressive. That wouldn't be good either.'"

And, recalled Luca, as the talks flitted from topic to topic, "almost unconsciously, small talk would turn into a confession." Letting down her guard, Audrey would discuss her childhood, speaking in depth about the loss of her father and the devastation his abrupt disappearance had wreaked upon her own self-image. Said Luca: "I learned to know her better at the breakfast table."

Over those early breakfasts, she talked about food, specifically her lifelong love of chocolate, explaining that she found it helped "banish sadness" and had done so since childhood. When her parents argued, she explained, she would eat—her own fingernails, bread, or best of all, chocolate. "Chocolate was my one true love as a child. It wouldn't betray me. I've always said it was either chocolate or my nails in those years. There was a lot of anxiety." The love of chocolate never did abate, and, explained Edith Head, after one of their intensive shopping expeditions, Audrey would set her eye on a chocolate reward: "'And now let's celebrate,' she'd say when we were exhausted, and that meant heading for the nearest confectionery to devour two of the biggest, fattest, most chocolatey French pastries."

Audrey often told the story of receiving seven chocolate bars from a British soldier at the end of the war, and how, after having nearly starved to death, she gorged on the chocolate until she became sick. Starvation, food, and self-image were all inextricably bound, and yet characteristically, she even found positives in the discipline resulting from the horrors of the war: "Being in Holland during the war—it was a terrible experience but it was finally enriching in ways. . . . Whatever I suffered has helped me later on." She refused to drown in bleakness, instead constantly moving forward and mending herself in a determination to accept all she had been given: "I'm a long way from the human being I'd like to be. But I've decided I'm not so bad after all."

Having turned sixty in 1989, she mused about the perpetual self-doubt with which she had finally made peace, in her own way seeming to accept the philosophy of Bruce Springsteen that "everybody's broken in some way." In her acute self-analysis: "I still feel I could lose everything at any moment. But the greatest victory has been to be able to live with myself, to accept my shortcomings and those of others."

She may have confided in Luca over those early morning breakfasts, but to the public in an autobiography? Never. In a 1990 television interview with Phil Donahue, she allowed as how "I might one day if I have time, have the urge write a book, about experiences, feelings, something I want to express, but it would never be a biography . . ." She had lived long enough to see several biographies of her life appear, and magazine articles purporting to tell the world about the "real" Audrey Hepburn continued unabated for decades, but there would be no reliving the war years or sharing of private pain. In short, as she explained to Luca, there would never be a summing up of her life written from her own perspective: "I would have to tell the whole truth Luchino, I could not speak only about the beautiful things. And I do not want to speak ill of others."

With the birth of Luca in 1970, Audrey proved happy to putter about the kitchen, and she liked having family and friends come to her home for meals. It all proved easier than going out and dealing with the paparazzi, whose continuous intrusion occasioned one of Audrey's rare complaints: "The only time my fame was a little hard for me was when my second son was born. I was living in Rome and I could not take him anywhere without paparazzi. It was bothering the child. That really drove me mad. To have photographers jump out from behind trees—he'd be howling because he was so startled. A dear friend who had a beautiful garden said bring him here as often as you want with other children and that solved the problem."

Having her picture snapped by the paparazzi was of no interest to Audrey, and yet a trace of the international superstar remained; she may not have liked the press, but her chef Florida Broadway observed that in some ways Audrey enjoyed the attention of being recognized: "Sometimes I think she made sure that they did, although she was subtle about it." In this respect Audrey resembled "the other" Hepburn, as the once fiercely private Katharine cagily devised new ways of keeping her name in the spotlight after leading lady roles dried up. Once a well-guarded private sanctum, Katharine's New York City townhouse was now graced by visits from select reporters and even television crews. Private letters to Spencer Tracy were read out loud on television, and a friendship with Michael Jackson was publicly discussed. The need for the oxygen of stardom had not abated.

But in the main, Audrey continued to guard her privacy fiercely, and in Luca's recall, so thoroughly did she cede the spotlight that when he was a little boy and journalists asked about Audrey Hepburn, he would reply: "'You are mistaken. I am the son of Mrs. Dotti. . . .' At home Dad was the center of attention."

So successfully had Audrey cut off her personal life from her Hollywood career that even the young Luca was not really sure what she had to do with the world of movies. Like any child, Luca loved his own birthday parties, and in those pre–home video days, his favorite part of the celebration would be the special treat of watching movies. He was a fan of *Chitty Chitty Bang Bang*, as well as *Mary Poppins* and *My Fair Lady*, and yet, in his smiling recall: "None of us, however, not even I, managed to completely connect Eliza Doolittle, who spoke in cockney on the screen, with the lady who oversaw the distribution of plates of pasta al forno."

Serving pasta appealed far more than did a glitzy Hollywood premiere, which was why her decision to walk away from Hollywood dovetailed so neatly with her new life as Mrs. Andrea Dotti. Grateful as Audrey was for all that acting had brought her, family and home brought her much greater fulfillment, and by the dawn of the 1970s, she continued to find reasons not to work.

Part of that choice lay in the fact that her modesty and refusal to take part in the Hollywood scene had given her a genuine private life, with public and paparazzi alike granting her more distance and greater respect than were ever accorded the Elizabeth Taylors and Marilyn Monroes of the world. And because she had been granted that privacy and developed a fulfilling life away from the cameras, it had proven that much easier to walk away from Hollywood after securing another Academy Award nomination for *Wait Until Dark*. The decision had developed in stages; there was no sentimental appearance at a retirement press conference to garner one last burst of adulation, not even a mention of the word "retirement." As in demand as ever, she had simply walked away. On her own terms.

Audrey wearing a favorite shearling fitted midi coat with passementerie trim while out on a stroll in Rome. She was photographed frequently in this coat, one which was typical of her practical, yeoman-like personal wardrobe, which featured certain favorite items worn repeatedly. INTERFOTO Personalities/Alamy Stock Photo.

Chapter Thirty-Seven

NINE YEARS OF SILENCE, 1967–1976

"I don't regret for one minute making the decision to quit movies for my children. If I just had movies to look back on, I'd not have known my boys."

—Audrey Hepburn

THE SEEDS FOR AUDREY'S NINE years of silence are easily discernible when placed in the context of her overall career: even in her 1950s and early 1960s heyday as one of the biggest movie stars in the world, she never displayed the drive for acting that she had regarding ballet: "Although I had great respect for the art and craft of acting, I never really cared for the business. They thought me inconsiderate. The fact is, I cared too much, but only about the things that really counted."

Audrey's refusal to prioritize making films is fully revealed by a consideration of the contrast between her rather slim twenty-two feature-length-film appearances from 1951 through 1993, and the bulging resumes of Meryl Streep and her fellow Academy Award winner, Nicole Kidman. As of 2023, Streep had appeared in seventy-eight feature films and television series with another nearly two dozen voiceover and narration credits to her name, while Kidman had compiled a staggering ninety feature film and television credits. Acting may have appeared to be the very stuff of oxygen for Kidman and Streep, but for Hepburn it held place as a nice but nonessential part of life.

Family and home only proved to be part of the story, however. Some of Audrey's reluctance to continue making movies came from the terrors she felt before filming a scene, terrors which never evaporated and ultimately took a cumulative toll: "I really die a million deaths every time. My stomach turns over, my hands get clammy. I do suffer. I really do. I wasn't cut out to do this kind of thing. I really wasn't."

Ironically, the more unavailable Audrey had made herself, the greater the public's interest in her. Would Garbo have maintained her powerful decades-long hold on the public imagination if she had remained in Hollywood or appeared in more films after 1941's flop *Two-Faced Woman*? The answer is unknown, but her passion for privacy informed her entire legend. Doris Day willingly walked away from Hollywood in the mid-1970s and never returned, yet remained an object of fascination, just as did Audrey's not-quite-kin Katharine Hepburn, who had mastered the art of selective disappearance. In the case of Katharine Hepburn, however, a canny strategy underlay her refusal to appear at premieres or ever attend a Hollywood party; unlike Audrey, she always wanted to keep working, and if the right role came along, suddenly a slew of "exclusive" interviews with Katharine Hepburn would spring forth, right alongside a canny appearance at a concert given by her friend Michael Jackson.

Audrey, however, would have been more than happy to never again deal with the press. She had, like Jackie Onassis, Garbo, and author Harper Lee, opted out of that all-consuming American church of fame. In their heyday, all four women carried a sense of mystery, an impossibility in today's age of Snapchat, Instagram, and X. Hard as it is to imagine in the internet age, Audrey personified the idea of a star who remained private at her essential core. Gracious and unfailingly polite, she had perfected the art of seeming open and accessible while revealing precisely nothing.

What Onassis, Garbo, and Harper Lee shared with Audrey was a simple yet deep desire for privacy—in Garbo's terms a desire not necessarily to be alone but to be left alone; said Audrey: "People who would rob you of your dearest possession—your privacy—aren't worth having as friends. . . . I feel each individual has the right to keep some things to himself." As she further explained: "I can spend time happily alone because I know somebody is going to walk in the door. I'm rather cheerful by nature—it's my best defense against the aches on the inside."

It was therefore not really a surprise that after the 1967 release of *Wait Until Dark*, Audrey undertook only two spots of work in the next four years, both of such a fleeting nature that the majority of the public did not even know about them. In the first, the globetrotting multinational 1971 television documentary *A World of Love* produced by UNICEF (with whom she did not yet have any formal association), Audrey filmed a brief appearance extolling life in Italy. In the second and even briefer turn before the cameras, she received a $100,000 payday for two days of work filming a television commercial for the Tokyo-based wig company Varie.

If, during the early days of her career, Audrey had rarely paused to catch her breath as she raced from *Gigi* to *Roman Holiday* to *Ondine*, by 1976, nine years had elapsed since her last starring role in *Wait Until Dark*. A lifetime in Hollywood years. Two lifetimes. Her absence was certainly not tied up in a fear of appearing old on camera. Said Luca: "She was actually happy about growing older because it meant more time for herself, more time for her family and separation from the frenzy of youth and beauty that is Hollywood." In Audrey's own reasoning: "I can't be a leading lady all my life. That's why I'd be thrilled if people offered me character parts in the future. I won't resent it. Either you have to face up to it and tell yourself you're not going to be eighteen all your life or be prepared for a terrible shock when you see the wrinkles and white hair."

Did she miss making movies? Some—not much: "I could survive without working but I couldn't survive without my family. That is why my private life has always taken precedence." She certainly did not apologize for her time away from the movies: "I worked from the age of 13 for 25 years straight. That's why I think I've deserved this time off."

The biggest reason for Audrey's absence from the screen may have been the desire to raise her children, but as the chief architect of her own career, she had also found almost all of the scripts submitted to her in the previous nine years severely lacking; not for Audrey the gargoyle roles foisted upon the aging likes of Joan Crawford and Bette Davis.

But just as she thought her nine years of silence might happily stretch out for at least another nine years, an intriguing script came her way: *Robin and Marian*—the story of the middle-aged

Robin Hood and Maid Marian. The film's Academy Award–winning screenwriter James Goldman (*The Lion in Winter*) was so interested in landing Audrey for the role of Marian that he personally left the screenplay right by her door at New York City's Plaza Hotel. And how did she react? Intrigued by the script, Audrey quickly signed on, embracing the chance to portray a three-dimensional woman her own age: "There's a great need in films today for mature women to be seen playing mature women. And this was one of the few stories where I could be my own age. I like that."

In Goldman's witty screenplay, the middle-aged Maid Marian, now the mother abbess of a nunnery, is entirely consumed by her vocation until, after a twenty-year absence, she once again crosses paths with Robin Hood. On some level that likely spoke to Audrey, the ultra-disciplined, self-effacing life of a nun seemed to resemble the life of self-denial required by the world of ballet, and Marian's voluntary immersion into the cloistered life seemed to echo Audrey's own retreat from Hollywood into the small, private world of Tolochenaz.

If *Two for the Road* (1967) examined the reality of a marriage after all the excitement has died down, then *Robin and Marian* would peel back the curtain to look at the reality behind the fairy-tale promise of "happily ever after." For Audrey, appalled as she was by the cynical violence permeating the screen, Goldman's script presented a rare opportunity for a mature woman to make a positive statement. Marian's decision to reunite with Robin and turn away from her religious vows is hers alone, a strong woman following her own internal compass. In Audrey's words: "Such a poetic idea."

On set Audrey would be surrounded by friends like producer Richard Shepherd (*Breakfast at Tiffany's*), and with her two sons now sixteen and six, the time, she admitted, might just be right to make another film: seventeen years following the release of *The Nun's Story*, Audrey would once again be appearing onscreen in a nun's robe.

A welcome return to the screen opposite Sean Connery in *Robin and Marian, 1976*. Photo by Douglas Kirkland/ Corbis via Getty Images.

Chapter Thirty-Eight

AS IF WE NEVER SAID GOODBYE, 1976

"I don't know why I'm frightened
I know my way around here"

—Andrew Lloyd Webber/Don Black, *Sunset Boulevard*

CERTAINLY, A PORTION OF AUDREY'S willingness to commit to *Robin and Marian* lay in the chance to work with the first-rate supporting cast anchored by Nicol Williamson, Ian Holm, and Robert Shaw, but the biggest enticement of all lay in the presence of her co-star, Sean Connery. Connery, whose determination to break out of the James Bond mold had already resulted in roles both suspenseful (*The Anderson Tapes*, 1971) and sweeping (*The Wind and the Lion*, 1975), appealed not only to Audrey but perhaps even more crucially, in her view, to her sons. All Sean and Luca needed to hear was that she would be making a movie with James Bond, and the desire for their mother to go back to work leapt upward.

Lucrative deals were signed: Connery would be paid $1 million and Audrey $750,000. The American-born but London-based Richard Lester, whose frenetic style had become famous with the Beatles films *A Hard Day's Night* (1964) and *Help!* (1965), signed on as director: after nine long years, Audrey Hepburn's return to movies had become a reality.

Trouble, however, lay dead ahead in Audrey's relationship with Lester, a situation which was clear from their very first meeting in the summer of 1975. At the appointed time for a meet-and-greet between star and director, Lester, who was playing tennis, greeted Audrey through the fence surrounding the court but did not take the time to interrupt his game. Said a Columbia Pictures producer: "Audrey could get along with Hitler, but Lester is not in her scrapbook of unforgettable characters."

Lester did, in fact, respect Audrey, calling her a good sport about her unflattering and volu-minous nun's habit: "After topping all the lists of the best dressed women in her career, here she was in her comeback film dressed in an over-large oven glove." He would not, however, bend his informal, speeded-up style of filmmaking to suit Audrey's needs, and in that refusal provided her with an abrupt introduction to the rapidly changing world of late twentieth-century film-making. Lester was not interested in reshoots and retakes, and instead used several cameras to capture each scene, often shooting only one take.

Used to William Wyler's endless retakes, Audrey underwent a somewhat trying adjustment to this informal, helter-skelter style of filming. Said son Sean: "She loved working with Sean Connery, but not with the director. Lester was introverted, not vocal, and rushed through things. Interestingly, when discussing the making of her various films, she said to me that the quality of the experience often has nothing to do with the outcome. Some of the films that were nightmares to make ended up the greatest successes, and some that were joys—filming in Paris, traveling the globe—turned out to be the duds of the century." For Audrey, in fact, it always had been about the journey more than the destination: "I think of my career as a happy blur of wonderful, very human experiences more than as jobs or work. There was always something marvelous—friendships, places."

Speaking to the press once location shooting had begun in Pamplona, Audrey confessed her anxiety: "I still find it terrifying to start a film. . . . Filming isn't like riding a bicycle, it doesn't just come back overnight after so long: even in the best artistic surroundings, in the end you are still alone."

Such uncertainty was exacerbated by Lester's unceasingly hectic pace, with filming completed after a mere thirty-six days. More used to the pace found on the four-and-a-half-month shooting schedule for *My Fair Lady*, Audrey grew uneasy, her feelings not helped by the fact that cinematographer David Watkin, a friend of Lester's, did not filter any of her close-ups. There would be no flattering lighting for a beautiful but nonetheless aging star, just straightforward, shoot-it-as-fast-as-you-can filmmaking. Ever tactful, Audrey spoke of Lester as "a whiz-bang with his many cameras and single takes." Author Charles Higham put it more bluntly: "He was in a hurry all the time, and his personality was grating, tough, and totally at odds with both Audrey and the subject matter of the film." When, during filming, Audrey was unexpectedly thrown off of a horse-drawn cart into a river, Lester did not even call "Cut" but let the filming continue, keeping the resulting shot in the final cut of the film.

She may have felt rushed and in her own words "still alone" on the set, but the finished film made it clear that Audrey Hepburn remained in full possession of her considerable acting skills. With the Spanish countryside standing in for England's Nottingham Forest, sweeping panoramas prove the order of the day until, a full thirty minutes after the movie has started, Maid Marian arrives on the scene. Her look of wonder as she sees Robin for the first time in twenty years instantly lays bare both her tenderness and her deepest desires. Her short but curly hair suits her gracefully aging face, and even the mother abbess's sack of a habit cannot camouflage Audrey's ease of movement. Her voice, still an elusive mix of smoke and fog, gives full value to Goldman's oft-times witty script:

Marian (to Robin): You never wrote.
Robin: I don't know how.

But it is in its depiction of middle-aged romance that the heart of the film truly lies, the setting almost irrelevant to the film's consideration of love, desire, and sacrifice. Hepburn and Connery play beautifully together, her dignified femininity matched step for step by his solid masculinity. When Marian tentatively asks Robin: "Am I old and ugly?" his response is simply to hug her. The words, when they do come, are precise and eloquent, touching in their simplicity. Fiercely declaring her love even after twenty years in a convent, Marian lays bare her heart: "I love you. I love you more than morning prayer, more than sunlight. I love you more than God."

Concerned about her acting after nine years away from the cameras, Audrey could not even judge her performance from the daily rushes, as Lester did not allow his actors to see the footage, and she saw the completed film for the first time alongside six thousand fellow spectators at the Radio City Music Hall premiere on March 11, 1976. Her reaction to the film remained mixed; pleased by her palpable onscreen rapport with Connery, she nonetheless felt frustrated by the fact that the romance between Robin and Marian remained curiously truncated: "With all these men I was the one who had to defend the romance in the picture. *Somebody* had to take care of Marian." She was, unsurprisingly, particularly upset with the fact that after Marian poisons herself as well as Robin, the film ends with shots of rotting fruit. Her disappointment was, as always, expressed in understated fashion, and she simply murmured: "I could've done without that last close-up of fruit turning rotten." Asked about her overall reaction to the film, she smiled and explained: "I shall have to see it again before I decide."

What was almost lost in all the talk of comebacks and the changing nature of Hollywood filmmaking was the fact that Audrey's skill as an actress had, if anything, deepened in the nine years since her last movie. Tenderness flickers across her face in a matter of seconds, as does the abrupt masking of emotions, and with nearly a decade of additional life experience under her belt, she imbues Marian with a hard-won wisdom, ultimately presenting a three-dimensional portrait of a mature woman who is by turns feisty, difficult, loving, and wise.

Commented Frank Rich in the *New York Post*: "This is a film about legends, and legends become even more beautiful with age. . . . The movie reminds us that legends never die—that they are, instead, perpetually reborn." Even more indicative of audience reaction was Jay Cocks's declaration in *Time* magazine: "The moment she appears on the screen is startling, not for her thorough, gentle command nor yet for her beauty, which seems heightened and renewed. It is rather that we are reminded of how long it has been since an actress has so beguiled us and captured our imagination. Hepburn is unique, and now almost alone."

Genuinely surprised by the enthusiastic standing ovation she received from the Radio City audience, Audrey agreed to a full round of press appearances in order to promote the film. With all of her customary politeness—John Isaac noted that on UNICEF trips she was "respectful to everyone. Most of the time she would address people as 'Sir' or 'Madam'"—she nonetheless kept her accustomed distance, accompanied by bodyguards and refusing an interview with Barbara Walters, whom she felt would ask too many personal questions. Her trademark tact had not deserted her and barraged with questions about her purported "comeback," she gracefully swatted away the very idea: "I keep hearing that I am making a comeback. I don't think of it as that. It is a homecoming."

Asked about her years away from Hollywood she explained: "I'm glad to have missed what's been happening in the movies these last eight years. It's all been sex and violence, and I'm far too scrawny to strip and I hate guns, so I'm better off out of it." Four years later she sounded the same note in an interview with the *New York Times*, explaining that she would not participate in the filming of violent, nihilistic films just for the sake of working: "I could never be cynical. I wouldn't dare. I'd roll over and die before that."

In that declaration of following the dictates of her own internal compass lay the explanation of exactly why audience affection for her had, if anything, only grown in fervor.

Audrey Hepburn, all of her fans understood, was as genuine and true to herself as they hoped. She could not lie.

A stylish jaunt through Rome with Andrea wearing a typical for the 1970s practical wool midi coat. Photo by Mondadori Portfolio via Getty Images.

Chapter Thirty-Nine

WHAT COULD GO WRONG, PART 2—1970s

"Doctors are great with their patients, but they never want to take care of their families."
—Audrey Hepburn

LIE, AUDREY WOULD NOT. BUT that did not mean that she would reveal all. Far from it. In fact clues as to the state of the Hepburn-Dotti marriage—the differing temperaments, divergent expectations, and contradictory life goals—had to be discerned in the subtext of the interviews Audrey so rarely granted. Polite as always, she would limit the interview to thirty minutes, knowing that any additional time would bring a barrage of personal questions about a host of topics she did not wish to discuss. Audrey was here displaying a technique she had perfected as far back as 1953 with *Roman Holiday* and *Sabrina*; having been politely bamboozled by Audrey's reticence, interviewer Kirtley Baskette reflected that "the Dutch treat with the English accent talks but tells nothing. If you ask a personal question she smiles sweetly and is as silent as the sphinx."

It's therefore all the more surprising that while living in Rome, Audrey and husband Andrea did grant one joint interview to *McCall's Magazine*. The interview reveals Dotti in a far more relaxed frame of mind than Audrey, even donning his psychiatrist's hat and offering rather keen insight into her psyche. After first expounding upon why he thinks the search for security and the search for love are intertwined, he goes on to say of his wife: "She's a perfectionist, with a strong need for security. She must have matters under control and she's afraid of surprises."

Hints of an unraveling can be glimpsed in Audrey's musings about the very nature of marriage: "Marriage should be only one thing: two people decide they love each other so much that they want to stay together. Whether they sign a piece of paper or not, it's still a marriage with a sacred contract of trust and respect. . . . So, if in some way I don't fulfill what he needs in a woman—emotionally, physically, sexually, or whatever it is—and if he needs somebody else, then I would not stick around. I'm not the kind to stay and make scenes."

A turning point in both the marriage and life in Italy now occurred for political, not personal, reasons. 1970s Rome was awash with rumors of kidnappings to be carried out by the militant, violently leftist Red Brigades, and the unsettled political atmosphere understandably made Audrey afraid for the very safety of her sons. Her general sense of unease came to a head when four masked men attempted to kidnap Andrea on the street, a kidnapping foiled only after

Dotti's screams for help reached two nearby security guards who ran over and chased the men away. Andrea was left with seven stitches in his head, and Audrey's nervous state was further exacerbated when she received a threatening phone call. A crisis point had been reached, leading Audrey to tell Sean: "You can stay with us and a bodyguard or you can go to Switzerland and have a normal life." Recalled Sean: "I was thirteen. I chose Le Rosey school in Switzerland and received my French baccalaureate when I was seventeen."

Although still based in Rome, Audrey now began spending more time in Switzerland, which meant that Andrea felt an increasing freedom to resume his jet-set lifestyle. Photographers began snapping pictures of him out on the town with a bevy of beautiful women; pictures of Dr. Andrea Dotti, philandering husband of Audrey Hepburn, proved marketable, and when the story of Andrea's partying was reported in the *National Enquirer*, Audrey felt humiliated. Arguments ensued. That the marriage was falling apart was painfully clear when Audrey stated: "My marriage is *basically* happy. . . . I can't measure it in percentages, because you can never do that with a relationship."

Said Mita Ungaro, a neighbor in Rome whose mother was a great friend of Audrey's: "She loved Andrea. But Andrea had a very destructive part of himself. He had a complicated personality. He was a serious doctor . . . and yet he was a typically Roman man." Putting the problem in blunter terms, granddaughter Emma stated: "He was committing a lot of adultery. He was photographed with over two hundred women by one of the Italian paparazzi." In the words of Dotti himself: "I was no angel. Italian husbands have never been famous for being faithful."

For a sensitive, love-starved woman like Audrey, the sense of betrayal proved overwhelming. In the view of Anna Cataldi: "It was devastating, totally devastating. Audrey was suffering a lot—she told me 'I suffer so much.'" Observed family friend Marilena Pilat: "If you see pictures of Audrey from that time, she lost a little bit of light in her eyes. . . . I couldn't understand why such a sweet lady like her had to find herself with a man who wouldn't deserve her, wouldn't understand her. . . . She struggled with the idea of a perfect family, with very simple things that make life easy. I don't think she had that—everything she had to fight for."

By now, husband and wife were leading separate lives and living in different countries. Said Audrey: "My husband and I had what you would call an open arrangement. It's inevitable when the man is younger. I wanted the marriage to last. Not just for our own sake, but for that of the son we had together." But her intimates all noted the strain, and in later years her two closest male companions, Hubert de Givenchy and Robert Wolders, both used the same word to characterize Audrey's reaction: "suffering." Recalled Hubert: "When she suffered—and she suffered a great deal—she kept it to herself. I sensed her in turmoil but naturally, I dared not ask any questions." Wolders echoed the observation in words which give insight into how deeply Audrey's feelings ran—a gift when it came to her acting, but a hindrance when personal life turned sour: "Once she sensed that she could trust somebody, she'd do anything for them. And if she were disappointed in them, it would be the end of the world for her. She suffered more than most of us."

The Dottis officially separated, and Audrey moved into a small house, albeit in the same Parioli district of Rome. In Luca's remembrance, during all this turmoil his mother consciously tried to distance herself from him "in order to hide her sadness from me." Sean methodically explains: "She realized that this charming simpatico Italian husband was just that—an Italian husband who was going out to clubs while she was pregnant with my little brother. He was not faithful. The marriage really lasted about three years: they were married in '69, my brother was born in 1970. When I was going to school in Switzerland in 1974, they were already leading basically separate lives. But she still had hopes, she still hoped that it would work out. . . Dotti had moved into his own place while my mother moved into a smaller place. He was living across the street so that he could see his son. This little boy would sit in the window waiting for his father to come—which he rarely did. . . . When Luca went to boarding school near Lake Geneva, two hours from La Paisible, my mother moved back to Switzerland."

Writing about his father and the family home in Switzerland, Luca bluntly stated: "La Paisible—the place of peace—seen through the filter of his sarcasm, soon became La Penible—the place of pain." But no matter the stresses and strains she felt, just as she had never spoken ill of Mel Ferrer to Sean, Audrey would never speak critically about Andrea to Luca, placing the value of her child's relationship with his father above any momentarily satisfying criticism of her spouse.

Sean has painted a dark picture of his mother's deteriorating marriage to Dotti, pointing out that the eroding of trust and security did not spring up overnight but continued year after year: "He did it over ten years—in the beginning when she was pregnant. When she found out. When they were separated. Then when she tried again to save the marriage." At the end of the marriage, the situation turned particularly upsetting, culminating when Sean came home in the spring of 1978: "When I came home, I found her in bed, and she had taken a bunch of sleeping pills. Dreadful. He killed the marriage every day, for ten years. The effect on my mother was absolutely devastating."

Ruminating upon the stresses of a failing marriage, Audrey explained: "Your heart just breaks, that's all. Men are human beings with all the frailties women have. Perhaps they are more vulnerable than women. I think you can hurt a man so easily. You cannot judge, you cannot point fingers, you cannot put anybody in a mold. You've just got to be lucky enough to find somebody who you can satisfy and then who pleases you if you're lucky."

Now spending all of their time apart, the Dottis' separation was announced in September 1980 by Vero Roberti; after thirteen years of marriage, the last three of which had been spent living apart, the divorce was finalized in 1982. In later years Audrey analyzed: "I clung on to both marriages very hard, for as long as I could, for the children's sake and out of respect for marriage. But I just couldn't manage that." Her childlike belief that loving and looking after others ensures that they will act in the same way had been shattered. Admitted Audrey: "Dotti was not much of an improvement on Ferrer."

Twenty-two by the time Audrey and Dotti divorced, Sean has cast a realistic view at both Dotti's failings and his mother's own wishful thinking: "My stepfather was a brilliant funny psychiatrist—but he was a hound dog . . . I think she knew from the beginning who [Dotti] was, yet I think she dreamed and hoped that somehow she could change that. And I think she was gravely disappointed when she realized she couldn't." In Sean's view though, "what she didn't do was to speak up and be heard when she needed to and she didn't put up healthy boundaries."

Commentators through the decades have rushed to draw a contrast between the authoritarian Svengali-like Ferrer, domineering and jealous of Audrey's success, and the charming, brilliant, compulsively unfaithful Dotti, but Sean, in fact, is the one person with firsthand knowledge who has pointed out the similarities between the two men that led to the failed marriages: "Both men had been emotionally scarred by equally powerful and brilliant mothers who, as a result of their backgrounds, their education, and the societal rules of their times, didn't connect with their children at a profound emotional level."

For his part, Luca summed up the failed marriage by explaining: "Growing up, I was struck above all by how different they were . . . Dad with his Latin male cynicism, and Mum with her rigid northern upbringing and difficulty speaking about feelings." From the perspective of his own adult years, Luca observed that with his mother being the older of his two parents, "it was my father who was too young, still immature. Sometimes I find myself thinking, completely irrationally, how different things would have been had they met later, when dad had changed." As it was, Dotti never remarried, continuing his practice and teaching until he died in 2007.

Two failed marriages. Disillusioned, hurt, and vulnerable, a downcast and chastened Audrey explained: "You always hope that if you love somebody enough, everything will be all right—but it isn't always true." Fifty years old, Audrey now spent her time puttering about in her garden. Looking after her boys when they were home. Cooking. But it wasn't enough after the breakup of her marriage, and she began thinking about a return to the world of moviemaking. It had been three years since the release of *Robin and Marian*, and a new film would take her mind off her troubles. Surrounded by cast and crew on location, she would have less time to ruminate.

Scripts were submitted. Offers were made, and Audrey Hepburn now signed on to headline the all-star film adaptation of Sidney Sheldon's best-selling novel *Bloodline*. On paper it all looked promising. In reality it proved to be the worst film of her career.

Audrey at age fifty in 1979's *Bloodline*, wearing the oversized sunglasses that became one of her signature looks. Audrey looks great—the film was anything but. Paramount Pictures/Photofest © Paramount Pictures.

Chapter Forty

FEATURE FILM MISTAKE #3—*BLOODLINE*, 1978–1979

"The movies that came after the breakup with Andrea Dotti are not a true reflection of the whole career."

—Sean Ferrer

ONCE ASKED IN AN INTERVIEW if she had ever made a film for the money, Audrey responded: "No, never. Never. I've never done that . . ." The answer was, as always proved the case with Audrey, entirely truthful. Making the tawdry pseudo thriller *Bloodline* got her out of the house, and the hefty $1 million payday she received for that film was the bonus, a substantial one. Who wouldn't want to earn $1 million to star in a film based on an international bestseller?

When she stepped away from Hollywood after *Wait Until Dark*, she had been only thirty-eight years old and had, she explained to an interviewer in flawless Italian, missed moviemaking "in an emotional way." Son Sean puts the decision in perspective: "After her retirement—the years away from the movies—my father wasn't around any longer, so she wasn't getting the proper advice and support. She needed to get out of the house because she was in the middle of a divorce from Dotti. She needed to be on the set thinking about something else."

Which is not to say Audrey instantly acquiesced to *Bloodline*. Director Terence Young, a fellow client of Kurt Frings, had direct personal and professional connections with Audrey, yet he found obtaining her approval as daunting a task as shooting the movie itself: "First of all you spend a year or so convincing her to accept even the principle that she might make another movie in her life. Then you have to persuade her to read the script . . . then you have to persuade her that she will not be totally destroying her son's life by spending six or eight weeks on a film set. . . . Then, more probably, she'll say she has to get back to her family and cooking."

Blame it on Audrey's restlessness, but whatever Young's specific blandishments, they worked, and she signed a lucrative deal calling for a $1 million guarantee against a percentage of the profits. After surviving the war with next to no money, a $1 million salary brought with it security, if not happiness, and yet the doubts about her own abilities had not abated: "Am I going to be able to do it? You don't gain more confidence, you gain a certain philosophy."

But, she figured, how bad could it be? Young was a friend, filming would take place relatively close to home in Sardinia and Copenhagen, interiors would be shot at Cinecitta in Rome, and no lengthy excursion to Hollywood would prove necessary. To top it off, for the first time since 1966's *How to Steal a Million*, her onscreen wardrobe would be designed by Givenchy. Perhaps an all-star international thriller could be the ticket to box office success.

Ironically, the film did not in fact really need to be a success, funded as it was by a German film syndicate, Geria, which only needed to spend the film's $10 million budget by the end of the year to lessen their tax liabilities. Expenditure was all, and quality, if there was any, simply a bonus.

Unsurprisingly, warning signs loomed from the start. *Bloodline* was now being billed as *Sidney Sheldon's Bloodline*, the potboiler novelist's status as an international best-selling author guaranteeing him star billing. It's unfortunate that Audrey did not read the Sheldon novel after director Young passed it along to her, because if she had, it likely would have given her more than a moment's pause. Aside from the contrived mechanics of the plot, in the novel "Elizabeth Rolfe" was twenty-three, and even now, her adjusted age of thirty-five registered like nothing so much as a wan acknowledgment of Audrey's own fifty years.

Of more import, however, Audrey either did not know or perhaps did not care that the underwritten part of cosmetics tycoon Elizabeth had already been rejected by Jacqueline Bisset, Candice Bergen, and Diane Keaton. But if Audrey wanted to return to the movies what exactly were her choices? As the wise old master Billy Wilder pointed out: "The difficulty with stars is, what do they do at fifty or fifty-five?" Or, in the even more trenchant words of Carrie Fisher: "There are not a lot of choices for women past twenty-seven."

In a 1978 interview with critic Rex Reed during filming, Audrey perhaps unintentionally revealed just why, in the wake of the breakup of her second marriage, she would take on flimsy material like *Bloodline*: "All I really want now is not to be lonely, and to have my garden." Two marriages, two beloved sons, and decades of adulation from adoring fans still could not fill the void of loneliness left over from childhood or the heartache of a second broken marriage. Although during filming the cast and crew left her alone out of respect, the distanced interactions proved so remote that she expressed the desire for more time with her fellow actors, not less: "It can be very lonely in a crowd. Why is everybody so worshipful?"

To those who asked, Audrey expressed contentment with the material: "I thought it was exciting. I'm not a snob about movies. They don't have to be high art, just enjoyable and fun. Besides, what woman wouldn't want a Givenchy wardrobe? You'd have thought after staying away so long that the public would forget me, not want me anymore. It's delightful to feel wanted."

It was a brave attempt at putting a positive spin on the second-rate material, but nothing really helped. According to Beatrice Straight, one of Audrey's co-stars, Audrey seemed to realize while still filming that she was stuck in a turkey: "Audrey, who'd come with her own bodyguard, but decided after a while that, on balance, she'd rather be kidnapped by the Mafia than have to complete the picture . . ."

And what of the film itself? Unfortunately, *Bloodline*, the only R-rated film of Audrey's career, unfolds like the television soap operas *Dynasty* and *Dallas*, but without the saving grace of the humor that made them guilty pleasures. It's a full and frustrating fifteen minutes before Audrey appears onscreen, still sporting the curled hair seen in *Robin and Marian*, her look accessorized by oversized sunglasses. Shot through filters and high-key lighting, she is given material of little substance to act, and what she is given is of such risible quality that the unthinkable happens: the viewer is embarrassed on Audrey's behalf. Repellent scenes from snuff movies are repeatedly shown as part of the plot, and one character's knees are nailed to the floor, resulting in a violence and tawdriness far worse than anything Audrey could have feared from her aborted Alfred Hitchcock film of twenty years earlier, *No Bail for the Judge*.

Top billed over Ben Gazzara, Omar Sharif, and James Mason, Audrey herself seems to know that for all the talk of Elizabeth being a successful business tycoon, this is just old-fashioned hokum dressed up with sex and violence. It was not only Audrey who was left stranded, however, and in some ways her inherent grace allowed her to survive the mess in better fashion than the others: Irene Papas is saddled with a bizarrely over-the-top wardrobe, Gert "Goldfinger" Fröbe is on hand as an absent-minded professor, and the movie screeches to a dead halt whenever Michelle Phillips appears. Even the score by the esteemed Ennio Morricone proves irritating, thundering along as if volume alone could help pump up the dismal proceedings. The entire experience is summed up by the fact that the most interesting scene in the film has nothing to do with stopping whoever is trying to murder Elizabeth Rolfe, but rather everything to do with Audrey's first appearance in a sparkling Givenchy gown. What else could one reasonably expect from a film where Audrey's jewels from Bulgari received a credit of their own?

The film flopped at the box office, and reviews were not kind, with the reception to Audrey's participation best summed up by the review in *Variety*: "Though it would take several pictures on the level of *Bloodline* to seriously damage her stature, it's a shame she picks something like this now that she works so seldom." Even hard-to-please critics seemed to await Audrey's rare onscreen appearances with anticipation, which undoubtedly led to the sense of disappointment running through all of the film's reviews. Added the *Variety* critic: "It's a shock to see Hepburn playing a role that even Raquel Welch would have the good sense to turn down."

Bloodline did, however, bring Audrey an unexpected romance with her co-star Ben Gazzara. The hyper-masculine Gazzara, one year younger, method trained, and unrelentingly intense, provided Audrey with a welcome lift up from the doldrums; when in the mood, he could be very charming, and with his assertiveness and take-no-prisoners attitude, he made Audrey feel protected. In the words of Alexander Walker: "He had the self-absorbed actor's unpredictability of response and played on it." For his part, Gazzara was taken with Audrey's elegant ladylike exterior: "I never heard a vulgar word come out of Audrey. I never heard anyone be vulgar in front of Audrey."

The last, and most humorous, word on that genteel behavior and beauty came from Liza Minnelli after Audrey and Gazzara spent one night during filming seeing Minnelli in concert. After compliments and gracious words were exchanged backstage and Audrey and Gazzara had departed, Liza turned to her assistant Bill Thomas and laughingly exclaimed: "That Audrey bitch was so fat! . . . Have you ever seen anyone thinner or more gorgeous? I felt like the ugliest stepsister in the world!"

Shown here with young Glenn Scarpelli, Audrey wore her own clothes in her last leading role—Peter Bogdanovich's *They All Laughed,* 1981. Courtesy of Photofest.

Chapter Forty-One

THEY ALL LAUGHED, 1980

"John Keats wrote, 'Beauty is truth, truth beauty,' and Audrey was living proof of that; watching her in a picture was seeing beauty and truth revealed at every shimmering moment."

—director Peter Bogdanovich

GORGEOUS AUDREY WAS. THIN SHE was. But also at loose ends, and more than a bit still in love with Ben Gazzara, which is why in 1980 she agreed to star alongside the actor in director Peter Bogdanovich's comedy/drama *They All Laughed*. In a year dominated by blockbusters like *Raiders of the Lost Ark*, *Body Heat*, and *Halloween*, Bogdanovich and Blaine Novak's screenplay for *They All Laughed*, a wry meditation on the foibles of love, represented a risky proposition. It was, Bogdanovich later explained, his attempt, after the large-scale failure of his Cole Porter musical *At Long Last Love* (1975), to "accept the question I had asked in *At Long Last Love*: What is falling in love?" Absent any explosions or wild action sequences, the film remained a dubious prospect for production until Audrey signed on; only then did Bogdanovich secure financing from Time-Life and begin shooting in April of 1980.

Audrey, for whom Kurt Frings had secured a salary of $1 million for six weeks of work in New York City, would play "Angela Niotes," a rich Italian industrialist's bored wife who unexpectedly falls for "John Russo" (Ben Gazzara), a detective specializing in cases of adultery. The *La Ronde*–like ensemble comedy of mismatched lovers would also co-star television's John Ritter and Bogdanovich's real life love, Playboy model Dorothy Stratten.

Unsurprisingly, Audrey had at first proved reluctant to sign on. Bogdanovich tried to interest her by explaining that he had crafted the script specifically for her, but, in his telling, she politely replied: "Oh, Peetah! Don't tell me that—I'll feel so *baaad* if I don't do it . . . !" Yes, the salary of $1 million helped, but in the director's view, Audrey largely agreed to make *They All Laughed* because he offered to make Sean, who had left the University of Geneva, his personal on-set assistant. It was not a mere case of pleasing his star, however, because in the director's own words, Sean "turned out to be not only the best on-set assistant I had ever had, but a damn fine actor in the supporting role entirely rewritten to suit him." Sean did indeed prove a pleasant onscreen presence, but holding little desire to continue acting, he eventually embarked upon a career in production.

Happy as Audrey was about Sean being a part of the film, and notwithstanding Bogdanov-ich's open-hearted admiration—"There's nobody greater at a romantic comedy than Audrey Hepburn"—the old doubts about her own talents persisted, a fact made clear in an interview conducted during the filming of the movie: "I'm not Laurence Olivier, no virtuoso talent. I'm basically rather inhibited and I find it difficult to do things in front of people. What my directors have had in common is that they've made me feel secure, made me feel loved."

She was always the first to put down her own abilities, doing so more frequently than any critics ever could, but the idea of Audrey as a non-actress burst forth most publicly some seventeen years after her death when a surprisingly self-serving Emma Thompson, then in the process of writing a never-filmed remake of *My Fair Lady* proclaimed: "I find Audrey Hepburn fantastically twee—twee is whimsy without wit, it's mimsy-mumsy sweetness without any kind of bite and that's not for me. . . . She can't sing and she can't act. I'm sure she was a delightful woman—and perhaps if I had known her I would have enjoyed her acting more but I don't and I didn't. I don't do Audrey Hepburn—I think that's a guy thing."

Says Sean Ferrer about the imbroglio: "Emma Thompson—she's an actress and a very good one. She has a very different persona from my mother's. My mother never criticized Emma or anyone else—in fact, she would have been the first to put herself down. All I can think is that Emma Thompson must have been going through something tough in her life at the time. To say she was mimsy-mumsy—it felt to me like throwing rocks at the Pope. My mother was not the greatest actress, dancer, or singer, not the most beautiful woman—but the combination of the high-level skills she did possess, and who she was as a person—all those qualities in one person made her unique."

In truth, the criticism was surprising coming from Thompson, who misread Hepburn's persona, missing the fact that she actually appealed to women even more than she did to men. The criticism bothered screenwriter Frederic Raphael enough that he rushed to the defense of his *Two for the Road* star, perceptively writing, "Audrey was just a little bit tougher than she seemed. That was her grace and her art and also during the war, her salvation."

Thompson's put-down ultimately mattered little, and it is Sean who offers a more nuanced assessment of his mother's abilities: "My mother was not of the ilk or capacity of Katharine Hepburn or Bette Davis. She never claimed to be. She was an actress but she was also a movie star. To be a star it takes a little more than being an actress, or being elegant, or being pretty. You have to wrap it all together with solid performances but when you're a star on that level it's also more like a beautiful presentation, not just about the ingredients. . . . My mother transcended the limitations of Hollywood stardom because she ended up with three components to her persona: movie star, icon of style, and her humanitarian work. Inner and outer elegance.

"She started out acting with the older generation, in the studio system that flourished in the 40s and early 50s, but as the years went by, she also worked in the much more natural way of acting that came out of Europe. She's not Anna Magnani, but she's one of the few whose acting transferred from one world of filmmaking to the next. Styles used to be very compartmentalized in people's minds, but my mother transcended that and remained as well-known in one era as in the next. *Two for the Road* represents a very different style of filmmaking and acting than *Sabrina*, but she mastered both and is remembered for both."

It was Audrey's own assessment—"it's not as if I'm the greatest actress. I'm not Bergman"—that proved most interesting, because genuine as this self-assessment was, she was actually wrong. In the very tough world of Hollywood, no actress maintains a decades-long star status without substance to back up the popularity. The camera doesn't lie, and while many are gifted with a flash-in-the-pan success, very few sustain stardom over the course of decades. Audrey's status as a worldwide icon was not a case of style over substance but rather a unique and winning combination of the two.

Bogdanovich clearly felt very differently than did Emma Thompson, and using his admiration for Audrey's talent as a springboard, he wrote the character of Angela specifically for and about her: "Audrey's backstory in the movie was very much the real backstory of what was going on in her life." Analyzing the movie with director West Anderson, Bogdanovich added: "She and Ben had had an affair during *Bloodline,* and I remember Ben coming back to my kitchen in Bel Air later that year and talking to me in my kitchen, saying: "Oh Peter, Peter—I'm in love with Audrey—Audrey, she's a saint."

Gazzara, not usually given to such overt emotionalism, had rhapsodized about how "lonely and fragile and saintlike she was." After speaking with Gazzara, Bogdanovich then drew upon the specifics of Audrey's life to create the character of "Angela," a woman devoted to her young son who endures life with an inattentive husband, and in the wake of a failing marriage embarks upon a brief but fulfilling affair. At movie's end, Angela leaves New York, flying away with her husband and son while true love John Russo remains behind—a deliberate echo of *Roman Holiday*'s Princess Ann choosing royal duty over love.

In the planning stages, *They All Laughed* may have sounded like a full-fledged and bittersweet Technicolor romance, but before production began, real life had intervened: while shooting *Inchon* (1981) immediately after *Bloodline*, Gazzara had fallen in love with Elke Stuckmann (soon to be his third wife). Analyzed Gazzara of his time with Audrey: "I was flattered that someone like that would be in love with me. But I didn't know how deeply she was in love with me until after I left. She told others, not me, that I had broken her heart. She was so kind and sweet. And I hurt her."

The relationship between Audrey and Gazzara may have registered as uncertain, but of Bogdanovich's affection for Audrey there was no doubt. Like nearly all of her previous directors, Bogdanovich found himself completely charmed by his star: "She was wonderful to work with. She was so unlike a movie star. . . . Never complained. Always knew the lines. Always improved the lines. You'd tell her 'That wasn't the line' and she'd say 'Isn't that the line? I thought it was—I'll say what you like.' And I'd find myself saying 'No, no Audrey—I like your version better.'"

Set in the present-day New York City of 1981, *They All Laughed* was deliberately planned by Bogdanovich to feature the casual, modern, Givenchy-less Audrey found in *Two for the Road*: "All of the clothes that Audrey wears in the film are her clothes—or imitations of the clothes that she herself wears. She wore blue jeans, silk shirts, and a pea jacket—so when I saw those were the clothes she wore, I asked her to wear those through the picture and she did."

With a minimal crew and no more than ten contracted extras—the crowds seen on the streets of Manhattan were simply New Yorkers going about their everyday business—production proved light years removed from Audrey's cosseted studio films of the 1950s. She remained unfazed by the lack of trailers and dressing rooms, patiently waiting inside stores until the call would come for the next shot. Enthused Bogdanovich: "Audrey was so wonderful. I remember her going into a store on 5th Avenue where we'd made her wait for that sequence on 5th Avenue, and she'd come out and say, 'Oh look, Peter—they gave me this lovely handkerchief.'

And she'd come out of another store, and she'd say, 'Oh look, Peter—they gave me this lovely umbrella.' I joked with her and said: 'Ok Audrey—after the next shot you can go to the other side of the street and work that side of the street.' She laughed. People just gave her things when they recognized her—and why wouldn't they?"

To Bogdanovich, Audrey's *Unforgiven* co-star Lillian Gish represented the first "virgin hearth goddess of the screen," and Audrey the last. In reality, however, Audrey seemed to more directly represent the last true innocent of the American screen; after directing Audrey in a bedroom scene with Gazzara, even Bogdanovich seemed surprised by the extent of her vulnerability. Although the scene in question proved rather tame in content and duration, the director was struck by one overwhelming element: "I got the impression she was pretty desperate for love." There was, he found, a lingering sadness surrounding his star: "She was a survivor, but it was painful. There was a sense of lost gaiety around Audrey that she could never quite recapture. I felt that it was from all the guys who had treated her badly."

As shooting progressed, Bogdanovich grew increasingly aware of the fragility that informed Audrey's life onscreen and off: "In life you'd think, 'How is she going to get through the day or even the hour?' Her hands are shaking, she's smoking too much, she's worried, she's being kind of desperately nice to everybody, she's so fragile. . . . But between the time she stepped in front of the camera and you said 'Action!,' something happened. She pulled it together. A kind of strength through vulnerability—strength like an iron butterfly."

She was, he realized, always scared. With all that talent and beauty, what exactly scared her so much? For starters, it seemed, of not being good enough. Of needing things to be perfect. Wanting, after the uncertainty of the war years, to control all situations. Wanting the love of a formidable mother and disappearing father. The irony, of course, lay in the fact that it was this nearly palpable, often beautiful uncertainty that continued to fuel the audience's love for her. In Sean's words: "When she cries, she really is feeling it, really living through it. She is believing—reliving—. . . She's actually there. And you want to take her in your arms and hug her."

And while the audience wants to protect Audrey/Angela, and roots for her happy ending with John/Gazzara, the rooting remains limp for the basic but important reason that her character's supposed onscreen romance with Gazzara seems rather tame and lacking in passion. They rarely seem to connect, an imbalance that may be a result of the fact that Audrey was at her best on the first takes while Gazzara improved with additional takes. In Sean's onset observation: "My mother was already a *print* on take one: the first and the second take were simply extraordinary. . . . Gazzara wasn't really good in that movie, or certainly he would have been better several takes later, when my mother might be just a bit tired, but Bogdanovich preferred to use my mother's better takes."

In fact, the rather tentative romance between Audrey and Ben pales in comparison to the genuinely affectionate relationship Audrey displays with young Glenn Scarpelli, who plays her son Michael. Her love of children is immediately apparent onscreen and warms up an otherwise tepid film.

Audrey finished her part six weeks before the rest of the cast, but at the end of shooting, 20th Century Fox pronounced themselves unhappy with the footage, causing Bogdanovich to buy back the film from the studio and release it himself under the banner of his own Moon Pictures.

It was all for naught, however, because the film could not overcome a basic, foundational problem: in struggling to be three films in one—comedy, drama, and bittersweet romance—it succeeded as none. Audiences remained confused, wondering—is the movie intended as a wry meditation on relationships? If so, why include the scenes suggesting abusive relationships? For that matter, why insert goofy scenes showing the characters roller-skating?

Bogdanovich, always at his best with films set in the past (*The Last Picture Show, Paper Moon*), seems uneasy with his valentine to present-day New York, and the different acting styles of Audrey, Gazzara, and John Ritter never mesh into a consistent tone. Matters are further complicated by Patti Hansen, who plays a cab driver in the manner of an insinuating Bacall-like Howard Hawks heroine, but registers only as exhausting.

Matters were not helped by the film's uneven editing, although Sean provides an interesting take on the rather unusual process involved: "Dorothy Stratten had died, and Peter was very distraught, understandably. So I helped Billy Carruth with the editing. In those days there was no digital editing. You had a movieola; the cutting room was in the screening room of Peter's house, where we would watch the day's work on the big screen. If you look at the film, there are a lot of over-the-shoulder shots in conversations, a lot of crosscuts. We were using the early takes in my mother's scenes, trying to blend with later takes of Gazzara."

By the time of the film's release in 1981, however, the biggest problem lay in the audience's knowledge that shortly after the end of principal photography, Dorothy Stratten had been murdered by her estranged husband Paul Snider. Her character, a sweet and beautiful young woman who comes home each night to a suspicious and jealous husband, simply contained too many uncomfortable parallels to Stratten's own life for the audience to separate the two. Compounding those difficulties was the wistful sadness pervading the entire film, Audrey's scenes included; the unspoken and not entirely welcome message conveyed to the audience seemed to be just how difficult and elusive true love always proves to be.

In the end, the film left viewers with the same reaction as did *Bloodline*: given how infrequently Audrey Hepburn chose to work, it's unfortunate that these pallid vehicles represented the best material available. It proved no surprise, then, that the critics were not impressed—what kind of Audrey Hepburn film did not allow Audrey to speak for the first thirty minutes? Sniffed Vincent Canby of the *New York Times*: "Mr. Bogdanovich treats Audrey Hepburn so shabbily that if this were a marriage instead of a movie, she'd have grounds for divorce." Zeroing in on the film's uneven tone, he continued: "Any way you look at it—as a comedy, as movie-making, as a financial investment—*They All Laughed* is an immodest disaster. It's aggressive in its ineptitude. It grates on the nerves like a 78 rpm record played at 33 rpm." *Newsweek* summed it up best with a simple declaration that the film represented "an aimless bust, unencumbered by a visual or structural scheme."

A handful of reviewers in trade publications such as *Variety* and the *Hollywood Reporter* seemed charmed, and the film subsequently acquired a small cult following, but box office returns at the time of initial release proved dismal, and Bogdanovich lost $5 million of his own money. The result was personal bankruptcy.

In later years, Bogdanovich did speak to Audrey about making another film together, one which would have found her playing the role of an addled leading lady in the backstage farce *Noises Off* (1992). She passed on the offer and the part was ultimately played by Carol Burnett. It proved a wise move by Audrey, with the role of a boisterous actress portraying a cleaning lady in a third-rate play not appearing to be a natural for her; in any event, the film proved a critical and financial flop.

Bogdanovich had not been surprised when she declined the role, sensing that *They All Laughed* would prove to be "her last film, which is why I did the ending as a montage of all those shots of her. I felt it was a farewell to that Audrey Hepburn. As the helicopter took her away, I thought, 'The world is taking her away." A saddened Bogdanovich philosophized "I had a strong sense that she didn't really enjoy making pictures anymore. The fun had gone out of it for her. She didn't think it was important anymore.'"

Always in demand from the press and studios alike, Audrey received dozens of scripts to consider each year. After starring in sixteen films from 1953 to 1967, she made only five more films during the next twenty-six years. Among those she turned down were *The Turning Point* (1977) and *Out of Africa* (1985). Photofest.

Chapter Forty-Two

MIGHT-HAVE-BEENS, 1950s through 1980s

"It's a shame to think about what the studio ended up killing for the movie-going audiences: a chance to see Hepburn and Olivier face off as Peter Pan and Captain Hook."

—Rafe Telsch, Cinemablend

GIVEN THE IMPRESSIVE NUMBER OF out-and-out triumphs in Audrey's career—among her twenty-two starring features she fully stumbled only with *Green Mansions*, *The Unforgiven*, *Bloodline*, and *They All Laughed*—an in-depth analysis of her filmography leads to a series of interesting questions regarding her career. Since everyone seemed to want in on the Audrey Hepburn film business (with the notable oft-times exception of Audrey herself), were there particular roles that she wanted and did not land? Which opportunities sounded great on paper only to fizzle in the planning stages? And perhaps most notably, which movies did she flat out turn down? As it happens, the list of films she was rumored to be considering during both her white-hot years in the 1950s and early '60s, as well as throughout her self-imposed retreat from 1967 onward, provides a tantalizing glimpse of both "If only" and "Thank goodness she didn't."

THE EARLY YEARS MIGHT-HAVE-BEENS

- *Twelfth Night*, with Audrey playing both Viola and Sebastian—to be directed by Joseph Mankiewicz.
- *L'Aiglon*, in which Audrey would have portrayed the tubercular son of Napoleon and Empress Marie Louise. Proposed director: William Wyler. In a 1955 interview Audrey explained: "We hope we can shoot *L'Aiglon* next year in Vienna and Schonbronn."
- *Rosalind*, based on the James M. Barrie play.
- A film version of her Broadway triumph *Ondine*. Audrey and Mel met with the English master filmmakers Michael Powell and Emeric Pressburger (*The Red Shoes*, *Black Narcissus*) about the proposed film, but Audrey and Mel were a package deal and, said Powell of Mel: "He had no warmth, nothing to give. Clever, yes—kind, no."

- *St. Joan*, to be directed by Otto Preminger, and a role subsequently played by Jean Seberg. At the time, there was some talk that Audrey turned down this notable role because of Preminger's refusal to cast Mel Ferrer as the Dauphin.
- Tennessee Williams's *Summer and Smoke*. As in *The Children's Hour*, Audrey would have taken on the role of a middle-aged schoolteacher in a small town. Such was the enthusiasm over Audrey that both producer Hal Wallis and Williams himself flew to Rome to pitch her the movie in person. Wallis, however, did not want Ferrer as the leading man, there was disagreement over Givenchy designing Audrey's wardrobe, and in the end, the film was made with Laurence Harvey and Geraldine Page in the starring roles.
- Henrik Ibsen's *Hedda Gabler*, with Mel directing. Financing never materialized.
- *The Diary of Anne Frank*. Scheduling problems and all, the role simply struck too close to home for Audrey, serving as an unwelcome reminder of her years spent living under Nazi rule.
- *Peter Pan*. A live-action film version of J. M. Barrie's play about the boy who refuses to grow up. Cukor expressed interest in directing, and the proposed cast was to include Audrey as Peter and Hayley Mills as Wendy, with either Peter Sellers or Laurence Olivier playing the villainous Captain Hook. It all seemed irresistible on paper, but London's Great Ormond Street Hospital for Sick Children, to which Barrie had bequeathed the rights, raised obstacles. So too did the Walt Disney Company, which had released a 1953 animated version and did not want competition in the form of a live-action mounting. With Audrey's androgynous vulnerability, as well as her playful inner spirit so reminiscent of Peter Pan (think Gregory Peck's description of her as a "cut up"), the idea struck many as near ideal casting. Perhaps for Audrey the film even represented a chance to recreate a childhood taken from her by the war. It's a tantalizing near miss, high on the list of "if only" Audrey Hepburn film projects, and a shame that such a star-studded possibility slowly drifted away.
- *Jane Eyre*. Audrey as Jane, playing opposite James Mason as "Rochester." The idea of Audrey and the equally velvet-voiced Mason exchanging dialogue straight out of Charlotte Brontë was enough to make any Anglophile swoon, but the film never progressed beyond the proposal stage. Perhaps it was because, as Mason himself smartly observed: "Audrey Hepburn just happened to be the most beautiful woman in movies. A head-turner. The whole point about Jane was that no one noticed her when she came into a room or left it."
- In the first iteration of the Audrey Hepburn–Julie Andrews mash-up, Audrey turned down a proposed 1950s English-language remake of the German-language *Die Trapp Familie*. That film's story of a singing family led by a former nun would emerge onscreen in 1965 as *The Sound of Music*, starring Julie Andrews.
- *The Doctor's Dilemma* (1958). Based upon the George Bernard Shaw play, the film was to be directed by Anthony Asquith. As was to happen with some frequency, after Audrey turned down the lead opposite Dirk Bogarde, her role was assumed by Leslie Caron.
- *A Certain Smile* (1958). This intergenerational soap opera romance would have found Audrey engaged to a law student but carrying on an affair with his uncle. Joan Fontaine and Rossanno Brazzi ultimately starred in a highly forgettable film notable only for the title tune sung by Johnny Mathis.

MIDCAREER MIGHT-HAVE-BEENS

- *West Side Story* (1961). A fortunate refusal. At the time of casting, Audrey was pregnant with son Sean but surely must have understood that whatever her formidable acting talents, she would have been unbelievable in the extreme as a Puerto Rican teenager. The role of "Maria" in this Academy Award–winning Best Picture went instead to the equally non-Hispanic Natalie Wood.
- *A Taste of Honey* (1961). Based upon the award-winning play by Shelagh Delaney, the script broke new ground in its depiction of teenage pregnancy, homosexuality, and interracial friendships. Audrey's interest in films exploring societal change would ultimately find expression two years later when she reunited with director William Wyler for *The Children's Hour*.
- *The Cardinal* (1963). Based upon the best-selling novel by Henry Morton Robinson, Audrey would have played the sister of a handsome American cardinal portrayed by Tom Tryon. Representing another attempt to team Audrey with director Otto Preminger, the film went on to receive several Academy Award nominations. Audrey's role was ultimately played by Carol Lynley.
- *In the Cool of the Day* (1963). Audrey's good sense prevailed, and she quickly turned down the role of Christine Bonner, an emotionally scarred young woman having an affair with her husband's best friend. Jane Fonda, who ultimately starred in the film, has publicly stated that it was the worst film of her career, one she wishes had never been made.
- *The Umbrellas of Cherbourg* (1964). Audrey was asked to play the role of "Madame Emery," mother of Catherine Deneuve, in the acclaimed through-sung musical directed by Jacques Demy. Her role was ultimately played by Anne Vernon.
- *The Greatest Story Ever Told* (1965). Preoccupied with both *Charade* and the looming *My Fair Lady*, and fearing a long location shoot, Audrey remained uninterested in playing the role of "Veronica" in George Stevens's retelling of the story of Jesus. Scheduled to be filmed in three months, the movie ultimately took nine months to shoot, with the role of Veronica undertaken by Carroll Baker.
- *Hawaii* (1966). A second casting crossover between Audrey and Julie Andrews. Based upon the monumental bestseller by James Michener, *Hawaii*'s leading female role, that of missionary wife Jerusha Bromley, would have necessitated months of location shooting. With son Sean only six years old at the time, Audrey never seriously considered taking on the role.

   Anxious to establish her dramatic credits after the one-two musical triumphs of *Mary Poppins* and *The Sound of Music*, Julie Andrews signed on instead. Given how often the two actresses were mentioned for the same role, what, one also wonders, could the sometimes-androgynous looking Audrey have done with Andrews's Oscar-nominated role as *Victor/Victoria*? With Andrews's part as Queen Clarisse Renaldi in the *Princess Diaries* movies? How would Julie have fared in Audrey's role as "Hap" the angel in Steven Spielberg's *Always*?

AND ON THROUGH THE YEARS

- *A Thousand Summers*. At times, the lengths to which some would go in order to secure Audrey's participation proved jaw-dropping; writer/director Garson Kanin (*Born Yesterday, Adam's Rib,*

My Favorite Wife) declared that he would give away the film rights to his novel *A Thousand Summers* if the purchaser would guarantee that Audrey would play the leading role of a diplomat's wife engaged in a romance with a country pharmacist. The prescription remained unfilled.

- *Romeo and Juliet* (1968). Directed by Franco Zeffirelli. With her tenderness, vulnerability, and iron will, Audrey would have made an intriguing Juliet, but she was thirty-nine at the time, and when she evinced no interest in the film, Zeffirelli reversed direction and cast the twenty-two-years-younger Olivia Hussey to great acclaim.

- *The Survivors* (1969). Based upon a Harold Robbins potboiler, the soapy plot did not interest Audrey, who was then in the first years of a self-imposed retirement; the story ultimately surfaced on television with Lana Turner starring as the matriarch of a rich Wall Street family.

- *Goodbye, Mr. Chips* (1969). A musical remake of the 1939 classic was bruited about as a possible co-starring vehicle for Audrey and Richard Burton. Cary Grant, with whom she had successfully co-starred in *Charade* six years earlier, was mentioned as another possible co-star for Audrey. Press items reported that Audrey would receive $1 million to take on the role of a former musical hall singer turned schoolmaster's wife. In the end, Audrey decided that she did not want to make another musical so soon after *My Fair Lady*, and the film was ultimately cast with Peter O'Toole and Petula Clark. Yet another attempt to cash in on the success of *The Sound of Music*, the film failed at the box office.

- *Father's Day* (1971), a comedy/drama about divorce, would have found Audrey playing a divorced woman alongside Elizabeth Taylor. Shirley MacLaine and Anne Bancroft were mentioned for other roles but the studios decided against filming a one-night Broadway flop, and the movie was never produced.

- *Jackpot* (1971) was to be directed by Audrey's old friend Terence Young. Audrey dropped out when she became pregnant with her second son, Luca. She was replaced by Charlotte Rampling (after leading man Richard Burton first asked Sophia Loren to take on the leading role). It proved a fortunate turn of events for both Audrey and Sophia, as the producers ran out of money after shooting commenced, and the film was abandoned midstream.

- *Nicholas and Alexandra* (1971). Based upon the highly successful book of the same name by Robert Massie, and with a screenplay by the Oscar-winning (*The Lion in Winter*) James Goldman, *Nicholas and Alexandra* was seriously considered by Audrey. With gowns, jewels, court intrigue, and a tragic death at the hands of a revolutionary firing squad, the role of Czarina Alexandra of Russia held juicy dramatic possibilities. Audrey, however, had doubts about whether she was age appropriate for the role, and when coupled with the fact that the film would be shot in Yugoslavia and Russia, and not Rome where she was then living, she regretfully turned down the film. British actress Janet Suzman landed the role and garnered an Academy Award nomination for her efforts.

- *40 Carats* (1973) would have starred Audrey as Anne Stanley, an upscale New York City realtor and "older woman" of forty, who is romanced by a younger man. Based upon the hit Broadway play of the same name, *40 Carats* was to co-star Edward Albert, the son of her *Roman Holiday* castmate Eddie Albert. William Wyler was slated to direct, and Audrey remained interested until the producers refused to film in Rome. When Audrey dropped out, so too did Wyler, and the film was ultimately and unmemorably produced with Liv Ullmann in the starring role and direction by Milton Katselas.

- *Family Portrait in an Apartment* (1974) was slated as an onscreen reunion with Burt Lancaster in a film to be directed by critical favorite Luchino Visconti. Hollywood columnists mentioned the film as a near certainty, with syndicated columnist Dorothy Manners explaining at the time that Audrey's decision to once again make movies had grown out of a discussion among her entire family. Husband Andrea Dotti, Manners reported, "has great admiration for her talent, their children are old enough not to need a mother's constant care, and besides, who ever said it's not fun being married to an active movie star?" Lancaster had already worked with Visconti on *The Leopard* (1963), and after *The Unforgiven* was eager to work again with Audrey, but while the film (eventually retitled *Conversation Piece*) reunited Lancaster and Visconti, Audrey, as usually happened at this point in her life, simply decided against a return to acting.
- *A Bridge Too Far* (1974), a World War II epic set in Audrey's native Netherlands. Audrey was approached about playing Kate ter Horst, the Dutch mother who turned her home just outside of Arnhem into a hospital for the Allies. Everything about the film rang too close to Audrey's own childhood memories of wartime violence; given her refusal to even watch war movies with her sons, the chances remained nonexistent that she would spend months of her life filming a war movie, let alone one set in her childhood backyard.
- *Lumiere* (1976), a film which Jeanne Moreau wrote expressly for Audrey. When Audrey declined the role of Sarah, a forty-ish actress living in Provence, Moreau played the role herself.
- *The Merry Widow*, to be directed by Ingmar Bergman. After proposed films with Otto Preminger and Luchino Visconti never materialized, Audrey was keen to work with the esteemed Bergman. She did not, however, like Bergman's script any more than she did the idea of shooting in Vienna while her young son Luca remained in Rome. Bergman subsequently approached Barbra Streisand, who liked the first half of the script but wanted the second half rewritten. Bergman declined, and the film was never produced.
- *Out of Africa* (1985). Approached to star in an adaptation of Isak Dinesen's *Out of Africa* (at that point titled *Silence Will Speak*), Audrey found the idea appealing enough to ask her friend Anna Cataldi, who had written the first draft of the film, to meet with her agent Kurt Frings. Said Cataldi of the meeting with Frings: "That was awful. He said 'You want to put my client in a stupid adventure movie? Forget it. Audrey will never do another movie.'" In the end, Cataldi ended up with a producer's credit when *Silence Will Speak*, retitled *Out of Africa*, was filmed with Meryl Streep, and went on to win the Academy Award for Best Picture. Says Sean: "My mother did later say to me that perhaps she should have done *Out of Africa*."

NEVER TALKED ABOUT BUT SHOULD HAVE BEEN

- Audrey as Daisy Buchanan in *The Great Gatsby*. With her throaty voice so full of hidden meanings, one can, even now, hear Audrey ruefully murmuring: "Rich girls don't marry poor boys, Jay Gatsby."

- A return to the theatre as the "Stage Manager" in Thornton Wilder's *Our Town*. Given her own life and personal philosophy, Audrey seemed to embody Wilder's thematic underpinnings that the aspects of daily life we take for granted represent the most precious parts of our lives.

INTERESTING MIGHT-HAVE-BEENS

- *No Bail for the Judge*, to be directed by Alfred Hitchcock for a 1959 release. Audrey would have starred as a lawyer working undercover as a prostitute in order to solve a murder involving her barrister father. The chance to work with Hitchcock intrigued Audrey and a contract was signed, but upon reading the completed script and realizing that she was to be nearly raped and strangled, she abruptly lost interest. With a fully executed contract already in place, it seemed impossible for Audrey to leave the film, but her subsequent pregnancy provided a loophole, as Hitchcock would have been forced to delay filming until Audrey had fully recovered from the birth of her child. This projected delay made the film impossible from both a scheduling and financial standpoint, and the production was permanently canceled.

  Audrey's aversion to violence was certainly the single biggest reason why the film was canceled, but other elements played a part as well: governmental powers in London told Paramount that the script's focus on prostitution ran counter to UK laws banning solicitation, and as a result, they would not allow location shooting in London. Leading man Laurence Harvey also dropped out, but a thoroughly dismayed Hitchcock continued to blame Audrey for the cancellation.

  In later years, Audrey mused to Sean that perhaps she should have done the film with as great a director as Hitchcock, but it's also likely that star and director might never have fully meshed. Analyzing Audrey's dislike of Hitchcock films, Robbie Wolders commented: "She thought they were too cynical."

- Kurt Frings proposed a sequel to *Roman Holiday* in which Audrey, now Queen Ann, and Gregory Peck, now a best-selling author, reconnect when her daughter and his son fall in love. However, the underlying rights proved to be extremely tangled, and the idea fell apart.

MOST INTRIGUINGLY OF ALL

- *The Turning Point* (1977). In a literate script by Arthur Laurents, Audrey would have played an aging prima ballerina who is replaced professionally by the daughter of her old friend (Shirley MacLaine). Set in the dance world that Audrey still loved, the film's mixture of ballet and romance, as well as the conflict between career and family, intrigued Audrey. However, she felt that at forty-eight she was too old for the part, and it was eventually played by Anne Bancroft. Son Sean shed light on Audrey's decision: "She loved the *Turning Point* script. But the film came along when she was feeling insecure after the breakup of her second marriage and she said to me that she was 'too young to be a grandmother but too old to be the love interest.' She no longer had the support system of discussing possible films with my father—that collaboration no longer existed. After seeing the film, she felt that Anne Bancroft did a terrific job, but that she also could have been very effective."

A critical and box office success, *The Turning Point* was ultimately nominated for eleven Academy Awards, including Best Picture.

TELEVISION

- At the time of *Gigi*, Audrey was asked to portray Gertrude Lawrence on Ed Sullivan's *Toast of the Town* television show. Lawrence's life story was eventually filmed as *Star!* with Julie Andrews in the leading role. Released in 1968 as the hoped for successful follow-up to *The Sound of Music*, *Star!* featured a hodgepodge of story and song which interested few, and the film bombed at the box office.
- Asked to star in a three-part television movie entitled *The Place to Be* (1979), Audrey seriously considered the offer, but NBC wanted her to sign a contract which included a provision for the movie to be turned into a weekly series. Uninterested in such a long-term commitment (which in any event never materialized), Audrey said no, and the role was played by Donna Reed.
- *The Thorn Birds* (1983). A highly publicized television "event" based upon the sprawling best-selling Colleen McCullough novel about life on an Australian ranch. Audrey turned down the role of family matriarch Mary Carson in the eight-hour miniseries because it would be shot in Hollywood, and Luca, not yet a teenager, was still living in Rome. The prime-time smash went on to score record high ratings, and Barbara Stanwyck, who played the role of Mary Carson, won an Emmy Award.

THEATRE

After working with Peter Bogdanovich on *They All Laughed*, there was some talk of Audrey returning to the theatre for the first time in thirty years, starring in a Bogdanovich-directed production of Noël Coward's *Private Lives*. The plan never came to fruition, nor did the idea of a film of Coward's *Hay Fever* co-starring Audrey and Michael Caine.

The idea of another Noël Coward stage production, *Blithe Spirit*, was also floated, and would have featured Audrey taking on the role of the dotty clairvoyant Madame Arcati. When Bogdanovich remarked that Margaret Rutherford had played that role, Hepburn smilingly replied: "Yes. She knew what the best part was." Bogdanovich may have been surprised by Audrey's interest in a role so different from those she normally played, but, he relayed, "she saw herself in it quite clearly." A hit 2009 Broadway revival of this sure-fire crowd pleaser saw Angela Lansbury win a fifth Tony Award for playing Madame Arcati, proof positive that Audrey's theatrical instincts remained undiminished.

There was simply no one else like her, a point underscored when millions of dollars were spent trying to recreate her star quality in both Audrey Hepburn biopics and feature film remakes of her greatest hits. To which the only possible reaction remained: Why?

Jennifer Love Hewitt portraying Audrey Hepburn as Holly Golightly. Hepburn's racer-back fitted-waist black evening dress became the gold standard for chic evening dresses after the film opened. Through no fault of her own, Hewitt proved no substitute for the real thing. ABC/Photofest © ABC.

Audrey, wearing one of Hubert de Givenchy's witty cocktail hats. Givenchy's early sense of humor was typified by his conversational fabric prints (often incorporating fruits and vegetables) and his amusing and unexpected cocktail hats. They gave a youthful air to the often stuffy world of French haute couture. Album/Alamy Stock Photo.

Chapter Forty-Three

ACCEPT NO SUBSTITUTES, 1987–2002

"Sydney Pollack's newly opened rehash of Sabrina seems not only superfluous but also painfully contrived."

—Michael H. Price, *Fort Worth Star-Telegram*

SUCH WAS THE DAZZLING EFFECT that Audrey had upon audiences from *Roman Holiday* right up through *Wait Until Dark*, that for the next sixty years Hollywood scrambled repeatedly and rather desperately to replicate her charm. Every one of the efforts was doomed to failure for the simple reason that no one stopped to analyze the one immutable truth at the heart of the enterprise: you can't clone a unique persona.

Exhibit number 1: a pedestrian 1987 television remake of *Roman Holiday* starring Catherine Oxenberg, a real-life Yugoslavian princess. The film might as well have carried the subtitle "just because you're a real princess playing a princess, doesn't mean it will work . . ." Tom Conti and Ed Begley Jr. in the Gregory Peck and Eddie Albert roles fared slightly better, but it all proved bland in the extreme. A hopeless undertaking from the get-go, it remains reminiscent of nothing so much as the extraordinarily unnecessary remake of *Ben-Hur* three decades later. Faced with these inferior remakes, audiences, understandably enough, had exactly one question: Why bother?

A 1995 remake of *Sabrina* directed by the estimable Sydney Pollack and starring Julia Ormond fell equally flat, and the presence of Harrison Ford and Greg Kinnear in the Bogart and William Holden roles made little difference. Kinnear came off the best of the trio by not forcing the issue, but Ormond registered as merely pleasant and vaguely charming, devoid of the necessary sparkle. She's beautiful, possesses a certain elegance and charm, and seems able to act, but she can't make it work. There is nothing in the least ethereal about Julia Ormond, and that lack flattens out the fable-like quality of the Cinderella story. Billy Wilder even came on board as a "consultant," but his idea that the screenplay should feature a bankrupt Larrabee company, with Sabrina's competition for David Larrabee's affections being the daughter of a prospective Japanese corporate raider, was ignored.

Wilder and Pollack did have lunch together, a meal during which Wilder provided an unasked-for review of Pollack's Oscar-winning *Out of Africa*: "That Africa movie you made—classy but boring." (Asked by Wilder how many Oscars he had won, Pollack replied "two," only to have Billy immediately shoot back: "I've got six.") Unlike *Out of Africa*, however, Pollack's remake of *Sabrina* proved no Oscar winner, and Wilder's distaste for the finished film was revealed in a conversation with director Cameron Crowe regarding remakes of his best-known films. After listening to a stranger's pitch about a proposed remake of *Sunset Boulevard*, Wilder offhandedly confided in Crowe: "Would Elizabeth Taylor be a good substitute for a new version of *Sunset Boulevard*, filmed against a fifties background? *I have no idea!!* I'm sure she would be no better or worse than the actress who played Audrey Hepburn in the remake of *Sabrina*."

In the end, this new version of *Sabrina* registered as nothing so much as a pro forma by-the-numbers copy. Ormond, who was touted in advance as the next big Hollywood star, never really recovered.

It proved the same story when Thandie Newton took on the role of Regina Lambert in *The Truth about Charlie* (2002), a very loose retelling of *Charade* (as well as partial homage to Truffaut's *Shoot the Piano Player*). It didn't help matters that Newton had Mark Wahlberg in the Cary Grant role, light charm not being Wahlberg's strong suit. Audiences remained resolutely uninterested.

Having failed with motion picture remakes of classic Audrey titles, Hollywood decided to take an even more direct step in 2000, with Jennifer Love Hewitt starring in the made-for-television *The Audrey Hepburn Story*. A slavish copy of the milestones in Audrey's life, it ultimately possessed little actual life itself, and audiences remained as indifferent to Hewitt playing Hepburn as they were to Nicole Kidman playing Princess Grace in 2014's *Grace of Monaco*.

Oxenberg, Ormond, Newton, and Love Hewitt—not without talent, but rather than float effortlessly, all four strode purposefully. The necessary quotient of magic was nowhere to be found.

Wearing a wing collar Givenchy skirt suit with three-quarter sleeves, Audrey takes a stroll with her mother, the always proper Baroness Ella van Heemstra. INTERPHOTO/Personalities/Alamy Stock Photo.

Chapter Forty-Four

WITH AND WITHOUT—LIFE WITH FATHER (AND MOTHER),
1929–1984

"I know my mother always used to say, 'Good things aren't supposed to just fall in your lap. God is very generous, but he expects you to do your part first.' So you have to make that effort."

—Audrey Hepburn

WHEN BEN GAZZARA HAD PROFESSED his love, only to disappoint and ultimately disappear, it all reopened wounds which had never fully healed, reminding Audrey once again that her father had neither attempted to contact her at the end of the war nor thought to even inquire about her welfare. Recollecting that difficult time decades later, Audrey said with tears in her eyes: "But maybe he didn't want to see me. His sense of discretion. . . . Perhaps I don't want to talk about it."

In a neat bit of self-analysis Audrey explained: "I do think there are things, experiences in childhood, that form you for the rest of your life," but it was Sean who summed up her fragile psyche with the greatest perception: "Well, she had feelings for all of us, yet she was never able to let go of her emotions or find peace within herself. She was truly scared on some level. The abandonment of her father was a wound that never truly healed. She never really trusted that love would stay."

In an attempt to heal that lingering wound, it was Mel who had, in the early 1960s, tracked down Joseph Ruston through the Red Cross. Finding Joseph in Ireland, Mel called him and arranged a private meeting between father and daughter at the famed Shelbourne Hotel in Dublin. Any fantasies Audrey might have still retained about a loving reunion with her father vanished in the face of the emotionally unavailable man she encountered. Said Sean about his mother's reaction: "I think she really hoped that like in a fairy tale he would jump from the seat in the hotel in Dublin with tears in his eyes and that would make up for what had happened. Instead, her father barely acknowledged her. She knew as soon as she saw him. I think she was devastated." It is a viewpoint echoed by Audrey's close friend John Isaac: "When she was telling me the story she was crying. She said he was so cold. He did not receive her. That really hurt her."

Writing further about the reunion in his own book, Sean explained: "It took my mother only a fraction of a second to understand. The man was frozen. He couldn't take a step, or lift an arm, let alone hug her. Not because of too much emotion—he was totally disconnected, as he had been for most of his life." The entire tale is summed up by a picture of Audrey with her father which appears in the family-approved *Audrey Hepburn Treasures*. Side by side with her father, she is smiling broadly, while he simply stares straight ahead at the camera. On the day of the reunion, when Mel returned to the Shelbourne at the agreed-upon time, Audrey simply told him: "We can go home now."

And yet, relates Sean, the reunion nonetheless created a sense of closure: "She realized it wouldn't have made a huge difference if he had been present in her life. He was an emotionally scarred man who couldn't express emotion and he never could have been the kind of father she wanted him to be. She realized that he was an emotional invalid, that he couldn't—he just didn't have the ability. She accepted it and that created closure. . . . She made peace with the whole experience."

So fractured had the relationship between father and daughter been throughout the years that it does raise the question of whether the rift had been made worse by Ella. Hepburn biographer Alexander Walker points out that Joseph himself claimed that throughout Audrey's childhood he had sent her letters which were never reciprocated, but also never returned to sender. If the letters had reached the intended address, had Ella intercepted the letters? Had she hoped to keep her daughter from suffering further disappointment in the face of James's unreliable nature?

At one point Joseph did state that Audrey sent him a telegram at Christmas of 1954, and that he had in fact visited La Paisible in later years. That claim is borne out by the recollection of Sean: "I did meet my grandfather when he came to Switzerland. I must have been five or six years old. He was a very serious man, very elegantly dressed—he wore a very nice, slightly tattered tweed jacket."

In the end, father and daughter did have intermittent contact after the difficult visit at the Shelbourne Hotel, and Audrey wrote him a letter in March of 1963 in which she talks of their too-long separation and how upset she was that her grandmother had given an interview about her to an Austrian newspaper: "I was terribly shocked to be somehow commercialized by my own grandmother at a time when I desperately wanted to be loved for myself."

For Audrey, such matters of the heart remained personal and not for public consumption. She undoubtedly would have been even more upset by the 2003 auction of a letter she wrote to her stepmother Fidelma in July 1980 during the last months of her father's life. Offered for sale by the Rendell Gallery in New York City, the letter is a rather open-hearted declaration of emotion by the fifty-one-year-old Audrey: "I have been struggling to find a way to come to see Daddy—but everything always happens at once! My mother is very ill too—I have been nursing her day and night, her heart is very bad and she has just had a third stroke. Added to all this my marriage is in bad shape so am suffering on all sides. I can only do the best I can."

Disappointment and all, Audrey quietly sent her father monthly checks for the final twenty years of his life. When word reached her that her father was dying, she did travel to Dublin once again, this time with Robert Wolders. Wolders related that Audrey found it "wonderfully ironic" that after a lifetime of looking down upon those of other races, her father was now being taken care of by a doctor from India. Even on his deathbed, however, this remote, austere man could not express any emotions to his daughter, talking instead about his horses. In Wolders's words: "It was very odd because he was on his deathbed, and when she went in to see him, she came out very disheartened—he had nothing really to say. And then he asked to see me. And then—and this was so miraculous—he proceeded to talk about Audrey and how proud he was of her. He knew I would be the conduit and that I would tell her, which I was more than happy to do."

His true feelings, it seemed, could only be expressed to and through others, only now able to explain "how much she meant to him, how he regretted not having been more of a father figure, and how proud he was of her."

Joseph Hepburn-Ruston died on October 16, 1980, at age ninety. The funeral was private, but in the view of Robbie Wolders, Audrey had by then made peace with her father's shortcomings: "What's important is that she had no bitterness toward him . . . She didn't hate him for his fascism, but she became what she was in reaction to it." As she told the *New York Times*: "I have hatred for no one, I must say. You can't if you have any common sense at all. You can hate any individual for what he or she does, but then we have to hate ourselves as well."

Just as her drive grew out of her father's absence, part of Audrey's self-effacement certainly seems to have stemmed from her complicated relationship with her mother. On the one hand, Audrey realized that without Ella's constant stage mother determination, she may not have accomplished all that she had on stage and screen. On the other, Ella's inability to express affection remained a constant frustration for her daughter. Only to others would Ella praise her daughter, albeit in a rather backhanded fashion; meeting Cecil Beaton at the time of *My Fair Lady*, she blithely told him that her daughter "lived on her nerves but was never any trouble: She just floats through life and learns everything herself."

Yes, it's praise, but being described as "never any trouble" is praise of a rather muted sort. This, after all, was a mother who commented upon her daughter's huge initial successes in *Roman Holiday* and *Sabrina* by exclaiming: "Considering that you have no talent, it's really extraordinary where you've got." Some young women would have crumpled under that smiling assault, but Audrey did not even feel her mother was putting her down, but rather helping to nudge her toward success: "And that's what I really believe to this day. I've always been self-conscious about interviews, about my thinness, my tallness, my unattractiveness. My success—it still bewilders me."

Pressed by a television interviewer about her mother calling her an ugly duckling, Audrey appeared startled and then smiled: "The ugly duckling grows into a swan—which didn't happen to me." To others she may have represented beauty and grace of the highest order, but in Audrey's own eyes, she remained an ugly duckling. The end result of Ella's edgy ugly duckling put-down? Audrey's smiling determination to show her mother that she was talented and deserving of both recognition and love.

It was, however, more than Ella's ill-chosen words and 1930s embrace of fascism that bothered her daughter throughout the decades. Instead, in the words of *Funny Face* screenwriter Leonard Gershe, who knew both women, it was Ella's natural inclination to walk into a room feeling superior to others that "embarrassed Audrey, who was exactly the opposite, and that was another one of the walls between them."

Whatever the conflicts between Audrey and Ella, and no matter the complications attached thereto, a loving bond nonetheless persisted, with Ella even moving into La Paisible in the latter part of her life. Explains Sean: "My grandmother lived in San Francisco until the 1980s when she couldn't live alone any longer. Unfortunately, in an attempt to save money, she did not renew her health insurance, so my mother had to pay for all of her medical care. She lived with us for the last ten years of her life." Ruminating further, Sean forthrightly explained: "It was strenuous when my grandmother came to live with my mother. How shall I put this? Their personalities were not well suited."

While she remained in good health, Ella managed the staff at La Paisible, and for all of her aristocratic exterior—in Sean's words Ella remained a "grande dame from another century"— she did prove a welcome, even exciting grandmotherly presence for the then still young Luca: "Ella was fantastic as a person. I grew up with her and I loved her. For a boy growing up, she was more fun than anything." Austere with Audrey, Ella proved anything but for her young grandson: "Ella was terrifying! When she would tell a creepy story, you would shake all night and love it, and ask her to tell it again the next day."

Whatever Audrey's problems with her mother, Ella had influenced her greatly, and nowhere more strongly than in Ella's insistence that even with her extraordinary worldwide fame, Audrey was no different, and certainly no better, than anyone else: "Never let yourself grow up believing that . . . anybody is any different from anybody else . . . we're all the same." It was advice Audrey carried with her for the rest of her life, and when the twenty-year-old Sean was leaving home in 1980 to work on the Terence Young film *Inchon*, Audrey put him on the plane with advice Sean remembers well: "Everybody is expendable and replaceable. So don't ever believe otherwise. Treat that job as if it's your last job and the most important one."

Audrey had lost her brothers Alex and Ian in 1979 and 2010, respectively (Alex's wife Miepje lived until 2006), but when Ella died on August 26, 1984, at age eighty-four, Audrey's reaction was one of gratitude for the extra time they had spent together in the last years of her mother's life: "I was very lucky to be able to take care of her, because I always think it's so sad when people have to die away from home."

In the end, said Sean, a definite bond existed between Ella and Audrey: "Close is not the way to describe it but they were tied to each other. They kept this daily pressure on each other. They had survived the war together . . . and when you go through something like that with whomever, you are sharing that for the rest of your life." Ella's death was, Audrey acknowledged, a devastating reversal: "I was lost without my mother. She had been my sounding board, my conscience. She was not the most affectionate person—in fact there were times I thought she was cold—but she loved me in her heart, and I knew that all along."

Love Among Thieves: A romantic Givenchy one-shouldered ruffled, long, evening beauty for Audrey's character, Baroness Caroline du Lac. This dress is a perfect example of Givenchy's late 1980s style of over-the-top femininity. Entertainment Pictures/Alamy Stock Photo.

Chapter Forty-Five

LOVE AMONG THIEVES, 1987

"Television's fast production pace is difficult but maybe it's better that way; you don't have time to think about things and ruin them!"

—Audrey Hepburn

AFTER ELLA'S DEATH, AUDREY DID make a brief return to the world of movies with a "talking head" appearance in 1986's fifty-eight-minute documentary *Directed by William Wyler*. The film, which featured her smiling recollection of how she had been scared into tears by Wyler on *Roman Holiday,* had been well received, was shown at film festivals and on Public Broadcasting System's *American Masters* television series, and even won honors at the Chicago Film Festival. But Audrey's appearance had been as blink-and-you'll-miss-her brief as those put in by other boldface names ranging from Bette Davis and Greer Garson to Laurence Olivier and Barbra Streisand, all of them eager to pay tribute to the famed director.

Now, however, with Sean age twenty-seven and Luca seventeen, Audrey acknowledged that it was not imperative she always stay at home, and she began perusing the scripts still continually coming her way. Although she did not land the role of New York society matron Alice Grenville in the television adaptation of her friend Dominick Dunne's *The Two Mrs. Grenvilles* (the role was played by Claudette Colbert), when the light romantic caper *Here a Thief, There a Thief* was proposed as a made-for-television movie, she said yes with little hesitation. Her co-star? The very popular Tom Selleck, then in the midst of an eight-year run in the hit CBS television series *Magnum P.I.*

When Selleck's participation proved impossible to schedule, an offer was made to Audrey's Gstaad friend and neighbor Robert Wagner. Recalls Wagner: "When Tom Selleck's participation didn't work out they came to me, and I jumped at it right away! I had known Audrey a long time—I actually met her when she first came to America. I was at Paramount working with Spencer Tracy on *Broken Lance* (1954) and she was working on *Sabrina*. I instantly liked her—in fact I adored her. Through the years I remained a big admirer of her work."

A devoted fan of Wagner's hit television series *Hart to Hart*, Audrey warmed to the idea of working with her friend in what she hoped would be a romantic caper in the vein of his earlier, popular series *To Catch a Thief*. Bolstered by a salary of $750,000, her role as classical pianist Baroness Caroline DuLac seemed to fit her own dictum that she would work again if it was "going to be fun, something cheerful." The picaresque plot featured the baroness stealing a Fabergé egg in order to save her kidnapped fiancé—and oh yes, somewhere in the midst of shootouts and concertizing, Caroline would be thwarted, saved, and romanced by the shadowy if attractive Mike Chambers (Wagner).

The plot did not bear close scrutiny, but all involved hoped that charm would rule the day. Audrey was game, not to mention top billed over Wagner and Jerry Orbach, but time away from the screen had not dimmed her self-deprecating take on her abilities: "I'm not a born actress, as such, but I care about expressing feelings." Co-star Wagner saw Audrey's talent in a much different light, enthusing: "Working with Audrey was one of the big highlights of my career. I thought she was a really exceptional actress. She was her own person, and her acting was an extension of that—she could access her own feelings. Incredibly professional. She was terrific."

If Audrey had found the filming of *Robin and Marian* rushed, it was downright leisurely in comparison to the August 1986 shoot for (the since-retitled) *Love Among Thieves*, a lightning-fast twenty-two days in Tucson, Hollywood, San Francisco, and the mountains of Dulce Agua, California. Said Wagner: "Fortunately we had rehearsed ahead of time, and we also had a terrific producer in Robert Papazian." The fast-paced schedule seemed to be reflected in the fact that Audrey did a lot of running throughout the movie; all that brisk walking in the Swiss Alps had served her well, but the plot was, to put it charitably, even weaker on film than on the page, with any chance of emotional involvement undercut by the comically evil stalker essayed by Jerry Orbach.

As happened with *Bloodline*, during *Love Among Thieves*'s slow patches, the main point of interest lies in Audrey's wardrobe. Although for most of the running time she is shown wearing one bland shirtwaist style dress, there are two Givenchy gowns onscreen during the opening and concluding scenes. The gowns are beautiful and Givenchy has not lost his touch, although one does idly wonder why a classical pianist would wear a hat throughout her concert. Said Wagner of the 1 a.m. filming of that concert scene in San Francisco's City Hall: "It was electric. When Audrey came to work, those two hundred people in the audience stood up and applauded before she even sat down at the piano. She was so beautiful. Such a marvelous, wonderful, woman."

As for the movie itself, Audrey proved a warm presence throughout, and Wagner, the star of three hit television series, remained a past master at pleasing an audience. The mechanics of the plot often proved forgettable, however, and while it was nice to see that Audrey could still float down imposing staircases with unearthly grace, the contrivances added up to a feeling that time had passed the genre by. In the end, *Love Among Thieves* registered as a junior varsity version of *Charade*, and while none of it was terrible, neither did any of it prove memorable.

When the film aired on February 23, 1987, the pairing of movie legend Audrey and television favorite Wagner proved a potent ratings draw. Reviews, however, were poor, with the *New York Post,* seemingly affronted by a lightweight television movie, loudly calling it "an unfortunate travesty." None of the harshness was directed at the two stars, and by this time critics, like the public, were simply glad for the chance to see Audrey once again on film; John O'Connor, writing in the *New York Times*, seemed to sum up the pervading feeling by writing: "Miss Hepburn, still lovely, though even more fragile than usual . . . deserves several more [Givenchy gowns] in a range of colors for having to trudge through this turkey."

Co-star Wagner continued his decades-long friendship with Audrey well after filming had wrapped: "I would see her a great deal—in Hollywood at Connie Wald's house, and in Switzerland with Julie Andrews and Blake Edwards. I loved her very much—she was one of the most extraordinary women I've ever known and Robbie Wolders, whom I'd known since he was under contract to Universal, was a very good person as well—a polite, genuinely nice man who was wonderful to Audrey. She was just such a good person, and her humanity was reflected in everything she did—in her clothes, her home, her flowers, her dogs and especially her children. I was not surprised in the least when she devoted herself to UNICEF—that's the kind of woman she was. She devoted so much of herself to that cause. In fact, she gave of herself so fully that I feel it affected her health and took a toll on her. There was so much travel and under such difficult conditions. But—she would do anything to help children all around the world."

Audrey had enjoyed herself making *Love Among Thieves*, and the film, whether critically acclaimed or not, had reintroduced her to tens of millions of viewers. But any lingering professional concern about *Love Among Thieves* soon vanished, because Audrey Hepburn was about to embark upon the hardest work and greatest achievement of her life.

ACT FOUR

WHAT MATTERS MOST

Her self-proclaimed "role of a lifetime" as a UNICEF ambassador, here in Ethiopia. Photofest.

Chapter Forty-Six

UNICEF, 1988–1993

"It's ironic that it was because of children that I stayed home all these years. Now it is for the sake of the children that I'm traveling all over the world."

—Audrey Hepburn

WITH MEMORIES OF HER OWN near starvation during the war still haunting the recesses of her mind, Audrey now began inching her way toward an increased commitment on behalf of poverty-stricken children, a commitment that accelerated after watching the 1985 Live Aid concert organized by rock star Bob Geldof. Startled and impressed by a worldwide audience of three billion donating $70 million, Audrey exclaimed to Luca: "This is a fantastic idea." She had in effect reached a tipping point: her name, she realized, could be used on behalf of the world's children, an illustration of the power of celebrity at its most potent.

In the Audrey Hepburn worldview, children constituted "our sacred charge." Her self-confessed need to give affection could now bear fruit on the widest possible stage: "I've always had enormous love of people—of children. I would pick babies up out of prams when I was young. . . . I had a desperate need to receive and give love. In fact, I think it is more important to give love than to receive it."

The adoring mother of two sons would now, through her efforts, seem as if she had "adopted the world's children." If years earlier, Billy Wilder had bluntly asked, "The difficulty with stars—what do they do if they are 50–55?," Audrey was now providing a thoroughly unexpected answer: embark upon the most meaningful work of one's life. Here, in Audrey's words, was the apotheosis of her own mother's training—"that wonderful, old-fashioned idea that others come first, and you come second. This was the whole ethic by which I was brought up. Others matter more than you do, so 'don't fuss dear; get on with it.'"

Explaining how his mother's commitment to UNICEF developed, Sean commented: "This decision grew first out of her own childhood under German occupation, with further seeds planted during her work on *Nun's Story*. The actual offer came about because my mother had a cousin Leopold (Quarles van Ufford) who was the consul for Holland in Macao. Every year they would hold an event to benefit UNICEF, and he'd ask her to attend. Finally she said yes, and agreed that she would serve as the host of their first International Music Festival. This was

October 1987—and the trip also included Hong Kong. She made a brief two-minute speech in Macao that was very well received.

"Jim Grant, whom I think of as the JFK of UNICEF—he took a postwar organization and brought it into the modern age while doubling the number of employees—had been in the audience in Macao. He said to my mother afterwards: 'You spoke so beautifully. Would you be interested in doing this again? You could make your own schedule.' That's how the actual offer came—she could now give back."

She traveled to Tokyo for a benefit concert given by the World Philharmonic Orchestra, her enduring appeal in Japan helping to ensure a highly successful turnout; audiences, she realized, might attend to see one of their favorite movie stars in person, but they would stay to learn about UNICEF's ability to transform the world, one child at a time.

Fluent in English, Dutch, French, Italian, and German, she was slowly but surely evolving into a citizen of the world, and her outlook on life changed accordingly; if an influential columnist wanted to discuss her classic films in a trip down memory lane, she'd comply—as long as it also meant publicity for UNICEF. "UNICEF means survival, development, and protection of children everywhere." She designed the first day of issue envelope for a set of UN stamps and would even sign photos of herself if the proceeds would flow to UNICEF: "It's now clear to me the reason I got famous all those years ago. It was to have this career, this new one." Said Sean: "My mother truly believed that the greatest crime was to rob a child of his or her childhood."

On Thursday, March 10, 1988, this devotion to giving back led her to follow in the steps of UNICEF activists Danny Kaye and Peter Ustinov and formally accept a job as special ambassador for UNICEF: "It's something I'd do for my child, so why not for others?"

Pronouncing herself thrilled with her new position, in a letter written to UNICEF chief of special events Horst Cerni, she enthused: "I am tickled pink by my little red U.N. passport!!!! UNICEF is keeping me going—and young." Her salary? One dollar per year. All expenses, except for travel and accommodations, were to be Audrey's. It was, she said, the greatest role of her career, the one she had "rehearsed for . . . all my life."

She was starting to harness the power which lay in both her worldwide fame and the enormous goodwill she had built up over thirty years. With an actor's instinct for the emotionally potent phrase, her trips began to generate worldwide press, a necessity for UNICEF, which did not receive any funds from the United Nations budget.

She undertook her first major trip in March of 1988, flying out of Geneva for a five-day tour of Ethiopia with only one carry-on and two suitcases—sufficient, she felt, for both field visits and press conferences. Audrey Hepburn, she of the jet set and ne plus ultra glamorous image, would be traveling by means of the most basic transportation: a Pilatus Porter PC-6 single-engine, single-wing, turboprop aircraft. In short, a utilitarian plane suited for the unpaved runways she and her fellow UNICEF workers would encounter on their flights throughout Ethiopia.

Accommodations were far from luxurious, but that proved to be of little concern. Recalling the hotel rooms in Ansara, Ethiopia, John Williams, executive secretary of the UNICEF board, noted: "She never complained [when] the hotel had no water." Nor did she balk at staying in a hotel that included armed guards in the lobby. Why, she was asked in interviews, would she put her life in danger by traveling to war zones. Her quick reply: "You just decide. Once you've decided, yes, I'll deal with it, then you don't think about it anymore." Audrey Hepburn was on a single-minded mission.

Her fame mattered to her only if it could help the children: "In the cities where there are some movie houses and people who have traveled abroad, they might be aware of who I am, but not where we went. I just hope that people at home will understand that once again there is a drought in Africa, in Ethiopia in particular, one which is potentially much worse than last time. UNICEF is already helping, is helping them to help themselves. What UNICEF wants to do is give them a spade to dig their wells, and not dig the graves of their children."

Politics did not interest her, and she refused to take sides in the grave political situation then ravaging Ethiopia, focusing instead upon how politicians could help the children in need. After the Marxist government launched into a critique of her efforts, she simply responded: "A child is a child is a child, whether his parents are Marxists or Nazis." The politics found in each country frustrated her: "Politics are something which are very hard for me to understand—the machinations are so complicated. . . . And responding to human suffering, that's finally what politics should be, ideally. That's what I dream about." Horrified by the fact that over forty thousand children a day died from preventable diseases and hunger, Audrey maintained one overarching goal: let the widest possible audience know about the unfolding disaster facing the world's children. "To save a child is a blessing: to save a million is a God-given opportunity."

It wasn't just politics she avoided but also organized religion; when offered the chance for an audience with Pope John Paul II, she turned it down because of her disagreement with the church's stance on birth control. Said Luca in later years: "She had never been a big fan of the Catholic Church—you know, give money so you can go to heaven." Instead, Audrey seemed to hold a deep belief in animism, telling Luca: "Nature is above the humans. We are not ruling the planet; we have to be *with* the planet."

The poverty she encountered in Ethiopia proved overwhelming, and the images of starving children seared themselves into her consciousness. When visiting a refugee camp, she glimpsed a young girl standing off by herself, and after slowly approaching the girl, asked what she wanted to be when she grew older: the answer came back: "Alive." The cumulative effect weighed on her: "The neglect and humiliation of a child by adults is a killer of trust, of hope, and of possibility." It was on this same trip, at an orphanage in Mekelee, that she met Father Chasade, a Catholic priest who spoke to Audrey with words that she came to repeat with increasing frequency over the years: "If you can't send me food for my children, then send me the spades to dig their graves."

Trip completed, Audrey undertook a grueling schedule of interviews to tell the world about the crisis in Ethiopia. After flying from Addis Ababa to New York City, she taped *Good Morning America*, spoke to two dozen reporters at UNICEF's New York headquarters, followed up the next day with appearances on *The Today Show*, *CBS This Morning*, *CNN Live*, and *Entertainment Tonight*, and topped off those efforts by taping four television appeals for the U.S. UNICEF Committee. As her commitment to UNICEF deepened, she could be counted on to rattle off statistics with precision and unending passion: there were, she forcefully stated, 5.6 billion people on earth, of whom 3 billion lived on less than 2 dollars per day, and 1.3 billion on under 1 dollar a day; 1.5 billion lived without clean water. In frustration she exclaimed: "Will it always be acceptable for their children to die of starvation and for our children to be fat?"

Traveling to Washington, DC, she met with U.S. senators and agreed to interviews with National Public Radio, the *Washington Post*, the *Washington Times*, and *USA Today*. Her energy seemed limitless when it came to UNICEF, and traveling to Canada the very next day, she agreed to interviews with two Toronto newspapers as well as the CBC, CBC radio, and CTV. Her globetrotting concluded with a trip to London, where in her numerous interviews she made her priorities clear: "I am not interested in promoting Audrey Hepburn these days. I am interested in telling the world about how they can help in Ethiopia and why I came away feeling optimistic."

Audrey Hepburn, movie star, fashion icon, and idol of millions, had found her purpose in life among the poorest and most neglected children on earth.

As an enormously effective public face for UNICEF, she helped raise heretofore unthinkable sums. Said the UNICEF photographer John Isaac: "Jim Grant told me they got $1 million in contributions every time she made an appeal on Barbara Walters or wherever. She made such a huge impression." Added Audrey's friend John Isaac, "that's what made her happy." Added Isaac pointedly: "Audrey had no color, no race." Said Sean: "She joined UNICEF and in 5 years UNICEF had doubled in size. I don't think that had happened since the war."

At the conclusion of her trip to Ethiopia, the United Nations reported that "during the Ethiopian crisis, a drive to raise $22 million for medicine, vaccines, and other non-food supplies was centered on her activities." In the words of former UNICEF USA CEO Caryl Stern: "There was a big rise in donations whenever she spoke. The American public—the whole world—was swayed by her voice, even after she died. In fact, after she died, when we had a huge gala in Dallas that was a tribute to Audrey and her legacy, it proved to be one of our most successful fundraisers ever. For quite some time we had an Audrey Hepburn Society, which was made up of those who gave gifts above a certain level. People would actually raise the amount of their donations just to become members of the Audrey Hepburn Society and have their own names affiliated with Audrey's."

Arriving home in Switzerland after her trip to Ethiopia, she spoke to a group of forty journalists from several different countries and gave one-on-one interviews to Swiss TV and France's Antenne2. She was exhausted, a bit depressed, full of stories, and in the words of close friend Doris Brynner, "completely done in." After only one trip, she already understood that she had arrived at a major turning point in her life: "I was so eager to go. I've been so privileged to be given this opportunity to do something for children. It's a marvelous happening for me that they are allowing me to do this. I'm happy to travel. For the children I'd go to the moon! It was a great relief for me because I've sat in front of the television and been frustrated. I had a pent up feeling of not doing anything, and now I can—it's a great relief."

Audrey had made the world pay attention to Ethiopia for the first time since Bob Geldof's Live Aid concert, and as a result, UNICEF promoted her from special ambassador to goodwill ambassador. Her star power, particularly at the black-tie galas designed to raise large sums of money, worked in ways that it never had for another celebrity, because part of what audiences responded to in her onscreen performances resulted from their knowledge of who she was as a person: sensitive, vulnerable, and genuinely caring. The audience collectively sensed that she understood issues of war, poverty, and health care because of her own childhood experiences, and they responded in kind with substantial donations.

Audrey Hepburn, people intuited, was the furthest thing from a celebrity dispensing help out of a distanced sense of noblesse oblige. In her own words: "The 'third world' is a term I don't like very much because we're all one world. I want people to know that the largest part of humanity is suffering."

Said Caryl Stern: "Audrey was, along with Danny Kaye, one of the original ambassadors, and everyone knew it was real—she had great credibility and set a standard for all future ambassadors. At UNICEF, we in effect want to date before marrying—we want to know the celebrity means it and is devoted. I would take them to the field, on an actual trip, before the affiliation became official; they had to speak 'kid'—they had to be real. Because you have to get on your hands and knees, not worry about makeup, and you have to deal with the heat of Africa. There are bugs, snakes, smells, flies—you must want to be there because when you're in the field, the field has no idea who the celebrity is, and there are no creature comforts. No one is carrying your bag, there is no five-star hotel, and you're not traveling on a private plane. I can tell on the first day whether or not they will make it, and Audrey's dedication was one thousand percent. We never want to diminish the honesty and integrity that Audrey brought to the organization. All those that followed had to rise to the level of commitment she set."

Although Audrey never could fully comprehend the nature of her appeal, in a lengthy 1990 television interview about her career, she came the closest she ever would to understanding how her persona appealed and helped to raise funds for UNICEF: "I have an enormous love for humanity and for the human qualities in people when they come out—that perhaps is what has come through off the screen to the public."

There was one additional key reason for Audrey's effectiveness as a UNICEF ambassador: she did her homework for each trip, studying the political, economic and agricultural situation in each country she would visit: "It's not even enough to know there has been a flood in Bangladesh and seven thousand people lost their lives. Why the flood? What is their history? Why are they one of the poorest countries of today?"

As she gained in experience, she hit upon a formula to further increase her effectiveness: she would travel to Guatemala or Bangladesh and then follow up with a trip to the United States, Canada, or Europe in order to speak out, raise funds, and stress the urgency of her mission. She still did not like speaking in public, and close associates from both UNICEF and Hollywood noted that her knees would literally knock before delivering a speech. Yet when it came time for her to speak about UNICEF, she would walk purposefully to center stage and quietly, with great command, deliver her message. Said Robbie Wolders: "Even though I knew the text of every speech she gave for UNICEF I was sometimes moved to tears when I heard her deliver it. She exuded such purity, innocence, and vulnerability, and at the same time, utter conviction. It made me tremendously proud."

Each of her trips placed her in extraordinarily difficult situations, yet her drive seemed unstoppable. The March 1988 trip to Ethiopia had been followed in October of that same year by trips to Ecuador and Venezuela. The whirlwind trip to Venezuela included stops at Barinas, Caracas, and Quito and culminated in a visit with the country's new president, Rodrigo Borja Cevallos. It proved an especially difficult trip for two reasons: (1) For the first time, Audrey found that there were limits to press interest in her UNICEF trips. In the view of the media, poverty in Venezuela simply did not merit the same attention as the unfolding famine in Ethiopia. (2) Audrey came face-to-face with the overwhelming issue of street children who had either been abandoned by parents or were forced to earn money for their families. Runaways preferred a life on the streets to homes plagued with violence, and, she learned, a horrifying sex industry for children as young as nine years old proved widespread. Said Robbie: "Eventually what affected her even more than those children who were suffering of hunger or disease were the thousands upon thousands of children that we saw who had lost their parents, who had nothing to relate to, who had no affection. That was something she could relate to even more."

As a follow-up to these trips, UNICEF scheduled Audrey for travel to Turkey. Though she had been well prepared for the trip to Ethiopia, she was determined to be even more thoroughly informed about Turkey, and to that end, UNICEF's Christa Roth came to Tolochenaz with briefing papers. It was, in essence, a combination tutorial, boot camp, and university exam, but Audrey Hepburn wanted facts and figures. Thoroughly prepared, she traveled to Turkey in April of 1989 to promote the benefits of immunization in combating the six main childhood diseases of measles, tuberculosis, tetanus, whooping cough, diphtheria, and polio. Striving to mix positive news in with the disheartening reports about widespread childhood illness, she noted that of the forty thousand children who die worldwide every day, thousands of those lives could be saved simply through immunization. Speaking proudly of her trip to Turkey she explained: "It took us ten days to vaccinate the whole country—not bad."

Audrey may not have liked politics, but savvy she was, and with an eye on future governmental help, she went out of her way to praise the Turkish government as well as the country's radio and television stations for the success of the inoculation campaign. (In an amusing sidenote to the trip, Turkish television was showing *My Fair Lady* in Audrey's honor, and since Robert Wolders had never seen the film, Audrey agreed that they would watch it; their viewing did not last long, given that the entire film—with the notable exception of Marni Nixon's singing—was dubbed in Turkish.)

Although her own suffering during World War II was an oft-told and well-known story, she refused to equate her own deprivations with those she observed firsthand in Africa, and she consistently downplayed her own childhood trauma: "My suffering is not comparable; yes, we had German occupation, long winters, malnutrition, in fact high degree of malnutrition, but my life was never in danger. It is if the war had gone on that my health might have been impaired." Her wartime experiences may have influenced her dedication to UNICEF, but, she emphasized, it constituted "more than paying a debt. I would have done the work even if I had not known war."

UNICEF had become the total focus of her working life, playing out if she had taken to heart the words of playwright Edward Albee while discussing his surprising admiration for Thornton Wilder's *Our Town* as the greatest play ever written by an American author: "When it is done properly it makes us understand that if we don't live our lives fully and completely, we've wasted everything we have." Audrey not only wanted to live her own life fully, but she was also insistent that the world's children be afforded the opportunity to do the same, that those in power not waste the abundance they had been given.

February 1989 found her making a trip to Guatemala, Honduras, El Salvador, and Mexico. The trip to Mexico included stops in remote villages where she could publicize both new water systems and oral rehydration therapies, but it was El Salvador that proved particularly daunting, with the trip coming at an unfortunately violent time in the country's history. Estimates of the number of men, women, and children—including priests and nuns—who had been murdered over the past decade ran as high as seventy thousand. And yet Audrey did not hesitate: the trip was necessary, end of discussion. Said Horst Cerni: "Audrey was never concerned about her personal safety. She felt being on a mission for UNICEF and the suffering children in a particular country provided an unseen shield from dangers. All her missions were dangerous."

It was all a long way from a pampered Hollywood set but fulfilled a need in Audrey that Hollywood never could, and in order to publicize her work for UNICEF, she finally agreed to an interview with Barbara Walters, one of several journalists who had relentlessly pursued her for years. In an interview which reached over ten million United States households, she talked a bit about Hollywood, but what she really wanted was to publicize UNICEF: "I can personally do very little, but I can contribute to a whole chain of events—which would be UNICEF. And that's a marvelous thing. It's like a bonus to me towards the end of my life."

In 1989 she flew with Robbie to Sudan, the biggest country in Africa and one racked by civil war, armed bandits, a measles epidemic, and starvation. A meeting with Prime Minister Sadiq al-Mahdi preceded a trip to the White Nile for the start of Operation Lifeline Sudan, but nothing had quite prepared Audrey for her next stop, the refugee camp El Meiram.

El Meiram, crammed with thousands of starving men, women, and children who were wracked by dysentery, represented a terrible new iteration of the famine that had plagued Ethiopia, and when Audrey spoke to the press, she did not hide her anger: "They have nothing left—not even their bodies. They are so emaciated. It seems that all they have left are their souls." Even her travel conditions, minimalistic at the best of times, grew worse in Sudan; flying on a Cessna at night with some journalists, Audrey was handed a flak jacket—not to wear, but to sit on, should bullets or rockets strike the plane directly through the fuselage.

After her trip to war-torn Sudan, she testified in April 1989 before the U.S. House Foreign Operations Sub-Committee and House Select Sub-Committee on World Hunger. She grew blunt: "There is no deficit in human resources. There is only a deficit of human will." Nervous but determined, she spoke from handwritten notes detailing the building of dams in Ethiopia and water systems in Ecuador, literacy efforts in Guatemala and immunization in El Salvador—all of the efforts funded by UNICEF: "So, Mr. Chairman, I am here today to speak for children who cannot speak for themselves, children who are going blind from lack of vitamins, children who are being slowly mutilated by polio, children who are wasting away through lack of water, for the estimated 100 million street children in the world . . ." In Sean's recollection: "When she testified before the U.S. Congress regarding a humanitarian crisis, she got $60 million in one hour from them. That showed how extraordinarily powerful she still was."

Two months later, on June 13, she delivered a powerful address to members of the United Nations staff in Geneva and once again pulled no punches: "When the impact becomes visible in the rising death rates among children, then what has happened is simply an outrage against a large section of humanity. Nothing can justify it." Yes, the vagaries of nature could and did exacerbate problems, but Audrey placed the majority of the blame squarely on the shoulders of her fellow man: "Whether it be famine in Ethiopia, excruciating poverty in Guatemala and Honduras, civil strife in El Salvador, or an ethnic massacre in the Sudan, I saw but one glaring truth: these are not natural disasters but man-made tragedies for which there is only one man-made solution: peace."

In her own words, Audrey was always willing to keep "talking my head off" in search of money because, in her memorable phrase, "The worst violence in Africa is widespread poverty."

In search of maximum impact, her message of urgency was stripped down to the most basic of analogies: "[If] a child has been hit by a car, at that moment you don't stop and wonder whose fault it is—was the driver going too fast, or did the child run after his ball? You just pick him up and run all the way to the hospital."

For field trips into poverty-stricken countries, Audrey wore a uniform of khaki slacks, Lacoste shirts, scarves and sunglasses, minimalism at work in service of the greater good. Dressed in basic black for media appearances, she wore the same outfit multiple times, pressed her own clothes, and did her own hair and makeup. One look at her television appearances to publicize her work for UNICEF tells even a casual viewer all they need to know about changed priorities: Givenchy's favorite model, the paragon of Parisian chic, was now dressed down in casual, comfortable clothes, with no sense of fuss in sight. She was uninterested in turning an interview into any sort of celebrity retrospective and spoke about her movies only as a quid pro quo for holding a conversation about the needs of children around the world. "Are we not reaping the mess we made so many years ago when we enriched ourselves? We didn't do a hell of a lot for those people, did we? That's why it's right that we do now."

After a lifetime of being pampered for life in front of the camera, she had ceased dwelling on her appearance. Age spots on her hands? Fine—let them show. Long gone were the days of traveling with fifty bags and trunks, all of them packed with her china, linens, and designer clothes. All personal trappings were subordinated in service of the message, a lesson unfortunately not learned by the well-meaning Sophia Loren in her work for the United Nations. Loren, who had herself suffered tremendous deprivation in Italy during the Second World War, seemed strangely oblivious to the optics of her UN work, and arrived for her appointment ceremony as a UN goodwill ambassador in a Rolls-Royce that matched the color of her fur coat.

Audrey remained modest about her own contribution, thinking of herself as a concerned citizen, nothing more. In fact, she was far more than a concerned citizen, and her reach and impact amongst Hollywood activists has been, through the years, rivaled only by Angelina Jolie's. Unlike Audrey, Jolie had not basically retired when she began her work for the UN, but she also possessed Audrey's skill at utilizing the press for the purposes of her charitable work. Jolie shared Audrey's rock-ribbed dedication to the safety and education of children, and with the honorary damehood personally bestowed upon her by Queen Elizabeth in 2014, she had completed a strikingly successful metamorphosis from a much-married woman who wore a vial of her ex-husband's blood around her neck to St. Angelina in khakis.

There was one caveat in all of Audrey's appeals, however. UNICEF could and would provide the necessary tools, but the key work for any project would be done by the citizens of the country in question: it was their land, their labor, and their pride of place. She had sounded this theme of self-sufficiency as far back as that first trip in Ethiopia: "I am very impressed by the people of Ethiopia, by their beauty, by their patience and by the enormous desire, their enormous will to help themselves." Of her Latin American trip in 1989, she noted with pride: "I watched boys build their own schoolhouse with bricks and cement provided by UNICEF."

In visiting as many countries as possible, touching and picking up endless babies no matter how gravely ill, in spreading the word before indifferent and often hostile governments, she had at last found the enormous family she had always wanted. Said John Isaac, who accompanied her on many of her UNICEF missions: "Often the kids would have flies all over them, but she would just go hug them . . . other people had a certain amount of hesitation, but she would just grab them. Children would just come up to hold her hand, touch her—she was like the pied piper." More than ever she fully led with her heart; on her trips, explained Isaac: "Dignity and love were what we always talked about. With the sufferings she went through, she always said, 'I love you' and would never hold back with the children."

Audrey was now routinely referred to as a saint for her efforts, a compliment she did not particularly enjoy; if she was thought of as a saint, then that made her code of conduct virtually unattainable for others, and she wanted everyone to know that they too could contribute to saving children. If she was a saint, then she was a saint who was riddled with self-doubt, one who could even occasionally grow short-tempered when faced with bureaucratic intransigence. Always considering herself a work in progress, she consistently brushed aside any praise for her work: "After all, I am doing only what any other human being would do." Most human beings did not, of course, travel the globe to work in war-torn countries, and as the months went by, she, like members of Doctors Without Borders and Partners in Health, succeeded in becoming part of a rare humanitarian band who neglected any personal comfort in order to help those lacking even the most elemental resources.

Following her trip to Latin America, October of 1989 found her flying to Australia to personally plea for continued UNICEF funding. Thanks to her presence at a dinner in Parliament House, $2 million was raised in a single day. Said Ian MacLeod of the Australian Committee for UNICEF: "It was like having your favorite aunt arrive. No airs, no pretenses; just an incredible amount of grace, sincerity, and love."

The trip to Australia and Asia included time in Bangkok for a meeting with human rights activist Prateep Ungsongtham Hata, and most notably, a stop in flood devastated Bangladesh. Henry Kissinger had famously termed Bangladesh a "basket case," and Audrey was determined to send a different message. Explained John Isaac: "With Bangladesh—people had given up and she said 'That's where I want to go. Those are the people I'd like to go and support.'" Visiting orphanages, a Dhaka slum, and the remote northern Bengali countryside, Audrey drove herself relentlessly. Close friend Anna Cataldi instantly understood her friend's motivation: "She realized the vastness of the tragedy. In a sense you're marked by that. She wanted to go back and back and back. In a way it's an addiction."

She still popped up with the occasional show business appearance, but it was always with UNICEF in mind. In September she served alongside Harry Belafonte as host of the first International Danny Kaye Awards in the Netherlands, and two months later, agreed to be the guest of honor at the Dutch Filmhuis Den Haag for a screening of *Funny Face*. Still underplaying her own extraordinary screen legacy, and calling herself "an actor by chance, nothing more, nothing less," it was her presence, along with a Sotheby auction of three dresses, including one designed by Givenchy, that raised $50,000 for UNICEF.

By now she was feeling the strain of her exhausting schedule and in 1990 reached out to Roger Moore, whom she had known since both had small parts in 1951's *One Wild Oat*, to see if he would possibly take over as UNICEF goodwill ambassador. Five years removed from his last outing as James Bond in *A View to a Kill*, Moore agreed, beginning his partnership with Audrey in August of 1990 when they co-hosted the Second Annual Danny Kaye Awards. Said

Moore: "When one of the world's great beauties calls you and asks if you would like to go somewhere with her, what do you say? No? Of course not! You ask where and when?"

Not yet well-informed about UNICEF, Moore tried to beg off the obligatory press conference, but a no-nonsense Audrey simply replied: "Roger. The Press will not want to talk about UNICEF; they will want to talk about movies!" Audrey was correct, but in Moore's admiring recount: "She wouldn't let them. Every question that was asked, Audrey turned around to the problems facing the world's children." Moore's admiration for Audrey soon grew to the point that he took to ending all of his own solo theatre appearances by reciting Audrey's favorite poem "The Beauty of a Woman," followed by an announcement that UNICEF collection buckets would be available in the theatre lobby.

Hope remained the currency in which she traded, and while her gracious manner may have remained intact, when speaking truth to power she refused to sugarcoat: "Donor fatigue and compassion fatigue just cannot apply to the monumental suffering in the developing world today—the only true fatigue is that of a mother seeing yet another one of her babies die."

Mustering the energy for a few final trips, on October 26, 1990, accompanied by *Time* magazine photographer Peter Charlesworth and two television cameramen, she hopped into an old Sikorsky helicopter and landed in Vietnam's northern province near the Chinese border. After touring a village water system—she was shown priming a pump, splashing her face with clean water, and pointedly noting that "the wells have all been made by the Vietnamese themselves"—she visited a school and spent time at a health center, more than happy to wear the skirt and blouse of the Tay people; no clothing could have been further from the rarified world of Givenchy, which is precisely why Audrey knew that photographs of her wearing a native outfit would generate widespread publicity. Emphasizing UNICEF's role in trying to provide sorely needed schoolbooks and medicines, she returned to one of the themes that underlay all of her work—UNICEF would help provide tools, but all of the hard work could and would be accomplished through self-determination: "What's extraordinary about Vietnam and its people is that unlike some of our countries, there may be a deficit of resources but not of will."

Always hungering to do more, she now admitted: "I'd like to be in the field and maybe vaccinate and operate like young doctors, but I can't." Operate she could not, but her contribution remained enormous and life altering: the widespread media coverage of her travels meant that during the years she worked for UNICEF, gifts to the U.S. Committee for UNICEF doubled.

The overwhelming irony underlying this unceasing work on behalf of UNICEF lay in the fact that stardom, the most narcissistic of occupations, now allowed her to perform the most selfless of acts. In the perfectly attuned words of one commentator: "The child became the adult who reached back to help the child."

Even as she grew increasingly exhausted, her endless drive derived from a determination to penetrate the world's indifference: "250,000 children die every week. It's the greatest tragedy of our time. It must stop." Asked by television talk show host Larry King why she didn't work, she instantly replied: "This is my work, Larry!" And while she always expressed gratitude for her time in Hollywood, it remained impossible to find her speaking about a film in the same excited tones she utilized when telling interviewers: "Last year we provided 52 million schoolbooks for Bangladesh, and in the last eight years we have sunk 250,000 tube wells."

Stanley Donen, so often ready with an acerbic comment, gave Audrey a rather backhanded compliment about her UNICEF work by exclaiming: "Never in a million years would I have predicted that Audrey would give so much, so selflessly and at such personal cost to a cause like UNICEF." It was, however, the equally opinionated Rex Harrison who surprisingly took the opposite viewpoint, explaining: "No, it's just the sort of thing she would do. . . . She understands the urgency of hunger and deprivation in a personal immediate way."

How did she keep going? How did she manage the sheer logistics of flying around the world into countries that often had no infrastructure? As Audrey was the first to admit, her constant travels on behalf of UNICEF were only possible with the help and support of Robert Wolders, who was soon appointed by UNICEF as her manager. By now Audrey and Wolders were life companions, and the pleasant irony underlying their devotion to UNICEF lay in the fact that when they first met, the last thing that would have been on either of their minds was globe-trotting work for UNICEF. Instead, their initial meeting proved to be a pleasant conversation between two Dutch survivors of World War II, each a disillusioned yet still hopeful romantic.

In meeting Robert Wolders, Audrey Hepburn, who craved control as much as she did love, who had organized and compartmentalized for decades on end, had for the first time in her life finally moved from one beat to the next without hesitation. After a lifetime of worry and care, she was, once and for all, about to exhale.

Audrey in Givenchy's bejeweled off-the-shoulder bodice cerise silk skirt gown. Givenchy's flair for color and drama was evident in this Spanish Infanta-inspired stunner. Media Punch Inc./Alamy Stock Photo.

Chapter Forty-Seven

ROBBIE, 1979–1993

"We were ready for each other. . . . At the time in our lives that we met, we had both made our mistakes."

—Robert Wolders

WHEN AUDREY MET ROBERT. A genteel Dutch-centric meeting of two sensitive, extraordinarily good-looking people that ended up providing Audrey with the love of a lifetime when she least expected it.

If *Gigi* and *Roman Holiday* had found Audrey Hepburn the right girl in the right place at the right time, then when he met Audrey, Robert Wolders was himself the right man at the right place at the right time. Nine years Audrey's junior, Wolders had lived happily with his twenty-five-years-older wife, the beautiful movie star Merle Oberon, until her death in 1979 at age sixty-eight. It had been a loving and fulfilling relationship, and when Oberon lay dying, she had said to Wolders: "You owe it to me to be happy, to restart your life."

In the many myths surrounding Audrey's life, Oberon's statement has been reshaped as "You owe it to me to be happy and remarry," as if Oberon had presciently ordained that Wolders would meet and marry Audrey. No, Oberon had not foreseen Audrey and Wolders falling in love, but she and Audrey had met several times and liked each other, and in a startling piece of Hollywood synchronicity, Audrey's role of Karen Wright in *The Children's Hour* had been played by Merle in *These Three*, the original film made from Lillian Hellman's play.

Audrey and Wolders's first meeting came in February 1980 over dinner at the home of Audrey's friend Connie Wald. Connie's home constituted home base for Audrey whenever she traveled to Los Angeles, and their friendship endured until Audrey's death. Said Wald: "She was such a fabulous lady. There was never anyone like her. I simply loved her. We had common tastes. We both loved our houses, our families. We both liked to cook. . . . All she really wanted was to have dinner in the kitchen, not even in the dining room." So comfortable did Audrey feel at Connie's home that, in Connie's recall, at one point while planning to build a home in Los Angeles, Audrey had an architect come to the Wald home "so he could design a smaller version of our house for her in L.A."

The comfortable setting of Wald's home had resulted in a conversation between Audrey and Robert Wolders that lasted throughout the entire dinner, leading to the discovery that they had lived within thirty miles of each other in Holland during the war. Said Wolders of that meeting: "The first night I met her I was struck by her wistfulness and her fragility." Audrey's memory was similarly guarded: "I was charmed with him that night but he didn't register that much. We were both very unhappy."

Six months later, Connie Wald stepped in as matchmaker, urging Wolders to call Audrey when he had to fly to New York, where Audrey was filming *They All Laughed*. Audrey and Wolders met for dinner at the Pierre Hotel, which led to long phone calls after Wolders returned to Los Angeles. Wolders humorously recalled that he "found out later that she had me in mind for her ex-sister-in-law." But their talks grew ever longer until "one day she called, and afterward I said, 'That's it, I have to go to New York.'"

With Audrey still officially married to Andrea Dotti, the relationship remained private. Wolders visited Tolochenaz, but it was only in 1981, after Audrey formally separated from Dotti, that they both decided Wolders should move into La Paisible. Explained Wolders: "When her divorce became final, we were together all the time. It seemed so natural." Looking back in later years he analyzed: "We had the good fortune to find each other, and I had gone through some bad stuff as well. We had no friction or hardships, really, except for some of the petty things which were easily settled." Their relationship was, he said, "a wonderful friendship. . . . We're both patient."

It was their mutual devotion to UNICEF that further helped to anchor their relationship, because Wolders, who years earlier had arranged a charity auction of the valuable jewelry left to him by Merle Oberon, spent nearly as much time on the charity as did Audrey. Explained Audrey: "Robert is just as passionate about children and UNICEF as I am." Wolders himself later analyzed their team effort: "For five years we did at least seven months of work for UNICEF—field trips and fund raising events all over the world."

It was Robert who took care of all travel arrangements, hotel reservations, booking of planes, and ground transportation, often in countries which possessed only the most rudimentary infrastructure. To that end, it remained a point of honor for both Audrey and Wolders to never fly first class; at best, they might buy each other business class tickets as a special treat, but, pointed out Sean: "Throughout our youth she had traveled economy all over Europe. She felt that in a day and age when so many people were going hungry, it was inappropriate to fly first class."

Sean and Wolders bonded easily, but Luca, ten years younger than his brother and used to having his father as the leading man in his mother's life, took longer to warm up to the actor. Wolders did, however, win over the toughest critic of all, Audrey's mother Ella. Said Audrey: "She opposed both my marriages, maybe knowing neither man was going to be totally good to me. But I must say, she adored Robbie."

Wolders's gentle manner and Dutch background softened Ella's formidably austere exterior, yet he too found it striking that even at this late juncture, Ella could not bring herself to freely express her love for Audrey, deep though it was. In the symbiotic relationship between mother and daughter, Ella now relied upon Audrey financially, but Audrey, still seeking her mother's approval, depended upon Ella from an emotional standpoint. The relationship remained complicated until the very end, not only because of Ella's emotional reticence and aristocratic manner but also because of Audrey's lingering resentment about her mother's flirtation with the Nazis. Said Luca: "Now I've come to understand that the underlying reason for all that was rooted in the political past of my grandmother. My mother had a very clear black-and-white, good-and-bad notion about the whole Nazi era."

It was Robbie who helped bridge the gap between mother and daughter: "[Ella] would use me as a conduit because she knew I would convey all that she felt to Audrey." At the same time, the relationship between Audrey and Robbie's mother Cemelia remained happily and noticeably uncomplicated, and Audrey took to calling Cemelia "Maman."

Life with Robbie provided Audrey with the romantic match she had been seeking throughout her life, but any thoughts of "if only I had met him sooner" were quickly pushed aside by her practical nature. With a perspective honed by five decades of living, she rationalized: "If I'd met him when I was 18, I wouldn't have appreciated him. I would have thought 'That's the way everyone is.'"

For the first time in Audrey's life there was now a day-in-and-day-out steadiness in her romantic relationship, one informed by a quality of trust and caring. In Audrey's view: "If a man has the indefinable quality that I can only call 'warmth' or 'charm' then I'll feel at ease with him." She found Wolders "very loving, he's a very affectionate man. I can trust him, I trust his love. I never fear that I'm losing it." Mel Ferrer had loved the Hollywood action, the hum and buzz of deal making, and Andrea Dotti thrived upon the glamorous circus that constituted life in Rome, but Wolders, like Audrey, felt most comfortable in the quiet rural life found at La Paisible.

So strong was their mutual attachment to home that Audrey planned each UNICEF trip to make sure that they were never away from their four Jack Russell terriers for more than two weeks; she had, in fact, given Robbie one of the terriers—"Tuppy"—for his fiftieth birthday because he had never had his own dog. Explained Audrey contentedly: "In the evenings we are very homey. We're mostly vegetarian because we don't need the protein at our age. I don't drink wine, but I like my little Scottish whisky before dinner. We have a television set in the bedroom and after dinner it's curl-up time, either watching a programme, a video or reading. I'm always asleep by 11 p.m."

Marriage was not in the cards because neither Audrey nor Wolders felt any need. Declared Audrey: "We're happy as we are," and Wolders bluntly analyzed her previous marriages as a cautionary tale: "Everyone knows how unhappy her marriage to Mel was, and the second, to Andrea, was even worse. It would be like asking someone who has just got out of an electric chair to sit back on it again." Fashioning a life in which they took care of, and seemed to complete, each other, Audrey and Wolders kept separate bank accounts and enjoyed nothing more than staying home. Peter Bogdanovich did write that "there reportedly were troubles toward the end," but Audrey seemed happy with Wolders, and in Sean's view, "although their relationship was not without small tensions and disagreements, what they had shared through the UNICEF years would probably have been enough to carry them through to the end of their lives."

Said Jeffrey Banks: "The extraordinary thing about Audrey was that men always wanted to protect her—to shield her from all the bad in the world. That was what I wanted to do starting at age eleven. But Rob's the one who truly did it."

Dressed simply in a white cotton Aran-like cable sweater and plain white cotton narrow slacks for her role as an angelic spirt in *Always*. To keep her wardrobe spotless, she was carried to the set, arriving, in the words of director Steven Spielberg, "like the princess she had always been in all of our dreams." Picture Lux/The Hollywood Archive/ Alamy Stock Photo.

Chapter Forty-Eight

ALWAYS, 1989

"And in a cameo as the heavenly sage who sends Dreyfuss back to earth, Audrey Hepburn is incandescent. Her dialogue is treacle, but she sells it with an effortless grace that shows why she is still a legend at sixty."

—Peter Travers in *Rolling Stone*

HAPPY IN HER LIFE WITH Robbie, and thoroughly devoted to her work on behalf of UNICEF, Audrey had made only one television movie—*Love Among Thieves*—in the six years since the 1981 release of *They All Laughed*. Which is why, in 1989, movie lovers were very pleasantly startled at the news that Audrey Hepburn was returning to films. And not just in any jerry-rigged vehicle, but rather in a remake of the beloved 1943 classic *A Guy Named Joe*. Who would be overseeing her return to the big screen? The king of Hollywood himself, Steven Spielberg.

A superstar in his own right, Spielberg courted Audrey unceasingly, and in June of 1989, with production of his film already underway, he plaintively wrote her: "In any case, whether or not you would decide to join our family in the last weeks of production, it is a tremendous thrill for me to make this offer." (Once a fan, always a fan—after working with Audrey, Spielberg purchased the rights to a script written by the then unknown Ryan Murphy, entitled *Why Can't I Be Audrey Hepburn?*; although never filmed, the story centered around a news anchor who idolizes Audrey Hepburn, gets left at the altar, and then starts a friendship with her ex-fiancé's best friend.)

No one knew it at the time, of course, but Audrey Hepburn's cameo role in this *Guy Named Joe* remake, now titled *Always,* would come to represent her last ever feature film appearance. In retrospect, concluding her movie career with Steven Spielberg made a certain kind of sense: she had started her feature film career under the guidance of golden age masters William Wyler and Billy Wilder, and she would now end it under the direction of their modern-day equivalent, Steven Spielberg.

Why did Audrey choose to appear as guardian angel "Hap" in Spielberg's remake of Victor Fleming's wartime fantasy? It turned out she had admired Spielberg's work ever since watching *E.T.*, exclaiming to Luca at the end of that movie: "This man is not just a director. He's the best storyteller I have ever experienced!" Yes, she still remained fully immersed in her work for UNICEF, but the chance to work with Spielberg also represented the fulfillment of a wish expressed in an interview two years earlier: "It would be fun to do another part before I roll over. People are inclined to send scripts to me for which the parts are too young. I'd love to do a picture with Michael Caine or Michael Douglas—actors who have style but aren't pompous about it."

She certainly wasn't desperate for the money, although she would receive an extraordinary $850,000 for ten days of work, most of which she donated to UNICEF. Nonetheless, her practical side asserted itself because, in the words of Robert Wolders, "she had to replenish her coffers." She never did let money rule her life, and when the financial crash hit in the mid-1980s, it was Robbie who was genuinely afraid of financial disaster, while Audrey reacted with great equanimity, exclaiming to him: "So what? Even if we were to lose everything, we have a garden; we can grow potatoes and eat them." In Luca's astute analysis, such acceptance spoke in large part to the primary place gardens held in his mother's heart and worldview: "Having a garden gave her reassurance, that in any event, she could produce her own fruit and vegetables. She also found that taking care of beautiful gardens was a way to fight her own demons. After a war like that, you are always left with the fear that it could happen again."

Audrey, who had lived through the horrors of Nazi occupation, would now be teaming with Steven Spielberg, who throughout his extraordinary career had never met a World War II trope he didn't like. The director had first watched *A Guy Named Joe* on television as a youngster in Phoenix, explaining it was "the second movie, after *Bambi*, that made me cry." The movie's plot centered around World War II pilot Pete Sandidge (Spencer Tracy) who dies in combat but comes back to earth in order to telepathically let his grieving girlfriend Dorinda (Irene Dunne) know that she must move on with her life. This, then, was a story that spoke to Spielberg's perennial exploration of loss: loss of innocence (*E.T.*), loss of childhood (*Hook*), and even, in his personal life at the time, the divorce/loss of first wife Amy Irving.

Based upon Dalton Trumbo's original 1943 screenplay, the script for *Always*, credited to Jerry Belson and Diane Thomas with an assist by adaptor Frederick Hazlitt Brennan, represented Spielberg's most concerted attempt yet at filming a boy-meets-girl romance, albeit one otherworldly in nature. In Spielberg's version, the story would now center around firefighting pilot Pete Sandich (played by Richard Dreyfuss, who stated he had seen *A Guy Named Joe* over thirty times); after dying in a crash, Sandich returns as a guardian angel to young flyer Ted Baker (Brad Johnson), who has fallen in love with Pete's old girlfriend Dorinda (Holly Hunter).

The part of Hap, Pete's guardian angel, had been played by Lionel Barrymore in the original, and this remake had been written with the idea of Hap again being played by a man. When first choice Sean Connery proved unavailable because of commitments on *The Hunt for Red October*, and with production already underway, Spielberg hit upon the notion of casting Audrey in the role. Audrey, in Spielberg's words, was "closer to the maternal side of nature," and intrigued by the chance to work with Spielberg in a major Hollywood production requiring a commitment of only ten days, she signed on. Even if limited to two brief scenes, the part was a good one, and garnered Audrey billing of "Special Appearance By."

Flying to the United States for the film's location shoot at an airbase in Libby, Montana, Audrey rented a house, where, it was reported in the papers, a neighbor brought her a large bowl of huckleberries as a welcome-to-the-neighborhood present. The very next day Audrey arrived at the neighbor's house with a pie made from the berries.

Happy she was, even if the exact nature of her role remained elusive. Confided Audrey mid-production: "Nobody knows what I am, even Steven Spielberg! I would say I'm a spirit.

But not an extraterrestrial. It's just plain old me with a sweater on." (It's an amusing comment which speaks to Audrey's essential modesty. Safe to say, no one else has ever referred to Audrey Hepburn as "plain old Audrey . . .") Because it was important that this heavenly spirit appear absolutely spotless and pristine onscreen, when it came time to film her first scene, which was set on an island of grass in the middle of a burned-out forest, four crew members carried Audrey in a chair from her car to the island. It was a fifty-yard trek, and in Spielberg's word, she was carried "like the princess she had always been in all of our dreams—right into her mark and into her key light." Said co-star Richard Dreyfuss: "She was love and humor and grace and open and knowing. She was perfect."

To the cast and crew, the airborne entrance seemed just right for a Hollywood queen, and yet glad as she was to be surrounded by co-workers of whom she appeared genuinely fond, even now she remained petrified of stepping before the cameras: "The last thing you want to be in acting is an introvert, which I am. I've never loved to perform. Oh, I liked it beforehand—all the preparation—and I liked it afterword, if it went well. But the thing itself is scary."

Analyzed Sean after his mother's death: "She was scared, man, scared." Reflecting upon those words in later years, he edited himself: "To say she was scared is the wrong word. It's too general. She was, however, insecure when it came to performing, and in there is the secret ingredient. If you're confident and self-assured at all times, you lose the connection—the walking of the razor's edge between performance and real life. She never lost that stage fright and it solidified the connection with her audience."

When interviewed by Jane Pauley about the film, Audrey herself enthused: "I had the best time. I had a ball. [Steven] is just the sensitive and humorous man I expected." Director and star engaged in numerous conversations on the set, talks which ranged from movies and children to history, and out of one of those talks came a key image which ultimately informed Spielberg's award-winning *Schindler's List*. At one point in that film, as Jewish people are being put onto the trains, a little girl in a red coat is startlingly visible, popping out, as she does, from a bleached-out black-and-white background. In Sean's words: "This comes from a story about her childhood that my mother told him during the filming of *Always*. She told him about seeing people being loaded on the trains at the Arnhem Station, and at some point, she saw a little girl with bright red-orange hair whose face was turned towards her as she was being loaded into one of those horrible railcars. That image stayed with her for her entire life. The color made it real—it could have been her. Spielberg took that story and transformed the girl with red hair into a girl wearing a bright red coat and put it into the movie." Speaking of those horrific scenes from her childhood, Audrey stated: "I was eleven or so, and all the nightmares I've ever had are mingled with that."

As for *Always* itself, while the idea of remaking a beloved film for present day-audiences sounded fine on paper, the resulting movie suffered from a pair of major casting flaws. Spielberg, generally so spot on with his choice of actors, thought of Richard Dreyfuss as a younger generation's Spencer Tracy, but Dreyfuss, for all of his talent, proved far too jittery an onscreen presence to ever channel Tracy's salt-of-the-earth persona. Similarly, Holly Hunter, her rat-a-tat-tat delivery and aggressive stance accentuated by endless gum chewing, misses the pathos inherent in Irene Dunne's original portrayal of Dorinda. Hunter's Dorinda does nothing so much as yell—often and loudly—and when this approach was combined with Dreyfuss's nervous tics, any sense of romance and wonder promptly flew out the window.

What spoke to the home front audience in 1943 when the fate of western civilization was hanging in the balance could not land with the same resonance when the pilots in question were fighting fires. In the end, *Always* is stuck in limbo between World War II and 1980s America, with the movie set in the present day yet using vintage World War II planes and archaic 1940s slang like "You big lug." The clothes may seem reminiscent of the 1940s but Dreyfuss and Hunter spell present-day America.

In the end, the constant verbal and visual references to World War II only make the stakes at play in *Always* seem that much smaller. Yes, the shots of firefighting are certainly more believable than the combat shots found in the 1943 original, but the overall effect rings false, because Spielberg's universe, exemplified by the self-conscious banter between the pilots and Dorinda, seems cribbed directly from vintage movies, not real life. If, as seems evident by *1941*, *Saving Private Ryan*, *Band of Brothers*, *Masters of the Air*, and *The Pacific*, Spielberg's heart truly lies in the 1940s, the last era in which the nation was united, then the question remains why he didn't keep the film set in that era.

It is therefore up to the character of Hap to supply the sense of genuine emotion missing from most of the film, and in the hands of Audrey Hepburn, that is precisely what happens. No one may have known exactly who and what Hap represented, but Hepburn's performance proves effortless and deeply moving, a summary of life experience and three decades of movie acting which lifts a leaden film into a realm where belief in the afterlife and guardian angels might actually prove possible.

Appearing forty minutes into the film, clad head to toe in white, her hair pulled back and hands clasped as she leans against a tree trunk, Audrey Hepburn's beauty is enhanced not just by her bone structure but also by her age. If, as Eleanor Roosevelt had it, "beautiful young people are an accident created by nature. Beautiful old people are works of art," then Audrey Hepburn's delicately lined face functions as proof positive of this aphorism. Her quiet, confiding delivery cuts right through all the attendant claptrap in a wonderful, all-too-brief performance that instantly makes you realize what the rest of the movie does not possess—charm and grace.

As the film lurches toward its finale, Audrey does appear again, instantly giving viewers a lift throughout the brief three-minute duration of the scene. Unfortunately, her all-too-quick sequence is followed by a bit of psychobabble nonsense meant to suggest an understanding of life's travails, with Richard Dreyfuss gravely informing Holly Hunter that "the love we hold back is the pain that follows us here." None of it registers, and a viewer's reaction to having pseudo-philosophy ladled out in such leaden fashion is likely to run along the lines of Woody Allen's putdown of pretension: "Did it achieve total heaviosity?"

The critics were not impressed, and while David Denby's review in *New York Magazine* referred to "Spielberg's long, long career as a boy," it was actually Pauline Kael who understood the film's failings best, saying of Spielberg: "He has caught the surface mechanics of '40s movies, but has no grasp of the simplicity that made them affecting. He overcooks everything, in a fast stressful style." Kael is on the money here, because even the music is of the "nudge-nudge" variety, with *A Guy Named Joe*'s theme of "I'll Get By" here replaced by the too-on-the-nose "Smoke Gets in Your Eyes."

Spielberg's frenetic, indeed at times bombastic style—as if yelling at the audience "See how touching this is?!"—only serves to heighten the effectiveness of Audrey's understated and heartfelt performance. Her portrayal of Hap provides the audience with both an overdue chance to relax into the film as well as an actual sense of wonder, the essential Spielberg quality found in his greatest films like *E. T.* A filmmaker of enormous talent and often exquisite sensitivity—witness *Schindler's List*—has here battered the audience into unwilling submission.

In the end, Audrey's all-too-brief scenes grant audiences a look at the film that might have been. In a lumbering, occasionally tedious film, she had triumphed in full, in the process providing a masterful coda to her life in movies.

Mel Ferrer's photo of Audrey with Anne Frank's father Otto and his second wife Elfriede. Otto urged Audrey to star in *The Diary of Anne Frank*. Photo Courtesy of Sean Hepburn Ferrer.

Chapter Forty-Nine

A RECKONING WITH ANNE FRANK, 1990–1991

"The most important thing I've carried through life is that whatever I've suffered has helped me later on. When I love, I love unconditionally."

—Audrey Hepburn

PERHAPS IT WAS BECAUSE SHE had enjoyed working with Steven Spielberg so much, or it may have been that she had rediscovered the joys of performing, but Audrey now agreed to return to the stage for the first time in forty years: not to appear in a play, but instead to narrate a symphonic tribute to Anne Frank. By 1990, the timing felt right—at long last, she could honor the young woman whose diary had circled, changed, and informed her own life for nearly fifty years.

That history with Anne Frank stretched back to 1946 when the seventeen-year-old Audrey had moved with her mother from Velp to Amsterdam. Mother and daughter settled into an apartment located directly below that of an editor working on the Dutch publication of *The Diary of Anne Frank*, and when the editor gave the book to Audrey, the teenager proved emotionally devastated: "There were floods of tears. I became hysterical."

In many ways, Audrey seemed the natural candidate to play Anne Frank in the George Stevens–directed movie based upon the Broadway play of the same name: the two dark-haired girls, only six weeks apart in age, were born outside of the Netherlands but raised Dutch, and lived only sixty miles from each other during the war. Furthering the connection between the two, Anne's diary actually contains a direct reference to Audrey's uncle Otto, Count van Limburg Stirum, one of the first five Dutch civilians executed after the occupation began. Said Audrey: "I've marked one place where she says, 'Five hostages shot today.' That was the day my uncle was shot. And in this child's words I was reading about what was inside me and is still there. It was a catharsis for me. Anne Frank's story was my own. . . . This child who was locked up in four walls had written a full report of everything I'd experienced and felt."

So keen was George Stevens for Audrey's participation that he asked Otto Frank, Anne's father, to travel from his home in Zurich to Bürgenstock in order to persuade Audrey to star in the film. Recalled Audrey: "He came to lunch and stayed to dinner. He came with his new wife who had lost her husband and her children. They both had the numbers on their arms. There was something so spiritual about his face. He had been there and back."

Audrey was hesitant, but at Stevens's request read the diary again. In her own recall, she "was so destroyed by it again that I said I couldn't deal with it. It's a little bit as if this had happened to my sister. I couldn't play my sister's life. It's too close and in a way, she was a soul sister." Did Audrey feel a bit of survivor's guilt? For such a sensitive, empathetic person it is certainly a possibility, and horrible as Audrey's war had been, she had moved about freely and not been locked up in an attic.

To a lesser extent, but very likely in the back of Audrey's mind, playing the role might also have given more publicity to her mother's one-time Nazi sympathies. It was all too much an unwelcome reminder of the horrible war years, and Audrey gracefully declined the role, which was subsequently played by Millie Perkins to great acclaim.

By 1990, however, enough time had passed for Audrey to feel more comfortable with Anne's story. The passage of forty-five years had even granted Audrey a perspective on the occasional good which occasionally arises out of one's own personal horror: "In the beginning it's an enemy, it's something that you don't want to face or think about or deal with. Yet with time it becomes almost a friend. . . . Being without food, fearful for one's life, the bombings—all made me so appreciative of safety, of liberty. In that sense, the bad experiences have become positive in my life."

It was time, Audrey felt, to pay tribute to her "soul sister" whose diary had by then sold over thirty million copies in dozens of languages. A plan was formulated: Audrey would select passages from the diary, and after he approved them, composer/conductor Michael Tilson Thomas would utilize them as the basis for composing a musical score. Audrey taped herself reading the passages she selected, and such was the power of those home recordings that Tilson Thomas readily admitted: "So much of the music, I realize now, was influenced by hearing the way she read, her voice, her personality. The piece is as much about Audrey as about Anne Frank."

The key to Audrey's participation lay in the fact that she would not have to act or sound like Anne Frank: "I'm just relaying her thoughts. I'm reading. I still wouldn't play her." The concerts, entitled *From the Diary of Anne Frank*, would benefit UNICEF. "Now I'm very happy to read her words," said the sixty-year-old Audrey. "I'm thrilled to do it because I think it's something very important. They're very deep and they're pure because she was a child, and she wrote them from her heart." For Audrey, Anne was "a symbol of the child in very difficult circumstances, which is what I devote all my time to. She transcends her death."

A schedule was set for a mini tour of the United States in March of 1990, followed by concerts in London two months later. Audrey had not appeared onstage in nearly forty years, but one constant remained: the genuine self-deprecation about her own abilities. After television talk show host Larry King told her she would have delivered a great performance as Anne Frank, she simply replied: "No, but then I'm not much of an actress . . . I could not have suffered through that again without destroying myself."

Each one of her appearances with Tilson Thomas sold out instantly, her appeal undiminished, indeed enhanced, after close to four decades away from the stage. Beginning with a March 19, 1990, concert at the Philadelphia Academy of Music, and continuing on to Chicago, Houston, and the United Nations General Assembly Hall, Audrey and Tilson Thomas raised hundreds of thousands of dollars at each concert. When the concert was repeated in May 1991 at London's Barbican concert hall, critic Sheridan Morley wrote of her appearance: "Heartbreakingly fragile, looking as though she were made of glass, she stood in front of that huge orchestra and gave a performance of such mesmerizing dramatic intensity that afterwards I was not alone in begging her to return to the stage she had left at the time of *Roman Holiday* almost forty years ago."

It was never to be.

For her PBS television *series Gardens of the World*, Audrey was dressed by Ralph Lauren. Here she is wearing a handkerchief linen poet's blouse, matching skirt, and pale blue shawl collared linen tailored vest. Pictorial Press Ltd./ Alamy Stock Photo.

Chapter Fifty

FOR THE LOVE OF GARDENS, 1990–1993

"I think that's what life is all about—children and flowers."
—Audrey Hepburn, *Gardens of the World*

WORN DOWN BY HER INCESSANT globetrotting on behalf of UNICEF, as well as the back-to-back appearances in *Always* and *From the Diary of Anne Frank*, Audrey was looking to remain at home, planning to only emerge periodically for UNICEF fundraising. With only one field trip scheduled in all of 1990, and none for 1991, she continued to think of herself as retired—if not entirely from UNICEF, then certainly from acting. Retired, that is, until an opportunity presented itself that proved irresistible: serving as the on-camera host for a public broadcasting series that would take her on a journey to the world's most famous and beautiful gardens.

The idea for a Public Broadcasting System (PBS) series about gardens had originated with documentarian and executive producer Janis Blackschleger, who first discussed the series as a multipart presentation without a host. When the production team began to talk about modifying the concept to include a host, it was Julie Leifermann who suggested Audrey, then reemerging in the public eye through *Always*. Said Blackschleger: "What fascinated me from the very beginning was, when you would just say 'Gardens of the World with Audrey Hepburn,' people's faces would light up."

Combining, as it did, her love of gardening and a chance to exercise her on-camera skills, the show proved irresistible to Audrey. Gardens had held an important place in her worldview from the time she was a youngster: "When I didn't have a dime, I held to the dream of one day having my own orchard with fruit trees and a place to grow vegetables." For Audrey, the gardens were indeed actual works of art: "The arts of the garden, like those of the theatre, painting, music and dance, nurture and comfort."

On September 14, 1989, producer Stuart Crowner flew with Blackschleger to meet with Audrey and Robert Wolders in Tolochenaz. Audrey had just returned from an overseas trip on behalf of UNICEF but yes, she informed them, she was definitely interested in their series. Said Blackschleger: "Hearing that beautiful voice, that unique cadence, in person, was extraordinary, and it was wonderful to see how much she cared right from the start. She wanted to play a role in selecting the gardens to be showcased, to consult with gardening expert Penelope Hobhouse and to work with the writers on the script. You can see Audrey's handwritten notes on script pages."

In that pre–cell phone era, multiple transatlantic phone calls transpired between the production team in the United States and Audrey and Robbie in Switzerland. Said producer Blackschleger: "The opening episode, with tulips and spring bulbs in Holland, was adapted from Audrey's own notes from those transatlantic calls. Sometimes during the conversations, you could hear cowbells in the background!"

Such was Audrey's enthusiasm for the project that the documentary's relatively low budget did not deter her in the slightest: "I had the time, and I was thrilled to do it. I love gardens and flowers. It interests me and it gives me an opportunity to see gardens I never would have otherwise. I think we're photographing what are the most beautiful gardens in the world. It's really all about the same things—children, flowers—it's life, it's survival, and like with flowers, it's the same with children: with a little help they can survive and stand up and live another day. . . . I put the same effort into helping a plant flourish as we do at UNICEF giving children a future and room to develop—the strength to have a future."

Her fee, she decreed, would be donated to UNICEF, and the gardens, not Audrey, were to be treated as the stars of the show. Her attractive, casual, and subtly eye-catching clothes would be provided by Ralph Lauren, with whom she had struck up a deep friendship. Each episode would find Audrey wearing two or three different outfits, ranging from a pink two-piece suit to a red silk shirt and white pants. This represented no turning of her back on Givenchy but rather simply a case of wearing different styles for different occasions. Said Audrey: "It's having the best of both worlds, Hubert, and Ralph. I don't want to compare them. I just want to wear them."

Mindful of the show's tight budget, Audrey suggested to producer Blackschleger that if the show could provide her with a hairdryer and iron, she'd do her own hair, makeup, and wardrobe. Twenty-six years earlier she had dozens of wardrobe personnel fussing over her on *My Fair Lady*, and now she was equally happy to be looking after herself. So happy, in fact, that Julie Leifermann, who worked on the show as a one-person production team/assistant to Audrey, related that Audrey insisted upon ironing Julie's clothes as well as her own. Said Leifermann: "She genuinely loved the beauty of small things. She was connected to the simplicity of how life could work and tried not to complicate it."

Her commitment to this show and to nature itself was plainly stated: "Perhaps if we now take a closer look at our gardens, we will better understand our lovely earth. Have we not lost sight of our only source of life? Or have we at last awakened to the fragility of our beautiful planet." Celebrating nature was a surefire way to enjoy herself and regain a sense of hope after the horrors she had faced down in war-torn, poverty-stricken countries. And yet, that UNICEF work all over the globe had actually served to deepen her commitment to preserving the natural world: "To plant a garden is to believe in tomorrow."

Audrey felt strongly that the gardens had to be presented not just in a beautiful style but also in a "poetic way." Blackschleger was not exactly sure what Audrey meant by the word "poetic," but she finally came to realize that the word tied in with the totality of Audrey's vision: "She meant a fusion of arts, garden, people, peace, quiet sky, light . . ."

Filming began on April 23, 1990, in the Netherlands, a segment highlighted by Audrey's tearful reunion with her wheelchair-bound aunt Jacqueline at the unveiling of the "Audrey Hepburn White Tulip." May found her filming in France and England, and in June there were trips to Japan, the Dominican Republic, and the United States. Laughed producer Blackschleger in later years, "In hindsight I realized that we built a schedule apropos to traveling as if we were still in our twenties—which none of us were! But Audrey, Robbie, and the crew were vigorous—real troopers. There was a shared sense of discovery and excitement."

Audrey downplayed her own gardening skills, but in fact proved knowledgeable about design, layout, color, and variety, all of which added to the program's effectiveness. Filming was limited to four hours per day: two in the morning and two in the afternoon, the hours when natural outdoor lighting was at its best. Limited shooting hours allowed Audrey to avoid exhausting herself, and the eight resulting twenty-five-minute minifilms showcased a relaxed and radiant star. Each segment was organized around a specific type of garden (rose, country), and while the off-camera narration was provided by Michael York, Audrey's own passion for the subject, what Blackschleger described as her "unerring sense of place," was made abundantly clear in her enthusiastic descriptions of everything from modern landscaping to the pleasure gardens inspired by the Islamic belief in a vast, peaceful heavenly garden.

There was a great rapport, onscreen and off, with Penelope Hobhouse, and in a charming sequence the two women discussed how difficult it was to travel and miss the latest changes in a home garden. Audrey tied that discussion back to the beginnings of her own career with a story about Colette: "I don't know if you've ever read that lovely story about Colette's mother being invited by Colette's husband to come and stay with them on a certain date. And she wrote back—'Thank you so much for your sweet invitation. You know how much I love my daughter. And my dearest wish is to see her. But on that very day my cactus will bloom. And it blooms only once every four years. And I must stay here.' And you know, Colette commented on how she adored her mother for that very quality, how much she loved her flowers. I can understand that. I really had a hard time leaving."

For those who followed the series, one extra bonus reminded everyone of just how extraordinary an actress Audrey Hepburn could be: at the end of the fourth episode, "Public Gardens and Trees," Audrey sat down on a bench and read an excerpt from *The Diary of Anne Frank* in which Anne writes about her love of nature. And there, in the midst of a beautiful garden setting, sixty-year-old Audrey Hepburn read with the enthusiasm and unbridled joy of a fourteen-year-old girl, never attempting to act fourteen, but rather conveying the essence of young Anne Frank. It served as a potent reminder of just how extraordinary an Anne Frank she would have been thirty-three years earlier in the George Stevens film.

Audrey completed voiceover work in January of 1991 in Los Angeles, the memory of her arrival at the recording studio etched in Blackschleger's mind thirty years later: "What I remember most vividly was Audrey arriving with Julie Leifermann in an Alfa Romeo convertible with the top down—it was just like Audrey on the Vespa in *Roman Holiday*!" Even at this late stage of her participation, Audrey's commitment remained absolute. Remembers Blackschleger: "Audrey was so involved that it was she who changed the script description of the orangery at Versailles from 'parade ground soldiers' to 'parade ground sentinels.' Every word mattered."

In the spring of 1991, an introductory version of *Gardens of the World* aired to great acclaim as a PBS fundraiser. It was only after a lengthy editing process that the first episode actually aired; the date was January 21, 1993, the day after Audrey died. Typical of the highly favorable reviews was Barbara Saltzman exclaiming in the *Los Angeles Times*: "Hard to imagine any [episode] more compelling than the half hour spent wandering through some of the world's most enchanting rose gardens with one of the world's most enchanting women."

At the 1993 Emmy Awards, Audrey was awarded a posthumous Emmy for "Outstanding Individual Achievement in Informational Programming," with her award being accepted by Janis Blackschleger. The series lived on in a 2006 reissue on DVD, as well as a CD release of music from the series, and Blackschleger proudly points to the prescient nature of the programs: "Many of the ideas Audrey most cared about introducing in the series thirty years ago are more relevant today than ever—the well-being of our planet, and what kind of natural world we are leaving for future generations."

Given Audrey's love of gardens, the series seemed a fitting conclusion to her life on camera, leading Robbie Wolders to state: "I know that for Audrey the making of *Gardens of the World* was not only a marvelous adventure, but also one of the most rewarding experiences of her life and career. It became an intensely personal and creative process for her." The program came to assume that same significance in Wolders's life as well: "Someone asked me recently if it's painful for me to watch film on Audrey, and I realized that in general it is, except for when it is *Gardens of the World*. That is, I think, because having gone to the locations with Audrey, having shared the experience, seeing the film becomes more like the revisiting of beautiful memories."

Yet for all the series' acclaim, it was not Audrey's on-camera skills that made production of the series so enjoyable. It was instead the warmth of a down-to-earth, international star who remained interested in others more than in talking about herself. In the words of Janis Blackschleger: "We all know Audrey Hepburn is a great legend. But what she was, more than a great legend, was a great human being. When you were with her you felt prettier, better about yourself and your own possibilities." Musing about Audrey's affect and impact years later, she added: "So many times I am asked, 'What was she really like?' And my answer is that she had such respect for life and for others. Audrey always looked forward. She possessed the most life-affirming way of living, of being wholeheartedly present in this world. She was extraordinary."

Said her good friend, photographer Bob Willoughby: "She left those who came into contact with her better for having known her. I miss her to this day."

Receiving the 1990 Cecil B. DeMille Golden Globe Award for Lifetime Achievement in a soft satin charmeuse Givenchy long-sleeve high-neck gown. Without being over the top or showy, the gown perfectly emphasized Audrey's beautiful face and figure. PictureLux/The Hollywood Archive/Alamy Stock Photo.

Chapter Fifty-One

TRIBUTES, 1990–1993

"She gives the distinct impression she can spell schizophrenia."
—Billy Wilder on Audrey Hepburn

AUDREY'S WELL-RECEIVED TURNS IN *ALWAYS* and *From the Diary of Anne Frank* had reawakened the film community to her unique charms, and lifetime achievement awards soon began to flow her way. Such evenings of celebration seemed a graceful way to pay tribute to a legendary star, and also provided a way of thanking Audrey for her own willing participation in galas honoring her great friends in Hollywood.

She had, along the way, participated in the 1981 American Film Institute (AFI) tribute to Cary Grant and attended no fewer than four galas honoring Givenchy in New York, Los Angeles, San Francisco, and Tokyo. In 1986 she took part in the AFI tribute to Billy Wilder and spoke at several benefits honoring her close friend Gregory Peck, even hosting the 1989 AFI tribute to her first co-star. All of which made it seem a logical progression that the biggest and most prestigious film organizations in the world decided it was time to pay homage to Audrey herself.

On October 21, 1987, she was honored at the New York City Museum of Modern Art's benefit for film preservation, and three years later, the Golden Globes awarded her the Cecil B. DeMille Award for lifetime achievement. In a charming acceptance speech Audrey rattled off the names of no fewer than thirty-five people who had helped her career, and in a sign of how difficult life remained for women in Hollywood, only two of those listed were women—Shirley MacLaine and Lillian Gish.

The biggest honor of all, however, took place at an April 22, 1991, tribute at the Film Society of Lincoln Center. Famous co-stars and directors lined up to pay tribute, not just to her beauty and talent, but above all else, her kindness. Said the supposedly tough Billy Wilder: "You looked around and suddenly there was this dazzling creature looking like a wild-eyed doe prancing in the forest. Everybody on the set was in love with her in five minutes, I included." Proving he had lost none of his trademark wit, he added: "My problem was that I am a guy who speaks in his sleep. I toss around and talk and talk . . . but fortunately my wife's first name is Audrey as well."

Fulsome tributes followed from Gregory Peck ("It was my good luck during that summer in Rome to be the first of her cinema swains"), Tony Perkins, Harry Belafonte, and ever the humorous cynic, Audrey's three-time director Stanley Donen, who added: "My passion for her has lasted through four marriages—two of hers and two of mine." If, in her modesty, Audrey always claimed, "I had to do it with feeling instead of technique," it was Alan Arkin who smilingly disagreed with the honoree: "She does not think of herself as a particularly good actress, but she is a consummate one, whether she likes it or not." Reflecting on that night decades later, Arkin added: "The only time I saw her after filming *Wait Until Dark* was at the Lincoln Center Tribute. I apologized to Audrey for having been as horrible as I was to her while playing the character of Roat. That role was actually depressing to me. And when I said this to Audrey she said: 'Nonsense! It was the role. Don't worry or even think about it.'"

Reflecting on his co-star's legacy, Arkin reflected: "I think she's revered, but for all her considerable skill, people seem to think about who she is more than about her acting chops. I disagree with that but it's understandable. She was of such impeccable character, so much greater than any person she was playing. Not many people in the business make it feel honorable, but she did. She really was what a human being should be."

As for Audrey herself, whether at the Lincoln Center tribute or that of the USA Film Festival in Dallas, the attention served to make her almost uneasy: "It's wonderful, but at the same time you don't know where to put yourself. You just die in a way. I mean, all those compliments . . . It's like eating too much chocolate cake all at once." What the tributes made clear, however, was that her small but substantial film career, encompassing twenty-two major roles, featured a range much larger than is often remembered: playing a nun, blind woman, quasi lesbian, princess, flower girl, prostitute, and guardian angel, she managed to convince audiences to accept her in every one of those varied guises. Said Stanley Donen: "She approached acting with determination, intelligence, and a lack of selfishness I have rarely seen."

In accepting all her honors, the closest she would ever come to acknowledging her own extraordinary talent was simply to humorously state: "I think it was quite wonderful that this skinny broad could be turned into a marketable commodity." Asked about her own favorite movie, she offered a somewhat surprising choice: After first demurring that "it's like asking if I like chocolate cake more than spaghetti," this time she selected *My Fair Lady*—"I loved working with music. The reason I wanted to dance was because I loved music. Music is the greatest helper in the world in all situations."

In March of 1992 she was presented with a special BAFTA Lifetime Achievement Award by Princess Anne, and that same year brought her the George Eastman Award for distinguished contribution to the art of film. But rather than bask in the glow of past achievements, she now remained focused upon one final piece of work that held special meaning for her as the climax of her performing career: Audrey Hepburn would narrate fairy tales in a special audio recording for children.

A lifelong love of children led to the recording of *Enchanted Tales* and a posthumous Grammy. PictureLux/The Hollywood Archive/Alamy Stock Photo.

Chapter Fifty-Two

SOLO VOCE, 1992

"Audrey's voice has always been rich with poignancy for me, a quiet yet lively sound tinged with a taste of sadness."

—Esperanza Miyake

WITH THE FILMING OF *Gardens of the World* completed, Audrey's last ever public appearance in a professional capacity occurred in March 1992, when she presented an honorary Academy Award to director Satyajit Ray. Said Vanessa Redgrave: "I was in Los Angeles at one of those hotels where they hold the awards ceremonies and I saw Audrey. I knew she had cancer and I think everyone knew it. What struck me again was that she was very, very humble."

Presenting the award to Satyajit Ray may have been Audrey's last ever public appearance in a professional capacity, but she had undertaken one last acting job—just not in front of a camera. Instead, she agreed to narrate a selection of four fairy tales for Dove Audio Books, with all royalties flowing to the ASPCA.

The idea for this recording had originated with pianist Mona Golabek and writer Mary Sheldon, with Sheldon writing adaptations of *Sleeping Beauty*, *Tom Thumb*, *Laidronette—Empress of the Pagoes*, and *Beauty and the Beast*. Audrey agreed very quickly to participate in these recordings—fairy tales, after all, were a source of comfort for children, and it turns out, for Audrey herself: "If I'm honest, I have to tell you I still read fairy tales and I like them best of all." It was no accident that Audrey always listed Frances Hodgson Burnett's *The Secret Garden* as her all-time favorite book.

It wasn't just Audrey's star power that Golabek wanted—it was the essence of the woman herself: "She had a quality I found in Eleanor Roosevelt. When Audrey said to you 'How are you, dear?' she looked in your eyes and wanted an answer. . . . There were differences between her and Eleanor, but they both built instant bridges to anyone they were with. What they wanted was your *soul*."

Audrey Hepburn's Enchanted Tales, as the recording came to be known, represented a near perfect fit of actress and material, with Audrey's soothing voice—comforting, all embracing, yet full of life—building nothing less than an aural cocoon. Such is the power of that unique voice that when she whispers the phrase "the softest of sheets" the very texture of those sheets proves near palpable. Said the *Los Angeles Times*: "Hepburn shapes the rich language with delicate clarity and her unique, captivating charm. The rest is pure magic." What Ernest Hemingway wrote about Marlene Dietrich here applied to Audrey Hepburn just as much: "If she had nothing more than her voice, she could break your heart with it."

When the successful release of the recording led to a 1994 Grammy Award for Best Spoken Word Album for Children, Audrey became the first actress to complete the EGOT (Emmy, Grammy, Oscar, and Tony Awards) posthumously. The first of her major awards had come in the 1950s with the Oscar and Tony, and now, forty years later, a year after her death, she had completed the grand slam of entertainment awards with an Emmy for *Gardens of the World* and a Grammy for *Enchanted Tales*.

This status as a beloved icon was far from just a posthumous honor; back in 1968, fourteen years after her last performance on Broadway, she had been honored with a special Tony Award for "Lifetime Achievement in the Theatre." In other words, Audrey was already so revered that she received the commercial theatre's highest award—for essentially turning her back on theatre for the world of films and Hollywood . . .

When she walked onstage to receive her special Tony, the theatre audience was clearly thrilled to see her in person, and she immediately captivated everyone in sight with a typically self-deprecating and thoroughly charming assessment of herself in *Gigi*: "A rather thin girl with a rather thin talent."

Audrey insisted upon one final UNICEF trip—a field visit to war-torn Somalia in 1992. Photofest

Chapter Fifty-Three

SOMALIA, 1992

> "My mother had a secret. . . . She was sad. My mother was sad because of what she saw happening to the children of the world."
>
> —Sean Hepburn Ferrer

BY 1992, AUDREY WAS EXHAUSTED, worn out, and alarmingly thin, with Roger Moore, who once again co-hosted the Danny Kaye Children's Awards with her, noting: "I should have been more aware of Audrey's failing health at that time. She was always desperately thin, but now she seemed to be very fragile too, and had to sit down quite often."

Exhaustion and all, Audrey had one final UNICEF trip in mind: if, in the aftermath of dictator Mohamed Siad Barre, Somalia had become the most broken country on earth, then she needed to visit Somalia. By 1992, one-quarter million Somalis had died of hunger and thirst, which meant that for Audrey there was no "if" about it—she had to see the living conditions facing the country's children for herself. In her own words, spoken directly to a reporter early in the year: "I'm not playing a role. Roles are imaginary and fantasy. There's no fantasy to this. It's tough, heartbreaking reality."

In the face of Somalia's marauding violent gangs and lack of a functioning government, it was far from a given that Audrey would even receive permission to visit. Which meant that after UNICEF fundraising trips to San Francisco, Chicago, Miami, Fort Lauderdale, Indianapolis, and Providence, she returned home to rest and, as the summer wore on, grew increasingly anxious about whether she would be permitted to visit Somalia. Finally, word arrived from UNICEF: she would be allowed into Somalia at the end of summer. The dangers she would face on the ground alarmed everyone but Audrey, and in the analysis of Ian MacLeod, who was tapped to accompany her on the trip: "We didn't publicize Audrey coming in advance or there could have been a security risk. . . . In terms of Audrey coming in, that information was on a need-to-know basis."

UN passport in hand, she boarded a flight on September 20 from Nairobi to the Somali city of Kismayo. There were, in fact, no visas provided for her visit because, she was told by a UNICEF official: "There is no government. You just fly in and hope you won't get shot down."

Audrey's flight touched down in a countryside filled with poisoned wells and thousands of armed men; outside the capital of Mogadishu there were neither schools nor hospitals, in fact nothing at all in the way of governmental institutions. Drought, civil war, nonexistent roads, and a total lack of sanitation were now the norm throughout the country.

When she visited feeding centers, she was confronted by the sight of listless children literally starving to death. Followed throughout by a UN video camera, it took an effort of will for her to keep moving forward, but she did not flinch. Said photographer Betty Press, who accompanied her on the trip: "What amazed me most of all was how she handled herself in these camps where they were desperate. . . . The situation at that point was so tragic, and she handled herself with such grace and such dignity. You'd see smiles on people who had nothing to smile about. . . . She really cared."

Arriving back in Mogadishu, Audrey was confronted with a capital city enveloped in total chaos. She had lived through the destruction of Arnhem, but this, she knew, was far worse: "I've never seen a whole city where there isn't a building that doesn't have holes in it or a roof on it. The city was a total battleground." She visited a hospital and school, and when the sound of machine guns rang alarmingly close to the hospital, such was the extent of the violence that no one even turned a head. No matter the psychic cost, she stayed the course, telling the clinical staff: "Wherever I go in the world I work for UNICEF, but I always talk about you, because I'm full of admiration, and your courage has been incredible." She seemed increasingly frail but refused to stop. Said Betty Press: "I could tell it was hard for her even to get down to the children's level. She would do that, but it was hard."

She did have one brief respite when she helicoptered onto the flight deck of the aircraft carrier *Tarawa* to thank those onboard for their help in protecting UNICEF workers. The servicemen and -women on board had collected $4,000 as a donation to UNICEF, a gesture which left Audrey in tears. She was to refer to this donation many times, as if reassuring herself that after the sights she was confronted with in Somalia, good people did still exist.

She had one more Somalian stop, in the city of Baidoa, ground zero for the country's devastating famine. Shops had been looted and deserted, dead bodies littered the ground, and in Audrey's own despairing words: "I walked into a nightmare." The children were now so weak that they could neither feed themselves nor make the slightest noise, and by Ian MacLeod's estimate, ten children died in the one hour he and Audrey spent watching the charity workers from "Concern" feed and tend Somalian children. Something inside of Audrey broke: "The silence is something you never forget." She felt haunted by the absence of joy: "And to see the children that quiet it's awful." Shaken to her core, she murmured "you really wonder if God hasn't entirely forgotten Mogadishu."

When pressed on French television for an explanation of that comment, she simply stated: "I have a tendency at times in my life, wonderful or awful, of turning to God." But as for God being responsible for the horrors, absolutely not—the blame, Audrey fiercely explained, lay entirely with man: "Drought is not what causes famine, it's man. . . . In the end, hate is the most evil thing in the world, and it begins with us. Children are born loving. They love. And racism, discrimination, hate are given by us. What's so bad in Africa is that they were given their independence without the tools, because in Somalia there is only ten percent of the population that is able to read and write."

Somalia pervaded her consciousness, and for the first time, the utter drenching loss of it all overwhelmed her. How, she wondered, could we have fashioned a world where war takes precedence over showing children that they are loved. She had reached her limit, the exhaustion caused by five years of work under the most wretched of conditions cracking her empathetic essence. In the apt words of Robert Matzen who chronicled her work for UNICEF in *Warrior: Audrey Hepburn*, "Drop by drop, she began to dole out her life force to those she met, a drop here and a drop there . . ."

She was fearful, terrified even, that nothing had been learned from the horrors of the Second World War. Forty-seven years after that war's end, she found herself surrounded once again by unwelcome reminders of the starvation and misery that had haunted her own adolescence: "The children . . . their eyes were like enormous pools of question . . . as if they are asking 'Why?' Some of the children have no light in their eyes. . . . I am becoming more raw, more hurt, more angry, feeling the pain more deeply. It's really not to be believed how these people live . . ."

The hypersensitivity which left her feeling like an open nerve had been noted as far back as 1960 by her friend and *Children's Hour* co-star Shirley MacLaine: "Audrey was the kind of person who when she saw someone else suffering, tried to take the pain on herself." By now, so widespread was the suffering that Audrey was far from the only relief worker who felt assaulted by the unrelenting misery: John Isaac reported that he found himself so upset after a trip to Rwanda that he went into therapy and "couldn't function. I was totally stunned."

Pictures of Audrey carrying a starving child now appeared around the world. Gone was even the slightest trace of weltschmerz, replaced instead by a fierce soldier. For the first time in her forty years of public life, Audrey Hepburn looked angry. More than angry: outraged and not caring who knew it—in fact wanting everyone to know it. Writing a *Newsweek* article after her trip to Somalia entitled "Unforgettable Silence," she painted a picture of abject hopelessness: "There were no small children. They had all been snuffed out like candles. . . . I'm filled with a rage at ourselves. I don't believe in collective guilt, but I do believe in collective responsibility."

The UNICEF footage in which she talks about Somalia revealed a different Audrey. She appeared so upset by the horrors she had witnessed, so touched in the deepest, most caring part of herself, that her face, nearly devoid of light, appears as a virtual mask of suffering. She is shown kissing the hands of emaciated children so bereft of nutrition that they remain virtually unrecognizable as little boys and girls: "I wanted to pick up the children and give them warmth but you're afraid you're going to break them. It is totally unacceptable to see children die before your eyes."

She had seen suffering and abject poverty on previous trips, but after the trip to Somalia, a watershed had been reached, as if the ground had crumbled beneath her and she was plummeting ever downward. In her own stunned words: "I have been to hell and back."

The horrors she felt she must describe in order to jolt people out of their indifference had rattled her to her core; disturbed himself by the trip, Robert Wolders understood why Audrey was so traumatized by what she experienced: "It's a love for people that goes beyond sympathy. It is perhaps more than empathy. An ability to project her imagination so that she could actually feel what others are feeling."

She confided to Anna Cataldi that she couldn't sleep: "I have nightmares. I'm crying all the time." She could no longer hide her despair: "I've always been fairly sensitive, but I think at this point I have had an overdose of suffering. That's why I do need to go home and do other things." Her emotional devastation seemed overwhelming, yet she determinedly told Cataldi: "War didn't kill me, and this won't either." But—the cumulative weight of bearing witness to so much tragedy could not help but take a toll, and in Cataldi's interpretation: "I had this feeling that sooner or later, war kills you. She was so skinny. I felt something was really wrong."

In a final irony, if a trip to hell can in any way ever be considered a success, Audrey's presence in Somalia had proved to be a fundraising triumph, and she followed the work in Somalia with a trip to Kenya, where she sat for interviews with two dozen journalists at an official press conference. This was, Audrey felt, her best chance to spread word of the Somalian disaster through the BBC, Reuters, and Visnews. Her overarching message remained one of urgency: "There is an immediate need for food, medicines and funds—right now!" She refused to let the world's wealthiest nations off the hook, bluntly stating of European colonialism: "We didn't help where education is concerned and now we're paying the price. We enriched ourselves on the back of these people. Drought is a tragedy of nature, but famine is not. . . . We all have blood on our hands."

After her trip she held further press conferences in Geneva, Paris, and London, with the United Nations reporting that her mission to Somalia had raised 1 million pounds in the United Kingdom alone. Her interview in Paris with Jean-Pierre Elkabbach for the television show *Reperes* laid bare her distress, the footage revealing a star who can barely speak above a whisper: "I think that in the end I won't be able to overcome this trip . . . to smell the death, seeing corpses . . . these tiny little faces. It's unbearable." When following up on British television she sadly confessed: "I haven't slept at night since then. I sometimes sleep during the day, but I'm having a hard time at night."

Perhaps she herself had a premonition of how sick she would soon become, and in an April 1991 interview at La Paisible, she told Alan Riding of the *New York Times* Paris bureau: "I'm running out of gas . . . I've done it on a constant basis because I know I cannot keep it up for long." She could pretend no longer: "Much as I love doing this for UNICEF, it's exhausting and it creates enormous stress . . . Because it's a huge responsibility. Lots of work, lots of physical work, traveling, fund-raising, but also lots of preparing."

She was worn out—by her travels, by the weight of caring for her mother, and by years of nonstop smoking. Her body was breaking down, and it started to become sadly and ironically clear that her greatest triumph as a humanitarian, drawing the world's attention to the nightmare of Somalia, had resulted in physical decline and emotional devastation. In an interview with Fairchild News Services she sadly admitted: "I'm scared."

Her work for UNICEF and her relentless advocacy on behalf of the world's most helpless children had changed her worldview. She looked politicians, warlords, and the military straight in the eye and found them all lacking. The Audrey of forty years earlier who floated through Hollywood, idolized by millions as proof that fairy tales did come true, would not have recognized the tough-talking soldier she had become: "Serenity—I don't think it exists. [You] can be perfectly serene, then you spend two minutes thinking about the Kurds and want to shoot yourself. I mistakenly thought that with age comes serenity, when your job is done. . . . Perhaps the only time you can be serene is when you are very small, when you don't know all these things."

Serene she wasn't. Brimming with happiness about the state of the world she wasn't. But clear in her understanding of what truly mattered in life, unflinching in her commitment to helping the world's most dispossessed, that she was.

In her search for a path toward healing, Audrey Hepburn had acquired wisdom.

Classic Audrey. A white bateau-neckline top and slim pant with pink obi-like sash. Daring and modern, it could be worn today with no changes. Timeless. Moviestore Collection Ltd./Alamy Stock Photo.

Chapter Fifty-Four

PRIORITIES, 1993

"If my world were to cave in tomorrow, I would look back on all the pleasures, excitements and worthwhilenesses I have been lucky enough to have had. Not the sadness, not my miscarriages or my father leaving home, but the joy of everything else. It will have been enough."

—Audrey Hepburn

WHILE IN SOMALIA, AUDREY HAD begun to feel ill, telling Anna Cataldi, "I have a lot of pain in my stomach. I think it's malaria." It was clear that her health was compromised, and in John Isaac's recall, "She knew something was wrong but she never talked about it. She kept it to herself."

Returning to Tolochenaz on September 30, she continued to feel run down, unable to bounce back the way she had from all her previous trips. She managed a flight to California in October, staying with Connie Wald and seeing Connie's doctor, and then flew to Rochester, New York, on October 24 for the Eastman Awards. Soldiering through the black-tie benefit, she attended a screening of *Breakfast at Tiffany's* the next night, but she was in great pain.

After receiving word from doctors in Los Angeles that tests confirmed she had contracted a parasitic infection, she nonetheless traveled to New York City with Robbie on October 27 to receive yet another honor for her humanitarian work, this one from the Casita Maria Settlement House.

Obligations fulfilled, she flew back to California for a series of doctor's appointments arranged with the help of Connie Wald, and exploratory surgery was scheduled for November 2, 1992. Recalled Sean: "It wasn't until she came to Los Angeles and none of the treatments were working that they did a small laparoscopy and found that the cancer had spread to her intestines." A malignant tumor was removed but the abdominal cancer had spread to her stomach: Audrey had contracted an extremely rare form of cancer-pseudomyxoma peritonei (PMP), which strikes only one person in every million. The cancer had metastasized around her intestines and colon, resulting in extreme pain and an inability to eat as the cancer strangled her small intestine. She was, just like the children in Somalia, starving to death, and was now placed on total parenteral nutrition, with liquids being fed to her intravenously.

Sean himself later made a perceptive analysis of the dichotomy between his mother's extraordinary ability to access emotions as an actress, a skill which had aided her career, and her emotional reaction to the suffering of children, which seemed to have now damaged her health. "The emotions would flood her. She was much more aware of people's pain than another person would be. Other people could somehow shut off the emotions, but she instinctively read the emotions of all those children who were suffering. She wanted to protect them."

In addition to feelings of vulnerability dating from her wartime experiences, there may, in fact, have been a biological basis for Audrey's extraordinarily high degree of empathy. Audrey, it seems, typified those examined by Dr. Abigail Marsh of Georgetown University for her study of minute structures in the brain known as amygdalae. Explained Dr. Marsh about the amygdalae: "One of the big things that we know they do is they're responsible for generating the experience of fear. What's interesting about that is that not only is the amygdala essential for giving *you* the experience of fear, it seems to allow you to empathize with other people's fear. . . . People who have given kidneys to strangers have an exaggerated response in the amygdala, which we think means that they are more sensitive than most people to others' distress." Studying the amygdalae's structure in people who immediately spring into action to help those in trouble, Dr. Marsh explained, "I was really pleased and gratified by what we found in the heroic rescuers, which is that, just like the altruistic kidney donors, their amygdalas [*sic*] were larger than average and significantly more responsive to the sight of somebody else in distress . . . you know these are the people who, when they saw somebody terrified because they thought they were about to die, they didn't just sit there."

Audrey had seen children suffering and starving to death in the world's poorest countries, and just as explained by Dr. Marsh, literally could not sit by and watch. Said Sean: "I'm sure it took a huge toll on her emotionally, physically, and in terms of her immune system. She had so many shots—too many shots—that she needed in order to travel to all those different countries. It's also possible that during the war she picked up something that triggered the cancer. There are environmental cancers, cancers of genetics, of bacteria; there are many different types but my mother's rare cancer—PMP—acts differently. There is no tumor mass because the cancer liquifies the tissues of the intestines."

Faced with the devastating news about her cancer, Audrey reacted just as she had when deserted by her father—she refused to indulge in self-pity. Which did not mean she simply shrugged and accepted her fate; as related in rather heartbreaking detail by Sean: "She had tears in her eyes, hugged me, sobbed, and whispered: 'Oh Seanie. I'm so scared.' I stood there, holding her with all my might as I felt huge chunks of me falling inside."

As the reality of her condition sunk in, it was not fear of death that consumed Audrey but a fear of unnecessary pain. The pain, Sean promised her, would always be managed. There would be no suffering. Givenchy, who noted her almost serene air, explained with an understandable touch of hyperbole, that she was able to accept her illness "because she accomplished everything with perfection."

There was no talk of God and heaven; Ella may have periodically embraced Christian Science, but Audrey never did practice a specific religion, stating: "My only religion is a belief in nature." In her worldview, it was an appreciation for the beauty of nature that approached the sacred, but even without an adherence to organized religion, a personal belief persisted: "I am no longer a Christian Scientist, but I believe in something—in the strength, maybe, of the human spirit." That belief had been tested by the war, by her travels on behalf of UNICEF, and now by her own suffering, yet she, like Anne Frank, persisted in a belief that "in spite of everything people are truly good at heart."

Very few were allowed to visit her in the hospital; besides Wolders, Sean, and Luca, Gregory Peck, Connie Wald, and Elizabeth Taylor constituted the inner Hollywood circle allowed access. The friendship with Taylor had deepened over the years, and different as the two screen legends were—one the epitome of conspicuous consumption and a private life lived through newspaper headlines, the other shy, reticent, and happiest out of the spotlight—the two women had bonded throughout the years, each sensing in the other a refusal to play the Hollywood game according to the rules of the day. They also shared a bawdy sense of humor, as when Audrey, taking note of a dazzling jewel Taylor was sporting, pointed to the bauble and, referring to a famous jeweler, inquired: "Kenny Lane?" "No," replied Taylor—"Richard Burton."

Both women were great beauties who had reached the peak of their onscreen popularity in the late '50s and early 1960s, both had demanding mothers who were Christian Scientists, and, most notably, both devoted the last years of their lives to charitable causes: Audrey to UNICEF, and Elizabeth Taylor to the fight against AIDS. In fact, explaining her fierce dedication to fighting the scourge of AIDS, Taylor utilized words remarkably similar in spirit to those used by Audrey to explain her devotion to UNICEF: "If people want to come to an AIDS event to see whether I'm fat or thin, pretty or not, or really have violet eyes, then great, just come. My fame finally makes sense to me."

But it was Robbie and her two sons who spent the most time with Audrey, and even during periods of great pain, her thoughtfulness remained undiminished; when she was still in the hospital, and Robbie spent nights sleeping on a cot in her room, she asked a nurse if they could please bring him a foam mattress to ease his discomfort.

Discharged from the hospital at her own request, she rested at the home of Connie Wald, and her devoted maid Giovanna Orunesu flew in with two of Audrey's dogs. It was at Connie's house that President George H. W. Bush reached Audrey by phone to tell her that he was awarding her the Presidential Medal of Freedom, the highest civilian honor granted in the United States. She managed to come to the phone to speak to the president, but it was clear that she would never be able to travel to Washington, DC, for the medal ceremony. Faced with intense pain, Audrey agreed to a second exploratory surgery on December 9, but the cancer had spread to such a degree that no further action could be taken.

There was a final conversation with great friend Billy Wilder, and deciding against any further chemotherapy she told Luca: "I'm sorry, but I'm ready to go." Sean, Luca, and Robert Wolders then banded together to fulfill her wish to be home for Christmas; too weak for a commercial flight, on December 21 she was transported home to Switzerland in Bunny Mellon's private jet, a flight which had been arranged through Givenchy's friendship with the wealthy Mellon.

Back in 1976, in that one joint interview with Andrea Dotti, Audrey had thought aloud about the very idea of existence: "Living is like tearing through a museum. Not until later do you really start absorbing what you saw, thinking about it, looking it up in a book and remembering—because you can't take it all in at once." And, as the end neared, what exactly did she see in the museum of her own life? Her two beloved sons. Robert Wolders. The neglected children of the world. Her mother and perhaps even her father. Close friends—the circle of people who had helped her avoid an end she had always feared: "I think it's one of the great tragedies in this world—the old who are lonely. It isn't age or even death that one fears, as much as loneliness and the lack of affection." Even as she lay dying, her concern remained for others more than for herself. Family friend Marilena Pilat noted: "She was very sick and yet she asked me how I felt. She was very peaceful. Usually you are afraid but she wasn't."

Ensconced at home, with Sean and Robbie administering the intravenous feedings and pain medications, Audrey was surrounded by family and cosseted in love. Explained Sean: "I would sit in a wicker chair next to her bed in the last few weeks of her life—we talked about those things that mattered to her. I think she always felt throughout her life that she had shortcomings. She felt the mistake was to sit there and hold a grudge. She had to make peace with life because she didn't have a choice. She often said it was fortunate to not have a choice—to have to move forward."

Although Audrey and Andrea Dotti had by now been divorced for over ten years, Dotti came to visit Audrey in her final days. Their shared love of Luca meant that mother, father, and son could spend some of her final days together. Wrote Luca of that sad time: "I only learned afterward that he fainted when he read my mother's medical charts. He had understood right away that there was nothing more to be done to save her life."

Still, attentive as they were, all three of Audrey's "boys"—Sean, Luca, and Robbie—held regrets. For Robbie, the self-perceived mistakes, especially when Audrey first fell ill, proved dark: "Neither the boys nor I could acknowledge that she was dying. We perhaps made a mistake in not telling her how ill she was. I think that was very unfair to her, because Audrey was as realistic about death as she was about life." With the hindsight of years, however, Wolders came to realize that Audrey was likely not only aware of the severity of her condition but in fact protecting her loved ones: "It's been my suspicion over the years that she wanted to hide her knowledge of her condition from us. She never feared death. She told Sean she was afraid only of pain."

Like all loving children, Luca and Sean regretted their inability to spend more time with their mother, angry and saddened that they were losing her when she was only sixty-three. The lack of time had, in fact, been on Audrey's own mind as far back as her 1987 television movie *Love Among Thieves*, when an interviewer asked her what she'd like to change about herself: "I'd like to be ten years younger. I don't care about getting older—but I'd like to have a little more time."

In Luca's words: "The only big regret I have and she would have had is not knowing her grandchildren. Because she would have been a fantastic grandmother—cooking cakes, keeping the grandchildren on every occasion, and telling them stories." In Sean's view, if Audrey had even one more day on earth, she'd hug both of her sons first and then "she would again talk about those children."

Audrey had made her understanding of the situation clear, gently issuing final instructions to her sons, insisting that they not be angry, and telling them that her ending was natural, "that death was a natural part of life." While Wolders could not accept such a cruel fate befalling "someone so precious," Audrey was, he related, much more realistic: "She'd say, 'Why *not* me?'" When he wondered aloud if it would have been wiser not to have traveled so relentlessly to the poverty-stricken countries where she faced extreme conditions, Audrey simply replied: "Think of all we would have missed."

Shortly before Christmas, there were last walks through her beloved garden, once with Givenchy, who had arrived for a final visit, and then again when accompanied by Robert, Doris Brynner, and her gardener Giovanni Orunesu. When Giovanni spoke hopefully of future plans for the garden—"Signora, when you get better, will you come and help me plant and trim again?"—Audrey simply replied that yes, she certainly would help him, "but not like before." Accepting her fate, and comforted by the knowledge that in the perennial cycle of death and rebirth her flowers would bloom yet again, she achieved a certain peace—an unspoken acknowledgment of the very circles of life.

She summoned a bit of strength on that final Christmas Eve and was, with her IV pole, able to come downstairs for a few hours. By now Audrey was on a constant morphine drip to ease the pain and could not leave the house. Explained Sean: "She couldn't go out and shop . . . so she went into her closet to find something in order to give us each something that was hers. That made it so touching, so magical."

She spoke of a favorite quotation from the Bengali poet Rabindranath Tagore: "Each child is a reminder that God has not lost hope in man." There was a final reading of a favorite text, "The Beauty of a Woman"; written as letters to his daughter and subsequently to his newly born granddaughter, Sam Levenson's words had been adapted into a poem by Audrey, who entitled it "Time Tested Beauty Tips" (after a line in Levenson's letter). Now more than ever it seemed to sum up her entire philosophy of life while encapsulating her own spirit:

> *For attractive lips, speak words of kindness.*
> *For lovely eyes, seek out the good in people.*
> *For a slim figure, share your food with the hungry.*

By now her life had come full circle, and in Sean's words: "I think she spent a large portion of her life thinking she wasn't worthy of all that affection and the love." And yet, in the end peace and self-acceptance had been achieved: "[But] that last Christmas, one of the great things she said was that she was sure that we loved her . . . after everything we had been through together. It meant a lot for us to know that she could go with that in her heart."

When she went to bed on her last Christmas Eve, she told Robbie Wolders it had been the best Christmas of her life.

Surrounded by family. With her faith in humanity restored.

She was now honored with the Screen Actors Guild (SAG) Lifetime Achievement Award, but by the time of the ceremony on January 10, 1993, she was far too ill to attend, and her graceful acceptance speech was read by one of her own favorite actresses, Julia Roberts: "I am proud to have been in a business that gives pleasure, creates beauty, and awakens our conscience, arouses compassion, and perhaps most importantly, gives millions a respite from our so violent world."

As the end approached, when Sean asked his mother if she missed "Granny," she made no reply. Her mind was still on UNICEF and the children, and in Sean's words: "She rallied for the last time and wanted to know if there had been any messages from UNICEF about the children in Somalia." Drifting in and out of consciousness she saw "the others. . . . She described them as 'Amish people in a field,' quietly waiting for her to the left of the bed." When asked to explain, Audrey, sounding remarkably like "Hap" in *Always*, softly replied: "You cannot understand. Maybe you'll understand later." Added Sean: "It felt good to know that she had a strong sense of the other side, that she wasn't scared."

Gently asked by Sean if she held any regrets, Audrey replied: "No . . . but I cannot understand why so much suffering for the children." After a pause, she added: "I do regret something. I regret not meeting the Dalai Lama. He's probably the closest thing to God we have on this earth. So much humour . . . so much compassion . . . humanity."

In Sean's detailed recall: "After she said that I sat down on the bed and held her hand and told her I loved her. . . . She was lying on the same bed to which I had been invited as a little boy to spend the night. I whispered that if she felt ready she should let go. I put her hand to my cheek to let her feel the warmth of my tears. Somewhere, I felt she could hear me."

A minister was called, and knowing that the end was near, last rites were administered.

Sean left his mother's room and walked downstairs to speak with each family member in turn. Luca was not present; at the urging of others, and against his better judgment, he had gone to the movies with his father. The intercom rang with an urgent message from Giovanna: "Come quickly."

Audrey Kathleen Hepburn died at 8 p.m., January 20, 1993, the day of President Bill Clinton's first inauguration. A mere seventy-nine days had passed since her operation in Los Angeles, and only six days since the official letter on White House stationery informing Audrey of her Presidential Medal of Freedom. At the end of the letter President Bush had taken the time to add a handwritten note of congratulations: "We are very proud of you."

In an act of sheer willpower, she had chosen to die when her room was empty of family. In Sean's recall: "She hadn't wanted to die with me in the room. To make it easier for me, I guess." Said Luca: "I always thought—but who knows the truth?—that she was too shy to die in front of me. Because for her I was always 'the little one.' I was 22–23 at that time, my brother Sean is 10 years older. And my mom was never worried about her condition, she was more worried about us, wondering if we were ready to cope without her being around us."

Love of family trumped all.

ACT FIVE

THE LAST GOLDEN AGE STAR

A final resting spot in her beloved Tolochenaz, Switzerland. Xinhua/Alamy Stock Photo.

Chapter Fifty-Five

ANNOUNCING THE NEWS, 1993

"Audrey was a lady with an elegance and a charm that was unsurpassed, except by her love for underprivileged children all over the world. God has a most beautiful new angel now that will know just what to do in heaven."

—Elizabeth Taylor

AUDREY'S DEATH WAS ANNOUNCED, FITTINGLY enough, not by a Hollywood publicist, but by James Grant, the director of UNICEF: "Children everywhere will feel her death as a painful and irreplaceable loss." Her passing was not the occasion for typical Hollywood-style obituaries—rise to fame, best movies, bad movies, peccadillos, and personal life. Instead, there was a straightforward acknowledgment of her talent and films, followed by in-depth looks at her life-changing work for UNICEF. Such was the nature of the tributes that even her extraordinary looks were now framed in terms of her honest—in other words, non-Hollywood—approach to life. Said the *New York Times*: "As unwilling to fake youth as she had been to fake voluptuousness, she looked like the 63 year old woman she was. Which is to say, better than any 63 year old woman who's pretending that she isn't."

Her death generated worldwide headlines and tributes from heads of state, but true to her wishes, her funeral on January 24 was to take place at Tolochenaz's small Evangelical church; Maurice Eindiguer, the same minister who had married Audrey and Mel and baptized Sean, came out of retirement to conduct the service before 120 invited guests.

Four days after Audrey's death, as the funeral procession slowly wound its way through the small Swiss village, people lined the street in order to pay their respects to "Madame Audrey." In fact it was only during his mother's illness and funeral service that Sean came to fully understand the extent of his mother's fame and what she meant to people around the world. "My mother didn't behave like a movie star in any way. I only connected to it when I saw the effect she had after she became ill; the cards and notes were so voluminous that it became a joke with the mail lady. In our small town she used a moped to get around and deliver the mail, but she had to get a truck to carry the big bags—the type you'd use for your leaf clean up—that were filled with get well wishes for my mother. We had to store them in the attic—we could never have answered all of them—I'd still be writing today. On the day of her funeral, in our little village of six hundred people, there were thousands of people . . . lining the streets to pay their respects. It was like a rock concert with cars parked everywhere along the road. People walked miles to come. It was very, very touching."

Those who could not find room in the tiny church listened to the brief service while standing outside, silent while the choir of St. George's International School in Montreaux sang a moving rendition of the twenty-third Psalm, "The Lord Is My Shepherd."

UNICEF's Prince Sadruddin Aga Khan, a friend of forty years stepped in to deliver an impromptu tribute when Givenchy broke down in tears. Sean read Sam Levenson's "The Beauty of a Woman" and delivered a eulogy in which he emphasized: "Mummy believed in one thing above all: She believed in love. She believed love could heal, fix, mend, and make everything fine and good in the end."

Her pale oak coffin rested upon a flower-bedecked catafalque but was itself adorned only by a cross and the words: "Audrey Hepburn 1929–1993." The coffin was carried to her gravesite by six men: Robert Wolders, Sean and Luca, Hubert de Givenchy, Audrey's brother Ian van Ufford, and former husband Andrea Dotti. Mel Ferrer attended the funeral, looking frail and distraught, hanging back until Sean called out to him: "Come, Papa." Hugged by Robert Wolders, and his eyes filling with tears, Mel followed the others as her coffin was carried to her gravesite at the top of a small hill overlooking Lake Geneva. Interviewed after the service, Alain Delon explained: "She brought joy and was loved by everyone." For an emotional Givenchy it was all "still unthinkable."

There were dozens of floral tributes from the household names with whom Audrey had crossed paths, but it is likely that nothing would have meant more to her than the flowers from UNICEF carrying the message: "From all the world's children." Surrounded by nature, she would rest for eternity in the town she loved above all others.

Four U.S. presidents sent condolence letters to Robbie Wolders, and Tiffany placed her photograph in store windows, alongside the evocative caption: "Audrey Hepburn—Our Huckleberry Friend 1929–1993."

Eight days before Audrey died, the Board of Governors of the Academy of Motion Picture Arts and Sciences had voted to honor her with the coveted Jean Hersholt Humanitarian Academy Award; two months after her death, on March 29, 1993, the award was presented by Gregory Peck and gracefully accepted by Sean. It was a well-deserved posthumous honor, but the most affecting tribute of all came from Anthony Lane in the *Independent on Sunday*, who simply wrote: "When Audrey Hepburn walked into the movies, all heaven broke loose."

Direct, straightforward, and always organized, Audrey left behind a detailed list of bequests for family and friends.
Pictorial Press Ltd./Alamy Stock Photo.

Chapter Fifty-Six

BEQUESTS, 1993–2000

"The Meaning of Life is to find your gift. The purpose of life is to give it away."

—Pablo Picasso

IN THE DAYS AND WEEKS after Audrey's death, as memorial contributions flowed into UNI-CEF, the public began asking questions about a will. Who were Audrey's beneficiaries? Was there even a will? Audrey Hepburn, the meticulously organized woman who had kept loose-leaf binders detailing every one of the possessions with which she traveled, dying intestate like Picasso, Abraham Lincoln, and Howard Hughes? Never.

The majority of her estate was divided equally between Sean and Luca in the form of properties and the extremely valuable film memorabilia, which meant that when it came to jewelry and furnishings, few specific bequests were left to the two young men: Sean received a pair of Bulgari gold and diamond earrings, a gift from Mel Ferrer to Audrey at the time of Sean's birth, while Luca received a pair of Bulgari pearl and diamond earrings. In a similar vein, knowing that Hubert de Givenchy and Robert Wolders were comfortably established on their own, the two men were simply gifted two Russian icons and two silver candlesticks, respectively.

Jewelry was, in fact, first left to relatives: Yvonne Quarles van Ufford received a diamond brooch in the form of a W, Sandra Quarles van Ufford a pearl solitaire ring, Evelyn Pinkerton (nee Quarles van Ufford) a pearl necklace with sapphire fastener, Michael Quarles van Ufford a small oil painting with butterfly, and Andrew van Ufford two silver candlesticks.

Close female friends were also included in the will, with Doris Brynner receiving a Bulgari emerald and sapphire brooch and earrings, Victoria Brynner a Tiffany diamond and platinum flowered brooch, and Christa Roth (UNICEF colleague) a platinum Tiffany brooch.

Maid, cook, and close friend Giovanna Orunesu received $25,000 (U.S.) as well as a pearl solitaire, small diamond solitaire, and Tiffany earrings, while monetary bequests of $25,000 were also left for Rucchita Orunesu, Engracia de la Rocha, Gina Cristoforetti, and gardener Giovanni Orunesu.

Of perhaps most interest was the disposition of Audrey's beloved La Paisible. There proved to be no difficulty with the distribution of the properties she owned in Saanen and Lully, but it was the sale of La Paisible in 2000 that seemed most fitting to the legacy of Audrey herself. The house was sold not to the highest bidder but instead to the people who seemed best suited to the spirit of the house. Explained Sean: "One family in particular came to us, they were friends and they had one little boy who had palsy and was in a wheelchair. We thought that would be the right thing: this garden that she loved so much, would play a very important part in his life and we felt that would be a good thing. He actually ended up in my room, and what used to be my second closet became the elevator."

Along with his brother Sean Ferrer, Audrey's younger son Luca Dotti carefully protects all use of his mother's image.
Anthony Devlin/PA Images/Alamy Stock Photo.

Chapter Fifty-Seven

PROTECTING THE LEGACY, 1993–2024

"Celebrity Net Worth reports that Hepburn was worth $55 million at the time of her death. . . .
This included a Los Angeles storage locker full of mementos and memorabilia."
—Leslie Veliz, "Here's Who Inherited Audrey Hepburn's Money after She Died"

VERY SOON AFTER AUDREY'S DEATH, her grave grew into a tourist destination for those wishing to pay their respects. Told by a cab driver that he and his fellow drivers undertake "sixty, seventy trips" there every day in the summer, Sean reflected in amazement: "That's in addition to the tour busses with people from all over the world that stop in front of the house and go to the cemetery. So that's hundreds of people per day that visit this little town of five hundred people. That's a lot of people passing through."

Given the popularity of her gravesite, and determined to protect their mother's image and legacy, Sean and Luca organized an exhibit entitled "Timeless Audrey," which traveled the world beginning in 2009. Two years later the "Audrey in Rome" exhibition ran from October to December at Rome's Ara Pacis Museum, and in 2019, the same year in which a statue of Audrey was erected in Velp, Sean organized "Intimate Audrey," an exhibition launched in Brussels in celebration of what would have been her ninetieth birthday. Featuring memorabilia, dresses, videos, her writings about UNICEF, and even the Vespa scooter from *Roman Holiday*, the exhibition, one Sean called a "living biography," proved to be a huge success, attracting forty thousand visitors.

As it became increasingly clear that Audrey's popularity was continuing to grow with each passing year, Sean and Luca began to jointly grapple with a looming problem: how to protect their mother's name and likeness and preserve the integrity of her legacy. This led to what Sean describes as the trademarking of "her name, signature, and image in every jurisdiction in the world, so it can't be misappropriated for commercial reasons." The Audrey Hepburn Estate was now able to protect Audrey's name from unlawful use, and yet, as explained by Sean in a 2016 interview, such was the reach and popularity of her image and brand that there were still "two, three dozen lawsuits going every year for medium to important unauthorized use of her name and likeness, or 'piracy.'"

Although Audrey had divided her estate equally between her two sons, difficulties arose regarding the distribution of career memorabilia, because her handwritten will failed to specify which items were to be Sean's, and which would pass to Luca; at stake were scripts, costumes, awards, and posters, as well as her personally annotated *Breakfast at Tiffany's* script. With some items valued well into six figures, the stakes for the memorabilia, which had been kept in a Los Angeles storage locker, grew high. The brothers ultimately came to an agreement that each would retain the personal items already in his possession, with the remaining items—specifically the extremely valuable film memorabilia—to be auctioned at Christie's, with profits split equally.

After Sean took on an additional position as the first ambassador for EURODIS, the European Organization for Rare Diseases, he left his top position at the Audrey Hepburn Children's Fund, and Luca assumed the position of chairman. Perhaps inevitably, given the scope and worldwide range of the name and image involved, intrafamily disagreements of varying strength and duration ensued. Explained Sean: "When I created this foundation, Hollywood for Children, I created a DBA so that we could control the intellectual property rights associated with my mother's image. I quit the board of the Audrey Hepburn's Children Fund because I wanted to implement some cost-cutting measures during the 2008 financial crisis, and I was outvoted by the rest of the board. My brother came in and had a very different vision for markets like China. I grew very concerned about protecting the identity and image."

Lawsuits were filed, and the matter went before Los Angeles Superior Court judge David Sotelo, who conducted a nonjury trial of the issues in the spring of 2019. In a ruling handed down in October of that year, the judge ruled that Sean and Luca are co-owners of the Hepburn right of publicity and that their joint unanimous consent is needed for any licensing of the Audrey Hepburn image taking place after March 2013. (The judge further ruled that either Ferrer or Dotti, acting alone, can terminate a license if there is no longer unanimous consent due to one of them removing his approval.)

Whatever their differences, what would have pleased Audrey is that both of her sons seem to have inherited her determination to combat the problems plaguing the world's poorest countries, utilizing the power of her image and legacy to specifically address the problem of dehydration. It remains a solvable epidemic thanks to oral rehydration therapy, and in the words of David Nalin, the first doctor to utilize that therapy: "No other single medical breakthrough of the twentieth century has the potential to prevent so many deaths over such a short period of time and at so little cost."

Wrote Sean in his memoir *Audrey Hepburn: An Elegant Spirit*: "The worst killer of all is dehydration from diarrhea caused by unclean drinking water and malnutrition. It costs five dollars to vaccinate a child for life, 6 cents will prevent death from dehydration and 84 cents per year will stop a child from going blind." In Luca's book of recipes and remembrances, he speaks directly of oral rehydration therapy as a tool which has saved over fifty million people from dysentery; in fact, what likely would have pleased Audrey most of all is that right alongside her favorite pasta recipes, Luca goes on to present the recipe for oral rehydration: eight teaspoons sugar and one-half teaspoon salt dissolved in one quart of drinkable water.

In their respective ways, both Sean and Luca continued to honor their mother's overriding concern to help the impoverished children of the world. Films and fashion? Fine, she would have said, but nonessential. Her sons using their books to let people around the world know about oral rehydration therapy? She would have found nothing more important.

Emma Ferrer continuing the family's legacy of giving back. Here in 2014 she packs UNICEF survival kits for children in Syria. Photo by Dave Kotinsky/Getty Images for UNICEF.

Chapter Fifty-Eight

GENERATIONS OF ACTIVISM, 1970–2024

> "She always used to say, 'If you ever have a doubt in life, do what's best for the other person. Take yourself out of the equation and you will see magically, everything will work out.'"
> —Sean Hepburn Ferrer

IN THE YEARS FOLLOWING HER death, Robert Wolders, Sean, and Luca focused on continuing Audrey's charitable endeavors, taking their first step through an Audrey Hepburn Pavilion, housed in a converted schoolhouse in Tolochenaz. From 1996 until 2002 when the museum closed, 30,000 people visited the pavilion, raising $275,000 for UNICEF.

The men then founded the Audrey Hepburn Foundation, and in the often byzantine ways of nonprofits, there was a concurrent creation of the Audrey Hepburn Memorial Fund at UNICEF; that fund morphed into the "All Children in School" project before growing into the Audrey Hepburn Society, termed by Sean "the big donor club of the US Fund for UNICEF."

Running these charities became a full-time job for Sean, and he had stopped his work as a film producer in 1993 to focus his attention on them. In his own evocative phrase: "I never got that wink from the entertainment industry. Certain projects didn't happen. Oh, I worked—I made a nice living. But after my mother died, I decided to take the baton and continue this extraordinary legacy of grace and generosity—that will be the focus and everything else will dance around it."

By then he had seemingly found the film industry not just frustrating but oft-times empty of purpose, filled with self-important players capable of losing all perspective in a pursuit of glory. Expanding on the topic in an interview, he explained: "And it's always the B minus and the B plus who behave the worst, and the superstars mostly . . . behave like princes. The really well-known people are nice."

Sean's time began to be taken up by the Audrey Hepburn Society for the US Fund for UNICEF, where he served as the first chairman and oversaw campaigns that raised over $140 million. "We have a full office, with lawyers, assistants, licensing directors, executive directors for the fund, bookkeepers, etc. We're like a small company, and we have agents and law firms all over the world."

This activism continued a family tradition which had begun with Ella's work on behalf of American soldiers returning from Vietnam in the 1970s. Explained Sean: "When my parents got married, Ella passed the baton of looking after my mother to my father. It was time for a new phase in my grandmother's life, and she decided she wanted to live in San Francisco. It was while living in San Francisco that she began working with Vietnam veterans who were encountering problems readjusting to civilian life." Although Ella's turn away from a youthful infatuation with fascism had certainly taken hold while the Second World War was still raging, her efforts in San Francisco represented the final fruits springing forth from a now much different worldview. In Audrey's words: "My mother always wanted to be useful, and she impressed that upon us."

From Ella to Audrey to Sean and Luca, and now on to Sean's children—a daughter, two sons and two stepchildren. Explained Sean proudly: "My daughter is already working with UNICEF and the UNHCR, the United Nations Refugee Agency. That is our family culture. I don't like the word charity because we're beyond charity now. The effort must be to restore people's rights."

Working with the Seoul-based Tree Planet organization, in April of 2015 Sean and his family traveled to Korea to help families devastated by the tragic ferry accident of April 16, 2014, in which three hundred died. "We went there as a family, not as official representatives of the Audrey Hepburn Children's Fund. We thought it would take two months to raise the necessary money to plant a forest of trees in honor of the victims, which we would name the Audrey Hepburn Memorial Forest. We held a big press conference, and within forty-eight hours we had raised the necessary money—$250,000. It was as meaningful for us as it was for the families of the people lost in the tragedy."

That family trip to Korea seemed to serve as impetus for Sean's daughter Emma's dedication to UNICEF, although Emma's awareness of service to others had started

As early as I can remember—because of my father and his work for the children's foundation. The idea that those of us who have been given so much should give back felt to me like second nature.

In 2016 I had a meeting with Caryl Stern at UNICEF USA. We met after I first moved to New York and I was instantly ready to press "go," but Caryl very smartly said "Wait—pause: if you want to make a difference you need to find the cause that you care about so much that not getting involved is simply not an option."

So, I waited a little bit. I was in Italy and Spain, and there had been a huge influx of refugees from Africa and the Middle East. I would watch the news and see harrowing images of young people who had drowned in their desperation. It was all very disturbing, and I realized that this was the cause that spoke so personally to me.

Through the United Nations High Commission on Refugees (UNHCR), I was able to put together a mission trip with a director of UNHCR and also with my good friend Michael Avedon, the grandson of Richard Avedon. We visited a refugee camp in Greece—Michael took photos and I conducted one-on-one interviews with refugees. These were families who had fled their homes and arrived in Greece or Turkey with almost nothing. The EU relocation scheme would then try to get them out of the refugee camps and into more stable situations. And yet—the staggering statistic I learned is that the average amount of time spent in a refugee camp is eighteen years!

I did some writing about the experience for the UNHCR and they made me a national ambassador in 2016. I then spoke at fundraisers in Washington, DC, Houston, and other cities.

There is a deep familial bond that only this kind of work makes me feel. Of course, I have had a connection to my grandmother through my father, but connection in other ways has not always been easy; her image, her success as an actor, her status as a fashion icon—it all seems like a larger-than-life entity. But this has let me feel an intimate bond with her legacy, a new way to understand who she was and what she did. Her field trips, the press, the raising of funds—it was revolutionary and changed the direction and dialectic of celebrity humanitarian work today.

Caryl Stern, who served as CEO and president of UNICEF USA from 2005 through 2019 feels that "Emma carries on Audrey's legacy in ways that trump everything else. She really does have the grace of her grandmother, her compassion and devotion to the cause, and has become iconic to the next generation who only know Audrey from her films. When she speaks, she speaks so genuinely and from the heart about what her grandmother did that it makes the legacy come alive all over again. She can capture full ballrooms with thousands of people with the same modesty and grace as her grandmother. In her own way and on her own terms, Emma is continuing Audrey's greatest and most important legacy."

In Emma's own words: "What I know in my heart is that my relationship with UNICEF will always be present." In the most personal of ways, "this work has also given me a feeling that I am at last truly in touch with my grandmother."

Luca Dotti and Sean Ferrer: a 2010 auction of a single sheet of misprinted stamps brought in 430,000 euros for UNICEF and the Audrey Hepburn Children's Fund. Abaca Press/Alamy Stock Photo.

Chapter Fifty-Nine

AUCTIONING HISTORY, 2017–2018

"It is with great joy that we seek to share her spirit, through this sale, and its related previews, with all of those who have enjoyed her films and her sense of style, and who have followed her humanitarian legacy."

—Sean Hepburn Ferrer and Luca Dotti

IN 1996, WHEN THE COSTUME jewelry hair ornament Audrey had worn in *Breakfast at Tiffany's* sold for $17,285, it became clear to all that her film memorabilia would only continue to grow in value each year. The idea of a memorabilia auction began to percolate; what Sean and Luca did not want was a repetition of the non-family-sanctioned 1998 Christie's auction of twelve letters from Audrey to her father and step-grandmother, which had brought in a cool $72,000. Referring to the 1998 sale of letters, Sean explained: "We were upset about that. These were personal items that belonged to my grandfather that were sold by my step-grandmother. I respect that people have needs in their lives, but she did not make an effort to speak to us first. We had always been there for her, helped her out when she needed it. We weren't thrilled about it."

Eight years later, worldwide press attention was generated by the announcement that Christie's would hold a Givenchy-approved auction of the black dress Audrey had worn in the first scene of *Breakfast at Tiffany's*. Of the three dresses Givenchy designed for the film, the first dress had remained in the Museum of Costume in Madrid, and the second in the archives at Maison Givenchy, but the third dress had been retained by Audrey. She subsequently returned the dress to Givenchy—in fact, before her death, she gave Givenchy twenty-five of his dresses that she had worn—and it was he who donated it for auction to benefit his friend Dominique Lapierre's City of Joy charity for children in India.

The charity waited until December 5, 2006, before auctioning the dress at Christie's, where it sold for $922,000, nearly seven times its presale estimate. (The $922,000 far surpassed the previous costume auction record holder, Judy Garland's blue gingham dress from *The Wizard of Oz*, which had sold for $226,000.) Said Sarah Hodgson, who was part of the Christie's team running the auction: "The dress—it was made of amazing Italian satin you can't get any more. It was incredible because the dress almost stood up on its own."

After the final bid had been entered on behalf of an anonymous European bidder, Lapierre exclaimed: "There are tears in my eyes. I am absolutely dumbfounded to believe that a piece of cloth which belonged to such a magical actress will now enable me to buy bricks and cement to put the most destitute children in the world into schools."

By this time, even errors regarding the Hepburn legacy could be turned into UNICEF fundraising possibilities. In 2001, the German Postal Service had printed fourteen million stamps featuring Audrey as Holly Golightly; the original image had depicted Audrey with a pair of sunglasses hanging from her mouth, but the postal system flipped the negative and the sunglasses were replaced by Holly's cigarette holder. When Sean refused to grant permission/copyright because of the alteration, the sheets were destroyed, with just a few retained—by the postal system archives and the German postal museum. Among the still extant stamps were those that the German Postal Service had sent Sean back in 2001 for his approval, and in 2010, he agreed to auction a sheet of ten stamps, with two-thirds of the proceeds flowing toward the Audrey Hepburn Children's Fund and one-third to UNICEF. That one sheet of stamps sold for 430,000 euros.

Having noted the extraordinary sums garnered by these auctions and wanting to take matters into their own hands regarding their mother's memorabilia, Sean and Luca now sanctioned an auction at Christie's to be held over the course of three days in 2017. Consisting of hundreds of items the brothers had personally approved for sale, the lot ranged from a hand-embroidered Givenchy gown designed for *Sabrina* to a Balthus drawing personally inscribed to Audrey.

With the provenance of each lot hand-signed by the two brothers, they explained the reasoning behind the auction: "We preserved our feelings for her as well as her belongings, each of which signified her life's choices and philosophy. After 24 years we have focused on those items that we wished to keep, as well as those we are pleased to pass on to future generations." Film footage of Audrey's two sons examining the exhibit is accompanied by recollections both poignant and practical; in Luca's words: "When you find out the world is in love with your mother, there's a hint of jealousy and then little by little you understand that it's a privilege." Noted Sean quietly: "Her entire estate was less than I think an actor gets paid for one film today."

Twelve thousand people visited the presale public exhibition of the collection, and the first of the three auctions, on September 27, 2017, attracted online, telephone, and salesroom bids from forty-six countries and six continents. In the process, a record was set for the highest online participation in the history of Christie's, and the frenzied bids by fans determined to own a piece of the Hepburn legacy seemed to take even seasoned auction observers by surprise. To wit:

- The *Breakfast at Tiffany's* blue satin sleep mask with lace-trimmed flowers attracted the highest number of bidders for any lot in the auction. The final price of 6,250 pounds proved to be fifty times the presale estimate.
- Audrey's personal *Gigi* script: 25,000 pounds.
- Audrey's script for *The Nun's Story*: 27,500 pounds.
- A tiara, worn to the London premiere of *The Nun's Story*: 43,750 pounds.
- Cartier lipstick holder: 56,250 pounds, nineteen times the presale estimate.
- Audrey's own three-quarter-length lined Burberry trench coat: 68,750 pounds, 10 times the estimate.
- A two-piece Givenchy cocktail gown made of black satin and worn in *Charade*, sold for 68,750 pounds—the same price as her Burberry trench coat.

- A 1963 Cecil Beaton photograph of Audrey in *My Fair Lady*: 93,750 pounds, thirty times the presale estimate.

As the auction continued, the pace of the bidding increased:

- Audrey's working script for *My Fair Lady*, dated June 24, 1963. Presale estimate: 30,000—50,000 pounds. Final price: 206,250 pounds.
- A 1969 painting by Audrey entitled *My Garden Flowers*. Winning bid: 224,750 pounds.
- A Tiffany bangle inscribed with the message "You are my inspiration," given to Audrey by her *Always* director Steven Spielberg: 332,750 pounds.

And:

- The ultimate show-stopper: Audrey's working script for *Breakfast at Tiffany's*. Final sale price: 632,750 pounds.

Total proceeds: 4,635,500 pounds/$6,202,299. Seven times the original estimate.

The second and third auctions, featuring movie memorabilia (a *Sabrina* call sheet—1,500 pounds) as well as personal mementos (a Bulgari cigarette case—11,250 pounds) raised another 648,625 pounds.

What, one wonders, would have been the reaction of Audrey herself to the extraordinary prices commanded at these three record-setting auctions? Most likely incredulity. A concern only for whatever portion of the proceeds would be given to UNICEF.

Because, in her own words: "Giving is living. If you stop wanting to give, there's nothing more to live for."

Audrey wearing the famous 128.54-carat canary Tiffany Diamond. Paramount Pictures/Photofest © Paramount Pictures.

Echoing Audrey's iconic *Breakfast at Tiffany's* black dress, Lady Gaga, here shown at the Academy Awards, went uncharacteristically demure in Alexander McQueen's hourglass strapless dress, accessorized, like Hepburn's, with black opera length gloves and an upswept hairdo. She is wearing the legendary canary Tiffany Diamond, here set in a new necklace. Photo by Frazer Harrison/Getty Images.

Chapter Sixty

EVERYTHING OLD IS NEW AGAIN, 1993–2021

"Now, 50% of her fan base are teens and tweens. She has replaced James Dean on that closet door in kids' bedrooms. It's quite extraordinary."

—Sean Hepburn Ferrer

AUDREY HEPBURN NOW SEEMS TO have transcended her own era, in the process journeying from postwar modern woman of the 1950s to timeless female ideal in the twenty-first century. In the thirty years since her death, her appeal appears not only undiminished but actually seems to increase with each succeeding year, with fan websites continuing to pop up in languages ranging from French, Dutch, and English to Polish, German, and Japanese. Her ever-growing presence is now so large that there is even an Audrey fan club within the Pokémon community.

Instagram now holds more than two million images hashtagged #Audrey Hepburn, and the iconic opening scene from *Breakfast at Tiffany's* has picked up more than eight million views; the clip of Audrey singing "Moon River" doubles that total. Her image, particularly from *Breakfast at Tiffany's*, appears on magazine covers, notepads, coffee mugs, calendars, and books.

That ubiquitous image has influenced how Emma Ferrer has processed the legacy of the grandmother she never knew:

My grandmother was such a beautiful woman, inside and out, and what she represents to me changes with time—what she represents to new generations is changing. I remember a conversation with my father when I was younger, and we passed a woman who was carrying a bag with my grandmother's face on it. He pointed to it and said: "That's your grandmother!" I knew it was something big but I didn't know exactly what it was. As time went by, I realized "She's really famous!" I'd go to friends' homes, and they had posters of her. It was really in high school that I started to realize I had a nuclear family member who was a worldwide icon. I'm actually still learning about her; I haven't seen all her films because I want to keep discovering her.

I've never tried to imitate my grandmother's look. She was the first to say everyone should be themselves, and certainly if I copied her look there would inevitably be a backlash. When I started modeling, I would sometimes read comments online—people were pretty tough. Some people wanted me to be a carbon copy of my grandmother and they would judge harshly on appearance, while others said I was my own person. I realized that her legacy and image are a bigger deal than I could have imagined.

People write to me today on Instagram about how much of an impact, a truly deep personal impact, she has made in their lives. It is very heartfelt—they talk about the values she represents, values they pine for and that we see in so few places nowadays. Over and over, they speak of what a huge influence she remains on how they want to live their lives.

That ever-growing influence has blossomed into a worldwide phenomenon, with a 1999 American Film Institute (AFI) poll rating her the third greatest female film star of all time, topped only by Katharine Hepburn and Bette Davis. The cult of Audrey is largest of all in Japan, where she has morphed into a legend; a 1990 Japanese poll taken by the television companies NHK and JSB found *Roman Holiday* voted the public's favorite foreign film of all time (*Gone with the Wind* placed second). Another Japanese poll rating the world's most well-liked historical figures found that Audrey ranked above Gandhi. The Japanese identified with Audrey in a way they could not with, say, Marilyn Monroe, because, in the words of Luca Dotti, Audrey was accessible, "tiny, elegant, and discreet, with dark hair and almond shaped eyes." For a country in which manners and politeness remain of paramount importance, Audrey's genteel and thoughtful style continues to prove eminently relatable.

The Audrey-centric cultural conversation, in which she morphed from symbol of nostalgia to cultural icon, had actually begun to take shape while she was still alive: Whitney Houston's 1990 video for "I'm Your Baby" referenced *Funny Face*, while in that same year, *People* magazine named Audrey as one of the fifty most beautiful people in the world. In June 1996, three years after her death, the cover of *Harper's & Queen* featured a photo of Audrey from *Breakfast at Tiffany's* with the headline: "The most alluring women in the world"; the article inside named Audrey the number-one most fascinating woman of the modern age.

Products ranging from clothing to liquor all want a connection to Audrey in hopes that her image will impart a sense of respectability and fun to their product. A 1990s ad for Gordon's gin used her image, as did one for Pantene shampoo, and by 2002 the product endorsements had traveled full circle, with the Parfums Givenchy marketing of a "modernized" version of L'Interdit perfume: "Created for Audrey Hepburn. Once Forbidden. Now Reborn."

She was honored with a Legends of Hollywood U.S. postage stamp in 2003, just as the rush of clothing companies wanting to be associated with her accelerated. The Racing Green clothing retailer dubbed their capri-style pants the "Audrey Trousers," while in the most high-profile of product associations, a 2006 Gap ad used the "Basal Metabolism" dance number from *Funny Face* to highlight their version of the little black pants. Thirteen years had passed since Audrey died, yet there on worldwide television screens was a computer-generated image of Audrey dancing across screens to rock group AC/DC's "Back in Black." The ad ended with the tagline "It's back. The skinny black pant," and even called the pant "the Audrey Hepburn pant."

In reality, the campaign was not a particular success. Television audiences had years to get used to Elizabeth Taylor's White Diamonds perfume ads because they began running while Taylor was still alive; seeing Audrey dance in an ad more than a decade after she died, however, proved more than a touch disconcerting. Then again, it may just be that the pants themselves looked impossibly skinny for ninety-nine percent of the population.

The relative failure of the Gap campaign did nothing to diminish her allure, however. Five years later, the queen of pop culture, Beyoncé, echoed those same *Funny Face* black pants in her video "Countdown," while in 2014, a computer-generated Audrey appeared in an ad replete with references to *Roman Holiday* and *Breakfast at Tiffany's* in order to tout the delights of Dove chocolate; by one account it took a full year of work to produce this sixty-second ad.

Unsurprisingly, it remained the references to *Breakfast at Tiffany's* which continued to echo most strongly. Ads for Elizabeth Arden fragrances featured a woman wearing a dress deliberately styled in the mode of *Breakfast at Tiffany's*, and in that same year, Oliver Goldsmith re-released sunglasses like those worn by Audrey in the film. By now, it seemed, her *Breakfast at Tiffany's* persona had become an industry unto itself.

References even abounded to Audrey on television, and she was name-checked in shows ranging from *The Simpsons* to *Seinfeld*. On *CSI: NY* three women dressed as Holly Golightly to rob a jewelry store, while on *Gossip Girl* the lead character fantasized herself as Holly. Whatever the show, her name was intoned with near reverence, and always in terms of style and grace. It therefore made a perfect kind of sense that on the very first episode of *Sex in the City* (1998), the main character of columnist Carrie Bradshaw (Sarah Jessica Parker) delivered a series-defining voiceover narration that referenced Audrey Hepburn, Deborah Kerr, and Cary Grant in two brief sentences: "Welcome to the age of un-innocence. No one has *Breakfast at Tiffany's,* and no one has affairs to remember." Three names, all of them instantly marking a bygone era of elegance and savoir faire.

It was in the season 4 finale of *Sex and the City* that the reference to Audrey as avatar of elegance was made even clearer. Arriving at Mr. Big's (Chris Noth) apartment, Carrie finds one of his parents' albums featuring "Moon River"; as Carrie and Big begin dancing, the sophisticated Mr. Big quietly recalls how his parents would listen to "Moon River" as they dressed up in their finest for Saturday night parties. As he describes the ritual and very look of his parents readying themselves for a night on the town, he encapsulates the entire distance traveled from *Breakfast at Tiffany's* to a modern-day world bereft of glamour and civility.

It was therefore no accident that before the largest possible worldwide television audience, Audrey and *Breakfast at Tiffany's* were even invoked in the opening ceremonies for the 2012 Olympic Games. The reference, courtesy of a recreation of the film-ending kiss in the rain, was executed without irony, comment, or subtext, with Audrey's graceful, romantic air acknowledged in a straightforward, nearly wistful manner.

Tributes continued, not just in fashion and television but also in music, with the song "Breakfast at Tiffany's" featured on a CD released by the rock group Deep Blue Something. The Hepburn allure remains especially evident in literature, where the homages began with a well-received 1996 novel by Alan Brown entitled *Audrey Hepburn's Neck*. Subsequently turned into a 2011 movie, the book centered around a Japanese boy who sees *Roman Holiday* at age nine and, overwhelmed by the beauty of Audrey Hepburn, forms a lifelong preference for Western girls. This was followed by the 2000 novel *In Beautiful Disguises* by Rajeev Balasubramanyam, a British-Indian author who fashioned the tale of a sixteen-year-old girl living in South India who escapes her difficult family life via fantasies about *My Fair Lady* and *Breakfast at Tiffany's*. Audrey even starred as herself in Sean's 2021 children's book *Little Audrey's Daydream*, as well as in 2011's *Just Being Audrey*, written by Margaret Cardillo, with illustrations by Julia Denos, the sweet natured-book features Audrey in episodes taken directly from her own life, and it even generated its own YouTube trailer.

The unending tributes in one medium after another lead to one overarching question: Why? What is it about Audrey Hepburn, a movie star whose career was all but finished a half century ago, that speaks to successive generations with a power that seems to grow with each passing year?

It is, Sean feels, her authenticity that underlines such continuing popularity: "People know instinctively that there is something real there, that besides the fashion and movies, she put her entire being into trying to save children through UNICEF. That's why the teens and tweens today look to her as their pied piper and that's how I'd like her to be remembered. Her outward elegance was matched by her inner beauty."

The epitome of glamour, wealth, and fame—the trifecta of life's goals according to the incessant messages on the social media that rules today—Audrey nonetheless figured out how to live an authentic life by turning her back on the church of fame. In a modern world where the once exalted position of star seems to have been usurped by the cheap currency of reality television, her persona, films, and way of life remain both current and effortlessly rewarding.

Not a flash in the pan, not a passing fancy, but a role model for the ages.

The very last Golden Age Hollywood star.

Icon upon icon. Richard Avedon's portrait of Audrey, projected onto the Empire State Building. UPI/Alamy Stock Photo.

Chapter Sixty-One

THE LAST GOLDEN AGE STAR

"How did we drift so far from Audrey Hepburn? Can we ever get back?"
—Tweet by CBS Television correspondent Mo Rocca

AUDREY HEPBURN REMAINS THE VERY last golden age larger-than-life movie star for one simple but important reason: careers like hers are no longer possible. From the late 1920s through the early 1960s, movie stars possessed a certain mystique, their images carefully curated by studio publicists whose job it was to shield the stars from overexposure. Stars appeared almost deliberately out of touch with the citizens of Main Street USA, and that behavior proved a crucial part of their appeal. Only occasionally descending from Mount Olympus to mingle with everyday citizens, these stars increased their allure through their very inaccessibility. No one, it is safe to say, would have demanded a selfie of Greta Garbo or Audrey Hepburn.

Tom Cruise, George Clooney, Denzel Washington, Meryl Streep, and Julia Roberts are names, stars even, but there is nothing otherworldly about them; theirs is a different type of stardom, one deliberately modeled upon a philosophy of "I'm just like you—you won't catch me putting on any airs." It is stardom as a reflection of life in the twenty-first century—we have lost the last vestiges of innocence that allowed the public to believe in the Hollywood dream factory.

It all plays out as a result of changing mores, increased cynicism, and different societal expectations, but when it comes to stardom, the ultimate game changer proved to be social media. When the movie star formerly glimpsed thirty feet high on the silver screen posts incessantly about his or her life, reasons to pay eighteen dollars to see them on that screen have vanished. Streaming the movie at home suffices.

It is the ever-tweeting, photo-posting public with whom actors now compete for bandwidth. As stars now proudly post Instagram photos of family and friends, straining to remain in the consciousness of a public saddled with an ever-shortening attention span, the very concepts of privacy and allure have vanished. Forever. Logically enough, the biggest stars of today are superheroes—the only figures who remain inaccessible.

Shifting standards of acceptable behavior further rocked the very concept of stardom; bad behavior from stars in Hollywood's golden age was usually covered up by studio fixers, but the same behavior today is now oft times publicized before being repositioned as a marketing opportunity for apology and redemption. Statements, tweets, and Instagram posts increase in dizzying profusion until the original offense fades away.

Publicists remain busy, but Sean Ferrer sees a possible day of reckoning coming as a result: "All these dramas about celebrities are going to embitter people about the very notion of celebrity. If they continue to disappoint us, we'll end up hating them all. I hope it won't happen to my mother because she was never about herself—she continually gave back. Black Lives Matter is an important movement, and my mother was fighting for that very idea thirty years ago in Africa through her work for UNICEF. I hope she'll survive any inevitable revisionism and attendant fall from the Hollywood pantheon."

What would Audrey have made of the social media which plays such a big role in maintaining a star's "brand" today? Never a snob, but definitely restrained beneath her gracious manner, Audrey would seem an extremely poor fit for an electronic world running on the fuel of oversharing. And yet she might well have embraced social media, not for the purposes of her acting career but instead to spread the word about UNICEF. Sean, in fact, posits that his mother would have adapted nicely to Instagram: "Well, she really was the queen of Instagram because she was more photographed than anyone else."

Fifty years ago, lasting movie stardom like Audrey's was helped by the fact that movies possessed a longer shelf life. There were no DVDs or streaming services, and a movie was likely five years old before it could be shown on television. Nowadays, even big budget movies like Martin Scorsese's *Killers of the Flower Moon* (2023) are streamed on television within weeks of release, and it seems a near truism that the more readily available the films, the briefer the career of the Hollywood star. Familiarity in this case does not breed contempt but rather indifference on the part of the public. With hundreds of films readily available at the flick of a switch, who really feels a personal connection with a star as the public did with Audrey? Where exactly are Hilary Swank, Marion Cotillard, and Brie Larson as box office draws today? All Academy Award winners in the twenty-first century, all talented, and none a galvanizing figure.

Audrey's time as a movie star—roughly 1953–1968—may read as somewhat truncated when compared to the Bette Davises and John Waynes of the world, but seventy years on, the power of her personality and image loom larger than ever. The images of her contemporaries like Marilyn Monroe and Elizabeth Taylor may often seem like remote relics from the past when viewed in the context of the twenty-first century, but Audrey's image still reads as current. Unlike the continuing fascination with the life and career of Monroe, the interest in Audrey has never focused upon either her death or any sense of tragedy. Instead, she is looked to as an inspirational source of life wisdom, a Hollywood star who is not the subject of tell-all biographies but instead the raison d'être of books entitled *What Would Audrey Do?*, *100 Reasons to Love Audrey Hepburn*, and in a nod to the twenty-first century, *How to Be Audrey in a Kardashian World*.

While Monroe's and Taylor's private lives were plastered all over newspapers and magazines, in Audrey the public found a star whose private life and screen image seemed to have achieved synchronicity while remaining pleasingly remote. A little time away in the mountains of Switzerland did a great deal to increase interest in the answer to the age-old question underlying true Hollywood stardom: What is she really like?

In some ways, Audrey's image as the last golden age star remains powerful precisely because of its mid-twentieth-century origins; in the 1950s and '60s, life may not have been any simpler than it is in the twenty-first century, but in retrospect it seems so to many, and Hollywood has always thrived on illusion. When it came to the sexual dynamic that fueled romantic comedies and dramas, no one in the middle of "the American century" spoke of heteronormatives, cisgender, or nonbinary identity. There were simply men, women, and, as the old joke had it, girl singers. Audrey, upper class but down to earth, the paragon of a certain type of femininity pitched at the burgeoning middle class, projected an image which flattered her audience's conception of itself.

Traditionally feminine on film, Audrey Hepburn nonetheless always spoke her mind and proved more than capable of holding her own in any onscreen battle of the sexes. Her persona, short on sex and long on romance, combined strength of character with an iron-tinged vulnerability that seemed to speak in a curiously modern way to the notion of having it all, impossible though that idea may be for men and women alike. In the words of one commentator, she remained "the only comedienne capable of brushing her teeth while still maintaining her glamour."

It was that glamour that actually has increased Audrey's appeal in today's decidedly dressed-down world. Her attention to appearance, whether swanning in Givenchy or walking in jeans and a Lacoste shirt, always registered, forming a marked contrast to the ever-informal stars of the twenty-first century. Says Sean:

> She always looked good, even at home where she dressed casually. She was never in sweats with her stomach sticking out. It was all very different from the actors and actresses of today. They go out wearing UGG boots and jeans and that's a reflection of the fact that it's a different time. Everybody has the right to be real, but as an actor you've chosen a career where you're supposed to project a certain style or persona. It plays out differently now, and it also plays out differently in terms of the length of your stardom.
>
> You don't get to be the most beloved actress and style icon of the last century, and now a pied piper for teens and tweens in the twenty-first century, without a tremendous respect for planning things and attention to details. My mother understood the importance of all this—I think she understood the importance of selling one ticket at a time. But now, maybe, the concept of movie star is finished. There are actors, not stars. You're on and you're off, beginning and ending with the performance.

In a particularly reflective moment, Audrey once mused: "How shall I sum up my life? I think I've been particularly lucky." But the luck, it seems, was not Audrey's but her audience's. Because when you're the most beautiful girl in school, the best-dressed cool kid who could ruthlessly rule the room but instead chooses to be the nicest person on the scene, then everyone wants to know you, to know how to live a more meaningful life like yours.

It is just such a meaningful life that was perfectly summed up by photographer Bob Willoughby in terms anyone, male or female, would wish spoken about them at the end of their days: "She was one of the most beautiful women I have ever photographed, and yet, I felt all her beauty came from inside and it radiated out to everyone around her."

Her greatest role: humanitarian. Derek Hudson/Hulton Archive/Getty Images.

Chapter Sixty-Two

AND IN THE END, 1929–1993

> "Love is action. It isn't just talk and it never was. . . . We are born with the ability to love yet we have to develop it like you would any other muscle."
>
> —Audrey Hepburn

If actions speak louder than words, then the Audrey Hepburn Life Lessons could be said to run as follows:

- Give of yourself.
- No matter the task at hand, put forth your best effort.
- Manners represent kindness. Remain humble.
- Leave the world improved in at least one small way.
- Stay true to your own inner compass and author a style of your own.
- No one will remember the latest dress or opening night, but everyone will remember generosity and a smile.
- Only connect.
- Ask yourself—how well have I loved?

The hard-won wisdom which allowed Audrey to separate the truly important—family, children, kindness—from the passing fancy of Hollywood stardom, had granted her a clarity of vision: the meaning of life, she stated, was "not to live for the day—that would be materialistic—but to treasure the day." Fame could not solve any problems except those of finance, but treasuring the day and helping others did pave the way to genuine happiness. In her own smiling acknowledgment, she exclaimed: "I heard a definition once: Happiness is health and a short memory! I wish I'd invented it, because it is very true."

In the case of Audrey Hepburn, the loss of her father and the suffering she witnessed in World War II combined to propel her away from the glittery surface toward an appreciation of the eternal verities. She took her family and UNICEF seriously, but never herself. For all the heft of her screen legacy, she left the lightest of footprints, refusing to draw attention to herself, and instead redirecting the spotlight toward others in need.

Emma Ferrer thinks of her grandmother's legacy as one of kindness, modesty, and virtue, adding, "Really, her legacy is contained in the Sam Levenson poem she loved so much. 'We have two hands—one for helping ourselves and one for helping others.' That's what she would say, and it sums up how she lived her personal life and conducted her professional career."

Caryl Stern has thought about the Hepburn legacy, but always in terms that stretch far beyond the years of Hollywood stardom: "I think her legacy is that there are things in the world more important than yourself. You can use whatever power you have to address them, and that's what she did. She is the epitome of 'I have a podium, and I can make a difference. I'm going to grab it and take it and use it.' I think about when I was a little girl, watching *Breakfast at Tiffany's* and wanting to grow up to be this beautiful actress—and then I grew into an older woman who looked again at Audrey and said 'I don't want *Breakfast at Tiffany's*—I want to go to Africa like she did. I want to make a difference.' That's her legacy. She set a standard for all of us."

Audrey herself always emphasized kindness above all else: "I feel so strongly that's where it all starts, with kindness. What a different world this could be if everyone lived by that." She was, in her own way, the living embodiment of the Henry James aphorism that "three things in human life are important: the first is to be kind; the second is to be kind; and the third is to be kind." In this she succeeded more fully than any other actress in the history of Hollywood.

Early in *Sabrina*, Audrey/Sabrina is shown writing in her diary: "I have learned how to live, how to be in the world and of the world, and not just stand aside and watch." It seems oddly prescient that those words, spoken at age twenty-five in only her second leading role, somehow came to define Audrey's own journey through life. After decades of striving, she had, through her sons, her work with UNICEF, and yes, her screen immortality, succeeded in fully living in and of the world, never standing aside just to watch.

Her best films—*Roman Holiday*, *Sabrina*, *The Nun's Story*, *My Fair Lady*, and *Two for the Road*—will continue to be shown for decades to come, and it is indisputable that Audrey herself remains the single most important factor in making those films endlessly watchable. In the words of Billy Wilder: "God kissed her on the cheek and there she was."

In the long run, however, her legacy remains far bigger and more important than that delivered by her films or fashion, and for the most personal and important of reasons: in gaining an understanding of her own pain and vulnerability, she used her fame to give back on the largest of international scales, literally saving lives and making the world a better place.

After years plagued by self-doubt and disappointment in her own best efforts, she had succeeded in living a generous yet perfectly human life, one that ultimately did nothing less than fulfill the ancient Greek definition of happiness so often quoted by President John F. Kennedy: "The full use of your powers along lines of excellence."

Time Tested Beauty Tips

Sam Levenson's letters to his daughter and granddaughter

Adapted into a poem by Audrey Hepburn

For attractive lips, speak words of kindness.
For lovely eyes, seek out the good in people.
For a slim figure, share your food with the hungry.
For beautiful hair, let a child run his or her fingers through it once a day.
For poise, walk with the knowledge that you never walk alone.
People, even more than things, have to be restored, renewed, revived,
    reclaimed and redeemed; never throw out anyone.
Remember, if you ever need a helping hand, you'll find one at the end of each of your arms.
As you grow older, you will discover that you have two hands, one
    for helping yourself, the other for helping others.
The beauty of a woman is not in the clothes she wears, the figure she carries, or
    the way she combs her hair. The beauty of a woman must be seen from in her
    eyes, because that is the doorway to her heart, the place where love resides.
The beauty of a woman is not in a facial mole, but the true beauty in a woman
    is reflected in her soul. It is the caring that she lovingly gives, the passion that
    she shows, and the beauty of a woman with passing years only grows!

APPENDIX A
SELECTED HONORS

1954—*Roman Holiday*
Best Actress: New York Film Critics Circle
Best Film Actress: British Academy of Film and Television Arts—BAFTA
Best Motion Pictures Actress: Golden Globe
Best Actress: Academy Award
1954—*Ondine*
Best Dramatic Actress: Tony Award
1955—*Sabrina*
Best Film Actress nomination: BAFTA
Best Actress: Academy Award nomination
1957—*War and Peace*
Best Actress Nomination: New York Film Critics Circle
Best Film Actress nomination: BAFTA
Best Motion Pictures Actress, Drama: Golden Globe nomination
1960—*Nun's Story*
Best Actress: New York Film Critics Circle
Best Film Actress: BAFTA
Best Foreign Actress: David di Donatello Award
Best Actress: Academy Award nomination
Best Motion Picture Actress, Drama: Golden Globe nomination
1962—*Breakfast at Tiffany's*
Best Motion Picture Actress, Musical/Comedy: Golden Globe nomination
Best Actress: Academy Award nomination
Best Foreign Actress: David di Donatello Award
1964—*Charade*
Best Motion Picture Actress, Musical/Comedy: Golden Globe nomination
Best Film Actress: BAFTA
1965—*My Fair Lady*
Best Actress: New York Film Critics
Best Foreign Actress: David di Donatello Award

Best Motion Picture Actress, Musical/Comedy: Golden Globe nomination

1968—*Wait Until Dark*

Best Actress nomination: New York Film Critics Circle

Best Actress: Academy Award nomination

Best Motion Picture Actress, Drama: Golden Globe nomination

1968—*Two for the Road*

Best Motion Picture Actress, Musical/Comedy: Golden Globe nomination

1968—Special Tony Award

1988—International Danny Kaye Award for Children: U.S. Committee for UNICEF

1989—International Humanitarian Award: presented by the Institute for Human Understanding—First ever recipient

1990—Golden Globe Awards: Cecil B. DeMille Lifetime Achievement Award

1991—Film Society of Lincoln Center: Gala Tribute Honoree

Variety Clubs International—Humanitarian Award

Children's Institute International: Champion of Children Award

1992—BAFTA: Lifetime Achievement Award

Presidential Medal of Freedom—Awarded for humanitarian efforts and contributions to the arts

Council of Fashion Designers of America: Lifetime of Style Award

1993—Screen Actors Guild of America: Lifetime Achievement Award

Academy Award—Jean Hersholt Humanitarian Award (posthumous)

Emmy Award—*Gardens of the World*—Outstanding Individual Achievement (posthumous)

Grammy Award—Best Spoken Word Album for Children: *Audrey Hepburn's Enchanted Tales* (posthumous)

Pearl S. Buck Women's Award, The Pearl S. Buck Foundation (posthumous)

2002—Spirit of Audrey Hepburn bronze sculpture, commissioned and donated by Robert Wolders (sculptor John Kennedy), unveiled at the public plaza, UNICEF headquarters in New York City

2003—Legends of Hollywood—US Postage Stamp released

APPENDIX B
CAREER SCORECARD

Feature film appearances, unless otherwise noted. Years refer to date of release.

YEAR	WORK	COMMENTS
1948	*Nederlands in Zeven Lessen*	A two-word role, playing a flight attendant in a short Dutch film.
1948	*High Button Shoes*	London's West End—Chorus girl Audrey dancing the famed Jerome Robbins "Mack Sennett Ballet."
1949	*Sauce Tartare*	Revue in London's West End. Dancing and comedy sketches. Salary: 10 pounds/week.
1950	*Sauce Piquante*	Revue in London's West End. Dancing and comedy sketches. Salary: 12 pounds/week.
1951	*One Wild Oat*	Two blink-and-you'll-miss-her snippets in a mediocre British farce.
1951	*Laughter in Paradise*	Miniscule role as "Cigarette girl." A screen credit of "Introducing Audrey Hepburn."
1951	*Young Wives Tale*	Forgettable sitcom of a film, but Audrey appears onscreen in seven scenes.
1951	*The Lavender Hill Mob*	Oscar-winning prestige film. Only one line as "Chiquita," but Audrey delivers it to Alec Guinness—who noticed.
1951	*Gigi*	Broadway—a star is born. Tony Award nomination as Best Actress.
1952	*Secret People*	Politics, intrigue, and love affairs. Third billed and playing a dancer.
1952/1953	*Nous Irons a Monte Carlo/Monte Carlo Baby*	Silly in both French and English. Notable for one reason: Audrey met Colette while shooting on location.
1953	*Roman Holiday*	An Oscar for her first starring role.
1954	*Ondine*	Broadway—Tony Award for Best Actress.
1954	*Sabrina*	Beautifully played. Oscar nomination.
1956	*War and Peace*	An international mish-mosh, but Audrey is touching as Natasha.
1957	*Funny Face*	Magical Gershwin musical with the great Fred Astaire.
1957	*Love in the Afternoon*	Reteaming with Billy Wilder. Prototypical young-Audrey-with-older-man plot.
1957	*Mayerling*	NBC Television—Co-starring with husband Mel Ferrer. Plodding.
1959	*Green Mansions*	Directed by Mel. Misfire.

YEAR	WORK	COMMENTS
1959	*The Nun's Story*	First-rate Fred Zinnemann film. Audrey's finest performance. A third Oscar nomination.
1960	*The Unforgiven*	Strange John Huston western. Miscast Audrey.
1961	*Breakfast at Tiffany's*	THE role. Iconic Audrey and a fourth Oscar nomination.
1962	*The Children's Hour*	Reunion with William Wyler. Not without interest but ultimately unsuccessful.
1963	*Charade*	A terrific teaming with Cary Grant.
1964	*Paris When It Sizzles*	Leaden whimsy. An unfortunate reunion with William Holden.
1964	*My Fair Lady*	The Oscar-winning Best Picture. Audrey soars in the film's second half.
1966	*How to Steal a Million*	Third and final film with Wyler. Should have been better.
1967	*Two for the Road*	First-rate bittersweet comedy-drama.
1967	*Wait Until Dark*	Audrey as terrorized blind woman in a suspenseful thriller. Fifth Oscar nomination.
1976	*Robin and Marian*	A welcome return to the screen. Beautifully judged performance.
1979	*Sidney Sheldon's Bloodline*	Audrey's worst film. Best and easily forgotten.
1981	*They All Laughed*	Ungainly Peter Bogdanovich film.
1986	*Directed by William Wyler*	Cameo; paying tribute to her great friend.
1987	*Love Among Thieves*	ABC Television—Disposable fluff.
1989	*Always*	Directed by Steven Spielberg. Audrey's cameo lifts the entire film.
1990–1991	*From the Diary of Anne Frank*	Striking, dramatically compelling concert narration of Anne Frank's diary, in conjunction with Michael Tilson Thomas's symphonic sketches.
1993	*Gardens of the World*	PBS Television—Sweet tour of the world's gardens. Posthumous Emmy Award.
1994	*Audrey Hepburn's Enchanted Tales*	Superb audio recording of four fairy tales. Posthumous Grammy Award.

Notes

ACT ONE—CODA/OVERTURE

One—A Closet, 1993

3   "She seemed so terribly different and sort of very angelic and sort of very ethereal": Harry Belafonte in Victoria Loustalot, *Living like Audrey: Life Lessons from the Fairest Lady of All* (Guilford, CT: Lyons Press, 2017), 131.

3   "not more than 20% full—with blue jeans, wool slacks, blazers, and t-shirts": Celia McGee, "Son Fondly Recalls 'Elegant' Hepburn," *New York Daily News,* November 4, 2003.

4   "Being away from home": "Luca Dotti: The Moment She Ended Her Career, My Mother Started to Be Happy Again," *Larevista.ro,* June 22, 2015.

4   "I love fashion, you know. Really love it. But fashion has nothing to do with *me*": Patricia Bosworth, *The Men in My Life* (New York: HarperCollins, 2017), 295

4   "The *me* in here . . . the private me, the interior me—inside I'm not fashionable at all": ibid.

Two—Beginnings, 1929–1948

7   "Her life really is like a fairy tale": *Darcey Bussell's Looking for Audrey Hepburn,* BBC Television, YouTube, uploaded by Charlotte Crosby, April 3, 2023, https://www.youtube.com/watch?v=kBJ01RrpinI.

7   "He was a true dilettante and a brilliant one at that": Sean Hepburn Ferrer, *Audrey Hepburn: An Elegant Spirit* (New York: Atria Books, 2003), 10.

7   "She saw life itself as a gift": Sue Robson, "Audrey Hepburn's Son: 'One Day We Will Find a Cure for the Cancer That Killed My Mother,'" *Express*, October 19, 2015, https://www.express.co.uk/life-style/life/613099/Audrey-Hepburn-son-cure-cancer-killed-awareness.

8   "I'm half-Irish, half-Dutch and I was born in Belgium": Alexander Walker, *Audrey: Her Real Story* (New York: St. Martin's Press, 1995), 43.

8   "I am convinced that, to her dying day, she believed she was a Hepburn": ibid.

8   "who have heard the call of Fascism, and have followed the light on the upward road to victory . . . ": ibid., 13.

8   "The Germany of today is a most present country": Robert Matzen, *Dutch Girl: Audrey Hepburn and World War II* (Pittsburgh: GoodKnight Books, 2019), 5.

8   "young Audrey took refuge in the one way that made sense to her six year old self": Walker, *Audrey: Her Real Story*, 10.

9   "She cried day in, day out. I thought that she never would stop": Matzen, *Dutch Girl*, 16.

9   "My mother would sob through the night": Audrey Hepburn in *Audrey: More Than an Icon*, Salon Pictures Head Gear Films, Universal Pictures, 2020.

9   "He was joyous—maybe not a warm father": "Audrey Hepburn . . . by Her Son," YouTube, posted by fisherclips123, January 9, 2013, https://www.youtube.com/watch?v=F-EouugFYq8&t=88s.

9   "the most traumatic event in my life . . . I was terrified": Donald Spoto, *Enchantment: The Life of Audrey Hepburn* (New York: Three Rivers Press, 2006), 14.

9   "(Children need) two parents for the equilibrium in life. I mean emotional equilibrium": Dominick Dunne, "Hepburn Heart," *Vanity Fair*, May 1991.

9   "turned out to be a good lesson in independence": Martin Abramson, "Audrey Hepburn," *Cosmopolitan*, October 1955.

9   "I liked the children and my teachers but": Matzen, *Dutch Girl*, 20.

9   "I loved it, just loved it": ibid., 22.

9   "I don't deal with words very well": "Audrey Hepburn Interview," *Good Morning America*, February 19, 1987, posted by You'reGonnaLoveTomorrow, May 4, 2016, https://www.youtube.com/watch?v=jmvDhPOy7EQ.

9   "to stay with a family (in England) whom I absolutely adored": Dunne, "Hepburn Heart."

10   "really one of the last planes out": Matzen, *Dutch Girl*, 25.

10   "There are so many images that will never go away": Majo Sato, "From Starving to Stardom: The Deleted Scenes of Audrey Hepburn's Life," *Rhētorikós: Excellence in Student Writing*, Fordham University (Fall 2022), https://rhetorikos.blog.fordham.edu/?p=1124.

10 "The second worst memory I have": Matzen, *Dutch Girl*, 43.

10 "From one day to the next": *Darcey Bussell's Looking for Audrey Hepburn*.

10 "more English than Dutch": Alan Riding, "25 Years Later Honor for Audrey Hepburn," *New York Times*, April 12, 1991.

10 "Every time I opened my mouth, everyone was roaring with laughter": Audrey Hepburn on the *Phil Donahue Show*, January 26, 1990.

10 "Maybe that's why I'm so attached to my own family. They are my roots": Mary Blume, "Audrey Hepburn Making Films," *International Herald Tribune*, July 11, 1975.

10 "I saw families with little children": Woodward, *Audrey Hepburn*, 34.

11 "Ella was a superior woman": Matzen, *Dutch Girl*, 31.

11 "Ella was her father figure": ibid., 195.

11 "My mother desperately wanted": Michael Heatley, *Audrey Hepburn in Words and Pictures* (New York: Chartwell Books, 2017), 26.

11 "I tried to obey my father": Ian Woodward, *Audrey Hepburn: Fair Lady of the Screen* (London: Virgin Books, 1993), 17.

11 "Ella was the frustrated prima donna, absolutely": Matzen, *Dutch Girl*, 75.

11 "My mother would have been better off": Heatley, *Audrey Hepburn in Words and Pictures*, 38.

Three—War and a Life of Dance, 1940–1947

13 "With her vivid style and incomparable elegance": "Dance, Expression and Audrey Hepburn," The Australian Ballet, May 5, 2010, https://australianballet.com.au/blog/dance-expression-and-audrey-hepburn.

13 "That discipline absolutely grew out of": Sean Hepburn Ferrer, interview with author, July 7, 2020.

13 "I was sixteen when the war finished": Woodward, *Audrey Hepburn*, 46.

13 "I was studying and dreaming": ibid., 41.

13 "I didn't think much of my looks": Matzen, *Dutch Girl*, 112.

14 "'Poezepas'–Dutch for cat-walk": ibid., 141.

14 "I was twenty-three years old behind the fragrance counter": Mo Rocca, interview with Larry King, *Larry King Now*, www.ora.tv, November 19, 2019.

14 "running around with food for the pilots": Matzen, *Dutch Girl*, 148.

15 "Stories about my contributions to the underground have been exaggerated": "Audrey Hepburn: *Sunday, Sunday*," host Gloria Hunniford, YouTube, posted by You'reGonnaLoveTomorrow, May 4, 2014, https://www.youtube.com/watch?v=W52UZU2oLVg&t=15s.

15 "we had thirty-seven people sleeping in our house as evacuees continued to arrive": Matzen, *Dutch Girl*, 204.

15 "We went for days at a time without anything to eat": Spoto, *Enchantment: The Life of Audrey Hepburn*, 30.

15 "Holland was one of the worst": Audrey Hepburn in *Audrey: More Than an Icon*.

15 "picked right off the street with a dozen others": *People* Extra: *A Tribute to Audrey Hepburn*, Winter 1993, 11.

15 "stayed indoors for a month": Matzen, *Dutch Girl*, 263.

15 "It was not on the scale of Somalia": ibid., 248.

15 "In those days I used to say to myself": Walker, *Audrey: Her Real Story*, 29.

15 "ran out to welcome the soldiers": Luca Dotti, *Audrey at Home* (New York: Harper Design, 2015), 208.

16 "that's why I say freedom has no price": "Audrey Hepburn Interview with Ivo Niehe," https://www.youtube.com/watch?v=3ubymGxbkys

16 "a white blouse with a Peter Pan collar": Robert Matzen, *Warrior: Audrey Hepburn* (Pittsburgh: GoodKnight Books, 2021), 37.

16 "One thing my mother always talked about": "Interview with Audrey Hepburn's Son," BBC One, YouTube, uploaded by uchubi, March 23, 2014, https://www.youtube.com/watch?v=A9sTOPmT0WY.

16 "I came out of the war thankful to be alive": Sheridan Morley, *Audrey Hepburn* (London: Pavilion Books, 1993), 19.

16 "I think when you have problems and so forth": Audrey Hepburn in *Audrey: More Than an Icon*.

16 "I've been often through hell": ibid.

16 "Having been arrested in July 1940 under Defense Regulation 18 B": Walker, *Audrey: Her Real Story*, 23.

16 "I didn't try to reach him": Jerry Vermilye, *The Complete Films of Audrey Hepburn* (Secaucus, NJ: Carol Publishing Group, 1997), 20.

17 "To fund her lessons": Loekie van Oven in "Prima Ballerina," *Audrey Hepburn: Her Life and Legacy*, A360 Media LLC, 2023, 22.

17 "Sonia taught me that if you really worked hard, you'd succeed": Barry Paris, *Audrey Hepburn* (New York: G. P. Putnam's Sons 1996), 35.

17 "I've been constantly in situations in my life and career": Matzen, *Dutch Girl*, 293.

17 "terribly strict": "Audrey Hepburn Interview," *Good Morning America*, February 19, 1987, https://www.youtube.com/watch?v=jmvDhPOy7EQ.

17 "I would train for two or three hours at a time": Woodward, *Audrey Hepburn*, 53.

17 "You'll have a lot more opportunities there": Paris, *Audrey Hepburn*, 37.

17 "the tall thin girl with the eyes": Woodward, *Audrey Hepburn*, 54.

17 "I am not an actress. You will regret it": Paris, *Audrey Hepburn*, 39.

Four—London, 1948

19 "Arthur Rubenstein had a difficult early life": Audrey Hepburn in *Audrey: More Than an Icon*.

19 "Miss Audrey Hepburn-Ruston is known to me": *Darcey Bussell's Looking for Audrey Hepburn*.

19   "She desperately wanted to be a dancer": "Interview with Audrey Hepburn's Son."
19   "The world was functioning again": Bob Willoughby, *Audrey Hepburn: Photographs 1953–1966* (Cologne: Taschen, 2012), 31.
19   "her dream had died": Pamela Keogh, *What Would Audrey Do? Timeless Lessons for Living with Grace and Style* (New York: Gotham Books, 2008), 167.
19   "I might have to slave for years (in ballet) to achieve only limited success": Robyn Karney, *Audrey Hepburn: A Charmed Life* (New York: Arcade Publishing, 1993), 31.
20   "bright colors overpower me and wash me out": Paris, *Audrey Hepburn*, 43.
20   "A powder base by day, a skin food by night": Vermilye, *Complete Films of Audrey Hepburn*, 24.
20   "Ella was a single Mom": Sean Hepburn Ferrer, interview with author, July 7, 2020.

Five—Chorus Girl, 1948–1949

23   "I tried always to do better": Ian Woodward, *Audrey Hepburn* (London: Virgin Published, 1993), viii.
23   "Lousy dancer. Great verve": Diana Maychick, *Audrey Hepburn: An Intimate Portrait* (Secaucus, NJ: Carol Publishing Group 1993), 54.
23   "I loved being in a musical show. For the first time, I felt the pure joy of living": Vermilye, *Complete Films of Audrey Hepburn*, 25.
23   "I saw a girl come running across the stage": *People* Extra: *A Tribute to Audrey Hepburn,* 14.
23   "in one she played a 'Boogie Woogie Yoga Follower,'" Spoto, *Enchantment*, 42.
23   "The trouble was that the sweater": Woodward, *Audrey Hepburn*, 76.
24   "A copy of the picture went into Mullally's office files": ibid.
24   "I was very ambitious and took every opportunity": Keogh, *What Would Audrey Do?* 13.
24   "Deep down, ballet was my dream": "Audrey Hepburn Interview," *Good Morning America*, February 19, 1987.
24   "Acting was in effect a default choice": Sean Hepburn Ferrer, interview with author, July 7, 2020.
24   "Only the absolutely determined people succeed": George Tiffin, *A Star Is Born* (London: Head of Zeus Ltd. 2015), 162.
24   "She struck me as being very alert, very smart, very talented, very ambitious": Keogh, *What Would Audrey Do?* 12.
24   "Everybody knew there was something totally remarkable about her": Paris, *Audrey Hepburn*, 48.

Six—A Star Is (Not Quite Yet) Born, 1950–1951

27   "Even in her early films": Alex Cox, "Audrey Hepburn—An Iconic Problem," *The Guardian*, 20 January 2011.
27   "utterly enchanting": Paris, *Audrey Hepburn*, 57.
27   "I thought she was going to make it": ibid.
28   "I'm sorry. I've just signed to do a short tour in a show": Woodward, *Audrey Hepburn*, 83.
28   "A battle royal ensued": Warren Harris, *Audrey Hepburn: A Biography* (New York: Simon & Schuster, 1994), 67.
28   "You start and finish on the same day": Woodward, *Audrey Hepburn*, 84.
28   "He had it in for me. It was the only unhappy experience I ever had making a picture": Spoto, *Enchantment*, 50.
28   "I was probably dreadful in it!": Ellen Johnson, "Will Hollywood Ever See Audrey Hepburn Again?" *Modern Screen*, April 1955.

Seven—A Single Line and Alec Guinness, 1951–1952

31   "We all have our blind spots": Woodward, *Audrey Hepburn*, 92.
31   "She only had half a line to say": Harris, *Audrey Hepburn*, 68.
31   "struck nobody as star material": ibid.
31   "made a total of one quick appearance": Sidney Fields, "Audrey Hepburn—Success Is Not Security," *McCall's*, July 1954.
31   "I never remember Guinness recommending anyone else to me": Maychick, *Audrey Hepburn*, 67–68.
31   "With the perfect bone structure of her face": Morley, *Audrey Hepburn,* 178.
32   "a beautiful thing, like a little deer, with this long neck and those big eyes": Paris, *Audrey Hepburn*, 55.
32   "Do you think I have a chance?": ibid.
32   "The ballet scenes were a great strain for her": Woodward, *Audrey Hepburn*, 94.
32   "With the young Audrey Hepburn in a sizable role, it's rather like seeing Cinderella before the transformation": Pauline Kael, quoted in Vermilye, *Complete Films of Audrey Hepburn*, 79.
32   "All right . . . you could then say": Woodward, *Audrey Hepburn*, 98.
32   "couldn't play Scene 42": ibid. 100.
32   "Petronilla is awake": *Brandy for the Parson*, screenplay by John Dighton, Walter Meade, and Alfred Shaughnessy, Associated British Film Distributors, 1952.
33   "The ladies in the script-typing pool": Woodward, *Audrey Hepburn*, 100.
33   "Think hard before you sign a long-term contract": Paris, *Audrey Hepburn*, 56.
33   "I said, 'If the cast is No. 1'": Valentina Cortese in "War and Peace," *Audrey Hepburn: Her Life and Legacy*, 22.
33   "She made this one before she became a (movie star) in reality": Oscar Godbout, *New York Times*, quoted in Vermilye, *Complete Films of Audrey Hepburn*, 82.

Eight—Discovery by Colette, 1951–1952

35 "With no actress cast": Robert Matzen, "Instincts," RobertMatzen.com.

35 "Voila! There is my Gigi!" Paris, *Audrey Hepburn*, 61.

36 "This would be a very good Gigi": Spoto, *Enchantment*, 62.

36 "Colette was very ill with arthritis or rheumatism and was in a wheelchair": Dunne, "Hepburn Heart."

36 "what a crazy thing to say": Melissa Hellstern, *How to Be Lovely: The Audrey Hepburn Way of Life* (New York: Dutton, 2004), 31.

36 "You're a dancer": ibid.

36 "Follow your instincts": Robert Matzen, "Instincts," *RobertMatzen.com.*

36 "It's a Cinderella story told in terms of sex": Harris, *Audrey Hepburn*, 74.

37 "She is greatly thought of by film people generally": Charles Higham, *Audrey: The Life of Audrey Hepburn* (New York: Macmillan, 1984), 41.

37 "Audrey didn't have much idea of phrasing, and even less of how to project": Harris, *Audrey Hepburn*, 83.

37 "blind the audience to her deficiencies": ibid., 85.

37 "He staged the play": ibid.

37 "the actors all followed me so completely": Higham, *Audrey: The Life of Audrey Hepburn*, 48.

38 "Once you're in a three-quarter-length dress, with a rustling petticoat underneath": Harris, *Audrey Hepburn*, 85.

38 "so that her high cheekbones slimmed the lower part of her face": Walker, *Audrey: Her Real Story*, 64.

38 "The delightful Miss Hepburn obviously is not an experienced actress": Higham, *Audrey: The Life of Audrey Hepburn*, 50.

38 "She was at ease on the stage as though she had been born to it": Elliot Norton, "Second Thoughts of a First-Nighter," *Boston Post*, March 28, 1954.

38 "a young actress of charm, honesty and talent": Morley, *Audrey Hepburn*, 48.

38 "Oh, dear, and I still have to learn how to act": Harris, *Audrey Hepburn*, 88.

38 "I'm halfway between a dancer and an actress": Heatley, *Audrey Hepburn in Words and Pictures*, 33.

38 "All I feel is a responsibility to live up to success": Walker, *Audrey: Her Real Story*, 99.

39 "An orgy of overacting and a vulgar script": Spoto, *Enchantment*, 72.

39 "To Audrey Hepburn, the treasure I found on the beach": Maychick, *Audrey Hepburn: An Intimate Portrait*, 76.

39 "I thought being the 'Toast of the Town'": Woodward, *Audrey Hepbur*n, 123–24.

ACT TWO—WHAT PRICE HOLLYWOOD

Nine—*Roman Holiday*, 1951–1953

43 "I was born with something that appealed to audiences at that particular time": *Audrey Hepburn Remembered.*

44 "You surprise me": Jan Herman, *A Talent for Trouble: The Life of Hollywood's Most Acclaimed Director, William Wyler* (New York: G. P. Putnam Sons, 1995), 344.

44 "I have no recollection of hesitating at all": ibid., 345–46.

44 "without an American accent": Axel Madsen, *William Wyler* (New York: Thomas Y. Crowell Co., 1973), 321.

44 "I have another candidate for *Roman Holiday*—Audrey Hepburn": Paris, *Audrey Hepburn*, 62.

44 "met with me for a few minutes": "Reflections on the Silver Screen: Audrey Hepburn Interview with Richard Brown," American Movie Classics, April 26, 1990. YouTube, posted by You'reGonnaLoveTomorrow, May 4, 2015, https://www.youtube.com/watch?v=v18G6K4MVjc.

44 "The minute you saw it, you knew she would get the part": Harris, *Audrey Hepburn*, 77.

44 "Oh, is it over now? Oh, good": ibid., 78.

44 "How was it? Was I any good?": Madsen, *William Wyler*, 321.

45 "Talking to Thorold I forgot about the camera": "Reflections on the Silver Screen Audrey Hepburn Interview with Richard Brown," American Movie Classics, April 26, 1990.

45 "I was so green I didn't really know what to do": Keogh, *Audrey Style*, 66.

45 "Acting, looks, and personality!" William Wyler, cited in Vermilye, *Complete Films of Audrey Hepburn*, 85.

45 "very intrigued": Herman, *Talent for Trouble*, 344.

45 "Please tell Dickinson he did an excellent job": ibid., 345.

45 "I remember him saying to me": ibid.

45 "When the war was over": "Audrey Hepburn Interview," *Good Morning America*, February 19, 1987.

45 "It's funny to think I might not have gotten the part": Lynn Haney, *Gregory Peck: A Charmed Life* (New York: Carroll & Graf, 2004), 217.

45 "Thick eyebrows, uneven teeth. She doesn't mind if her hair is disheveled": *People* Extra: *A Tribute to Audrey Hepburn* 53.

45 "self-conscious": *People* Extra: *A Tribute to Audrey Hepburn,* 23.

45 "absolutely delicious": ibid.

45 "Lord, help me live up to all of this": Keogh, *What Would Audrey Do?* 21.

46 "Now I know what it's like": Woodward, *Audrey Hepburn*, 129.

46 "She's a darling girl, enchanting, just adorable": Hugo Vickers, *Malice in Wonderland: My Adventures in the World of Cecil Beaton* (New York: Pegasus Books, 2021), 254.

46 "I never saw anyone misbehave in her presence": Pamela Fiori, "Forever Audrey," *Town & Country*, May 2003.

47 "Almost everything": Paris, *Audrey Hepburn*, 79.

47 "He was so dear to me": Herman, *Talent for Trouble*, 348–49.

47 "These directors realized there was enough": "Reflections on the Silver Screen Interview with Richard Brown," American Movie Classics, April 26, 1990.

47 "We can't stay here all night. Can't you cry, for God's sake?" Audrey Hepburn in *Audrey Hepburn Remembered*.

47 "It was embarrassing and frightened her": Gregory Peck as cited in Vermilye, *Complete Films of Audrey Hepburn*, 88.

47 "No, Greg, don't get upset": Roger Moore, *One Lucky Bastard: Tales From Tinseltown* (Guilford, CT: Lyons Press, 2014), 152.

47 "one of the defining moments of his career": ibid.

48 "Willy sensed the interplay": Herman, *Talent for Trouble*, 349.

48 "You should always wear my clothes": *Roman Holiday*, screenplay by John McClellan Hunter, and John Dighton (Dalton Trumbo—originally uncredited), Paramount Pictures, 1953.

48 "(She) had the assurance of a veteran": Higham, *Audrey: The Life of Audrey Hepburn*, 53.

48 "of the ten hour, not ten minute, kind": Keogh, *What Would Audrey Do?* 141.

48 "What I liked best about her is that she calculated all her business decisions": Maychick, *Audrey Hepburn*, 90.

48 "Audrey knows more about fashion than any actress, save Dietrich": Edith Head, *The Dress Doctor: Prescriptions for Style, from A to Z* (New York: HarperCollins, 2008), 7.

49 "only one person ever looked good in all thirty-six mirrors": Nora Ephron in Mo Rocca, *Mobituaries* (New York: Simon & Schuster, 2019), 237.

49 "Audrey was the perfect figure model": Head, *Dress Doctor*, 7.

49 "In a sense I reversed her face by emphasizing her temples": Keogh, *Audrey Style*, 119.

49 "I remember her saying when he died": Ferrer, *Audrey Hepburn: An Elegant Spirit*, 62.

50 "If there was anything going on, it didn't last long": Haney, *Gregory Peck: A Charmed Life*, 224.

50 "Greg . . . was the gentlest person I'd ever known": Glenn Paskin, "Audrey Hepburn," *Us Weekly*, October 17, 1988.

50 "It was my good luck, during that wonderful summer in Rome": Haney, *Gregory Peck: A Charmed Life*, 223.

50 "Everyone on the set of *Roman Holiday* was in love with Audrey": ibid.

50 "It was the only scene Wyler ever did in one take": Lawrence Cohn, "Turnaway Crowd Honors Audrey Hepburn," *Film*, April 19, 1991.

50 "Audrey had it in her to be the sugar coating on a bad-tasting pill": Sam Wasson, *Fifth Avenue, 5 A.M.: Audrey Hepburn, Breakfast at Tiffany's, and the Dawn of the Modern Woman* (New York: Harper Perennial, 2010), 24.

51 "The real star of this picture is Audrey Hepburn": Paris, *Audrey Hepburn*, 78.

51 "they realized this was a delicate matter because of the actor's contract": Spoto, *Enchantment*, 85.

51 "She was adamant that she would change nothing in her appearance": ibid., 96.

51 "What a burden she lifted from women": David Willis, *Audrey: The 60s* (New York: HarperCollins, 2012), 49.

51 "For quite a while, especially at the beginning": Jeanine Basinger, interview with author, September 11, 2020.

51 "alternately regal and childlike": Bosley Crowther in the *New York Times*, cited in Higham, *Audrey: The Life of Audrey Hepburn*, 69.

52 "bittersweet legend with laughs that leave the spirits soaring": A. H. Weiler, "Roman Holiday at Music Hall Is Modern Fairy Tale Starring Peck and Audrey Hepburn," *New York Times*, August 28, 1953.

52 "Amid the rhinestone glitter of *Roman Holiday*'s make-believe": "Princess Apparent," *Time*, September 7, 1953.

52 "President Kennedy requested be screened at the White House": Herman, *Talent for Trouble*, 355.

52 "when you are introduced in a high-quality film like *Roman Holiday*": Jeanine Basinger, interview with author, September 11, 2020.

52 "I was given an Academy Award for a story that was clearly not mine": Gabriel Miller, *William Wyler: The Life and Films of Hollywood's Most Celebrated Director* (Lexington: The University Press of Kentucky, 2013), 315.

53 "the best Oscar dress of all time": de la Hoz, *Audrey and Givenchy*, 173.

53 "It's too much": "Audrey Hepburn Wins Best Actress: 1954 Oscars," March 25, 1954, https://www.youtube.com/watch?v=p-vR7D21wqI-.

53 "She was always very real": Loustalot, *Living like Audrey*, 9.

53 "It's easier to be a shy dancer than a shy actress": Keogh, *Audrey Style*, 54.

Ten—Right Girl, Right Place, Right Time, the 1950s

55 "With her skinny waist": Alex, "How Audrey Hepburn Changed the Way Hollywood Looked at Women," *medium.com*, December 28, 2019.

56 "It took the rubble of Belgium, an English accent, and an American success": Cecil Beaton, "Audrey Hepburn by Cecil Beaton": *Vogue*, November 1, 1954.

56 "wacky and funny, a very lovable girl": Morley, *Audrey Hepburn*, 51.

56 "a sophisticated elf": Maychick, *Audrey Hepburn*, 4.

56 "Her sense of appropriateness and decorum was happily mixed": Robert Wolders as quoted in Loustalot, *Living like Audrey*, 105.

Eleven—A First Love, 1950–1952

59 "For a year I thought": Julie Miller, "Audrey Hepburn Reveals Heartbreak and Discusses Secret Wedding in Never-before-Seen Letters," *Vanity Fair*, June 14, 2016, https://www.vanityfair.com/style/2016/06/audrey-hepburn-love-letters.

59 "net worth . . . in the tens of millions of pounds sterling": Spoto, *Enchantment*, 55.

59 "17 billion dollar global conglomerate": Paris, *Audrey Hepburn*, 52.

59   "Everybody saw in her this wonderful life and brightness and terrific strength of character": ibid.

59   "thought we were well suited": ibid., 53.

59   "daughter of Baroness Ella van Heemstra": Woodward, *Audrey Hepburn*, 120.

59   "Baroness Ella van Heemstra much regrets to announce": Heatley, *Audrey Hepburn in Words and Pictures*, 44.

60   "The engagement between Mr. James Hanson and Miss Audrey Hepburn has been broken": Harris, *Audrey Hepburn*, 97.

60   "Jimmy and I talked it over two weeks ago": "Audrey Admits Romance with Jimmy Is Over," *New York Daily News*, November 18, 1952.

60   "Our work kept us apart more and more": ibid.

60   "When I found out that I didn't even have time to attend to the furnishing of our London flat": Anita Loos, "Everything Happens to Audrey Hepburn," *American Weekly*, September 12, 1954.

60   "I really don't think I want to get married at this time": *New York Daily News*, November 18, 1952.

60   "Had she married me, Audrey would have continued with her career": Paris, *Audrey Hepburn*, 81.

60   "I want my dress to be worn": Roberta Correia, "TBT: Audrey Hepburn's Three Wedding Dresses," *Brides.com*, October 30, 2019, https://www.brides.com/story/tbt-audrey-hepburn-wedding-dress.

60   "I have had a happy marriage": ibid.

61   "a little smile and said, 'Haven't we done well!'": Paris, *Audrey Hepburn*, 258.

61   "Anything positive you have heard is not an exaggeration": "Interview about Audrey Hepburn with Michael Butler (Former Boyfriend)," YouTube, posted by Rare Audrey Hepburn, May 26, 2017, https://www.youtube.com/watch?v=osXcpg-wkemw. *Michael Butler's Memoirs—The Podcast*, Audacy.com, January 6, 2015.

61   "I have admired and loved you at a distance": Matzen, *Warrior*, 166.

Twelve—*Sabrina*, Bogie, and William Holden, 1953–1954

63   "This girl, singlehanded, will make bosoms a thing of the past": "Princess Apparent," *Time*, September 7, 1953.

63   "We first saw a test": Crowe, *Conversations with Wilder*, 219.

63   "Once upon a time": *Sabrina*, screenplay by Billy Wilder, Samuel Taylor, and Ernest Lehman, Paramount Pictures, 1954.

64   "Look, you have to fumble a line": Crowe, *Conversations with Wilder*, 52.

64   "After so many drive-in waitresses": Ed Sikov, *On Sunset Boulevard: The Life and Times of Billy Wilder* (Jackson: University Press of Mississippi, 2017), 348.

65   "Great. . . . She was a good *everything*": Crowe, *Conversations with Wilder*, 305.

65   "The one thing I dreamed of in my life": Ferrer, *Audrey Hepburn: An Elegant Spirit*, 140.

65   "The constant talk of marriage and babies": Woodward, *Audrey Hepburn*, 149.

65   "I was in a jealous rage": ibid.

65   "I was talking to Bud Fraker, waiting for the arrival of the subject": Bob Willoughby, *Remembering Audrey: LIFE Great Photographers Series* (New York: Time Inc., 2008), 29.

65   "She took my hand and dazzled me": ibid., 30.

65   "To Audrey Hepburn. With sincere love and great admiration": Erwin and Diamond, *Audrey Hepburn Treasures*, 79.

66   "She's OK if you like to do 36 takes": Maychick, *Audrey Hepburn*, 100.

66   "Twenty-six takes? Audrey Hepburn?": Cameron Crowe, *Conversations with Wilder*, 159.

66   "Dad also did not care for Audrey Hepburn": Stephen Bogart, *Bogart: In Search of My Father* (New York: Dutton, 1995), 181.

66   "Even on this movie which he was unhappy about": ibid.

66   "'Look, this guy is shooting the back of my head,'": ibid., 180.

66   "went to Billy Wilder": ibid.

66   "What happened in that scene is that Billy Wilder fell in love with Audrey's image onscreen": Amy Fine Collins, "When Hubert Met Audrey," *Vanity Fair*, December 1995.

66   "I adored Bogie. If he didn't like me": Paskin, *Us Weekly*, October 17, 1988.

66   "Like Audrey, Lauren Bacall was one of the very few others": Jeanine Basinger, interview with author, September 11, 2020.

66   "With Audrey it's kind of unpredictable": Paris, *Audrey Hepburn*, 95.

66   "She's disciplined, like all those ballet dames": Joanna Benecke, *100 Reasons to Love Audrey Hepburn* (London: Plexus Publishing, 2016), 30.

67   "I was rather terrified of Humphrey": Paskin, *Us Magazine*, October 17, 1988.

67   "jovial roughness": Paris, *Audrey Hepburn*, 95.

67   "okay": Ferrer, *Audrey Hepburn: An Elegant Spirit*, 67.

67   "looked straight at me and said he probably had reason to": ibid.

67   "Nazi son of a bitch": Maurice Zolotow, *Billy Wilder in Hollywood* (London: W. H. Allen, 1977), 251.

67   "I look at you, Bogie, and beneath the surface of an apparent shit, I see the face of a real shit": ibid.

67   "Bogart thought that a director must humble himself before Bogart": ibid., 252.

67   "Unfortunately, Bogart knew he was my second choice": Robert Horton, ed., *Billy Wilder Interviews* (Jackson: University Press of Mississippi, 2001), 187.

67   "He always played the hero": Crowe, *Conversations with Wilder*, 343.

67   "I absolutely wouldn't let Billy do it": Kevin Lally, *Wilder Times: The Life of Billy Wilder* (New York: Henry Holt and Company, 1996), 233.

68   "But in the remake": Crowe, *Conversations with Wilder*, 94.

68   "The scene needed a concept, a gimmick, a trick": Collins, "When Hubert Met Audrey."

68   "Would you like to kiss me": *Sabrina*, screenplay by Billy Wilder, Samuel Taylor, and Ernest Lehman, Paramount Pictures, 1954.

69   "I am beginning to believe she is not the easiest actress in the world to cast": Walker, *Audrey: Her Real Story*, 109.
69   "You'll feel like buying Paramount stock": Louis Sobol, "Along the Broadway Beat," *New York Journal American*, September 26, 1954.
69   "*Sabrina* would not work without Audrey": Jeanine Basinger, interview with author, September 11, 2020.
70   "Audrey Hepburn is here sporting a totally original and spectacular look": ibid.
70   "What has always helped me are the clothes": "Reflections on the Silver Screen Interview with Richard Brown.," American Movie Classics, April 26, 1990.

Thirteen—Soul Mates, 1953–1993

73   "They were just way up there in the sky": Crowe, *Conversations with Wilder*, 219.
73   "very smart French day dress": Wasson, *Fifth Avenue, 5 A.M.*, 35.
73   "Obviously we cannot afford to give any screen credit": ibid., 36.
74   "This is too much!": Collins, "When Hubert Met Audrey."
74   "like a very fragile animal": Keogh, *Audrey Style*, 26.
74   "(She) was like the arrival of a summer flower": Collins, "When Hubert Met Audrey."
74   "The change from the little girl who arrived that morning was unbelievable": ibid.
74   "an Oxford-gray wool-ottoman tailleur with a cinch-waisted, double-breasted scoop-neck jacket": Keogh, *Audrey Style*, 42.
75   "jazzy": ibid.
75   "I always wanted a neck like Audrey Hepburn's": Neil Simon, *Only When I Laugh*, Columbia Pictures, 1981.
75   "She always puts the finishing touch on my work": Patricia Bosworth, *The Men in My Life* (New York: HarperCollins, 2017), 294.
75   "Givenchy always said": "Audrey Hepburn . . . by Her Son."
75   "the secret of elegance is elimination": Hellstern, *How to Be Lovely*, 151.
75   "She was attracted by the image he could give her": Collins, "When Hubert Met Audrey."
75   "Yes, it was heaven. An angelic bouffant layered gown": Bosworth, *The Men in My Life*, 294.
75   "The slim boyish figure with the airborne femininity": ibid.
75   "Somehow his clothes have always been right for me": Matzen, *Warrior*, 106.
76   "There's a wonderful French word": Audrey Hepburn in *Audrey: More Than an Icon*, 2020.
76   "In film after film, Audrey wore clothes with such talent and flair": de la Hoz, *Audrey and Givenchy*, 10.
76   "His are the only clothes in which I am myself": Benecke, *100 Reasons to Love Audrey Hepburn*, 16.
76   "Audrey was almost more about fashion than movies or acting": David Dresser and Garth S. Jowett, eds., *Hollywood Goes Shopping* (Minneapolis: University of Minnesota Press. 2000), 159.
76   "Hubert and I are very much alike": Audrey Hepburn in *Audrey: More Than an Icon*, 2020.
76   "They consulted with each other": Sean Hepburn Ferrer in ibid.
76   "and then she'd say bye-bye and hang up": Collins, "When Hubert Met Audrey."
76   "She shared her joy with friends, but kept her unhappy moments to herself": Givenchy quoted in Leslie Caron, "Audrey, Darling," *Vogue* (UK), April 1993.
77   "It's hard work, really": Matzen, *Warrior*, 88.
77   "Edith was very good about it": David Chierichetti, *Edith Head: The Life and Times of Hollywood's Celebrated Costume Designer* (New York: HarperCollins, 2003), 134.
77   "Edith was a better actress than most": ibid.
77   "Unknowingly I used a picture of the ballgown in *Hollywood Costume Design*": ibid., 135.
77   "I lied. So what?" ibid., 136.
77   "an oversight": Keogh, *Audrey Style*, 37.
77   "Imagine if I had received credit for *Sabrina* then": Collins, "When Hubert Met Audrey."
77   "the single person I know with the greatest integrity": Keogh, *Audrey Style*, 30.
77   "She kept her promise": Harris, *Audrey Hepburn*, 129.
78   "I don't replace clothes until they can't be worn": Gloria Emerson, "Co-stars Again: Audrey Hepburn and Givenchy," *New York Times*, September 8, 1965.

Fourteen—Meeting Mel, 1953–1968

81   "When I fell in love and married": Edward Klein, "One Woman's Search for Love: A Profile of Audrey Hepburn," *Parade*, March 5, 1989.
82   "light years ahead": Paris, *Audrey Hepburn*, 89.
82   "I still consider it the best movie I was ever lucky enough to be in": ibid.
82   "I saw you in *Lili*—I loved it": ibid., 83.
82   "The thing I remember most about that first meeting": David Stone, "My Husband Mel!" *Everybody's Weekly*, March 10, 1956.
82   "She was in part attracted to Mel because he was like a father figure to her": Sam Wasson, *Fifth Avenue, 5 A.M.*, 48.
82   "It ate away at me": Simon Edge, "Audrey Hepburn's Obsessive Tormentor," *express.co.uk*, June 6, 2008.
83   "I think marriage and art can develop together": Karney, *Audrey Hepburn: A Charmed Life*, 67.
83   "American women have a tendency to take over too much": Rosalind Massow, "Audrey's Advice: Have Fun, Let Hubby Wear the Pants," *New York Journal American*, August 19, 1957.

83 "carried my own bags": ibid.

83 "When she would get time off, between her UNICEF trips": "Audrey Hepburn Interview with Ivo Niehe."

84 "He is a protective husband, and I like it. Most women do": Sidney Solsky, "Audrey Hepburn," *New York Post*, March 24, 1957.

84 "I'm fortunate to be married to a fashion-conscious man by the name of Mel Ferrer": "Audrey Hepburn's Fashion Formula," *New York Herald Tribune*, November 11, 1962.

Fifteen—Exhibits A-B-C, 1954–1957

87 "Mel's success in Lili did not bear the fruits": Simon Edge, "Audrey Hepburn's Obsessive Tormentor," *express.co.uk.*, June 6, 2008.

88 "She could not understand why people wanted her . . .": Loustalot, *Living like Audrey*, 177.

88 "Ferrer used Audrey's crush on him": Julia Molony, "Audrey's Glittering Career Hit Star's Secret Heartache," *Irish Independent*, June 7, 2015.

88 "I loved watching her rehearse and act": Paris, *Audrey Hepburn*, 100.

88 "She was very correct": Spoto, *Enchantment*, 122.

88 "irresistible": Richard Watts Jr., "Two on the Aisle," *New York Post*, February 28, 1954.

88 "She gives a pulsing performance that is all grace and enchantment": Brooks Atkinson, "MAGICAL ONDINE; Audrey Hepburn Stars in English Version of Giradoux Play," *New York Times*, February 28, 1954.

88 "She is every man's dream of the nymph he once planned to meet": Maychick, *Audrey Hepburn*, 2.

88 "six weeks later, Audrey was once again taking solo curtain calls": Spoto, *Enchantment*, 122.

89 "I have learned the little I know about acting": Woodward, *Audrey Hepburn*, 163.

90 "I'm not worth it. It's impossible. Please don't tell anyone": David Willis, *Audrey: The 50s* (New York: HarperCollins 2016), 95.

90 "Her problem is the jawline": Woodward, *Audrey Hepburn*, 262.

90 "Audrey has made a symbol of her eyebrows": ibid.

91 "She has steel determination": ibid.

91 "like a manager with her": ibid., 178.

92 "I had no technique so I had to make believe like children do": *Audrey Hepburn Remembered*.

92 "dramatic sense of theatre": Sean Hepburn Ferrer, interview with author, July 7, 2020.

93 "When I was in Vienna in the '20s": Billy Wilder in Horton, *Billy Wilder Interviews*, 191.

93 "The lovers seemed more fated to bore each other to death": Sheilah Graham quoted in Vermilye, *Complete Films of Audrey Hepburn*, 123.

93 "I'm not sorry I did it": Bob Thomas, "Audrey Hepburn's Secret of Bliss; Must Be More Giving than Taking," *New York Post*, March 25, 1957.

Sixteen—Bonjour, Paris! 1956–1957

95 "Paris is always a good idea": Maggie Parker, "13 of Audrey Hepburn's Most Inspiring Quotes," https://time.com/4316700 /audrey-hepburn-inspiring-quotes/, May 4, 2016.

95 "love to do a musical one day": Stephen M. Silverman, *Dancing on the Ceiling: Stanley Donen and His Movies* (New York: Knopf, 1996), 223.

95 "I read it in Paris and I fell in love with it. It was a charming story": ibid., 227.

95 "Miss Hepburn was all shrewd businesswoman till the deal was signed": ibid., 230.

95 "By the estimation of director Donen": ibid., 230.

96 "They had her and she said, well, I'll do it if you get Fred Astaire": Sarah Giles, *Fred Astaire: His Friends Talk* (New York: Doubleday, 1988), 56.

96 "Who cares how old he is? He's Fred Astaire!": Curtis Bill Pepper, "Audrey Keeps Park in a Stir," *New York World Telegram and Sun*, August 16, 1957.

96 "Was Fred good looking? I think so": Giles, *Fred Astaire*, 48.

96 "I learned how to be me by pretending to be him": Norma Stevens and Steven M. L. Aronson, *Avedon: Something Personal* (New York: Spiegel & Grau, 2017), 177.

96 "it's every woman's dream to dance with Fred Astaire": *Audrey Hepburn Remembered*, Janson Media, 2008.

96 "One look at this most debonair and elegant and distinguished of legends": Giles, *Fred Astaire*, 80.

96 "Come on, let's have a little go together": Warren Harris, *Audrey Hepburn,* 138.

96 "It was such fun, it was so divine." ibid.

96 "suddenly I felt a hand around my waist": Giles, *Fred Astaire*, 80.

96 "He gave me such confidence": Harris, *Audrey Hepburn*, 138

97 "They were two very special individuals. The talent was so unique": "The Fashion Designer and His Muse—Audrey Hepburn and Hubert de Givenchy": *Funny Face*, 50th Anniversary Edition DVD, Paramount Pictures 2007.

97 "They were both modern masters of their métier": Jeffrey Banks, interview with author, August 25, 2020.

97 "Soft, gentle, but dear": Silverman, *Dancing on the Ceiling*, 236.

97 "She took off on a dance whirlwind that had been bottled up for years": Cindy De La Hoz, *Audrey and Givenchy: A Fashion Love Affair* (Philadelphia: Running Press, 2016), 63.

97 "But what I did not tell Stanley until years later was that there was something": Pamela Clarke Keogh, *Audrey Style* (New York: HarperCollins, 1999), 97.

97 "I'd like to have had smaller feet. My friends have pretty feet and wear such pretty shoes": "Audrey Hepburn Interview," *Good Morning America*, February 19, 1987.

98 "Years ago my mother said": ibid.

98 "You were right about the socks": Keogh, *Audrey Style*, 97.

98 "When she realized you appreciated her gifts and were doing all in your power": ibid., 133.

98 "The white pants, the little cropped top and pink sash": "The Fashion Designer and His Muse—Audrey Hepburn and Hubert de Givenchy," *Funny Face*, 50th Anniversary Edition DVD, Paramount Pictures 2007.

98 "while Avedon focused on the mirror, and the lab later matched the still photo with the film frame": Joseph Andrew Casper, *Stanley Donen*, Scarecrow Filmmakers Series Book 5 (Metuchen, NJ: Scarecrow Press, 1995), 96.

98 "I did it once and I didn't break my neck. Just good luck": *Audrey Hepburn Remembered*.

99 "It had a dropped torso": Jeffrey Banks, interview with author, August 25, 2020.

99 "I can't dance in that. Fix it": Harris, *Audrey Hepburn*, 141.

99 "What are you doing?": Silverman, *Dancing on the Ceiling*, 238.

99 "remember the camera is on you": ibid., 239.

99 "Yes, well, it is a bit of a strain": Peter J. Levinson, *Puttin' On The Ritz: Fred Astaire and the Fine Art of Panache* (New York: St. Martin's Press 2009), 211.

99 "I never saw him cross, never. I've never even heard he was difficult": Giles, *Fred Astaire*, 185.

99 "very serious. There was no coziness": Silverman, *Dancing on the Ceiling*, 235.

99 "Here I have waited twenty years to dance with Fred Astaire, and what do I get? Mud!": Ferrer, *Audrey Hepburn: An Elegant Spirit*, 57.

99 "my favorite remark of all time": ibid.

99 "It soon became apparent": Stanley Donen, "Audrey in Funny Face: Cinderella of Fashion," *New York Times*, February 10, 1957.

100 "the most original screen musical": John Cutts, *Films and Filming*, cited in Vermilye, *Complete Films of Audrey Hepburn*, 110.

100 "Too chic . . . I didn't think it had any muscle in it": Paris, *Audrey Hepburn*, 132.

100 "(Working with Audrey) is still an unfulfilled ambition of mine": George Hadley-Garcia, "Audrey Hepburn 30 Years of Stardom," *Hollywood Studio Magazine* 16, no. 4 (1983).

100 "Miss Hepburn has the meek charm of a wallflower turned into a rueful butterfly": Ellen Erwin and Jessica Z. Diamond, *The Audrey Hepburn Treasures* (New York: Atria Books, 2006), 94.

Seventeen—*Love in the Afternoon*, 1957

103 "An over-long and only spasmodically amusing romantic comedy . . .": Geoff Andrew, *Love in the Afternoon*, *Time Out*, as quoted in *RottenTomatoes.com*, March 18, 2007.

104 "*Ariane* without you": Sikov, *On Sunset Boulevard*, 390–91.

104 "But the mistake there was that my beloved friend Gary Cooper": Horton, *Billy Wilder Interviews*, 155.

104 "I've been in pictures over thirty years": Woodward, *Audrey Hepburn*, 197.

105 "It's cheerful, charming": "1961: Hollywood, Audrey Hepburn read a poem called 'What is a Gary Cooper?' (January 9)," YouTube, posted by Gerard Henry soogen, September 19, 2017, https://www.youtube.com/watch?v=0sOQTuq2zzU.

105 "His only topic of conversation from morning to night was himself": Higham, *Audrey: The Life of Audrey Hepburn*, 109.

105 "She made it so clear that her acting partners had to react the proper way": Billy Wilder in *Audrey Hepburn Remembered*.

105 "Not much meat on her": *Pat and Mike*, screenplay by Ruth Gordon and Garson Kanin, MGM, 1952.

105 "I'm too thin": *Love in the Afternoon*, screenplay by Billy Wilder and I. A. L. Diamond, Allied Artists, 1957.

106 "Wyler said": Crowe, *Conversations with Wilder*, 190.

106 "Yes. I would have had her start to follow": ibid., 191.

106 "They are now married": *Love in the Afternoon*, screenplay by Billy Wilder and I. A. L. Diamond, Allied Artists, 1957.

Eighteen—Feature Film Mistake #1—*Green Mansions*, 1958–1959

109 "Filmization of W. H. Hudson's novel has been approached with reverence": Variety Staff, "Green Mansions," *Variety*, December 31, 1958.

110 "She never forgave herself": Dotti, *Audrey at Home*, 226.

111 "She was wonderful to work with": Boz Hadleigh, *Hollywood Gays* (New York: Barricade Books, 1996), 207.

111 "because it was good but unusual": ibid.

111 "In some ways it seems": Sean Hepburn Ferrer, interview with author, July 7, 2020.

111 "Even so, Miss Hepburn conducts herself all through it with grace and dignity": Bosley Crowther "Delicate Enchantment of 'Green Mansions'; Audrey Hepburn Stars in Role of Rima," *New York Times*, March 20, 1959.

111 "A piece of irritating and often risible hokum": "D.B.," *Monthly Film Bulletin* quoted in Vermilye, *Complete Films of Audrey Hepburn*, 127.

Nineteen—*The Nun's Story*, 1959

113 "A transcendent film, comparable more to Bergman or Bresson": Arthur Nolletti Jr., "Conversation with Fred Zinnemann," *The Films of Fred Zinnemann: Critical Perspectives*, ed. Arthur Nolletti Jr. (Albany: State University Press of New York, 1999), 25–26.

113 "If I am not for myself": *The Nun's Story*, screenplay by Robert Anderson, Warner Bros., 1959.

114 "someone who had the courage": Sean Hepburn Ferrer, interview with author, July 7, 2020.

114 "not a crisis of faith, but a crisis of worthiness": Paris, *Audrey Hepburn*, 152.

114 "work out a schedule whereby *Anne Frank* could possibly be done": J. E. Smyth, *Fred Zinnemann and the Cinema of Resistance* (Jackson: University Press of Mississippi, 2014), 159.

114 "self-knowledge that enables": Gene D. Phillips, "Fred Zinnemann: Darkness at Noon," *Major Film Directors of the American and British Cinema* (Bethlehem, PA: Lehigh University Press, 1990), 115.

114 "Unhappily, my enthusiasm . . ." Fred Zinnemann, *Fred Zinnemann: An Autobiography* (New York: Charles Scribner's Sons, 1992), 155.

115 "With the exception of Ingrid Bergman": Vermilye, *Complete Films of Audrey Hepburn*, 41.

115 "I was very fortunate to fall into a period of moviemaking": *Audrey Hepburn Remembered*.

115 "In the end, twenty dancers were borrowed": Zinnemann, *Fred Zinnemann: An Autobiography*, 162.

115 "great character and personality": ibid.

115 "A lot of principessas and contessas": ibid.

115 "It seemed important to keep an objective approach": ibid. 163.

115 "and then realize she no longer has that kind of skirt": Nolletti Jr., "Conversation with Fred Zinnemann," 27.

116 "It took many hours of going into lots of details": ibid., 29.

116 "obedience remained the hardest vow of all to follow": Zinnemann, *Fred Zinnemann: An Autobiography,* 158.

116 "Dear Lord, forgive me": *The Nun's Story*, screenplay by Robert Anderson, Warner Bros., 1959.

116 "In a way, it's a life against nature": ibid.

116 "The story is not pro-catholic nor is it anti-catholic": "Miss Hepburn: One Jungle after Another," *New York Herald Tribune*, August 31, 1958.

116 "In the story we find examples of the Order trying to make her conform": Letter from Audrey Hepburn to Mel Ferrer, January 20, 1958, facsimile included in Erwin and Diamond, *Audrey Hepburn Treasures*, 102.

117 "became an erotic barometer": Peter Ustinov, *Dear Me* (Boston: Little Brown and Company, 1977), 307.

117 "I've seen nuns come and go": *The Nun's Story*, screenplay by Robert Anderson, Warner Bros., 1959.

117 "You have less risk of getting leprosy here": Zinnemann, *Fred Zinnemann: An Autobiography*, 168.

117 "Of course you have to understand": ibid.

117 "all the chicken-wire and cement": ibid, 167.

117 "too tricky and too far ahead of popular imagination": ibid., 166.

117 "In the Congo, a cool day was 100 and the temperature was often 130": "Miss Hepburn: One Jungle after Another," *New York Herald Tribune*, August 31, 1958.

118 "How and where would you hook it up?": Paris, *Audrey Hepburn*, 146.

118 "I have never seen anyone more disciplined": Zinnemann, *Fred Zinnemann: An Autobiography*, 166.

118 "a brilliant grasp of the end result wanted": Robert F. Hawkins, "Seen on the Italian Screen Scene," *New York Times*, April 7, 1958.

118 "My character would never do these things": Bosworth, *Men in My Life*, 282.

118 "seemed almost transfixed": ibid.

118 "There might be some things I can still correct": Audrey Hepburn in *Audrey: More Than an Icon*, 2020.

118 "Audrey drifted over to me and took my hands in hers": Bosworth, *Men in My Life*, 291.

119 "obedience without question, without inner murmuring": *The Nun's Story*, screenplay by Robert Anderson, Warner Bros., 1959.

119 "What I didn't know": Zinnemann, *Fred Zinnemann: An Autobiography*, 169.

119 "every Warner Brothers picture": ibid.

119 "Warner Brothers congratulate": ibid.

119 "Is that what you want?": ibid.

119 "partly because of the tension and the war": Nolletti Jr., "Conversation with Fred Zinnemann," 30.

120 "I'm never going to see it again because if I do": David Zeitlin, "A Lovely Audrey in Religious Role," *Life*, June 8, 1959, 141–44.

120 "in a close race between Audrey and Simone Signoret . . .": Joe Pihodna, "N.Y. Film Critics Select Ben-Hur as Best of 1959," *New York Herald Tribune*, December 29, 1959.

120 "Audrey Hepburn here gives one of the great performances by an actress": Jeanine Basinger, interview with author, September 11, 2020.

120 "Looking at the film again, after more than twenty-five years": Zinnemann, *Fred Zinnemann: An Autobiography*, 163.

121 "Fred Zinnemann is a perfectionist": "Audrey Hepburn Interview," *Good Morning America*, February 19, 1987.

121 "forever silence those who": Henry Hart, "The Nun's Story," *Films in Review*, June–July 1959.

121 "I think my mother was proudest of": "Forever Audrey," *Town & Country*, May 2003.

121 "What I see in the film and in the character is so close to Audrey": Spoto, *Enchantment*, 186.

Twenty—Feature Film Mistake #2—*The Unforgiven*, 1960

123 "Some of my pictures I don't care for": John Huston, *An Open Book* (New York: Alfred A. Knopf, 1980), 284.

124 "I never seen you before": *The Unforgiven*, screenplay by Ben Maddow, United Artists, 1960.

124 "They jest fly a mite higher": ibid.

124 "makes the artist take a lot of responsibility and that is like a challenge": Higham, *Audrey: The Life of Audrey Hepburn*, 141.

124 "lay unconscious for five minutes": "1959: Audrey Hepburn Falls from White Stallion on the Set of 'Unforgiven,' on January 28," YouTube, posted by Gerard Henry sooge, July 30, 2012, https://www.youtube.com/watch?v=QLUjOPI7q78.

125 "the overall tone is bombastic and overinflated. Everybody in it is bigger than life": John Huston, *An Open Book* (New York: Alfred A. Knopf, 1980), 284.

125   "She is not an actress, she is a model": Dwight MacDonald, *Esquire*, June 1960.

125   "She's as good as the other Hepburn": Paris, *Audrey Hepburn*, 162.

Twenty-One—Motherhood, 1960

127   "My mother wanted to have a kid because she wanted to right the wrongs of her childhood": Sam Wasson, *Fifth Avenue, 5 A.M.*, 217.

127   "My greatest ambition is to have a career without becoming a career woman": Alexander Walker, *Audrey: Her Real Story* (New York: St. Martin's Press, 1995), 101.

127   "the loss of a little girl": *Darcey Bussell's Looking for Audrey Hepburn*.

127   "From the earliest time I can remember, the thing I most wanted was babies": Erwin and Diamond, *Audrey Hepburn Treasures*, 101.

127   "I think it was part of the healing": *Darcey Bussell's Looking for Audrey Hepburn*.

127   "I must work to forget. Only work can help me": Paris, *Audrey Hepburn*, 168.

128   "I would like to mix Sean with all kinds of people in all countries": Higham, *Audrey: The Life of Audrey Hepburn*, 147.

128   "I'm sure it's wonderful when you're eighteen": *People* Extra: *A Tribute to Audrey Hepburn,* 38.

128   "I think when she finally had me": Alexander Kacala, "Beyond the Glamour: Audrey Hepburn's Son Opens Up about Her Struggles in New Interview," *Today,* October 9, 2010, https://www.today.com/popculture/audrey-hepburn-s-son-opens -about-her-struggles-new-interview-t193670?cid=sm_npd_td_fb_ma.

128   "To step inside this Swiss doll's house": Cecil Beaton, *Diaries: The Parting Years 1963–74* (Leeds: Sapere Books, 2018), 16–17.

Twenty-Two—When Audrey Met Holly, 1961

131   "Everything you have read, heard or wished to be true about Audrey Hepburn": Richard Shepherd quoted in Wasson, *5th Avenue, 5 A.M.*, 160.

132   "Only Mae West could have made a bigger production out of his entrance than did Capote": Sarah Gristwood, *Breakfast at Tiffany's: The Official 50th Anniversary Companion* (New York: Rizzoli, 2011), 31.

132   "'worked up' two scenes to play only for Capote": Paris, *Audrey Hepburn*, 170.

132   "Marilyn Monroe will not play a lady of the evening": Wasson, *Fifth Avenue, 5 A.M.*, 78.

132   "Marilyn Monroe would probably have been allowed to play": Gristwood, *Breakfast at Tiffany's: The Official 50th Anniversary Companion*, 61.

132   "She had a way of showing us who she really was": "Documentary on Breakfast at Tiffany's Movie," YouTube, posted by r-e-t-r-o-g-a-l, July 22, 2011, https://www.youtube.com/watch?v=xyA__0GJqhs.

132   "an elongated carving of a head": Truman Capote, *Breakfast at Tiffany's and Three Stories* (New York: Random House, 1958), 6.

133   "slim cool black dress": ibid., 10.

133   "We wanted someone who was no-nonsense": Gristwood, *Breakfast at Tiffany's: The Official 50th Anniversary Companion*, 72.

133   "a woman who defied definition": ibid., 43.

133   "I have often thought of myself as quite ugly": Bill Tusher, "Candy Pants Princess," *Motion Picture*, February 1954.

134   "Audrey still had qualms about playing the role until I said": Harris, *Audrey Hepburn: A Biography*, 172.

134   "since Givenchy had not before designed period costumes": Chierichetti, *Edith Head*, 137.

134   "Why Edith, you haven't changed a bit": ibid.

134   "Audrey could have been a designer herself": ibid.

134   "I have no opinion of the film script, never having had the opportunity to read it": Truman Capote, letter to Audrey Hepburn dated July 23, 1960, facsimile included in Erwin and Diamond, *Audrey Hepburn Treasures*, 109.

134   "I was fired because of course she had never heard of me": John Frankenheimer quoted in Vermilye, *Complete Films of Audrey Hepburn*, 149.

135   "I would have done it if I had to crawl": "Documentary on Breakfast at Tiffany's Movie."

135   "in Audrey's mind it was a big jump from Capote's Holly to our film's Holly": ibid.

135   "purified by the style in which he would shoot the picture": "Holly at 50: How Breakfast at Tiffany's Came to the Screen and Changed Everything," *George's Journal*, October 13, 2011, https://georgesjournal.org/2011/10/13/holly-hits-50-how -breakfast-at-tiffanys-came-to-the-screen-and-changed-everything/.

135   "We liked each other as human beings": "Documentary on Breakfast at Tiffany's Movie."

135   "(New York City) is like living inside an electric light bulb": Gristwood, *Breakfast at Tiffany's: The Official 50th Anniversary Companion*, 12.

136   "Kook is not, as everybody associated with *Breakfast at Tiffany's* knows, a beatnik term": Wasson, *Fifth Avenue, 5 A.M.*, 179.

136   "It's true we've left sex ambiguous in the script": Eugene Archer, "Playgirl on the Town," *New York Times*, October 9, 1960.

137   "After Tiffany's anyone, no matter what their financial situation": Wasson, *Fifth Avenue, 5 A.M.*, 129.

137   "It was as if God said, I'm going to give you a break now": Gristwood, *Breakfast at Tiffany's: The Official 50th Anniversary Companion*, 11.

137   "Audrey and I never had a disagreement that I can remember": "Documentary on Breakfast at Tiffany's Movie."

137   "She was funny, dear, disciplined, joyous, a hard worker": *Audrey Hepburn Remembered*.

137 "We got along superbly at the Actors Studio": "Documentary on Breakfast at Tiffany's Movie."
137 "I must say there wasn't a human being that Audrey Hepburn didn't have a kind word for": Wasson, *Fifth Avenue, 5 A.M.*, 147.
137 "The script didn't delineate that much in terms of party shenanigans": "Documentary on Breakfast at Tiffany's Movie."
137 "She's a phony, but she's a real phony": *Breakfast at Tiffany's*, George Axelrod, screenwriter, Paramount Pictures, 1961.
137 "so nice. She would sit around and talk to us": *Darcey Bussell's Looking for Audrey Hepburn.*
137 "Audrey was amazing": ibid.
137 "the most innocent call girl you ever saw": *Audrey Hepburn Remembered.*
138 "I didn't really think it out": "Documentary on Breakfast at Tiffany's Movie."
138 "downright ashamed": Gristwood, *Breakfast at Tiffany's: The Official 50th Anniversary Companion*, 165.
138 "I was too cute. And the whole damn movie was just too, too precious": ibid.
138 "She elevates the part out of typecasting": Sean Hepburn Ferrer in *Audrey: More Than an Icon*, 2020.
138 "*Breakfast at Tiffany's* is treated as her most sacred film": Sean Hepburn Ferrer, interview with author, August 4, 2020.
138 "beloved and charming . . . in other ways": Gristwood, *Breakfast at Tiffany's: The Official 50th Anniversary Companion*, 165.
138 "you'd explain the painful historical context and how stereotypes prevent people from seeing reality": ibid.
138 "slight sadness": ibid., 145.
138 "Very, very simple . . . a sophisticated country song": Paris, *Audrey Hepburn*, 171.
139 "Despite the difficulties of life": "Lovely Audrey," *Timelessexclusive.blogspot.com*, June 14, 2011.
139 "the fucking song": Wasson, *Fifth Avenue, 5 A.M.*, 176.
139 "Over my dead body": "Documentary on Breakfast at Tiffany's Movie."
139 "You'll cut that song over my dead body!": Wasson, *Fifth Avenue, 5 A.M.*, 177.
139 "To this day, no one has done it": Ferrer, *Audrey Hepburn: An Elegant Spirit*, 83–84.
139 "We're after the same rainbow's end": "Moon River," music by Henry Mancini, lyrics by Johnny Mercer, 1961.
139 "A movie without music is a little bit like an aeroplane without fuel": Wasson, *Fifth Avenue, 5 A.M.*, 175.
140 "Man, did that cat smell!": "Documentary on Breakfast at Tiffany's Movie."
140 "The sheer pain of letting love in is written on her face": Gristwood, *Breakfast at Tiffany's: The Official 50th Anniversary Companion*, 138.
140 "A completely unbelievable but wholly captivating flight into fancy": A. H. Weiler, "The Screen: 'Breakfast at Tiffany's' Audrey Hepburn Stars in Music Hall Comedy": *New York Times*, October 6, 1961.
140 "Audrey Hepburn may not be your (or Truman Capote's) notion": Judith Crist, quoted in Vermilye, *Complete Films of Audrey Hepburn*, 153.
140 "The book was really rather bitter": ibid., 163.
141 "Although I'm very fond of Audrey Hepburn": Wasson, *Fifth Avenue, 5 A.M.*, 188.
141 "rather than subject the public to an excruciatingly boring evening": Gristwood, *Breakfast at Tiffany's: The Official 50th Anniversary Companion*, 169.
141 "Film history works in mysterious ways": Jeanine Basinger, interview with author, September 11, 2020.
142 "Please Doc, please understand": *Breakfast at Tiffany's*, George Axelrod, screenwriter, Paramount Pictures, 1961.
142 "I so wanted to be like you in *Breakfast at Tiffany's*": Miller, *Fan Phenomena—Audrey Hepburn*, 83.
142 "With that film we became grownups": Judith Crist quoted in Tom Santopietro, *The Sound of Music Story* (New York: St. Martin's Press, 2015), 174.
142 "This is the best thing I've ever done, because it was the hardest": Rowland Barber, "The Delightful Riddle of Audrey Hepburn," *Good Housekeeping*, August 1962.
142 "I'm an introvert . . . playing the extroverted girl in *Breakfast at Tiffany's*": Tiffin, *A Star Is Born*, 162.
142 "It's the easiest of my pictures for me to look at": "Audrey Hepburn Interview," *Good Morning America*, February 19, 1987.
143 "The two things": Paris, *Audrey Hepburn*, 170.
143 "I had very little real youth, few friends": Hellstern, *How to Be Lovely*, 124.
143 "Oh dear, Blackie": *People* Extra: *A Tribute to Audrey Hepburn*, 74.
143 "Obviously I'm not the first or last person": ibid.

Twenty-Three—From Holly to Karen, 1961

145 "She knew how to love": Shirley MacLaine, "Quotes About Audrey Hepburn," https://londonmumsmagazine.com/shopping-guides/movies-tested-recommended/quotes-about-audrey-hepburn, 18 May 2015
145 "I'm just thrilled": Herman, *Talent for Trouble*, 414.
145 "her salary burnished by substantial perks": ibid., 417.
146 "I had plenty of qualms": Woodward, *Audrey Hepburn*, 241.
146 "I tried to teach her how to be eloquently profane": *People* Extra: *A Tribute to Audrey Hepburn*, 77.
146 "Audrey, like most actresses": Madsen, *William Wyler*, 372.
146 "fell in love with her. She was quiet and demure, a very proper lady": James Garner and Jon Winokur, *The Garner File* (New York: Simon & Schuster, 2011), 79.
146 "I could never figure out how she could have married that guy Mel Ferrer": ibid.
146 "She would just disappear, and when I went looking": *LIFE* magazine, *Audrey: 25 Years Later* (New York: LIFE Books, January 5, 2018), 47.
146 "chickened out": Miller, *William Wyler*, 332.
146 "gutted scenes in the middle of the picture": ibid.
146 "I should have fought more with Willie Wyler": Harris, *Audrey Hepburn: A Biography*, 182.
147 "(It is) mostly workable, but": Herman, *Talent for Trouble*, 416.

147 "You can never give her such a stage direction": Arthur Mizener, *The Far Side of Paradise: A Biography of F. Scott Fitzgerald* (New York: Houghton Mifflin, 1949), 279.

147 "The Lesbian Said the Better": Herman, *A Talent for Trouble*, 417.

147 "But Audrey Hepburn gives her standard frail, indomitable characterization": *Time* magazine review of *The Children's Hour* quoted in Vermilye, *Complete Films of Audrey Hepburn*, 160.

148 "a disaster": Miller, *William Wyler*, 327.

148 "too faithful to the original": Madsen, *William Wyler*, 374.

148 "If I was taking part at this moment": Herman, *Talent for Trouble*, 417.

Twenty-Four—Paris When It Fizzles, 1962–1964

151 "The trouble is that *Paris When It Sizzles*": "Paris When It Sizzles Strong in Marquee Power," *Hollywood Reporter*, April 8, 1964.

152 "Audrey's strong, very strong": Higham, *Audrey: The Life of Audrey Hepburn*, 155.

153 "in the image of Audrey Hepburn as a tribute to her beauty": de la Hoz, *Audrey and Givenchy*, 116.

153 "She didn't care much for *Paris When It Sizzles*": Fiori, "Forever Audrey."

153 "Audrey . . . was the charmer of the world": Higham, *Audrey: The Life of Audrey Hepburn*, 158.

Twenty-Five—*Charade*, 1962–1963

155 "Cary Grant and Audrey Hepburn are two people who will never be bettered on the screen": *Audrey Hepburn Remembered*.

155 "Don't persist. Look, I like you, Wilder": Scott Eyman, *Cary Grant: A Brilliant Disguise* (New York: Simon & Schuster, 2020), 320.

155 "I'd heard he didn't like actors very much": ibid., 321.

155 "might make a very interesting suspense action film": ibid., 384–85.

156 "I don't know anyone who lived in those years who doesn't think of Audrey and Cary as the most enchanting people": Stanley Donen in *Audrey Hepburn Remembered*.

156 "How do you shave in there?": *Charade*, screenplay by Peter Stone, Universal Pictures, 1963.

156 "While you might not think it, Cary was a vulnerable man": Harris, *Audrey Hepburn: A Biography*, 194.

156 "You've got to learn to like yourself": ibid.

157 "In spite of her fragile appearance she's like steel": Keogh, *What Would Audrey Do?* 3.

157 "Best on the bill" "Charade": music by Henry Mancini, lyrics by Johnny Mercer, 1963.

157 "I think *Charade* is the best work John (Mercer) and I ever did together": Silverman, *Dancing on the Ceiling*, 304.

157 "feel in on the joke": "Audrey Hepburn," *The Seventh Art* 2, no. 2 (Spring 1964).

157 "I was bloody lucky, let's face it": Silverman, *Dancing on the Ceiling*, 298.

157 "Of course the directors listened to her input": Sean Hepburn Ferrer, interview with author, August 4, 2020.

157 "I longed to get closer, to get behind whatever was the invisible": Silverman, *Dancing on the Ceiling*, 298–99.

158 "probably the best American film of last year": Pauline Kael, quoted in Michael Newton, "Charade: The Last Sparkle of Hollywood," *The Guardian*, December 13, 2013.

158 "All I want for Christmas": *LIFE* magazine, *Audrey: 25 Years Later*, 94.

158 "Cary was a lovely souvenir in my life": *Audrey Hepburn Remembered*.

158 "Do you know what's wrong with you?" *Charade*, screenplay by Peter Stone, Universal Pictures, 1963.

Twenty-Six—Home, 1963–1993

161 "It's going to sound like a thumping bore, but my idea of heaven . . .": Dotti, *Audrey at Home*, 124.

161 "She had the ability to keep people at a distance without being in the least bit rough or unkind": Hellstern, *How to Be Lovely*, 108.

162 "She ended up on the wrong side of the house": "Audrey Hepburn . . . by Her Son."

162 "remembered feeling butterflies in her stomach and felt she had come home": Ferrer, *Audrey Hepburn: An Elegant Spirit*, 208.

162 "When my parents found the house": Sean Hepburn Ferrer, interview with author, July 7, 2020.

162 "Simple, homey, cottagey": Matzen, *Dutch Girl*, 316.

162 "My mother chose to keep the acknowledgements she received for her humanitarian work": Dotti, *Audrey at Home*, 10–11.

163 "This was the single most romantic thing": Miranda Evans, "Luca Dotti: Memories of My Mother, Audrey Hepburn the Gardener," *The Telegraph*, 15 September 2015.

163 "beautiful . . . because they are a deep pink": ibid.

163 "The more there is, the less I want": Pamela Keogh, *What Would Audrey Do* (New York: Gotham Books, 2008), 88.

163 "My mother was at the very deep of her heart a farm girl": Laura Jacobs and Luca Dotti, "Audrey's Dolce Vita," *Vanity Fair*, May 2013.

163 "We had a lot of fruit trees": Evans, "Luca Dotti: Memories of My Mother."

163 "hate anything that crowds me": Jim Watters, "Audrey Hepburn: A Star Is Reborn and Romance Lives in Robin and Marian," *People*, April 12, 1976.

163 "She loved going to the market herself": Luca Dotti, *Larevista.ro*, June 22, 2015.

163 "She had a true passion for enormous supermarkets": Dotti, *Audrey at Home*, 179.

163 "My mother didn't order people around": Fiori, "Forever Audrey."

163 "Throughout her formative years": "Audrey Hepburn . . . by Her Son."

163 "I just want to get there": Ferrer, *Audrey Hepburn: An Elegant Spirit*, 95.

163 "She was a wonderful, talented, very healthy cook": "Audrey Hepburn . . . by Her Son."

164 "I get nervous. I smoke too, you know": Bosworth, *Men in My Life*, 286.

164 "One of the most brutal, heartless things I've ever had to sit through": Walker, *Audrey: Her Real Story*, 229.

165 "the film that meant the most to me emotionally": Matzen, *Warrior*, 31.

165 "darker, less secure place. . . no longer very funny": Walker, *Audrey: Her Real Story*, 229.

165 "Cher has an enormous scale of emotions and total lack of inhibition": Paris, *Audrey Hepburn*, 308.

Twenty-Seven—*My Fair Lady*, 1963–1964

167 "And, finally, my thanks to a man": Cassidy Stephenson, "Why Julie Andrews Wasn't Chosen for My Fair Lady," *cbr.com*, February 18, 2023, https://www.cbr.com/julie-andrews-my-fair-lady-audrey-hepburn/.

167 "That's easy to answer. I'd do anything to play Eliza Doolittle in *My Fair Lady*": *Audrey Hepburn Remembered*.

167 "More tears are shed over answered prayers": Gloria Steinem, "Go Ahead and Ask Me Anything' (And So She Did): An Interview with Truman Capote," *McCall's*, November 1967.

167 "Screen test? You've seen me do the part. You know I can do a good job": Paris, *Audrey Hepburn*, 195.

167 "You've never made a movie and I'm investing a lot of money in this": ibid.

168 "She actually hosted a dinner party for some of the studio executives": Erwin and Diamond, *Audrey Hepburn Treasures*, 117.

168 "If I turned it down they would offer it to another movie actress": Paris, *Audrey Hepburn*, 195.

168 "It was a plum role, the script was terrific, and so I accepted the offer": Joan Kramer and David Heeley, *In the Company of Legends* (New York: Beaufort Books, 2015), 285.

168 "Thank God I didn't get that part": Sean Hepburn Ferrer, interview with author, July 7, 2020.

168 "Audrey sold her percentages": ibid.

168 "enormously successful": Walker, *Audrey: Her Real Story*, 187

168 "two of the songs": ibid.

169 "I am not mean spirited or envious but me no like": Emanuel Levy, *George Cukor: Master of Elegance* (New York: William Morrow 1994), 292.

169 "earthbound and prim": ibid.

169 "I hope O'Toole was liked": Alexander Walker, *Fatal Charm: The Life of Rex Harrison* (New York: St. Martin's 1993), 260.

170 "when I flew into Los Angeles": Rex Harrison, *Rex: An Autobiography* (New York: William Morrow 1975), 195.

170 "Nobody was interested in the girl. They were only interested in *him*": André Previn quoted in Paris, *Audrey Hepburn*, 204.

170 "In the three years we played together": Harrison, *Rex: An Autobiography*, 162.

170 "we had had an extremely good working relationship": ibid., 197.

170 "I think there's a lot of steel": ibid.

170 "The difference between talking to (Julie) and talking to Audrey Hepburn": Vickers, *Malice in Wonderland*, 281.

170 "Why the musicians will have to follow me": Hugo Vickers, *Cecil Beaton: A Biography* (Boston: Little Brown & Company, 1985), 470.

170 "Audrey is just as marvellous": ibid.

170 "My feeling about Cecil—I really did love him": Vickers, *Malice in Wonderland,* 230.

171 "She loved Audrey Hepburn": ibid., 314.

171 "Filming *My Fair Lady* was not at all": Rex Harrison, *A Damned Serious Business: My Life in Comedy* (New York: Bantam Books, 1991), 156.

171 "As I was just off for a few days in Madrid with Mel": Rocky Land and Barbara Hall, eds., *Letters from Hollywood: Inside the Private World of Classic American Moviemaking* (New York: Abrams, 2019), 283.

171 "The reason I even dare to make the suggestion": ibid., 285.

171 "I worked on the accent, worked on the lines": "Audrey Hepburn My Fair Lady Interview."

171 "after lunch we accompanied": Cecil Beaton, *Cecil Beaton's Fair Lady* (New York: Henry Holt, 1964), 47.

172 "Marni had this peculiar, chameleonlike quality": Marni Nixon, *I Could Have Sung All Night* (New York: Billboard Books, 2006), 139.

172 "We can't have any native 'Californian' to do *this* dubbing": ibid., 146.

172 "The only one who can do this part is Marni Nixon": ibid.

172 "Fine, it's done! Hire her!" ibid.

172 "I'll understand if you do, but in any case, I'll work hard on my voice": Beaton, *Cecil Beaton's Fair Lady*, 62.

172 "Having worked on it": ibid.

172 "it wasn't such a crime. But you can imagine how Lerner and Loewe felt": Paris, *Audrey Hepburn*, 200.

172 "unprofessional": Vickers, *Malice in Wonderland*, 316–17.

172 "The most crucial criterion was for the basic timbre of the voice": Nixon, *I Could Have Sung All Night*, 146.

173 "Audrey seemed to have a lower, wider-shaped hard palate than mine": ibid., 151.

173 "Who had ever heard of such a thing? Audrey Hepburn had!": ibid., 147.

173 "The more I know a person the more chameleonlike I can be": ibid.

173 "trying to sing it as I thought she would have": Paris, *Audrey Hepburn*, 201.

173 "An American who probably knows London": Nixon, *I Could Have Sung All Night*, 148.

173 "Ultimately Audrey (and I) listened carefully to all the opinions": ibid., 149.

173   "She felt that now that she heard how it *should* be done, she could actually do it": ibid., 151.

173   "an ordeal": Nixon, ibid., 150.

174   "the mayor of Miami": Harrison, *Rex: An Autobiography*, 198.

174   "(Audrey) didn't get into the right groove": Beaton, *Cecil Beaton's Hollywood*, 74.

174   "hung a sign on the white picket fence erected around her dressing room": Harris, *Audrey Hepburn: A Biography*, 202.

174   "claiming it threw her 'off balance'": "The Two Audrey Hepburns," *Silver Screen*, August 1964.

174   "an extraordinary array of long-out-of-style hats": "Cecil Beaton's Own Story of *My Fair Lady*," *New York Journal American*, October 18, 1964.

174   "He makes you look the way you have always wanted to look": "Audrey Hepburn's Glorious Whirl in *My Fair Lady*," *Vogue*, December 1963.

174   "are like those in a Flemish painting and are even more appealing—young and sad": "Cecil Beaton's Own Story of *My Fair Lady*," *New York Journal American*, October 18, 1964.

174   "I really adored him": Hugo Vickers, *Cecil Beaton: A Biography* (Boston: Little Brown & Company, 1985), 174v.

174   "every time he mentioned you": Vickers, *Malice in Wonderland*, 233.

175   "We did understand each other": ibid.

175   "The coolly detached and the fanatically involved": Vickers, *Cecil Beaton*, 529.

175   "Both women were marvelous at conveying this earthiness": Anne Edwards, *Streisand: A Biography* (New York: Little, Brown and Company, 1997), 281.

175   "Beaton took upwards of one thousand photos": Vickers, *Cecil Beaton*, 529.

175   "the combination of Audrey and these exaggerated clothes": Beaton, *Cecil Beaton's Fair Lady*, 52.

175   "she spent a combined total of two years of her life shooting magazine covers": Benecke, *100 Reasons to Love Audrey Hepburn*, 80.

175   "Dearest C.B.": Beaton, *Cecil Beaton's Fair Lady*, 52.

175   "He created the look of the film": Sean Hepburn Ferrer, interview with author, August 4, 2020.

176   "The glittering capes": Beaton, *Cecil Beaton's Fair Lady*, 65.

176   "Mr. Cukor doesn't want you to take pictures": ibid., 106.

176   "I was later told that it took George Cukor": ibid.

176   "it was something I was not aware of during the picture": Vickers, *Malice in Wonderland*, 231.

176   "I have begun to feel like a trespasser": Beaton, *Cecil Beaton's Fair Lady*, 115.

176   "He was unrelenting": *LIFE* magazine, *Audrey: 25 Years Later*, 74.

176   "three days longer": Beaton, *Cecil Beaton's Fair Lady*, 115.

176   "Dearest, dearest, Audrey": "Consoling Audrey," *Stars and Letters: Letters from Hollywood's Golden Age*, November 30, 2017, https://starsandletters.blogspot.com/2017/11/consoling-audrey-hepburn.html.

176   "I hope all this praise": ibid.

177   "wicked' behavior": Paris, *Audrey Hepburn*, 203.

177   "I felt used. And I was angry. I was really angry": Maychick, *Audrey Hepburn*, 183.

177   "Rudi Fehr, who was with Warner all the time": Nixon, *I Could Have Sung All Night*, 152.

177   "Marni blabbed all over town that she was going to more or less 'save' the movie": Paris, *Audrey Hepburn*, 211.

177   "Having to really play the whole role": Nixon, *I Could Have Sung All Night*, 166–67.

177   "felt bad for Audrey: she could tell that she wasn't quite getting it": Marc Santoro, "Is That Really Her Voice?" *New York Times*, January 2, 2003.

177   "He told me that his mother admired me": Nixon, *I Could Have Sung All Night*, 166–67.

177   "I used to think that *My Fair Lady* had aged": Sean Hepburn Ferrer, interview with author, August 4, 2020.

178   "I've forgotten her name, a lovely girl": *Larry King Extra*, "Audrey Hepburn," October 21, 1991.

178   "I sang a *bit* of it Larry!": ibid.

178   "hated (Andrews) with a passion": Moore, *One Lucky Bastard*, 170.

178   "wary at first": Alexander Walker, *Fatal Charm*, 267.

178   "Audrey is a very gentle and sweet person": Harrison, *Rex: An Autobiography*, 197.

178   "Audrey also had to weather a great deal of adverse press publicity": Harrison, *Damned Serious Business,* 158.

178   "gave one of the most transcendental performances ever": Paris, *Audrey Hepburn*, 204.

178   "(Audrey) had to be dubbed, and she mouthed the words": Harrison, *Damned Serious Business,* 158.

178   "The only thing I was not delighted with": ibid., 159.

178   "outward self-assurance was only a cover-up": Paris, *Audrey Hepburn*, 203.

178   "What's the matter, what are you looking at?": ibid., 218.

179   "Audrey you're just so beautiful": ibid.

179   "I gave Audrey's coat seven different dyeings to make it look as old as that": David Thomas, "The Year of My Fair Lady," *Ladies Home Journal*, January–February 1964.

179   "It is remarkable that this scraggy little girl": Vickers, *Cecil Beaton*, 470.

179   "'I may look dirty,' she'd say": Willoughby, *Audrey Hepburn: Photographs 1953–1966*, 247.

179   "quite as beautiful as snow and ice on trees in Switzerland": Vickers, *Cecil Beaton*, 463.

179   "When she entered the set for the first time in it, she looked so beautiful . . .": Scott Anthony, "A Film to Remember: *My Fair Lady*," *Medium*, April 24, 2019, https://medium.com/@sadissinger/a-film-to-remember-my-fair-lady-1964-2d9ecb3b25d1.

179   "In that absolutely sublime dress, with my hair dressed to kill": Harris, *Audrey Hepburn: A Biography*, 201.

179   "All I had to do was walk down the stairs": "Reflections on the Silver Screen Interview with Richard Brown."

179   "The little princess of *Roman Holiday* had grown into a queen's estate": Cecil Beaton as quoted in Walker, *Audrey: Her Real Story*, 193.

180 "They've made a superlative film from the musical stage show *My Fair Lady*": Bosley Crowther, "Lots of Chocolates for Miss Eliza Doolittle," *New York Times*, October 22, 1964.

180 "Audrey Hepburn is an enchanting Eliza Doolittle": Rose Pelswick, *New York Journal-American*, quoted in Vermilye, *The Complete Films of Audrey Hepburn*,179.

180 "That's all very nice—but can we please get back to the story?": Jeanine Basinger, interview with author, September 11, 2020.

180 "What's to become of me?": *My Fair Lady*, screenplay by Alan J. Lerner, Warner Bros., 1964.

180 "She doesn't belong in a mansion": *Sabrina*, screenplay by Billy Wilder, Samuel Taylor, and Ernest Lehman, Paramount Pictures, 1954.

181 "almost unbearably poignant in the later scenes when she hungers for love": Bosley Crowther, *New York Times*, October 22, 1964.

181 "Let's put up our feet and just sit and enjoy it": Levy, *George Cukor*, 288.

182 "I think this may have been why": Harrison, *Rex: An Autobiography*, 196.

182 "She never considered ours a business relationship": Collins, "When Hubert Met Audrey."

182 "Julie Andrews Chosen, Audrey Hepburn Omitted": Donald Lyons, "Slicing the Tony Baloney," *Wall Street Journal*, May 14, 1996.

182 "Hepburn did the acting, but Marni Nixon subbed for her in the singing department": Nixon, *I Could Have Sung All Night*, 152.

182 "blabbed too much to the press": ibid.

182 "One thing I never wanted": ibid.

182 "dreamed last night that I made a date with Audrey Hepburn": ibid., 172.

182 "I'm happy for Julie but sad and disappointed for myself": Gene Grove, "Julie Very Sad that Audrey Didn't Get It," *New York Post*, February 26, 1965.

183 "I think Audrey should have been nominated": Harris, *Audrey Hepburn: A Biography*, 210.

183 "I think I am the only one": Spoto, *Enchantment*, 243.

183 "little daughter": Erwin and Diamond, *Audrey Hepburn Treasures*, 119.

183 "Don't worry about not being nominated": Harris, *Audrey Hepburn: A Biography*, 210.

183 "Darling C.B. Just to say how happy, happy, happy, happy": Vickers, *Cecil Beaton*, 476.

183 "a deep bow": George Cukor Academy Award acceptance speech, April 5, 1965, "My Fair Lady and George Cukor Win Best Picture and Directing: 1965 Oscars," YouTube, posted by Oscars, August 29, 2013, https://www.youtube.com/watch?v=Q_ntrUBJTHk.

183 "I feel in a way I should split this in half": "Rex Harrison Wins Best Actor: 1965 Oscars," April 5, 1965, YouTube, posted by Oscars, September 27, 2011, https://www.youtube.com/watch?v=0aL5W0dxoQY.

183 "You deserve it all": ibid.

183 "Deep love": ibid.

183 "There he was having wanted to recast the whole thing for the film": Harrison, *Damned Serious Business*, 159.

183 "a little hurt and disappointed": "Pat Neal Hurt by Oscar's Snub," *New York Post*, April 8, 1965.

184 "She and Audrey have known each other a long time": ibid.

184 "with Audrey proclaiming 'I'm thrilled for her, of course'": Harris, *Audrey Hepburn: A Biography*, 212.

184 "All the winners and presenters were asked to pose for photographs together": Julie Andrews, *Home Work: A Memoir of My Hollywood Years* (New York: Hachette Books, 2019), 135.

184 "I wouldn't consider it poetic justice": Harris, *Audrey Hepburn: A Biography*, 212.

184 "Actually I think that in the end, Audrey gave an enchanting performance on film": Karney, *Audrey Hepburn: A Charmed Life*, 143.

184 "There are very few similarities between the two girls, except that they both have extraordinary charm": David Willis, *Audrey: The 60s*, 131.

184 "much better than Julie Andrews": Spoto, *Enchantment*, 240.

184 "Julie Andrews put everyone at ease": Dotti, *Audrey at Home*, 156.

184 "Hello, everyone, I'm Marni Nixon!" Nixon, *I Could Have Sung All Night*, 252.

Twenty-Eight—What Could Go Wrong? 1960s

187 "I knew how difficult it had to be to be married to a world celebrity": Julia Molony, "Audrey's Glittering Career Hit Star's Secret Heartache," *Irish Independent*, June 7, 2015.

187 "You won't believe this": Woodward, *Audrey Hepburn*, 189.

187 "Based on what I saw": Sean Hepburn Ferrer, interview with author, August 4, 2020.

187 "People conveniently forget that they made a lot of good choices together": Paris, *Audrey Hepburn*, 241.

188 "I think Audrey allows Mel to think he influences her": Walker, *Audrey: Her Real Story*, 116.

188 "Gradually and then suddenly": Ernest Hemingway, *The Sun Also Rises* (New York: Scribner; Hemingway Library Edition, 2016), 136.

188 "Your father was the producer of my career": "Sean Hepburn Ferrer on 'Intimate Audrey': You Walk Around Like It's a Personal Visit and Personal Experience," *FilmTalk.org*, November 2, 2019, https://filmtalk.org/2019/11/02/sean-hepburn-ferrer-on-intimate-audrey-you-walk-around-like-its-a-personal-visit-and-a-personal-experience/.

188 "He was a good producer": Sean Hepburn Ferrer, interview with author, July 7, 2020.

188 "I'm sure that, above everything, Mel was jealous of her success": Higham, *Audrey: The Life of Audrey Hepburn*, 187.

188 "Finally she couldn't take it any longer": Harris, *Audrey Hepburn*, 231.

188 "I don't think anybody could compete with Audrey": Paris, *Audrey Hepburn*, 241.

188 "I was not competitive nor was I controlling": Spoto, *Enchantment*, 259.

188 "It's a problem when the wife outshines the husband as Audrey does me": Paris, *Audrey Hepburn*, 240.

188 "Rarely did I ever see her happy": Henry C. Rogers, *Walking the Tightrope* (New York: William Morrow and Co., 1980), 216–17.

189 "Mel was so incensed at this profanity": Wasson, *Fifth Avenue, 5 A.M.*, 106.

189 "I also told myself . . . if you have a grain of energy or thought or emotion left in you": Audrey Hepburn as told to Henry Gris, "A Man to Hold—A Child to Love—I Won't Let Them Be Taken Away," *Modern Screen*, January 1965.

189 "I would love to do another play or musical": "Audrey Hepburn My Fair Lady Interview 1964," YouTube, posted by Rare Audrey Hepburn, August 5, 2014, https://www.youtube.com/watch?v=k-u4v8f9asM.

189 "through every part of Europe": Higham, *Audrey: The Life of Audrey Hepburn*, 170.

Twenty-Nine—For the Love of Animals, 1957–1993

191 "I walk my dogs": Olivia O'Bryan, "Audrey Hepburn's Love for Dogs Became Part of Her Aesthetic," *Forbes.com*, July 25, 2021.

191 "Mr. Famous was already on tranquilizers": Woodward, *Audrey Hepburn*, 202.

191 "Whenever we saw cats or dogs she would straight away go and pet them": Matzen, *Warrior,* 66.

191 "you know what they say about tomorrow": Woodward, *Audrey Hepburn*, 77.

191 "Audrey was rather good": ibid.

192 "She was kind of a little frivolous": Crowe, *Conversations with Wilder*, 173.

192 "Who thinks you're as fantastic as your dog does?": Keogh, *What Would Audrey Do?* 99.

192 "No person, and few children . . . are as unpremeditated, as understanding": ibid., 100.

Thirty—A Beautiful Uncertainty

195 "I'm terribly uncomfortable seeing myself onscreen": "Audrey Hepburn Interview," *Good Morning America*, February 19, 1987.

195 "Miss Hepburn would like you to join her for tea tomorrow": Bosworth, *Men in My Life*, 292.

195 "And you sort of don't believe any of it, and yet you're terribly grateful": Dunne, "Hepburn Heart."

196 "You can tell more about a person by what he says about others": Loustalot, *Living like Audrey*, 40.

196 "After five minutes with Audrey you forgot who she was for everybody else": ibid., 46.

196 "Being around her was like traveling with a rock star": Andrew Wald in *Audrey: More Than an Icon*, 2020.

196 "I had been in love with Audrey since I was nine or ten years old": Jeffrey Banks, interview with author, August 25, 2020.

198 "There are moments when the world seems suddenly to stand very still": Vickers, *Malice in Wonderland*, 229.

198 "I think she was chasing unconditional love her whole life": Emma Ferrer, interview with author, September 23, 2020.

198 "She's something of a mystery": Bosworth, *Men in My Life*, 270.

198 "I watched spellbound as she glided across the floor": ibid., 280–81.

198 "It's as if she's from another world": ibid., 270.

ACT THREE—ICON

Thirty-One—The Nature of the Appeal, 1953–1993

201 "Over the years we chose three style icons": Pamela Fiori, interview with author, September 16, 2020.

202 "There is no speech I can relax into when I'm tired": Spoto, *Enchantment*, 21

202 "the quality of heartbreak": Beaton, *Vogue*, November 1954.

202 "To me, Ella Fitzgerald has the most tranquilizing singing voice on earth": Silverman, *Dancing on the Ceiling*, 236.

202 "Her voice was enough to soothe your jangled nerves": Walker, *Audrey: Her Real Story*, 110–11.

202 "Happy girls are the prettiest girls": Benecke, *100 Reasons to Love Audrey Hepburn,* 22.

202 "Nothing's impossible. The word itself says 'I'm possible!'" ibid., 87.

203 "Doris exuded sex": Tom Santopietro, *Considering Doris Day* (New York: St. Martin's Press, 2007), 9.

203 "I'm not as well-stacked as Sophia Loren or Gina Lollobrigida": Keogh, *Audrey Style*, 82.

203 "When she stood before the cameras, she became Miss Audrey Hepburn": Crowe, *Conversations with Wilder*, 51.

204 "If I can do it, anyone can do it": *Doris Day: A Sentimental Journey*, PBS, 1991.

204 "I see the problems when I get up in the morning": Audrey Hepburn in *Audrey: More Than an Icon*, 2020.

204 "I'm not in love with my looks": Sidney Solsky, "Hollywood Is My Beat," *New York Post*, August 26, 1956.

204 "Oh I'd like to be not so flat chested": Woodward, *Audrey Hepburn*, 76.

204 "Actually I'm very grateful": ibid.

204 "No, I don't think girls would like to look like me": Frank Quinn, "Mel Will Direct Audrey," *New York Mirror*, August 1, 1957.

204 "I've always wanted really feminine shoulders that sort of slope down": Keogh, *What Would Audrey Do?* 132.

204 "Oh, there's nothing terribly unusual about me . . .": Vickers, *Malice in Wonderland,* 314.

204 "Audrey Hepburn was something special": Crowe, *Conversations with Wilder*, 172.

204 "(She was) the perfect package of imperfections": Jacqui Miller, ed., *Fan Phenomena—Audrey Hepburn* (Bristol UK: Intellect Books 2014), 80.

204 "The definition of beauty": ibid.

205 "Her style was born as we now know it": *People* Extra: *A Tribute to Audrey Hepburn*, 50.

205 "For me Jackie was the Audrey Hepburn of *War and Peace* and *My Fair Lady*": Carly Simon, *Touched by the Sun: My Friendship with Jackie* (New York: Farrar, Straus, and Giroux 2019), 52.

205 "She felt honored and thankful for the attention": Ferrer, *Audrey Hepburn: An Elegant Sprit*, xiii.

Thirty-Two—Fashionista, 1953–1993

207 "She created her very own style": Hubert de Givenchy in *Audrey Hepburn: A Life In Pictures*, 5.

207 "Beautiful evening dresses by Givenchy and Valentino": "Audrey Hepburn . . . by Her Son."

207 "emotionally accessible": Keogh, *What Would Audrey Do?* 70.

207 "My look is attainable": Loustalot, *Living like Audrey*, 55.

207 "according to playwright Anita Loos": "Glamour & Grace," *Audrey Hepburn: Her Life and Legacy*, 61.

207 "a friend once used Audrey's belt": Eleanor Harris, "Audrey Hepburn," *Good Housekeeping*, August 1959.

208 "Never, ever did Audrey speak with her": Paris, *Audrey Hepburn*, 375.

208 "Audrey's favorite: my chicken salad": Fiori, "Forever Audrey."

208 "She would eat anything and everything": Jeffrey Banks, interview with author, August 25, 2020.

208 "When you have had the strength to survive starvation": Paris, *Audrey Hepburn*, 161.

208 "She could eat us both under the table!" "Audrey Hepburn . . . by Her Son."

208 "especially her thoracic cage": Ferrer, *Audrey Hepburn: An Elegant Spirit*, 34.

208 "fake thin": ibid.

208 "she possessed the same figure as her paternal grandmother": Keogh, *Audrey Style*, 53.

209 "The underthings, the shoes, the hats, the gloves": Harris, *Audrey Hepburn: A Biography*, 131.

209 "She was so disciplined, so organized, she never was once late for a fitting": Collins, "When Hubert Met Audrey."

209 "I prepare a clothes chart for the coming season": "Audrey Hepburn's Fashion Formula," *New York Herald Tribune*, November 11, 1962.

209 "You have to look at yourself objectively": Keogh, *Audrey Style*, 61–62.

209 "Elegance starts within": Sean Hepburn Ferrer, interview with author, July 7, 2020.

209 "Casually dressed in capri pants and ballet flats": Pamela Fiori, interview with author, September 16, 2020.

209 "truly small eyes": Damiani Ludovica and Luca Dotti, eds., *Audrey in Rome* (New York: Harper Design, 2012), 33.

209 "was only a trick of makeup": ibid.

209 "I like to wear very little jewelry": Bernadine Morris, "Actress Has Influential Fashion Role," *New York Times*, December 15, 1963.

209 "warm": Jacobs and Dotti, "Audrey's Dolce Vita."

209 "I often cheat on my armholes and collars": "Audrey Hepburn's Fashion Formula," *New York Herald Tribune*, November 11, 1962.

209 "My coloring lacks definition": ibid.

209 "walking the mountains": Bernadine Morris, "Actress Has Influential Fashion Role," *New York Times*, December 15, 1963.

211 "It sounds terribly snobby, but fur is much warmer when it is against you": Gloria Emerson, "Co-Stars Again: Audrey Hepburn and Givenchy," *New York Times*, September 8, 1965.

211 "Look for simplicity of line": "Audrey Hepburn's Fashion Formula," *New York Herald Tribune*, November 11, 1962.

211 "Beauty Regimen": Paris, *Audrey Hepburn*, 256.

211 "nothing wrong with that": Curtis Bill Pepper, "Audrey Hepburn at 46," *McCall's*, January 1976.

211 "My mother thought everybody should be allowed to make their own choices": Benecke, *100 Reasons to Love Audrey Hepburn*, 90.

211 "Put me in furs and jewels and I look like": "Audrey Hepburn," *Movie D.V. Album*, July 1957.

211 "(She was) almost like a child": Keogh, *What Would Audrey Do?* 132.

211 "The beauty of a woman": Sam Levenson, "Time Tested Beauty Tips" (retitled and adapted by Audrey Hepburn) from Sam Levenson, *In One Era and Out the Other*, reprinted in Ferrer, *Audrey Hepburn: An Elegant Spirit*, 217.

Thirty-Three—Once More with Feeling, 1966

213 "As a child I was taught that it was bad manners to bring attention to yourself": Audrey Hepburn in David Willis, *Audrey: The 60s* (New York: HarperCollins, 2012), 100.

213 "Willy took that picture at that moment": Herman, *Talent for Trouble*, 432.

213 "he deliberately asked for Audrey": ibid., 433.

214 "stern and formidable": *People* Extra: *A Tribute to Audrey Hepburn*, 33.

214 "There was a modesty and a sadness about her": ibid.

214 "She was the one—and I think only": Maychick, *Audrey Hepburn*, 190.

214 "cracked the safe and escaped with the following week's French payroll": Madsen, *William Wyler*, 396.

214 "He knew his lines and knew what he was doing": Herman, *Talent for Trouble*, 435.

214 "at a total cost of $100,000": ibid., 433.

215 "That does it!": *How to Steal a Million*, screenplay by Harry Kurnitz, 20th Century Fox, 1966.

215 "Did this ruffian molest you in any way?": ibid.

215 "wholly ingratiating film": Bosley Crowther, "Screen: How to Steal a Million Opens at Music Hall: Audrey Hepburn Stars with Peter O'Toole," *New York Times*, July 15, 1966.

215 "If every picture that Fox made": Herman, *Talent for Trouble*, 437.

Thirty-Four—*Two for the Road*, 1967

217 "Donen and his associates": Roger Ebert, "Two for the Road," *rogerebert.com*, October 2, 1967.

217 "I'm sending you a treatment": Stanley Donen, audio commentary, *Two for the Road* DVD, 20th Century Fox, 2005.

217 "It's too complicated": ibid.

217 "You have to make this film": ibid.

217 "I'll do it. It's wonderful. I was wrong": ibid.

217 "gracious, entirely sweet, and unassuming": Silverman, *Dancing on the Ceiling*, 302.

217 "one-hundred percent pain in the ass, very boring": ibid., 302–3.

217 "Audrey usually makes up her own mind about what she's going to do": Spoto, *Enchantment*, 249.

217 "overtake ourselves—pass our old selves": Alexander Walker, *Audrey: Her Real Story*, 205.

217 "Yes, the Albert Finney role": Chris Chase, "At the Movies; Michael Caine and Roles He Wishes He Got," *New York Times*, March 19, 1982.

218 "The entire lunch Audrey's jaw kept dropping": Silverman, *Dancing on the Ceiling*, 308.

218 "a confidence I don't have on my own": *People* Extra: *A Tribute to Audrey Hepburn*, 49.

218 "I buy just as many things from Hubert as ever": Anne Anabl, "Audrey Hepburn Sees the Dark," *New York World Journal Tribune*, February 1, 1967.

218 "You two know what's right for me, you do the shopping": "Is This Really Audrey Hepburn," *Ladies Home Journal*, January 1967.

218 "no bright colors, no prints": ibid.

218 "extremely rigid": Paris, *Audrey Hepburn*, 233.

218 "the 'vinyl girl,' who designed for the ready to wear French house of V de V": Angela Taylor, "Audrey Hepburn Tries on a Swingin' Image": *New York Times*, December 27, 1966.

219 "Audrey's eyebrows are twice as thin now": Woodward, *Audrey Hepburn*, 281.

219 "She was so free, so happy. I never saw her like that. So young!": Maychick, *Audrey Hepburn*, 193.

219 "I love people who make me laugh. It's probably the most important thing in a person": Loustalot, *Living like Audrey*, 89.

219 "I was on the set": Sean Hepburn Ferrer, interview with author, July 7, 2020.

219 "Audrey cared for Finney a great deal": Keogh, *Audrey Style*, 153.

219 "Performing with Audrey was quite disturbing, actually": *People* Extra: *A Tribute to Audrey Hepburn*, 34.

219 "She and Albie had this wonderful thing to see": ibid., 43.

219 "They don't look very happy": *Two for the Road*, screenplay by Frederic Raphael, 20th Century Fox, 1967.

220 "a lot of dialogue and lots of moving at the same time": Stanley Donen, audio commentary, *Two for the Road*, DVD, 2015.

220 "By removing all transitions": Jeanine Basinger, *I Do and I Don't: A History of Marriage in the Movies* (New York: Alfred A. Knopf, 2012), 46.

220 "You don't give me everything I want": *Two for the Road*, screenplay by Frederic Raphael, 20th Century Fox, 1967.

220 "Most of Audrey's pictures were about the euphoric feeling of falling in love": Stanley Donen in *Audrey Hepburn Remembered*.

220 "Are you sure you remember which one I am?": *Two for the Road*, screenplay by Frederic Raphael, 20th Century Fox, 1967.

220 "All of us had things in our lives that it reminded us of, so we really suffered": Stanley Donen, audio commentary, *Two for the Road*, DVD, 2015.

220 "It was very courageous of her to do it. Twice": ibid.

221 "They worked well as a team": ibid.

221 "I remember hearing her give Stanley eight different readings of the words 'Hello, darling'": Walker, *Audrey: Her Real Story*, 213.

221 "I don't think it's right for the movie": Stanley Donen, audio commentary, *Two for the Road*, DVD, 2015.

221 "If you listen to those songs—('Moon River,' 'Charade,' 'Two for the Road')": Ferrer, *Audrey Hepburn: An Elegant Spirit*, 83.

221 "Love had always issued out of the places that hurt the most": Pat Conroy, https://www.pinterest.com/pin/442337994628617791/?d=t&mt=login/

221 "On earlier pictures I camera cut the film—there was virtually no film left over after editing": Stanley Donen, audio commentary, *Two for the Road*, DVD, 2015.

221 "The role required a depth of emotion, care, yearning and maturity": Silverman, *Dancing on the Ceiling*, 305.

221 "Bitch," "Bastard": *Two for the Road*, screenplay by Frederic Raphael, 20th Century Fox, 1967.

221 "It really is one of the greatest, most fully realized": Jeanine Basinger, interview with author, September 11, 2020.

222 "new (mod and non-Givenchy) Audrey Hepburn": Judith Crist, *New York World Journal Tribune*, quoted in Vermilye, *Complete Films of Audrey Hepburn*, 192.

222 "Helped partially by variations in her hairdos": "Robe," *Variety*, quoted in Vermilye, *Complete Films of Audrey Hepburn*, 195.

222 "It came out a little one-sided, like he's a shit, and he wasn't supposed to be": Silverman, *Dancing on the Ceiling*, 299.

222 "sublime": ibid., 305.

222 "This isn't happily ever after": Stanley Donen, audio commentary, *Two for the Road* DVD, 2015.

222 "Stanley had his career when he was a young man": Silverman, *Dancing on the Ceiling*, 333.

223 "Who are you?": *Two for the Road*, screenplay by Frederic Raphael, 20th Century Fox, 1967.

Thirty-Five—Alone in the Dark, 1967–1968

225 "When the lights go out at the end of the film": *Slant Magazine,* as cited in metacritic.com.

226 "a blessing. . . . I said, 'Do something for me, find your way around this room'": Karney, *Audrey Hepburn: A Charmed Life,* 162.

226 "draw attention to the fact": "Reflections on the Silver Screen: Audrey Hepburn Interview with Richard Brown."

226 "I was coming out of a rough period in Chicago": Alan Arkin, interview with author, September 8, 2020.

226 "An umbrella would be placed outside the set": ibid.

226 "She had a regality about her": ibid.

227 "At the time I certainly had no idea": ibid.

227 "in his book *Danse Macabre*": Benecke, *100 Reasons to Love Audrey Hepburn,* 83.

227 "I was nominated for *Wait Until Dark* when I liked myself better in *Two for the Road* that year": "Life Imitates Film Art as Audrey Meets Press," *Dallas Morning News,* March 30, 1976.

228 "Audrey Hepburn, thirty-eight, and Mel Ferrer, fifty, have separated after thirteen years of marriage": Maychick, *Audrey Hepburn,* 197.

228 "She sat me down in the bedroom": Fiori, "Forever Audrey."

228 "My parents never argued in front of me": Lina Das, "Another Audrey," *Mail on Sunday,* November 7, 1999.

228 "I hung on in there as long as I could": Audrey Hepburn in *Audrey: More Than an Icon,* 2020.

228 "The feeling of family is terribly important": ibid.

228 "I don't hear from Audrey and I respect that. Audrey asked for the divorce": *People* Extra: *A Tribute to Audrey Hepburn,* 43.

228 "I still don't know what the difficulties were": J. D. Podolsky, "Life with Audrey," *People,* October 31, 1994.

228 "My father spent the rest of his life regretting": Sean Hepburn Ferrer in *Audrey: More Than an Icon,* 2020.

228 "Audrey and Mel did dance together as parents of the groom": Harris, *Audrey Hepburn,* 275.

228 "For obvious dramatic and strangely romantic reasons": Peter Bogdanovich, *Who the Hell's in It: Conversations with Hollywood's Legendary Actors* (New York: Alfred A. Knopf, 2004), 268–69.

228 "She was an exceptional person, kind, caring, involved and strong": Richard Corliss, *Time.com,* "Audrey Hepburn: Still the Fairest Lady," January 20, 2017, https://content.time.com/time/arts/article/0,8599,1580936-2,00.html.

229 "spiritual biographer": Sean Hepburn Ferrer, interview with author, July 7, 2020.

229 "They were both responsible for the failed marriage": Spoto, *Enchantment,* 259.

229 "He was a perfectionist": Ferrer, *Audrey Hepburn: An Elegant Spirit,* 12.

229 "She was hoping that real love would come in the form of flowers": "Audrey Hepburn . . . by Her Son."

229 "Mostly—it's on both sides": ibid.

229 "What she didn't do was to speak up and be heard when she needed to": Ferrer, *Audrey Hepburn: An Elegant Spirit,* 13.

229 "She stayed too long in the marriage": Spoto, *Enchantment,* 259.

229   "each strand . . . blunt cut, then thinned diagonally": Keogh, *Audrey Style,* 160.

Thirty-Six—A Different Roman Holiday, 1969–1979

231 "She took her dogs for walks, navigated the city's grocery stores": Asia London Palamba, "A Glimpse into Audrey Hepburn's Life in Rome,"*Americadomani.com,* July 10, 2023.

232 "To become part of a family was extremely important to her": Paris, *Audrey Hepburn,* 247.

232 "lost her mind": Matzen, *Warrior,* 140.

232 "For once in your life": ibid., 141.

232 "Suddenly there was room": ibid., 142.

232 "he made her laugh, he made her feel good about herself": ibid.

232 "At the beginning of the marriage she was so happy": Anna Cataldi in *Audrey: More Than an Icon,* 2020.

232 "Every spring, especially here in Rome, you have this smell of orange blossom in the air": Laura Jacobs and Luca Dotti, "Audrey's Dolce Vita," *Vanity Fair,* May 2013.

232 "People in Rome, they were not nice to Audrey . . .": Matzen, *Warrior,* 27.

232 "She loved Rome and Rome loved her": Andrew Wald in *Audrey: More Than an Icon,* 2020.

232 "I'd give anything to eat in the kitchen": "Audrey Hepburn . . . by Her Son."

232 "We didn't grow up in 'Hollywood,' not the place, but the state of mind": Ferrer, *Audrey Hepburn: An Elegant Spirit,* 131.

232 "Remember, there was no VHS": Sean Hepburn Ferrer, interview with author July 7, 2020.

233 "(It) had high ceilings and frescoes. It must have been 12,000 to 15,000 square feet": Fiori, "Forever Audrey."

233 "When she needed things that I did not make": Collins, "When Hubert Met Audrey."

233 "We never together had an argument": ibid.

233 "for their political and social views": Matzen, *Dutch Girl,* 317.

234 "I didn't think was the best idea": Andrew Wald in *Audrey: More Than an Icon,* 2020.

234 "I began to resent the time I spent away from him on location": Morley, *Audrey Hepburn,* 103.

234 "Her success is astonishing": Beaton, *Diaries,* 17.

234 "Not at all. Not at all": "Audrey Hepburn Interview," *Good Morning America,* February 19, 1987.

234 "He is my best friend": "Audrey Hepburn Interview with Ivo Niehe."

234 "We had a tremendous relationship": "Audrey Hepburn—Documentary and Interview with Son Sean Ferrer," https://www.youtube.com/watch?v=Y2N2Kzl9L2s.

235 "showed her displeasure. And she knew how to make you feel really bad": Dotti, *Audrey at Home,* 201.

235 "She was, as some like to call her": Ferrer, *Audrey Hepburn: An Elegant Spirit,* 14.

235 "Behind the spritely persona": Sean Hepburn Ferrer, interview with author, July 7, 2020.

235 "It applied to her both professional and personally": Sean Hepburn Ferrer, interview with author, August 4, 2020.

235 "kitchen table biography": Dotti, *Audrey at Home*, 14.

235 "She completely flipped out": Matzen, *Warrior*, 33.

235 "and from that day she started talking more": ibid.

235 "We talked about so many things, even politics or euthanasia or prostitution": Luca Dotti, *Larevista.ro,* June 22, 2015.

235 "almost unconsciously, small talk would turn into a confession": Dotti, *Audrey at Home*, 45.

235 "I learned to know her better at the breakfast table": ibid., 46.

235 "banish sadness": ibid.

235 "Chocolate was my one true love as a child": Maychick, *Audrey Hepburn*, 15.

236 "'And now let's celebrate,' she'd say": Head, *Dress Doctor*, 7.

236 "Being in Holland during the war—it was a terrible experience": "Audrey Hepburn Interview," *Good Morning America*, February 19, 1987.

236 "I'm a long way from the human being I'd like to be": Klein, *Parade*.

236 "everybody's broken in some way": Ken Jaworoski, "Western Stars Review: Bruce Springsteen and Broken Cowboys," *New York Times*, October 24, 2019.

236 "I still feel I could lose everything at any moment": Klein, *Parade*.

236 "I might one day, if I have time": Audrey Hepburn on *Donahue,* January 31, 1990.

236 "I would have to tell the whole truth Luchino": Dotti, *Audrey at Home*, 14.

236 "The only time my fame was a little hard for me": "Reflections on the Silver Screen Interview with Richard Brown."

236 "Sometimes I think she made sure that they did, although she was subtle about it": Paris, *Audrey Hepburn*, 257.

237 "You are mistaken. I am the son of Mrs. Dotti": Dotti, *Audrey at Home*, 10.

237 "None of us, however, not even I, managed to completely connect Eliza Doolittle": ibid., 195.

Thirty-Seven—Nine Years of Silence, 1967–1976

239 "I don't regret for one minute": Carissa Mosness, "Six Audrey Hepburn Quotes That Prove She Remains a Timeless Hollywood Icon," www.womansworld.com/entertainment/celebrities/audrey-hepburn-quotes-131670, July 9, 2024.

239 "Although I had great respect for the art and craft of acting": Maychick, *Audrey Hepburn*, 9.

239 "I really die a million deaths every time": Wasson, *5th Avenue, 5 A.M.*, 107.

240 "People who would rob you of your dearest possession—your privacy": Martin Abramson, "Audrey Hepburn," *Cosmopolitan*, October 1955.

240 "I can spend time happily alone because I know somebody is going to walk in the door": Keogh, *What Would Audrey Do?* 82.

240 "She was actually happy about growing older because it meant more time for herself": Laura Jacobs and Luca Dotti, "Audrey Hepburn in Rome," *Vanity Fair*, May 2013.

240 "I can't be a leading lady all my life": Harris, *Audrey Hepburn: A Biography*, 268.

240 "I could survive without working but I couldn't survive without my family": *People* Staff, "The Private Audrey," *People.com*, https://people.com/archive/the-private-audrey/.

240 "I worked from the age of 13 for 25 years straight": Watters, "Audrey Hepburn: A Star Is Reborn."

241 "There's a great need in films today for mature women to be seen playing mature women": *Audrey Hepburn Remembered*.

241 "Such a poetic idea": Paris, *Audrey Hepburn*, 260.

Thirty-Eight—As If We Never Said Goodbye, 1976

243 "I don't know why I'm frightened": music by Andrew Lloyd Webber, lyrics by Don Black, "As If We Never Said Goodbye," *Sunset Boulevard*, 1993.

243 "Connery would be paid $1 million": Walker, *Audrey: Her Real Story*, 232.

243 "Audrey could get along with Hitler": Spoto, *Enchantment*, 276.

243 "After topping all the lists of the best dressed women in her career": Walker, *Audrey: Her Real Story*, 233.

244 "She loved working with Sean Connery": Sean Hepburn Ferrer, interview with author, July 7, 2020.

244 "I think of my career": "Audrey Hepburn Interview," *Good Morning America*, February 19, 1987.

244 "I still find it terrifying to start a film": Morley, *Audrey Hepburn*, 154.

244 "a whiz-bang with his many cameras and single takes": Matzen, *Warrior: Audrey Hepburn*, 4.

244 "He was in a hurry all the time": Higham, *Audrey: The Life of Audrey Hepburn*, 204.

244 "still alone": Paris, *Audrey Hepburn*, 263.

244 "You never wrote": *Robin and Marian*, screenplay by James Goldman, Columbia Pictures, 1976.

244 "Am I old and ugly?": ibid.

244 "I love you. I love you more than morning prayer": ibid.

245 "With all these men": Karney, *Audrey Hepburn: A Charmed Life*, 170.

245 "I could've done without that last close-up of fruit turning rotten": *Film Facts*, vol. 20 (Los Angeles: Division of Cinema University of Southern California, 1977), 26.

245 "I shall have to see it again before I decide": *Time*, March 22, 1976.

245 "This is a film about legends, and legends become even more beautiful with age": Frank Rich, *New York Post*, quoted in Vermilye, *Complete Films of Audrey Hepburn*, 204.

245 "The moment she appears on the screen is startling": *Time*, March 22, 1976.

245 "respectful to everyone": Matzen, *Warrior*, 68.

245 "I keep hearing that I am making a comeback": Erwin and Diamond, *Audrey Hepburn Treasures*, 141.

245 "I'm glad to have missed what's been happening in the movies these last eight years": Morley, *Audrey Hepburn*, 158.

245 "I could never be cynical. I wouldn't dare": Michiko Kakutani, "Why Has She Done So Few Films in Recent Years," *New York Times*, June 4, 1980.

Thirty-Nine—What Could Go Wrong, Part 2—1970s

247 "Doctors are great with their patients": Nosheen Iqbal, "The Best-Kept-Secret about Audrey Hepburn Is That She Was So Sad": *The Guardian*, November 15, 2020, https://www.theguardian.com/culture/2020/nov/15/the-best-kept-secret-about-audrey-hepburn-is-that-she-was-so-sad.

247 "the Dutch treat with the English accent talks but tells nothing": Matzen, *Dutch Girl*, 306.

247 "She's a perfectionist, with a strong need for security": Pepper, "Audrey Hepburn at 46."

247 "Marriage should be only one thing": ibid.

248 "You can stay with us and a bodyguard": Fiori, "Forever Audrey."

248 "I was thirteen": Sean Hepburn Ferrer, interview with author, July 7, 2020.

248 "My marriage is *basically* happy": Woodward, *Audrey Hepburn*, 327.

248 "She loved Andrea": Mita Ungaro in *Audrey: More Than an Icon*, 2020.

248 "He was committing a lot of adultery": Emma Ferrer in ibid.

248 "I was no angel. Italian husbands have never been famous for being faithful": Matzen, *Dutch Girl*, 315.

248 "It was devastating, totally devastating": Anna Cataldi in *Audrey: More Than an Icon*, 2020.

248 "If you see pictures of Audrey": Marilena Pilat in ibid.

248 "My husband and I had what you would call an open arrangement": George Haddad-Garcia, "Hepburn's Back!" *Sacramento Bee*, January 10, 1982, as quoted in Paris, *Audrey Hepburn*, 277.

248 "When she suffered—and she suffered a great deal—she kept it to herself": Harris, *Audrey Hepburn: A Biography*, 264.

248 "Once she sensed that she could trust somebody, she'd do anything for them": Keogh, *What Would Audrey Do?* 70.

248 "in order to hide her sadness from me": Dotti, *Audrey at Home*, 112.

248 "She realized that this charming simpatico Italian husband": Sean Hepburn Ferrer, interview with author, July 7, 2020.

249 "La Paisible—the place of peace—seen through the filter of his sarcasm": Dotti, *Audrey at Home*, 90.

249 "He did it over ten years": "Sean Hepburn Ferrer Talks about Audrey Hepburn."

249 "When I came home I found her in bed": ibid.

249 "Your heart just breaks": Audrey Hepburn in *Audrey: More Than an Icon*, 2020.

249 "I clung on to both marriages very hard, for as long as I could": *People* Extra: *A Tribute to Audrey Hepburn*, 44–45.

249 "Dotti was not much of an improvement on Ferrer": Lynn Barber, "Hepburn's Relief," *Sunday Express*, May 1, 1988.

249 "My stepfather was a brilliant funny psychiatrist—but he was a hound dog": Sean Hepburn Ferrer in "Audrey," *The Age*, November 29, 2003.

249 "What she didn't do was to speak up and be heard": Ferrer, *Audrey Hepburn: An Elegant Spirit*, 13.

250 "Both men had been emotionally scarred by equally powerful and brilliant mothers": ibid., 11.

250 "Growing up, I was struck above all by how different they were": Dotti, *Audrey at Home*, 113.

250 "it was my father who was too young, still immature": ibid.

250 "You always hope that if you love somebody enough, everything will be all right": Erwin and Diamond, *Audrey Hepburn Treasures*, 145.

Forty—Feature Film Mistake #3—*Bloodline*, 1978–1979

253 "The movies that came after the breakup with Andrea Dotti": Sean Ferrer, interview with author, July 7, 2020.

253 "No, never. Never. I've never done that": Keogh, *What Would Audrey Do?* 187.

253 "in an emotional way": "Italian Interview with Audrey Hepburn," YouTube, posted by Arranging_Matches, May 6, 2006, https://www.youtube.com/watch?v=5p78PFW2aNg&t=73s.

253 "After her retirement": Sean Hepburn Ferrer, interview with author, July 7, 2020.

253 "First of all you spend a year or so convincing her": Dotti, *Audrey at Home*, 85.

253 "Am I going to be able to do it": Woodward, *Audrey Hepburn*, 331.

254 "The difficulty with stars is, what do they do at fifty or fifty-five?": Billy Wilder in *Audrey Hepburn Remembered*.

254 "There are not a lot of choices for women past twenty-seven": Sheila Waller, *Carrie Fisher: A Life on the Edge* (New York: Farrar Straus Giroux, 2019), 320.

254 "All I really want now is not to be lonely, and to have my garden": Morley, *Audrey Hepburn*, 158.

254 "It can be very lonely in a crowd": M. George Haddad, "It's a Sexy New Audrey Hepburn in Bloodline," *Us Weekly*, July 10, 1979.

254 "I thought it was exciting. I'm not a snob about movies": ibid.

254 "Audrey, who'd come with her own bodyguard": Karney, *Audrey Hepburn: A Charmed Life*, 175.

255 "Though it would take several pictures on the level of *Bloodline*": "Cart," *Variety*, quoted in Vermilye, *Complete Films of Audrey Hepburn*, 206.

255 "It's a shock to see Hepburn playing a role": "Cart," Variety, as quoted in Harris, *Audrey Hepburn*, 264.

255 "He had the self-absorbed actor's unpredictability of response": Walker, *Audrey: Her Real Story*, 242.

255 "I never heard a vulgar word come out of Audrey": *People* Extra: *A Tribute to Audrey Hepburn*, 75.

255 "That Audrey bitch was so fat!": Harris, *Audrey Hepburn: A Biography*, 262

Forty-One—*They All Laughed*, 1980

257 "John Keats wrote 'Beauty is truth'": Bogdanovich, *Who the Hell's in It*, 443.

257 "accept the question": Thomas J. Harris, *Bogdanovich's Picture Shows* (Metuchen: The Scarecrow Press Inc., 1990), 229.

257 "Oh Peetah!": Bogdanovich, *Who the Hell's in It*, 441.

257 "turned out to be": ibid., 441–42.

258 "There's nobody greater at a romantic comedy": ibid.

258 "I'm not Laurence Olivier, no virtuoso talent": Michiko Kakutani "Why Has She Done So Few Films in Recent Years?" *New York Times*, June 4, 1980.

258 "I find Audrey Hepburn fantastically twee": Emma Thompson in "Emma Thompson: Audrey Hepburn Couldn't Act," *Belfast Telegraph*, August 9, 2010.

258 "Emma Thompson—she's an actress and a very good one": Sean Hepburn Ferrer, interview with author, August 4, 2020.

258 "Audrey was just a little bit tougher": Frederic Raphael, "Audrey was a Writer's Dream: Frederic C. Raphael," *Gulfnews.com*, August 23, 2010.

258 "My mother was not of the ilk and capacity": Sean Hepburn Ferrer, interview with author, July 7, 2020.

258 "it's not as if I'm the greatest actress": Audrey Hepburn *Audrey Hepburn Remembered*.

259 "Audrey's backstory in the movie": director's commentary, *Peter Bogdanovich's They All Laughed*, 25th Anniversary Edition DVD, HBO, 2006.

259 "She and Ben had had an affair during Bloodline": "Director to Director: A Conversation with Peter Bogdanovich and Wes Anderson," *Peter Bogdanovich's They All Laughed*, 25th Anniversary Edition DVD, HBO, 2006.

259 "lonely and fragile and saintlike": Bogdanovich, *Who the Hell's in It*, 430.

259 "I was flattered that someone like that would be in love with me": Spoto, *Enchantment*, 282.

259 "She was wonderful to work with": director's commentary, *Peter Bogdanovich's They All Laughed*, 25th Anniversary Edition DVD, HBO, 2006.

259 "All of the clothes that Audrey wears in the film": ibid.

259 "Audrey was so wonderful": ibid.

260 "virgin hearth goddess": Bogdanovich, *Who the Hell's in It*, 41.

260 "I got the impression she was pretty desperate for love": Walker, *Audrey: Her Real Story*, 246.

260 "She was a survivor": Peter Bogdanovich in *Audrey Hepburn: A Life in Pictures*, 17.

260 "In life you'd think, 'How is she going to get through the day or even the hour?'": Paris, *Audrey Hepburn*, 283.

260 "When she cries": Paris, *Audrey Hepburn*, 371.

260 "My mother was already a *print* on take one": "Sean Hepburn Ferrer Talks about Audrey Hepburn: The Actress, the Mother, the Style Icon and the Humanitarian," *FilmTalk.org*, December 8, 2016, https://filmtalk.org/2016/12/08/sean-hepburn-ferrer-talks-about-audrey-hepburn-the-actress-the-mother-the-style-icon-and-the-humanitarian/.

261 "Dorothy Stratten had died and Peter was very distraught": Sean Hepburn Ferrer, interview with author, August 4, 2020.

261 "Mr. Bogdanovich treats Audrey Hepburn so shabbily that": Vincent Canby, "Film: They All Laughed," *New York Times*, November 20, 1981.

261 "Any way you look at it": ibid.

261 "an aimless bust": *Newsweek* review of *They All Laughed*, as quoted in Paris, *Audrey Hepburn*, 284.

262 "her last film": Peter Bogdanovich in *Audrey Hepburn: A Life in Pictures*, 17.

262 "I had a strong sense that she didn't really enjoy making pictures anymore": Paris, *Audrey Hepburn*, 285.

Forty-Two—Might-Have-Beens, 1950s through 1980s

265 "It's a shame to think about what the studio ended up killing for the movie-going audiences": Rafe Telsch, "What Could Have Been: Hepburn as Peter Pan," *Cinemablend.com*, December 28, 2008, https://www.cinemablend.com/new/What-Could-Have-Been-Hepburn-Peter-Pan-11382.html.

265 "We hope we can shoot": "La Voix d'Audrey Hepburn (Audrey's Voice): French Interview with Simone Dubreuilh, February 22, 1955, https://www.rts.ch/YouTube, posted by Rare Audrey Hepburn, November 8, 2017, https://www.youtube.com/watch?v=ouMf6OOwQao.

265 "He had no warmth, nothing to give. Clever, yes—kind, no": Walker, *Audrey: Her Real Story*, 107.

266 "Audrey Hepburn just happened to be the most beautiful woman in movies": Woodward, *Audrey Hepburn*, 175.

269 "has great admiration for her talent": Dorothy Manners, "Audrey in Comeback," *Boston Herald American*, October 23, 1973.

269 "That was awful. He said 'You want to put my client in a stupid adventure movie?'": Paris, *Audrey Hepburn*, 270.

269 "My mother did later say to me": Sean Hepburn Ferrer, interview with author, August 4, 2020.

270 "She thought they were too cynical": Paris, *Audrey Hepburn*, 168.

270 "She loved the *Turning Point* script": ibid.

271 "Yes. She knew what the best part was": Walker, *Audrey: Her Real Story*, 247.

271 "she saw herself in it quite clearly": Bogdanovich, *Who the Hell's in It*, 445.

Forty-Three—Accept No Substitutes, 1987–2002

273 "Sydney Pollack's newly opened rehash of Sabrina": Michael H. Price, "*Sabrina* Remake Not Even Close to the Original Version," *Fort Worth Star-Telegram*, December 15, 1995.

273 "That Africa movie you made": Ed Sikov, *On Sunset Boulevard: The Life and Times of Billy Wilder* (Jackson: University Press of Mississippi, 2017), 590.
274 "I've got six": ibid.
274 "Would Elizabeth Taylor be a good substitute": Cameron Crowe, *Conversations with Wilder* (New York: Knopf, 1999), 220.

Forty-Four—With and Without—Life with Father (and Mother), 1929–1984

277 "I know my mother": "Audrey Hepburn and Salvatore Ferragamo," https://artsandculture.google.com/story/audrey-hepburn-and-salvatore-ferragamo-museosalvatoreferragamo/bAXhc2L06jr9Lw?hl=en.
277 "But maybe he didn't want to see me": Edward Klein, *Parade*, March 5, 1989.
277 "I do think there are things, experiences in childhood, that form you for the rest of your life": Hellstern, *How to Be Lovely*, 95.
277 "Well, she had feelings for all of us": Ferrer, *Audrey Hepburn: An Elegant Spirit*, 32.
277 "I think she really hoped that like in a fairy tale": *Darcey Bussell's Looking for Audrey Hepburn*.
277 "When she was telling me the story": John Isaac in *Audrey: More Than an Icon*, 2020.
277 "It took my mother only a fraction of a second to understand": Ferrer, *Audrey Hepburn: An Elegant Spirit*, 9.
278 "We can go home now": ibid., 10.
278 "She realized it wouldn't have made a huge difference": "Audrey Hepburn . . . by Her Son."
278 "At one point James did state that Audrey sent him a telegram at Christmas of 1954": Walker, *Audrey: Her Real Story*, 255.
278 "I did meet my grandfather": Sean Hepburn Ferrer, interview with author, August 4, 2020.
278 "I was terribly shocked to be somehow commercialized by my own grandmother": Nourmand, *Audrey Hepburn: The Paramount Years*, 60.
278 "I have been struggling to find a way to come to see Daddy": Wendy Noonan, "To Daddy Dearest from Audrey," *New York Times*, August 22, 2003.
278 "wonderfully ironic": Matzen, *Warrior*, 93.
278 "It was very odd": *Darcey Bussell's Looking for Audrey Hepburn*.
279 "how much she meant to him": Ferrer, *Audrey: An Elegant Spirit*, 11.
279 "What's important is that she had no bitterness toward him": Paris, *Audrey Hepburn*, 292.
279 "I have hatred for no one, I must say": Matzen, *Warrior*, 94.
279 "lived on her nerves but was never any trouble": Vickers, *Cecil Beaton*, 467.
279 "Considering that you have no talent, it's really extraordinary where you've got": Klein, *Parade*, March 5, 1989.
279 "And that's what I really believe to this day": ibid.
279 "The ugly duckling grows into a swan": "Audrey Hepburn Interview with Ivo Niehe."
279 "embarrassed Audrey, who was exactly the opposite": Paris, *Audrey Hepburn*, 294.
279 "My grandmother lived in San Francisco": Sean Hepburn Ferrer, interview with author, July 7, 2020.
280 "It was strenuous when my grandmother came to live with her": ibid.
280 "grande dame from another century": ibid.
280 "Ella was fantastic as a person": Matzen, *Dutch Girl*, 316.
280 "Ella was terrifying!" ibid.
280 "Never let yourself grow up believing that . . . anybody is any different from anybody else": Hellstern, *How to Be Lovely*, 101.
280 "Everybody is expendable and replaceable": "Sean Hepburn Ferrer Talks about Audrey Hepburn."
280 "I was very lucky to be able to take care of her": Dunne, "Hepburn Heart."
280 "Close is not the way to describe it": *Darcey Bussell's Looking for Audrey Hepburn*.
280 "I was lost without my mother": Martin Gitlin, *Audrey Hepburn: A Biography* (Westport, CT: Greenwood Press, 2009), 92.

Forty-Five—*Love Among Thieves*, 1987

283 "Television's fast production pace is difficult but maybe it's better that way": Robert Bianco, "Fun of 'Thieves' Lures Hepburn Back," *Chicago Tribune*, February 22, 1987.
283 "When Tom Selleck's participation didn't work out": Robert Wagner, interview with author, September 17, 2020.
284 "going to be fun, something cheerful": Paris, *Audrey Hepburn*, 301.
284 "I'm not a born actress, as such, but I care about expressing feelings": Heatley, *Audrey Hepburn in Words and Pictures*, 161.
284 "Working with Audrey was one of the big highlights of my career": Robert Wagner, interview with author, September 17, 2020.
284 "Fortunately we had rehearsed ahead of time": ibid.
284 "It was electric": ibid.
284 "an unfortunate travesty": Ricardo Hunter Garcia, "No Love for Thieves That Steal Your Time," *New York Post*, February 23, 1987.
284 "Miss Hepburn, still lovely, though even more fragile than usual": John O'Connor, "ABC and NBC Movies on Romance and Crime": *New York Times*, February 23, 1987.
285 "I would see her a great deal": Robert Wagner, interview with author, September 17, 2020.

ACT FOUR—WHAT MATTERS MOST

Forty-Six—UNICEF, 1988–1993

289 "It's ironic that it was because of children that I stayed home all these years": Hellstern, *How to Be Lovely*, 173.

289 "This is a fantastic idea." Matzen, *Warrior*, 49.

289 "our sacred charge": ibid., 71.

289 "I've always had enormous love of people—of children": Audrey Hepburn in *Audrey Hepburn: In Her Own Words*.

289 "adopted the world's children": Erwin and Diamond, *Audrey Hepburn Treasures*, 180.

289 "The difficulty with stars—what do they do if they are 50–55?": Billy Wilder in *Audrey Hepburn Remembered*.

289 "that wonderful, old-fashioned idea that others come first": *People* Extra: *A Tribute to Audrey Hepburn*, 65.

289 "This decision grew first out of her own childhood": Sean Hepburn Ferrer, interview with author, July 7, 2020.

290 "UNICEF means survival" Audrey Hepburn in *Audrey Hepburn: In Her Own Words*.

290 "It's now clear to me the reason I got famous all those years ago": Maychick, *Audrey Hepburn*, 228.

290 "My mother truly believed that the greatest crime was to rob a child of his or her childhood": Fiori, "Forever Audrey."

290 "It's something I'd do for my child, so why not for others?": Paris, *Audrey Hepburn*, 332.

290 "I am tickled pink by my little red U.N. passport!!!!": Spoto, *Enchantment*, 296.

290 "rehearsed for . . . all my life": Luca Dotti, "Audrey Forever," *Audrey Hepburn: Her Life and Legacy*, 7.

290 "She never complained": Matzen, *Warrior*, 64.

290 "You just decide." ibid., 58.

291 "In the cities there are some movie houses": "Audrey Hepburn on Ethiopia and UNICEF," March 25, 1988, YouTube, posted by Global News, November 8, 2012, https://www.youtube.com/watch?v=zorxr3IaksM.

291 "A child is a child is a child": Paris, *Audrey Hepburn*, 336.

291 "Politics are something which are very hard": Ferrer, *Audrey Hepburn: An Elegant Spirit*, 187.

291 "To save a child": *Audrey Hepburn: In Her Own Words*.

291 "She had never been a big fan of the Catholic Church": Matzen, *Warrior*, 49.

291 "Nature is above the humans": ibid., 216.

291 "after slowly approaching the girl": Hellstern, *How to Be Lovely*, 182.

291 "The neglect and humiliation of a child by adults is a killer of trust, of hope, and of possibility": Ferrer, *Audrey Hepburn: An Elegant Spirit*, 187.

291 "If you can't send me food for my children, then send me the spades to dig their graves": Erwin and Diamond, *Audrey Hepburn Treasures*, 167.

291 "Will it always be acceptable for their children to die of starvation": Ferrer, *Audrey Hepburn: An Elegant Spirit*, 181.

292 "I am not interested in promoting Audrey Hepburn these days": Matzen, *Warrior*, 74.

292 "Jim Grant told me they got $1 million in contributions every time she made an appeal": Paris, *Audrey Hepburn*, 344.

292 "That's what made her happy": John Isaac in *Audrey: More Than an Icon*.

292 "Audrey had no color, no race": Paris, *Audrey Hepburn*, 346.

292 "She joined UNICEF and in five years UNICEF had doubled in size": Sean Hepburn Ferrer in *Audrey: More Than an Icon*.

292 "during the Ethiopian crisis, a drive to raise $22 million": Andrew F. Cooper, *Celebrity Diplomacy* (Boulder, CO: Paradigm Publishers, 2008), 19.

292 "There was a big rise in donations": Caryl Stern, interview with author, September 16, 2020.

292 "completely done in": Matzen, *Warrior*, 76.

292 "I was so eager to go": "Audrey Hepburn on Ethiopia and UNICEF."

293 "The 'third world' is a term I don't like very much because we're all one world": Willoughby, *Remembering Audrey*, 140.

293 "Audrey was, along with Danny Kaye, one of the original ambassadors": Caryl Stern, interview with author, September 16, 2020.

293 "I have an enormous love for humanity": "Reflections on the Silver Screen Interview with Richard Brown."

293 "It's not even enough to know there has been a flood in Bangladesh": Hellstern, *How to Be Lovely*, 178.

293 "Even though I knew the text of every speech she gave for UNICEF": Fiori, "Forever Audrey."

294 "Eventually what affected her even more than those children who were suffering of hunger or disease": Matzen, *Warrior*, 101.

294 "It took us ten days to vaccinate the whole country—not bad": *LIFE* magazine, *Audrey: 25 Years Later*, 124.

294 "My suffering is not comparable": "Audrey Hepburn on *Sunday, Sunday*," host Gloria Hunniford.

294 "more than paying a debt": "Audrey Hepburn Interviewed on French Current Affairs TV Show 'Repéres' (1992)," YouTube, posted by Daniel Archers, March 7, 2013, https://www.youtube.com/watch?v=_hP1KXdu2bA.

294 "When it is done properly": Howard Sherman, *Another Day's Begun: Thornton Wilder's Our Town in the 21st Century* (New York: Methuen Drama, 2021), 3–4.

295 "Audrey was never concerned about her personal safety": Ferrer, *Audrey Hepburn: An Elegant Spirit*, 123.

295 "I can personally do very little": ibid., 126.

295 "They have nothing left": Matzen, *Warrior*, 146.

295 "There is no deficit in human resources. There is only a deficit of human will": Audrey Hepburn statement to members of the United Nations Staff, Geneva, Switzerland, June 13, 1989.

295 "So, Mr. Chairman, I am here today to speak for children who cannot speak for themselves": Matzen, *Warrior*, 133.

295 "When she testified before the U.S. Congress": Sean Hepburn Ferrer in *Audrey: More Than an Icon*.

295 "When the impact becomes visible": Audrey Hepburn statement to members of the United Nations Staff, Geneva, Switzerland, June 13, 1989

295 "Whether it be famine in Ethiopia": ibid.

295 "talking my head off": Cooper, *Celebrity Diplomacy*, 20.

295 "The worst violence in Africa is widespread poverty": ibid., 19.

296 "(If) a child is hit by a car you don't stop and wonder whose fault it is": Ferrer, *Audrey Hepburn: An Elegant Sp*irit, 146.

296 "Are we not reaping the mess we made so many years ago when we enriched ourselves?": Paris, *Audrey Hepburn*, 352.

296 "I am very impressed by the people of Ethiopia, by their beauty": Erwin and Diamond, *Audrey Hepburn Treasures*, 167.

296 "I watched boys build their own schoolhouse with bricks and cement provided by UNICEF": *LIFE* magazine, *Audrey: 25 Years Later*, 124.

297 "Often the kids would have flies all over them, but she would just go hug them": Erwin and Diamond, *Audrey Hepburn Treasures*, 172.

297 "Dignity and love were what we always talked about": John Isaac in *Audrey: More Than an Icon*, 2020.

297 "After all, I am doing only what any other human being would do": Keogh, *Audrey Style*, 217.

297 "It was like having your favorite aunt arrive": Matzen, *Warrior*, 175.

297 "With Bangladesh people had given up": John Isaac in *Audrey: More Than an Icon*.

297 "She realized the vastness of the tragedy": Anna Cataldi in ibid.

297 "an actor by chance": Matzen, *Warrior*, 170**.**

298 "When one of the world's great beauties calls you": Roger Moore, *My Word Is My Bond: A Memoir* (New York: HarperCollins, 2008), 265.

298 "Roger. The Press will not want to talk about UNICEF": ibid., 266.

298 "She wouldn't let them": ibid.

298 "Donor fatigue and compassion fatigue just cannot apply": Ferrer, *Audrey Hepburn: An Elegant Spirit*, 140.

298 "the wells have all been made by the Vietnamese themselves": Paris, *Audrey Hepburn*, 348.

298 "What's extraordinary about Vietnam": Matzen, *Warrior*, 209.

298 "I'd like to be in the field": "Audrey Hepburn Interviewed on French Current Affairs TV Show 'Repéres' (1992)."

298 "The child became the adult who reached back to help the child": Baron Wormser, *Legends of the Slow Explosion: Eleven Modern Lives* (North Adams, MA: Tupelo Press, 2018), 111.

298 "250,000 children die every week": *Audrey Hepburn: In Her Own Words*.

298 "This is my work Larry!": *Larry King Live*, "Interview with Audrey Hepburn," April 19, 1989.

298 "Last year we provided 52 million schoolbooks for Bangladesh": Dunne, "Hepburn Heart."

298 "Never in a million years would I have predicted that Audrey would give so much": Natalie Gittelson, "Personalities: Audrey Hepburn," *McCall's*, August 1989.

299 "No, it's just the sort of thing she would do": ibid.

Forty-Seven—Robbie, 1979–1993

301 "We were ready for each other": Ale Russian, "Audrey Hepburn's Last Love Robert Wolders Dies at 81," *people.com*, July 16, 2018.

301 "She was such a fabulous lady": Fiori, "Forever Audrey."

301 "so he could design a smaller version of our house for her in L.A": ibid.

302 "The first night I met her": *Darcey Bussell's Looking for Audrey Hepburn*.

302 "I was charmed with him that night": Matzen, *Warrior*, 82.

302 "one day she called": Fiori, "Forever Audrey."

302   "found out later that she had me in mind for her ex-sister-in-law": ibid.

302 "When her divorce became final, we were together all the time. It seemed so natural": ibid.

302 "We had the good fortune to find each other": Keogh, *What Would Audrey Do?* 211.

302 "a wonderful friendship. . . . We're both patient": *People* Extra: *A Tribute to Audrey Hepburn*, 46.

302 "Robert is just as passionate about children and UNICEF as I am": "Audrey Hepburn: *Sunday, Sunday*": host Gloria Hunniford.

302 "For five years": *People* Extra: *A Tribute to Audrey Hepburn*, 46.

302 "Throughout our youth": Ferrer, *Audrey Hepburn: An Elegant Spirit*, 145.

302 "She opposed both my marriages": Erwin and Diamond, *Audrey Hepburn Treasures*, 154.

302 "Now I've come to understand that the underlying reason": Matzen, *Dutch Girl*, 317.

303 "(Ella) would use me as a conduit": Keogh, *Audrey Style*, 188.

303 "Audrey took to calling Cemelia 'Maman'": *Audrey: More Than an Icon*.

303 "If I'd met him when I was 18, I wouldn't have appreciated him": Klein, *Parade*.

303 "If a man has the indefinable quality that I can only call 'warmth' or 'charm'": Loustalot, *Living like Audrey*, 16.

303 "In the evenings we are very homey": Woodward, *Audrey Hepburn*, 349.

303 "We're happy as we are": Morley, *Audrey Hepburn*, 166.

303 "Everyone knows how unhappy her marriage to Mel was": ibid.

303 "there reportedly were troubles toward the end": Bogdanovich*, Who the Hell's in It*, 441.

303 "although their relationship was not without small tensions and disagreements": Ferrer, *Audrey Hepburn: An Elegant Spirit*, 14.

303 "The extraordinary thing about Audrey": Jeffrey Banks, interview with author, August 25, 2020.

Forty-Eight—*Always*, 1989

305 "And in a cameo as the heavenly sage who sends Dreyfuss back to earth, Audrey Hepburn is incandescent": Peter Travers, "Always," *RollingStone.com*, December 22, 1989, https://www.rollingstone.com/tv-movies/tv-movie-reviews/always-100579/.

305 "In any case, whether or not you would decide to join our family": Matzen, *Warrior*, 165.

305 "This man is not just a director": ibid., 161.

306 "It would be fun to do another part before I roll over": Klein, *Parade*.

306 "she had to replenish her coffers": "Audrey," *Christian Science Monitor*, March 11, 1999.

306 "So what? Even if we were to lose everything, we have a garden": Dotti, *Audrey at Home*, 135.

306 "Having a garden gave her reassurance": Evans, "Luca Dotti: Memories of My Mother."

306 "the second movie, after *Bambi*, that made me cry": Joseph McBride, *Steven Spielberg: A Biography*, 2nd ed. (Jackson: University Press of Mississippi, 2010), 406.

306 "closer to the maternal side of nature": ibid., 407.

306 "Nobody knows what I am, even Steven Spielberg!": Paris, *Audrey Hepburn*, 312.

307 "like the princess she had always been in all of our dreams": Keogh, *Audrey Style*, 212.

307 "She was love and humor and grace and open and knowing. She was perfect": Loustalot, *Living like Audrey*, 88.

307 "The last thing you want to be in acting": Klein, *Parade*.

307 "She was scared, man, scared": Keogh, *What Would Audrey Do?* 246.

307 "To say she was scared is the wrong word": Sean Hepburn Ferrer, interview with author, July 7, 2020.

307 "I had the best time. I had a ball": Matzen, *Warrior*, 170.

307 "This comes from a story about her childhood that my mother told him": Sean Hepburn Ferrer, interview with author, July 7, 2020.

307 "I was eleven or so": Hartley, *Audrey Hepburn in Words and Pictures*, 22.

308 "beautiful young people": Megan Staggs, "Eleanor Roosevelt Once Said," *Huffpost*, updated December 14, 2013, https://www.huffpost.com/entry/eleanor-roosevelt-once-sa_b_4088528.

308 "the love we hold back": *Always*, screenplay by Jerry Belson and Diane Thomas Universal/United Artists, 1989.

308 "Did it achieve total heaviosity?": *Annie Hall*, screenplay by Woody Allen and Marshall Brickman, United Artists, 1977.

308 "Spielberg's long, long career as a boy": David Denby, "Always," *New York Magazine*, January 8, 1990.

308 "He has caught the surface mechanics of '40s movies": Pauline Kael, *New Yorker*, January 8, 1990.

Forty-Nine—A Reckoning with Anne Frank, 1990–1991

311 "The most important thing I've carried through life": Audrey Hepburn in *Audrey: More Than an Icon*.

311 "There were floods of tears. I became hysterical": Matzen, *Dutch Girl*, 120.

311 "I've marked one place where she says, 'Five hostages shot today,'" ibid.,121.

311 "He came to lunch and stayed to dinner": Jane Wooldridge, "At This Stage of Her Life Hepburn's Still a Fair Lady," *Miami Herald*, December 3, 1989.

312 "was so destroyed by it again that I said I couldn't deal with it": Matzen, *Dutch Girl*, 122.

312 "In the beginning it's an enemy": Paris, *Audrey Hepburn*, 317.

312 "So much of the music, I realize now": Matzen, *Warrior*, 189.

312 "I'm just relaying her thoughts. I'm reading. I still wouldn't play her": Wooldridge, "At This Stage of Her Life."

312 "Now I'm very happy to read her words": Matzen, *Dutch Girl*, 123–24.

312 "I'm thrilled to do it": ibid.

312 "a symbol of the child in very difficult circumstances, which is what I devote all my time to": *LIFE* Magazine—*Audrey: 25 Years Later*, 126.

312 "No, but then I'm not much of an actress": *Larry King Extra*, October 18, 1991.

313 "Heart-breakingly fragile, looking as though she were made of glass": Morley, *Audrey Hepburn*, 10.

Fifty—For the Love of Gardens, 1990–1993

315 "I think that's what life is all about—children and flowers": *Gardens of the World with Audrey Hepburn*, DVD Special Tribute Edition, Kultur Video, 1993.

315 "What fascinated me from the very beginning": Paris, *Audrey Hepburn*, 321.

315 "When I didn't have a dime": *Garden Design*, January/February 1991.

315 "The arts of the garden, like those of the theatre, painting, music and dance, nurture and comfort the human spirit." *Gardens of the World with Audrey Hepburn*.

315 "Hearing that beautiful voice": Janis Blackschleger, interview with author, August 18, 2020.

316 "The opening episode": ibid.

316 "I had the time": Audrey Hepburn, promotional interview for *Gardens of the World with Audrey Hepburn*.

316 "It's having the best of both worlds, Hubert and Ralph": *People Extra: A Tribute to Audrey Hepburn*, 57.

316 "She genuinely loved the beauty of small things": Paris, *Audrey Hepburn*, 324.

316 "Perhaps if we now take a closer look at our gardens": Heatley, *Audrey Hepburn in Words and Pictures*, 171.

316 "To plant a garden is to believe in tomorrow": *losttheplotdesign.com*, March 18, 2020.

316 "poetic way": Janis Blackschleger, interview with author, August 18, 2020.

316 "She meant a fusion of arts, garden, people": Yoshiko Kashuga, "Interview with Janis Blackschleger": *Bises*, November 2001.

316 "In hindsight I realized": Janis Blackschleger, "Gardens of the World—Presentation Notes: Talking Points," for the Audrey Hepburn Children's Fund and Gardens of the World exhibition, Tokyo Seibu Stadium, May 2013.

317 "unerring sense of place": Janis Blackschleger, interview with author, August 18, 2020.

317 "I don't know if you've ever read that lovely story": Audrey Hepburn with Penelope Hobhouse, *Gardens of the World*.

317 "What I remember most vividly": Janis Blackschleger, interview with author, August 18, 2020.

317 "Audrey was so involved": ibid.

317 "Hard to imagine": Barbara Saltzman, "Tulips, Roses on View in Debut of Gardens," *Los Angeles Times*, January 21, 1993.

318 "Many of the ideas Audrey most cared about": Janis Blackschleger, interview with author, August 18, 2020.

318 "I know that for Audrey, the making of *Gardens of the World*": Blackschleger, "Gardens of the World—Presentation Notes."

318 "Someone asked me recently": Robbie Wolders, "HGTV premiere of 'Tropical Gardens,'" *Gardens of the World*, March 27, 1996.

318 "We all know Audrey Hepburn is a great legend": *People Extra: A Tribute to Audrey Hepburn*, 77.

318 "So many times I am asked": Janis Blackschleger, interview with author, August 18, 2020.

318 "She left those who came into contact with her better for having known her": Willoughby, *Remembering Audrey*, 106.

Fifty-One—Tributes, 1990–1993

321 "She gives the distinct impression": Billy Wilder, as quoted in Nourmand, *Paramount Years*, 8.

321 "You looked around and suddenly there was this dazzling creature": *People Extra: A Tribute to Audrey Hepburn*, 28.

321 "My problem was that": "Billy Wilder . . . Genius," *The Classic Hollywood Blog*, June 22, 2013, https://classichollywood.wordpress.com/2013/06/22/billy-wilder-genius/.

321 "It was my good luck during that summer in Rome": Matzen, *Warrior*, 221.

322 "My passion for her has lasted through four marriages—two of hers and two of mine": Paris, *Audrey Hepburn*, 328.

322 "I had to do it with feeling instead of technique": Morley, *Audrey Hepburn*, 172.

322 "She does not think of herself as a particularly good actress": *People Extra: A Tribute to Audrey Hepburn*, 35.

322 "The only time I saw her after filming": Alan Arkin, interview with author, September 8, 2020.

322 "I think she's revered": ibid.

322 "It's wonderful, but at the same time you don't know where to put yourself": Harris, *Audrey Hepburn: A Biography*, 284.

322 "She approached acting with determination, intelligence, and a lack of selfishness": Keogh, *What Would Audrey Do?* 202.

322 "I think it was quite wonderful that this skinny broad": *People* Extra: *A Tribute to Audrey Hepburn*, 28.

322 "it's like asking if I like chocolate cake more than spaghetti": Riding, "25 Years Later."

322 "I loved working with music. The reason I wanted to dance was because I loved music": ibid.

Fifty-Two—Solo Voce, 1992

325 "Audrey's voice has always been rich with poignancy for me": Esperanza Miyake, "Fan Phenomenon Audrey Hepburn," *rareaudreyhepburn.com*, April 22, 2014.

325 "I was in Los Angeles at one of those hotels": *Darcey Bussell's Looking for Audrey Hepburn*.

325 "If I'm honest, I have to tell you I still read fairy tales and I like them best of all": Miller, *Fan Phenomena—Audrey Hepburn*, 11.

325 "Audrey always listed Frances Hodgson Burnett's *The Secret Garden* as her all-time favorite book": "Funny Facts," *Audrey Hepburn: Her Life and Legacy*, 90

325 "She had a quality I found in Eleanor Roosevelt": Paris, *Audrey Hepburn*, 357.

325 "Hepburn shapes the rich language with delicate clarity": Erwin and Diamond, *Audrey Hepburn Treasures*, 178.

326 "If she had nothing more than her voice": "Hemingway's Dietrich Letters Published," *The Telegraph*, March 30, 2007, https://www.telegraph.co.uk/news/worldnews/1547140/Hemingways-Dietrich-letters-published.html.

326 "A rather thin girl with a rather thin talent": Spoto, *Enchantment*, 256.

Fifty-Three—Somalia, 1992

329 "My mother had a secret. . . . She was sad . . .": Ferrer, *Audrey Hepburn: An Elegant Spirit*, x–xi.

329 "I should have been more aware": Moore, *My Word Is My Bond*, 277.

329 "I'm not playing a role": Matzen, *Warrior*, 231.

329 "We didn't publicize Audrey coming in advance": ibid., 246.

329 "There is no government. You just fly in and hope you won't get shot down": Ferrer, *Audrey Hepburn: An Elegant Spirit*, 179.

330 "What amazed me most of all": Matzen, *Warrior*, 250.

330 "I've never seen a whole city": ibid., 253.

330 "Wherever I go in the world": ibid., 259.

330 "I could tell it was hard for her": ibid., 261.

330 "I walked into a nightmare": ibid., 276.

330 "The silence is something you never forget": Walker, *Audrey: Her Real Story*, 276.

330 "And to see the children that quiet, it's awful": "Audrey Hepburn Interviewed on French Current Affairs TV Show 'Repéres' (1992)."

330 "You really wonder if God hasn't entirely forgotten Mogadishu": Walker, *Audrey: Her Real Story*, 276.
330 "I have a tendency at times in my life": "Audrey Hepburn Interviewed on French Current Affairs TV Show 'Repéres' (1992)."
330 "Drought is not what causes famine": ibid.
331 "Drop by drop, she began to dole out her life force to those she met": Matzen, *Warrior*, 60.
331 "The children . . . their eyes were like enormous pools of question": Spoto, *Enchantment*, 310.
331 "Audrey was the kind of person who when she saw someone else suffering": Benecke, *100 Reasons to Love Audrey Hepburn*, 70.
331 "couldn't function. I was totally stunned": Paris, *Audrey Hepburn*, 359.
331 "There were no small children": Erwin and Diamond, *Audrey Hepburn Treasures*, 178.
331 "I wanted to pick up the children and give them": *Audrey Hepburn: In Her Own Words* DVD.
331 "I have been to hell and back": Ferrer, *Audrey Hepburn: An Elegant Spirit*, 146.
331 "It's a love for people that goes beyond sympathy." Matzen, *Warrior*, 278.
331 "I have nightmares. I'm crying all the time": Paris, *Audrey Hepburn*, 359.
331 "I've always been fairly sensitive": Matzen, *Warrior*, 282.
331 "War didn't kill me, and this won't either": Matzen, *Dutch Girl*, 346.
331 "I had this feeling that sooner or later, war kills you": ibid.
332 "There is an immediate need for food, medicines and funds—right now!" Matzen, *Warrior*, 283.
332 "We didn't help where education is concerned": ibid., 284.
332 "her mission to Somalia had raised one million pounds in the United Kingdom alone": Cooper, *Celebrity Diplomacy*, 19.
332 "I think that in the end I won't be able to overcome this trip": "Audrey Hepburn Interviewed on French Current Affairs TV Show 'Repéres' (1992)."
332 "I haven't slept at night since then": Matzen, *Warrior*, 287.
332 "I'm running out of gas": Riding, "25 Years Later."
332 "Much as I love doing this for UNICEF": ibid.
332 "I'm scared": Matzen, *Warrior*, 196.
332 "Serenity—I don't think it exists": Riding, "25 Years Later."

Fifty-Four—Priorities, 1993

335 "If my world were to cave in tomorrow": Audrey Hepburn quoted in Heatley, *Audrey Hepburn in Words and Pictures*, 162.
335 "I have a lot of pain in my stomach": Anna Cataldi in *Audrey: More Than an Icon*.
335 "She knew something was wrong": John Isaac in ibid.
335 "It wasn't until she came to Los Angeles": "Audrey Hepburn—Documentary and Interview with Son Sean Ferrer."
335 "one person in every million": "Sean Hepburn Ferrer Talks about Audrey Hepburn."
336 "The emotions would flood her": Sean Hepburn Ferrer, interview with author, August 4, 2020.
336 "One of the big things that we know they do": Dr. Abigail Marsh in Scott Pelley, "Carnegie Heroes and the Neuroscience behind Acts of Heroism," CBS News, June 5, 2022, https://www.cbsnews.com/news/andrew-carnegie-hero-fund-commission-60-minutes-2022-06-05/.
336 "I was really pleased and gratified by what we found in the heroic rescuers": ibid.
336 "I'm sure it took a huge toll on her emotionally": Sean Hepburn Ferrer, interview with author, August 4, 2020.
336 "She had tears in her eyes, hugged me, sobbed . . .": Ferrer, *Audrey Hepburn: An Elegant Spirit*, 149.
336 "because she accomplished everything with perfection": Hubert de Givenchy in *Audrey Hepburn Remembered*.
336 "My only religion is a belief in nature": Hellstern, *How to Be Lovely*, 139.
336 "I am no longer a Christian Scientist, but I believe in something": ibid.
337 "in spite of everything": *The Diary of a Young Girl: Anne Frank; The Definitive Edition* (New York: Bantam, 1997), 328.
337 "Kenny Lane?": Dunne, "Hepburn Heart."
337 "If people want to come to an AIDS event to see whether I'm fat or thin": Boze Hadleigh, *Elizabeth Taylor: Tribute to a Legend* (Guilford, CT: Lyons Press, 2017), 61.
337 "I'm sorry, but I'm ready to go": Podolsky, "Life with Audrey."
337 "Living is like tearing through a museum. Not until later do you really start absorbing": Pepper, "Audrey Hepburn at 46."
338 "I think it's one of the great tragedies in this world—the old who are lonely": ibid.
338 "She was very sick and yet she asked me how I felt": Marilena Pilat in *Audrey: More Than an Icon*, 2020.
338 "I would sit in a wicker chair next to her bed": Sean Hepburn Ferrer in ibid.
338 "I only learned afterward that he fainted when he read my mother's medical charts": Dotti, *Audrey at Home*, 113.
338 "Neither the boys nor I could acknowledge that she was dying": Spoto, *Enchantment*, 312.
338 "It's been my suspicion over the years": Fiori, "Forever Audrey."
338 "I'd like to be ten years younger": *Good Morning America*, February 19, 1987.
338 "The only big regret I have and she would have had is not knowing her grandchildren": Laura Jacobs and Luca Dotti, "Audrey's Dolce Vita," *Vanity Fair*, May 2013.
338 "she would again talk about those children": Ferrer, *Audrey Hepburn: An Elegant Spirit*, 140.
338 "that death was a natural part of life": Erwin and Diamond, *Audrey Hepburn Treasures*, 182.
338 "someone so precious": Fiori, "Forever Audrey."
338 "She'd say, 'Why *not* me?'": ibid.
338 "Think of all we would have missed": ibid.
339 "Signora, when you get better": Walker, *Audrey: Her Real Story*, 280.

339 "But not like before": ibid.

339 "She couldn't go out and shop": *Darcey Bussell's Looking for Audrey Hepburn.*

339 "Each child is a reminder that God has not lost hope in man": Walker, *Audrey: Her Real Story*, 280.

339 "For attractive lips": "Time Tested Beauty Tips" (retitled and adapted by Audrey Hepburn) from Sam Levenson, *In One Era and Out the Other* , reprinted in Ferrer, *Audrey Hepburn: An Elegant Spirit*, 217.

339 "I think she spent a large portion of her life": *Darcey Bussell's Looking for Audrey Hepburn.*

339 "(But) that last Christmas, one of the great things she said": "Audrey Hepburn—Documentary and Interview with Son Sean Ferrer."

339 "it had been the best Christmas of her life": Robert Wolders, *Audrey Hepburn Remembered.*

339 "I am proud to have been in a business that gives pleasure, creates beauty": Gitlin, *Audrey Hepburn: A Biography*, 108.

339 "She rallied for the last time": *People* Extra: *A Tribute to Audrey Hepburn*, 78.

339 "the others . . . she described them as 'Amish People in a field'": Ferrer, *Audrey Hepburn: An Elegant Spirit*, 212.

339 "You cannot understand. Maybe you'll understand later": ibid.

340 "It felt good to know that she had a strong sense of the other side, that she wasn't scared": ibid.

340 "No . . . but I cannot understand why so much suffering for the children": ibid., 211.

340 "I do regret something. I regret not meeting the Dalai Lama": ibid.

340 "After she said that I sat down on the bed": Sean Hepburn Ferrer in "Audrey," *The Age*, November 29, 2003.

340 "Come quickly": Ferrer, *Audrey Hepburn: An Elegant Spirit*, 213.

340 "We are very proud of you": Letter from President George H. W. Bush, reprinted in Dotti, *Audrey at Home*, 237.

340 "She hadn't wanted to die with me in the room": Sean Hepburn Ferrer in "Audrey," *The Age*, November 29, 2003.

340 "I always thought—but who knows the truth?": Luca Dotti, *Larevista.ro*, June 22, 2015.

ACT FIVE—THE LAST GOLDEN AGE STAR

Fifty-Five—Announcing the News, 1993

343 "Audrey was a lady with an elegance and a charm that was unsurpassed": Elizabeth Taylor quoted in Vermilye, *Complete Films of Audrey Hepburn*, 62.

343 "Children everywhere will feel her death as a painful and irreplaceable loss": Harris, *Audrey Hepburn: A Biography*, 290.

343 "As unwilling to fake youth": "Audrey Hepburn's Perfection," *New York Times* Opinion Piece, January 23, 1993.

343 "My mother didn't behave like a movie star in any way": Sean Hepburn Ferrer, interview with author, July 7, 2020.

344 "Mummy believed in one thing above all": Ferrer, *Audrey Hepburn: An Elegant Spirit*, 217.

344 "Come, Papa": *People Extra*, 70.

344 "She brought joy": "Farewell to Audrey Hepburn," YouTube, posted by Gerard Henry soogen, January 22, 2017, https://www.youtube.com/watch?v=fykS-wZPuOw.

344 "still unthinkable": ibid.

344 "When Audrey Hepburn walked into the movies, all heaven broke loose": Anthony Lane, "You Dream-Maker. You Heartbreaker: Audrey Hepburn Died on Wednesday at the Age of 63. An Appreciation by Anthony Lane," *Independent on Sunday*, January 24, 1993.

Fifty-Six—Bequests, 1993–2000

347 "The Meaning of Life is to find your gift": "Pablo Picasso: The Meaning and the Purpose of Life," *Excellence Reporter*, January 9, 2020, https://excellencereporter.com/2020/01/09/pablo-picasso-the-meaning-and-the-purpose-of-life/.

348 "One family in particular": "Sean Hepburn Ferrer Talks about Audrey Hepburn."

Fifty-Seven—Protecting the Legacy, 1993–2024

351 "Celebrity net worth reports that": Leslie Veliz, "Here's Who Inherited Audrey Hepburn's Money after She Died," *grunge.com*, December 6, 2021.

351 "sixty, seventy trips": Sean Hepburn Ferrer, interview with author, July 7, 2020.

351 "That's in addition to the tour busses": ibid.

351 "living biography": "Sean Hepburn Ferrer on 'Intimate Audrey.'"

351 "forty thousand visitors": ibid.

351 "her name, signature, and image": "Sean Hepburn Ferrer Talks about Audrey Hepburn."

351 "two, three dozen lawsuits": ibid.

352 "When I created": Sean Hepburn Ferrer, interview with author, July 7, 2020.

352 "the judge ruled that Sean and Luca are co-owners of the Hepburn right of publicity": Contributing Editor, "Proposed Decision Favors Actress' Eldest Son in Dispute with Charity," *mynewsla.com*, October 18, 2019.

352 "The judge further ruled": ibid.

352 "No other single medical breakthrough of the twentieth century": Dotti, *Audrey at Home*, 241.

352 "The worst killer of all is dehydration from diarrhea caused by unclean drinking water": Ferrer, *Audrey Hepburn: An Elegant Spirit*, 197.

Fifty-Eight—Generations of Activism, 1970–2024

355 "She always used to say": Kacala, "Beyond the Glamour."

355 "the big donor club": Sean Hepburn Ferrer, interview with author, July 7, 2020.

355 "I never got that wink": ibid.

355 "And it's always the B minus and the B plus who behave the worst": "Sean Hepburn Ferrer Talks about Audrey Hepburn."

355 "raised over $140 million": ibid.

355 "We have a full office": Sean Hepburn Ferrer, interview with author, July 7, 2020.

355 "When my parents got married": Sean Hepburn Ferrer, interview with author, July 7, 2020.

356 "My mother always wanted to be useful": "Audrey Hepburn Interview with Ivo Niehe."

356 "My daughter is already working for UNICEF and the UNHCR": "Sean Hepburn Ferrer on 'Intimate Audrey.'"

356 "We went there as a family": Sean Hepburn Ferrer, interview with author, July 7, 2020.

356 "as early as I can remember": Emma Ferrer, interview with author, September 23, 2020.

357 "Emma carries on Audrey's legacy": Caryl Stern, interview with author, September 16, 2020.

357 "What I know in my heart," Emma Ferrer, interview with author, September 23, 2020.

357 "This work has also given me the feeling," ibid.

Fifty-Nine—Auctioning History, 2017–2018

359 "It is with great joy": Sean Hepburn Ferrer and Luca Dotti, "Audrey Hepburn: Exhibition, Flagship Live and Online Auction," *christies.com*, July 25, 2017.

359 "sold for $17,285": Nourmand, *Audrey Hepburn: The Paramount Years*, 58.

359 "We were upset about that": "Audrey Hepburn—Documentary and Interview with Son Sean Ferrer."

359 "The dress—it was made of amazing Italian satin": *Darcey Bussell's Looking for Audrey Hepburn.*

359 "There are tears in my eyes": Cahal Milmo, "The Price of 'Breakfast At Tiffany's': Hepburn's Dress Is Sold for £467,200," *Independent*, December 6, 2006, https://www.independent.co.uk/news/uk/this-britain/the-price-of-breakfast-at-tiffanys-hepburns-dress-is-sold-for-163467200-427258.html.

360 "We preserved our feelings": "Audrey Hepburn: Exhibition, Flagship Live and Online Auctions—September 2017," Christie's, July 25, 2017, https://www.christies.com/features/The-Personal-Collection-of-Audrey-Hepburn-8382-3.aspx.

360 "When you find out the world is in love with your mother": "Audrey Hepburn's Personal Items to be Auctioned in London," YouTube, posted by AP Archive, September 27, 2017, https://www.youtube.com/watch?v=Trp1raPhWiI.

360 "Her entire estate was less than, I think": ibid.

360 "In the process, a record was set for the highest online participation in the history of Christie's": Katie Frost, "One of Audrey Hepburn's Personal Belongings Just Broke World Auction Records," Harper's Bazaar, September 28, 2017, https://www.harpersbazaar.com/uk/culture/culture-news/a44039/audrey-hepburn-personal-collection-auction-sales-totals/.

361 "You are my inspiration": Haroon Siddique and agencies, "Audrey Hepburn's Breakfast at Tiffany's Script Sells for £630,000," *The Guardian*, September 28, 2017, https://www.theguardian.com/culture/2017/sep/28/audrey-hepburn-breakfast-at-tiffanys-script-sells-auction-630000.

361 "Total proceeds: 4,635,500 pounds/$6,202,299": Hannah Schweiger, "Results: The Personal Collection of Audrey Hepburn (Part I) Realised £4,635,500 / $6,202,299 / €5,270,563," Christie's, September 27, 2017, https://www.christies.com/about-us/press-archive/details?PressReleaseID=8818&lid=1.

361 "Giving is living. If you stop wanting to give, there's nothing more to live for": Audrey Hepburn, interview with Harry Smith, *CBS This Morning*, June 3, 1991.

Sixty—Everything Old Is New Again, 1993–2021

363 "Now, 50% of her fanbase are teens and tweens": Hannah Marriott, "Audrey Hepburn Exhibition Celebrates Star's Enduring Appeal," *The Guardian*, September 22, 2017, https://www.theguardian.com/fashion/2017/sep/22/audrey-hepburn-exhibition-celebrates-film-star-enduring-appeal-fashion.

363 "Instagram now holds more than two million images hashtagged #Audrey Hepburn": "Under Her Influence," *Audrey Hepburn: Her Life and Legacy*, 84.

363 "the iconic opening scene from Breakfast at Tiffany's has picked up more than eight million views": ibid., 85.

363 "My grandmother was such a beautiful woman": Emma Ferrer, interview with author, September 23, 2020.

364 "tiny, elegant, and discreet, with dark hair and almond shaped eyes": Dotti, *Audrey at Home*, 173.

365 "By one account it took a full year of work": "Audrey Hepburn Resurrected in New TV Commercial—Creepy or Cool?" YouTube, posted by EverythingAudrey.com, January 10, 2015, https://www.youtube.com/watch?v=eJt9narRaf4&t=9s.

365 "Welcome to the age of un-innocence": Darren Star, *Sex and the City*, season 1, episode 1, aired June 6, 1998.

Sixty-One—The Last Golden Age Star

369 "How did we drift so far from Audrey Hepburn?": Rocca, *Mobituaries*, 245.

370 "All these dramas about celebrities": Sean Hepburn Ferrer, interview with author, August 4, 2020.

370 "Well she really was the Queen of Instagram": Kacala, "Beyond the Glamour."

370 "the only comedienne capable of brushing her teeth while still maintaining her glamour": Mosley, *Growing up with Audrey Hepburn*, 42.

371 "She always looked good, even at home": Sean Hepburn Ferrer, interview with author, July 7, 2020.

371 "How shall I sum up my life?" "Audrey Hepburn and Salvatore Ferragamo," https://artsandculture.google.com/story/audrey-hepburn-and-salvatore-ferragamo-museosalvatoreferragamo/bAXhc2L06jr9Lw?hl=en

371 "She was one of the most beautiful women I have ever photographed": Nourmand, *Paramount Years*, 150.

Sixty-Two—And in the End, 1929–1993

373 "Love is action. It isn't just talk and it never was": Ferrer, *Audrey Hepburn: An Elegant Spirit*, 12–13.

373 "not to live for the day—that would be materialistic—but to treasure the day": Keogh, *Audrey Style*, 225.

373 "I heard a definition once: Happiness is health and a short memory!" Hellstern, *How to Be Lovely*, 4.

373 "Really, her legacy is contained in the Sam Levenson poem she loved so much": Emma Ferrer, interview with author, September 23, 2020.

374 "I think her legacy is that there are things in the world more important than yourself": Caryl Stern, interview with author, September 16, 2020.

374 "I feel so strongly that's where it all starts, with kindness": Erwin and Diamond, *Audrey Hepburn Treasures*, 182.

374 "three things in human life are important": Lev Raphael, "Henry James' Killer Kindness Quote," *Huffpost*, January 24, 2017, https://www.huffpost.com/entry/a-killer-kindness-quote_b_9063666.

374 "I have learned how to live, how to be in the world": *Sabrina*, screenplay by Billy Wilder, Samuel Taylor, and Ernest Lehman, Paramount Pictures, 1954.

374 "God kissed her on the cheek and there she was": Billy Wilder in *Audrey Hepburn Remembered*.

374 "The full use of your powers": *Public Papers of the Presidents of the United States: John F. Kennedy* (Washington DC: U.S. Government Printing Office, 1963), 380.

Bibliography

Books

Andrews, Julie. *Home Work: A Memoir of My Hollywood Years*. New York: Hachette Books, 2019.
Basinger, Jeanine. *I Do and I Don't: A History of Marriage in the Movies*. New York: Alfred A. Knopf, 2012.
Beaton, Cecil. *Cecil Beaton's Fair Lady*. New York: Henry Holt, 1964.
Beaton, Cecil. *Diaries: The Parting Years 1963–74*. Leeds: Sapere Books, 2018.
Benecke, Joanna. *100 Reasons to Love Audrey Hepburn*. London: Plexus Publishing, 2016.
Billman, Larry. *Fred Astaire: A Bio-Bibliography*. Westport, CT: Greenwood Press, 1997.
Bogart, Stephen. *Bogart: In Search of My Father*. New York: Dutton, 1995.
Bogdanovich, Peter. *Who the Hell's in It: Conversations with Hollywood's Legendary Actors*. New York: Alfred A. Knopf. 2004.
Bosworth, Patricia. *The Men in My Life*. New York: HarperCollins, 2017.
Brown, Alan. *Audrey Hepburn's Neck*. New York: Pocket Books, 1996.
Capote, Truman. *Breakfast at Tiffany's: A Short Novel and Three Stories*. New York: Random House, 1958.
Cardillo, Margaret, and Julia Denos. *Just Being Audrey*. New York: Blazer&Bray, 2011.
Cartwright, Angela, and Tom McLaren. *Styling the Stars*. San Rafael: Insight Editions, 2014.
Casper, Joseph Andrew. *Stanley Donen*. Scarecrow Filmmakers Series Book 5. Metuchen, NJ: Scarecrow Press, 1995.
Chierichetti, David. *Edith Head: The Life and Times of Hollywood's Celebrated Costume Designer*. New York: HarperCollins, 2003.
Christy, Jordan. *How to Be a Hepburn in a Kardashian World*. New York: Center Street, 2017.
Cooper, Andrew F. *Celebrity Diplomacy*. Boulder, CO: Paradigm Publishers, 2008.
Crist, Judith. *Take 22: Moviemakers on Moviemaking*. New York: Viking, 1984.
Crowe, Cameron. *Conversations with Wilder*. New York: Knopf, 2001.
Damiani, Ludovica, and Luca Dotti, eds. *Audrey in Rome*. New York: Harper Design, 2012.
De La Hoz, Cindy. *Audrey and Givenchy: A Fashion Love Affair*. Philadelphia: Running Press, 2016.
De La Hoz, Cindy. *So Audrey: 59 Ways to Put a Little Hepburn in Your Step*. Philadelphia: Running Press, 2011.
Dherbier, Yann-Brice, ed. *Audrey Hepburn: A Life in Pictures*. London: Pavilion Books Company Ltd, 2007.
Dotti, Luca (with Luigi Spinola). *Audrey at Home*. New York: Harper Design, 2015.
Dresser, David, and Garth S. Jowett, eds. *Hollywood Goes Shopping*. Minneapolis: University of Minnesota Press. 2000.
Edwards, Anne. *Streisand: A Biography*. New York: Little, Brown and Co., 1997.
Erwin, Ellen, and Jessica Z. Diamond. *The Audrey Hepburn Treasures*. New York: Atria Books, 2006.
Eyman, Scott. *Cary Grant: A Brilliant Disguise*. New York: Simon & Schuster, 2020.
Ferrer, Sean Hepburn. *Audrey Hepburn: An Elegant Spirit*. New York: Atria Books, 2003.
Ferrer, Sean Hepburn, and Karin Ferrer. *Little Audrey's Daydream: The Life of Audrey Hepburn*. New York: Princeton Architectural Press, 2021.
Film Facts. Vol. 20. Los Angeles: Division of Cinema University of Southern California, 1977.
Frank, Anne. *The Diary of a Young Girl: Anne Frank; The Definitive Edition*. New York: Bantam, 1997.
Garner, James, and Jon Winokur. *The Garner Files*. New York: Simon & Schuster, 2011.
Giles, Sarah. *Fred Astaire: His Friends Talk*. New York: Doubleday, 1988.
Gitlin, Martin. *Audrey Hepburn: A Biography*. Westport, CT: Greenwood Press, 2009.
Gristwood, Sarah. *Breakfast at Tiffany's: The Official 50th Anniversary Companion*. New York: Rizzoli, 2011.
Hadleigh, Boze. *Elizabeth Taylor: Tribute to a Legend*. Guilford, CT: Lyons Press, 2017.
Hadleigh, Boze. *Hollywood Gays*. New York: Barricade Books, 1996.
Handey, Lynn. *Gregory Peck: A Charmed Life*. New York: Carroll & Graf, 2004.
Harris, Thomas J. *Bogdanovich's Pictures Shows*. Metuchen, NJ: The Scarecrow Press, 1990.
Harris, Warren. *Audrey Hepburn: A Biography*. New York: Simon & Schuster, 1994.
Harrison, Rex. *A Damned Serious Business: My Life in Comedy*. New York: Bantam Books, 1991.
Harrison, Rex. *Rex: An Autobiography*. New York: William Morrow, 1975.
Head, Edith. *The Dress Doctor: Prescriptions for Style, From A to Z*. New York: HarperCollins, 2008.
Heatley, Michael. *Audrey Hepburn in Words and Pictures*. New York: Chartwell Books, 2017.
Hellstern, Melissa. *How to Be Lovely: The Audrey Hepburn Way of Life*. New York: Dutton, 2004.
Hemingway, Ernest. *The Sun Also Rises*. New York: Scribner; Hemingway Library Edition, 2016.

Herman, Jan. *A Talent for Trouble: The Life of Hollywood's Most Acclaimed Director, William Wyler.* New York: G. P. Putnam's Sons, 1995.

Higashi, Sumiko. *Stars, Fans, and Consumption in the 1950s: Reading Photoplay.* New York: Palgrave Macmillan, 2014.

Higham, Charles. *Audrey: The Life of Audrey Hepburn.* New York: Macmillan, 1984.

Hobhouse, Penelope, and Elvin McDonald, consulting eds. *Gardens of the World: The Art and Practice of Gardening.* New York: Macmillan, 1991.

Holliday, Lucy. *A Night in with Audrey Hepburn.* London: HarperCollins, 2015.

Horton, Robert, ed. *Billy Wilder Interviews.* Jackson: University Press of Mississippi, 2001.

Huston, John. *An Open Book.* New York: Alfred A. Knopf, 1980.

Kakutani, Michiko. *The Poet at the Piano: Portraits of Writers, Filmmakers, Playwrights and Other Artists at Work.* New York: Times Books, 1988.

Karney, Robyn. *Audrey Hepburn: A Charmed Life.* New York: Arcade Publishing, 1993.

Keogh, Pamela Clarke. *Audrey Style.* New York: HarperCollins, 1999.

Keogh, Pamela. *What Would Audrey Do? Timeless Lessons for Living with Grace and Style.* New York: Gotham Books, 2008.

Kramer, Joan, and David Heeley. *In the Company of Legends.* New York: Beaufort Books, 2015.

Krenz, Carol. *Audrey: A Life in Pictures.* New York: Barnes & Noble Books, 2001.

Lally, Kevin. *Wilder Times: The Life of Billy Wilder.* New York: Henry Holt and Company, 1996.

Lang, Rocky, and Barbara Hall, eds. *Letters from Hollywood: Inside the Private World of Classic American Moviemaking.* New York: Abrams, 2019.

Levenson, Sam. *In One Era and Out the Other.* New York: Simon & Schuster, 1973.

Levinson, Peter J. *Puttin' on the Ritz: Fred Astaire and the Fine Art of Panache.* New York: St. Martin's Press, 2009.

Levy, Emanuel. *George Cukor: Master of Elegance.* New York: William Morrow, 1994.

Loustalot, Victoria. *Living like Audrey: Life Lessons from the Fairest Lady of All.* Guilford, CT: Lyons Press, 2017.

Madsen, Axel. *William Wyler.* New York: Thomas Y. Crowell Co., 1973.

Marsh, June. *Audrey Hepburn in Hats.* London: Reel Art Press, 2013.

Matzen, Robert. *Dutch Girl: Audrey Hepburn and World War II.* Pittsburgh: GoodKnight Books, 2019.

Matzen, Robert. *Warrior: Audrey Hepburn.* Pittsburgh: GoodKnight Books, 2021.

Maychick, Diana. *Audrey Hepburn: An Intimate Portrait.* Secaucus, NJ: Carol Publishing Group, 1993.

McBride, Joseph. *Steven Spielberg: A Biography.* 2nd ed. Jackson: University Press of Mississippi, 2010.

Miller, Gabriel. *William Wyler: The Life and Films of Hollywood's Most Celebrated Director.* Lexington: University Press of Kentucky, 2013.

Miller, Jacqui, ed. *Fan Phenomena—Audrey Hepburn.* Bristol UK: Intellect Books, 2014.

Mizener, Arthur. *The Far Side of Paradise: A Biography of F. Scott Fitzgerald.* New York: Houghton Mifflin, 1949.

Moore, Roger. *My Word Is My Bond: A Memoir.* New York: HarperCollins, 2008.

Moore, Roger. *One Lucky Bastard: Tales From Tinseltown.* Guilford, CT: Lyons Press, 2014.

Morley, Sheridan. *Audrey Hepburn.* London: Pavilion Books, 1993.

Moseley, Rachel. *Growing Up with Audrey Hepburn.* Manchester: Manchester University Press, 2002.

Nixon, Marni. *I Could Have Sung All Night.* New York: Billboard, 2006.

Nolletti, Arthur, Jr., ed. *The Films of Fred Zinnemann: Critical Perspectives.* Albany: State University of New York Press, 1999.

Nourmand, Tony. *Audrey Hepburn: The Paramount Years.* San Francisco: Chronicle Books, 2007.

Palmer, R. Barton, ed. *Larger Than Life: Movie Stars of the 1950s.* New Brunswick, NJ: Rutgers University Press, 2010.

Paris, Barry. *Audrey Hepburn.* New York: G. P. Putnam's Sons, 1996.

Phillips, Gene D. "Fred Zinnemann: Darkness at Noon." *Major Film Directors of the American and British Cinema.* Bethlehem, PA: Lehigh University Press, 1990.

Public Papers of the Presidents of the United States: John F. Kennedy, Washington DC: U.S. Government Printing Office, 1963.

Randall, Tony, and Michael Mindlin. *Which Reminds Me.* New York: Delacorte Press, 1989.

Rocca, Mo. *Mobituaries.* New York: Simon & Schuster, 2019.

Rogers, Henry C. *Walking the Tightrope.* New York: William Morrow and Co., 1980.

Rollin, Lucy. "Audrey Hepburn." In *American Icons,* edited by Dennis R. Hall and Susan Grove Hall. Westport, CT: Greenwood Press, 2006.

Rosen, Marjorie. *Popcorn Venus.* New York: Coward, McCann & Geoghegan, 1973.

Santopietro, Tom. *Considering Doris Day.* New York: St. Martin's Press, 2007.

Schickel, Richard. *Steven Spielberg: A Retrospective.* New York: Sterling Publishing, 2012.

Shaw, Mark (photographs by). *Charmed by Audrey: Life on the Set of Sabrina.* San Rafael: Insight Editions, 2009.

Sherman, Howard. *Another Day's Begun: Thornton Wilder's Our Town in the 21st Century.* New York: Methuen Drama, 2021.

Sikov, Ed. *On Sunset Boulevard: The Life and Times of Billy Wilder.* Jackson: University Press of Mississippi, 2017.

Silverman, Stephen M. *Dancing on the Ceiling: Stanley Donen and His Movies.* New York: Alfred A. Knopf, 1996.

Simon, Carly. *Touched by the Sun: My Friendship with Jackie.* New York: Farrar, Straus, and Giroux, 2019.

Smyth, J. E. *Fred Zinnemann and the Cinema of Resistance.* Jackson: University Press of Mississippi, 2014.

Spoto, Donald. *Enchantment: The Life of Audrey Hepburn.* New York: Three Rivers Press, 2006.

Stevens, Norma, and Steven M. L. Aronson. *Avedon: Something Personal.* New York: Spiegel & Grau, 2017.

Tiffin, George. *A Star Is Born: The Moment an Actress Becomes an Icon.* London: Head of Zeus Ltd., 2015.

Ustinov, Peter. *Dear Me.* Boston: Little Brown and Company, 1977.

Vermilye, Jerry. *The Complete Films of Audrey Hepburn.* Secaucus, NJ: Carol Publishing Group, 1997.

Vickers, Hugo. *Cecil Beaton: A Biography.* Boston: Little Brown and Company, 1985.

Vickers, Hugo. *Malice in Wonderland: My Adventures in the World of Cecil Beaton.* New York: Pegasus Books, 2021.

Walker, Alexander. *Audrey: Her Real Story.* New York: St. Martin's Press, 1995.

Walker, Alexander. *Fatal Charm: The Life of Rex Harrison.* New York: St. Martin's Press, 1993.

Waller, Sheila. *Carrie Fisher: A Life on the Edge.* New York: Farrar, Straus, and Giroux, 2019.

Wasson, Sam. *Fifth Avenue, 5 A.M.: Audrey Hepburn, Breakfast at Tiffany's, and the Dawn of the Modern Woman.* New York: Harper Perennial, 2010.

Willis, David. *Audrey: The 50s.* New York: HarperCollins. 2016.

Willis, David. *Audrey: The 60s.* New York: HarperCollins, 2012.

Willoughby, Bob. *Audrey: An Intimate Collection.* London: Vision on Publishing Ltd, 2002.

Willoughby, Bob. *Audrey Hepburn: Photographs 1953–1966.* Cologne: Taschen, 2012.

Willoughby, Bob. *Remembering Audrey. LIFE* Great Photographers Series. New York: Time Inc., 2008.

Woodward, Ian. *Audrey Hepburn: Fair Lady of the Screen.* Rev. ed. London: Virgin Publishing, 1993.

Wormser, Baron. *Legends of the Slow Explosion: Eleven Modern Lives.* North Adams, MA: Tupelo Press, 2018.

Xu Xi. "Crying with Audrey Hepburn." In *Manhattan Noir,* edited by Lawrence Block. New York: Akashic Books. 2006.

Zinnemann, Fred. *Fred Zinnemann: An Autobiography.* New York: Charles Scribner's Sons, 1992.

Zolotow, Maurice. *Billy Wilder in Hollywood.* London: W. H. Allen, 1977.

Audiobooks

Sheldon, Mary (author/adaptor), and Audrey Hepburn (narrator). *Audrey Hepburn's Enchanted Tales.* Audible Audiobook. Phoenix Books, 1993.

Periodicals

Abramson, Martin. "Audrey Hepburn." *Cosmopolitan,* October 1955.

Alexander, Ron. "A Glittering Tribute to Audrey Hepburn at the Modern." *New York Times,* October 22, 1987.

"A Little Bit of Audrey for Everyone." *New Yorker,* May 17, 1999.

Anabl, Anne. "Audrey Hepburn Sees the Dark." *New York World Journal Tribune,* February 1, 1967.

Anderson, John. "Head of the Class." *Newsday,* April 22, 1991.

Ansen, David. "A Princess in Disguise." *Newsweek,* January 31, 1993.

Archer, Eugene. "Playgirl on the Town." *New York Times.* October 9, 1960.

"Ask Voice—Doubles Forego Publicity; Did Marni Cost Audrey an Oscar?" *Variety.* February 28, 1968.

Atkinson, Brooks. "MAGICAL ONDINE; Audrey Hepburn Stars in English Version of Giradoux Play." *New York Times,* February 28, 1954.

"Audrey." *The Age,* November 29, 2003.

"Audrey." *Christian Science Monitor.* March 11, 1999.

"Audrey Admits Romance with Jimmy Is Over." *New York Daily News,* November 18, 1952.

"Audrey Hepburn." *Garden Design,* January/February 1991.

"Audrey Hepburn." *Movie D.V. Album,* July 1957.

"Audrey Hepburn." *New York World Telegram and Sun,* August 16, 1957.

"Audrey Hepburn." *The Seventh Art* 2, no. 2 (Spring 1964).

"Audrey Hepburn." *Vogue,* October 15, 1961.

"Audrey Hepburn and Rex Harrison in My Fair Lady." *Screen Stories,* December 1964

"Audrey Hepburn by Cecil Beaton." *Vogue,* November 1954.

"Audrey Hepburn, Chevalier, Spark Love in the Afternoon." *New York World Telegram,* August 15, 1957.

"Audrey Hepburn: The Dainty Dish Hollywood Can't Digest." *Confidential,* April 1964.

"Audrey Hepburn Dress Fetches Nearly a Million." *New York Times,* December 6, 2006

"Audrey Hepburn Enchants Broadway." *Look,* April 20, 1954.

"Audrey Hepburn's Fashion Formula." *New York Herald Tribune,* November 11, 1962.

"Audrey Hepburn Flown Home; To Walk in 3 Weeks." *New York Herald Tribune,* February 3, 1959.

"Audrey Hepburn Gets Her Lesson From Meticulous Director William Wyler." *Newark Evening News,* November 7, 1965.

"Audrey Hepburn's Glorious Whirl in My Fair Lady." *Vogue,* December 1963.

"Audrey Hepburn: The Heart Is a Lonely Hunter." *Photoplay,* September 1956.

"Audrey Hepburn: Princess Apparent." *Time,* September 7, 1953.

"Audrey Hepburn's Perfection." *New York Times* Opinion Piece, January 23, 1993.

"Audrey Hepburn's Weird Marriage." *National Enquirer,* April 25, 1978.

"Audrey Hepburn: World's Highest Paid Actress." *Parade,* August 21, 1955.

"Audrey Stars in Givenchy Styles." *Life,* May 11, 1962.

"Audrey Waits for Academy Decision." *Life,* April 5, 1954.

"Audrey Will Attend the Oscar Awards." *New York Post,* March 5, 1965.

Barber, Lynn. "Hepburn's Relief." *Sunday Express,* May 1, 1988.

Barber, Rowland. "The Delightful Riddle of Audrey Hepburn." *Good Housekeeping,* August 1962.

Basinger, Jeanine. "Audrey Hepburn." *American Movie Classics,* May 2001.

Bean, Robin, ed. "Robin and Marian." *Films and Filming* 22, no. 7 (April 1976).

Beaton, Cecil. "Audrey Hepburn by Cecil Beaton." *Vogue,* November 1954.

Bernstein, Richard. "When Everyone's in Love with Audrey Hepburn." *New York Times,* April 24, 1991.

"Best Kept Secret about Audrey Hepburn Is That She Was So Sad." *The Guardian,* November 15, 2020

Bianco, Robert. "Fun of 'Thieves' Lures Hepburn Back." *Chicago Tribune,* February 22, 1987.

Blackschleger, Janis. "Gardens of the World—Presentation Notes: Talking Points." Tokyo, Seibu Stadium for the Audrey Hepburn Children's Fund and Gardens of the World Exhibition, May 2013.

Blair, W. Granger. "On the Seine in the Rain with Funny Face." *New York Times,* July 15, 1956.

Blume, Mary. "Audrey Hepburn: The Family, Making Films." *International Herald Tribune*, July 11, 1975.

Braunstein, Peter. "Neck and Neck." *Village Voice*, April 27, 1999.

Brett, Simon. "Audrey Hepburn." *Films and Filming*, March 1964.

"Brog." "Funny Face." *Variety*, February 13, 1957.

Cameron, Kate. "Funny Face: A Gay and Charming Film." *New York Daily News*, March 29, 1957.

Canby, Vincent. "Mr. Chips Stars to Share Gross." *New York Times*, January 13, 1966.

Caron, Leslie. "Audrey, Darling." *Vogue* (UK), March 1993.

"Cecil Beaton's Own Story of My Fair Lady." *New York Journal American,* October 18, 1964.

Chapman, John. "Hepburn's Ondine Sheer Magic." *New York Daily News*, February 18, 1954.

Clement, Carl. "Look Where You're Going, Audrey!" *Photoplay,* June 1957.

Cohn, Alan. "Turnaway Crowd Honors Audrey Hepburn." *Variety*, April 29, 1991.

Coleman, Robert. "Giradoux's Ondine Is Fascinating Fantasy." *New York Daily Mirror*, February 19, 1954.

Collins, Amy Fine. "When Hubert Met Audrey." *Vanity Fair*, December 1995.

Contributing Editor. "Proposed Decision Favors Actress' Eldest Son in Dispute with Charity." *Mynewsla.com*. October 18, 2019.

Cook, Alton. "A Nun's Painful Ordeal Retains Impact." *New York World Telegram*, June 19, 1959.

"Cook." "Mansions Offered at Music Hall." *New York World Telegram and Sun*, March 26, 1959.

Corliss, Richard. "Audrey Hepburn: Still the Fairest Lady." *Time*, January 20, 2007.

Corliss, Richard. "Tribute to Audrey Hepburn." *Stagebill*, April 1991.

Cox, Alex. "Audrey Hepburn, An Iconic Problem." *The Guardian*, 20 January 2011.

Crowther, Bosley. "Audrey Hepburn and Grant in Charade." *New York Times*, December 6, 1963.

Crowther, Bosley. "Delicate Enchantment of 'Green Mansions'; Audrey Hepburn Stars in Role of Rima," *New York Times*, March 20, 1959.

Crowther, Bosley. "Lots of Chocolates for Miss Eliza Doolittle." *New York Time*s, October 22, 1964.

Crowther, Bosley. "Mellow Season." *New York Times*, August 25, 1957.

Crowther, Bosley. "The Screen: Audrey Hepburn Stars in 'Wait Until Dark.'" *New York Times*, October 27, 1967.

Das, Lina. "Another Audrey." *Mail on Sunday*, November 7, 1999.

Denby, David. "Always." *New York Magazine*, January 8, 1990.

"Detention Home Shooting: Audrey Hepburn Films Scene in Village." *New York World-Telegram.* October 7, 1960.

Donen, Stanley. "Audrey in Funny Face: Cinderella of Fashion." *New York Herald Tribune*, February 10, 1957.

Dunne, Dominick. "Hepburn Heart." *Vanity Fair*, May 1991.

Egan, Cy, Jr. "Ferrer Tells How Audrey Broke Her Back." *New York Journal-American*, January 31, 1959.

Emerson, Gloria. "Co-Stars Again: Audrey Hepburn and Givenchy." *New York Times*, September 8, 1965.

"Emma Thompson: Audrey Hepburn Couldn't Act." *Belfast Telegraph*, August 9, 2010.

Evans, Miranda. "Luca Dotti: Memories of My Mother, Audrey Hepburn the Gardener." *The Telegraph*, September 15, 2015.

"Fans in Oscar Drive for Audrey Hepburn." *New York Journal-American*, February 28, 1965.

Fields, Sidney. "Audrey Hepburn—Success Is Not Security." *McCall's*, July 1954.

Fiori, Pamela. "Forever Audrey." *Town & Country*, May 2003.

Foley, Bridget. "The Scene." *Women's Wear Daily*, April 2, 1990.

Garcia, Ricardo Hunter. "Love Among Thieves." *New York Post*, February 23, 1987.

Garrett, Diane. "Enchantment." *Variety*, October 2, 2006.

George, Eliot. "The Two Audrey Hepburns." *Silver Screen*, August 1964.

Gittelson, Natalie. "Personalities: Audrey Hepburn." *McCall's*, August 1989.

"Givenchy-Hepburn." *Vogue*, November 1964.

Gold, Sylviane. "Hearts Beneath the Tinsel." *New York Times*, November 4, 1984.

Graham, Sheilah. "Audrey Mel in Chalet." *Newark Evening News*, January 1, 1961.

Graham, Sheilah. "Star on the Move." *Newark Evening News*, November 20, 1965.

Grove, Gene. "Julie 'Very Sad' That Audrey Didn't Get It." *New York Post*, February 26, 1965.

Guarino, Ann. "And One Happy Return of the Day." *New York Daily News*, March 13, 1976.

Haber, Joyce. "Astaire's Way to the Stars," *Los Angeles Times*, May 1, 1975.

Haddad, George. "It's a Sexy New Audrey Hepburn in Bloodline." *Us Weekly*, July 10, 1979.

Hadley-Garcia, George. "Audrey Hepburn: 30 Years of Stardom." *Hollywood Studio Magazine* 16, no. 4 (1983).

Hale, Wanda. "Hollywood Visitor: She Lights Up the Hall." *New York Daily News*, December 30, 1964.

Harris, Eleanor. "Audrey Hepburn." *Good Housekeeping*, August 1959.

Harris, Paul. "The Tarnished Truth beneath Hollywood's Golden Age Glitter." *London Observer*, October 8, 2006.

Hart, Henry. "The Nun's Story." *Films in Review*, June–July 1959.

Haskell, Molly. "Our Fair Lady." *Film Comment*, March–April 1991.

Haun, Harry. "That's Our Fair Audrey." *New York Daily News*, April 21, 1991.

Heffernan, Harold. "Not Slipping By." *Newark Evening News*, May 17, 1966.

Hepburn, Audrey, as told to Henry Gris. "A Man to Hold—A Child to Love—I Won't Let Them Be Taken Away." *Modern Screen*, January 1965.

"Hepburn and Ferrer Preview of TV Mayerling." *LIFE*, February 4, 1957.

Hipp, Edward Sothern. "Wacky Charm." *Newark Evening News*, December 7, 1961.

"Hollywood's Snub to Its Fair Lady." *New York Post*, February 24, 1965.

"Hooky From the World." *Motion Picture*, October 1955.

Hunter Garcia, Ricardo. "No Love for Thieves That Steal Your Time." *New York Post*, February 23, 1987.

Hyams, Joe. "Audrey Hepburn is Signed for Italian War and Peace." *New York Herald Tribune*, April 6, 1955.

"Is This Really Audrey Hepburn?" *Ladies Home Journal*, January 1967.

Jacobs, Laura, and Luca Dotti. "Audrey's Dolce Vita." *Vanity Fair*, May 2013.

Jaworoski, Ken. "Western Stars Review: Bruce Springsteen and Broken Cowboys." *New York Times*, October 24, 2019.

Jefferson, Margo. "A Princess Whose Life Was No Fairy Tale." *New York Times*, July 27, 1994.

Johnson, Ellen. "Will Hollywood Ever See Audrey Hepburn Again?" *Modern Screen*, April 1955.

Johnson, Diane. "The Thoroughbred." *New York Times*, November 24, 1998.

Johnson, Erskine. "Audrey's in the Pink—Her Lovers are Graying." *New York World Telegram*, July 2, 1957.

"Just Mel's Wife." *Screen Album*, May–June 1965.

Kael, Pauline. "The Current Cinema." *New Yorker*, January 8, 1990.

Kakutani, Michiko. "Why Has She Done So Few Films in Recent Years." *New York Times,* June 4, 1980.

Kanour, Gilbert. "Some Notes on Audrey Hepburn, of the Popular Roman Holiday." *Baltimore Evening Sun*, September 18, 1954.

Klein, Edward. "One Woman's Search for Love: A Profile of Audrey Hepburn." *Parade*, March 5, 1989.

Kasuga, Yoshiko. "Interview with Janis Blackschleger," *Bises*, November 2001.

La Ferla, Ruth. "Front Row." *New York Times*, February 18, 2003.

Lane, Anthony. "You Dream-Maker. You Heartbreaker: Audrey Hepburn Died on Wednesday at the Age of 63. An Appreciation by Anthony Lane." *Independent on Sunday.* January 24, 1993.

"Last Fifties Picture Show." *Films and Filming* 20, no. 12 (September 1974).

"Life Imitates Film Art as Audrey Meets Press." *Dallas Morning News*, March 30, 1976.

LIFE. "Audrey Waits for Academy Decision." April 5, 1954.

LIFE. "On an Italian Farm with Audrey Hepburn." July 18, 1955.

LIFE. "Audrey: 25 Years Later." January 5, 2018.

Lombardi, Margaret. "They Dared to Love." *Motion Picture,* February 1955.

"Look at Audrey Hepburn Now." *Ladies Home Journal*, July 1966.

Loos, Anita. "Everything Happens to Audrey Hepburn." *American Weekly*, September 12, 1954.

"Luca Dotti: The Moment She Ended Her Career, My Mother Started to be Happy Again," *Larevista.ro*, June 22, 2015.

Lyons, Donald. "Slicing the Tony Baloney." *Wall Street Journal*, May 14, 1996.

Mallon, Thomas. "Hepburn & Hepburn." *New York Times*, October 8, 2006.

Manners, Dorothy. "Audrey in Comeback." *Boston Herald American*, October 23, 1973.

Manners, Dorothy. "A High Tea Welcomes Audrey Hepburn Back." *New York World Journal Tribune*, January 18, 1967.

Mansfield, Stephanie. "Audrey Hepburn, Eternal Waif." *New York Post*, August 31, 1985.

Marin, Rick. "Ever a Goddess, Ever a Dream." *New York Times*, April 25, 1999.

Maslin, Janet. "Audrey Hepburn's Party." *New York Times*, April 21, 1991.

Massow, Rosalind. "Audrey's Advice: Have Fun, Let Hubby Wear the Pants." *New York Journal American*, August 19, 1957.

Masters, Dorothy. "Love in Afternoon Debut at 2 Theaters." *New York Daily News*, August 24, 1957.

"Mayerling Lives Again—On TV." *New York Times*, January 27, 1957.

McClain, John. "After Starring in First Play Audrey Wants to Learn Acting." *New York Journal American*, February 6, 1954.

McDonald, Marci. "The Torture of Being a Star." *San Francisco Chronicle*, May 3, 1979.

McGee, Celia. "Son Fondly Recalls 'Elegant' Hepburn. *New York Daily News.* November 4, 2003.

"Miss Hepburn in One Jungle after Another." *New York Herald Tribune,* August 31, 1958.

Molony, Julia. "Audrey's Glittering Career Hid Star's Secret Heartache." *Irish Independent*, 7 June 2015.

Moonan, Wendy. "Antiques—To Daddy Dearest from Audrey." *New York Times*, August 22, 2003.

Monmaney, Terence. "Taking Stock of Hepburn." *Smithsonian,* January 2003.

Morris, Bernadine. "Actress Has Influential Fashion Role." *New York Times*, December 15, 1963.

Muir, Florabel. "Hollywood: The New Hepburn." *New York Daily News,* July 1, 1966.

"My Fair Lady's Dream Comes True." *Look,* February 25, 1964.

Newton, Michael. "Charade: The Last Sparkle of Hollywood." *The Guardian,* December 13, 2013.

Norton, Elliot. "Second Thoughts of a First-Nighter." *Boston Post*, March 28, 1954.

"The Nun's Story." *Movie Mirror*, July 1959.

O'Connor, John. "ABC and NBC Movies on Romance and Crime." *New York Times*, February 23, 1987.

"Ondine." *Gotham Guide.* February 18, 1954.

"Oscar Write-In Can't Help Audrey.*" Variety,* March 3, 1965.

"Paging Audrey Hepburn for a Thousand Summers." *Entertainment Today.* November 9, 1973.

"Paris When It Sizzles Strong in Marquee Power," *Hollywood Reporter*, April 8, 1964.

Parsons, Louella O. "Audrey Hepburn: What's in a Name." *Pictorial TV View*, January 31, 1960.

Paskin, Glenn. "Audrey Hepburn." *Us Weekly*, October 17, 1988.

"Pat Neal Hurt by Oscar Snub." *New York Post*, April 8, 1965.

Pepper, Curtis Bill. "Audrey Hepburn at 46." *McCall's*, January 1976.

Pepper, Curtis Bill. "Audrey Keeps Park in a Stir." *New York World Telegram and Sun*, August 16, 1957.

Pepper, Curtis Bill. "War & Peace Settled in Two Speeding Autos." *New York World Telegram*, August 11, 1956.

People Extra. "A Tribute to Audrey Hepburn." Winter 1993.

Pihodna, Joe. "N. Y. Film Critics Select Ben-Hur as Best of 1959." *New York Herald Tribune*, December 29, 1959.

Podolsky, J. D. "Life with Audrey." *People.* October 31, 1994.

Price, Michael H. "Sabrina Remake Not Even Close to the Original Version." *Fort Worth Star-Telegram*. December 15, 1995.

Pryor, Thomas. "Audrey Hepburn Home to Recover." *New York Times*, February 3, 1959.

Quinn, Frank. "Mel Will Direct Audrey." *New York Mirror*, August 18, 1957.

Quinn, Frank, and Fred Zepp. "The Rise of Audrey Hepburn." *New York Mirror*. March 26, 1954.

"Radd." "Audrey." *Variety*, November 28, 1984.

Riding, Alan. "25 Years Later, Honor for Audrey Hepburn." *New York Times*, April 22, 1991.

Rittersporn, Liz. "Audrey Hepburn's Clotheslines." *New York Daily News*, July 6, 1979.

Roach, Margaret. "The World's Gardens." *Newsday*, March 7, 1991.

"Robin and Marian." *Films and Filming* 22, no. 7 (April 1976).

Rush, George, and Joanna Malloy. "Crying Foul over Fair Lady's Memory." *New York Daily News,* October 28, 2002
Saltzman, Barbara. "Tulips, Roses on View in Debut of Gardens." *Los Angeles Times*, January 21, 1993.
Santoro, Marc. "Is That Really Her Voice?" *New York Times*, January 2, 2003.
Scheuer, Philip K. "Audrey's Face Launched Era." *New York Journal-American*, August 8, 1965.
Schumach, Murray. "Audrey Hepburn Is Wary on Roles." *New York Times,* June 16, 1961.
"Sentimental Trip." *Newark Evening News*, January 6, 1993.
Sheppard, Eugenia. "Gigi Shops for Easter Bonnets." *New York Herald Tribune*, April 4, 1952.
Smith, Liz. "Audrey Hepburn: A Return of Elegance." *New York Daily News*, September 7, 1975.
Sobol, Louis. "A Day With Audrey and Mel." *New York Journal American,* June 11, 1955.
Sobol, Louis. "Along the Broadway Beat." *New York Journal American*, September 26, 1954.
Solsky, Sidney. "Audrey Hepburn." *New York Post*, March 24, 1957.
Solsky, Sydney. "Enchantress." *New York Post*, March 29, 1964.
Solsky, Sydney. "Hollywood Is My Beat." *New York Post*, August 26, 1956.
Speck, Gregory. "Legends: Audrey Hepburn." *Cable Guide*. October 1989.
Steinem, Gloria. "'Go Ahead and Ask Me Anything' (And So She Did): An Interview with Truman Capote." *McCall's*, November 1967.
Stone, Laurie. "In Thin Air." *Village Voice*, April 23, 1993.
Suzy. "How Liz Gives In. Why Audrey Holds Out." *Movie Stars*, April 1964.
Taylor, Angela. "Audrey Hepburn Tries on a Swingin' Image." *New York Times*, December 27, 1966.
"Their Divorce Is for Real Now." *New York Daily News*, November 21, 1968.
Thirer, Irene. "Audrey Hepburn and Her Old Men." *New York Post*, August 23, 1957.
Thomas, Bob. "Audrey Hepburn's Secret of Bliss; Must Be More Giving than Taking." *New York Post*, March 25, 1957.
Thomas, David. "The Year of My Fair Lady." *Ladies Home Journal*, January–February 1964
"Together Again: Audrey and Givenchy." *Life*. May 1979.
Tusher, Bill. "Candy Pants Princess." *Motion Picture*. February 1954.
Van Horne, Harriet. "Mayerling Shines as All TV Should." *New York World Telegram*, February 17, 1957.
Variety Staff. "Green Mansions." *Variety*, December 31, 1958.
Warga, Wayne. "Roll 'Em . . . On a Real Live Movie." *Los Angeles Times*, April 18, 1976.
Watters, Jim. "Audrey Hepburn: A Star Is Reborn and Romance Lives in Robin and Marian." *People*. April 12, 1976.
Watts, Richard, Jr. "Two on the Aisle." *New York Post*, February 28, 1954.
Weiler, A. H. "Hepburn to Reign in Spain." *New York Times*, April 11, 1965.
Weiler, A. H. "Roman Holiday at Music Hall Is Modern Fairy Tale Starring Peck and Audrey Hepburn." *New York Times*, August 28, 1953.
Weiler, A. H "The Screen: 'Breakfast at Tiffany's' Audrey Hepburn Stars in Music Hall Comedy." *New York Times*, October 6, 1961.
Whipp, Glen. "This Interview with Cher Is Many Things. Cathartic Isn't One of Them." *Los Angeles Times*, October 2, 2020.
"Why Audrey Hepburn." *Interview*. August 1990.
Wilson, Earl. "It Happened Last Night." *Newsday,* October 6, 1966.
Wilson, Liza. "Audrey." *American Weekly*, September 29, 1957.
Wooldridge, Jane. "At This Stage of Her Life Hepburn's Still a Fair Lady." *Miami Herald*, December 3, 1989.

DVDs

Audrey Hepburn: In Her Own Words. Produced by TVE.Org. UNICEF, 1993.
Audrey Hepburn in the Movies. Wildwood Films. MVD Entertainment Group, 2009.
Audrey Hepburn Magical. Shami Media Group, 2016.
Audrey Hepburn: The Magic of Audrey Hepburn. The Documentary Channel, 2016.
Audrey Hepburn Remembered. Janson Media, 2008.
Audrey: More Than an Icon. Universal Pictures, 2021.
Discovering Audrey Hepburn. 3DD Productions, 2015.
Gardens of the World with Audrey Hepburn. DVD Special Tribute Edition—Kultur Video, 1993.
The Life & Work of Jack Cardiff. Strand Releasing LLC, 2011.

Television

CBS This Morning. Audrey Hepburn, interview with Harry Smith, June 3, 1991.
Donahue. Interview with Audrey Hepburn, January 31, 1990.
Gardens of the World. BHS interview, reel 3.
Hitler's British Girl. Channel 4 UK Television Corporation, 2007.
Larry King Extra. Interview with Audrey Hepburn, October 21, 1991.
Larry King Live. Interview with Audrey Hepburn, April 19, 1989.
Larry King Now. Interview with Mo Rocca, www.ora.tv, November 19, 2019.
Spielberg. HBO, 2017.
Today. Audrey Hepburn Interview with Bryant Gumbel, September 29, 1992.

Radio

Fresh Air on Stage and Screen with Terry Gross. "Interview With Audrey Hepburn." April 15, 1998.

Websites

"1959: Audrey Hepburn Falls from White Stallion on the Set of 'Unforgiven,' on January 28." YouTube, posted by Gerard Henry sooge, July 30, 2012, https://www.youtube.com/watch?v=QLUjOPI7q78.

Alex. "How Audrey Hepburn Changed the Way Hollywood Looked at Women." *Medium.com*. December 28, 2019.

Andrew, Geoff. "Love in the Afternoon." *Time Out* as reported in *Rottentomatoes.com*, March 18, 2007.

Anthony, Scott. "A Film to Remember: *My Fair Lady*." *Medium*, April 24, 2019. https://medium.com/@sadissinger/a-film-to-remember-my-fair-lady-1964-2d9ecb3b25d1.

"Audrey Hepburn . . . by Her Son." YouTube, posted by fisherclips123, January 9, 2013. https://www.youtube.com/watch?v=F-EouugFYq8&t=88s. https://www.youtube.com/watch?v=F-EouugFYq8&t=141s

"Audrey Hepburn—Documentary and Interview with Son Sean Ferrer." https://www.youtube.com/watch?v=Y2N2Kzl9L2s&t=3s.

"Audrey Hepburn: Exhibition, Flagship Live and Online Auctions—September 2017." Christie's, July 25, 2017, https://www.christies.com/features/The-Personal-Collection-of-Audrey-Hepburn-8382-3.aspx.

"Audrey Hepburn Interviewed on French Current Affairs TV Show 'Repéres' (1992)." YouTube, posted by Daniel Archers, March 7, 2013. https://www.youtube.com/watch?v=_hP1KXdu2bA.

"Audrey Hepburn interviewed by Arne Weisse (1958)." YouTube, posted by Rare Audrey Hepburn, May 4, 2019. https://www.youtube.com/watch?v=D0LOqw9WC7k.

"Audrey Hepburn—Interview with Ivo Niehe at her home La Paisible in Switzerland." https://www.youtube.com/watch?v=3ubymGxbkys, 1990.

"Audrey Hepburn My Fair Lady Interview." YouTube, posted by Rare Audrey Hepburn, August 5, 2014. https://www.youtube.com/watch?v=k-u4v8f9asM.

"Audrey Hepburn on Ethiopia and UNICEF." March 25, 1988. YouTube, posted by Global News, November 8, 2012. https://www.youtube.com/watch?v=zorxr3IaksM.

"Audrey Hepburn: The Personal Collection, Part iii." Onlineonly.Christies.com/s/audrey-hepburn-personal part iii, May 2–9, 2019.

"Audrey Hepburn's Personal Items to be Auctioned in London." YouTube, posted by AP Archive, September 27, 2017. https://www.youtube.com/watch?v=Trp1raPhWiI.

"Audrey Hepburn Resurrected in New TV Commercial—Creepy or Cool?" YouTube, posted by EverythingAudrey.com, January 10, 2015. https://www.youtube.com/watch?v=eJt9narRaf4&t=9s.

"Audrey Hepburn and Salvatore Ferragamo." https://artsandculture.google.com/story/audrey-hepburn-and-salvatore-ferragamo-museosalvatoreferragamo/bAXhc2L06jr9Lw?hl=en

"Audrey Hepburn: *Sunday, Sunday*." Host: Gloria Hunniford. https://www.youtube.com/watch?v=W52UZU2oLVg&t=15s.

"Audrey Hepburn Tribute/UNICEF Goodwill Ambassador." YouTube, posted by UNICEF Canada, May 4, 2016. https://www.youtube.com/watch?v=u2wgU94FLCg.

"Audrey Hepburn Wins Best Actress: 1954 Oscars." March 25, 1954, https://www.youtube.com/watch?v=p-vR7D21wqI-.

"Billy Wilder . . . Genius." *The Classic Hollywood Blog*, June 22, 2013. https://classichollywood.wordpress.com/2013/06/22/billy-wilder-genius/.

"Brothers in Dispute Over Handwritten Will." Inheritancedisputes.co.uk. https://www.inheritancedisputes.co.uk/news-articles/brothers-dispute-over-audrey-hepburns-handwritten-will.html December 2020.

"Consoling Audrey." *Stars and Letters: Letters from Hollywood's Golden Age*, November 30, 2017. https://starsandletters.blogspot.com/2017/11/consoling-audrey-hepburn.html.

Corliss, Richard. "Audrey Hepburn: Still the Fairest Lady." *Time*, January 20, 2007. https://content.time.com/time/arts/article/0,8599,1580936-2,00.html.

Correia, Roberta. "TBT: Audrey Hepburn's Three Wedding Dresses." *Brides.com*, October 30, 2019. https://www.brides.com/story/tbt-audrey-hepburn-wedding-dress.

"Darcy Bussell's Looking for Audrey." BBC Television. https://www.youtube.com/watch?v=2fW-PfC3DiY.

"Documentary on Breakfast at Tiffany's Movie." YouTube, posted by r-e-t-r-o-g-a-l, July 22, 2011. https://www.youtube.com/watch?v=xyA__0GJqhs.

Ebert, Roger. "Two for the Road." *rogerebert.com*, October 2, 1967.

Edge, Simon. "Audrey Hepburn's Obsessive Tormentor." *express.co.uk*, June 6, 2008.

EverythingAudrey.com.

"Expression and Audrey Hepburn." *Australianballet.com.au*, May 5, 2010.

Fabaudrey.blogspot.com.

"Farewell to Audrey Hepburn." YouTube, posted by Gerard Henry soogen, January 22, 2017. https://www.youtube.com/watch?v=fykS-wZPuOw.

"The Fashion Designer and His Muse—Audrey Hepburn and Hubert de Givenchy." *Funny Face*, 50th Anniversary DVD, Paramount Pictures, 2007.

Frost, Katie. "One of Audrey Hepburn's Personal Belongings Just Broke World Auction Records." *Harper's Bazaar*, September 28, 2017, https://www.harpersbazaar.com/uk/culture/culture-news/a44039/audrey-hepburn-personal-collection-auction-sales-totals/.

"Hemingway's Dietrich Letters Published." *The Telegraph*, March 30, 2007. https://www.telegraph.co.uk/news/worldnews/1547140/Hemingways-Dietrich-letters-published.html.

Hernandez, Chino R. "Hubert de Givenchy and Audrey Hepburn: A Love Story." *Lifestyle Asia*, January 15, 2018. https://lifestyleasia.onemega.com/hubert-de-givenchy-audrey-hepburn-love-story/.

"Holly at 50: How Breakfast at Tiffany's Came to the Screen and Changed Everything." *George's Journal*, October 13, 2011. https://georgesjournal.org/2011/10/13/holly-hits-50-how-breakfast-at-tiffanys-came-to-the-screen-and-changed-everything/.

"Interview about Audrey Hepburn with Michael Butler (Former Boyfriend)." YouTube, posted by Rare Audrey Hepburn, May 26, 2017. https://www.youtube.com/watch?v=osXcpgwkemw.

"Interview with Audrey Hepburn's Son." BBC One, YouTube, uploaded by uchubi, March 23, 2014. https://www.youtube.com/watch?v=A9sTOPmT0WY.

Iqbal, Nosheen. "The Best-Kept-Secret about Audrey Hepburn Is That She Was So Sad." *The Guardian*, November 15, 2020. https://www.theguardian.com/culture/2020/nov/15/the-best-kept-secret-about-audrey-hepburn-is-that-she-was-so-sad.

"Italian Interview with Audrey Hepburn." YouTube, posted by Arranging_Matches, May 6, 2006. https://www.youtube.com/watch?v=5p78PFW2aNg&t=73s.

Kacala, Alexander. "Beyond the Glamour: Audrey Hepburn's Son Opens Up about Her Struggles in New Interview." *Today*, October 9, 2010. https://www.today.com/popculture/audrey-hepburn-s-son-opens-about-her-struggles-new-interview-t193670?cid=sm_npd_td_fb_ma.

"La Voix d'Audrey Hepburn (Audrey's Voice): French Interview (1955)." YouTube, posted by Rare Audrey Hepburn, November 8, 2017. https://www.youtube.com/watch?v=ouMf6OOwQao.

"Lovely Audrey." *Timeless* (blog), June 14, 2011. http://timelessexclusive.blogspot.com/2011/06/lovely-audrey.html.

"Audrey Hepburn: The Magic of Audrey—UNICEF." YouTube, posted by Inception Media Group, February 16, 2012. https://www.youtube.com/watch?v=1SvddNIlRaw.

MacLaine, Shirley. "Quotes About Audrey Hepburn." https://londonmumsmagazine.com/shopping-guides/movies-tested-recommended/quotes-about-audrey-hepburn.

Marriott, Hannah. "Audrey Hepburn Exhibition Celebrates Star's Enduring Appeal." *The Guardian*, September 22, 2017. https://www.theguardian.com/fashion/2017/sep/22/audrey-hepburn-exhibition-celebrates-film-star-enduring-appeal-fashion.

Matzen, Robert, "Instincts." *RobertMatzen.com*. https://robertmatzen.com/2019/01/30/instincts/, January 30, 2019.

Miller, Daniel. "Audrey Hepburn: Dead is the New Alive." *Huffington Post*, September 15, 2006. https://www.huffpost.com/entry/audrey-hepburn-dead-is-th_b_29484.

Millier, Julie. "Audrey Hepburn Reveals Heartbreak and Discusses Secret Wedding in Never-Before-Seen Letters." *Vanity Fair*, June 14, 2016. https://www.vanityfair.com/style/2016/06/audrey-hepburn-love-letters.

Milmo, Cahil. "The Price of 'Breakfast At Tiffany's': Hepburn's Dress Is Sold for £467,200." *Independent*, December 6, 2006. https://www.independent.co.uk/news/uk/this-britain/the-price-of-breakfast-at-tiffanys-hepburns-dress-is-sold-for-163467200-427258.html.

"My Fair Lady and George Cukor Win Best Picture and Directing: 1965 Oscars." April 5, 1965. YouTube, posted by Oscars, August 29, 2013. https://www.youtube.com/watch?v=Q_ntrUBJTHk.

O'Bryon, Olivia. "Audrey Hepburn's Love for Dogs Became Part of Her Aesthetic." *Forbes.com*, July 25, 2021. https://www.forbes.com/sites/oliviaobryon/2021/07/25/audrey-hepburns-love-for-dogs-became-part-of-her-aesthetic/.

O'Malley, Sheila. "Singlehandedly." *The Sheila Variations* (blog), May 13, 2004. https://www.sheilaomalley.com/?p=831.

"Pablo Picasso: The Meaning and the Purpose of Life." *Excellence Reporter*, January 9, 2020. https://excellencereporter.com/2020/01/09/pablo-picasso-the-meaning-and-the-purpose-of-life/.

Palamba, Asia London. "A Glimpse into Audrey Hepburn's Life in Rome."*Americadomani.com*, July 10, 2023. https://americadomani.com/audrey-hepburns-life-in-rome/.

Pelley, Scott. "Carnegie Heroes and the Neuroscience behind Acts of Heroism." CBS News, June 5, 2022. https://www.cbsnews.com/news/andrew-carnegie-hero-fund-commission-60-minutes-2022-06-05/.

People Staff. "The Private Audrey." *People*, January 1, 1993. https://people.com/archive/the-private-audrey/.

"Proposed Decision Favors Actress' Eldest Son in Dispute with Charity." NBC Los Angeles, October 19, 2019. https://www.nbclosangeles.com/news/proposed-decision-favors-actress-eldest-son-in-dispute-with-charity/1963157/#:~:text=In%20a%20dispute%20over%20the,actress%20Audrey%20Hepburn's%20eldest%20son.

Raphael, Fredric. "Audrey Was a Writer's Dream." *Gulfnews.com*, August 23, 2010, https://gulfnews.com/entertainment/audrey-was-a-writers-dream-frederic-raphael-1.671646.

Raphael, Lev. "Henry James' Killer Kindness Quote." *Huffpost*, January 24, 2017, https://www.huffpost.com/entry/a-killer-kindness-quote_b_9063666.

"Rare Audrey Hepburn Stamps Sold at Berlin Auction." BBC News, October 17, 2010. https://www.bbc.com/news/entertainment-arts-11550814#:~:text=A%20rare%20sheet%20of%2010,the%20film%20Breakfast%20at%20Tiffany's.

"Rare Footage of Audrey Hepburn on *We The People* in 1951." *CBS Sunday Morning* on Facebook, February 7, 2019. https://www.facebook.com/watch/?extid=SEO——&v=244515853125749.

"Reflections on the Silver Screen: Audrey Hepburn Interview with Richard Brown." YouTube, posted by You're Gonna Love Tomorrow, May 4, 2015. https://www.youtube.com/watch?v=v18G6K4MVjc.

"Rex Harrison Wins Best Actor: 1965 Oscars." April 5, 1965. YouTube, posted by Oscars, September 27, 2011. https://www.youtube.com/watch?v=0aL5W0dxoQY.

Robson, Sue. "Audrey Hepburn's Son: 'One Day We Will Find a Cure for the Cancer That Killed My Mother.'" *Express*, October 19, 2015. https://www.express.co.uk/life-style/life/613099/Audrey-Hepburn-son-cure-cancer-killed-awareness.

Ruiz, Karen. "EXCLUSIVE: Audrey Hepburn's will revealed!" *Daily Mail*, December 15, 2017. https://www.dailymail.co.uk/news/article-5181153/Audrey-Hepburns-revealed-sons-lawsuit.html.

Russian, Ale. "Audrey Hepburn's Last Love Robert Wolders Dies at 81." *People.com*, July 16, 2018. https://people.com/movies/audrey-hepburns-last-love-robert-wolders-dies-at-81/.

Sato, Majo. "From Starving to Stardom: The Deleted Scenes of Audrey Hepburn's Life." *Rhētorikós: Excellence in Student Writing*. Fordham University (Fall 2022). https://rhetorikos.blog.fordham.edu/?p=1124.

Schweiger, Hannah. "Results: The Personal Collection of Audrey Hepburn (Part I) Realised £4,635,500 / $6,202,299 / €5,270,563." Christie's, September 27, 2017. https://www.christies.com/about-us/press-archive/details?PressReleaseID=8818&lid=1.

"Sean Hepburn Ferrer on 'Intimate Audrey': You Walk Around Like It's a Personal Visit and Personal Experience." *FilmTalk.org*, November 2, 2019. https://filmtalk.org/2019/11/02/sean-hepburn-ferrer-on-intimate-audrey-you-walk-around-like-its-a-personal-visit-and-a-personal-experience/.

"Sean Hepburn Ferrer Talks about Audrey Hepburn: The Actress, the Mother, the Style Icon and the Humanitarian," *FilmTalk.org*, December 8, 2016. https://filmtalk.org/2016/12/08/sean-hepburn-ferrer-talks-about-audrey-hepburn-the-actress-the-mother-the-style-incon-and-the-humanitarian/.

Siddique, Haroon, and agencies. "Audrey Hepburn's Breakfast at Tiffany's Script Sells for £630,000." *The Guardian*, September 28, 2017. https://www.theguardian.com/culture/2017/sep/28/audrey-hepburn-breakfast-at-tiffanys-script-sells-auction-630000.

Staggs, Megan. "Eleanor Roosevelt Once Said." *Huffpost*, updated December 14, 2013. https://www.huffpost.com/entry/eleanor-roosevelt-once-sa_b_4088528.

Stephenson, Cassidy. "Why Julie Andrews Wasn't Chosen for My Fair Lady." Cbr.com. Updated February 18, 2023. https://www.cbr.com/julie-andrews-my-fair-lady-audrey-hepburn/.

Telsch, Rafe. "What Could Have Been: Hepburn as Peter Pan." *Cinemablend.com*, December 29, 2008. https://www.cinemablend.com/new/What-Could-Have-Been-Hepburn-Peter-Pan-11382.html.

"Test Pattern: Hepburn Falls into the Gap." *Today*, October 4, 2006. https://www.today.com/popculture/test-pattern-hepburn-falls-gap-wbna14854161.

Torello, Peggy. "Lessons Learned from Audrey Hepburn's Sons Dispute over Her Estate." February 19, 2021. https://lifepathma.org/stories/legal-notes-lessons-learned-from-audrey-hepburn-s-sons-dispute-over-her-estate/#:~:text=She%20did%20not%20name%20which,in%20litigation%20over%20her%20estate.

Travers, Peter. "Always." *RollingStone.com*, December 22, 1989. https://www.rollingstone.com/tv-movies/tv-movie-reviews/always-100579/.

Veliz, Leslie. "Here's Who Inherited Audrey Hepburn's Money after She Died." *grunge.com*, December 6, 2021. here's-who-inherited-audrey-hepburn's money-after-she-died.

"What Is a Gary Cooper." "1961: Hollywood, Audrey Hepburn read a poem called 'What is a Gary Cooper?' (January 9)." YouTube, posted by Gerard Henry soogen, September 19, 2017. https://www.youtube.com/watch?v=0sOQTuq2zzU.

Personal Interviews

Alan Arkin—September 8, 2020
Jeffrey Banks—August 25, 2020
Jeanine Basinger—September 11, 2020
Janis Blackschleger—August 18, 2020
Emma Ferrer—September 23, 2020
Sean Hepburn Ferrer—July 7, 2020; August 4, 2020
Pamela Fiori—September 16, 2020
Caryl Stern—September 16, 2020
Robert Wagner—September 17, 2020

Acknowledgments

MY FIRST THANKS MUST GO to Sean Hepburn Ferrer for his willingness to sit for several lengthy interviews. Insightful, polite, clear-eyed, yet always loving in his recollections, he does his mother proud. A similar thanks to Sean's daughter Emma Ferrer, who took time away from her busy life to answer my questions with endless patience.

Jeffrey Banks provided not only his fashion expertise regarding Audrey's extraordinary influence as a fashion icon but also detailed photo captions that deepened understanding of the remarkable relationship between Audrey Hepburn and Hubert de Givenchy.

Thanks as well to the late Alan Arkin, who provided me with a terrific interview beginning with his opening exclamation: "I hear you're looking for me!" A similar thank you to Robert Wagner, who proved the gentleman of reputation and then some.

Producer Janis Blackschleger, editor Pamela Fiori, and former UNICEF executive Caryl Stern all proved generous with their time while providing insight into the essence of Audrey Hepburn's life and work. A special thank you, as always, to film scholar/historian/author Jeanine Basinger, whose knowledge and insight remain peerless.

Many thanks to my agent Malaga Baldi and editor John Cerullo, as well as to Chris Chappell and Jessica Thwaite of Applause Books; a special thank you to Barbara Claire at Applause for her help with the multitude of photos, and even more so for her endless patience with my technical ineptitude. Thank you to production manager Keerthika Purushothman, copyeditor Ryan Mastellar, and proofreader June Sawyers.

Similar thanks to the staff at the New York Public Library's Performing Arts Division; the library's unparalleled collection of books, articles, and clippings remains one of the many reasons I am glad to live in New York City.

Of the dozens of books that deal with the life and career of Audrey Hepburn, I found books by two authors to be particularly helpful in terms of background information: *Audrey*, by Barry Paris, which provides a graceful, detailed biographical insight into Audrey's psyche; and two books by Robert Matzen—*Dutch Girl* and *Warrior*—which provide, respectively, extraordinarily detailed and definitive accounts of Audrey Hepburn's childhood and work for UNICEF. Although all three books utilize a different approach to Audrey's legacy than that which I have undertaken, they were especially helpful to my own study. I hope that I have fully acknowledged their insights with all appropriate citations and recommend all three books for additional understanding of Audrey Hepburn's extraordinary life.

I am very fortunate, in fact downright lucky, to have a terrific group of friends and colleagues who not only make living in New York City stimulating and entertaining but also provided great encouragement during these past four years. Too numerous to mention, they know who they are, and fearful of leaving someone out, I hope they understand that I mention only two by name: my sister Sarah and nephew Parker.

Index